PERENNIAL GARDEN PLANTS
or The Modern Florilegium

Perennial Garden Plants

or The Modern Florilegium

A concise account of herbaceous plants,
including bulbs, for general garden use

Third Edition

Written and illustrated by

GRAHAM STUART THOMAS OBE, VMH, DHM, VMM

Gardens Consultant to the National Trust

With 32 plates in colour and
79 in black-and-white

SAGAPRESS, INC./TIMBER PRESS, INC.
Portland, Oregon

Printed in Great Britain
for
J. M. DENT & SONS LTD
91 Clapham High Street, London SW4 7TA
© Graham Stuart Thomas 1976, 1982, 1990
First published 1976
Second edition (revised) 1982
Reprinted 1984, 1985, 1986
Third edition (revised) 1990
Reprinted 1994

Published in North America in 1990 by
Sagapress, Inc./Timber Press, Inc.
The Haseltine Building
133 S.W. Second Avenue, Suite 450
Portland, Oregon 97204, U.S.A.

ISBN 0–88192–167–X

Contents

Illustrations

Pencil Drawings (scale of reduction $\frac{2}{3}$ actual size)

Between pages 144 and 145

Many of the photographs have been taken in our leading botanic gardens which are indicated by citing their cities only throughout the captions.

Photographs in Colour

Between pages 240 and 241

Photographs in Monochrome

Between pages 336 and 337

Gratitude

It would have been beyond me, as a gardener, to have attempted this book without the help of a skilled botanist to guide me through the more intricate nomenclatorial tangles which have piled up in certain genera, decade by decade. I want therefore to register my infinite indebtedness to Christopher Brickell, Director of the Royal Horticultural Society's garden at Wisley, who has so often placed his wide knowledge of botanical writings and plants at my disposal. For much work of this kind during his few spare hours daily I want to give my best thanks and also for his kindness in reading through the manuscript. To the staff of the Botany Department at Wisley and also to the Society's Librarian and staff at Vincent Square, London, my sincere thanks are due, likewise to Dr C. E. Hubbard for checking the chapter on grasses and to Dr P. F. Yeo for help with the genus *Geranium*. Dr F. M. Jarrett and Wessel Marais at the Herbarium of the Royal Botanic Gardens, Kew, have kindly assisted me with some ferns and monocotyledonous plants respectively. The staff in the Herbaceous Department at Kew have been consistently helpful, as have the Regius Keeper and staff at the Royal Botanic Garden, Edinburgh.

It has been a wonderful experience making several visits over the years to the great collection of perennials at Bressingham Gardens, Diss, Norfolk, so well grown and grouped by Alan Bloom, our leading British hardy plant nurseryman, and to share experiences with him. My thanks are due to him and also to another friend of long standing, James Russell, who has been dropping hints and making valuable suggestions ever since the early days of the manuscript. To Mrs Margaret Neal, who has brought order out of the confusion of the manuscripts of all my books by her impeccable typing, I am exceedingly grateful. I also acknowledge with thanks help by John Lloyd of Kelway's Nurseries, about peonies, Lawrence Neel of the Orpington Nurseries about Siberian irises, Leslie Slinger of the Slieve Donard Nurseries about *Dierama* hybrids and by Mrs Knox Finlay in regard to *Meconopsis* and *Codonopsis*. Many similar acts of kindness through the freemasonry of gardening enabled me to approach with confidence this big task, while the interest of the staff of Messrs Dent—and particularly that of Miss L. M. Mont-Clar, who acted as editor for me—enabled me to finish it.

1990 Edition

Kind correspondents have pointed out a few errors and omissions since the first edition appeared, and I tender to them my best thanks. Apart from these, many additions have been made to this new edition and it has been thoroughly revised and reset with improvements designed to help the reader. Special thanks go to John E. Elsley for providing the USA Hardiness Zones throughout and a lot of useful advice, and to Peter G. Barnes for much careful help, especially botanical.

G. S. T.

Introduction

Reminiscences can be boring, but I feel I must explain the reason for my subtitle. It all started in the early 1950s after my book *The Old Shrub Roses** had appeared. In 1955 I paid a third visit to Ireland and found *Morina longifolia, Veratrum viride* and the rare *Hosta tokudama* 'Variegata' in Lady Moore's garden, Willbrook House, near Dublin, and *Cirsium eriophorum, Digitalis grandiflora* and a strange geranium in Miss Freeman's garden at Leixlip. I met several other plants for the first time during my tour and realized that keen gardeners were treasuring the rarer hardy plants in the same way that various enthusiasts had cared for the Old Shrub Roses. I immediately began to think how I could write some catalogue or list which would help to keep these rare plants to the fore. There were plenty of books and catalogues dwelling on the more popular plants—the irises, the delphiniums, and the like—but the stress was never on these stalwart beauties of Nature, unadulterated by man's hybridizing—the equivalents of the species and unusual hybrid roses. I felt that the collecting of such plants and writing a list and record of them would be absorbing and I should discover new beauty and in some measure be able to pass it on. There is no doubt that "the rich power which breeds so many and many a flower" is there to lead one on from one group of plants to another during one's life.

The opportunity came when, a few years later, I gave up managership of a large wholesale nursery and joined James Russell at Sunningdale Nurseries. He has always been an ardent collector of good things and together we amassed a considerable number of hardy and tender herbaceous plants, with the result that a year or two later I wrote and produced *The Modern Florilegium*, in the same format as *The Manual of Shrub Roses*, from the nursery.

We had cast about for a title which would convey that it was something more than a catalogue, and *Florilegium*—the Latin equivalent of the Greek *Anthology*—seemed appropriate. An anthology is a collection of flowers, though it is more usually applied to a collection of poems. But can we not say that just as poems are flowers of thought, flowers are poems of beauty? The word "Modern" was added because I believed that while the appreciation of beautiful plants was presented in its pages, the collection was also aimed at keeping garden work to a minimum by the use of ground-cover plants and the almost total exclusion of plants requiring support; in addition the publication stressed the importance of foliage and sought to help the modern movement of flower arranging by the inclusion of lists of special plants for this and for other purposes.

Over the next twelve years or so some twenty-five thousand copies each of the *Florilegium* and the *Manual* were sent out, and I have received many letters of appreciation about these little publications, proving that they were referred

---

*Published by Phoenix House, an associate company of J. M. Dent & Sons Ltd, who since then have published most of my other books.

to again and again by keen gardeners, and had in fact become "bedside books" for many.

Since then the picture has somewhat changed; Sunningdale Nurseries passed into the Waterer Group in January 1969, and after giving a helping hand in various ways for three years, I parted company with them. Meanwhile two things had happened. One was that *The Manual of Shrub Roses* and *The Modern Florilegium* had gone out of print. The other was that I had been working on *Plants for Ground-Cover*, which Messrs Dent published for me in 1970. I therefore decided I would re-write and enlarge the *Florilegium*, but would exclude all the purely ground-covering plants. But the more work I did upon it the more I felt it was inadequate; the exclusion of many of the popular races and also plants which need staking in one form or another would result in a book that could not be used as a work of general reference by gardeners. And this was really my aim—to list most plants that could be grown in this country, to present in particular the basic species and also to put the herbaceous plant into the perspective of horticulture from all points of view. I also wanted to sort out the nomenclature, which had become dreadfully confused by nurserymen's faulty catalogues and busy botanists.

Therefore I have produced this bigger volume, which I hope will be a guide and help to all who garden, because a garden without herbaceous plants is almost non-existent. The book seeks to embrace the vast majority of good plants—with warning notes about some bad ones; not only the normal or rare "border" plants, but many bulbs, grasses, ferns, woodland and bog plants, with some notes on biennials, but excluding annuals and aquatics. It was obvious that ferns and grasses should be numbered among herbaceous perennials; likewise there seemed no point in adhering to the time-honoured horticultural separation of fibrous-rooted perennials from those with rhizomes, corms or bulbous roots. Even so I have had to exclude the big popular genera of bulbs and corms for the simple reason that they could not be contained with all the other plants in one volume. Hence I have omitted such genera as *Narcissus*, *Tulipa* (except one species), *Crocus*, *Hyacinthus*, *Colchicum*, but these are well covered by books and catalogues specially concerned with bulbs. *Chrysanthemum*, *Dahlia* and *Gladiolus* cultivars are also excluded.

The other self-imposed limit I have accepted is one of height. The upper limits obviously presented no difficulty; I have excluded none on account of height. Visualizing the many smaller gardens of today, with their necessarily small beds and borders, it was essential to include plenty of small- and short-growing plants. But where does one draw the line between small perennials and the larger rock plants? Many are interchangeable for either site. To include hundreds of these little plants and little bulbs would, once again, have swelled the book too much. The little bulbous plants are very much the lesser fry of the garden and I had no compunction about excluding them. The low-growing perennials are, many of them, plants of substance, often evergreen, and invaluable for finishing of frontal areas. Instead of putting them into the main alphabetical part of the book I have compromised by listing some of the more important in Cuttings from My Notebook (No. 1) at the end of this book. I hope this will satisfy; many of them are in addition fully documented in my *Plants for Ground-Cover*.

This matter of size has proved very difficult. I have erred and strayed and made inclusions and exclusions for which there are no real reasons and I must ask your indulgence. In short, I have at times flatly refused to be bullied by my own rules.

The original *Florilegium* tried to stress the many beautiful flower-forms other than that of the daisy, but I realized that, to make a comprehensive survey, I must include all the Compositae or Daisy Family, as they contribute so much colour to the garden through the year.

It has been a formidable task. It is, when all is said and done, my selection and a personal record. The title was another matter. Messrs Dent and I felt that *Florilegium* was too much of a tongue-twister, too rarefied for a general book on perennials of all kinds, and so it has been deposed and turned into a subtitle.

Is there room for another book on garden perennials? Comprehensive reviews of these plants have been produced from decade to decade, particularly in Germany, as will be seen from the bibliography. Frances Perry and Alan Bloom have contributed to our store of knowledge and more recently Dr B. K. Boom has given us a major botanical work. There is always room, however, for a new presentation, I think, a new record of experience with plants, a new personal approach, even if it only seeks to keep up to date with recent research and nomenclature.

There are more reliable comprehensive books on trees and shrubs than there are on herbaceous plants. Further, there is no shortage of good shrub catalogues today, but garden plants—perennials, herbaceous plants, call them what you will—have always been rather neglected, the main reason being that from a nurseryman's point of view there is less profit to be made out of them and in consequence there is less capital available for catalogues. It is also true that there are more great gardens devoted to shrubby plants than herbaceous plants.

An evil that creeps in upon us today is that in the interests of "economy" specific names are often omitted from catalogues of named cultivars. We are given the genus, followed by 'Pink Delight' or 'Giant White'. We cannot tell from what it is derived, and in consequence, to me, much of the interest is lost. We do not know what country has given us this gem, nor what its botanical status is.

I write from Surrey, which perhaps may be taken as half-way house when it comes to hardiness in Britain. Some tender plants will grow on the coast of Northumberland or in the north of Scotland which would not be hardy in Surrey. There are many gardens in the south and west from Cornwall to the west of Scotland, and in Ireland, where tender plants thrive. I have therefore deliberately included in these pages many plants that would not be hardy in Surrey. Hence my title, which does not include the word "hardy"; nor does it include the word "border". They are perennials for every part of the garden, in sun, in shade, in different soils and climates, clump-forming or spreading, and of every size. They are not all even "herbaceous", since some are evergreen and woody. I have tried, in vain perhaps, to survey every likely genus and to bring forth a "bottomless cornucopia" from which the collector-gardener, the garden artist, and the flower arranger can each select the most appropriate plant for any given spot.

In writing the descriptions I have tried to bear all this in mind. This is not a botanist's book but a gardener's, written for gardeners, though from time to time a botanical point has been included to indicate how two similar or confused plants differ.

The book is designed to be useful to the millions of amateur gardeners through these islands and also to the curators of our public parks, to landscape architects and planners and to nurserymen. Many of the same details which I am told have made my ground-cover book useful are included—heights, seasons of flowering, distances apart for planting, culture and other fundamentals. The flower arrangers will I hope also derive some help from the notes on flowers, seed-heads and foliage for cutting.

Here then is my contribution. I have tried to be truthful, concise and at the same time appetizing; appetizing because it is my desire to encourage you to grow these lovely things; the smaller ones among them may be called garden toys, while many of the larger kinds are plants of great personality. To whichever class they belong they are growing things, of a beauty unsurpassed among the passive things of this world and worthy of our reverence and awe, to be treasured and enshrined in our gardens.

"It has been frequently observed that flower gardens have been on the decline for the last half century; and the cause of this appears to have been the influx of new plants during that period, by which gardeners have been induced . . . to be more solicitous about rarity and variety, than well disposed colours and quantity." J. C. Loudon: *An Encyclopaedia of Gardening*, 1827.

Chapter 1

A General Survey

Of the plants mentioned in this book I have grown some nine-tenths, either handled personally in my own garden, in the University Botanic Garden, Cambridge, or in nurseries, or only by proxy in such places or in the gardens of the National Trust, and have been closely observing plants since school days. In my garden today are direct descendants of plants I was brought up with— *Hemerocallis flava*, *H. fulva*, Lily-of-the-Valley, *Iris pallida dalmatica*, Japanese Anemones, Montbretia and *Aster tradescantii*—which says much for their longevity.

From old notebooks I can with amusement look back on early efforts at colour effects, noting in 1928 for instance a grouping of four pretty strong colour-givers—*Erigeron* 'Mesagrande', *Achillea filipendulina*, *Salvia nemorosa*, and *Chrysanthemum maximum*. These four genera are still the backbone of many a border. The next year the contrast of the purple *Iris × fulvala* caught my eye alongside the orange-yellow *Buphthalmum salicifolium*. These were all in the splendid herbaceous borders at Sidney Sussex College, Cambridge, arranged by my old friend Dr B. T. D. Smith.

In a totally different vein I noted *Arisaema candidissimum* and *Meconopsis grandis* on one of the wonderful exhibits staged by Lord Aberconway at Chelsea. My notes also tell me I thought *Iris* 'Lord of June' had poor standards—as indeed it had!

There was also a traditional herbaceous border at the University Botanic Garden at Cambridge where I was a student at the time. It was annually double-trenched and good manure was put below. In those days clumps of summer-flowering annuals were replaced in early September by groups of chrysanthemums, renowned old varieties like 'Goacher's Crimson'—after the famous Sussex firm—and 'Perle Chatillonaise'. The two best Michaelmas Daisies were 'October Dawn' and 'Climax' and the last has not been superseded in its own class today.

Having been given Gertrude Jekyll's *Colour Schemes for the Flower Garden* by Dr Smith, to help to educate me, I remember making with a length of cardboard and some coloured papers an imaginary border, following her colour schemes, as a basis for a talk I gave to my fellow workers. Naturally on arrival in Surrey one of my first objects was to try to visit Munstead Wood, Miss Jekyll's home. I did not realize how lucky I was to be allowed to see her and to walk around her garden. "Pick a piece of anything you would like to talk about and come back and have some tea with me." This privilege was the more greatly appreciated when I read later that at the time, September 1931, she had almost given up seeing visitors. She died a little over a year later. (I have never ceased to marvel, of late years, that we in this country could let such a work of art as her garden disappear as it has done. She worked at it and polished it until her painting with flowers and foliage as her media satisfied her. Gardening, particularly with perennials, is transient, but it would have been something to have ensured that the garden design at Munstead Wood was not lost.)

My notes from my visit included *Aster corymbosus* and *Gentiana asclepiadea*: *Lilium krameri* (*L. japonicum*) with *Delphinium* 'Blue Fairy'. But to see in reality those wonderful borders of graded colour was like an entry into a new world, or walking through a static rainbow. Her borders glowed with a plenitude of flowers, in an effortless colour progression—a poem of colour.

Gertrude Jekyll was our greatest exponent of the artistry of gardening. Concurrently William Robinson sought mainly through his writings—he lived in Sussex and was a celebrated horticultural and silvicultural journalist—to bring to the notice of gardeners the great wealth of plants that was awaiting intelligent use. He also misguidedly sought to sweep away all formal designs. These two great gardeners, with Ellen Willmott, another expert, at Great Warley, Essex. revolutionized gardening and ushered in the greater awareness of the uses and beauty of plants, which has resulted in twentieth-century gardening. Every possible style of gardening is practised today, but if one style is specially relevant to this century, apart from the formless woodland garden, it is the Jekyll or Hidcote style: beautiful plants used in an artistic way in a garden of firm and good design.

The reasons behind Gertrude Jekyll's tremendous flair for the artistry of gardening were that she had spent half a lifetime absorbing and practising other arts before she took to gardening, and also that she was a lover of the craft of gardening; we should be thankful that she was also an able writer and photographer. Few gardeners have passed on more of their knowledge and experiences.

The Place of Perennials in the Garden

Nowadays people speak of the "herbaceous border" as an extravagant Edwardian addition to gardens. This is indeed the path up which Gertrude Jekyll led us for many years, and her type of herbaceous border with its attendant colour schemes is still practised in some gardens. More often it is a great collection of herbaceous plants graded to size but not to colour. The normal answer to the question implied in the title to this paragraph of most gardeners would be, undoubtedly, "in the herbaceous border". But this opens up vast suppositions and arguments and is not really what this book is about. It is about perennial plants for varied uses in our gardens. Perennials have always been grown, ever since gardens began. In our own country in Renaissance days they would have been grown mixed with bulbs, annuals, herbs both culinary and medicinal, and a few shrubs in the knot gardens and patterned parterres, that is, in *beds*, and also in surrounding *borders*. Over the next two centuries or more fashion decreed that the prospects from great houses should be laid out without flowers, but in the walled kitchen gardens there were always borders of treasured flowers and plants, in mixture.

Sometimes a garden may be a mere plot in which to grow plants; if it should have any pretence to design, however, one must arrange the cultivated areas in some way so that one can walk in it to admire and tend the plants. In order to do this plants have to be grown in *beds* or *borders*, because a garden is mainly, shall we say, a *space* around which interests can be accumulated. Even if one has a woodland garden the plants will be arranged in certain areas or borders— strips or areas, that is, bordering onto clumps of solid shrubs and trees or paths, ponds or banks. I have written this because, elementary though it may sound, it is the reason why perennial herbaceous plants acquired the title of "border plants". What else are they?

In the seventeenth century a great collection of perennial herbaceous plants was made by the Laird of Livingstone; after his death his plants were conveyed to the Physic Garden at Edinburgh and in due course to the ultimate Royal

Botanic Garden. No doubt they were grown, for purposes of study, in beds and borders. In *The Florist's Manual*, 1822, Mrs Maria Elizabeth Jackson was rather severe. She considered that the area given to flowers (as opposed to fruit, vegetables and shrubberies) "should in no case be of great extent", also that where the ground is sloping or undulating the parterre [*sic*] should have borders of various shapes intermingled with grass, "but such a flower-garden partakes more of the nature of pleasure ground than of the common parterre and will admit of a judicious introduction of flowering shrubs."

The "common parterre" of the nineteenth century was usually filled with bedding plants (note: not border plants) due to the numberous tender exotics which were raised under glass by means of cheap labour and cheap coal. It was not long before William Robinson sought to call a halt to this "artificial gardening"—which Mrs Ruby Fleischmann always described, so aptly, as "in-and-out gardening". He pleaded that rather than going to all this annual trouble of planting out and taking up, hardy perennials should be used *as bedding plants*. Towards the end of the century Nicholson's *Dictionary of Gardening* extolled the growing of herbaceous perennials in borders by themselves, and, as we have seen, what Robinson and Nicholson recommended, Jekyll carried on, bringing the pure culture of these plants to an unprecedented height of artistry.

Today's accepted term "herbaceous border" is therefore not old as gardens go. The replanting, staking, tying, disbudding and dead-heading, coupled with the popping in of potsful of other plants to cheer up portions of the border in late summer, made an immense amount of work, and the result, so glowing for two or three months, was poor for most of the year. It is far better to limit our choice to real permanencies, which do not require staking, and return to the style of earlier gardening when plants of all kinds were grown together. Inevitably we have to grow our plants in beds and borders, but my own preference is for mixed ones, where there are some trees giving retreats for shade-loving shrubs and plants, and casting their dappling of shade across the lawn; groups of larger shrubs on corners and elsewhere to give shape to the views and to create surprises; and a general mixture throughout of dwarf shrubs, perennials and ground-covers, with bulbs to provide added interest. This has been called gardening in four layers, and I believe it to be the most satisfying form of gardening. It provides the greatest enjoyment over the longest period with the least work. I devoted some pages to it in *Plants for Ground-Cover*. One often hears garden owners claiming that they are scrapping their herbaceous borders and planting shrubs instead, to save work. In my opinion this saves no work and deprives one of that richness of contrast that can only be obtained from a mixture of shrubs and plants. There is no doubt that a combination of shrubs *and* suitable ground-covering plants gives the very minimum of work. (Strangely enough many people actually *like* working in their gardens!) Shrubs require pruning and cutting back—because one always plants them too closely; perennials only require cutting down once a year. Perennials give us almost immediate beauty and are easy to move if they are unsuccessful or in unpleasant contrast the one with another; shrubs take several years to develop, and provide a back-breaking job if it comes to transplanting. And finally, to my mind, a garden border of nothing but shrubs can be nearly as boring sometimes as a garden solely filled with perennials.

The place of perennials in the garden, then, is *everywhere*, to act as complements to the greater or lesser things around them. Alan Bloom has been the archpriest of the cult of the island bed; by using short-growing plants in isolated beds—set in grass lawn perhaps—he achieves a long display with comparatively short and labour-saving plants without interrupting the eye from travelling around the shrubs which make the background of any good garden. This sort

3

of scheme has much to commend it and the plants, growing isolated and exposed to full light and wind, tend to remain compact and pright. It is the herbaceous-plant-specialist's ideal. It is an excellent means of *growing* plants, but from a design point of view can easily destroy the peace of a garden by filling up the principal space.

Perennials are indeed very much concerned with background. Unless one's garden is large enough to have an area devoted to them where the winter emptiness will not pall, it is absolutely essential to have not only some shrubs to give height and solidity, but also some shorter evergreen plants or low shrubs to help to furnish the area in winter. This is assuming you will cut down most of your perennials in the autumn, although some people like to see the dead stems standing, a perch for hoar frost until they are knocked down by wind and snow.

There are perennials for those hot borders under the house, such as nerines, *Liriope muscari* and *Chrysanthemum nipponicum*; their cold counterparts on the north side provide homes for hostas, perhaps, and bergenias. Hot sloping banks for *Sedum* 'Autumn Joy', shady areas for a host of beautiful things, Solomon's Seal, ferns, meconopsis; damp ground for primulas, and sunny places for all the old favourite flowers. I hope the cultural directions I have given will enable intending planters to make their selections, whatever may be their soil and whatever their purpose. Some plants will even naturalize in rough grass. Others need the delight of a cool root run in the peat bed or under rocks; some are hardier when protected by overhead tree branches and some will actually wander among tree and shrub roots. If you garden on chalk there is no need for despair, and if your garden is permanently damp your neighbours will wish they could grow certain things as successfully as you do. Dry sand can be covered, untidy ditches can be made beautiful with the aid of perennials; your deciduous shrubs will provide homes for hellebores and you will enjoy the flowers under the leafless branches.

In one way we have come full circle since the days of Elizabeth I. In those days gardeners and botanists were keen to acquire and grow plants, and grew them without much thought of their arrangement in the garden. Today, having learnt from the examples of garden design and plant associations through the intervening centuries, we are able to enhance a good design with a better understanding of the use of plants in general. Though equally keen on assembling plants in our gardens we can even, by making a right choice among them, not only extend our seasons of beauty and flower, but also actually save ourselves work.

On the other hand it is important, I think, not to go too far in the use of plants for contrast. Today's garden designers are apt to produce a bizarre effect by the use of too much contrast of form and, at times, of colour. The most restful gardens are those where there is a careful blend of colour even though there may be some contrast of form. There is no doubt that too much contrast of form—"plant texture" is another term—can be unrestful, especially when a lot of bright-coloured foliage, grey, copper and variegated, is included. In fact one is beginning to see this superabundance overdone. The Jekyll idea was colour-blending and plant contrast *within the idea*; we should do well to reconsider this and not to use a fresh piece of variegation at every turn.

The Basic Plants and Their Development

Although I have tried to indicate good plants among the vast numbers of garden varieties with "popular" names I must stress that I am mainly concerned with species. It is the old theme, about which I have written before, whether you like *plants* or just *flowers*; whether you are interested in a plant's beauty through the year—or at least during the whole of its growing season—or only in its actual flowers. To my mind the foliage and growth of a plant (known in horticultural circles as its "habit") are of equal importance to its flowers; we have the latter usually for only a few weeks whereas the plant, to be a worthy denizen of our gardens, should look attractive before and, if possible, after flowering. And this is what many species contrive to do. There are of course exceptions. It so happens that the bulk of perennials that have been "improved" by our hybridizers belong to the Daisy Family or Compositae, and the bulk of these have rather uninteresting foliage. Take *Helenium, Aster, Gaillardia, Erigeron, Solidago, Chrysanthemum, Heliopsis,* for example; add to them popular genera of other Families such as *Phlox, Fuchsia, Monarda, Campanula* and *Veronica.* Compare them with yet other genera which have been freely hybridized like *Paeonia, Lupinus, Astilbe, Iris* and *Hemerocallis,* and the difference will at once be apparent. These few latter genera together with *Dianthus, Hosta, Bergenia, Sedum,* and less favoured plants like *Trollius,* Japanese Anemones, *Kirengeshoma, Crambe, Echinops, Helleborus, Geranium, Peltiphyllum, Rodgersia* and the like, with contrasting grasses and ferns, present a range of leaves that is at once surprising, inspiring and gratifying. Their presence in the garden both before and after the flowering period is a great asset.

There is another motive for reassessing the species. As a general rule they are free from diseases, if their simple wants can be studied, and more likely than not they require no support nor staking. On the other hand overbred and inbred strains seem to offer an open door to diseases and pests—eelworm, root-rot, mite and mildew are just a few—and with their ever larger and more plentiful flowers they frequently need support. If a plant does not remain healthy in my garden, out it goes; likewise I grow practically nothing that needs staking, and thus save myself a lot of work and disappointment.

A further reason for favouring species is that the growing of plants from many different countries, all over the world, provides an added interest to the garden.

Breeders' varieties have come and gone with alarming rapidity as one looks back over the years, and a book concerned with these man-made plants would soon be out of date. That is why I prefer to leave you to make your own choice of them, if you desire them, but have indicated the range of colours, seasons and sizes available as far as possible. I have never been one for collecting varieties; I have preferred to *collect species* and to *select varieties*—apart from my lengthy researches into the Rose.

Supply and Demand

Not only is gardening changing today, but nurseries are changing even faster. During the last twenty-five years or so we have watched one renowned firm after another disappear—either finished or taken under the wing of a bigger combine. Most firms today are curtailing their collections and fewer and fewer items are for sale through mail order or in garden centres. There is so much at stake today: costly labour, and most of it unskilled; costly machinery and costly overheads of all kinds; so that a nurseryman can grow only those items which sell well and regularly. It is easier for them to cope with many varieties of one sort and size than a lot of individuals: machine-planting and rule-of-thumb are more easily applied. In addition the older generations of nurserymen were content with smaller profits. Small personally run firms dealing with perennial and rock plants are likely to increase, though this cannot be expected with trees and shrubs. Fortunately there will always be the dedicated growers of plants, both amateur and commercial. It is these who have helped horticulture along in the past and they will always be with us.

Many people do not realize how difficult it is to maintain stock of a plant for sale every year. The weather, human error and erratic demand are all against the nurseryman. If too many are sold each year, it may be two or more years before stock is available again, and in these days of less hand work and personal touch, the young plants run the gauntlet of errant machines, sudden drought, carelessly handled weed-killers and other hazards. Intending purchasers are not finding it easy to obtain the individual plants they require to complete certain schemes. We have the choice of accepting a substitute or waiting a year for stock to become available. The choicer plants, the old varieties and the species, are difficult to find. But whatever we do we must continue to ask for them, to bolster the demand and keep them in commerce, however frustrating it may be.

The progress of horticulture, together with other pursuits, has taken big knocks during this century through two world wars. Plants became scarce but with a return to peace both amateurs and professional growers were avid to regain the plants that had disappeared. We are now witnessing something far more fundamental and insidious because, except for a few dedicated specialists, the nursery trade as a whole is only interested in the best sellers.

To be a best seller a plant should be easy to propagate, showy and gay, should have a compelling and easy name, succeed in untoward conditions and be given lots of publicity. It is unnecessary to state the opposite; no true gardener would be persuaded to purchase against his will and he should reserve his own judgment.

In the days between the two world wars a reliable and comparatively cheap rail and postal service was the foundation on which all nurseries built their trade. The car changed all this, gradually at first but with acceleration since the last war, and is of course the whole *raison d'être* of the garden centre of today. And with the bulk of the trade being achieved through this sort of cash and carry, it is manifest that plants have to be distinctive and attractive while in containers. The persuasive catalogue has, in the main, had its day.

Many of the choicer plants are like antiques. We should not go to the multiple store to pick up an odd Chippendale chair, much less a suite; rather should we search and search through suitable shops. This is what is happening to us who seek for choicer plants; we have to go on inquiring until success crowns our efforts. Collections are always being built up in the gardens of specialists, and at the end of the collector's life they often become redistributed. In the meanwhile he has given many roots away which have gone into the younger collections. There is no doubt that to many of us this "seek and ye shall find" pursuit is the spice of life. Others may prefer to send their order to a nursery and put up with what can be delivered. I write all this to point out the difficulty of acquiring the noted heirlooms, the individual species and the off-the-beat varieties.

We all know how the intrepid (they are always described as "intrepid" as indeed they are) plant hunters have scoured the earth for us; shall I predict that in future years a new kind of plant hunting will come to the fore? Unless the economics of nursery work change we shall all be seeking the gems and scarce items among ourselves in the future. Fortunately gardening has ever been a freemasonry, and many a good plant has been brought back into circulation by exchange.

The Flower Arrangers

Some of the most eager seekers after beauty are those who prefer their flowers cut. During the last thirty years or so we have watched the astonishing rise in membership of the National Association of Flower Arrangers. This movement has had a profound effect on nurserymen's catalogues, and has resulted in many obscure plants coming to the fore, not only for arranging indoors but also for arranging in the garden. The members' taste for beauty of flower and leaf and seed-head will, when history is written, be shown to have altered the trend of horticulture to no small degree. Isn't this a splendid thing? The tentative enlightenment of Gertrude Jekyll in her *Flower Decoration*, followed by the dynamic enthusiasm and originality of Constance Spry and of many others since, were no small flames—they were beacons which have linked county to county and town to town, and show no signs of dying out. The fact that these enthusiasts rob their gardens to beautify their homes matters not at all. In order to cut their flowers they must grow them, and thus they help to keep up the demand, which benefits us all. However, there is a good deal more to this matter than just the growing and picking of flowers; Beverley Nichols, in his *The Art of Flower Arrangement*, explains this to the full. His is a profound and basic book for everyone to study.

The Year's Pageant

The Lungworts and Lenten Roses flower in early spring, followed closely by Fair Maids of France, Globe Flowers, Bleeding Heart, doronicums and *Smilacina*. Peony species start in May also, and go on into June, with the many popular genera like irises, pyrethrums, poppies and lupins, columbines and Burning Bush (though it doesn't "burn" until August). Full summer arrives with its wealth of flowers, the popular delphiniums, sages and numerous members of the Daisy Family—*Anthemis* and *Achillea* for instance. There are so many easily grown sun-lovers that one is apt to forget the shady or moist nooks where orchids and primulas are already fading. August is the month of the *Phlox*, *Helenium*, *Sidalcea* and others of the Mallow Family, the Day Lilies, astilbes and the neglected montbretias. Late phloxes linger into September, when it is the turn of the Monkshoods, Willow Gentian, the Toad Lilies and the Michaelmas Daisies; there are still flowers to be seen in October, from *Nerine*, Kaffir Lilies, *Cimicifuga*, Fortune's Saxifrage and *Liriope*. In between there are flowers of every colour, height and shape, and for every week. The last display comes from the berried pods of the Gladwyn iris, which can to advantage be grown under *Mahonia* 'Charity' to brighten the November garden—and at that time too the Algerian iris may start to flower, spanning the winter months.

With all this to our hand could a garden be conceived satisfactorily without perennial plants?

> "What we want to encourage is a greater variety, contrasted or grouped to show off habit and colour to more advantage than could be done by any one set of plants set down in juxtaposition."
>
> James Anderson: *The New Practical Gardener*, 1873

Chapter 2

Interlude: The Gathering of the Plants

Infinite numbers, delicacies, smells,
With hues on hues expression cannot paint,
The breath of Nature and her endless bloom.
James Thomson, *The Seasons,* 1730

A glance through the plant list will quickly show how very few of our garden favourites are natives of Britain. Lily-of-the-Valley, Monkshood, Yarrow, Columbine, Marsh Marigold, Meadow Buttercup, Sea Holly, a few geraniums and a couple of Hellebores, Absinth, the Pasque Flower, Dropwort and *Veronica spicata* are some which are grown in their natural state, or as double or specially coloured forms. There are as many more among lesser plants, and a number of ferns and variegated forms of grasses.

Since early gardens were mostly given to fruits and vegetables and herbs for cooking or medicine, with them we can imagine a number of ornamental natives being grown. The Globe Flower, from northern and western Britain, was recorded as arriving in London gardens in the late sixteenth century, together with the newly discovered double form of *Ranunculus acris*, and it is at this time that gardening as we know it today began to take shape.

Though no gardens remain, in this country, of the Renaissance period, we have contemporary pictures to help us realize the inventiveness that had given rise to the geometrically designed beds and borders, of "curious design", surrounded by arched alleys. Here we may note that the profession of architect in this country was also established, and this prepared the way for the design of gardens. These knot-gardens as they were called—from the intricacy of the patterns of the beds—formed a repository for all kinds of plants. The new desire for beauty in all things led people to study and copy foreign art; much of the learning and the plants came from countries that lay around the Mediterranean. Herbs and simples having already arrived for the sake of their value to life, the purely ornamental plants followed, though all kinds of magic properties were conjured up for them. Versed in the study of all sorts of living creatures and plants, men travelled far and wide seeking for the rare and new. Plants, bulbs and seeds reached the gardens of north-western Europe, particularly England.

The date 1596 is often quoted for the introduction of plants. This is due to the publication in that year of John Gerard's *Catalogus* of the plants grown in his garden near London. The next year he published his *Herball*; this was served up as his own work whereas he had really used and unblushingly published under his own name an original work by Dodoens, a great Belgian botanist. These were some of the first books which called attention to the numerous "new" plants which had reached northern Europe.

The Oriental Poppy was one of the early arrivals from the Middle East, secured by Joseph de Tournefort, whose name is commemorated in *Origanum tournefortii, Eryngium tournefortii* and *Echinops tournefortii*. The Tulip arrived in Holland at some early date, and subsequently the raising and propagating of

8

new kinds reached such a pitch that fortunes were made and lost over them in the seventeenth century. At the same time hitherto unknown plants in Europe were introduced from the new Spanish Empire in the West. One of these was the potato.

During the eighteenth century many good plants reached our gardens from the East, via the Imperial Academy of Sciences at St Petersburg. *Nepeta mussinii* commemorates Mussin Puschkin, after whom, again, is named *Puschkinia scilloides*. Bieberstein, Maximowicz, Mlokosewitsch (*Paeonia mlokosewitschii*) were collectors continuing into the beginning of the twentieth century whose names are preserved in our plants. Plants also reached Europe from the Far East in early days over the routes which the merchant caravans took to bring silk and spices to the European courts. Wherever trade was carried on, in between wars and other upheavals, so plants also travelled, until today certain plants which have for long been treasured in our Western civilization, like some of the archetypal Bearded Irises, can no longer be ascribed as definitely wild to any precise spot.

Some important garden plants were brought from the hinterland of China in the first half of the nineteenth century by Nathaniel Wallich, Edward Madden and Lady Amherst, such as *Podophyllum emodi, Bergenia ciliata ligulata, Cardiocrinum (Lilium) giganteum, Geranium wallichianum* and *Anemone hupehensis*.

As time goes on the diaries of these travellers become more interesting and full of detail, and those who are desirous of tracing the romantic history of the discovery of plants could not do better than read *The Quest for Plants* by that painstaking historian Alice M. Coats. Through the many pages we can gain an idea of the difficulties of travel in those days, the slow sea journeys and shipwrecks, the hazards and dangers, the suspicions of the native peoples of the mad English (and other nationalities) who travelled regardless of personal discomfort to take home these weeds of other countries. Some returned for a second journey, others perished in foreign jungles and on mountainsides, either cherished or forsaken by their native helpers. And for hundreds of years this has been going on, all over the world.

Soon after the colonies were established in Virginia plants began to travel across the Atlantic into England, some of the earliest being the hardy Maidenhair Fern, *Adiantum pedatum*; the sweetly scented Solomon's Seal relative, *Smilacina racemosa*; *Yucca filamentosa* and *Echinacea purpurea*. Famous travellers and collectors in the eastern coastal areas were the Tradescants, father and son (*Tradescantia virginiana, Aster tradescantii*), Catesby, Bartram (who sent over *Monarda didyma*) Fraser, and Michaux, all of whom are immortalized in different species. The parents of our garden penstemons, *P. cobaea* and *P. hartwegii*, were introduced by Thomas Nuttall (of *Cornus nuttallii* fame) and Theodore Hartweg. In California Thomas Coulter found *Romneya coulteri*.

The strawberry has a nice story. *Fragaria chiloense*, from the Island of Chiloe off the coast of Chile, was discovered *c.* 1717 by one Amédée Frézier, a Frenchman with Scottish Frazer ancestors. Miss Coats calls attention to the fact that the French *fraise* and the Scots heraldic 'Frazier' may have some connection.

David Douglas, for ever to be remembered in the Douglas Fir, was the agent in bringing over *Gaillardia aristata, Sidalcea malviflora* and *Lupinus polyphyllus*—the latter to become the parent of one of the most popular of all plants—from his collecting around 1827.

In much later times, some fifty years ago, both Harold Comber and Clarence Elliott brought back good things from Chile, *Alstroemeria ligtu angustifolia, A. haemantha* and the near-white fuchsia. E. K. Balls was one of my workmates at Clarence Elliott's famous Six Hills Nursery in the early 1930s, and he discovered

Salvia haematodes in Greece in 1937. This is one of the daintiest salvias for the June garden.

Since early times our travellers used the routes via Cape Horn or South Africa to make their journeys round the world. In this way, while the storms and dangers of the Magellan Straits would hardly be conducive to botanizing, a spell under the lee of Table Mountain would be inviting. Perhaps this is the reason why many of our favourite bulbous plants from South Africa crept in without any record of their arrival—a *Gladiolus* or two, *Agapanthus, Crocosmia* and *Crinum*. It was comparatively easy to transport seeds and dormant bulbs, but imagine what precautions would be needed to send living plants safely home, perhaps through the tropics and with months at sea. But succeed they did, partly through the use of Wardian Cases. These were made like miniature greenhouses, and stood on deck, the plants being protected from wind, cold and salt spray. They were kept closed, even in heat, and the moisture around the roots did not evaporate but condensed on the glass and returned later to the soil. These cases were the invention of Dr Nathaniel Ward, and they solved in great part the transportation of living plants around the world. Such details, together with reproductions of ancient pictures, letters and diagrams, are to be found in Kenneth Lemmon's *The Golden Age of Plant Hunters*. This also, no less than Miss Coats's book, is an enthralling account of plant discovery, and carries one in thought to those journeys by sea, so fraught with difficulty and hardship.

I have saved until last a paragraph or two concerning the treasure house of the Far East. Very early travellers were already paying visits to Japan and the seaboard towns of China, and in fact two well-known plants from China, the so-called "Persian" Lilac (*Syringa persica*) and "Syrian" Hibiscus (*Hibiscus syriacus*) had reached us from the Middle East, and hence their misleading names. Trade prospered with China and travellers went farther inland as the centuries passed. The Chinese people, followed of course by the Japanese, had been keen cultivators of flowers for far longer than the peoples of Western Europe, and had brought the culture of chrysanthemums and a few other flowers to a considerable level. Chinese plants reached Japan and vice versa, and the naming of these garden discoveries consequently could not be based on a knowledge of which plants were natives of one country or the other. This is why several plants with a specific name of *japonica* are really natives of China.

By the middle of the seventeenth century practically all trade with Japan was stopped by the Emperor's edict, after troubles with Europeans. The doors were not fully opened for a long time, though certain Dutch travellers, Engelbert Kaempfer, Carl Thunberg and Philipp von Siebold, are commemorated in the names of plants they sent back: *Iris kaempferi, Hemerocallis thunbergii, Primula sieboldii* and many others. William Kerr is remembered in *Kerria* and also for the gift of *Lilium tigrinum* (now to be called *L. lancifolium*). By 1860 things had improved and Robert Fortune collected *Saxifraga fortunei* and the splendid *Primula japonica*.

From then onwards China and its western states, neighbouring countries and the Himalayas, have been combed and combed again by a stream of illustrious plant collectors. With the genus named after d'Incarville of mid-eighteenth century and the specific name commemorating Père Jean-Marie Delavay, *Incarvillea delavayi* is rich in association. Père Armand David is remembered by *Lilium davidii* and *Davidia involucrata*. E. H. Wilson has many plants to his name but *Lilium regale* must rank with his best. George Forrest, Reginald Farrer, William Purdom, Euan Cox, Kingdon Ward and George Sherriff are conspicuous by the many splendid plants they discovered or introduced, many of which have been named after them. Kew and other institutions, and syndicates of private individuals, subscribed to the expenses of their journeys.

It is a long story of toil, disappointment and triumph. And I think people of our generation can look back with intense satisfaction to having lived in a century which was without doubt the climax of the pouring in of foreign plants, never to be equalled again. In this small island, whose climate is so much maligned, it is amazing that we should be able to keep so many plants in health from so many countries all over the world. I have omitted Australia, New Zealand and Tasmania as they have not contributed so many perennials as woody plants for these islands, but they have played their part too. The British climate can accommodate plants from the swamps of ice-cold Alaska, to tropical mountain tops, and south to further extremes. While many have thrived, many have been lost and need to be reintroduced for further trial, and journeys of exploration and collecting are going on in various parts of the world today.

These pages have indicated a mere tithe of the fascinating history of plants. At Cambridge Botanic Garden you will find a series of beds planted to illustrate some of the story. At Kew in the Queen's Garden is a demonstration of the type of garden that was created in the seventeenth century with plants of the period. In the National Trust a smaller effort is at Moseley Old Hall, Wolverhampton, a house treasured because Charles Stuart stayed there for a night after the disastrous battle of Worcester: only plants in cultivation at the time are used. At Westbury Court, Gloucestershire, the Trust has reinstated the same assortment of plants that the records show were used in 1700. There are also period gardens, created mainly by one generation of owners, illustrating garden fashions through the centuries in various countries. Plants were arriving from abroad all the time and had an immense influence on garden design. Just as the medicinal and culinary plants had caused the making of little beds whence they could easily be culled, so we find in the nineteenth century two great new gardening pursuits opening up—the creation of the great arboreta or collections of foreign trees and also the use in beds on the lawn of the numerous, tender, dwarf-growing plants, nursed along for spring planting in the also new greenhouses. Complementary to these two gardening styles for growing the new plants no doubt sprang the borders where the new perennials were grown; mere collections at first, awaiting the appraisal and artistry of Gertrude Jekyll and others. But this really belongs to the previous chapter.

The influence of plants upon gardening in general is not of course solely concerned with the botanical institutions and the wealthy amateurs sending their men abroad for plants to beautify their gardens. Leading nurserymen also sent collectors abroad or took shares in the expeditions. Nurserymen were foremost in propagating and distributing the results, and also devoted much time and energy and expense to raising successive crops from seed, selecting good forms or hybridizing.

So far back as the seventeenth century we hear of firms who became famous; part of the garden at Hampton Court was laid out by London & Wise of Brompton Park in the reign of William and Mary. The great landscapists of the next century, Kent, Brown and Repton, would have been able to turn to Kennedy & Lee of Hammersmith, and Lucombe & Pince of Exeter, for their supplies of trees. The first partner of the latter firm is best remembered in the hybrid oak, *Quercus × hispanica* 'Lucombeana', good specimens of which grow at Killerton, Devon. Kennedy & Lee were instrumental in popularizing the then new fuchsias.

Many great firms started when the arrival of plants from abroad became a high tide, even a flood, and Conrad Loddiges & Sons of Hackney were to the forefront as vendors of many of the newer trees, shrubs, orchids and other tender plants which became so much a fashion of Victorian times. The vast walled kitchen gardens of the period would have had their trained fruit trees

11

supplied by Rivers of Sawbridgeworth, whose name is commemorated in many good fruits, Jackman of Woking, Standish & Noble of Sunningdale (*Lonicera standishii* and *Rhododendron × nobleanum*) and Bunyard of Maidstone. Seeds of bedding plants were supplied by Sutton & Sons and Thompson of Ipswich. Farther north we hear of Artindale of Sheffield—*Eremurus* was a speciality— also Fisher of Sheffield, Backhouse of York and Dickson of Edinburgh. Abroad some well-known firms were Lemoine, Vilmorin and Van Houtte, and their names are found attached to many plants. The great firm of Veitch of Chelsea was to the forefront towards the end of the nineteenth century and this firm, Barr & Sons of Covent Garden and James Kelway of Langport bring us nearer to the present day. The last two firms have always been closely associated with perennials and we will return to them later.

I am always hoping that one of our garden historians will give us a full history of nurseries, before all the records disappear to make way for the ubiquitous Garden Centres. What an absorbing tale that would make—the reception of plants, the shares in explorers' journeys, the early hybrids, the fluctuating demand for plants, quickly in fashion and as quickly out of it. Miles Hadfield has given us enough information in his *Gardening in Britain* to make us ask for more. In a lighter vein, the names alone would open up amusing thoughts, as for instance the firm of Rich & Cooling of Bath; did they by chance also sell tobacco? and Messrs Peach and Stone—were they growers of fruit trees? I have recently seen a garden shop called Laurel & Hardy. But that is a subject for much research, and we are concerned with the herbaceous plant.

I have been collecting nursery catalogues since my youthful days; many a halfpenny of pocket money went on postcards which in return brought me much information and delight. Looking again at some of them and also those in the wonderful collection of catalogues at the Lindley Library, Vincent Square, and at Wisley, I came across one of the now defunct firm of Forbes of Hawick, dated 1901, a compact little volume, not illustrated but containing a vast number of plants. There were no less than 100 varieties of penstemon, 60 gaillardias, 120 pyrethrums, 37 montbretias and—believe it or not—350 phloxes. A year later a Barr & Sons catalogue, illustrated by line drawings and photographs, contained an astonishing array of hardy plants: over 260 irises—one of the firm's longstanding specialities—10 cypripediums and 200 peonies; they also called special attention to *Iris pallida* 'Princess Beatrice', a name which crops up repeatedly in old publications, and I believe it to have been identical to *I.p. dalmatica*. They listed both the green and the variegated forms of *Hemerocallis fulva* and *H.f.* 'Kwanso Flore Pleno'. They had 15 bergenias and 16 funkias (hostas) and later went in for hellebores, in 1937 listing 36 species and varieties, mostly named forms of the *H. orientalis* complex.

Kelway of Langport always produced sumptuous catalogues and it is little short of amazing that their catalogue of 1910, a fat, bound manual with *art nouveau* drawing on the cover, contains 14 large pages of gladioluses, 10 pages of pyrethrums, 38 pages of peonies—one of their prime specialities through the years—and hosts of delphiniums. They included some beautiful coloured photographs, and I have a large peony catalogue of theirs of 1928 of 32 pages similarly illustrated. Looking at the Enfield catalogue of Perry for 1910 we find an interest being taken in Day Lilies—19 of them—over 30 ornamental grasses and 50 hardy terrestrial orchids. Those were the days! Orders would have been from the big private gardens for one or more dozens of a kind, not the collectors' miniature orders of today, often limited to one of a kind.

In Ireland much the same occurred. The Lissadell firm at Sligo in 1913 provided 12 species of *Meconopsis* including *M. punicea*, only one funkia, *Myosotidium nobile* (now *M. hortensia*) and 60 kinds of *Primula*. At Newry,

Tom Smith's famous Daisy Hill Nursery a year earlier listed 12 funkias, 9 euphorbias, 8 ferulas, 18 eryngiums including *E. proteiflorum* (considered rather a treasure trove today); he made a great speciality of 24 kinds of megaseas (bergenias) and I am pretty certain that Miss Jekyll must have had supplies from him. His list also abounded in the big and the coarse moisture-loving plants and grasses, much admired and advocated by William Robinson. The firm that did as much as any to foster interest in the grand type of plant was Gauntlett's of Chiddingfold; their massive volumes of trees, shrubs and plants are a constant source of delight, with innumerable photographs and descriptions which reveal a deep interest in the plant as opposed to just the flowers. Half an hour spent in browsing through the 400 pages is as good as any refresher course, and makes one realize yet again the wonderful variety that is available among garden plants. I coveted one of these fat catalogues as a youngster and wrote asking for one. The reply came back that they were 10s. each ... "but if you have a country seat we shall be pleased to send one free of charge". Alas! I had no country seat, and it was many, many years before I acquired a second-hand copy, after the firm had ceased to function.

Later on, in the 1930s, there were many good firms growing hardy plants, and the excellent collections of Waterers of Twyford, Maurice Prichard of Christchurch and Wells of Merstham may be remembered. It comes somewhat as a surprise that in 1936 Wells listed 31 Oriental Poppy forms. Prichard showed the way with many hardy geraniums; he also listed 40 montbretias and 40 *Iris kaempferi*. In a more catholic sphere we can recall Ernest Ladhams' remarkable lists from Elstead. He was a great seeker after the choice and rare.

With the ever-growing interest in gardens, it is obvious that the wealthy, during late Victorian and Edwardian times, caused a really remarkable number of plants to be grown and catalogued. And with such an influx of plants it is not surprising that gardeners have been imbued with enthusiasm for collecting, selecting and breeding their new-found plants. The great conifers of North America have taken their permanent place in the grounds of stately homes of the British Isles, and remain more or less static, but during the last hundred years or more many generations of perennial plants have been raised.

Not only can we visualize the lucky head gardeners who could order to their heart's content but also the lucky nurserymen whose static, ill-paid staff knew every plant by name, by leaf and almost by touch. The trend has always been towards great collections of "improved" varieties within certain genera, leaving the individual plants to follow on with less care. All we can say in defence of the modern trend towards drastically reduced collections is that it is far easier to select from say twelve kinds than from a hundred or more. There is no doubt that the proliferation of varieties during the early part of this century was quite unnecessary, and it only happens in certain very popular genera today, to a much smaller degree. Unfortunately in their haste to reduce collections, the nurserymen very often discard a variety that is unique in colour, time of flowering or is shorter or taller than most.

Today the most carefully arranged, comprehensive, informative and best printed catalogues of plants are produced in Germany. Several great firms with long traditions continue to provide us with quite remarkable treatises. It would seem that the Germans in particular have realized that garden perennials are of importance and Hagemann of Hanover, Arends of Ronsdorf and Kayser & Siebert of Darmstadt are well to the fore. Herr Richard Hansen has contributed to our knowledge with his *Namen der Stauden* and his list of plants grown in the trial grounds at Weihenstephan, München. In Holland the firm of B. Ruys had also a long and detailed catalogue, and Dr B. K. Boom in his *Flora der Geweekte Kruidachtige Gewassen* has attempted at last a basic and exhaustive

13

review of plants in general cultivation in Holland in an endeavour to get some uniformity into catalogue nomenclature.

We have seen the rise and fall of some big collections during this century. Certain genera have been taken up, many hybrids or forms have been raised and then, like the Earlham Montbretias, have been dropped. The great day of Michaelmas Daisy raising is past and the Korean chrysanthemums, starting life as a hardy strain, have been so hybridized with other groups that they can no longer be safely regarded as true perennials.

Through many decades the Royal Horticultural Society's Trials at Wisley have helped to sift through the dross and pick out the nuggests. Trials of hardy plants and vegetables were started in 1905, and ever since then a constant and growing stream of information regarding the genera on trial has reached us through the invaluable *Journal*. In addition we have been able to visit Wisley and select our own favourites. This is one of the many benefits that the Society provides for its members and the general public. The trials are mainly concerned with man-made varieties. We are lucky also to have the list of plants which have been given the Award of Garden Merit to help us sort out the species and isolated cultivars. (See No. 22 in Cuttings from My Notebook.) There is of course a great number of perennials growing at Wisley and at Kew, Oxford and Edinburgh and many other botanical and horticultural institutions, to say nothing of the splendid selection at Bressingham, Norfolk, and at Beth Chatto's, Elmstead Market, Colchester.

You might ask why I constantly stress the value of the original species, when possibly they have never been great sellers since their introduction, perhaps three hundred years ago. Has this not been long enough for them to prove their worth? It is not quite so simple as that. When once a new hybrid is raised and a strain develops the nurserymen find it easy both to cultivate and catalogue a string of varieties, all variations on the one theme. They "catch on" with the buying public. They make a "noise" in the horticultural world. They become the fashion, but their in-breeding often causes weaknesses as fast as the strain "improves". In spite of this disadvantage, these new races with their popular and collective appeal tend to drive the individuals which have not been "selected" and "improved" into obscurity. In the desire to put the new seedlings on the market, testing is all too short. Many a variety is claimed to be an "improvement" on another whereas, after it has been grown *throughout the country* for some years, it is found to have as many fresh disadvantages as it has advantages. Particularly is this true of roses, though it also occurs in the popular genera of herbaceous plants, which include bulbs. But every now and again some outstanding and invaluable cultivar is named, and so perhaps a steady but slow advance is made.

The public too seem to like all flowers to be not only larger and brighter but also more obvious, flatter and more staring. This is why the marvellous shape of the daffodil has been degraded into a circle of ever wider, thicker, broader perianth segments, and even the protruding trumpet, the joy of the whole flower, is more than just degraded and turned into another flat circle: it is perhaps even slit into lobes. It is why, also, the falls of an iris—another exquisite three-dimensional flower—have to be "flaring"—that is, raised and flat rather than recurved and drooping; the consequence is that the flower is less conspicuous at a distance. It is why the beautiful lily-shape of a hemerocallis has to be made broader and flatter and more open—resulting, I presume, in one bright orange, extremely broadly segmented and widely open variety being given the derogatory name of 'Cartwheels'; or was it named after something quite unconnected? If so I tender my apologies to him who named it. The daisy flowers have this wide, circular, upturned form of flower; they look one in the face and leave nothing to the imagination. Why should other flowers of such highly differing character be made like them? And even the poor daisies are almost invariably turned into doubles, as if it were shameful to have a yellow central disc. Another example is the new strain of antirrhinum, in which the amusing monkey-mouth flower has been down-graded into a segmented circle.

We cannot place all this entirely at the nurserymen's door; many amateurs have also had a hand in it. It is in my opinion a deplorable trend and something which will eventually rebound on us and turn our attention back to the many entrancingly different flower shapes available. It is a blind age with horrors on every side; we have buildings, not architecture; sound not music; words not poems; and unfortunately the greater the number of blatant flowers that are sold the more money accrues from them, and the more will be raised. It is a vicious circle.

By going back to nature's classical forms we may therefore do ourselves a good turn; we shall certainly have a more varied and interesting garden, possibly at the expense of some vivid colouring. We shall not achieve the huge blaze of colour at one time that many varieties of one species can provide; rather will our garden have many smaller highlights through the season. We shall learn what an inexhaustible fund of plant variation there is among the species, which are of timeless beauty.

At the same time I should not like it to be thought that I eschew all hybrids; far from it indeed. As you go through my list you will find extolled many a hybrid. There are some superb plants among them which, because they have not been developed into an in-bred strain, still maintain their poise, balance and good health. Fortunately our leading hybridist among perennials today, Alan Bloom, realizes this, and spreads his hybridizing and selecting over a great number of genera. A few of his most successful plants are *Gaillardia* 'Mandarin', *Aconitum* 'Ivorine' and 'Bressingham Spire', *Dicentra* 'Adrian Bloom', *Echinacea purpurea* 'Robert Bloom', some heucheras, veronicas, erigerons and *Achillea* 'Moonshine'. There are many more. Some older hybrids of other origin that I could not do without are *Aster × frikartii* 'Mönch', the Japanese *Anemone* 'Honorine Jobert', *Primula* 'Rowallane Rose' and *Hosta* 'Royal Standard'. It is when breeding goes on and on through the years that trouble starts to occur and boredom sets in.

There is another and totally unrelated reason for certain plants just remaining in cultivation, but neglected, and that is the changes in fashion that keep occurring. I need only cite some *Hosta* species which have been in cultivation for 150 or more years, and *Smilacina*, introduced in 1640. These have only recently become popular due to the interest of flower arrangers and also to the modern liking for woodland gardens.

"We spare no expense in sending out collectors to gather all that is interesting or beautiful in nature, from the humble inhabitant of the arctic regions to the magnificent and lofty productions of the torrid zone; from the humble Linnaea to the lofty Palm; with many thousand intervening species and varieties of nature's choicest gifts, with which our gardens abound."

James Anderson: *The New Practical Gardener*, 1873

15

Chapter 3

Display

Some of us grow plants for their individual interest, be it botanical or economic, biological or historical, or just to amass a collection. We could not do without such enthusiasts: it is they who keep plants in cultivation. Others of us use plants to create a special effect, by their sympathetic affinities or their intriguing contrast of colour, height, density or line. Knowing that it takes many years not only to assess plants and to acquire skill in their cultivation but also to find out how to group them for best effect, I have been at pains to recall here and there in the Alphabetical Lists particular associations which have pleased me in various gardens. There is a further list in Cuttings from My Notebook, No. 16. I am convinced that this is the best way to start; by gathering a number of mental pictures of plant association one can then fit them into a more coherent whole when it comes to planting a larger area. Alternatively, I hope that some of the examples I have suggested will perhaps be food for thought when it is desired to plant, say, a group of three or four kinds in a small area between shrubs.

Some of us, again, have to start gardening on a rough plot without any dominating feature or any shade. Others are luckier in refurbishing older gardens. Wherever and whatever the garden is, though, plants can be found to fill it satisfactorily; it is one of the aims of this book to show how this may be done. Whatever the area is like you will have to decide on what kind of garden you wish to achieve. If you desire a full-blooded herbaceous border in it you could not do better than study Gertrude Jekyll's *Colour Schemes for the Flower Garden*. A number of the plants she used have been superseded by newer varieties, but the basic planning is there and could hardly be improved upon.

Before attempting any such task it would be worth while to visit a few gardens where fine herbaceous borders are still to be seen. The following gardens are in the hands of the National Trust and the National Trust for Scotland or other organizations, and I have listed these because they are likely to be maintained in excellence indefinitely. Others which are in private hands, good though they may be at the moment, come and go with successive generations or ownership.

1. Some gardens where there are borders mainly of Herbaceous Plants grouped and graded according to colour:
    Barrington Court, Somerset.* Garden designed by Gertrude Jekyll.
    Blickling Hall, Norfolk. Colour schemes originally conceived by Mrs Norah Lindsay.
    Bodnant, Gwynedd.
    Cliveden, Buckinghamshire. Two borders of contrasting colours.
    Crathes Castle, Kincardineshire. Several borders of different tints.
    Dunham Massey, Cheshire. Courtyard beds of soft colours.
    Lyme Park, Cheshire. Double borders with graded colour scheme.

* Much of the garden is private and permission to visit should be sought from the Secretary.

Mottisfont Abbey, Hampshire. Double borders.
Overbecks, Devon. Strong colours.
Powis Castle, Montgomeryshire. Four long borders.
Sizergh Castle, Cumbria. Graded colour schemes.
Tatton Park, Cheshire. Various colour schemes.
Upton House, Oxfordshire.

2. Some gardens where there are borders mainly of Herbaceous Plants not grouped and graded according to colour:
Anglesey Abbey, Cambridgeshire.
Arlington Court, Devon.
Carnell, Ayrshire.
Castle Drogo, Devon.
Castle Fraser, Aberdeenshire.
Falkland Palace, Stirlingshire.
Hampton Court, Surrey.
Inverewe, Ross and Cromarty.
Killerton, Devon. Buddleias are included to add self-reliant height in this windy border.
Lanhydrock, Cornwall.
Oxburgh Hall, Norfolk.
Pitmedden, Aberdeenshire.
Packwood House, Warwickshire.
Petworth Park, Sussex.
Polesden Lacey, Surrey.
Royal Botanic Garden, Edinburgh.
The Savill Garden, Windsor Great Park, Berkshire.
University Botanic Gardens, Cambridge and Oxford.
The Vyne, Hampshire.

It is manifest that if herbaceous plants are used with shrubs the resultant mixture will have more interest through the year than if perennials are used alone. The shrubs can be chosen perhaps to give flower, berry and foliage in autumn, winter and spring, before the bulk of perennials start to flower; this is the way to achieve continuity of interest. As a further embellishment, spring or autumn bulbs can be planted under deciduous shrubs which do not clothe the ground too closely themselves, together with hellebores and other shade-loving spring plants. This is the best way to keep up interest in a small garden, repeating the same sort of close-knit scheme in each area.

Sometimes early-flowering plants such as irises, lupins and Oriental Poppies can be grown rather at the back of a bed or border, so that when out of flower they will be obscured by plants that have grown up to produce their later crops. In an area to be set aside for real colour-giving for a specified period of the year, shrubs can be chosen which will enhance the groupings of flower colour and at the same time—notably when they are shrubs with more than one season of colourful beauty—provide not only solidity but further beauty when the perennials are not performing.

Because they are closely connected with the Jekyll colour schemes let us look at the sort of results that can be achieved by the liberal mixture of shrubs and plants in some more of the Trust's gardens. My mind instinctively goes to the purple border at Sissinghurst Castle, Kent, where flowering plants of every tint of mauve-pink, magenta, violet and purple are grouped against a wall covered with purplish clematis, *Solanum crispum* and other climbers. This is in beauty for about three months, from late June to September. Of even longer duration is the display in the renowned white garden, where white and off-white flowers are supplemented by dark green foliage for contrast, and grey foliage for blending. Another area is devoted to sharper colours, salmon, orange and coppery red. The garden devoted to old shrub roses is done in very soft pinks and mauves; irises and *Allium christophii* precede the roses, which are augmented by *Kolkwitzia* and followed later by the soft-toned acanthus, *Hydrangea villosa*, indigoferas and Japanese Anemones.

At Hidcote there are just as many examples. By the house is a garden of soft colours, leading to the Red borders, where orange, red and purple flowers are grown. The display starts with red tulips and polyanthus under shrubs, red *Rheum*, and ends with dahlias and roses in strong colour, while all the time shrubs and plants with purplish foliage and a dusky pine soften the colour clashes. The little enclosure known as Mrs Winthrop's garden has yellow and blue flowers enhanced by the foliage of golden-leafed hop, variegated plants, the fresh green of *Paeonia lutea ludlowii* and a copper beech hedge; bluish foliage accrues from *Thalictrum speciosissimum*, and there is an edging of *Alchemilla*. On a smaller scale are the borders at Tintinhull, Somerset. One area has two borders flanking a long formal pool; the east-facing border wakens one up with a piercing colour scheme of white, scarlet and yellow blended with Mount Etna broom and *Philadelphus*; the western border contains evening tones of soft yellow, pink and mauve. The two are brought into one scheme by the use of clumps of silvery plants and grey-leafed shrubs and by a reiteration of grassy leaves. Another border echoes the Red borders at Hidcote in that it has lots of coppery-leafed shrubs and red flowers, mostly roses, but also yellow-variegated *Cornus*.

Such schemes as these are in big gardens which few of us can hope to achieve or maintain. Even so, they provide inspiration to us mortals with lesser gardens, rather than despair and discontent. At whatever time one goes to these gardens in spring, summer or autumn there will be food for thought and examples to be seen of clever plant association and colour scheming. Although I have had the honour of helping to keep these and other gardens in good heart I feel no hesitation in recommending them as excellent examples because most were schemed long before I came on the scene and are tended in detail by devoted gardeners. Some further examples come to mind.

HARDWICK HALL, DERBYSHIRE. Various colour schemes.

ICKWORTH, SUFFOLK. A colour scheme of purple, blue, white and yellow.

LYTES CARY, SOMERSET. A border of rich colours.

At MONTACUTE, SOMERSET, the borders flanking the old walls are planted with strong colours and coppery-leafed shrubs, yuccas, roses and *Philadelphus*; they are of sufficient strength not to be overpowered by the deep ochre of the Ham Hill stone of the buildings.

MOTTISFONT ABBEY, HAMPSHIRE, has a long raised border on harsh limy soil composed entirely of catmint, hardy crimson fuchsias, and low-growing species of yuccas, which flower very freely in August. Borders of soft colours in the rose-garden.

MOUNT STEWART, ULSTER. Beds and borders in various tints; purple, blue, orange and yellow; pink, mauve, white and grey; red, orange, blue and yellow.

NYMANS, SUSSEX. Here the summer borders are backed by summer-flowering shrubs, *Aesculus parviflora, Styrax hemsleyana, Buddleia* and the like, adding greatly to the floral display of the perennials.

ROYAL HORTICULTURAL SOCIETY, WISLEY, SURREY. Borders of graded colours.

SALTRAM HOUSE, DEVON. Linked with a blue-grey cedar, the colour scheme is of blues, mauves and pinks with some pale yellow perennials, bolstered by ceanothuses, roses, escallonias and the grey of *Rosa soulieana* and other shrubs, together with climbers on the wall at the back.

WALLINGTON HALL, NORTHUMBERLAND. In this cold part of the country it is surprising what grows well. A cool-coloured border starts with the silvery-leafed *Cytisus battandieri* from Morocco, and has Sea Buckthorn, *Rosa fedtschenkoana* and other grey things in the border and on the wall at the back, to grow forward and break the lower plantings of white, pink, mauve and pale blue perennials. A further big border runs through the spectrum from light mauve and yellow, on to crimsons and purples, finishing with strong reds and yellows. A pair of narrow borders is devoted to blue, purple and yellow flowers overhung by yellow climbers on arches.

These are all pretty big schemes, where a large-scale deliberate effect has been envisaged. But in these and other gardens are innumerable small groups—separate from or within the bigger schemes—which can act as reminders to us. I find many people are afraid of colour and they fall into two categories: those who do not understand it and those who are so aesthetic in outlook that they prefer just white with greenery. It is possible that some in the second group really belong to the first group. If one has not played about with a water-colour paint-box, or is colour-blind or is insensitive to the colour-side of beauty, it can well be understood that to try to arrange garden colour schemes would be a daunting task. Such garden owners often fall back on the old idea that flower colours in the garden never strike a discordant note. This is true up to a point, but depends upon how far apart the colours are in the spectrum and what bulk there is.

White, off-white and all pale colours are certainly easier to handle and arrange in gardens than strong colours. There is little chance of a strident clash. After having walked through a garden of all sorts of colour schemes it is a relief and delight to come to an area devoted to greenery, perhaps with some white flowers and silvery foliage. It is like cooling drinks and ices after a hot day. And fortunately there are very few dead-white flowers; we need the off-tints to support their flatness. In the evening very pale colours provide a new delight: when the richer colours fade into the gathering dusk the whites take on a luminous quality. Then does *Eryngium giganteum* assume its ghostly character.

The least satisfactory and satisfying, perhaps, are borders devoted to yellow flowers. Yellow is too near to green for the green to act as a good foil for the flower colour. A better contrast is needed, and this can be attained by including creamy white flowers with or without blue flowers and blue-grey foliage; alternatively an excursion into the other portion of the spectrum would call for the inclusion of orange and red flowers with coppery purple foliage.

No two gardens are alike and we all have our preferences, and while the majority of colours blend happily in the garden with its background of greenery, there is one basic rule which I like to apply wherever and whenever possible. It is that we must carefully place the reds and pinks which have yellow in their composition away from those which have a hint of blue. It is as simple as that, and it will quickly register with the inexperienced after half an hour with a paint-box. It is the basis of all good colour-scheming, whichever sort of red or pink may be your favourite. If we are sensitive to colours we find the difficulty particularly when coming upon orange azaleas growing near to pink and crimson rhododendrons; it occurs as much again later with flaming modern roses trying to look well against the Rugosa roses; it repeats through the season with other plants, dahlias in their own range of colours, for instance, and crocosmias with Japanese Anemones, heleniums with phloxes.

This is no new thought, having been powerfully argued by Gertrude Jekyll. A colour scheme of brilliant orange-reds, flames, salmons and strong yellows is best associated with sharp yellowish greens and some coppery foliage, while the softer colours, the crimsons, pure pinks, magentas, mauves, together with lavender, blue, palest yellow and white assort well with the bluish greens, the silvers and greys—and sometimes with coppery foliage again.

We do not all have large enough gardens to have borders devoted to separate schemes, but it is a safe move in small gardens to group colours in this way even in one border. It is so much easier when wanting to include a new plant to know that by thoughtful placing into its rightful colour scheme it will not upset the plants already there. At the same time if one's garden is small it may be somewhat boring to have one assortment of colours per border; a method of creating more interest is by causing the borders to change colour half way through the season. Thus in May and June it might be of soft tones with *Nepeta, Baptisia, Dictamnus*, hardy geraniums, etc., and burst into yellow and orange in July and August. The shrubs would have to be suitable for either scheme, in which case some copper might not come amiss; otherwise they could be simply of green foliage, producing their flower, berry or autumn colour at other times.

Plants in the garden must fulfil an object—to make it beautiful of course, but at the same time to augment the quality of the neighbouring plants, or to act as a contrast to them. Most plants can be classed as dominant or complementary when it comes to assessing their garden value, and they should be used accordingly. We should take a leaf out of the book of the Japanese gardeners and spend time contemplating the beauty which is spread around us, and it is my belief that the time required for this enjoyable occupation is best provided by using those plants which are permanencies. Being perennials they give us the same display year by year and we can watch it carefully and often improve it by some small alteration or new planting.

The value of good foliage cannot be overstated or overestimated; flowers come and go, but the leaves—whether green or grey, coppery or variegated—last for the whole season and supplement the floral display. In Cuttings from My Notebook, No. 5, will be found some lists of tinted leaves.

It is not generally appreciated that leaf colouring is affected by sunshine and shade. In considering the placing of plants and shrubs whose foliage is other than plain green, we have first the category of densely felted—"silvery"—foliage and those of glaucous hue, all of which almost invariably prefer full sunshine. Both surface-coverings are invented by nature as an antidote to hot sunshine. (Even the glaucous hostas will tolerate more sun than the green kinds.) Some of us like to arrange two borders opposite each other, and perhaps want both to include some grey foliage. So long as the borders both get full sun this is easy, but if one is in sun and the other in shade it is difficult to make them a balanced pair. Real stalwarts like *Artemisia ludoviciana* will do in either, but the only grey-leafed perennials that prefer some "coolth" are one or two hostas and *Anaphalis* species, articularly *A. triplinervis*. This same matter should be borne in mind when using variegated or purplish foliage. Leaves of the last tint need sun to bring them to full colour; in the shade they only acquire a purplish-tinted green. As a general rule all yellow-variegated leaves require full sunshine, but we have the useful deciduous yellow-flushed ones (as opposed to striped or otherwise marked) which are best where the sun's strength is broken. All white-variegated leaves are best in partial or full shade; in a way they are helpful in shady borders, therefore, where silvery foliage is not successful. All of these recommendations are generalizings; there are a few exceptions, as will be realized on considering the needs of the different species.

With all this wealth of material at hand for our mixed plantings and combinations of colour and shape our gardens might easily become a magpie jumble of plants, mere collectors' gardens. I am a bit this way inclined myself, but realize more and more that if one is to have a garden where one can gain refreshment for the mind, its colours and contrasts must be carefully considered.

Just think of the beauty that is available in leaves alone. We can use the big, fingered foliage of peonies, *Acanthus*, anemones, filipendulas, astilbes and hellebores to offset the sword-like leaves of phormiums, the tall irises, the arching Day Lilies and the invaluable range of ornamental grasses. We can plant solid clumps of the bold, rounded leaves of bergenias, hostas and brunneras to contrast with the filigree of ferns. We can get untold satisfaction from the convoluted and scalloped glaucous grey of the Seakale, the woolly grey of Mullein and *Stachys*, the silvery lace of Absinth. No less valuable are the white- or yellow-variegated hostas, the yellow-flushed Marjoram and Meadow-sweet, and the gorgeous coppery purple of *Sedum, Tellima* and others. Considering that even those leaves which are deciduous remain in beauty for four to six months it is small wonder that these varied attractions are so much sought for the augmenting of colour schemes. At the same time these grey, variegated and purple tints should never be planted to excess; true green, in all its varied tones, is the best for creating a restful garden.

Once again a thought occurs which I read somewhere—it sounds like Miss Jekyll—"people forget that green is a colour". Not only is it a colour but it is the most important colour in the garden. It is with us for longest, and without it the garden would be nothing; it would be as well to fill it with plastic flowers.

In the winter the evergreens and the colour of the lawns give us a satisfying background to the winter flowers and the bare twigs of tree and shrub. I love the earliest rich greens—the Lords and Ladies and the *Colchicum* foliage, which are both invaluable for growing between the clumps of daffodils in the sere grass or bare border. At the same time appears one of the brightest tints of the year, the young leaves of the Day Lilies which have affinity to *Hemerocallis fulva*. Their light golden green will charm away a cold spring quicker than anything else. A little later Bowles's Golden Grass (*Milium*) is even brighter. Meanwhile many good greens have appeared, darkly tinted in aconitums and pale and glaucous in *Sedum spectabile*, irises and alliums.

Green during the summer is deep and at times too fulsome, but after being satiated with colourful flowers, as a relief even from white schemes, green is the panacea into which we all need to withdraw at times for refreshment: a pause in life. The long corridor of green hedges and lawn at Hidcote does this; not only is the green a rest, but the undeviating lines are a relief from the many enclosures of colour and interest. One of the most complete changes in a garden is to enter green woodland; everything is there: proportion, contrast, shape and poise, with the soft path of decaying brown leaves. To be able to walk through this sort of scheme in going from, say, one's rose beds to the mixed border is not given to many of us, but to walk under the shade of even a small group of trees is a perfect antidote, with green as amorous as Andrew Marvell's.

Colour schemes for areas devoted to perennials alone are not much use until June. Before then, with the help of shrubs and the larger rock plants, much can be done. The traditional Jekyll-type border does not come into its own until June, when there is a mass of colour to use—irises, Oriental Poppies, *Nepeta*, peonies, *Eremurus*, aquilegias and geraniums; the palette is not lacking. The most productive time of the year is from July to August, when the bulk of perennials flower. True blue and pale yellow are scarce. Strong yellow abounds, also lavender, mauve and purple, but true pink is scarce until the phloxes and anemones appear. Pure orange is a rarer tint than any through the year. In making a definite decision to adhere to certain colour schemes for given periods difficulties are bound to crop up. There is not necessarily a plant of every colour in every height for every week of the year. That is what we should like to find, but in order to achieve just the right colour we may have to put up with a second-class plant. The alternative is to grow an annual plant to give the desired tone, a method employed by many. But I would rather let the nicety of colour go, and be content with the rich mixture of shrub and plant so long as a harsh colour combination did not break the peace of the garden.

"The Chinese ... reject all that are of straggling growth, of harsh colours, and poor foliage, choosing such only as are of some duration ... of beautiful forms, well-leaved, and of tints that harmonise with the greens that surround them."

James Anderson: *The New Practical Gardener*, 1873

Chapter 4

Shade and Moisture

Apart from an undrained swamp no planting problem can be more difficult than that of dry soil in a shady place. When first confronted with these conditions they seem impossible. Yet there are more than just a few plants which will thrive, and I have made suggestions in Cuttings from My Notebook, No. 7. There are, however, places under certain hungry-rooted trees which are hopeless for anything but ivy and periwinkle and common ferns, together with some bulbs and spring-flowering annuals which will come and go before summer. Old beech trees are the worst offenders; little but moss will grow under their shade owing mainly to the roots being so close to the surface. Elm, chestnuts, ash and pine are nearly as bad; birch and oaks are more tolerable, but any tree that is densely leafy creates problems. The best solution for the driest deep shade, if the area lends itself to such treatment, is to strew it with sawdust, which in time will make a foothold for moss on the trodden earth and provide a pleasant spot for sitting. Moss seems to be encouraged by occasional applications of a normal dilution of one of the Paraquat weedkillers.

Usually the higher the canopy the easier is the gardening, though this only applies to normally high trees. Garden shade is often from fruit trees and what we call flowering trees as opposed to forest trees, and these smaller types provide often the only patches of overhead shade in today's garden, apart from high walls and buildings.

If your shade is of this less troublesome kind you will find a host of plants in this book which can be used. If I acquired a shadeless garden my first act would be to provide some shade in order to grow some of the exquisite things which prefer it, and whose charms are not owned by sun-lovers. It is, indeed a prevalent misconception that perennials must be grown in full sun, and this has sprung from the old herbaceous border ideal.

It is true that most shade-loving plants enjoy a cool, somewhat moist, rooting medium. The suitable plants are natives of the rocky sides of hills and mountains, or woodland, and we have to provide some substitute for these conditions in the garden. As a rule they have less of a mass of flowers than the sun-lovers; their often tall but wiry stems lean gracefully and their flowers often nod as well. Their beauty is more easily spoiled by stakes and canes than are the sun-lovers' more flamboyant attractions. The fact of overhead shade, or shade from a wall, often causes them to lean but only the most disastrous lean must make you fly to the shed for a stake. As a rule they will persevere at their chosen angle for the whole season.

The spring season would open with all sorts of hellebores. The plum-coloured sorts would provide a lovely contrast to the cream-flowered shrubs *Stachyurus praecox* and *Corylopsis pauciflora*. The cream and green hellebores could be offset by purple crocuses, and early rhododendrons such as *R.* Praecox Spring-flowering bulbs of course thrive in shade but I have been unable to permit myself the luxury of writing about *Narcissus, Erythronium, Crocus* and the like in this volume. Endless lovely colour schemes are imaginable.

The snow-white *Dentaria pinnata* (*Cardamine heptaphylla*) would overlap with the blue of *Brunnera*, the near-white of *Lunaria rediviva* and the deep mauve-crimson of the biennial *L. annua*; two of the Honesty plants which are so valuable in spring, to say nothing of their later pods. Pale yellow epimediums, *Uvularia grandiflora* and the invasive *Euphorbia robbiae* would present a cool tonic to blue scillas of many kinds.

In the choicer, moister spots some of the most beautiful of spring and early summer flowers should be gathered, all requiring ample humus in the soil. *Glaucidium* and *Trillium*, *Dodecatheon*, *Dicentra* and *Speirantha* would be sprinkled through with Bowles's Golden Grass and the unfurling croziers of choice ferns. *Meconopsis* in glorious blue, white, lavender and yellow will follow.

Where there is room, Lilies-of-the-Valley could be tried, their waywardness alone telling where they might grow or fail, and over and around them clumps of *Smilacina racemosa* and the great yellow leaves of *Hosta* 'Shade Fanfare', *H. fortunei* 'Albopicta' and 'Aurea' would bring a touch of sunlight to the shadiest spot.

Now let us visualize summer approaching and the soil becoming drier. *Campanula latifolia*, with its deep roots, will thrive almost anywhere—often too well!—and *Aruncus* in two sizes is easy to please in shade or sun. The blue, white and cream of these plants could be accentuated by the giant grey leaves of *Hosta sieboldiana* and the mauve of *Geranium nodosum*. *Anemonopsis* would nestle at one end of the bed, away from the coarse growers; lilies of shade-loving types— particularly *Lilium martagon* in plum, pink or white—could be interplanted. In a well-prepared moist patch at the far end *Cardiocrinum* might dominate the whole and later colour could be provided by the wiry *Phlox paniculata* (the species).

Woodland gardens are essentially for spring, but there are several good late flowers which can be used. I would have as many *Gentiana asclepiadea* as I could spare room for; the blue flower sprays last for weeks in September, and need the white-variegated *Hosta* 'Thomas Hogg' for a contrast, with perhaps *Fuchsia magellanica* 'Gracilis Versicolor' nearby. Fuchsias are sun-lovers but do well also in shade, and this one's leaves are a warm mauve-grey in sun but true grey in shade. The alternative would be the grey fern *Athyrium niponicum* 'Pictum'. This group for late summer beauty could be given *Corydalis lutea* and *C. ochroleuca* as a ground cover but kept away from the fern, and columbines could be put in to provide some early summer colour. *Deinanthe caerulea* would give a strange bluish colour.

The gentian would also contrast well with pale yellow *Tricyrtis*, white *Eupatorium ageratoides* and scarlet-berried *Actaea*. By the time autumn arrives the dignity and beauty of *Kirengeshoma* stand revealed and *Saxifraga fortunei* finishes the season with a fluff of white. The beautifully marbled leaves of *Arum italicum* 'Pictum' appear, the pods of *Iris foetidissima* burst to show their orange seeds, and *Galax urceolata* takes on its winter colour. Meanwhile silvery honesty pods flutter in the breeze.

But it may be that you want a green oasis in your shady area; if so ferns are the ideal, with the contrast of hostas and *Carex pendula*, the great-fingered leaves of the shrub *Fatsia japonica* and the grace of non-spreading bamboos.

It is an obvious fact that plants grow in woodland conditions because they need protection from drying winds. Apart from *Glaucidium*, *Deinanthe* and *Meconopsis* all of the above plants will grow for you if their soil requirements are studied, with just a small tree, a good shrub or a wall to protect them from hot sunshine. Those who garden in the drier east and south of England will find such methods least satisfactory, but in the moister west and north many plants will grow in the open without continuous shade.

We can read into this that, if a plant liking cool conditions is moist at the root, it will put up with at least some sun. This would be true of all the plants noted for shade in Cuttings from My Notebook, No. 7, except those specially marked. There is thus a great range of plants which will add beauty to gardens in our counties of heavy rainfall, with or without shade.

Now let us consider some true moisture-lovers, bog-plants, plants for the margins of streams and ponds, or just damp borders. All prefer full sunshine. There is a great range of foliage shapes from *Gunnera* through *Rodgersia* and *Peltiphyllum*, down to the much smaller but still bold leaves of *Caltha*. An equal range is found in grasses and rushes from *Miscanthus* down to *Carex*, and in ferns—which do best away from hot sun—from *Osmunda* down to *Thelypteris palustris*. The flowering season extends from the spring King Cups and Globe Flowers, the early summer primulas and irises, followed by *Filipendula* and *Astilbe* in pinks and crimsons. These assort well with *Lythrum* and *Lysimachia*, but not with the orange and yellow of ligularias and senecios; these blend with the citron of *Primula florindae*, orange-red *Lilium pardalinum* and white astilbes. *Primula florindae* is cool enough in its invaluable pale yellow to assort with the magenta lythrums and the purple lobelias. I prefer to keep the tall red lobelias by themselves, but they can merge into pink and red *Schizostylis*, with whose season they frequently overlap, thus carrying on the colour into October.

Many of us pine for moisture in our gardens. It may sound strange on reading it, but moisture-loving plants thrive where there is good drainage. Ill-drained stagnant soil will kill them more quickly than drought, and before making a damp area, or planting an existing one, it is best to spend a year contemplating the conditions. Many good plants can be made to thrive in a bed that is too dry for them by the simple expedient of sinking a clay flower pot or land-drain alongside; it can be filled up with water from time to time, thus carrying moisture straight to the roots. There are gardeners who will want oozing pipes laid beneath the surface, and spray-lines overhead; who will revel in the idea of excavation and the laying of clay or polythene sheets. To these I would recommend *Moisture Gardening* by Alan Bloom and *The Damp Garden* by Beth Chatto, which discuss in detail every difficulty and eventuality of the project and provide also splendid lists of plants. There is a lushness and magnificence of foliage among the moisture-loving plants which makes them irresistible. With their lush growth comes the exuberance of lush weeds, but many of the semi-bog plants are capable of holding their own against all but the most invasive of weeds, and this aspect of the matter is treated fully in my *Plants for Ground-Cover*. Even the lush grass of a wet ditch can be overcome by establishing *Lysichitum, Peltiphyllum* and the bigger filipendulas.

So there is no need to despair if your garden has no obviously moist place, nor shade. An old friend who gardened on a hot slope in Devon achieved miracles by planting her *Kirengeshoma, Deinanthe*, hellebores, small ferns and the like to the north of small bushes and rocks, thus ensuring a cool root-run on which they throve amazingly.

"Anyone can cultivate an herbaceous border but to grow a natural garden is an art and a science."

F. S. Smythe: *The Valley of the Flowers*

Chapter 5

Tender Plants

We have seen how economics have imposed difficulties upon the commercial production of plants in this country, and that the reduction of varieties in catalogues is one method of combating these perplexities. To a certain extent this procedure will inevitably result in gardens becoming more like one another. The bulk of genera which have been extensively hybridized and selected belong to those of reliable hardiness, proved in gardens through all our counties. Many books have been written about these hardy plants, but in very few of them has much space been given to the more tender genera and species. In addition to my endeavour to call attention to the less known hardy kinds, I decided to devote a chapter to plants which would be regarded as tender in Surrey.

It is a strange characteristic of gardeners in the British Isles that they always seek to achieve success with plants which are not quite hardy in their gardens or which present difficulties in regard to soil or moisture. As soon as we are possessed of a sunny wall we cast around for some tender plants which might be tempted to thrive on it; a gardener on limy soil makes up beds of lime-free compost in which to grow rhododendrons; the shade of a wall or small tree makes us yearn for a bed of *Meconopsis* and *Nomocharis*, and a dry hill slope sets us pondering where a pool and attendant bog garden would look least out of place. Such are the gardener's hurdles, to be overcome if possible, and in the resulting triumph a great satisfaction lies; at the same time I must point out that if we garden with Nature, rather than against her, our life will be easier and the result more restful in every way.

Our climate varies enormously, county by county; my work has taken me into most of them. There are very few generalizations which will hold against criticism. One, however, may be fairly stated: the south-east of Britain is drier than the north-west. Maps showing differences in rainfall and temperature should be perused by all who contemplate serious gardening. Less valuable is a geological map, because neighbouring gardens and the plants that thrive in them reveal quickly the limits of the soil factor. The concentration of heavy rainfall is on high land mostly to the west and north. For instance, parts of north Somerset, north Flint, County Dublin and areas around the Moray Firth are as dry as much of the Midlands. From clouds approaching from the Atlantic rain is precipitated on mountains and high ground, but the western coasts are often comparatively dry. Similarly the beneficent Gulf Stream which protects us from cold brings warmth, particularly to our western coasts, but also flows around the north of Scotland and down to Lincolnshire. For this reason maritime districts of most coastal counties provide places where tender plants will thrive. As a general rule frost is not so severe by the sea. There are plants thriving in Morayshire maritime gardens and coastal Northumberland that would suffer from frost in Surrey. There are, as is well known, tropical plants growing well in gardens in the south-west of Ireland, Cornwall, the Channel Islands and as far north as Wigtownshire and Argyllshire.

It struck me that were I living in some of these favoured coastal districts, I should want to grow plants other than the perennials and shrubs of proved hardiness. Given such a wonderful opportunity I should not want to be dependent on Floribunda roses, forsythias and lilacs, and all the fully hardy perennials. My garden would be "different", with Cape bulbous plants, tender South Americans, plants from Southern Europe and Asia and the Antipodes. For this reason I have omitted the word "hardy" from my title, have included many plants which will only suit the warmer counties and am devoting a chapter to this idea. After all a book on garden perennials should include anything that can be grown in gardens in the country for which it is written. But it would require several volumes to make it thoroughly comprehensive and I have perforce had to be selective.

There is one further aspect of the matter. Many gardeners today have greenhouses; modern techniques have made their maintenance simple and not too expensive. It follows therefore that many of us who garden in the colder counties will be growing plants which need this protection and encouragement. Here again I would bring out my well-worn theme: why be content with growing just the conventional things in your greenhouse when there are so many beautiful individuals to choose from? Many of the Cape bulbs for instance—nerines, agapanthus and others—thrive in pots and delight us with their flowers. In larger greenhouses open borders can contain perennials of many tender sorts, a delightful change from the ubiquitous chrysanthemums, the inevitable carnations and cinerarias.

Because I think there may be some adventurous spirits who will want to pick out tender plants from the Alphabetical Lists, I have marked these W, indicating warmth, in the Lists. Little has been written about their artistic use in the garden and we are therefore on unexplored ground; and so I will indicate a few suggestions of plant associations, to which you can add after visiting some of the gardens in Devon, Cornwall and other districts where these plants are grown in the open. To these can be added of course beautiful examples in warm corners of gardens in our colder counties.

In soft climatic conditions plants scarcely cease growing in the winter, and the usual geraniums and fuchsias almost span the year with their flowers. The urge of spring is evident in the early appearance of *Helleborus lividus*. I should like plants of this to be perched on a retaining wall if possible, so that their sweetly fragrant flowers were not far from the nose. Below, *Bergenia ciliata* would produce flowers in earliest spring. Its huge hairy leaves would not have to run the gauntlet of late frosts as they do at Hidcote, Gloucestershire. Some dry positions would provide homes for the coral-red of *Erythrina* and those two irises of spectacular foliage and growth—to say nothing of their exquisite flowers—*I. confusa* and *I. wattii*, with the lily-white *Pancratium*, the astonishing blue yucca-relative *Puya alpestris, Hippeastrum pratense*, and some of the less hardy alstroemerias. To give them solidity the large leaves of a yellow-flowering canna would be a useful contribution, and under them all could be sprinkled the little mauve flowers of *Tulbaghia*. If behind them a great tuft of *Beschorneria yuccoides* could be settled, its huge arching sprays of rose-pink and green flowers would contribute magnificently. But it does this wherever it is planted, and to see a dozen spikes growing from one clump of its grey yucca-like leaves is worth a June journey to Mount Stewart in Northern Ireland.

Silvery foliage loves sun and warmth and my favourite silvery plant—*Artemisia arborescens*—is not hardy in Surrey, but its inimitable aluminium filigree would enhance any grouping of soft colours as would be provided by *Agastache, Hibiscus moscheutos, Crinum moorei* interspread by the soft mauve of *Dahlia merckii*.

I can imagine the graceful stems of dieramas, swinging their bells of pink and

27

mauve, purple and white, over agapanthuses; not just the usual Headbourne hybrids, which are pretty hardy anywhere, but the big blue *Agapanthus umbellatus* (of gardens), its handsome white form, and astonishing navy-blue tubes of *A. inapertus pendulus*. Below could be the daisies of several tints of *Osteospermum jucundum* and hybrids, and large-flowered fuchsias of pink and white would complete the picture.

Some plants, like fuchsias, penstemons and *Dahlia merckii*, seem to flower incessantly through the summer, and with some silvery foliage, perhaps from *Senecio cineraria* 'White Diamond', would provide as much gaiety as any hardy shrub or plant.

If your choice is towards the sharper colours I would suggest using *Asclepias tuberosa* in orange, coral *Kniphofia snowdenii* and others (they thrive on warmth), the soft salmon-orange of *Mimulus glutinosus*, the purple of *Linaria triornithophora* and some salmon or orange watsonias. With them perhaps could be placed the maroon *Cosmos atrosanguineus*, and some of the red *Canna* varieties which have large leaves nearly as dark as those of a copper beech. There are several gorgeous red salvias, both herbaceous and shrubby, for such a colour scheme as this, to which the yellow arum *Zantedeschia elliottiana* would be a striking addition. Crocosmias, which do so well in damper sunny gardens, would provide yellow and orange, and here again the rather tender 'Solfatare' with soft coppery brown leaves would be admirable. If a wall is at the back of such a grouping *Eccremocarpus*, followed by *Bomarea*, would add to the general scheme. *Gladiolus × colvillei*, to tone, could be added here and there. All these plants will flower during summer months, some early and some later, and most of them will take reasonable exposure so long as they are not at the mercy of the ocean gales.

In sheltered gardens we might give an area to tropical luxuriance. Here *Myosotidium* would take the place of bergenias for a solid foreground, and the huge grey divided leaves of *Melianthus major*, a shrubby plant, would contrast with the smooth broad blades of that most majestic of cannas, *C. iridiflora*. The nodding crimson flowers would be perfect as a complement to the general soft colour. The great white arum, *Zantedeschia*, would be a worthy companion. Under trees, or with suitable shelter, the tree fern (*Dicksonia*) would provide further shade for the great arching fronds of *Woodwardia radicans* and the dark holly-like fronds of *Cyrtomium falcatum*. Among them, still in shelter, we could grow the orchid *Calanthe* and enjoy the intriguing broad leaves of *Begonia evansiana* and *Arisaema consanguineum*.

If you hanker after the tropical effect and your garden is much exposed to wind, *Phormium tenax*, in its green, purplish or variegated forms, will astonish all at flowering time.

A narrow border could take francoas, around whose spires of pinky white would weave the erect stalks of *Commelina coelestis*, bearing flowers of very true and splendid blue. I am very fond of blue and yellow together and I should try to arrange to have the translucent amber berries of *Coriaria terminalis xanthocarpa* somewhere near to the *Commelina* or *Agapanthus*. *Mirabilis jalapa* would, in its various tints, blend with all these, and also *Salvia farinacea* and *S. patens*.

While all these plants are in flower fuchsias are with us and carry on, until in the autumn they will still be available for all the softer colour schemes and a few of the sharper ones. There is an astonishing range of colours, sizes and shapes available among the large-flowered tender sorts today. These are flamboyant, but I visualize an area of subdued tone nearby, to be created with the two species of all-green *Eucomis*, white crinums and watsonias and the strange greeny-grey-mauve *Gladiolus papilio*.

We should have a burst of pink in September from *Nerine, Amaryllis, Amarcrinum* and *Crinodonna* and I should use lots of silver foliage with them. In between the clumps, dianellas would provide violet-blue berries, and at the back the deep violet-blue of *Salvia guaranitica* (*S. ambigens*) and the sky-blue of *S. uliginosa* would look very beautiful with the yellows of some hedychiums. The contrast in heights might be too much and some 90-cm (3-ft) high plant which had flowers earlier could be interposed, or some *Gladiolus callianthus*. A short distance away the red *Schizostylis coccinea* 'Major' with some of the salmon-red fuchsias could interweave some good tints; by October the watery blue flowers of *Vinca difformis* would carry on flowering into late autumn.

These notes have called attention to just a few of the many tender plants which can be enjoyed in favoured gardens; there are of course hosts of true shrubs, more woody than fuchsias, which can join them through the year.

With regard to soils and manures for tender plants, it is as well to remember that our summers are often not warm enough to hurry the autumn-flowering plants and bulbs into bloom. This is one reason why we plant them against sunny walls. Certain plants—crinums in particular—like rich soil, but if this contains too much nitrogen flowering will not be encouraged. It is better to apply one of the balanced fertilizers containing plenty of potash and phosphate, such as we should apply to tomatoes and fruit trees.

My last point is that where the setting of tender plants against sunny walls is recommended, it should be remembered that these places tend to dry out in hot weather. Water must be given so that not only do the plants grow and flower well but also so that they can complete their growth and absorb goodness through their leaves after the flowers are over. Even so, just to make matters really difficult I must remind you that some plants die off earlier than others; some like a dry summer and others a dry winter....

"Subtropical gardening is quite a modern idea, capable of being carried out to only a limited extent in the gardens of this country."
James Anderson: *The New Practical Gardener,* 1873

Chapter 6

Some Thoughts on Small Gardens

This chapter runs the risk of repeating several of the points I have already enlarged upon. However, this may be excused as it is intended to gather all these points under one heading, for consideration by the owners of gardens of less than a quarter of an acre. Small gardens require as much care and forethought as large ones—or even more, considering that we are probably concerned with one main view for every day of the year.

In other publications and in lectures I have claimed that my idea of a garden is a place which should be as large as possible with the least work and the longest display. Perennials can play an important role in achieving this if chosen carefully. But first I want to put forward a few thoughts on the ordering of small gardens.

To achieve an impression of size in a small garden two things are necessary. One is that the boundaries should be disguised or softened by plant growth of an informal and permanent kind—shrubs or climbers on fence or wall—and the other that the whole area should not be seen in one glance from the windows or major viewpoint. It would be irrelevant to enter here into the general design of small gardens but my second point above can be ensured by allowing a clump of shrubs—or even one shrub of some size—to stand forth and screen a portion of the garden from immediate view. This gives a sense of mystery and interest to even a very small plot.

In a small garden we should try to keep up a display of flower and interest for the whole year, and this is best done by what is known as gardening in four layers—a tree or two, shrubs, plants and bulbs. To achieve continuity of interest through the year it is well to plant one (or more) small trees, such as an Apple or Crab Apple, which will give beauty when in flower and again when in fruit, and will provide some shade for plants that need it. This can be balanced on the other side of the plot by a handsome evergreen shrub, perhaps *Mahonia japonica* or *Fatsia japonica* or *Aucuba japonica*. Green is the best thing to look at daily; variegation can be tucked away to effect a surprise.

The test of a garden comes when the autumn colour has fallen and the birds have gobbled the berries in late November. Just then the Autumn Cherry takes over with *Mahonia* 'Charity' and the berries of *Iris foetidissima*. If we put in some winter-flowering shrubs, such as *Hamamelis mollis* 'Pallida', and other shrubs for winter and autumn colour or berry, and underplant them with hellebores, pulmonarias, winter and spring bulbs, this will see us through until spring really begins, and from April until early June there are plenty of shrubs to screen the boundaries and to provide not only early flower but perhaps a further bonus of autumn colour or berry.

From June until September the bulk of perennials flower, with Kaffir Lilies and nerines keeping the colour going often into November. Meanwhile roses and fuchsias, potentillas and hydrangeas extend their flowering season from mid summer onwards also into autumn, when the brightly tinted leaves and berries once again take over.

Fortunately there are many short and compact perennials to choose from and the list is always lengthening, thanks to Alan Bloom's efforts. He sees the necessity for raising new varieties which not only have good flowers and colours but are also self-reliant and need no staking. Hence his shorter sidalceas and monkshoods and his preoccupation with heucheras, veronicas and erigerons, to name but a few.

This book contains much about tall plants, but the shorter ones, down to at least 300 mm (1 ft) are also included; in Cuttings from My Notebook, No. 1, I record some more short plants. It would be pointless to include here a list of plants for small gardens because the Alphabetical Lists show clearly the approximate height of each. A glance at the "line of facts" will quickly prove this, but perhaps even more important is the width of each plant. It is wise in small gardens to avoid the wide-spreading plants unless one knows how to cope with their flopping branches or incursive roots.

The smaller the garden the more important is the relationship between the scale of the plant and the size of the bed or border, and also the size of each clump. Small gardens tend to be fussily planted, for we gardeners are apt to try to grow as many different plants as possible. This disquieting impression can be minimized by the use of larger patches of dwarf ground-cover plants in frontal positions. And do not cut out ground-cover plants on the score that they only provide leaves; there are many that can play their part nobly in the provision of seasonal flowers. The fourth layer, that of bulbs, comes into its own not only under the shrubby background but also among roses, peonies and dwarf ground-cover.

A trap for the unwary is that many of the smaller plants and shrubs have small foliage. One cannot make a satisfactory garden picture without some big foliage of a rounded nature, like that of bergenias, Japanese Anemones and hostas, contrasted with the erect lines of irises and grasses. Further, if these more conspicuous leaves are kept in the foreground of a view, and the small-leafed shrubs and plants at the end, it will help to make the garden appear larger.

This chapter is not meant to be a blueprint for the small garden; a writer would be unwise to attempt such a thing. Rather is it a broad indication of some possible lines of design and thought, upon which each individual can build while his appreciation of, and experience with, plants increase. Whatever type of garden is contemplated it would indeed be a poor one that could not accommodate some perennials; moreover it is difficult to visualize any garden that perennials would not improve in colour, shape and form, so long as they do not obscure the shrubs which provide a background for them. Here is another point of scale and another reason for the use of short-growing plants: the shrubs should always be dominant, because they are there through the year while perennials are only in growth for a few months. These therefore play a lesser but essential part in the design of every garden, and can unite the bigger isolated features.

Chapter 7

Some Practical Points

This book is not about garden design, nor is it a practical "how to do it" sort of book; rather is it meant to be a help in cultivating a very diverse collection of plants and a guide to the artistry of arranging them in the garden. Even so, I feel I must devote a few paragraphs to the design of the areas—beds or borders—into which are to be put a number of perennials. It will be clear by now that I favour mixing them with shrubs; whether your garden be formal or informal in design shrubs will soften it, give it character and shape throughout the year, which very few perennials can do.

The advantage of growing perennials in isolated beds is that the plants keep more compact and do not tend to draw away from the background, thus needing staking. On the other hand if a border has a good background of shrubs, or climbers on wall or fence, or ornamental hedge, this adds immeasurably to the possibilities of scheming for colours or seasons, or both. Likewise an island bed is all the better for a shrub or two to give a height and solidity through the year. If there is a hedge, wall or fence at the back of the border, a narrow way should be left behind the shrubs and perennials to clip the hedge, sever its encroaching roots every few years, or to prune and tie climbers and shrubs.

It is very rarely that one sees a garden where there is nothing planted around the boundaries at all—where hedge or fence or wall stand nakedly and uncompromisingly in view. It is surely better to soften the line with shrubs of various sizes and seasons of flowering. Perhaps the borders surround a lawn large enough to allow for an island bed in it; if so it will provide a tour around even the smallest plot.

The planting of any given area will depend entirely upon taste and ability. I cannot help you with your taste, but in the Alphabetical Lists I have given the approximate height of each perennial when in flower and the approximate distance apart for planting, having in mind its growth both above and below ground. Apart from plants whose root growth is described as "running" or "invasive" or "questing", which should be used very circumspectly and only in aeas bounded by shrubs which they can scarcely defeat, the combination of the given height and the width will provide a mental picture of the size of the plant. As a general rule one obviously puts the taller plants behind those of shorter growth, but there are two exceptions. They are (a) splendid plants whose whole deportment—basal leaves, stem leaves and duration of respectable growth—is so good and lasting that whatever their height they should have nothing over 300 mm (1 ft) in height in front of them, (b) those plants which have a dwarf basal clump of leaves and tall slender flower stalks: whatever their flowering height they too should be kept in forward positions. Examples of (a) are *Macleaya cordata*, *Crambe cordifolia* and *Verbascum vernale* and (b) *Eryngium eburneum*, *Asphodeline lutea* and pyrethrums.

It is pretty obvious too that plants renowed for their good clumps of foliage, such as *Crambe maritima*, *Hosta* and *Clematis heracleifolia*, should be given positions in the foreground.

Although it is unwise to make hard and fast rules, the relationship of the height of the perennial to the width of the border should be considered. A rough guide is that the plants should not exceed in height much more than half the width of the border. A formal border of one width will therefore present less opportunity for dramatic contrast of heights than a border which is informally designed, with both wide and narrow sections.

In planting isolated beds on lawn or gravel areas, rather less than the above relationship is needed except where the plants can build up, perhaps, to the height of a shrub or two. The only exceptions to these rules are the plants in groups (a) and (b) above; these are invaluable for giving height in certain places.

The width of a plant, apart from those with freely spreading roots, will dictate how many are needed for a square metre (yard), and I hope that this information will be useful to all who have to cope with this fundamental subject, whether amateur or professional. Some plants will more than fill such a square in a year or two; others can be planted thickly, nine to a square. The latter are mostly quite dwarf plants for the front; some bulbs would require even closer planting. In between are the rank and file of perennials awaiting your choice and deliberation. Coupled with the decision you will have to take about quantities per given area lies the varying size and shape of each group. Here again the collector of plants will acquire one of each, and will presumably be satisfied with the spotty effect, but the planting of perennials with or without shrubs acquires its greatest distinction and interest when groups are of different sizes and shapes. Once again those in group (a) above can perhaps be used singly; others with less majesty of port and foliage need several together to make any effect. Just as it is necessary to give and take a little over height, so the size and shape of a group must be a matter of taste. Plants which die away early, like Oriental Poppies, and plants of thin effect, such as bulbs and those in group (b) above are perhaps best in long slender groups, as a round group would create a bigger void when they are out of flower. Miss Jekyll used groups of all sizes but she specially favoured longish drifts of one thing sloping away after another, as will be seen in some of the border designs in her books. It is all a matter of scale in design, coupled with personal preferences.

If a border is to remain in flower for a long time, it is a good idea to put in some of the early plants right at the back, so that, when untidy in late summer, they will be somewhat obscured by later growth in front. The other way of extending the flowering season of a border is to grow what may be called large rock plants, such as *Aubrieta, Arabis*, thrift, pinks, achilleas, etc. along the immediate verge; these will flower early and make a green finish to the front of the border for the rest of the year. There is a big range of such dwarfs, enough to supplement by their summer foliage colour schemes of all kinds. Some suggestions are in Nos. 1 and 2 in Cuttings from My Notebook.

Those whose borders and beds are arranged along a gravel or paved path have an easier task than where they are fronted by grass. Over the paths the frontal plants can flop prettily forward; over the lawn they are a nuisance when mowing. There are certain small plants, *Ajuga, Mitella, Potentilla alba, Sedum spurium* 'Green Mantle', London Pride and the little plants I have already mentioned which can be introduced along the very verge to save hand weeding, but one still has the grass edge to cut. It is a help to have a row of flagstones or bricks laid just under the grass level, among which and over which plants will grow without interfering with mowing. A width of 30–60 cm (1–2 ft) according to the width of the bed or border is ample for the paving.

And so we come to the actual digging and planting. All plants benefit from clean, well-dug soil, enriched with humus and the right nutrients, or old manure, and no amount of work afterwards can equal the value of this initial preparation.

The whole subject was treated at some length in my *Plants for Ground-Cover* to which I will ask you to refer. Perennials transplant best from the end of August until April, according to the variety; those which flower in spring or early summer should be planted or divided in late summer or very early autumn. A lot will depend on the texture of the soil; a sticky soil—heavy or of a clay nature—should be left alone until it is drier. To avoid a lot of footmarks and compacting of the soil surface it is best to use a plank as a platform. If plants arrive when the soil is unsuitable they should be stored in peat or other damp loose material until the time is propitious. If the soil is too dry, it is a good plan to take out the holes with a trowel or spade, fill them with water, and when it has drained away, to put in the plant and surround it with the damp soil. Plants should be made firm with pressure from hand or heel. After planting, prick up the soil surface and do the same after using a hose or sprinkler.

If the right plants are chosen for each spot, subsequent watering is usually unnecessary, except in periods of extreme drought. Even at these times it will be found that a mulch of dead leaves, peat or other compost will be of almost equal value. With a permament thick mulch and a good admixture of ground-covering types of plant, I find it quite unnecessary to dig or hoe; nor are there any weeds except along the lawn verges, which can be removed when attending to the grass edges. Perennials are thus a joy and labour-saving, simply requiring one operation of cutting down in autumn or spring, and occasional division or replanting.

Staking and Supports

Because I grudge the time and effort required for staking or otherwise supporting plants that need it—and it never improves their appearance though safeguarding the growth and blooms—I have added a note where support is usually necessary. All the other plants, in a normal garden and season, unless drawn up by high buildings and trees or bowed by storms, will usually stand up on their own.

To my mind a plant gracefully leaning, or given room to flop, is far more pleasing than a plant which is restrained by canes and string, pea-sticks or wire cages. In some of the gardens of the National Trust for Scotland, notably at Crathes Castle and Pitmedden, a wide-mesh, black plastic netting is suspended tautly over the entire border—except for the very front—60 cm (2 ft) or so above the ground. The plants grow through the netting, which thereby makes it invisible and the growth is natural without being stiff; to all intents the plants are unsupported. This method is admirable for large borders filled solely with herbaceous plants, but is not of course suitable for borders and beds of mixed shrubs and plants. The support provided is similar to that resulting from the use of the excellent old wire-mesh circles used for each plant. A combination of netting and wire supports for isolated groups in a small garden would be easily constructed. In my own garden—apart from an isolated stake which is needed after a gale—the only support I provide is from permanent, thick galvanized hoops which I put round clumps of peonies, and a few other plants. These remain in place from one year to the next. The two legs are about 60 cm (2 ft) long, and they connect to each other by a horizontal half-circle. Two hoops are thus needed for each clump. Those who live in country districts may be able to get branched stems of elder; besides having good forked growth, the stems last for years in the ground, as has been proved at Hidcote.

Soils and Conditions

One important point to bear in mind is that it is useless to attempt too much. It is far better to grow plants which are suited to your garden conditions, soil, aspect and climate, than to try to grow others in untoward conditions. A plant

34

that is healthy gives of its best; the opposite is true of an unsuitable plant and it is prone to diseases and pests. Particularly does this apply to the numerous highly bred cultivars; they are far more susceptible than the tougher species, which is another point in the latter's favour. For instance, the dreaded phlox root-eelworm, iris root-rot, the mite which attacks asters, to name but a few, seldom trouble species of phlox, iris and aster, but the cultivars are highly prone.

We are all apt to think that our soil is "normal", "ordinary", "reasonable" and fertile until we see other gardens or have the opportunity to garden elsewhere. It is really astonishing how plants from countries all over the world will settle down in our different soils. The two most important things about soil are that it shall be well drained and fertile. Fertility can be gauged by the growth throughout the garden and district, and provided that this is at a satisfactory level, and that the drainage is also satisfactory, most plants will settle down happily in most soils. I have added to the descriptions a note about abhorrence of lime or chalk or any special likes or dislikes. Thin acid sands and very heavy soils and clay have great disadvantages, but each can be improved, funnily enough, by the admixture of humus. We will take it, then, that the plants mentioned in this book can be satisfactorily cultivated in reasonable soil, with reasonable fertility and drainage, subject to the requirements noted for each genus or species.

Shade and Moisture were considered in Chapter 4 and the problems of all kinds of soils and conditions will be minimized by consulting the lists in Cuttings from My Notebook.

Chapter 8

A Guide to the Alphabetical Lists

Plants, whether trees, shrubs or herbaceous plants, British or foreign, have been classified according to certain floral characteristics and are broadly grouped into Families. Since this book is so much concerned with plant description I thought it might be helpful to include the Family after the generic name. It will reveal some surprising as well as some obvious affinities.

NOTES ON THE ALPHABETICAL LISTS

The different printer's type faces used in the names of plants in the Alphabetical Lists indicate as follows:

CAPITALS, bold face, for the genus or generic name.

small letters, bold face, for the species or specific name, or recognized botanical variety, form or strain.

'Single quotes', bold face, for a fancy name given to a cultivar or garden form or variety.

(While single quotes are retained for fancy names in the text, generic and specific names and botanical varieties, etc. are set in *italic* face.)

★ Indicates those plants which I consider really good garden plants, judged from the general standpoint of habit, foliage and flower.

● Indicates plants with exceptional or unusual beauty of flower.

× Denotes a recognized hybrid between two genera, if placed before the generic name, and between two species if placed before the specific epithet (or second name).

SPORT ("mutation" in genetic parlance)
A shoot which is different in growth from the parent plant; these shoots usually remain constant when vegetatively propagated and are then termed a "garden variety", "form" or "cultivar".

CULTIVAR (contraction of "cultivated variety")
The vegetatively reproduced progeny of a hybrid, garden form or sport, variety, or of a strain of natural or hybrid origin which when raised from seed breeds reasonably true to type. "Clone" is also used and refers specially to vegetatively reproduced garden forms.

These two terms tend to supplant the old use of "variety" or "form", but not wishing to be too technical I have often contented myself with the older terms.

The Line of Facts

This is designed to enable the reader to pick out quickly plants of certain size, colour, period of usefulness, without having to read through the detailed descriptions.

NOMENCLATURE

I am not going to apologize for the use throughout the book of Latin names. They are essential to avoid confusion and are internationally understood. We have no difficulty over *Dahlia, Chrysanthemum* or *Delphinium*; *Hosta* has rapidly become second nature to gardeners, and other names like *Gypsophila* and *Physalis* are soon accepted by the uninitiated. All of these names have a meaning and significance, recorded in the Royal Horticultural Society's *Dictionary of Gardening*. For further insight we can refer to Dr W. T. Stearn's *A Gardener's Dictionary of Plant Names*.

It has been difficult in many instances to know what botanical name to use. As more species and more variants of species become known from the wild, more and more research goes on so that nomenclature is permanently in a state of flux and there is no single book that is up to date. The *Dictionary of Gardening* has been a useful basis, but I have had recourse to numerous specialized or more recent publications to get as near to correct nomenclature as possible. Even so, I have retained some names simply because they are so well known, and have contented myself with adding the modern synonyms. The trouble is that next week another assiduous and expert botanist, in the light of further evidence, may decide that the new name is wrong and go back to the old! This has happened with several plants. Botany is not an exact science.

The true, old vernacular names are interesting and acceptable, but many of the freshly coined popular names such as "Fairy Bells" and "Fleeceflower" have no real grounding, and merely pander to those who think that Latin names are a nuisance.

DATE OF INTRODUCTION AND COUNTRY OF ORIGIN

As an extra bonus to the species I have given when possible the date of their introduction from abroad into cultivation, which usually means England or Europe. There are many gaps which I should like to fill, but it is a start. These dates are a study on their own, visualized in Chapter 2, and are approximate.

Whenever possible the date of introduction of cultivars has also been given; in all cases the dates cited must be taken with leniency; records differ, and with a number of plants I have only been able to arrive at an approximate date. Corrections and additions will be welcomed.

I have added too the country of origin because this is linked to the date of introduction and the march of events and discoveries through history; in addition it has some bearing upon cultivation, if the world's rainfall and temperature be taken into account, together with the sort of altitude that would be required in a hot country to produce a plant hardy enough for our gardens.

HEIGHT AND WIDTH

The first figure indicates the approximate height of the plant when in flower, the second indicates the distance apart for planting, envisaging its spread in a few years. Today's approved measurements are given in metres and centimetres.

PLANT HARDINESS ZONES IN THE UNITED STATES

The figures in square brackets [] denote the hardiness zones for each species. The zones are based on the average annual minimum temperature for each zone. All plants are designated with a number spread, the lower number indicating the most northerly area where they will reliably survive the winter, and the higher number the most southerly area where they will perform consistently. Many factors, such as altitude, degree of exposure to wind, proximity to bodies of water, snow cover, soil types and the like can create variations of as much as two zones in winter hardiness, while cool nights, shade and amount of water received can extend the southern limits. For map, see pp. 42–3.

COLOUR

Just one word of colour for quick reference, pending examination of the more detailed description.

FLOWERING SEASON

A plant's season of flowering varies greatly through the country. A given plant might produce blooms in Devon in early June, in Surrey ten days later, high up in the Cotswolds another week later; another week would be required for Derbyshire and another for Northumberland, finishing up in August in Aberdeenshire. And so I felt it useless to try to give the months of flowering in Surrey, and have contented myself with a broad indication of its period of flowering. Most plants are responsive to warmth and season in the same way and so a rough guide is thereby obtained.

Nurserymen's catalogues were written mostly according to experience in the field, where young plants are put out in spring for sale in the autumn. The majority of these will flower later and for much longer than an established clump in a garden. In fact, if one has the time and the energy, one should treat certain plants likewise; very long-flowering seasons can thus be obtained from perennials like *Erigeron, Gaillardia, Scabiosa caucasica, Anthemis tinctoria* and *Buphthalmum salicifolium* by planting young divisions each year. The plants so treated will tend to be shorter. Freshly planted pinks, grown from cuttings, will tend to produce successive crops of flower.

W   denotes plants not reliably hardy in Surrey, which have been included because they are good perennials in the south and west, though they may need Warm corners.

FLOWER ARRANGERS' NOTES

P   denotes that the flowers, when Picked for the house, will last for a while in water.

F   denotes that the ripening Fruits or seed-heads have some beauty and use for cutting, even though the flowers do not last in water. The descriptions call attention to the quality and size of the foliage; as a general rule this can also be cut.

Further notes for Flower Arrangers are in Cuttings from My Notebook, Nos. 5 and 17.

PROPAGATION

Many of us want to increase our stock for fresh plantings or to offer in exchange for other choice plants, and the normal methods of propagation are shown by the following letters.

C   CUTTINGS. I have only called attention to this method where cuttings can be taken of *portions of stems during the growing season*; it must be understood that practically all herbaceous plants, other than Monocotyledons, Ferns and Grasses, can be increased by means of short basal cuttings, preferably taken with a heel, and rooted in a frame of sandy soil in spring. Stem cuttings can be treated likewise.

D   DIVISION (AND PLANTING). Many plants when lifted pull apart quite easily, the best growth being made by the outer shoots with young roots. Some very thick, heavy clumps, such as *Hemerocallis* and *Hosta*, can be chopped up with a spade, or portions removed by cutting out sections as one might dissect a round cake. Peonies and woody-rooted plants need lifting bodily and separating with the help of a knife. Two forks levering back to back will force apart plants with matted roots. Unless otherwise stated in the descriptions, divisions can be made in autumn or spring, or during the winter with very hardy, easy plants; this also applies to *planting* generally. Greyleafed plants and grasses are most successful when planted in late spring.

G   GRAFTING. Though gypsophilas can be rooted from cuttings the larger kinds are usually grafted onto pieces of root of *G. paniculata* in a greenhouse in spring.

     LAYERING.

R   ROOT CUTTINGS. Many plants with fleshy thongs or woody roots can be propagated by cutting the roots into 25–75-mm (1–3-in) lengths and inserting flat or upright in sandy soil, barely covered. Some of the thickest of roots will sprout if put into nursery beds; the thinner ones require the aid of a frame or greenhouse. Late winter is best.

S   SEEDS. Any genuine species can be propagated from seeds, perhaps showing some variation—or even a chance new hybrid—but the cultivars and forms, in the event of their setting good seeds, will be likely to show much more variation and should only be increased vegetatively. Hellebores, gentians and primulas should be sown when ripe; they may not germinate until the spring or even a year later. Most will germinate well if sown in prepared soil in early spring in cool greenhouse or frame; the more ordinary and hardy, big-seeded plants can be raised like peas and carrots in the open ground by sowing in March, or as soon as ripe in late summer. To get good germination of *Baptisia* and *Lupinus* it is usually necessary to chip the seed-coats—a laborious job.

The Descriptions
I have tried hard to avoid clichés, principally those which are careless and give a wrong impression. To say, for instance, of *Campanula rapunculoides* (a notorious but very decorative weed) that "its roots must be watched" is a masterpiece of understatement. I have been frank about plants which are invasive. I have also tried to avoid silly colour descriptions like the ubiquitous "golden yellow"; the word "gold" cannot enhance the brilliance of strong yellow. On the other hand I find terms like salmon, emerald, citron and wine helpful—and I hope you will too. Terms of the paint-box and spectrum are more generally useful than those of scientific colour charts, which we do not all possess. Colour is a difficult subject, no two people seeing it alike, and it can also vary a lot with the time of day, the soil, climate and season; also with altitude and latitude, some colours being much richer as one goes north.

In the descriptions, either generally following the introduction to the genus, or more particularly following the discussion on each species, there are notes about culture, staking and like matters. These are amplified in Chapter 7.

The Quotations
Since several of these appeared in the original *Modern Florilegium*—along with the line of facts for quick reference—I thought it would be pleasant to continue with them. I have therefore added many more and have included some other authors. Here are some details about them.

GH   Gerard's Herball, 1597. This happened to be on my shelf with other books and I have included some quotations from his book which show how, at that time, people were more interested in what they thought plants meant and did and were; there are some amusements as well.

WR   William Robinson, *The English Flower Garden*. First published 1883; Fifteenth Edition, reprinted 1934. Robinson, through his voluminous writings in his periodicals *The Garden* and the *Flora and Sylva*, and also his articles and books, was one of the first of the new people at the end of the nineteenth century who laid before us the infinite variety of plants and their uses in the garden landscape. He was dead against "in-and-out gardening" (annual bedding), loved trees and the wilder, *picturesque* landscape and admired grand herbaceous plants with fine foliage. He wrote from Sussex.

CWE   Mrs Earle, author of *Pot-pourri from a Surrey Garden*, 1897. She was an observant lady and as many quotations as I have used for plants could have been found as corroboration to a book on cooking or on other pursuits. She is ever practical and enlightened.

GJ   Gertrude Jekyll. The quotations are almost entirely from *Colour Schemes for the Flower Garden*, 1910. Her books reflect truthfully and simply her gardening. Though she was deeply interested in the Surrey countryside, crafts, and the varied beauties of plants, it was the effect they gave that was her main occupation. To the end of her life she was painting border after border, garden after garden, with the well-tried favourites with which she conjured up such satisfying schemes.

RF   In *The English Rock Garden*, 1918, Reginald Farrer produced some of his most graphic and flowery prose. Magenta was anathema to him but his admiration was reserved for the new and ravishing rather than the impressive (William Robinson) and was scarcely concerned with effect (Gertrude Jekyll). He had white-hot likes and dislikes, but his outpourings of words drew many into the arms of horticulture. He was of course mainly concerned with the gems of alpine regions, which he cultivated in Yorkshire.

EAB   Edward Augustus Bowles, the writer of that charming trilogy *My Garden in Spring, Summer, Autumn and Winter*, 1914, was a collector and appreciator of plants as well as a gardener fond of looking into the scientific side of things. In his traditional garden in Middlesex there seemed to be a corner for everything, which he described simply but entertainingly.

ATJ   Arthur Tysilio Johnson and his wife Nora together gardened in North Wales; he concerned himself with writing about them in characteristic prose, packed with words and well-turned phrases, revealing his close association with plants. Together they produced a garden in the modern trend, of woodland without a straight line, with natural-looking groupings of plants.

Since this is meant to be a personal book, reflecting my approach to gardening and choice of plants, you may well ask why I have chosen to include all these quotations. There are several reasons. Like Pooh Bah, I felt a little corroborative detail would add verisimilitude and let you know I am not alone in some of my enthusiasms, and indeed often these writers have provided a turn of phrase which I could not hope to equal. For this reason they add leavening to an interminable catalogue of plants. They help likewise to break up the page. And lastly, well, it follows *The Modern Florilegium* and I believe that the success of that little publication was due as much to its literary entertainment as to its cultural facts.

So come with me and let me show you these lovely plants, page by page, with as fair descriptions as I can manage, amplified here and there with a word of appreciation from some great gardeners who first showed the way. We will deal first with the general run of flowering plants, and pass on to grasses and ferns, and finally to Cuttings from My Notebook.

"True ornamental gardening consists ... in making selections from all [types of plants] and grouping them together so as to have, when the details are complete, a finished and charming effect."

James Anderson: *The New Practical Gardener*, 1873

Chapter 9

Plant Hardiness Zones in the United States

HARDINESS ZONE
TEMPERATURE RANGES

°F	ZONE	°C
below −50	1	below −45
−50 to −40	2	−45 to −40
−40 to −30	3	−40 to −34
−30 to −20	4	−34 to −29
−20 to −10	5	−29 to −23
−10 to 0	6	−23 to −17
0 to 10	7	−17 to −12
10 to 20	8	−12 to −7
20 to 30	9	−7 to −1
30 to 40	10	−1 to 5

Map developed by the Agricultural Research Service of the U.S. Dept. of Agriculture.

Plant hardiness can be broadly interpreted as the genetic potential for a plant to survive under an existing range of climatic and environmental conditions. Cold tolerance is the major factor governing plant hardiness and the Hardiness Zones beside each entry indicate the geographical survival range for this specific factor. The accompanying Hardiness Zone Map compiled by the U.S.D.A. (United States Department of Agriculture) is based on average winter minimum temperatures and indicates the geographical extent of each Zone. In addition to cold hardiness, other factors are critical to the success of various herbaceous perennials. Summer hardiness is influenced by high day time and nighttime temperatures, a factor closely linked with humidity levels. Soil type critically influences both drainage and water retention—poor drainage being lethal to many perennials. In more northerly Zones the presence or absence of a winter snow cover is of vital significance each year—a presence negating the adverse effects of low temperatures.

It is important to realize that within each Zone considerable climatic and environmental variations can prevail. For example, considerable variations exist between a given Zone in the southeast USA and those experienced in the same Zone in the southwest USA. The presence of microclimates within each Zone is critical at both local and regional levels. Thus any Zone hardiness re-commendations should be interpreted in the broadest sense, always allowing adjustments for prevailing local conditions.

Hardiness recommendations in this book are somewhat conservative especially at their northern limits due to the snow-cover factor. Hardiness recommendations should be considered a guide rather than an absolute because statistically valid, practically based information on the performance of many of the plants included in this book is yet to be recorded from numerous areas of North America.

The Hardiness Zones were kindly furnished by John E. Elsley, Director of Horticulture, Wayside Gardens.

Chapter 10

Alphabetical List of Plants excluding Grasses and Ferns

● **ACANTHUS**, Acanthaceae. Bear's Breeches. Statuesque plants of classical dignity, whose great basal leaves form a good podium to the prickly flower spikes, stiff and imposing. Their leaves are so handsome that they are most appreciated in frontal positions, where there is enough space, in spite of their floral height. They will on the other hand dominate any area which they will colonize with their invasive roots. Although they will grow in shade, they are most at home in sun, which encourages them to flower. Any fertile soil suits them so long as it is reasonably well drained, and they are best planted in spring and protected by a mulch for the first winter in cold districts, or until thoroughly established. The flower spikes of all are useful for drying for the winter, but beware of handling them for they are interspersed with hooded calyx lobes ending in sharp prickles.

caroli-alexandri

30 × 90 cm	*[7–9]*	*Pinkish*	*Summer*	PF	DRS
1 × 3 ft					

Greece. 1887. An invasive root-stock produces four narrow spiny leaves and spikes of white, pink-tinted flowers with the usual thorny bracts.

dioscoridis

46 × 60 cm	*[7–9]*	*Pink*	*L.Summer*	PF	DRS
18 in × 2 ft					

Middle East. 1893. Deeply toothed, grey-green leaves; the flowers vary from purplish to clear pink; the latter colour is sometimes given the name of *A. perringii* in gardens, a highly desirable plant.

"like some pink prunella glorified unimaginably, and taught to look well-bred."—RF

hungaricus

90 × 60 cm	*[6–10]*	*Mauve*	*L.Summer*	PF	DRS
3 × 2 ft					

Balkans. 1869. *A. balcanicus*. In gardens often labelled *A. longifolius*. The deeply lobed sinuate leaves, of a rather dull green, and tall spikes of flowers are in the *A. mollis* persuasion. This is simply a collector's piece and not to be compared with *A. spinosus* and *A. mollis* from a foliage point of view, though it is free-flowering. The leaves have long gaps between the lobes, connected with a flange of leaf parallel to the central stalk. In *A. mollis* the gaps are much shorter or almost missing and the the short flange is bowed between each lobe, not parallel to the stalk. The lobes are sometimes angled like those of the ivy. (Both species are very variable.) It thrives at Trelissick, Cornwall.

mollis

1.2–1.5 m × 90 cm   [8–10]   Mauve   L.Summer   PF DRS
4–5 × 3 ft

Italy. 1548. Bear's Breeches. For long in our gardens, this is a good plant, with dull green long leaves, cut deeply into almost pinnate lobes. The flowers are handsome, like those of all other species, and are fairly freely borne in the south of the country. It is a less common plant than its variety *A.m. latifolius* [6–10]. In this the leaves are very large, of rich shining green, limp and arching. The usual flower spikes of mauve-pink foxglove-like flowers are sparingly produced. Surprisingly it breeds true from seeds. It is probable that this species was the inspiration for the leaves on Corinthian capitals; it has long been grown and become naturalized in Greece; cf. *A. spinosus. A. mollis latifolius* thrives at Cliveden.

spinosus ★

1.2–1.5 m × 60 cm   [7–10]   Mauve   L.Summer   PF DRS
4–5 × 2 ft

S. Europe. 1629. The leaves of this species are very handsome, dark green, about 60 cm × 90 cm (2–3 ft) long, deeply divided, with spiny points, erect but arching. The spires of soft mauve foxglove-like flowers are striking and far more freely borne than those of *A. mollis latifolius*. Splendid with *Rosa glauca* at Sissinghurst, Kent. Long known in Ireland, where it was treasured by Lady Moore, is a form whose leaves are so dotted with creamy white in spring that they appear to be silvery grey. It is proposed to call this 'Lady Moore'.

> "*A. spinosus* is the species of classical reknown and architectural fame in the Corinthian capitals, and is one of the best to grow, its leaves adding the beauty of their finely-cut tracery to the colossal size of mollis."—EAB

—**spinosissimus** [7–10]. 1629. With leaves more finely cut than those of *A. spinosus* and with silvery points, an established clump of this looks like a grey and green porcupine. It is not over-free with its flowers except when well roasted, though it thrives under a stone on the Edinburgh rock garden. The flower spikes have long spines. Both this and *A. spinosus* provide marked contrast for bergenias.

ACHILLEA, Compositae. The flower heads of the achilleas here described are flat, close and solid arrays of tiny daisy-flowers, mostly without ray-petals. They are borne on stout stems, last a long time in flower and are excellent for cutting and drying for the winter. The foliage is feather-like except in *A. ptarmica*. They need good drainage, but are probably best suited to the more retentive soils in full sun. It is safest to transplant in spring. Sun.

clypeolata

of gardens

46 × 30 cm   [4–8]   Yellow   Summer   PF D
18 in × 1 ft

Hybrid. The leaves are some of the most silvery imaginable and are ideal for cutting with pinks, etc. They are just like palest jade-green feathers. The flat heads of clear yellow tansy-flowers, on silvery leafy stems, appear in June, or throughout the summer on freshly divided plants. Short-lived unless pulled apart and replanted in spring. Evergreen. This seems to have been lost in gardens, but Alan Bloom's 'Anthea' is very silvery with bright yellow flowers.

'Coronation Gold' ★

90 × 46 cm   *[4-8]*   *Yellow*   *Summer*   PF   D
3 ft × 18 in

Hybrid. 1952. *A. filipendulina* × *A. clypeolata* (of gardens). A self-sown seedling from Miss R. B. Pole. Fairly near to *A. filipendulina* in its yellow heads, but is not so tall and has somewhat greyish leaves. A useful and beautiful plant for the smaller garden and an ideal companion to *Salvia nemorosa* 'Lubeca' or 'East Friesland'. Also from Miss Pole are 'Lye End Lemon' and 'Lye End Ivory' progressively paler, and very beautiful with their greyish-green leaves. Evergreen winter rosettes.

decolorans

60 × 60 cm   *[4–8]*   *White*   *Summer*   PF   D
2 × 2 ft

Switzerland. 1798. *A serrata*. It might be said to come half way between *A. millefolium* and *A. ptarmica*, but without running roots. 'W. B. Child' is the only noted variety; it has flat heads of small white daisies with ray-florets and dark green eyes. An attractive cut flower.

filipendulina ★

1.2 m × 46 cm   *[4–8]*   *Yellow*   *Summer*   PF   D
4 ft × 18 in

Caucasus. 1803. *A. eupatorium*. A well-known and most handsome plant whose stout leafy stems, springing from a clump of feathery green leaves, each support a flat head of yellow flowers—like a yellow plate, some 12.5 cm (5 in) in diameter. It is in spectacular contrast to *Salvia nemorosa* 'Superba'. Long-lasting, and retains its colour when cut for the winter. 'Parker's Variety' and 'Gold Plate' are fine forms, but all are good. Excellent in the dry borders at Polesden Lacey, Surrey.

● **'Galaxy Hybrids'.** [4–8]. With parents *A. millefolium* ranging from white to red, and *A. × taygetae* in light yellow, a range of four named seedlings appeared in 1986 from Wilhelm Kikillus in Germany. 'Appleblossom' ('Apfelblute') light pink; 'Great Expectations' ('Hoffnung') light yellow; 'Beacon' ('Fanal') red, and 'Salmon Beauty' ('Lachsschoenheit') salmon-pink. 60 × 60 cm. 2 ft × 2 ft.

grandifolia

90 × 60 cm   *[4–8]*   *White*   *Summer/*   PF   DS
3 × 2 ft   *Autumn*

S.E. Europe, Asia Minor. The tiny white daisy flowers, held in good flat heads, are carried on stout stems all over the beautiful clump of grey foliage, lacy and deeply pinnatisect. A rare and neglected plant. Constantly in flower if old heads are cut off. Evergreen.

millefolium

60 × 60 cm   *[3–8]*   *Crimson*   *Summer*   PF   D
2 × 2 ft

Europe, Britain. The common Yarrow, a noxious lawn weed, has usually been represented in our gardens solely by its colour form *A.m.* 'Cerise Queen' (Harkness). The invasive roots produce a mat of feathery dark green leaves. The wide flat heads borne on stout stalks are of cerise-crimson, each floret with a paler centre. 'Sammetriese' is larger, and 'Fire King' and 'Red Beauty' are richer in colour, but otherwise are no improvement. 'Martina' [3–8] is a good yellow hybrid with long-lasting, non-fading flowers. *A. millefolium* may well be the parent of *A. taygetea* (of gardens), and others of similar qualities. Gerard discovered a reddish form of the common yarrow:

"... saving that his spokie tufts are of an excellent red crimson colour ... in a field by Sutton in Kent."—GH

★—'Coleen Keesing'

White   Summer   PF   D

Our native yarrow is always a dull grey-white. This form, collected in Greece by Messrs Cook and Keesing of Kew, has large flat heads of clear creamy white. An excellent new plant. 90 cm (3 ft).

—'Lilac Queen'   Cool lilac, not pink. Also desirable. 75 cm (2½ ft).

'Moonshine' ★
60 × 46 cm   [4–8]   Sulphur   Summer   PF   D
2 ft × 18 in
Hybrid. An excellent hybrid of Alan Bloom's, combining good points from the two garden clones *A. clypeolata* and *A. taygetea*. The flat heads are of bright light yellow over copious grey-green feathery foliage. An ideal foil for this and the others is *Salvia officinalis* 'Purpurascens'. Evergreen.

ptarmica
60 × 60 cm   [4–9]   White   Summer   P   D
2 × 2 ft
Europe, England. Here again this is an invasive weed, but two double-flowered varieties are useful for their pure white branched heads and stout stalks. 'The Pearl', a good white with neat double button-flowers in branching heads, was raised by Lemoine and originally christened 'Boule de Neige'. 'Perry's White' (1912) is whiter and larger but somewhat less upstanding. Double forms have been known since the sixteenth century. Poor foliage.

"... the clean white Achillea 'The Pearl' and the grey-white clouds of *Gypsophila paniculata*."—GJ

sibirica
46 × 46 cm   [3–9]   White   Summer   PF   DS
18 × 18 in
Northern Temperate Regions. 1811. A pleasing green plant with narrow leaves and flat heads of flowers, lasting for several weeks.

× taygetea ★
of gardens
60 × 46 cm   [5–8]   Sulphur   Summer   PF   D
2 ft × 18 in
Hybrid. The leaves are equally as feathery as those of *A. clypeolata*, but are less silvery, deriving their greener tone perhaps from *A. millefolium*, since these two species are believed to be its parents. It is more vigorous than the first and has flat heads of cool sulphur-primrose tint; it is therefore an ideal foil for many flowers. A similar plant is 'Schwefelblüte' ('Flowers of Sulphur') (1935), of rather brighter sulphur tone. Evergreen.

ACIDANTHERA, see **Gladiolus callianthus**

ACIPHYLLA, Umbelliferae. New Zealand species delighting in sunshine and mild rather damp air, and good drainage. Few of us would want the great tufts of stiletto-like, but divided, leaves in our gardens. Massive thorny flower spikes arise in suitable years. *A. scott-thompsonii* [8–10] grew well at Crathes Castle, Kincardineshire and *A. colensoi* [8–10], the Wild Spaniard, at Rowallane, Northern Ireland. *A squarrosa* [8–10], the Bayonet Plant, is more often seen. The flowers of all are individually small, of yellowish white. Evergreen. WS

ACONITUM, Ranunculaceae. Monkshood, Helmet Flower, Wolf's Bane. Poisonous-rooted plants. The significant, hooded flowers may suggest deliquium with a little imagination. The hoods contain nectaries on long stalks. Though they are stalwart plants the taller, branching kinds do sometimes need staking unless well nourished. The roots are tuberous except in *A. vulparia* and its relatives, and need thinning and replanting 125 mm (5 in) deep every few years to encourage good stems. As they start into growth very early (often in February) autumn or winter transplanting is best. They are easily satisfied as regards soil but grow best on those soils of a retentive nature; full sun suits them though they will also grow well in part or full shade—when the darkened colours of some kinds appear to increase in their evil beauty. For all their poison, there is no doubt that their unique floral shape contributes much to the garden.

"They should not be planted where the roots could be by any chance dug up by mistake for edible roots, as they are deadly poison."—WR

anglicum

90 × 46 cm	*[4–8]*	*Violet-blue*	*E.Summer*	PS	DS
3 ft × 18 in					

England, Europe. Though this is a conventional Monkshood, it has the merit of flowering in early summer and the added interest of being a native.

× bicolor

1.2 m × 46 cm	*[4–8]*	*Various*	*Summer*	P	D
4 ft × 18 in					

A name under which it is convenient to class a number of garden plants, supposedly hybrids between *A. variegatum* and *A. napellus*. Synonymous with *A. stoerkianum, A. cammarum,* and *A. napellus bicolor.* The garden plants with stiff upright spikes derive this character from *A. napellus*; the wider-branching plants, often with two-toned flowers, are derived from *A. variegatum.* All have dark green, glossy, deeply fingered leaves.

With dense erect spikes are 'Newry Blue', navy blue, 1.5 m (5 ft); some sturdy short plants by Alan Bloom are about 90 cm (3 ft); 'Blue Sceptre', violet-blue and white, and 'Bressingham Spire', violet-blue. These two have spikes as straight as Salisbury steeple, with small subsidiary steeples to carry on the display.

Wide-branching stems are found in two excellent garden plants: 'Bicolor' (of gardens) particoloured in violet-blue and white, which may be the original hybrid, and 'Spark's Variety', Prichard (*c.* 1898), intense dark violet-blue; this latter is admirable for dusky colour schemes and also for associating with vivid yellows. It is also known as *A. henryi.* These two are 1.2–1.5 m (4–5 ft).

carmichaelii ● ★

1.2 m × 30 cm	*[3–8]*	*Blue*	*E.Autumn*	PF	DS
4 × 1 ft					

Kamchatka. 1886. *A. fischeri* (of gardens). A beautiful erect plant whose rich green divided foliage is respectable from spring to autumn, when its flowers make such a notable contrast to *Kniphofia triangularis* (*K. galpinii,* of gardens). The hooded blooms are borne in short spikes and are of light Wedgwood blue. About the same height, but of richer colouring, is 'Arendsii' (1945), so called by the raiser when *A. fischeri* and *A. wilsonii* (of gardens) were considered distinct species. *A. wilsonii* (1903) was a name given to a very tall variant of *A. carmichaelii* now known as *A.c. wilsonii*. A good type is 'Barker's Variety', which breeds true from seeds; 'Kelmscott' is a richer colour, violet-blue. Both achieve 1.8 m (6 ft) and are highly attractive and valuable for contrasting with *Cimicifuga ramosa* and *Chrysanthemum uliginosum*.

'Ivorine'

| 60 × 30 cm | [5–8] | Cream | E.Summer | P | D |
| 2 × 1 ft | | | | | |

It is not stated to what species this garden form owes its early flowering habit (with *A. anglicum*) nor its colouring, though *A. septentrionale* (a relative of *A. vulparia*) is often cited; the fibrous roots suggest this.

japonicum ● ★

| 90 × 30 cm | [5–8] | Lavender | L.Summer | P | DS |
| 3 × 1 ft | | | | | |

Japan. 1790. A variable species, recently re-introduced. Its stems, well clad in pale, divided leaves, have good subsidiary flower heads as well as the terminal one, giving it a long flowering period. Luminous lavender-blue in best forms.

napellus ★

| 1.5 m × 30 cm | [5–8] | Blue | L.Summer | PF | DS |
| 5 × 1 ft | | | | | |

Europe, Britain, Asia. The common Monkshood has, like the others, a poisonous root, and has been cultivated since the sixteenth century. Many of the garden monkshoods are derived from this species; see under *A × bicolor*. While the light indigo-blue flowers on this stately plant are not to be despised the soft flesh-pink 'Carneum' is a noteworthy plant and brings a new tone to this genus. In the south in dry gardens it may be a washed-out tint but in the north and particularly in Scottish gardens it is a plant of rare beauty and great value. There is also a fine white form★ 'Album Grandiflorum'.

orientale

| 1.5 m × 30 cm | [4–8] | Greyish | Summer | PF | DS |
| 5 × 1 ft | | | | | |

Caucasus, etc. While the flowers resemble the blooms of *A. vulparia*, this is a more erect plant, with longer spikes of smoky lilac or pinkish flowers.

paniculatum

| 1.5 m × 60 cm | [5–8] | Blue | E.Summer | PF | DS |
| 5 × 2 ft | | | | | |

S. Europe. An elegant plant with stems freely branching into a wide paniculate head of flowers with high helmets whose tops project forwards; they may be soft blue but are variable. The leaves are dark green and well divided. It thrives at Wallington, Northumberland. A form which does not need support is named *A.p.* 'Nanum'.

variegatum

| 1.5 m × 60 cm | [4–8] | Blue/ | L.Summer | PF | DS |
| 5 × 2 ft | | Yellowish | | | |

E. Alps. 1597. One of the parents of the garden hybrids described under *A. × bicolor*. The blue or yellowish or particoloured flowers have helmets similar in shape to those of *A. paniculatum*. Finely divided leaves on stately, wiry, branching stems.

volubile

Climbing   *[6–8]*   *Lilac*   *L.Summer*   DS

Altai Mountains. 1780. An amusing plant which will annually pleach through a shrub, surprising one by producing its hooded lilac-mauve flowers among the alien foliage. There is also a desirable dark blue form. *A. stapfianum* [5–8] is a strong climber with hooded flowers of dark blue, whitish below.

vulparia

1.2–1.5 m × 30 cm   *[4–8]*   *Yellowish*   *Summer*   PF   DS
4–5 × 1 ft

Europe, E. Asia. *A. lycoctonum.* The use of the poisonous roots as a bait for wolves in olden days earned it the name of Wolf's Bane. *A. lamarckii* [4–8] (*A. pyrenaicum*) and *A. anthora* [4–8] are similar. They all have deeply divided dark green leaves and the hood or helmet—the top segment of the flower—is narrow and tall. The flowers are of parchment- or straw-yellow, or nearly white, borne in branching spikes. They need some support, especially *A. vulparia*, and can be placed to lean over low shrubs. A wonderful contrast to wine-purple phloxes. The roots are fibrous in this group.

ACORUS, Araceae. For stream and pond verges, damp and boggy ground.

calamus

90 × 30 cm   *[4–10]*   *Variegated*   *Summer*   D
3 × 1 ft

Europe, Britain. The green-leafed type was used in the past for strewing the floor; it is the Sweet Flag. (A pleasant cinnamon scent emanates from the leaves when crushed, and no doubt helped to counteract the smell of garbage thrown to the dogs, long before vacuum cleaners were invented.) In effect this is a waterside rush; the flowers are insignificant greenish yellow but I have included it for the sake of 'Variegatus', whose long leaves are neatly striped with cream. Much smaller, *Acorus gramineus* is useful for damp spots, particularly *A.g.* 'Variegatus', whose narrow dark green grassy leaves are freely striped with cream.

ACTAEA, Ranunculaceae. Poisonous berries, hence the name Baneberry. Though not difficult to please and quite hardy, they grow best in cool or part-shaded positions in somewhat moist and retentive, fertile soils.

alba

90 × 46 cm   *[4–9]*   *Berries*   *L.Summer*   PF   DS
3 ft × 18 in

E. North America. 1656. *A. pachypoda.* White Baneberry. Fresh green leaves, like those of *Astilbe*, form an elegant clump. The flowers are fluffy, white, borne in small heads, but by August they have turned into most intriguing spires of pea-sized white berries supported on thickened scarlet stalks. There is nothing like it—a real August treasure; it thrives at Powis Castle, Montgomeryshire. The "Indian branched wolf's bane with white fruits" of Tradescant.

"The white berried ... I like best of all ... its more finely cut leaves and curiously swollen pedicels being so distinct. It is a pity these plants are so dreadfully poisonous."—EAB

rubra

46 × 30 cm	*[4–8]*	*Berries*	*E.Autumn*	PF	DS
18 × 12 in					

North America. 1635. Red Baneberry. An unusual plant whose spikes of clustered, glistening, scarlet berries are carried well above the clumps of ferny green leaves. A useful plant for cool places, among shrubs. There is an attractive and rare form, *A.r. neglecta*, whose berries are pure white. At Sissinghurst, Kent, this achieves 90 cm (3 ft).

spicata

46 × 46 cm	*[3–8]*	*Berries*	*E.Autumn*	PF	DS
18 × 18 in					

N. Old World, Britain. 1596. The Herb Christopher resembles *A. rubra* except for the colour of its shining berries, which are black—suitable to bring alive the most subdued of flowers, like those of *Tricyrtis*. *A. erythrocarpa* has much smaller maroon berries and achieves greater height.

ADENOPHORA, Campanulaceae. Forming deep-questing fleshy roots, these prefer a good well-drained soil in full sun. The species resemble each other considerably, all having good basal leaves, and tall branching spires of pale or dark lavender-blue, cup-, or wide bell-shaped flowers, rather small, in summer. *A. bulleyana* (1908) [4–8] is one of the tallest, achieving 1.2 m (4 ft) and most satisfactory; *A. tashiroi* [4–8] (*A. polymorpha tashiroi*), 60 cm (2 ft), is a good second. There are many others.

ADONIS, Ranunculaceae. There are several species whose height just allows me to include them in this book, natives of Europe and the Far East. They all grow very early in the year; achieve 23–46 cm (9–18 in); their stems are densely clad in leaves deeply divided into narrow lobes, and bear at the top large buttercup-like flowers in yellow, red or white. The European *A. vernalis* [4–7], yellow, is one of the most reliable; others to be tried in sheltered corners are *A. amurensis* [4–7] (of which there are variously coloured Japanese cultivars), *A. volgensis* [4–7], *A. pyrenaica* [4–7]. The last flowers in summer. Increased by division and seeds. The vivid green feathery foliage of *A. vernalis* lasts until summer.

> "Slugs love its fat round flower-buds . . . and they often lose their hearts as early in the day as the heroine of a penny novelette."—EAB

AGAPANTHUS, Liliaceae. Blue African Lily. Botanically a confusing genus, with several species which have not yet been introduced to British gardens. The favourite old plant for tubs, known for long as *A. umbellatus*, is a magnificent kind for our warmest counties, but may be dispensed with elsewhere since there are good hardy strains available, though these are not all so deep a blue. They all require full sun in any fertile soil, moist rather than dry, but not boggy. They increase slowly, eventually needing division and replanting, which is best done in spring, avoiding planting too deeply. They blend with all softer coloured schemes and also contrast well with yellow flowers. Excellent for cutting. It will be seen from the notes below that those with deciduous, narrow, greyish-green leaves are more hardy than those with more or less evergreen, broad rich green leaves. An important point should be borne in mind when planting: in enclosed gardens nearly all the varieties lean towards the sun, which can be troublesome in borders facing east or west; north-facing borders are not usually chosen for them. The exceptions to this leaning habit are found in *A. inapertus*, and some hybrids therefrom, whose stems remain always erect.

africanus

| 60–90 × 46 cm | [9–10] | Blue | L.Summer | PF | W | DS |

2–3 ft × 18 in

Cape Province. 1679. Although this was the first species to be introduced, it is seldom seen in gardens; *A. umbellatus* (of gardens) sometimes does duty for it, and the names are confused. It would be best grown under glass. Usually deep blue. Evergreen.

campanulatus ★

| 60 cm– | [8–10] | Blue | L.Summer | PF | DS |

1.2 m × 46 cm
2–4 ft × 18 in

E. South Africa, etc. *c.* 1870. *A. umbellatus globosus, mooreanus* and *minor* are names which have been used for forms of this species. It seems to be perfectly hardy in all our counties, though it might be wise to give it a winter mulch in coldest districts. I have had a clump since 1927, first in Cambridge and latterly in Surrey, which has flowered freely every year. Clones grow as far north as Wallington, Northumberland. It has wholly deciduous, narrow greyish-green leaves. The stalwart stems support rather flat (not spherical) heads of flowers of soft blue, variable in tint; as pale as Spode or dark as Wedgwood. Excellent value for the August border and a lovely contrast to clones of *Potentilla fruticosa* and grey-leafed plants.

—**campanulatus** Natal, etc. The perhaps typical subspecies, or hybrids therefrom, is in many gardens. A dwarf form, which became known as *A. umbellatus mooreanus* (commemorating Sir Frederick Moore of Glasnevin, in 1879) is now seldom seen. It had dense heads of dark blue flowers and achieved about 46 cm. (18 in).

—**patens** Orange Free State, Basutoland, etc. This achieves about 1.2 m (4 ft), has the same stout stems and greyish leaves of the above and appears to be perfectly hardy. It is distinguished by its wide-open flowers (scarcely trumpet-shaped as in the above), which create thereby a round dense head earning its earlier name of *A. globosus*. It is an effective garden plant for associating with *Fuchsia magellanica* 'Versicolor', but its small heads are less conspicuous than most.

caulescens

| 90 cm– | [8–10] | Blue | L.Summer | PF | DS |

1.2 m × 60 cm
3–4 × 2 ft

Swaziland, Natal, Transvaal, etc. Prior to 1914. *A. umbellatus caulescens* or *insignis*. Another deciduous hardy species, with very broad, ribbed, green leaves, up to 60 cm (2 ft) high. Large open heads of large trumpet-shaped flowers of varying shades of blue. Two sub-species have been named, *A.c. gracilis* and *A.c. angustifolius*.

inapertus

| 90 cm– | [8–10] | Blue | L.Summer/ | PF | DS |
| | | | E.Autumn | | |

1.5 m × 60 cm
3–5 × 2 ft

Transvaal, etc. Prior to 1914. This has been known as *A. weillighii* and is characterized by stiffly erect stems (see introductory paragraph above) and pendulous, more or less tubular flowers. These bring quite a different outline to the heads. The leaves may be rich green or glaucous; they are deciduous, and the species is proving hardy. All the forms flower in September or October. It has been divided into several subspecies of which the following are distinct:

—**'Albus'**   This is a pleasing creamy white form with small heads of tubular flowers.

—**hollandii**   Rather more open flowers; blue. Attractive. 1.2 m (4 ft).

★ —**inapertus**   May achieve as much as 1.5 m (5 ft) in height, but the head of tubular drooping flowers is hardly in scale. Light to mid-blue, produced before October in warm summers. Leaves glaucous.

—**pendulus**   Rich green, broad leaves. 90 cm (3 ft) stems bear flowers of almost navy blue, very striking when seen against grey-leafed plants, but their strictly pendulous disposition creates a dense, small, mop-like head. An excellent companion for *Nerine bowdenii*.

nutans

| 90 × 46 cm | [8–10] | Blue | L.Summer | PF | DS |
| 3 ft × 18 in | | | | | |

Natal, Transvaal, etc. A lesser species, deciduous, hardy, often with greyish leaves. The flowers are long-trumpet-shaped, carried lightly in an open head. Soft blue.

praecox

| 1.2 m × 60 cm | [9–10] | Blue | L.Summer/ | PF | W | DS |
| 4 × 2 ft | | | E.Autumn | | | |

Cape Province, Natal, etc. Prior to 1800. *A. umbellatus maximus, giganteus.* One of the more tender species, with large spherical heads of beautiful trumpet-shaped flowers, rich blue, above handsome clumps of broad usually dark green leaves, more or less evergreen. One or more clones have been popular for a century or more for growing in pots and tubs for late summer effect and bringing under shelter for the winter. It seems sensible to continue to call these *A. umbellatus* (of gardens) since they have for ages been grown from division of the original importations; they are the well-known Blue African Lily. They thrive out of doors in our mildest maritime districts and are even known to naturalize themselves on the seashore. They flower late in the season and need all the sun they can get. There are two subspecies of note:

—**orientalis**   Large dense heads of flowers on a plant of shorter stature.

● —**praecox**   The largest and tallest version, with very large heads of flowers. There is a double-flowered form, not of much value. 'Maximus Albus' and 'Albatross' (from Oakhurst Nurseries, California) are two large white varieties of great vigour which probably belong here.

Several old garden forms lurk in specialists' collections, such as the old *A. umbellatus* 'Albus', and forms with variegated leaves, such as 'Aureovittatus'.

The Blue African Lily can be seen in tubs at Ickworth, Suffolk; Saltram, Devon; it is grown in the open ground at Mount Stewart, Northern Ireland.

"They have to be rather pot-bound and kept dry in the winter, to flower well; as the flower buds form they want to be well watered and given a weekly dose of liquid manure."—CWE

★ GARDEN FORMS AND HYBRIDS. During the 1950s and '60s the Honourable Lewis Palmer distributed seeds from his garden at Headbourne Worthy near Winchester, mainly from light and dark blue forms of *A. campanulatus*, under the name of Headbourne Hybrids [8–10]. Many selected clones have received names from various raisers, such as the tiny dark blue 'Lilliput' (Jackman); rather larger 'Isis' (Bloom), 'Molly Howick' (Palmer), and 'Midnight Blue' (Slieve Donard), all about 60 cm (2 ft), and 'Dorothy Palmer' (Jackman) 90 cm (3 ft), all of rich colouring. 'Cherry Holley' (Palmer) 75 cm (2½ ft) is noted for the secondary flower stems it produces after the main crop; it is a very dark blue. The most magnificent I have seen is ● 'Loch Hope' (Savill Garden, Windsor) 1.2 m (4 ft), a valuable late-flowering clone with large heads. Among light blues are 'African Moon' 60 cm (2 ft) with subsidiary bunches of flowers around each head, a doubtful advantage; 'Blue Moon' (Plantsmen) very dense heads, stout stems. ● 'Luly' (Palmer) is a magnificent light blue 90 cm (3 ft) named after the raiser. 'Rosemary' 90 cm (3 ft) may almost be called pale grey. ● 'Blue Giant' 1.2 m (4 ft) is a fine product of Bressingham.

There are some excellent whites. The finest so far is ● 'Alice Gloucester' (Palmer) a large head and early flowering; the pedicels and buds are purplish, a tint shared by 'Ardernei Hybrid', a doubtful name (known as *A. orientalis albus*, erroneously, in Holland), giving the plants a warm white tone, 90 cm (3 ft). 'Victoria' (Palmer) is creamy white. 'Snowy Owl' (Palmer) is first class also.

Some further hybrids came to light in the Trials at Wisley which were started in 1972, showing the influence of *A. inapertus* and other species, and these will be worth watching.

A point to observe in assessing these new seedlings is the colour of the fading flower. Many of the earlier dark blues turn to reddish purple, which is a great disadvantage. 'Cherry Holley' and 'Loch Hope' do not do this, and it is not usually noticeable in those of paler colouring.

The dark blues look particularly well with *Crocosmia* 'Solfatare'; all assort well with silvery-leafed plants, and the whites give a good contrast to *Clematis viticella* 'Abundance'.

AGASTACHE, Labiatae. Sun-loving plants with fragrant leaves like Bergamot. They are happy in well-drained fertile soil and are erect and self-reliant.

anisata
90 × 30 cm	*[7–10]*	*Violet*	*Summer*	P	S
3 × 1 ft					

S. United States. 1829. *A. anethiodora, Agastache foeniculum, Lophanthus anisatus, Cedronella foeniculum.* A bushy, thrifty, hardy plant with fragrant mint-like leaves, and dense fat spikes of mint-like flowers on the top of every branch, of a dusky dull indigo-violet. It is useful for late and soft colour schemes, particularly with Japanese Anemones.

mexicana
60 × 30 cm	*[8–10]*	*Pink*	*Summer*	P	W	S
2 × 1 ft						

Mexico. 1938. *Brittonastrum mexicanum, Cedronella mexicana.* The slender spires of sage-like flowers vary from dark pink to crimson, and a good tint should be sought. Oval, pointed leaves. This is not long-lived and is best suited to our warmest and driest counties. *A. cana (Cedronella cana)* is similar.

AGAVE, Amaryllidaceae.
americana

6 × 2.4 m	*[8–10]*	*Yellowish*	*Summer*	W	D
20 × 8 ft					

Mexico. The American Aloe grows well in Cornish and other favoured gardens. At Glendurgan its immense rosette of dangerously pointed grey-green leaves creates an exotic note in the valley. The rosette may achieve 1.8 m × 1.8 m (6 ft × 6 ft). It produces its immense flower spike after thirty or forty years' growth. *A. parryi* is barely half the size and is usually considered hardier; from S.W. United States. There are several smaller species which might be tried in warmest gardens, with full sun, perfect drainage and protected from winter wet. Evergreen.

ALBUCA, Liliaceae. There are several smaller species worth trying (if your garden is warm and sheltered), such as *A. altissima* [8–10] and *A. major* [8–10], but they are seldom seen, the following being the most noteworthy.

nelsonii

1.2 m × 60 cm	*[8–10]*	*White*	*Summer*	W	DS
4 ft × 2 ft					

Natal. 1880. The white nodding flowers are smoothly chiselled, each with a green-brown stripe on the outer segments. The whole inflorescence may contain a dozen or more of these beauties, over long, lax, bright green leaves. Plant 8 in deep.

ALCHEMILLA, Rosaceae. Easily grown in any fertile soil in sun or shade.

mollis ★

46 × 60 cm	*[4–8]*	*Yellow*	*E.Summer*	PF	DS
18 in × 2 ft					

Asia Minor. 1874. Apart from the beauty of the downy, rounded leaves, a copious, airy display of tiny greeny-yellow stars in feathery sprays is produced, remaining long in beauty. The ideal foil for white, yellow, blue and purple flowers. The Lady's Mantle grows anywhere, except in a bog, and is a splendid ground cover, but it is best to remove the flower-heads before the seeds ripen, as it can become a nuisance.

"... of a very tender shade of greyish green and covered with fine silky hairs, which help their cuplike shape to hold raindrops which glitter like quicksilver."—EAB

ALLIUM, Liliaceae. The Onion tribe has some very decorative plants for the garden. Many are quite small but the following are large enough to create good effect in the garden bed or border. They enjoy full sun and are not difficult to please in any reasonably drained, fertile soil. The leaves of the following species are unremarkable, soon dying away. They are all apt to seed themselves like cress, when suited. Their bulbs should be planted in permanent positions in early autumn, about 12.5 cm (5 in) deep.

"The Onion requireth a fat ground well digged and dunged, as Palladius saith."—GH

aflatunense
90 cm–1.2 m   *[4–10]*   *Lilac*   *L.Spring*   PF   DS
× 30 cm
3–4 × 1 ft

China. This is like an early-flowering *A. giganteum*, producing its fine spherical heads, about 5–7.5 cm (2–3 in) across, of tiny rich deep lilac flowers in late May. The leaves die away early. This could well be grown among some late-flowering plant such as *Agapanthus*. There is a good white variety, 'Album'. A similar but even earlier species is *A. stenopetalum* (*A. atropurpureum*).

beesianum
46 × 15 cm   *[5–10]*   *Blue*   *Summer*   PF   DS
18 × 6 in

W. China. Included for its beautiful blue colour; small flowers in rounded heads over grassy leaves. *A. caeruleum* [4–10] is similar, but is sometimes tender. Both are lovely for planting in a carpet of silvery foliage such as *Artemisia stelleriana*.

bulgaricum ●
90 × 30 cm   *[4–10]*   *Mauve and*   *L.Spring*   PF   DS
3 × 1 ft   *green*

Balkans. *A. dioscoridis*, *A. siculum dioscoridis*, *Nectaroscordon bulgaricum*. A *siculum* itself occurs in other southern Mediterranean countries; its flowers are plum-coloured while those of *A. bulgaricum* are creamy green with purple flush. The flowers of all are large, bell-shaped, hung from drooping stalks at the top of the stout stems, and after fertilization stand erect. These plants have stoloniferous bulbs which quickly increase; they can become a nuisance, but the flowers are of great beauty, also the seed-heads. Try it with *Paeonia broteroi* or *P. arietina*. From the Crimea hails another similar plant, sometimes called *A. dioscoridis*, but correctly *A. meliophilum* [4–8].

"... I enjoy breaking a leaf in half and getting my friends to help in deciding whether it most resembles an escape of gas or a new mackintosh."—EAB

carinatum pulchellum
60 × 15 cm   *[6–9]*   *Purple*   *Summer*   PF   DS
2 ft × 6 in

Mediterranean Region. *A. pulchellum*. Inclined, like many others, to sow itself too freely. Slight grassy foliage. The flowers nod in bud, turning upwards after pollination; they are rich amethyst purple and there is a beautiful white form, 'Album'.

cernuum
46 × 15 cm   *[3–8]*   *Amethyst*   *Summer*   PF   DS
18 × 6 in

United States. *c.* 1800. One of the smaller species but just large enough for inclusion, especially as its flowers are borne in such pretty drooping heads, like an exploding rocket, and are of rich amethyst or deep lilac-pink, assorting well with *Zygadenus elegans*. The seed-heads are exquisite too. The good form that is usually grown today has been distributed from seeds given to me by John Wall, one time curator of the rock garden at Wisley. May be seen at Hidcote, Gloucestershire, and is sometimes called 'Hidcote'.

christophii ●

| 60 × 46 cm | [4–10] | Violet | Summer | PF | DS |
| *2 ft × 18 in* | | | | | |

Turkestan. 1901. *A. albopilosum*. The leaves die away almost before the stout stems have developed their wonderful spherical heads of bloom, about 25 cm. (10 in) across, an array of amethystine-violet glossy stars. The seed-heads are superb and last well. Grown successfully among Bearded Irises at Sissinghurst, Kent, where the flowers appear in late June with the last of the irises and benefit from the grey-green iris foliage.

giganteum ★

| 1.2–1.5 m × 30 cm | [6–10] | Lilac | Summer | PF | DS |
| *4–5 × 1 ft* | | | | | |

Central Asia, etc. 1883. A superb, stately plant carrying handsome knobs of bloom, the size of an orange, on stout glaucous stems. The many tiny flowers are of a rich warm lilac. The leaves appear very early. *A. elatum* is similar, but usually paler.

macranthum

| 60 × 23 cm | [4–10] | Purple | L.Summer | PF | DS |
| *2 ft × 9 in* | | | | | |

Sikkim. 1883. This rapidly forms fresh green, grassy hummocks from the almost tuberous roots, above which the stems ascend, each with a drooping mop of small rich red-purple flowers. May be likened to a much larger *A. cyathophorum farreri* [4–8]; it is effective for some weeks.

neapolitanum

| 60 × 15 cm | [6–10] | White | Summer | PF | DS |
| *2 ft × 6 in* | | | | | |

Mediterranean Region. 1828. For sunny, well-drained positions. The form in commerce known as 'Grandiflorum' is a beautiful, dainty plant with a profuse display of snow-white flowers in good heads, each with a dark eye. It spreads freely and can be a nuisance when well suited.

odorum

| 46 × 23 cm | [4–9] | White | L.Summer | P | DS |
| *18 × 9 in* | | | | | |

Far East. *A. tuberosum*. Chinese Chives. The flat heads of white flowers have dark eyes which give a greyish effect to the whole head. *A. ramosum* [4–9] is similar.

rosenbachianum ★

| 1.2 m × 30 cm | [4–10] | Mauve | E.Summer | PF | DS |
| *4 × 1 ft* | | | | | |

Central Asia. 1894. In the *A. giganteum* class but it is shorter and flowers earlier, usually at the end of May. Maroon pedicels. This and *A. elatum, A. stipitatum* and *A. afflatunense* are similar species [4–10]; all bring a unique and decorative form to the garden.

schoenoprasum

| 30 × 23 cm | [3–9] | Mauve | Summer | P | DS |
| *1 ft × 9 in* | | | | | |

Northern Hemisphere. Chives is an old and valued garden herb, whose tight heads of rosy lilac blooms give good effect in the border front or as an edging to a herb garden. It increases freely in the clump. A taller plant, flowering in late summer, is *A. angulosum*; *A. wallichianum* from a garden point of view is an excellent midsummer-flowering, larger species. 'Forescate' [3–9] has rich deep rose flowers. It was found by Mr Dalfsen and commemorates the town of Voorscholten in Holland for which Forescate is a historical name.

schubertii ●

60 × 46 cm *2 ft × 18 in*	*[4–10]*	*Pink*	*Summer*	PF	DS

E. Mediterranean and Central Asia. Like *A. christophii*, but the flowers are smaller and of lilac-pink. The huge spherical head of blossom has stalks of different lengths and it looks like a bursting firework. The seed-heads are unique.

senescens

30 × 15 cm *1 ft × 6 in*	*[4–8]*	*Lilac*	*L.Summer*	P	DS

Central Europe, N. Asia. There are some good late-flowering dwarf plants under this name in gardens, though they may be variants of *A. montanum* [4–8]. The dwarf tuft of curly greenish leaves makes a ground cover; the heads of flowers give the effect of a giant Thrift. Plant next to *Sedum spectabile* or *S.* 'Ruby Glow'.

sphaerocephalum

60 × 23 cm *2 ft × 9 in*	*[6–10]*	*Purple*	*Summer*	PF	DS

Europe, etc. 1594. A slender plant with insignificant leaves. Its value in the garden and for cutting is in the knobby flower-heads, densely filled with small blooms of rich wine-purple. There are good white forms. They all increase freely at the root, whereas the closely related *A. descendens* [6–10] is less inclined this way.

> "*A. sphaerocephalum* is also in flower ... and is much sought after by Bumble-bees."—EAB

unifolium

60 × 23 cm *2 ft × 9 in*	*[4–10]*	*Pink*	*E.Summer*	PF	DS

California. 1873. It is seldom single-leafed, but is a highly attractive plant. The flowers are of old rose-pink, in a generous spherical head. A well-drained sunny position is required.

victorialis

46 × 30 cm *18 in × 1 ft*	*[7–9]*	*Whitish*	*E.Summer*	PF	DS

Mediterranean Region. 1739. When in bud it is a plant of promise on account of its broad leaves. The flowers, greenish white in a small head, are disappointing.

ALOE, Liliaceae. The only species I have seen growing out of doors in England is *A. aristata*, which throve for many years at Highdown, Sussex, and also flowers at St Michael's Mount, Cornwall.

aristata

60 × 30 cm	*[9–10]*	*Orange*	*Summer*	**W**	**D**
2 × 1 ft					

Cape Province. Dense dark green rosettes of acutely pointed fleshy leaves, white marked. Lily-like flowers in slender spires. It is extremely difficult to keep out of doors, needing perfect drainage, hot sun and a dry winter. Evergreen.

ALSTROEMERIA, Amaryllidaceae. Peruvian Lily. The small lily-like flowers are beautifully marked and are borne in large heads on erect wiry stems set with limp, narrow leaves. An established clump in early summer presents a fine leafy mass. They spread freely from running fleshy roots but are not always easy to establish, needing a warm sunny position in well-drained soil. *A. aurantiaca* is so prolific that large clumps can be dug up in late summer for re-establishment. Growers usually send out *A. ligtu* and its hybrids as young seed-raised pot plants in spring, or when dormant in late summer. The young shoots are frail and I favour dormant planting, but whichever method is chosen it is advisable to plant 23 cm (9 in) deep; this is easy with dormant roots, but young growing plants can be set in a hollow and be earthed up as they grow or when they have died down. They can also be increased by sowing seeds where they are to be established. All young plants should be protected by a thick mulch for their first winter or two. They wither away by the end of July but the seed-heads are usually ornamental. The hybrid strain is well established at Oxford Botanical Garden.

aurea ★

90 × 30 cm	*[7–10]*	*Orange*	*Summer*	**PF**	**DS**
3 × 1 ft					

Chile. 1831. *A. aurantiaca.* Peruvian Lily. All species are apt to be a nuisance because of their running roots, but this is easier to establish and more invasive than the next. It grows well at Powis Castle, Montgomeryshire. Some gardeners curse it, others love it for its orange colouring; most like it for cutting, and the discriminating admire its yellow form *A.a.* 'Lutea'. Those who like rich orange should try 'Dover Orange' (1935) or 'Moerheim Orange'. All grow well when once established, with wiry stems each bearing narrow leaves and a head of daintily marked small lily-flowers. Long-lasting in water. They will all thrive in partly shaded positions.

> "They do not mind moving in August after flowering, and they are best increased as Lilies of the Valley are—by digging out square pieces, filling in with good soil and dropping in the pieces cut out where they are wanted ... without disturbing the earth that clings to them."—CWE

chilensis

75 × 46 cm	*[8–10]*	*Red*	*E.Summer*	**PF**	**W**	**D**
2½ ft × 18 in						

Chile. 1842. The flower-heads vary from reddish pink to creamy white. It needs a warm, sunny, sheltered position. Very seldom is the genuine species seen since it readily hybridizes with others.

haemantha

90 × 46 cm	*[8–10]*	*Red*	*E.Summer*	**PF**	**DS**
3 ft × 18 in					

Chile. *A. simsii.* Closely related to *A. ligtu*, this has flowers whose outer segments are reddish orange while the inner ones may be deep yellow streaked with maroon or purple; like most of the others it is variable. A hundred years or more ago hybrids were raised by the Belgian firm of Van Houtte, with the dwarf form of *A. ligtu* (possibly a distinct species) known as *A. hookeri* [8–10], but its present population in this country is mainly due to seeds collected by Clarence Elliott and Balfour Gourlay in 1927. However, these became so freely hybridized with *A. ligtu angustifolia* that one seldom sees either species now. I have not seen the white form that is recorded.

ligtu ● ★

| 1.2 m × 46 cm | [6–10] | Pinkish | E.Summer | PF | DS |
| 4 ft × 18 in | | | | | |

Chile. 1838. A variable species with flowers from reddish pink to blush. A dwarf form (possibly a distinct species) was known as *A. hookeri*. *A. ligtu angustifolia*, a form with bright, though variable, rose-pink flowers was introduced by Harold Comber in 1925 and bears—on top of its leafy wiry stems—heads of the usual small lily-flowers beautifully marked. It is not until one sees the clarity of its pink colouring that one realizes the superb beauty of this plant. The two erect coral-tinted segments with orange marks light up the flowers in a remarkable way. Unfortunately it is a rare plant; its hybrids with *A. haemantha*, which produce a wonderful blend of forms from pink through coral to salmon and orange, are better known. This strain was started by bees at the Six Hills Nursery, Stevenage, Hertfordshire. Attractive with *Philadelphus* 'Sybille' and 'Belle Etoile'.

pelegrina

| 30 × 30 cm | [8–10] | Pinkish | E.Summer | P | W | DS |
| 1 × 1 ft | | | | | | |

Chile. 1754. Lilac-pink, with dark spots and yellow throat. *A.p.* 'Alba', the Lily of the Incas, is a beautiful white form with dark markings. The flowers are large for the size of the plant. To be treasured in warm borders.

pulchella

| 90 × 30 cm | [8–10] | Reddish | Summer/ | P | W | DS |
| 3 × 1 ft | | | Autumn | | | |

Brazil. 1829. *A. psittacina*. As might be expected of a Brazilian plant, it is only hardy in sheltered positions in our warmest counties, where its flowers of strange colouring—rich red-brown with bright green tips to the segments—earn it the name of Parrot Lily. *A. braziliensis* is another tender Brazilian species with red and yellow flowers, produced for several months.

violacea

| 46 × 30 cm | [8–10] | Violet | E.Summer | P | W | DS |
| 18 in × 1 ft | | | | | | |

Chile. The warm violet-mauve tint of the flowers, with the forward central segments nearly white but spotted with purple, puts this in a class apart. It may be tried in our most favoured climates.

HYBRIDS. Many of the species cross readily, but division of selected clones is a chancy business. Apart from the *A. ligtu* × *A. haemantha* strains, *A. chilensis, A. violacea* and probably *A. pulchella* have all been used. 'Walter Fleming', known in the cut-flower trade also as 'Orchid', is a noted sterile hybrid of *A. violacea*; raised at Borde Hill, Sussex, prior to 1948. The other parent is variously described as *A. aurantiaca* or *A. chilensis*. In Holland J. A. M. Goemans has raised a series of lovely hybrids of *A. aurantiaca*. They are grown for the cut-flower trade, but have not reached nurseries yet. 'Ballerina', pale pink;

'Afterglow', deep reddish orange; 'Parigo Charm', salmon, primrose and deep coppery pink; 'Sonata', deep pink; are a few of them; their colourings are rich, varied by greenish and brownish overtones, and spiced by yellow flash and dark markings. Some of the above have become known as 'Princess Lilies'. Some dwarf hybrids probably derived from *A. chilensis* are of various lovely colourings, but are of doubtful hardiness. [Hybrids all 8–10].

ALTHAEA, Malvaceae. Sun-loving plants for any reasonable fertile soil.

cannabina

| 2.1 × 1.5 m | [3–9] | Pink | Summer/ | | PF | S |
| 7 × 5 ft | | | Autumn | | | |

Europe. 1597. It is seldom that this tall wiry plant needs staking. The stems are lightly clad in lobed leaves. The flowers, small, cupped, rosy lavender with dark eyes, project from the leaf axils on long stalks. The whole plant is light and graceful.

ficifolia

| 1.2 m or taller | [3–9] | Yellow | Summer | | PF | S |
| 4 ft or taller | | | | | | |

Siberia. 1597. Antwerp Hollyhock. Though so long known in gardens—where it has been used in hybridizing with *A. rosea*—a short-growing form has recently appeared in gardens as *A. rugosa*, a synonym of it. If only it would remain short and lemon-yellow, all would be well; unfortunately it readily hybridizes with other Hollyhocks. Not reliably perennial.

rosea

| 2.7 m × 90 cm | [3–9] | Various | Summer/ | | PF | S |
| 9 × 3 ft | | | Autumn | | | |

Orient. 1573. *Alcea rosea*. The Hollyhock started life as a perennial. Only the garden strains are seen today, but they need renewing frequently. This so-called species is of ancient lineage but of indefinite origin.

"Bee Keepers would do well to grow a few, for bees are fond of their flowers."—WR

ALYSSOIDES, Cruciferae. Sun-loving plant, perennial for a few years, easily raised from seeds. It requires a well-drained soil, such as would suit wallflowers.

utriculatum

| 46 × 46 cm | [4–7] | Yellow | Spring | | PF | S |
| 18 × 18 in | | | | | | |

Europe, Asia Minor. 1739. *Vesicaria utriculata*. A wallflower-like plant with small yellow flowers. The real interest lies in the elegant spires of seed-pods, which are pale green until ripe and sere. Fragrant.

AMARYLLIS, Amaryllidaceae. These beautiful bulbs need lots of sun and good soil, also patience, for flowers are only produced freely when the bulbs are well established. Plant at least 12.5 cm (5 in) deep, and protect from frost. They are beautiful when grouped near *Caryopteris mastacanthus* and *Vitex agnus-castus*.

belladonna ●
> 60 × 30 cm   [8–10]   Pink   L.Summer/   P   W   D
> 2 × 1 ft   E.Autumn

South Africa. 1712. The Belladonna Lily may be seen flowering freely in Cornish gardens, such as Trengwainton and Glendurgan, wherever they are happily growing in full sun. Up country they need the encouragement and protection of a sunny wall, and in colder districts (Surrey) will flower well when planted along a south- or west-facing exterior wall of a heated greenhouse. They need rich deep soil for their large bulbs, and a good soak of rain or water in, say, late July to start them into growth. The stout purple stems each bear a fine head of warm-pink, broad-petalled, trumpet flowers, deepening with age to crimson. A good form should be sought such as 'Purpurea', 'Spectabilis' or 'Rosea'. Of late years, Van Tubergen has launched some selections, 'Barberton' and 'Jagersfontein', dark rose-pink; 'Capetown', deep rose-red; 'Johannesburg', light rose-pink; and all of these have fine heads of large blooms. 'Hathor' is an excellent white. The leaves of all are broad, rich green, strap-shaped, and appear after the flowers, which is one reason why they need areas with mild winters or suitable protection. 'Beacon' is a fine crimson. Sweetly fragrant.

> "See what a lovely way they have of flushing a deeper and richer pink every hour of their floral life till they expire in a finish of crimson."—EAB

Hybridists are busy producing intergeneric hybrids between *Amaryllis, Crinum, Brunsvigia, Nerine,* etc., many of which have considerable beauty. These are seldom seen as yet, either in gardens or lists. One of the most celebrated is *Crinodonna × corsii* (*Crinum moorei × Amaryllis belladonna*) a plant of great beauty and warm colouring. Another is *Amarine × tubergenii* (*Nerine bowdenii × Amaryllis belladonna*); it has 60–cm (2–ft) stems carrying large *Nerine*-style blooms of deep pink; crimson-pink in the clone 'Zwanenburg'. *Brunsdonna × parkeri* (*Amaryllis belladonna × Brunsvigia josephinae*) is yet another. It is a fine, large, free-flowering plant, resembling the first parent; the reverse cross, known as 'Tubergen's Variety' has smaller flowers of a rich purplish rose. All kinds should have the tops of their bulbs about 12.5 cm (5 in) below the surface of the soil. [All hybrids 8–10].

AMICIA, Leguminosae. A tender, sun-loving, tall plant mainly for foliage effect in warm spots in the south and west. Any fertile soil.

zygomeris
> 2.1 × 1.2 m   [8–10]   Yellow   Autumn   CS
> 7 × 4 ft

Mexico. 1826. Stout stems and lush greenery; the large pea-flowers are yellow with maroon marks on the keel, borne in small spikes in the leaf axils. Big pale green stipules with purplish veins enclose the young leaves, which are in pairs, with a notch at the end: the leaf when folded in the bud thus gives space for the next shoot.

AMSONIA, Apocynaceae. A sun-loving genus for any fertile soil.

tabernaemontana
> 60 × 40 cm   [4–9]   Blue   Summer   P   DS
> 2 ft × 18 in

North America. 1759. *A. salicifolia.* Closely allied to *Rhazya orientalis,* this is of a more compact root-stock producing a sheaf of stems clad in narrow leaves with somewhat drooping heads of pale periwinkle-blue stars. On the whole I prefer *Rhazya. A. angustifolia* is similar but of less garden value.

ANAPHALIS, Compositae. Pearl Everlasting. The "everlasting" flowers are small, but are borne in large heads, white with yellow eyes. They are useful for cutting and drying. In the garden they are pleasing and thrifty plants, quickly making large clumps. They are useful for creating a grey-white effect in borders which are too moist for the average run of silvery, drought-loving plants; they thrive in sun and will also grow well in the shade of a building, but preferably not under trees. Few plants create a better complement to Japanese Anemones. Any reasonably retentive soil suits them but they droop and look miserable if they get too dry at the root. The following species are closely related, and are described as known in gardens.

cinnamomea

60 × 60 cm	[4–8]	White	L.Summer	PF	D
2 × 2 ft					

India, Burma. Felted, white, erect stems well clad in broad green leaves, white-felted beneath. The flat flower heads are conspicuous, and each "everlasting" flower is white with a yellow eye. *A. margaritacea* (1596) [3–8] from Eastern N. America and its forms are usually narrower in the leaf, the flowerheads more loose. These are all very beautiful when used with *Sedum spectabile* and red fuchsias, and are long-lasting. Sometimes confused with *A. yedoensis*, which is not in cultivation.

triplinervis ★

38 × 60 cm	[4–9]	White	L.Summer/	P	D
15 in × 2 ft			E.Autumn		

Himalaya. 1824. A tufted plant with copious greyish leaves, making a dome of foliage, which is covered with a galaxy of flowers from July onwards. The starry "everlasting" blooms are white with small yellow centres and borne in wide-branching heads. Excellent for cutting, white borders, and general planting, it is easily grown, but does not tolerate drought. It is used with tremendous success in the great parterre at Drummond Castle, Stirlingshire. *A. nubigena* [4–8] is similar but smaller; *A. cuneifolia* (1930) [4–8] is smaller still.

ANARRHINUM, Scrophulariaceae.

bellidifolium

60 × 46 cm	[7–8]	Blue	Summer	P	S
2 ft × 18 in					

S. Europe. 1629. This meek little plant with its undistinguished pointed leaves is pretty enough when it bursts into slender spires of small lilac-blue tubular flowers. For the front of the bed or border, in any fertile soil in full sun.

ANCHUSA, Boraginaceae. The most reliable garden member of this genus, *Anchusa myosotidiflora*, is now called *Brunnera macrophylla, q.v.* The forms of *A. azurea* provide the richest and truest blues for June together with veronicas, but are unreliable perennials and usually need staking. Full sun is best. Young plants are most satisfactory and are easily propagated from root cuttings, and succeed in any reasonable soil. Lovely with Bearded Irises and lupins.

azurea

90 cm–1.2 m	[4–8]	Blue	E.Summer	DR
× 60 cm				
3–4 × 2 ft				

Caucasus, etc. 1597. *A. italica*. There are several named forms, 'Opal' being a pleasing light blue, while 'Loddon Royalist' (1957), 'Royal Blue' (1954) and 'Little John'—a dwarf 46 cm (18 in)—are of deep glorious colour and improvements on the old 'Dropmore' (1905). Their flowers are borne in heavy, branching spikes, like giant forget-me-not, over coarse, hairy leaves, but severally the genera and species do give us good true-blue colouring, which is rare. *A. barrelieri* (1820) [4–8] is a smaller species with toothed leaves, achieving about 60 cm (2 ft). Blue flowers with white eye. Eastern Europe.

"In the yellow border is one patch of clear pale blue, the *Anchusa* Opal, grouped with pale yellows and white."—GJ

sempervirens
> *60 × 60 cm*   *[3–8]*   *Blue*   *E./L.Summer*   RS
> *2 × 2 ft*

Europe, Britain. *Pentaglottis sempervirens.* A rather coarse plant with flaccid hairy basal leaves and erect or flopping stems carrying small, good blue flowers. New stems arise during the growing season. It thrives in sun or shade, anywhere except in a bog, and seeds itself freely in waste places. Sometimes called Alkanet, but this belongs to a much shorter, related plant, *Alkanna tinctoria.*

ANEMONE, Ranunculaceae. Windflower. The anemones listed under *A. hupehensis, A. hybrida, A. tomentosa* and *A. vitifolia* are sound perennials with colonizing roots which can be invasive, particularly in light soils. One sees them growing in shade or sun, but an open position suits them best, and on the whole a retentive soil—even sticky and limy—produces the tallest stems and best flowers. The broad, vine-like foliage, rough and of dark green, is handsome throughout the summer, and the clumps are overtopped by the wiry stems, bearing at their branching extremities large rounded flowers of satisfying quality with a central green knob surrounded by yellow stamens. The little green knobs stay after the flowers have fallen and are sometimes cut, but the flowers are rather unreliable in water. Few plants look so satisfying in leaf and flower for so long a period. *A. canadensis, A. sylvestris* and *A. lesseri* are easy sun-lovers; *A. narcissiflora* and *A. rivularis* are small-flowered and need some coolth. *A. nemorosa* is best in shade under trees and shrubs or in thin grass. *A. pavonina* and its hybrids require full sun and good drainage with fertile soil.

canadensis
> *60 × 30 cm*   *[3–7]*   *White*   *E.Summer*   DS
> *2 × 1 ft*

W. North America. 1768. *A. pennsylvanica.* The Meadow Anemone is a pleasing small plant, with divided leaves and small flights of starry white flowers. For a sunny spot, but it will also flower in shade. Spreader.

hupehensis ★
> *60 × 46 cm*   *[5–9]*   *Pink*   *L.Summer*   DR
> *2 ft × 18 in*

W. China. 1908. A beautiful but rare species whose pleasing flowers have five or sometimes six rounded segments. The outer ones are crimson on the reverse, but all contribute to a rounded pink flower within. The colouring is slightly sharper than in the hybrid Japanese Anemones. The leaves are divided into three deeply toothed leaflets. In nature it varies from soft pink to a rich rubious tone. In all the outer segments are darkest but also smallest; even so they all contribute to a pleasing rounded flower. A good form from Germany bears the name 'Superbum' and I place highly 'Hadspen Abundance', raised by Eric Smith; it is of rich deep colour. With *A. tomentosa* this ushers in the flowering period of those distinguished plants, the so-called Japanese Anemones. *A. hupehensis* 'Superba' is a more common and prolific clone; 'September Charm' is a close hybrid of great merit: see below.

—japonica

60 × 46 cm	*[5–8]*	*Pink*	*L.Summer*	DR
2 ft × 18 in				

China. 1844. [5–8]. In earlier editions of this book I published a drawing of this plant, sketched at Kew, also one of *A.* × *hybrida* 'Prinz Heinrich' from my own garden. It now appears that they may be one and the same thing, and the differences in the drawings due to different soils and conditions. The matter must remain unsolved until we can obtain plants from the wild in Japan, where *A.h. japonica* is reported to be abundant.

★ —'September Charm' 1932 (Bristol Nurseries). With perhaps an extra petal or two, this is a close hybrid of *A. hupehensis* and, from a garden point of view, may be described as a superior and colourful type of it. A first-class plant, very free-flowering and clump-forming. 75 cm (2½ ft). It thrives at Peckover House, Cambridgeshire.

● ★ × hybrida

1.5 m × 60 cm	*[5–8]*	*Pink*	*E.Autumn*	DR
5 × 2 ft				

1848. *A. hupehensis japonica* × *A. vitifolia. A. elegans*; *A. japonica* of gardens. Raised at the Horticultural Society's (R.H.S.) garden, Chiswick. This is the wonderful, common pink Japanese Anemone of gardens. Beautiful rounded rose-pink blooms are produced for many weeks on ascending branching stems, over fine clumps of three-lobed, pointed, dark green leaves. There is no doubt that it is one of the highlights of the year, surpassed only by its superb white sport ● ★ 'Honorine Jobert' (*c.* 1858); in this the contrast of the bunch of yellow stamens and the dark green leaves raises it to a very high place. (It is amusing to note that on many modern Christmas cards this flower does duty for a Christmas rose, with the inevitable holly.) They are both hearty perennials when once established, but are invasive, and are perhaps most suited to the foreground of large shrub borders, etc. In spite of their height these two plants seldom require staking, nor do the parents or the subsequent hybrids. They flower best in full sun but will tolerate shade. These flowers can compete in beauty with all the flowers that have gone by during the season—daffodils, iris, lily or rose—as if Nature decided on a final fling.

> " 'Honorine Jobert' will give nearly three months' display of its well-shaped pure-white flowers, which have the most lovely of golden centres, both for form and colour, of any flower I can think of except *Rosa bracteata*."— EAB

It is remarkable that the above two varieties, raised so long ago, are still by far the most common of all Japanese Anemones, despite numerous named clones having been put on the market since. 'Whirlwind' (1887), from America, is a good semi-double white. A seedling of 'Honorine Jobert' called 'Lady Ardilaun' was raised in Ireland and this proved a prolific parent in the hands of Messrs Lemoine and others in France: 'Mont Rose' (1899), 'Géant des Blanches' ('White Queen'), prior to 1914, are two varieties which are still grown. The former is a good rich pink, the latter a sumptuous white of large proportions throughout. In Germany Wilhelm Pfitzer and others carried on, and some famous varieties are 'Prinz Heinrich' ('Prince Henry'), 1902, 'Luise Uhink', 'Königen Charlotte'

('Queen Charlotte'), 1898, 'Krimhilde', 1909, and 'Lorelei'. 'Prinz Heinrich' bears a remarkable resemblance to the original *A. hupehensis japonica*. Of late years 'Prinz Heinrich' has appeared in some lists under the name 'Profusion', a totally different variety with paler pink flowers and only an occasional extra segment to the flowers; it was raised in 1898 (Lemoine). More recent varieties are 'Lady Gilmour', semi-double, light pink; the rich deep pink 'Margarete', rather more than semi-double, and Alan Bloom's 'Bressingham Glow'. These are all unquestionably first-class garden plants, about 90 cm (3 ft) high, invasive but valuable, and needing no staking. They give their main display after *A. hupehensis* and *A. tomentosa* and their immediate cultivars. 'Queen Charlotte' is a favourite of mine and of Mr Bowles.

"It has taken possession of rather more of the garden than I desired, but it is so lovely that I cannot bring myself to root any of it out."—EAB

× lesseri

| 46 × 30 cm | [5–8] | Various | E.Summer | D |
| 18 in × 1 ft | | | | |

1932. *A. multifida* × *A. sylvestris*. The form most usually seen has flowers of deep rose-carmine, small but plentifully borne on erect stems above ferny leaves. A large rock-plant or frontal plant for the border.

narcissiflora

| 60 × 46 cm | [5–8] | White | E.Summer | S |
| 2 ft × 18 in | | | | |

Europe, Asia, North America. 1773. The buttercup-shaped white flowers are often flushed with mauve on the outside, and are held in a branched head over a tump of handsome, divided, dark green leaves. It is in fact much like a May-flowering miniature version of a Japanese Anemone. The root is fibrous. A plant of breeding, preferring the softer west and enjoying rich humus-laden soils; it does well at Bodnant, Gwynedd. See also *A. rivularis*. *A. virginiana* (1722) [3–8] from North America is similar.

"... always and everywhere a well beloved friend ... foot high heads of six to ten lovely flowers exactly like so many Apple-blossoms."—RF

nemorosa★

| 15 × 30 cm | [4–8] | Various | Spring | D |
| 6 in × 1 ft | | | | |

Europe, Britain. Wood Anemone. Refusing to be bullied by my self-imposed rules about height I am including this species because it is a woodland gem, and so few of the numerous forms are seen in gardens. They are of the easiest culture—preferably in part shade under shrubs perhaps—in light or heavy soil. They colonize quickly, having invasive roots. They flower from late March to early May in Surrey and by July the foliage has died down. The species is a common native, usually white in the east, or with pinkish buds, but in the western counties, Wales and Ireland, it produces rich blue and pink flowers, whence most of the named forms originate. Most have six to eight petals, usually seven. Lovely for intermingling with miniature daffodils in thin grass. Most of these are established at Cliveden, Buckinghamshire.

● ★ **'Allenii'** Raised by James Allen, Shepton Mallet prior to 1890. Maroon petioles and brownish flower-stalks. The largest and most richly tinted of the lavender-blues, a most lovely flower. Outside a deep rich lilac, inside rich lavender-blue. It thrives at Trelissick, Cornwall.

—**'Blue Bonnet'** Brownish green flower stalks, darker petioles. The flowers are of pale grey-blue outside, deep azure blue inside, faintly tinted with lavender with a pale base around the stamens.

● ★—**'Leeds' Variety'** According to E. A. Bowles this was found in Ireland by Lady Doneraile, and distributed by Leeds; there is a figure of it in *The Garden*, 15th October 1887. It is sometimes called 'Dr Lowe's Variety', and also, I believe, 'Wilks' Giant'. It seems to have a habit of seeding itself about the garden. The flowers are at least twice the size of any other variety, faintly flushed with pink outside as they fade, but otherwise of pure milk-white. The stalk is green, but brownish at the base of the petioles. It is one of the first to flower.

—**'Lismore Blue'** Stems darkest at base, but brownish up to the petioles, which are rich red-brown. Outside pale grey-blue, inside light lavender-blue. This is about midway between 'Allenii' and 'Blue Bonnet' in colour.

—**'Lismore Pink'** Stems and petioles as in 'Lismore Blue'. This is the only variety I have met in which the petals are a uniform pale pink inside and outside. It thrives at Hidcote, Gloucestershire. The colour outside deepens with age.

—**'Robinsoniana'** Named after William Robinson, who recorded in 1883 that he had found it in the Botanic Garden at Oxford, but it had been sent from Ireland. Dark maroon stalk, petioles paler. Petals pale creamy grey outside, light lavender-blue inside; with slightly undulate edges.

—**'Rosea'** Many forms are pink or rosy lilac in bud but the colour is reserved to the outside of the segments and often intensifies as the flowers age. They are white within.

DOUBLES. Whereas all of the above have usually seven petals, there is a form with usually ten petals of a size approaching 'Leeds' Variety', but it cannot really be described as a double. The petals are flushed with pale rosy mauve outside. The base of the stem is beetroot-tinted, becoming paler and brownish upwards; the petioles are reddish-brown. The following are true doubles, white.

—**'Bracteata'** is figured in old books, as early as the sixteenth century. In this variety the flower is full of narrow petals, all much the same length and width, but some of the outer ones are often green.

● ★ —**'Vestal'** is figured from about 1870 onwards. It opens its flowers when all the others are beginning to fade. It is pure white, with the usual seven outer petals, but with a dense button of tiny petals in the centre. An exquisite and valuable plant. Leaves more or less glabrous.
　　Another fully double form grows at Knightshayes Court, Devon. It flowers earlier than 'Vestal', has hairy leaves, and the flowers are larger, but with an equally dense middle. Around this the circlet of bright yellow stamens is noticeable. Both kinds have brownish green stalks. Another prolific grower has fully double white flowers, dizened with a tuft of lilac-blue segments in the centre.
　　There are many other forms mentioned in books, and no doubt a lot of unnamed forms are grown as well. The above are some of the more distinct. A smaller plant of the same nature is *A. ranunculoides* [4–8], and a good form, 'Superba', is a bright buttercup yellow. There is a charming double, 'Pleniflora'. A primrose-yellow hybrid with *A. nemorosa* is *A.* × *seemanii* or *A* × *intermedia* [4–8], a dainty charmer. I have to resist going further into these small species, such as *A. apennina* [5–8] and *A. blanda* [4–8]; their charms are sufficiently described in bulb catalogues.

"Fairest among all the lesser flowers of the early year are the wood anemones. Is there anything more affecting in the records of spring than its ripple of laughter which trembles across the crystal whiteness of some woodland glade in answer to the breezes of March?"—ATJ

"The stocke or kindred of the Anemones or Winde-floures ... are without number, or at least not sufficiently knowne unto any one that hath written of plants."—GH [This is still true]

pavonina

38 × 23 cm	[8–10]	Various	Spring	P	DS
15 × 9 in					

Balearic Islands, S.E. Europe. It thrives and seeds itself in heavy soil in full sun, with good drainage. The parsley-like frilly leaves cover the ground in spring, when for many weeks the gorgeous blooms with their indigo centres appear. They vary from almost white through pink to scarlet, and purple and blue to opalescent tints. The tuberous roots should be planted about 5 cm (2 in) deep in autumn. Cottony seed-heads.

This species is closely allied to *A. coronaria* [8–10] and *A. hortensis* [6–9]; the de Caen, St Bavo, St Brigid and other strains of anemones grown in Cornwall, France and elsewhere for the cut-flower trade are derived from them. These highly bred strains seem to me to be less perennial and less easy to grow than *A. pavonina*. *A.* × *fulgens* [7–9] (*A. pavonina* × *A. hortensis*) comes into this group; it is blazing scarlet with dark centre.

rivularis

60 × 30 cm	[6–8]	White	Summer	S
2 × 1 ft				

N. India, etc. 1840. A close relative of *A. narcissiflora*. This appears to favour the moister parts of the country, but is not difficult to grow in humus-laden soil. The rounded root-stock gives good divided dark green leaves and stiff stems, branching freely, with several white flowers whose sepals are metallic blue outside and have blue anthers. The colour is variable. *N. tetrasepala* [5–8] from the W. Himalaya is a similar plant.

sylvestris

46 × 30 cm	[4–9]	White	Spring	DR
18 in × 1 ft			onwards	

Europe, etc. 1596. The Snowdrop Anemone runs freely in light soil, but is more static in heavy soil, in sun or shade. The larger-flowered form 'Macrantha' or 'Grandiflora' should be sought; in this the fragrant, nodding, white flowers are of good size, set off by a cluster of yellow stamens, and held well above the deeply cut leaves. Gossypine white seed-heads mature. There is a double form.

"... White flowers come in Spring, then the ripe seeds like lumps of cotton-wool follow, and are very white and ornamental, and till late in the autumn the plant is continually throwing up a fresh flower stem or two."—EAB

tomentosa ★

1.2 m × 60 cm	[5–9]	Pink	L.Summer	F	DRS
4 × 2 ft					

Tibet, etc. 1909. *A. vitifolia* and *A. vitifolia* 'Robustissima' (1900) of gardens. A handsome and extremely vigorous plant which produces sheaves of soft pink blooms rather earlier in the season than those of the hybrid Japanese Anemones. The leaves are large, divided, deeply veined and grey-green beneath. It will colonize large areas fairly quickly; it thrives at Hidcote, Gloucestershire. A good companion for *Hydrangea villosa*.

vitifolia

1.2 m × 46 cm	[5–9]	White	E.Autumn	F	DRS
4 ft × 18 in					

Upper Nepal, etc. 1829. A rare plant whose name is usually applied to *A. tomentosa*. This is a comparatively small, compact plant, with leaves lobed but not divided into sections, and truly vine-like. The flowers are usually pure white and have yellow stamens. A garden plant known as 'Alba Dura' (1937) is probably a form or hybrid of this species; it is of similar height and its white flowers are purplish in the bud.

ANEMONOPSIS, Ranunculaceae.

macrophylla ●

75 × 46 cm	[5–8]	Lavender	Summer	DS
2½ ft × 18 in				

Japan. 1869. This is a plant of unusual refinement for cool humus-laden soils. It also needs a cool climate because dry summer winds inhibit the growth of its fresh green, divided ferny leaves which make a decorative clump. Purple without, the lavender flowers are meek and forlorn, nodding, cup-shaped, borne in airy sprays.

"... their effect is rather that of big belated Columbines, spurless and very waxy, white centred and of a rich lavender-blue."—RF

ANIGOZANTHUS, Amaryllidaceae. Tuberous or swollen roots and sword-like leaves; tall stems with branching heads of tubular blooms with starry mouths. These need the very warmest and best-drained corners in our warmest and driest climates.

flavida

1.2 m × 30 cm	[9–10]	Yellowish	L.Summer	P	W	DS
4 × 1 ft						

W. Australia. 1808. The downy flowers are of yellowish green, usually tinged with red-brown on the exposed surface. A very good reddish form is known as *A. coccinea*. Several other rare species may be tried.

ANTHEMIS, Compositae. All grow best in full sun, in well-drained soil. Divide and replant in spring to keep them in health if they appear to have suffered from the winter.

cupaniana

30 × 90 cm	[5–8]	White	E.Summer	P	D
1 × 3 ft					

Italy. Sometimes dying back in winter, the dense silvery mats spread freely and are covered with pure white daisies for several weeks; they accentuate the silvery grey-white foliage, and create a scintillating effect. Lovely with Bearded Irises. A useful edging plant at Saltram and Overbecks, Devon.

sancti-johannis

| 60 × 60 cm | [4–9] | Orange | Summer | P | DS |
| 2 × 2 ft | | | | | |

Bulgaria. 1928. The true species bears rich orange daisies and the ray-petals are notably short, surrounding the large orange centre. Dainty foliage. A rare, hot colour, of value in the garden. Unfortunately it freely hybridizes with *A. tinctoria* and is apt to lose its colour and identity thereby.

tinctoria

| 90 × 90 cm | [4–8] | Yellow | Summer | P | D |
| 3 × 3 ft | | | | | |

Europe. 1561. Golden Marguerite. Both *A. sancti-johannis* and *A. tinctoria* suffer from over-exuberant flowering at times, and it is advisable to cut down the old flowering stems as soon as they are over so as to encourage basal growth, without which the plants are apt to fade away. A showy and highly satisfactory garden plant producing a basal clump of parsley-like leaves over which are sheaves of upturned yellow daisies, on show for many weeks. The plants usually need support. 'Grallach Gold' (1946) is a vivid and glorious yellow, superior to 'Perry's Variety', but less perennial. ★ 'E. C. Buxton' is cool lemon-yellow, invaluable in the garden and for picking. This variety stands out as the most useful and admirable of all the (very few) light yellow summer-flowering plants, and a summer border without it is difficult to conceive. Specially good with *Campanula lactiflora* and other blue and purple flowers, and all colours of phloxes. Raised at Betws-y-Coed, Caernarvonshire, in the garden of E. C. Buxton. 'Wargrave' is of more creamy colouring. A good white-rayed, yellow-centred form has originated at Powis Castle, Powys; named 'Powis White' (1973).

ANTHERICUM, Liliaceae. Easily grown, clump-forming plants for any fertile soil in sun.

liliago ★

| 60 × 30 cm | [5–9] | White | E.Summer | PF | DS |
| 2 × 1 ft | | | | | |

S. Europe. 1596. St Bernard's Lily. Quickly makes itself at home, seeding about here and there. It is a prolific plant when established and the flowers are trumpet-shaped. Highly decorative and a lovely contrast to *Dictamnus albus purpureus*. Good seed spikes. The larger-flowered relative, *Paradisea liliastrum*, St Bruno's Lily, is a less good garden plant in my experience, nor is it so tall.

"Bulbous plants of the Lily family ... among the most beautiful of hardy flowers."—WR

—major ● ★

| 90 × 30 cm | [5–9] | White | E.Summer | P | DS |
| 3 × 1 ft | | | | | |

(*A. algeriense* of gardens) I consider this and the above plant the most decorative for the garden, and both are happy in any sunny border that is not boggy. Grassy, grey-green basal leaves through which arise wiry erect stems with small snow-white, lily-flowers, opening flat, with yellow stamens. Try planting it in front of *Baptisia australis*, with *Geranium sanguineum lancastriense* in the foreground. It always flowers well at Hidcote, Gloucestershire, but seldom sets seeds. Lovely with early peonies.

ramosum

90 × 30 cm	*[5–9]*	*White*	*Summer*	P	DS
3 × 1 ft					

W. and S. Europe. 1570. *A. graminifolium* (of gardens). While the tuft of grassy leaves remains the same in this species the flowers are tiny, borne in much divided airy spikes, like an early, airy *Gypsophila*. A good contrast for *Geranium pratense* forms. It does well at Benthall Hall, Shropshire.

AQUILEGIA, Ranunculaceae. Both aquilegia and columbine refer to the shape of the flowers, the petals being like the extended wings of eagle or dove below the spurs of the flowers, which resemble neck and head.

alpina

60–90 × 30 cm	*[4–7]*	*Blue*	*E.Summer*	PF	S
2–3 × 1 ft					

Switzerland. 1731. Deep blue nodding flowers, or sometimes blue and white.

—'Hensol
★ Harebell'

90 × 30 cm	*[4–8]*	*Various*	*E.Summer*	PF	S
3 × 1 ft					

A. alpina × A. vulgaris. Raised at Mossdale, Castle Douglas, Kirkcudbrightshire, by Mrs Kennedy, early twentieth century. This strain is of deep Wedgwood blue, but several keen gardeners, notably A. T. Johnson, gradually selected a variety of tints; several of us have continued to distribute this Bulkeley Mill strain. Besides the blue—sometimes blue-and-white—rich plum-mahogany, soft pink, lilac and pure white occur, no doubt inherited from the old 'Granny's Bonnets', *A. vulgaris*, of the Welsh valleys. They will seed themselves about mildly and give a splendid display for several years. The foliage is handsome for months, dying off to tones of lilac and purple. They thrive almost anywhere in ordinary soil, and seed themselves freely. They help to fill the gap made by the demise of the daffodils and tulips, with Honesty and Bluebells.

> "As for the rest of the tribe which fringe our ferny woodland walks most of them are mongrels ... which at one time we made gallant efforts to 'improve'."—ATJ

canadensis

60 × 30 cm	*[4–9]*	*Red/Yellow*	*E.Summer*	PF	S
2 × 1 ft					

North America. 1640. Noted for its dainty blooms with lemon-yellow petals, guarded by forward-pointing sepals and spurs of deep red. It is an elegant plant for well-drained sunny places. Typical foliage, dark green.

chrysantha ●

90 × 60 cm	*[4–9]*	*Yellow*	*E.Summer*	PF	S
3 × 2 ft					

S. North America. 1873. One of the species from which the Long Spurred Hybrids were raised. A vigorous elegant representative of long-spurred *Aquilegia*, whose flowers are rich yellow with paler spurs. Pretty divided foliage. A fairly reliable plant, when grown in a sunny well-drained position, and spectacular in flower.

flabellata

30 × 30 cm	*[4–9]*	*White*	*Spring*	PF	S
1 × 1 ft					

Japan. 1887. Lacking in grace, this plant has compensation in its stocky growth, its rounded, rather glaucous leaves and chubby, short-spurred nodding flowers of white, tinged more or less with lilac-blue. There is a much shorter white form, *A.f.* 'Nana Alba' (1909).

formosa

60–90 × 46 cm	*[4–8]*	*Red and Yellow*	*E.Summer*	PF	S
2–3 ft × 18 in					

W. North America. This is similar to *A. chrysantha* and *A. canadensis*, and also a parent of the garden hybrids. The flower colour is bright, the petals being yellow and the spurs from pale coral-red to bright red. A short-lived but easily grown plant in well-drained soil in sun.

HYBRID STRAINS ●

60–90 × 46 cm	*[3–9]*	*Various*	*E.Summer*	PF	S
2–3 ft × 18 in					

There are many popular strains of Long Spurred aquilegias, probably mainly derived from *A. chrysantha, A. canadensis* and perhaps *A. caerulea* [3–8]. They all have elegant, divided, rather glaucous foliage at the base, and wiry branching stems on which are poised nodding flowers of beautiful shape. (See above.) The colours range from yellow to pink and rich red, to purple and mauve; usually the petals are paler than the spurs. Separately coloured strains, such as 'Crimson Star', or mixed colours, can be easily raised from seed. They are not long-lived but thrive in any well-drained fertile soil, preferably in sun. In their numerous colours they blend or contrast well with Bearded Irises, Catmint, Lupins and Oriental Poppies. There is a dwarf strain 'Biedermeier' which loses the essential grace of the usual strains, of which the 'McKana' and 'Monarch' hybrids are vigorous and elegant. These seem to have superseded the one-time excellent 'Mrs Scott Elliott' strain, but they are no doubt derived from it. There is also a beautiful white strain 'Schneekonigen', or 'Snow Queen'. The 'Dwarf Fairyland' strain is an abomination, having lost all beauty of floral shape. 'Clematiflora' is a name given to a race of spur-less hybrids, mostly in pale tints, *c.* 1930.

longissima ●

60 × 46 cm	*[4–9]*	*Yellow*	*E.Summer*	PF	S
2 ft × 18 in					

S. North America. 1888. A dainty plant, again short-lived but easy in sun on well-drained soil. The leaves are finely divided and the length of the spurs exceeds all others; they are bright yellow while the petals are paler. This has been bred with the Long Spurred Hybrids and the resulting strain, 'Longissima Hybrids', has absorbed the greater range of colours.

skinneri

60 × 46 cm	*[4–9]*	*Red*	*E.Summer*	PF	W	S
2 ft × 18 in						

Mexico. 1840. Very neatly divided glaucous leaves and flowers, whose red, erect spurs seem very large for the downward-pointing greenish-yellow small petals. This needs a warm well-drained position and is short-lived. *A. × jaeschkanii* [3–8] is a race derived from crosses between this species and *A. chrysantha*.

vulgaris

90 × 46 cm	*[5–9]*	*Various*	*E.Summer*	PF	S
3 ft × 18 in					

Europe. The Common Columbine has dumpy, short-spurred flowers in great profusion, indigo or violet, crimson, pink and plum colour. The lovely white *A.v. nivea*, the 'Munstead White Columbine', was a favourite of Miss Jekyll. It has the greyest foliage among aquilegias, pale green stems and buds, opening pure white. It remains true to type if grown in reasonable isolation, and seeds itself as do all the others. A valuable garden plant.

"... white foxgloves, the great white Columbine and the tall stems of white Peach-leaved Campanula rise at the back of this eastern border."—GJ

ARALIA, Araliaceae. Easily grown plants, for the connoisseur of the elegant. Sun or part-shade in any fertile soil.

cachemirica

1.8 × 1.8 m	*[6–9]*	*Green*	*Summer*	PF	DS
6 × 6 ft					

Kashmir. 1888. *A. macrophylla*. A symphony in green. Large, deeply cut, hand-like leaves of rich green borne copiously up the arching stems, which carry a long open panicle of creamy flower-heads. They are like ivy blossoms and are followed by maroon-black berries. A massive plant for larger gardens, suitable for a specimen on a lawn or in a wild area. Leaves have 5–9 segments.

"... which in size and beauty of leaf are far before many 'fine foliaged plants' grown in hothouses."—WR

racemosa

1.5 × 1.2 m	*[5–9]*	*Green*	*Summer*	PF	DS
5 × 4 ft					

North America. 1658. Similar to the above, but more refined and upright, with brownish stems and greenish white flower-umbels in a large spike. Leaves have 3–5 leaflets. A similar species is *A. californica* [6–9].

ARISAEMA, Araceae. See also *Arum*. The Arum Family provides some choice beauties for the outdoor garden. These tuberous-rooted species are hardy in all but our coldest counties, preferably in retentive, fertile soil with some humus and part shade—or full sun. They should be planted about 10 cm (4 in) deep. There are many other species of *Arisaema* which are intriguing even if not of overpowering beauty; they prove fascinating to their devotees. Though all species produce spikes of colourful berries, some clones in cultivation appear to need other clones to ensure pollination. They are mainly distinguished from species of *Arum* by their divided foliage.

"... large handsome foliage waves impressively, and among them are seen the dingy great Arum-flowers, often hooded over and ending in a long rat-tail wisp."—RF

amurense

46 × 46 cm	*[5–9]*	*Green/brown*	*E.Summer*	DS
18 in × 18 in				

subsp. *robustum*. Far East. 1884. A smaller plant than most others on these pages; the neat green or brown spathe has elegant white stripes and a small hood. The leaves are five-parted, fresh green. Plant 6 in deep.

candidissimum ● ★

   30 × 46 cm   *[7–9]*   *White*   *Summer*   PF DS
   1 ft × 18 in

W. China. 1924. Mark its position with a good stake. The first thing you will see is the flower appearing in June or later: a hooded pure white spathe beautifully striped with pink in the throat but outside with pale green. There is also a pure white form. The leaves which follow are splendid, broad and three-lobed. This is a great beauty, to be treasured, but is easy when once established and carries orange seeds in later summer. Excellent at Hidcote, Gloucestershire, at the Savill Garden, Windsor, and at Wisley, Surrey.

consanguineum ●

   90 × 30 cm   *[8–9]*   *Greenish*   *Summer*   P W DS
   3 × 1 ft

China, etc. 1893. A slender, remarkably elegant plant. The erect stems, mottled green and brown, bear one or two leaves divided, umbrella-like, into many long fine points. Just under them, modestly, a hooded green arum stands, striped with brown and with a long brown tail from the tip of the spathe hanging down in front. Red berries sometimes mature. It requires a warm corner.

costatum ●

   90 × 60 cm   *[8–9]*   *Purple*   *E.Summer*   DS
   3 × 2 ft

Nepal. 1831. Though known in the 19th century it was introduced again recently by A. D. Schilling. The hooded spathe is decorated with white stripes and has a long tip. The spadix is elongated to a curly thread which reaches the ground. While these characters do not add up to a highly decorative flower, the leaves, with their three immense, ribbed lobes, are of great character. For woodland conditions. Plant 6 in deep.

dracontium

   30–90 × 46 cm   *[4–9]*   *Green*   *E.Summer*   PF DS
   1–3 ft × 18 in

E. North America. The Green Dragon earns its name from the very long yellow spadix (30 cm or more long) which projects from the small green hooded spathe. The leaves have many segments, carried on tall stems. Very often showy orange-red berries mature. Moist shady ground.

ringens

   46 × 30 cm   *[7–9]*   *Purplish*   *E.Summer*   P DS
   18 in × 1 ft

Japan. Each shoot produces two handsome, three-lobed, attenuated leaves on stout stalks. The flower is astonishing—the green-striped spathe curves over with lips of maroon-purple. Plant mimicry?—well, it *is* rather like a fat snail!

sikokianum ●

   46 × 46 cm   *[5–9]*   *White*   *Spring*   P DS
   18 × 18 in

Japan. 1938. Again with handsome three-lobed leaves this flowers earlier and like *A. candidissimum*, before the leaves are fully developed. Of variable colouring, but usually seen with the black-maroon spathe, the hooded portion green and brown striped, over a pure white knobbed spadix and throat. All arums are handsome; this and *A. candidissimum* are exquisitely beautiful too.

speciosum
> *60–90 × 46 cm*   *[8–9]*   *Maroon*   *Spring*   PF W DS
> *2–3 ft × 18 in*

Himalaya. 1872. Splendid foliage, three-lobed, of rich green rimmed with red-brown, borne on a stout green stem freely mottled with brown. The large spathes are of velvety maroon-purple within, while without the tint is tempered by green striping. A purple string, some 50 cm (20 in) long, extends from the tip of the creamy spadix. These remarkable blooms are on short stems held below the leaves. It needs a sheltered position.

triphyllum
> *30 × 30 cm*   *[4–9]*   *Purplish*   *E.Summer*   PF DS
> *1 × 1 ft*

E. North America. 1664. *A. atrorubens.* Jack in the Pulpit—from the appearance of the greenish-brown spadix hooded over with the arching, beautifully fashioned green spathe, which is purplish, striped with white inside and flushed with a similar dark tint outside, also at the base. An amusing fellow, with three-lobed, beautiful leaves. Orange-red berries borne in spikes sometimes follow.

ARISTEA, Iridaceae. Grassy-leafed South African plants for the sunniest, best-drained positions in our warmest counties. The flowers live but a day but are produced for many days, from branching stems; they are a beautiful pure blue, small, of six segments and rather like those of *Sisyrinchium striatum.* They are tricky to move except as seedlings, and their fibrous roots should be grown in pots while young. *A. eckloni* [9–10] is one of the best-known species; it flowers in early summer, as also does *A. ensifolia* [9–10]. Others are worth trying. 46 cm (18 in).   W S

ARISTOLOCHIA, Aristolochiaceae. A genus renowned for its unusual flowers, often shaped like a tobacco pipe, with a bulbous base.

clematitis
> *90 × 60 cm*   *[5–9]*   *Yellow*   *L.Summer*   D
> *3 × 2 ft*

Europe. A plant with an invasive root system, easily grown in any fertile soil, preferably in sun. Leafy erect stems with small pale yellow flowers held in the leaf axils. Intriguing, hardly showy, but it can puzzle a know-all visitor. Pollination is effected by insects entrapped in the hairy throat of the flower.

ARMERIA, Plumbaginaceae. Thrift or Sea Pink. Useful plants for edging, or for small borders, in full sun and well-drained soil. *Armeria maritima* [4–8] and its forms and *A. corsica* (of gardens) [6–9] are useful dwarfs.

leucocephala
> *30 × 25 cm*   *[6–9]*   *White*   *L.Summer*   DS
> *1 ft × 10 in*

Corsica, Sardinia. Included because it is the tallest among white-flowered species.

plantaginea
> *46 × 30 cm*   *[4–9]*   *Pink*   *E.Summer*   DS
> *18 in × 1 ft*

Europe. 1740. *A. pseudoarmeria, A. cephalotes, A. latifolia; A. formosa* and *A. alliacea* (of gardens). Variable from carmine to the white form, *A.p. leucantha* or 'Alba'. The broad, long leaves make good clumps; the large flower-heads are borne on stout stalks. The most noted colour form is 'Bees' Ruby', whose flowers are of brilliant, deep, "shocking" pink, glorious with *Linum narbonense* and *Iris pallida dalmatica*. If you dislike this sort of colour there is a hybrid strain called 'Formosa Hybrids' or 'Plantaginea Hybrids', probably the result of crossing with *A. corsica* (of gardens), in a strange range of tints from deep carmine to terracotta. Evergreen.

ARNICA, Compositae. The following plant is one of the glories of the alpine meadows, but takes kindly to ordinary border cultivation.

montana

30 × 30 cm	*[6–9]*	*Orange*	*Summer*	DS
1 × 1 ft				

Europe. 1731. Tufts of tongue-shaped hairy green leaves. The wide orange-yellow daisies are held aloft on stout stems. It thrives at Rowallane, Northern Ireland. *A. cordifolia* from Eastern N. America (1898) [5–9] is similar but with heart-shaped basal leaves.

ARTEMISIA, Compositae. All species need full sun and well-drained soil and are valued more for foliage effect than for their flowers, except *A. lactiflora*.

abrotanum

90 cm–1.2 m	*[5–8]*	*Grey foliage*	*Summer*	P	CD
× 46 cm					
3–4 ft × 18 in					

S. Europe. 1548. Southernwood, Old Man, Lad's Love. A shrubby plant, densely bushy, with very feathery sage-green, strongly aromatic foliage. The flowers are insignificant. A good plant for sunny position in any poor or medium soil. It should be planted near the path or seat, so that one can brush by or otherwise savour its foliage. It is best to prune it back every spring to keep it compact.

absinthium

60–90 × 60 cm	*[4–9]*	*Greyish*	*Summer*	P	CD
2–3 × 2 ft					

Europe, Britain. Wormwood or Absinth. Margery Fish selected two excellent forms: 'Lambrook Silver', 75 cm (2½ ft), 'Lambrook Giant', rather taller. They are both a shimmer of silky grey much-divided leaves; the stems carry tiny grey flowers in long, branched spikes. Perfect against shrubs with coppery leaves, or with *Sedum maximum atropurpureum*. Evergreen. *A. maritima*, the Sea Wormwood, is a smaller edition of the above and frequents sand dunes and salty marshes around our coasts.

arborescens

60–90 × 60 cm	*[9]*	*Grey foliage*	*Summer/*	P	W	CD
2–3 × 2 ft			*Autumn*			

S. Europe. 1640. The most silky and lacy of all the grey-foliage plants. Best planted at the foot of a warm wall in full sun; with a red-brick wall at its back the contrast is wonderful. Dry soil. It needs protection in the winter even in very sheltered gardens and should be planted in spring; a reputedly hardier form is called 'Faith Raven', collected from high ground in Crete by John Raven. It is a marvellous contrast to *Nerine bowdenii*. In cold areas *A. absinthium* 'Lambrook Giant' will prove a worthy substitute. Evergreen.

canescens
of gardens
46 × 30 cm	*[5–9]*	*Grey foliage*	*Summer/*	P CD
18 in × 1 ft			*Autumn*	

Extremely lacy filigree leaves of silver-grey make this a most beautiful dense ground-covering plant, one of the best of all silverlings, freely branching and making a mass of curling divided leaves on ascending stems. Ideal with the old shrub roses. Sun, ordinary soil. *A. splendens* (of gardens) [5–9] is similar; both plants are confused with *A. armeniaca* [5–9].

lactiflora
1.8 m × 60 cm	*[4–9]*	*Cream*	*L.Summer*	P D
6 × 2 ft				

China, India. 1901. The "odd-man-out" of this group. A stalwart garden plant, greedy but erect, bearing jagged green leaves and conspicuous sheaves of tiny creamy flowers, long-lasting, and suitable for cutting when mature. It is seen at its best when grouped with yellow, purple, or blue flowers; it appears to be of a "dirty" tint when placed near white flowers or silvery foliage.

ludoviciana ★
1.2 m × 60 cm	*[4–9]*	*Grey-White*	*Summer/*	PF D
4 × 2 ft			*Autumn*	

North America. *A. gnaphaloides, A. purshiana; A. palmeri* (of gardens). A pretty plant, with willow-leaves of silvery grey-white all up the slender erect stems, sometimes bending outwards, and bearing slender plumes of tiny grey-white flowers above, in July and August. It has running roots, forming a thicket of stems in any sunny position in drained soil. An effective contrast for crimson roses, and any varieties of phlox, particularly the pink ones. The form grown under this name in gardens has entire leaves, but sometimes they have jagged margins. Of these the following have been named.

★ —**latiloba** [4–8]   This short growing, 60 cm (2 ft) plant has spectacular grey-white leaves with jagged edges. It creates an excellent pale effect in the White Garden at Sissinghurst. It comes from higher altitudes than the taller *A. ludoviciana.*

—**'Silver Queen'**
90 × 60 cm	*[6–9]*	*Grey foliage*	*Summer/*	P D
3 × 2 ft			*Autumn*	

A similar plant, less tall and less reliably erect than *A. ludoviciana.* But the leaves are profuse and prettily cut. It does not flower so much, relying upon its foliage for effect. Since there are many silverlings with divided foliage, I rank the clean-cut effect of *A. ludoviciana* higher.

pontica
60 × 46 cm	*[5–9]*	*Grey foliage*	*Summer*	P D
2 ft × 18 in				

Central Europe. 1570. Roman Wormwood or Small Absinth. Sometimes confused with *A. maritima.* It is a rapid, dense, invasive colonizer, a fluff of feathery sage-green foliage in slender, erect sprays; tiny greyish blooms. Effective for months. Sun; ordinary soil. A smaller edition of *A. abrotanum.*

'Powis Castle' ★

90 cm × 1.2 m	*[5–8]*	*Silvery*	*L.Summer*	P	C
3 × 4 ft					

c. 1978. A hybrid raised and distributed by Mr A. J. Hancock. Its parentage is thought to be *A. arborescens* and *A. absinthium* and it combines the beautiful filigree foliage of the former with the greater hardiness of the latter. Flowers are seldom produced. It suffers in cold wet winters but as a general rule comes through unharmed in Surrey. A first rate shrubby plant.

stelleriana ★

60 × 90 cm	*[4–8]*	*Grey foliage*	*Summer*	P	CD
2 × 3 ft					

N.E. Asia, E. North America. 1865. The Dusty Miller makes a splendid clump or carpet of broad, deeply fingered, grey-white leaves, and is a shrubby evergreen in mild districts. The tiny yellow flowers are borne on grey stems swathed in grey leaflets. A first-rate silver-grey foreground for *Aster × frikartii*. This is a good plant for maritime or cold gardens. Evergreen.

From Japan came recently a new form, originating apparently with Mr Kazuo Mori, which is completely prostrate and even more silvery white in leaf than the usual type.

"... the whole is carpeted and edged with the white foliage of Artemisia stelleriana, the quite hardy plant that is such a good substitute for the tenderer *Cineraria maritima.*" [*Senecio cineraria*]—GJ

valesiaca

46 × 46 cm	*[8–9]*	*Grey foliage*	*Summer*	P	CD
18 × 18 in					

S. Europe. 1739. As silvery in its filigree as *A. canescens*, and as hardy, but in this all the leaves and the flower spikes arch prettily. *A. nutans* is just as silvery and about the same size, but is more erect-growing.

ARTHROPODIUM, Liliaceae. A tender plant for sunny borders in good soil in our warmest counties.

cirratum

90 × 30 cm	*[8–9]*	*White*	*E.Summer*	P	W	DS
3 × 1 ft						

New Zealand. 1821. Narrow sword-like leaves; the nodding flowers are produced in airy branching sprays on wiry stems; white, enlivened by the orange and mauve pointel in the centre.

ARUM, Araceae. See also under *Arisaema, Dracunculus, Lysichitum* and *Zantedeschia*. All the species of *Arum* bear flowers which in general outline resemble the Arum Lily of our greenhouses (see *Zantedeschia*), often with strange colouring and very elegant hastate leaves. They are all hardy in our warmer counties and should be given sunny places, except where stated otherwise, in good fertile retentive soil if possible, but will also grow in lighter mediums. Their tubers should be planted about 10 cm (4 in) deep. All of the following produce their new leaves—markedly spear-shaped with strong reverse lobes—in the late autumn or during early winter, unlike the late spring-leafing of *Arisaema* and *Dracunculus*.

creticum ● ★

46 × 30 cm	*[7–9]*	*Yellow*	*Spring*	PF	D
18 in × 1 ft					

Crete. 1928. A remarkable, hardy plant for full sun. The spear-shaped leaves are of lustrous green, and over these appear the striking yellow arums: goblet-shaped spathes with drooping hood, and erect, projecting yellow spadices. Always excites the imagination ... and envy. It has thriven in the open at Hidcote, Gloucestershire, for many years, on raised beds which must have been frozen solid on many occasions. In good seasons spikes of dark red berries mature.

dioscoridis

30 × 30 cm	*[7–9]*	*Green/Purple*	*Spring*	PF	DS
1 × 1 ft					

E. Mediterranean. *A. spectabile*. The spathe-colour is very variable and a number of forms have been named; usually green at the base, they are often striped, spotted or flushed with maroon-purple or may be wholly purplish. Handsome triangular foliage in rich green.

italicum

46 × 30 cm	*[6–9]*	*Greenish*	*Spring*	PF	D
18 in × 1 ft					

S.E. Europe, Canary Islands, etc. 1683. A very variable plant—of wide distribution in nature—of which the two forms mentioned below are fairly well known in gardens. The leaves are produced in autumn and brave the winter successfully in the confines of the average garden; the flowers (spathes) are greenish-white "Lords and Ladies" with purplish staining at the base and creamy spadices. The flowers are fleeting in spring, but in late summer stout stalks support columns of orange-red berries, at which time a group is made highly conspicuous, though bare of leaves.

"... we are glad of the lucky accident that provides such a bright colour from the fruits in the beds of Bearded Irises."—EAB

—**'Marmoratum'** (of gardens) [7–9]. Very broadly spear-shaped, the green leaves are somewhat marbled along the veins with grey.

—**'Pictum'** (of gardens) [7–9]. *A. italicum italicum*. The narrowly spear-shaped leaves are conspicuously marbled with grey and cream. They are much sought by flower arrangers and in the garden they can make an effective winter foliage group, particularly if near to *Iris foetidissima* 'Citrina'. This form is not to be confused with *A. pictum* L. (*A. corsicum*, Loisel).

orientale

30 × 30 cm	*[7–9]*	*Purplish*	*E. Summer*	P	DS
1 × 1 ft					

Orient. Another of these dingy flowers which, however, have much beauty when examined closely. The handsome maroon-to-greenish spathes are lightened by cream spadices, and are held under the three-pointed leaves. It is a species with many forms and geographical variants.

ARUNCUS, Rosaceae.
dioicus ★

1.8–2.1 × 1.2 m	*[3–8]*	*Cream*	*Summer*	F	DS
6–7 × 4 ft					

Northern Hemisphere. 1633. *Aruncus sylvester, Spiraea aruncus.* Goat's Beard. An extraordinarily handsome plant whose broad fern-like leaves make an elegant hummock 1.2 m (4 ft) high, beautiful for many months, and are over-topped at midsummer by great cream plumes of minute starry blossoms. Beautiful with *Campanula latiloba*. It thrives in any soil, dry or moist, in sun or shade. Grand enough to stand on its own as a lawn specimen or in the wilder parts of the garden, but is also excellent for general use. The male plants are usually the most feathery and are not so troublesome in regard to self-sown seedlings, but the females have of course lasting ornamental seed-heads which are useful for drying. *A. dioicus* flowers with the main flush of shrub roses and is a lovely companion for them.

"... the husbands are ... very much handsomer in their plumes than the more drooping, tasselled ladies, and they are happy enough unconsciously waving their magnificent beards to an unresponding world."—ATJ

—astilboides

60 × 46 cm	*[3–8]*	*White*	*E.Summer*	DS
2 ft × 18 in				

Japan. *Aruncus astilboides*, not to be confused with *Astilbe astilboides*. Few gardens today can provide room for the species, but this variety and the next are good substitutes. This is an exact miniature of the species.

—'Kneiffii' ★

90 × 46 cm	*[3–8]*	*Cream*	*Summer*	D
3 ft × 18 in				

1889. A dainty, small-growing form, whose leaves are finely divided into threadlike ferny segments. Though so much smaller it is equally beautiful, and a delightful miniature for smaller gardens.

ASCLEPIAS, Asclepiadaceae. Silk Weed (they have silky seeds). Plants with fleshy, wandering roots which should be planted about 10 cm (4 in) deep. The flowers are of intriguing shape, with small reflexed petals, five projecting honeyhorns and five-parted stigma.

speciosa

60–90 × 60 cm	*[3–9]*	*Pink*	*Summer*	DRS
2–3 × 2 ft				

North America. 1846. *A. douglasii*. There are several species fairly closely related to this, *A. hallii* [4–9] and *A. incarnata* [3–9] included; all are stout plants with good broad leaves and stems ascending to branching heads of starry flowers carried in somewhat drooping clusters. They are in soft tones of creamy lilac-pink. The stems are filled with milky juice and the fleshy roots ramble widely through any porous soil, in a sunny position. The greyish leaves of *A. speciosa* tone well with the flowers.

tuberosa

46 × 30 cm	*[4–9]*	*Orange*	*E.Autumn*	P W	DRS
18 in × 1 ft					

E. North America. 1690. This unreliable plant is grown, and included here, for the sake of its heads of brilliant brick-orange. It is not easy to establish—or to keep—but thrives best in deep sandy soil in full sun in sheltered gardens in our warmer counties. A richly coloured form has been named 'Vermilion'.

"The Butterfly Silk-weed is the prettiest species, with its clusters of showy bright orange-red flowers in the autumn."—WR

ASPARAGUS, Liliaceae. The asparagus of the kitchen garden, *A. officinalis* [2–9], is a beautiful plant with waving, fine greenery, as everyone knows; the female plants are hung with shining red berries amongst the yellowing foliage. It is a plant of beauty, but I have never seen it used in the flower garden. There is a form, *A. officinalis pseudoscaber* known in Germany as 'Spitzenschleier', which is grown for ornament. *A. filicinus* [7–9] is a rare and charming, hardy plant about 46 cm (18 in) high. Neither this nor *A. tenuifolius* [7–9] is often seen in gardens, though this last, of about 90 cm (3 ft) in height, has highly ornamental berries, as large as those of a cherry. *A. filicinus* hails from India and China, *A. tenuifolius* from South Europe; both need a warm sunny position in any fertile soil. *A. verticillatus* [8–9] is a vigorous climber achieving 3 m (10 ft) or more, from S.W. Asia. All need full sun.

ASPHODELINE, Liliaceae. Stately plants, easily grown in sunny, well-drained soils.

liburnica
90 × 30 cm	*[6–8]*	*Yellow*	*Summer*	PF	DS
3 × 1 ft					

S. Europe. Less known than the next, with narrower grassy leaves, and more slender spires of paler yellow flowers, with recurving stamens; it is later-flowering too.

lutea
90 × 30 cm	*[6–8]*	*Yellow*	*L.Spring*	PF	DS
3 × 1 ft					

Sicily. 1596. Asphodel or King's Spear. The stiffly erect flower spikes are set at the base with a cluster of blue-grey grassy leaves 23 cm (9 in) high. The flowers are closely disposed among buff-coloured bracts, and are bright straw-yellow, silky and fragrant. Excellent seed-spikes. It grows well at Powis Castle.

ASPHODELUS, Liliaceae. Closely related to *Asphodeline* and requiring the same conditions.

albus
90 × 30 cm	*[5–9]*	*White*	*E.Summer*	PF	DS
3 × 1 ft					

S. Europe. 1596. A clump of grassy leaves produces a sparsely leafed erect stem the top of which develops into a spike of white flowers. The brownish tint of the calyx and vein of the petal warms the white to a pale mushroom-tinted effect. It is a useful early flower to be interplanted with something to bloom later, such as *Agapanthus*.

cerasiferus ★
1.2 m × 60 cm	*[5–9]*	*White*	*Summer*	PF	DS
4 × 2 ft					

S. Europe. 1829. Apart from the colour of its flowers—which are white warmed with brown reverse, salmon filaments and orange anthers—it differs from the above and the two species of *Asphodeline* listed because of its longer, broader, grey-green leaves and much branched flower-spikes. A highly decorative plant. *A. microcarpus* [5–9] is a similar plant, and the name *A. ramosus* has been used for both.

ASPIDISTRA, Liliaceae. To many this must be the Cinderella of Liliaceous plants, with its stemless maroon flowers which are pollinated by slugs. Though the common species is usually seen indoors, I know of a clump which has grown in Worcestershire under shrubs for over thirty years.

lurida
46 × 46 cm   [8–10]   E.Summer   W   D
18 × 18 in
China. 1822. The broad glossy dark green leaves are too well known to need much description. It prefers shade, in any fertile soil, in our warmer counties. The beautiful variegated form might also be tried. Evergreen.

ASTELIA, Liliaceae. The flowers of the various species are small, in dense or open panicles, resembling those of *Veratrum*, but usually are short spikes in the centre of the loose rosette of leaves. It is in their leaves that the garden value of the following two species lies. They make large open tussocks of arching rapier-like leaves. Several species thrive in the Royal Botanic Garden, Edinburgh; also at Wakehurst Place, Sussex, Knightshayes Court, Devon, and Rowallane, Northern Ireland. They grow best in full sun or part shade in any good soil, not too dry. The sexes are on separate plants, but the flowers are short and inconspicuous.

nervosa
60 cm × 1.5 m   [8–9]   Brownish   Summer   DS
2 × 5 ft
New Zealand. 1853. *A.n. montanta, A. cockaynei.* Beautiful silvery grey leaves. Evergreen.

petriei
60 cm × 1.5 m   [8–9]   Purplish   Summer   DS
2 × 5 ft
New Zealand. 1899. Pale grey-green leaves, silvery white beneath. Evergreen.

ASTER, Compositae. Michaelmas Daisy is a loose term which is often used to cover most of the taller species listed here, though it strictly refers only to *A. novi-belgii.* The garden forms of this species have been multiplied to excess, to the unfortunate and unmerited exclusion of the many other decorative species which linger in obscurity. There are some first-rate but neglected species among them. All kinds thrive in sunny or part-shaded places in any reasonably fertile soil, but many will also grow and flower satisfactorily in poor conditions. Division is best in spring.

amellus ★
30 × 46 cm   [5–8]   Violet/Pink   L.Summer/   P   D
1 ft × 18 in   E.Autumn
Europe, Asia Minor, etc., 1659. A tough short plant with rough leaves and stems which stand erect or flop unattractively, bearing clusters of large flowers at the top. The wild type is seldom seen but 'Ultramarine' and 'Violet Queen' approximate it; they are plants of some refinement, but as so often happens the

nurserymen's selections—like 'King George'—are larger and heavier in the flower, and sometimes downright coarse and clumsy. However, they give good colour value in the garden; the violet shades—'Bessie Chapman', 'Rudolph Goethe' (1914), 'Moerheim Gem' (1933)—are striking plants in full flower but are inelegant for picking, and they can compare in no way favourably for length of flowering season and beauty with the taller plant, *A. × frikartii* 'Mönch'. On the other hand we can forgive the pink varieties these shortcomings for the sake of their tints—valuable at that time of the year; good clones are 'Nocturne', 'Sonia', 'Mrs Ralph Woods', and 'Lady Hindlip' (1954). It is best to select varieties when in bloom, to suit your tastes, or from a reliable catalogue. They are excellent at the border front with *Sedum spectabile* and *Anaphalis triplinervis*.

canus

60 × 30 cm	[4–8]	Lavender	E.Autumn	P	D
2 × 1 ft					

Hungary. This is a similar plant to the well-known *A. sedifolius* but it is to my mind of better effect, with good greyish foliage and dense twiggy growth. Flowers lavender-blue, with widely spaced rays around yellow centres.

divaricatus

60 × 60 cm	[4–8]	White	Autumn	PF	D
2 × 2 ft					

North America. *A. corymbosus*. Wiry, nearly black stems, and a profusion of white stars. A pretty plant which needs staking to hold it erect, and then it looks horrible. Gertrude Jekyll found the answer; she let its graceful clouds of tiny flowers flop over her edging of bergenias (depicted on p. 97 in her *Colour Schemes for the Flower Garden*).

> "I find it, in conjunction with Megasea, one of the most useful of these filling plants for edge spaces that just want some pretty trimming but are not wide enough for anything larger."—GJ

ericoides ★

75 × 30 cm	[3–8]	Pale	Autumn	PF	D
2½ × 1 ft					

North America. 1732. *A. multiflorus*. The several varieties of this small-flowered Michaelmas Daisy deserve more consideration. They provide interest and colour late in the season; the wiry, twiggy stems and branches of the shorter varieties require no support and their flowers last a long time. They do not suffer from wilt and will go on for many years without division, besides looking respectable through the summer while just green and, indeed, dainty and starry in winter. (Varieties of *A. cordifolius* (1759) [3–8] are similar but usually need staking. Good varieties are 'Ideal' and 'Silver Spray'; both 90 cm–1.2 m (3–4 ft)). A fair range of varieties is at Peckover, Cambridgeshire. Some excellent short and compact varieties are 'Blue Star', pale blue; the effect of 'Brimstone' is creamy yellow; 'Pink Cloud', pale lilac-pink; 'White Heather', white. 'Golden Spray' and 'Ringdove' are taller and usually need support.

× frikartii
'Mönch' ● ★

90 × 38 cm	[5–8]	Lavender-	Summer/	P	D
3 ft × 15 in		blue	Autumn		

(*A. amellus × A. thomsonii*) Without doubt this, one of the original hybrids, is the finest Aster for long display; it lasts twice as long as any *Amellus* variety, and is far more elegant and refined, is stout and upright, and freely branching.

The individual blooms are beautifully rayed, in clear lavender-blue, appearing from July to October. It prefers sun, and is worth good soil and the very best position in the garden. Its colour is so gentle that it blends with any other colour; if placed next to flowers of like colour it shames them by its cool quality.

There were three seedlings originally raised by Frikart in Switzerland around 1920; they were named after the three famous mountains, Eiger, Jungfrau and Mönch. The last is by far the best; the other two are nearer to *A. amellus*. A subsequent seedling was named 'Wunder von Stäfa'; this is less blue than 'Mönch' with less perfect flowers, and usually needs staking. 'Mönch' is not only the finest perennial aster; it is one of the six best plants, and should be in every garden. (Please do not ask for the names of the other five!) Try it in front of *Lavatera olbia* 'Rosea'.

—'Flora's Delight' ★

50 × 30 cm.	*[4–9]*	*Lilac*	*Summer/*		P	D
20 in × 1 ft			*Autumn*			

A new hybrid, like a dwarf *A. × frikartii*, or perhaps I should say a lilac-coloured *A. thomsonii* 'Nanus'. It has greyish leaves and makes a dense bushy plant with good light lilac flowers for weeks and weeks. One of Alan Bloom's best efforts, it is an ideal front-line plant, but has obtrusively large yellow centres.

laevis

60 × 30 cm	*[4–8]*	*Lavender-blue*	*L.Summer*	P	DS
2 × 1 ft					

North America. Prior to 1761. A distinct plant with narrow dark green leaves and freely branching heads of clear-tinted daisies.

lateriflorus

60 × 30 cm	*[4–8]*	*Mauve*	*Autumn*	P	D
2 × 1 ft					

North America. 1829. In the form 'Horizontalis'—the plant is better known than its name—it is unique on account of its tiny foliage, which becomes coppery purple by September, and the tiny palest lilac flowers with pronounced rosy stamens, giving a general effect of rosy mauve. It is erect, twiggy, with dense horizontal branching and assorts with the varieties of *A. ericoides*. Sometimes labelled *A. diffusus*.

Some seventy years ago a garden hybrid was raised by Archer Hind and named after his home 'Coombe Fishacre'. This has something of the horizontal branching habit of the type, and thus is distinct from the other small-flowered forms and hybrids of *A. ericoides* and *A. cordifolius*. Palest lilac with the rosy brown centres of the parent species. It flowers in early autumn and achieves 1.2 m (4 ft).

linosyris

60 × 30 cm	*[3–8]*	*Yellow*	*L.Summer*	P	DS
2 × 1 ft					

Europe, Asia Minor. 1596. *Linosyris vulgaris*. An undistinguished plant, also known as 'Goldilocks' on account of its heads of yellow rayless flowers. Its chief claim to fame is its part in producing × *Solidaster, q.v.*; there is also a hybrid with *A. sedifolius* of little garden merit.

macrophyllus

60 × 60 cm	*[4–8]*	*Lilac*	*Autumn*	D
2 × 2 ft				

North America. 1739. The invasive roots create good ground cover with handome, large heart-shaped leaves. The palest lilac rather poor starry flowers come as something of a disappointment, until one remembers it will grow and spread in rooty, shady places.

novae-angliae

1.5 m × 60 cm	*[4–8]*	*Mauve*	*L.Summer/*	D
5 × 2 ft			*E.Autumn*	

North America. 1710. One of the toughest aliens that has established itself in our gardens though it seldom seeds itself like *A. novi-belgii*. It seems to thrive anywhere, short of a bog. I have little use for the stiff old pinky mauve varieties—which do not open properly when cut—but the clear pink, September-flowering, 'Harrington's Pink' has much garden charm, 90 cm (3 ft). 'Lye End Beauty' is rich cerise-lilac, August flowering, 1.2 m (4 ft). This cropped up in Miss R.B. Pole's garden, *c.*1958, near to *A.n.* 'Crimson Beauty' and 'Harrington's Pink'. After many years of neglect from breeders (while the market was glutted with forms of *A. novi-belgii*, so prone to mildew) two striking cultivars have been named in Germany: 'Herbstschnee' ('Autumn Snow') and the dazzling 'Alma Potschke' with enough colour in its glowing cerise-scarlet to warm the most drear autumn day.

novi-belgii

90 cm–1.2 m.	*[4–8]*	*Violet-blue*	*E.Autumn*	P D
× 46 cm				
3–4 ft × 18 in				

E. United States. 1710. The species or ancient garden forms may often be seen adorning waste areas, railway embankments and pond sides, and very pretty they look too in October along the sidings near London. There is no doubt that with their dense questing roots they make admirable and beautiful subjects for holding banks of ponds and streams—even against things that quack. But the large modern varieties suffer from flowers that are too large (often resulting in the taller clones needing support), wilting of the leaves and whole plant, and from a horrid insect which attacks the buds, preventing them from opening. Their colours are, however, very lovely, ranging from white, pale and deep pink, crimson, to purple, dark and pale lavender-blue. It is best to see them in flower to make a selection. They range in height from 75 cm–1.2 m (2½–4 ft). They need division and thinning out every few years and this is best done in spring. Many famous varieties were raised by Ernest Ballard of Colwall, Malvern.

—'Climax' ★

1.8 m × 46 cm	*[4–8]*	*Spode*	*E.Autumn*	P D
6 ft × 18 in				

Prior to 1908. A variety raised at Aldenham, Hertfordshire, which has never been surpassed for vigour and elegance. Good broad foliage and huge pyramid-shaped panicles of Spode blue, evenly shaped, single flowers. The typical garden Michaelmas Daisy, I have singled it out for special mention because I feel that no others equal its quality. The tall willowy stems need staking only in very tidy gardens. Mrs Thorneley of Devizes, Wiltshire, raised 'Blue Gown' in the 1930s, which is much the same but it flowers, usefully, a fortnight later. There is a useful race of dwarfs for the border front derived in part from *A. dumosus* [4–8], ranging from 15–46 cm (6–18 in), and should be planted 30 cm (1 ft) apart. They vary from pink to lavender-blue and there is also a white. They should be seen in flower for selection, and assort well with *A. sedifolius* 'Nanus', and are of similar quality and stature but rather later.

"There is a quiet beauty about the more select Starworts, which is charming in the autumn days."—WR

pyrenaeus
60 × 30 cm	*[4–8]*	*Lilac*	*L.Summer*	P	DS
2 × 1 ft					

Pyrenees. This makes a good tuft of grey-green leaves, and the stems stand well aloft each with one or more wide-rayed lilac daisies with bold yellow eyes. It is in the *A. tongolensis* group but much later flowering.

sedifolius
90 × 60 cm	*[4–7]*	*Lavender-blue*	*L.Summer*	D
3 × 2 ft				

S. Europe. 1731. *A. acris*. The lanky species is seldom seen, giving way to the compact 46–cm (18–in) high dome of blossom provided by *A. sedifolius* 'Nanus'. Unfortunately, though the colour is clear and insistent, the blooms of all forms are poor and starry. For *A. sedifolius canus*, see *A. canus* above.

sericeus
60 × 60 cm	*[6–9]*	*Violet*	*L.Summer/*	DS
2 × 2 ft			*Autumn*	

United States. 1801. *A. argenteus*. Silky Aster. Both names call attention to the grey leaves, like silvery silk. Nothing could so well complement the single violet-blue daisies, produced all over a wide bushy plant. For hot sunny places.

spectabilis
30 × 46 cm	*[4–9]*	*Violet*	*E.Autumn*	P	DS
1 ft × 18 in					

United States. 1777. Another example of a first-rate plant suffering from long neglect. It is of the *A. amellus* persuasion, with tufts of broad leaves. Wiry branching stems carry a long succession of vivid violet-blue flowers.

thomsonii
60–90 × 46 cm	*[4–9]*	*Lilac-blue*	*Summer/*	P	D
2–3 ft × 18 in			*Autumn*		

W. Himalaya. 1887. I have never seen this plant, but should much like to do so, particularly the selected form or hybrid raised by Amos Perry called 'Winchmore Hill'.

—'Nanus' ★
46 × 23 cm	*[4–9]*	*Lilac-blue*	*Summer/*	P	CD
18 × 9 in			*Autumn*		

Perpetually in flower, this is just like *A. × frikartii* in miniature but with more starry flowers. Plant in spring in sunny places and leave undisturbed. It flowers from July onwards and is valued at Gunby Hall, Lincolnshire. Though it is a colour-giver for so long, with no trouble, I could wish for a flower better set with petals. Nobody who wants a garden to be in beauty for months on end can afford to neglect this and *A. × frikartii* 'Mönch'.

tongolensis

46 × 30 cm	*[5–8]*	*Violet*	*Summer*	P	D
18 in × 1 ft					

W. China. 1901. *A. subcaeruleus*. A good plant, forming mats of hairy dark green leaves. 'Napsbury' (*A. yunnanensis* 'Napsbury' of gardens) raised in the 1930s, and 'Wendy' and the more recent 'Berggarten' (1953) are good clones with large lavender-blue daisies, singly borne on stout stalks, with vivid orange centres. Division after flowering or in late summer or early autumn keeps them in good health in any well-drained fertile soil. Sun. *A. farreri* [5–8], also from W. China, is a similar but less good plant; *A. forrestii* [5–8] and *A. souliei* [5–8] are both in the same class horticulturally.

tradescantii ★
of gardens

1.2 m × 46 cm	*[4–8]*	*White*	*Autumn*	P	D
4 ft × 18 in					

North America. 1633. Perhaps this is the plant introduced in 1633 by John Tradescant, gardener to Charles I; at least it is a well-established clone, but botanically it may be assigned more correctly to *A. pilosus demotus*. It is one of the last flowers of autumn and a valuable, erect, pyramidal, wiry plant with very small narrow leaves, but freely set with tiny white daisies, yellow centred. It is like a gypsophila in its airiness, a larger version of *A. ericoides*. First rate for cutting with red-berried shrubs and a good contrast for autumn leaf colour.

"... a stream of them [late summer Daisies] flows on that will not run dry until the last of the *Aster tradescantii* flowers are overwhelmed by December frosts."—EAB

turbinellus ★

1.2 m × 60 cm	*[3–8]*	*Violet*	*Autumn*	P	D
4 × 2 ft					

United States. An unusual species, with the normal narrow leaves, and wiry, dark-tinted stems bearing particularly airy sprays of refined violet-blue daisies. The absolute antithesis of the overbred modern varieties of *A. novi-belgii*. First rate.

"... even if it were to flower during the reign of the best varieties it would still be indispensable, for there is no other like it."—EAB

umbellatus

1.2 m × 60 cm	*[3–8]*	*White*	*E. Autumn*	P	D
4 × 2 ft					

North America. 1759. *A. amygdalinus*; *Doellingeria umbellata*. The merit of this little-known species is its long-flowering period in September and October, when the wiry, dense, round-topped bushes are covered with small white daisies with yellow eyes. It produces a creamy yellow effect. Good green leaves.

"... a stately, white flowered species of striking appearance ... a pleasing way of turning white again in old age ... when covered with silvery seeds ..."—EAB

ASTILBE, Saxifragaceae. These are often confused with the herbaceous Spiraeas (*Filipendula*), which belong to a different botanical family and whose flowers are borne in flat-topped branching heads. The flowers of *Astilbe* are in tapering panicles. The plants are imperturbably hardy, thriving in moist or even boggy ground and effectively making their own ground cover; they last long in flower and never require support. They enjoy full sun or part shade—the latter is best if the soil is on the dry side—and grow satisfactorily in any medium except excessive chalk, or clay which bakes or cracks. They are most decorative in the winter landscape too, holding aloft their rich brown plumes, and should never be cut down therefore until the spring, unless prematurely flattened by heavy snow. The early-flowering cultivars are superb with Japanese Irises.

× **arendsii**

60 cm–1.2 m	*[4–8]*	*Various*	*Summer*	F	D
× *60–90 cm*					
2–4 × 2–3 ft					

Hybrid. *c.* 1900. A group name, commemorating Georg Arends of Ronsdorf, covering many garden hybrids, raised since 1907, between four species. These are the Chinese *A. davidii* (magenta-pink or purplish flowers borne in long slender upright panicles with erect side-stalks) [4–8] and three Japanese species: *A. astilboides* (white flowers borne in panicles with branched horizontal side-stalks; hairy leaves) [4–8], *A. japonica* (white flowers borne in short panicles with densely packed side-stalks which are branched, erect, but arching outwards) [4–8]; and *A. thunbergii* (white flowers in open panicles with unbranched side-stalks gracefully recurving) [4–8]. In height they vary from the last, about 46 cm (18 in) to the 1.5 m (5 ft) of *A. davidii*. The foliage of this last is often dark and purplish with dark stems, and *A. japonica* sports to a form with coppery leaves. It will be seen therefore that efforts were made to unite the colouring of *A. davidii* with the other elegant shorter species having white flowers. The hybrids made by Lemoine of Nancy and later by Arends do just this, but in years of selection some very brilliant reds have been raised. The following clones appeal to me most though there are many more. My selection has been influenced by the range of colours and shapes of the flower sprays, the range of foliage tints, and also the extra early and extra late cultivars which do so much to prolong the display. In general these plants seem to have every possible good point except a sweet fragrance. A number of kinds are established at Trelissick and Trengwainton, Cornwall. I have listed the hybrids at length for the reason that they are stalwart perennials and are not quickly superseded by successive raisings.

> "Lofty wavy shoots which are the last word in elegance of form and poise … and derive no little pleasure from the crimson-bronze and amber of their spring shoots, while the dried mahogany stems and ruddy brown seed-heads afford a glow of warm colour through the winter."—ATJ

TALL GARDEN HYBRIDS★; Plant about 90 cm (3 ft) apart, according to height.   F   D

By using early, mid-season and late varieties and finishing with *A. taquetii*, a very long season of flower can be enjoyed.

WHITE VARIETIES, whose foliage is bright green.

'Bergkrystall', 1920. Elegant open sprays, pure white. Later than 'Bridal Veil'. 1.20 m (3½ ft).

'Bridal Veil', 1929 ('Brautschleier'). Elegant open sprays, pure white, opening from bright green buds and turning to creamy yellow as they fade. 75 cm (2½ ft).

'Professor van der Wielen', 1917. Large, graceful, open, arching sprays, handsome foliage. 1.2 m (4 ft). A big plant in all its parts, suitable for large gardens where the arching plumes can give full effect, with cultivars of similar quality like 'Betsy Cuperus' and 'Ostrich Plume'. These three flower at mid season.

'White Gloria', 1924. Dense erect spikes of white. 60 cm (2 ft). Early.

89

PALE PINK VARIETIES, mostly with green foliage.

'Betsy Cuperus', 1917. A pale pink counterpart to 'Professor van der Wielen'. 1.2 m. (4 ft).

'Ceres'. Clear light pink, elegant open sprays. 90 cm (3 ft). Late.

'Erica'. Erect spikes of clear bright pink. 90 cm. (3 ft).

'Europa', 1930. Pale pink, heavy elegant spikes. Very early. 60 cm (2 ft)

DEEP PINK TO CORAL VARIETIES. The foliage of most is brownish-tinted when young, turning to dark green.

'Cattleya', 1953. Fine, elegant, open spikes of rose-pink. 90 cm (3 ft).

'Lilli Goos', 1930. Handsome open sprays of rose-pink. Dark foliage, tinted with brownish purple. 90 cm (3 ft). Very late.

'Ostrich Plume', 1952 ('Straussenfeder'). Rich coral-pink; large, open, arching plumes. A counterpart to 'Professor van der Wielen' and 'Betsy Cuperus'. These arching varieties probably owe some of their grace to *A. thunbergii*. 90 cm (3 ft).

'Rheinland', 1920. Compact, dense upright spikes of bright clear pink. 60 cm (2 ft). Early.

RED VARIETIES. The leaves are mostly mahogany-tinted in spring, and dark-toned during the summer.

'Fanal', 1933. Dark crimson-red; dense short spikes. 60 cm (2 ft). Early.

'Fire', 1940 ('Feuer'). Coral-red. Feathery spikes. 90 cm (3 ft). Late.

'Glow', 1952 ('Glut'). Deep ruby-red. Feathery spikes. 90 cm (3 ft). Late.

'Koblenz', 1938. Deep salmon-red, open, elegant. 90 cm (3 ft) Early.

'Red Sentinel', 1947. Deep crimson-red, open, elegant. 90 cm (3 ft). Early.

'Spinel', 1955. Vivid salmon-red. Open, elegant. 90 cm (3 ft).

MAGENTA VARIETIES. Green leaves.

'Amethyst', 1920. Open, elegant sprays, clear lilac-pink. 90 cm (3 ft). Early.

'Jo Ophorst'. Dense, erect spikes of deep rosy lilac. 90 cm (3 ft). Very late.

There are two very late varieties, probably descended from *A. davidii*:

'King Albert'. Warm-white flowers in arrow erect spikes.

'Salland'. Magenta-purple; flowers in long slender erect spikes. Both of these have dark brownish stems and dark green leaves, and achieve 1.8 m (6 ft) in good conditions.

"These plants group well together and the handsome foliage makes healthy undergrowth over which the tall plumes ... of flowers tower with good effect."—WR

DWARF GARDEN HYBRIDS. ★ Plant 46 cm (18 in) apart.   F   D

An increasing number of these are being raised. They are admirable for the front of the border and the larger rock garden, pond- and stream-side. They are the results of hybridizing the *A.* × *arendsii* or *A.* × *rosea* (*A. chinensis* × *A. japonica*) [4–8] group with the dainty little *A. simplicifolia* [4–8] from Japan, whose tiny 20–cm (8–in) plumes arch prettily. This character has been passed on to the following—all of great charm and just as easy to grow as the *A.* × *arendsii* hybrids. The first to appear in lists was *A.* 'Hybrida Rosea' which has been superseded by 'Atrorosea'. The latest flowering cultivars extend the season into August.

'Atrorosea', 1934. Pretty arching sprays of deep flesh-pink. 46 cm (18 in).

'Bronze Elegance'. This ranks very high in beauty. Pretty foliage and arching sprays of clear pink with a creamy salmon hint. 30 cm (1 ft). Late.

'Dunkellachs'. Coppery foliage is added to a plant of charm; rich salmon-pink, small arching sprays. 30 cm (1 ft). Very late.

'Praecox Alba'. White. 30 cm (1 ft).

'**Serenade**'. Feathery spikes of clear pink. 46 cm (18 in). Very late.
'**Sprite**'. Completes the series in pale shell-pink. 46 cm (18 in).

chinensis

90 × 60 cm	*[4–8]*	*Pink*	*L.Summer*	F	D
3 × 2 ft					

China. 1892. A variable plant in the wild. The dwarf form or hybrid 'Pumila' is usually seen in gardens, forming a creeping, dense mat of leaves over which the stiff, branched, chalky mauve-pink flower spikes appear in August and September. Excellent in cool moist soil under shrubs or pool-side. First class ground-cover and just tall enough for inclusion in these pages. 46 × 60 cm (18 in × 2 ft).

—taquetii

1.2 m × 90 cm	*[4–8]*	*Purple*	*L.Summer*	F	D
4 × 3 ft					

E. China. 1914. A unique plant, flowering when other astilbes except *A. davidii* and some dwarfs have finished, in August. Dark-tinted, rounded leaves and mahogany stems support long erect spikes of vivid magenta-purple. It is a very tough plant, and though it is not so dependent on "coolth" as the others and will stand in full sun so long as the soil is moist, its strong colour never looks so well as in shade—perhaps with pale yellow *Lysimachia ciliata* and pale Day Lilies. ★'Superba' (1932) is a noted form, and a newcomer from Germany is 'Purpurlanze' ('Purple Lance').

grandis

1.5 m × 90 cm	*[4–8]*	*White*	*Summer*	F	DS
5 × 3 ft					

China. A handsome downy-leafed plant of considerable port, carrying large panicles of white flowers.

koreana

60 × 60 cm	*[4–8]*	*Creamy*	*Summer*	F	DS
2 × 2 ft					

Korea. 1932. A useful early-flowering species with widely divided green foliage, and neat, branching, nodding flower panicles, usually pink in bud opening to creamy white. It is one of the very few astilbes which will thrive in dry conditions, and therefore may make a useful parent.

rivularis

1.8 × 1.2 m	*[4–8]*	*White*	*Summer*	F	DS
6 × 4 ft					

Nepal, W. China. 1825. A grand foliage plant with leaves deeply divided into many lobes, making a large basal clump, and also extending up the stems. Large, arching plumes of tiny greenish white flowers develop into brown seed-heads 60–90 cm (2–3 ft) long, borne on 1.2–1.5 m (4–5 ft) stems. Increases by vagrant underground shoots. Sometimes listed as *A. biternata*.

ASTILBOIDES, Saxifragaceae. Formerly included in *Rodgersia*.
tabularis ★

| 90 × 90 cm | [5–7] | White | Summer | F | DS |
| 3 × 3 ft | | | | | |

China 1887. This might be described as the poor man's *Gunnera*. The great circular slightly lobed leaves (resembling somewhat those of the smaller *Peltiphyllum peltatum*) are 90 cm (3 ft) wide and of light green. The leaf stalk supports the middle of the leaf. The white-cream flowers are most conspicuous in contrast, borne well aloft, to 1.5 m (5 ft). A superb plant. Formerly *Rodgersia tabularis*; though now known as *Astilboides*, it bears no resemblance to *Astilbe*.

"A bold growing and handsome species with huge peltate leaves and plumes of creamy-white flowers."—WR

ASTRAGALUS, Leguminosae. For well-drained soil in full sun.

galegiformis

| 1.5 m × 90 cm | [5–8] | Creamy | Summer | P | S |
| 5 × 3 ft | | | | | |

Asia Minor, Caucasus. 1729. Wiry erect stems have pinnate leaves like a galega's, and axillary spikes of creamy yellow vetch flowers. It creates an unusual effect, is open, airy, and has the invaluable pale yellow that is so scarce in garden plants.

ASTRANTIA, Umbelliferae. Masterwort. These plants have flowers of very interesting and beautiful shape. The wiry stems branch into several flower-heads, each a posy of tiny florets, arranged in a dome, with a "plate" or "collar" of bracts. They have good basal divided foliage, which makes a dense clump and they spread by underground runners. Happy in any drained soil, in sun or partial shade.

major

| 60 × 46 cm | [4–8] | White | Summer/ | P | DS |
| 2 ft × 18 in | | | Autumn | | |

Austria. 1597. The heads of flowers are greenish white with a pale green "collar" composed of narrow segments. A distinct botanical form is *A.m. involucrata*, which has an extra long and large "collar" around the flower; a good type of this is known in gardens as 'Shaggy'. There is a plum-coloured relative called 'Rubra', which is useful for a sombre effect amongst grey foliage. *A. major* is often wrongly ascribed to *A. carniolica* [4–8], which is a dwarf species.

"The Astrantias have a quaint beauty of their own."—WR

—**'Sunningdale Variegated'** (1966). The flowers are as above, borne well above the divided leaves, which are elegantly splashed and striped with yellow and cream. The leaves colour best in sun, and are at their best in spring. *Viola labradorica* makes a good purplish ground-cover for it.

maxima ● ★

| 60 × 30 cm | [4–8] | Pink | Summer | P | DS |
| 2 × 1 ft | | | | | |

Europe. 1804. *A. helleborifolia*. Exquisite flowers, pinkish with a pronounced "collar" of broad segments of pure rose-pink, above bold tripartite foliage. (*A. major* has more divisions.) This needs a good soil to give of its best; it is not successful in poor sandy soils. It is a very beautiful plant.

minor

| 23 × 30 cm | [4–8] | White | Summer | P | DS |

9 in × 1 ft

Europe. 1686. Diminutive edition of *A. major*. Leaves usually divided into seven lobes. A charmer for tiny bouquets. *A. pauciflora* [4–8] and *A. bavarica* [4–8] are closely related. Some hybrids have been named in Germany; one is 'Rosensymphonie', 2 ft.

ATHAMANTA, Umbelliferae.

turbith

| 60 × 30 cm | [5–8] | White | Summer | P | DS |

2 × 1 ft

Carinthian Alps. 1802. *A. matthioli*. A mass of feathery, fragrant green is the main asset of this plant, which is easily grown in sun in any fertile soil. Small heads of small white flowers, cow-parsley like.

BALSAMORRHIZA, Compositae. A genus of few species, native to North America with fleshy edible roots.

hookeri

| 30 × 30 cm | [5–9] | Yellow | E.Summer | P | DS |

1 × 1 ft

Central N. America. 1915. In sunny positions, benefiting its greyish broad leaves, this plant can be of outstanding beauty with its comparatively large yellow daisies, one or three to a stem.

BAPTISIA, Leguminosae. Full sun in deep soil, preferably free from lime. Deeply rooted plants, which should be left undisturbed when once established.

australis ★

| 1.2 m × 60 cm | [3–9] | Blue | E.Summer | PF | S |

4 × 2 ft

E. United States. 1724. *B. exaltata*. This plant is beautiful from June when the blue-green leaves cover the grey-green stems, through summer and autumn while it is a waving mass of soft green, until the frosts turn the leaves to coal-black, at which time the dark grey seed-pods make it useful for drying. The bonus of good flowers is added to all this; they are borne in spikes, like those of a lupin, of a unique, soft, blue-tinted indigo. There are several other species, mostly with yellow or white flowers, but they are not often seen in British gardens: *B. alba* [5–9], *B. leucophaea* [5–9], *B. leucantha* [5–9], *B. tinctoria* [5–9] and *B. perfoliata* [6–9], all from the United States, may be worth trying, *B. leucantha* achieves some 1.5 m (5 ft), has white flowers and frequents moist ground in nature.

pendula

| 90 × 60 cm | [5–9] | White | E.Summer | P | S |

3 × 2 ft

S.E. United States. A pleasing counterpart in creamy-white.

BEGONIA, Begoniaceae.

grandis

30 × 46 cm	*[6–9]*	Blush	Summer/	W	D
1 ft × 18 in			Autumn		

Malay, China, Japan. 1804. Also known as *B. evansiana; B. discolor*. Who ever thought of the luxury of a hardy begonia? Yet here it is and it thrives (increasing by means of bulbils) in sheltered corners in our warmer counties, in sun or part shade. Beautiful, glistening, large leaves, red-tinted beneath, and sprays of glistening, pale pink flowers opening from reddish buds. *B.e.* 'Alba' has white flowers; there is also a large-flowered form, 'Simsii'.

BELAMCANDA, Iridaceae. Bulbous plants which are usually lifted annually, but they should be successful against a sunny wall in our warmer counties, in well-drained soil.

chinensis

90 × 30 cm	*[5–10]*	Orange	E.Summer	PF	W	DS
3 × 1 ft						

China. 1823. Good sword-shaped leaves of rich green enclasp the stems, iris-fashion. The stems branch in a zigzag way, displaying gay flowers of six segments, bright yellow heavily spotted with orange-red. The seed-pods open to show a mass of black seeds, earning its name of "Blackberry Lily". Hybrids with *Pardanthopsis dichotoma* are called × *Pardancanda norrisii*. These are like *Belamcanda* but with larger flowers in a wide range of colours. They will achieve 90 cm (3 ft) in good soil and have a long, late flowering period.

BERGENIA, Saxifragaceae. Megasea or Saxifrage. These plants provide the ideal evergreen ground-cover* with bold outline and are a godsend to those dry, windy gardens where hostas do not thrive. The slowly creeping rhizome sends up great, round, leathery blades of rich green, which are invaluable as a contrast for vases indoors, especially when in the autumn, winter or spring some of the dying leaves turn to yellow and scarlet. They last a month or more in water. Many of them assume burnished tones and retain them through the winter, turning green in the spring. The stalwart red stems bearing the dense heads of magenta pink or white flowers in the spring are often a grand sight and blend well with the pink and white of Japanese Cherries. Apart from their value in contrast to sword-like and other foliage, few plants look so well when spreading in firm bunches over the edges of paving, etc. They grow in any soil, in sun or shade, but for the best winter colouring of the leaves they should be grown in full exposure in not-too-rich soil. Evergreen.

> "I am never tired of admiring the fine solid foliage of this family of plants, remaining as it does in beauty both winter and summer."—GJ

ciliata

30 × 46 cm	*[5–8]*	Pink	Spring	P	W	DS
1 ft × 18 in						

Nepal, Kashmir, W. Pakistan. 1819. This has large rounded leaves, densely hairy on *both* surfaces, extremely handsome, and large heads of clear blush flowers from ruddy calyces, in early spring. Though the rhizome is hardy the leaves and flowers are apt to be damaged by frost except in sheltered gardens, where it is a plant of unusual beauty. Thrives at Hidcote, Gloucestershire.

*Several kinds are illustrated in my book *Plants for Ground-Cover*.

—ligulata

| 30 × 46 cm | [5–8] | White | E.Spring | P | D |
| 1 ft × 18 in | | | | | |

E. Afghanistan to Assam, etc. 1820. The leaves have a hairy margin and are broad, rounded, and not resistant to severe frost. The flowers appear early in dense heads, opening out into graceful sprays; they are nearly white but have a pretty contrast in the rosy red calyces.

cordifolia

| 46 × 60 cm | [3–8] | Magenta | Spring | P | D |
| 18 in × 2 ft | | | | | |

Siberia. 1779. Rounded, bullate leaves, crinkled at the edges, usually remaining constantly green. The light mauve-pink flowers are borne in good heads.

—'Purpurea' ★

| 60 × 75 cm | [3–8] | Magenta | Spring | P | D |
| 2 × 2½ ft | | | | | |

1879. One of Gertrude Jekyll's favourites among these plants; she planted it at Barringon Court and elsewhere. It is spectacular in foliage, with large hardy rounded leaves, becoming purplish in winter. Vivid magenta flowers on tall red stalks.

crassifolia

| 30 × 46 cm | [3–8] | Magenta | Spring | P | DS |
| 1 ft × 18 in | | | | | |

Siberia, Mongolia. 1765. The fine large spoon-shaped leaves (recurved, with the back of the spoon to the front) become mahogany-tinted in winter, and are less large than *B. cordifolia*. Flowers light lavender-pink in graceful strays. This is E. A. Bowles's 'pig-sqeak', from the sound made by finger and thumb rapidly drawn up the leaf blades.

purpurascens ★

| 30 × 30 cm | [3–8] | Pink | Spring | P | DS |
| 1 × 1 ft | | | | | |

Himalaya, etc. 1850. *B. delavayi*. This has a slender graceful reddish flower-stem, bearing flowers of good rich colouring. But it is for the winter colour of its leaves that it is specially prized. They are narrow and held erect; dark green in summer, by the end of November they have turned to a magnificent beetroot colour while the backs are mahogany-red. The ideal plant for contrasting with variegated forms of *Euonymus fortunei radicans*—and of course, hamamelis and snowdrops; it imparts an air of warmth to the winter garden. Forms have been separated and given the names *B. beesiana* and *B. yunnanensis*.

stracheyi

| 23 × 30 cm | [4–8] | Pink | Spring | P | DS |
| 9 in × 1 ft | | | | | |

Afghanistan, W. Himalaya. 1851. This pretty minikin has quite small rounded leaves, and short heads of substantial flowers in white or clear pink. They nestle among the mass of short foliage. The pink form is to the fore at Mount Stewart, Northern Ireland.

HYBRIDS. Species of *Bergenia* intermarry with great fecundity and many of the garden clones, unless raised from original plant- or seed-introduction from the wild, may well be somewhat hybridized. The above descriptions, however, apply to well-known garden clones. Several of the following should be classified under

B. × *smithii* (*B. cordifolia* × *B. purpurascens*) [3-8], for example 'Bressingham Bountiful' and 'Pugsley's Purple'; but as the result of *B. ciliata* × *B. crassifolia* is well known under the name of *B.* × *schmidtii* [4–8], I have omitted the confusing name *B.* × *smithii*, even though—together with a synonym *B.* × *newryensis*—it commemorates Tom Smith of Daisy Hill Nurseries, Newry, Northern Ireland, one of the earliest admirers of these useful plants. He raised 'Profusion' among others but their colours are outclassed by the newer hybrids.

'Abendglut'

23 × 30 cm	[3–8]	Crimson-	Spring	P	D
9 in × 1 ft		purple			

1950. 'Evening Glow'. The tufts of rounded, nearly prostrate leaves are particularly richly maroon-coloured in winter, the backs being plum-red. The flowers are inclined to be semi-double, on stems shorter than most, of deep magenta-crimson and lovely when grown next to *Omphalodes cappadocica*. This cultivar, together with 'Morgenröte' and 'Silberlicht', was raised by G. Arends in the late thirties from a parentage involving the old T. Smith hybrids, *B. purpurascens, B. ciliata* and others. 'Abendglocken' [4–8] and 'Purpurglocken' [4–8], both raised and introduced by G. Arends in 1971, are as yet on trial. 'Admiral', 'Beethoven', 'Brahms', 'Wintermärchen' are further excellent German-raised varieties [all 4–8].

'Ballawley' ●

60 × 60 cm	[4–8]	Crimson	Spring	P	D
2 × 2 ft					

'Delbees'. An extremely fine hybrid. Raised at Ballawley Park, Dublin, prior to 1950. The leaves are less tough and evergreen than those of most kinds; they are shining, green, round, flabby, 23 cm (9 in) or more across, and turn to the colour of liver in the winter. The red stems, sparingly produced, gracefully bear sheaves of wide bright crimson blooms. It deserves a sheltered position away from cold winds and in partial shade, in good fertile soil.

'Bressingham Bountiful'

46 × 30 cm	[4–8]	Magenta	Spring	P	D
18 in × 1 ft					

c. 1972. One of Mr Pugsley's raising; a compact plant with good dark leaves trimmed with maroon; and good, clear rose-pink nodding flowers in branching heads, deepening with age. The foliage is rather susceptible to frost.

'Distinction'. [3–8] One of T. Smith's old hybrids, referable to *B.* × *smithii*, like 'Profusion'. It leans much more towards *B. cordifolia*, with its rather light green bullate leaves and tall heads of clear pink flowers.

'Eric Smith' ★ ●

46 × 46 cm	[4–8]	Pink	Spring	P	D
18 × 18 in					

Well noted for its large crinkly leaves and winter colour and the upstanding heads of deep coral-pink flowers. Undoubtedly a winner.

'Margery Fish'

46 × 30 cm	[4–8]	Magenta-	E. Spring	P	D
18 in × 1 ft		purple			

Named by the raiser, Mr Pugsley, in honour of one who helped to popularize these useful plants. It is very early-flowering, with excellent broad foliage and branching heads of large rich red-purple. A cross between *B.* 'Ballawley' and *B. ciliata*.

'Morgenröte' ★

46 × 30 cm	*[3–8]*	*Pink*	*Spring/*	P	D
18 in × 1 ft			*Summer*		

1950. 'Morning Blush'. To good foliage and fine flower-stems, supporting large deep carmine-pink flowers, this adds the unique asset of invariably producing a second crop of flowers in June after its early spring crop.

'Profusion'

30 × 46 cm	*[3–8]*	*Pink*	*Spring*	P	D
1 ft × 18 in					

c. 1880. Rounded green leaves somewhat deeply veined and leaden-tinted, allied to *B. cordifolia*, and good pale pink flowers. In sunny open positions the foliage is interspersed in autumn with the scarlet tint of old dying leaves.

'Pugsley's Purple'

60 × 46 cm	*[4–8]*	*Purple*	*Spring*	P	D
2 ft × 18 in					

An extra vigorous new clone with large, dark green, red-margined leaves and stout reddish stems, beautifully crowned with arching sprays of deep crimson-magenta. Late-flowering.

× schmidtii ★

30 × 60 cm	*[4–8]*	*Pink*	*E.Spring*	P	D
1 × 2 ft					

Hybrid. 1878. *Saxifraga ligulata speciosa, Bergenia ornata.* There is a well-known clone in gardens which, to distinguish it from similar hybrids, has been given the name of 'Ernst Schmidt'. This is another of Gertrude Jekyll's favourites; she used it exclusively at Hestercombe, Somerset. It is the outcome of a cross between *B. ciliata ligulata* and *B. crassifolia*. The leaves have toothed margins, and are broad, roundish, flat, of bright rich green and borne on long stalks; the bases scarcely cordate. The flowers are in dense short heads, growing up to 30 cm (1 ft) and opening out into graceful sprays; they are clear pink with rosy red calyces. A showy, early plant, often in flower in sheltered positions as early as February.

'Silberlicht' ● ★

30 × 46cm	*[3–8]*	*White*	*Spring*	P	D
1 ft × 18 in					

1950. 'Silver Light'. Pure white flowers, developing a pinkish tinge with age. A splendid stalwart variety with dark calyces and handsome foliage. Those who cannot bear the purplish varieties fortunately have this and 'Ballawley' to delight them. Ideal with *Brunnera macrophylla*.

'Sunningdale' ● ★

30 × 60 cm	*[3–8]*	*Carmine*	*Spring*	P	D
1 × 2 ft					

1964. Inheriting some of the magnificent winter colour of *B. purpurascens*, this is a better ground-cover and in general a better plant, which I picked out from a batch of seedlings. The rounded leaves assume deep burnished tones in winter, with mahogany-red reverses. As with all these winter-colouring varieties, full exposure to sun and wind is necessary to achieve the richest tones. The flowers are of good, rich lilac-carmine, on red stalks.

BERKHEYA, Compositae. South African plants requiring full sun in good fertile soil in our warmer counties. They are not in the first rank of hardy plants, but are gay in flower.

macrocephala
90 × 90 cm	[9–10]	Yellow	Summer	P	DS
3 × 3 ft					

Natal. A spiny-leafed plant whose flowers are borne on much branched stems. Each is protected by spiny bracts and calyx. Vivid yellow daisies appear for many weeks. Even larger is *B. adlamii* (1897) [9–10] from the Transvaal, with large yellow daisies. 1.8 × 1.2 m. (6 × 4 ft).

purpurea
90 × 60 cm	[9–10]	Purple	L.Summer	P	DS
3 × 2 ft					

South Africa, prior to 1872. *Stobaea purpurea.* Heads of daisy flowers over clammy prickly leaves, grey beneath. This is a handsome plant for sunny positions. White forms are recorded.

BESCHORNERIA, Amaryllidaceae.

yuccoides
2.4 m × 90 cm	[9–10]	Coral-pink	Summer	W	D
8 × 3 ft					

Mexico. Sword-like leaves of grey-green—like those of a yucca but less fierce—create a beautiful rosette up to 60 cm (2 ft) high and wide from which, in occasional years, a great arching spike appears, clothed in coral-red and pink bracts, shooting forth nodding green bells. It needs a warm, sunny place, and is only successful, outdoors in the south and west. It is best planted in spring. Gives a very exotic effect at Mount Stewart, Northern Ireland. Evergreen.

> "... in warm shore-gardens ... create an effect unlike any other ... the great arching stems themselves are of so vivid a crimson as to make a striking picture."—WR

BLETILLA, Orchidaceae. Tuberous roots, which should be planted 5 cm (2 in) deep.

striata
38 × 23 cm	[5–8]	Purple	E.Summer	P W	D
15 × 9 in					

China. 1802. *Bletia hyacinthina.* The rich green sword-shaped pleated leaves spring from the ground and over them wave the dainty sprays of rosy purple orchid-flowers. There is also a white form. Though usually recommended for cool humus-laden soil with a loose surface, it thrives against a hot wall at Kew in full sun and flowers freely. There are forms with creamy margins to the leaves. The bulbous roots should not be covered deeply.

BOLTONIA, Compositae. Easily satisfied plants for any fertile soil, in sun or shade but not overshadowed by trees. The two following species are very large, branching, overpowering and need stout stakes. They produce vast quantities of small Michaelmas Daisy flowers in the manner of a giant *Gypsophila.* They have small and insignificant leaves.

asteroides

2.1 × 1.2 m	*[4–9]*	*Pale lilac*	*Autumn*	P	D
7 × 4 ft					

North America. 1758. *B. glastifolia*. Sheaves of neat daisies from white to lilac. If staked firmly to 1.2 m (4 ft) it will make a great cloud of blossom like a giant gypsophila. 'Snowbank' is shorter and more manageable, but less effective.

latisquama

1.8 × 1.2 m	*[4–9]*	*Lilac*	*Autumn*	P	D
6 × 4 ft					

North America. 1879. This is a superior garden plant to *B. asteroides*, with larger flowers of more decisive lilac.

Two East-Asian species are of shorter growth; *B. indica* [4–9] from Japan is rather small-flowered for our purpose, but *B. incisa* [3–9] from Siberia has good flowers; both are lilac-white, and flower in late summer or early autumn.

BOMAREA, Amaryllidaceae. A genus from South America, usually with tuberous roots. They closely resemble *Alstroemeria* (from the same continent) having similar leaves and very similar flowers, starry trumpet-shaped and carried in heads, but they are climbing plants. They are usually grown in greenhouses but will thrive against hot sunny walls in our warmest counties; plant about 12.5 cm (5 in) deep.

● × **cantabrigiensis** [9–10], a hybrid between *B. caldasiana* and *B. hirtella*, has grown out of doors at Cambridge Botanic Garden for more than forty years, nestling against the greenhouse wall and protected by a winter mulch. This twining plant should be hardy in parts of Devon and Cornwall, and possibly also the following species:
B. andimarcana (non-twining) [9–10], *B. caldasii* [10], *B. kalbreyeri* [10], all with flowers in varying combinations and tones of red, green and yellow; *B. carderi* [10], pink and purplish brown. The last three are twiners and all flower usefully late in the summer and early autumn.
hirtella, 1801 (*B. edulis*) [8–10]. The heads of bell-shaped flowers are of coral-orange outside while within they are green with crimson spotting. A slender climber which seems to be perfectly hardy and thrives at Kew in semi-woodland. Plant 6 in deep.

BORAGO, Boraginaceae. Lovers of stony or poor soil in sun or shade.

laxiflora

46 × 60 cm	*[5–9]*	*Blue*	*E.Summer/*	S
18 in × 2 ft			*Autumn*	

Corsica. 1813. Once again the borage family gives us exquisite blue flowers, this time of a pale azure, gracefully nodding in branching sprays, but marred by large rosettes of coarse hairy foliage. It seeds itself freely in rough places. (*B. pygmaea*).

"This gentle woodlander is never out of bloom from spring to winter."— ATJ

BOYKINIA, Saxifragaceae. Compared with most of the plants in this book the species mentioned are second-rate. They have some value in their pleasant leaves and ability to produce flowers in cool places, sunny or partly shaded, preferably in lime-free or neutral soil.

aconitifolia

60 × 30 cm	*[5–9]*	*White*	*Summer*	DS
2 × 1 ft				

E. United States. Forming clumps of rounded leaves, deeply cut or lobed, this plant throws up stalwart stems branching into heads of small creamy white flowers with yellow eyes. *B. major* [5–9], *B. occidentalis* [5–9] and *B. rotundifolia* [5–9] are similar but less often seen; none is exciting. *B. tellimoides* (*Peltoboykinia tellimoides*) [5–9] has the same dull flowers but handsome round leaves deeply divided. Japan.

BRUNNERA, Boraginaceae.

macrophylla ★

46 × 60 cm	*[4–8]*	*Blue*	*Spring*	P	DRS
18 in × 2 ft					

W. Caucasus. 1713. *Anchusa myosotidiflora*. Vivid forget-me-not flowers are held on 46 cm (18 in) stems in April and May, after which the large heart-shaped leaves assume greater proportions and create attractive greenery through the summer. An admirable ground-cover plant, easily satisfied regarding soil, but preferring some moisture and half or full shade. Some forms have spots of silvery grey on their leaves; one is named 'Langtrees', commemorating Dr Rogerson's garden in Devon. There is a very beautiful form with leaves handsomely particoloured with creamy white, 'Variegata' (brought from a garden in Holland by Douglas Dawson prior to 1969), but it needs a cool sheltered spot out of the wind in soil that does not dry out, because its white variegation easily bruises and turns brown. The contrast at flowering time is very appealing. With care all kinds can be made to last in water when fairly mature.

> "... indulging in a summer leafage to which 'Cabbagy' would be flattering. But this is surely a matter of placing ... for it becomes elevated from an ugly nuisance to a woodlander of distinction."—ATJ

—**'Hadspen Cream'.** A form recently raised by Eric Smith. The dark leaves are broadly bordered with cream, a pleasing background to the blue flowers.

BULBINE, Liliaceae. For well-drained soil in warm sheltered gardens.

bulbosa ●

60 − 90 × 30 cm	*[9–10]*	*Yellow*	*E. Summer*	P	W	DS
2 − 3 × 1 ft						

E. Australia. Green grassy leaves make a basal tuft. The slender flower-stems are set with many flowers, well spaced, making an open spike; each resembles a bloom of Winter Jasmine, clear yellow and starry. A plant of charm and quality.

BULBINELLA, Liliaceae. Easy to grow so long as it is in a cool peaty soil that does not dry out; sun or part shade.

hookeri

60 × 30 cm	*[8–9]*	*Yellow*	*Summer*	PF	DS
2 × 1 ft					

New Zealand. 1850. *Chrysobactron hookeri*. A pretty foreground plant, or for the peat bed or rock garden, where its grassy tufts will be decorated with spires of starry deep yellow flowers, much like our native Bog Asphodel. *B. gibbsii* [8–9] and *B. modesta* [8–9] are rather taller and sound desirable. *B. rossii* [8–9] is a rare relative with larger individual flowers, broader, shorter spikes and broader leaves.

BUPHTHALMUM, Compositae. Vigorous hardy plants for sun or part shade in any reasonable soil. *B. speciosum* is an incurable runner and should only be used in moist places where it can naturalize itself in grass, or in very large borders and beds.

salicifolium

60 × 60 cm	*[4–9]*	*Yellow*	*Summer*	P	DS
2 × 2 ft					

Austria. 1759. *B. grandiflorum*. Usually seen staked, it is far more beautiful when allowed to flop and make a large mass of neat, narrow, dark green leaves and slender stems carrying gay deep yellow daisies for weeks on end. Planting 90 cm (3 ft) apart is not too wide on well-nurtured soils, but it is more attractive when starved. Sometimes called *Inula* 'Golden Beauty'. It makes a good contrast with *Iris × fulvala* and a good foreground to heleniums.

speciosum

1.5 m × 90 cm	*[4–9]*	*Yellow*	*Summer*	P	D
5 × 3 ft					

S.E. Europe. 1739. *B. cordifolium, Telekia speciosa*. A gross plant whose aromatic, large leaves and wide, deep yellow daisies create a fine effect for many weeks. But beware its spreading habit. *B. speciosissimum* [4–9] is smaller and less ornamental.

"It is a very fine thing to grow in an isolated group in turf."—EAB

BUPLEURUM, Umbelliferae. Sun-loving plants for any fertile soil, not florally very wonderful but noted for their green colouring. There are several small species.

falcatum

90 × 60 cm	*[4–9]*	*Yellowish*	*Summer*	P	DS
3 × 2 ft					

Europe to Himalaya. 1739. Small heads of yellowish Cow-Parsley flowers, and small narrow leaves. The miniature features of the plant give a *Gypsophila*-like effect, for many weeks from midsummer onwards.

CACCINIA, Boraginaceae. A plant for well-drained soil in sun. Rather coarse, like so many of the Borage Family.

macranthera

60 × 60 cm	*[4–8]*	*Blue*	*L.Spring*	DRS
2 × 2 ft				

Armenia, Afghanistan. The form *crassifolia* (1880) has broad hairy glaucous foliage. The flowers are in big branching heads, of true blue, emerging from pinkish buds, and with white centres. It is a lax plant, with a beautiful colour scheme of its own. Blends well with old roses.

CALAMINTHA, Labiatae. Well-drained soil in sun.

grandiflora

46 × 46 cm	*[5–9]*	*Pink*	*E.Summer*	DS
18 × 18 in				

S. Europe. 1596. *Satureja grandiflora*. Small aromatic leaves on dense bushy plants, covered all over with small lilac-pink sage-like flowers. A lovely verge-plant to grow among white pinks and *Sedum spectabile* foliage.

nepetoides

| 30 × 30 cm | [5–9] | Lilac-white | L.Summer/ | DS |
| 1 × 1 ft | | | E.Autumn | |

S. Europe. An imperturbable little plant with a long flowering season, and of delicious minty odour when crushed. The tiny thyme-like flowers are beloved by bees and are borne in such profusion that they make good effect. Lovely with *Berberis thunbergii* 'Atropurpurea Nana'.

CALANTHE, Orchidaceae. The following few species—and I believe several more of greater rarity—may be grown out of doors successfully in our warmer counties in part shade in well-drained soil full of humus. The bulbous roots should be scarcely covered when planting in autumn.

discolor

| 30 × 60 cm | [8–9] | Pinkish | E.Summer | P | W | D |
| 1 × 2 ft | | | | | | |

Japan. 1837. It needs a cool position in peaty soil. The bulbous root throws up large oblong leaves, and tall stems carry several chocolate or purplish flowers with white lips. Sweetly fragrant. *C. discolor bicolor* (1840) (*C. striata*) [8–9] may be regarded as equally desirable: the five upper segments are of orange brown, the lip yellow.

reflexa

| 30 × 30 cm | [8–9] | Lilac | L.Summer | PW | D |
| 1 × 1 ft | | | | | |

Japan, W. China. 1912. Apart from the charm that all these species have, the pale lavender upper segments and rich lilac lip mark it apart from others of these semi-hardy species.

tricarinata

| 60 × 30 cm | [8–9] | White | E.Summer | P | W | D |
| 2 × 1 ft | | | | | | |

Nepal. 1879. This is an elegant and delightful plant. Stout basal leaves and airy sprays of greeny cream flowers with a striking purplish brown lip. Similar cultivation to *C. discolor*.

CALTHA, Ranunculaceae. These are related to the Buttercups and need very moist or boggy soil, preferring full sunshine unless the soil is on the drier side, when some shade will help them in the summer. The petals shine, as glib as glass.

leptosepala

| 30 × 30 cm | [5–9] | White | Spring | DS |
| 1 × 1 ft | | | | |

N.W. America. Although it does not hold a candle to the calthas of the Old World, this white-flowered species has some value. It has small leaves and flowers.

minor

| 30 × 30 cm | [4–9] | Yellow | Spring | DS |
| 1 × 1 ft | | | | |

N. Britain. *C. palustris minor, C. radicans.* This flowers well after the others are over. It is a pleasing smaller edition of *C. palustris* and needs the same cultivation. It is somewhat stoloniferous. 1982: correctly *C. palustris flabellifolia.*

palustris ★

| 30 × 46 cm | [4–9] | Yellow | Spring | DS |
| 1 ft × 18 in | | | | |

Europe, North America, Britain. The Marsh Marigold or King Cup is a plant for moist soil or the waterside. One of the most beautiful of British wild plants, it is well worth a place in the garden for the sake of its handsome, rounded leaves and gorgeous, large, deep yellow, buttercup-like flowers in early spring. But keep it well away from *Primula rosea*, whose "shocking pink" flowers appear at the same time! There is a white form *C.p.* 'Alba', which, while not conspicuous, is rewarding and has a long flowering season.

—'Flora Pleno'

| 30 × 46 cm | | Yellow | Spring | D |
| 1 ft × 18 in | | | | |

C.P. 'Multiplex' or 'Monstrosa Plena'. One of the showiest of plants in March and April. Its full double, ranunculus-like, golden yellow flowers contrast well with glossy rounded leaves which later grow into handsome ground-cover. This plant has been cultivated since early in the seventeenth century. A garden form known as 'Semi-plena' or 'Pleurisepala' has two rows of petals of a lighter colour.

polypetala

| 60 × 90 cm | [4–9] | Yellow | E.Spring | DS |
| 2 × 3 ft | | | | |

Caucasus etc. Much larger in leaf and growth, and also somewhat larger in flower than the Marsh Marigold, this is not a clump-former, but spreads over wet ground by means of its rooting stems. It will even make a mass of shoots over water. A gay but rampageous plant whose foliage stands up well during the summer; to the fore at Gunby Hall, Lincolnshire, and at Stourhead, Wiltshire. It flowers a good fortnight earlier than *C. palustris*. Legend has it that this plant owes its introduction to our gardens by being stolen from the Vatican Gardens. While quite likely somebody's "green fingers" itched while visiting there, it grows freely in its native habitat. *C.p.* 'Tyermanii' has dark-tinted procumbent flower-stems and clear yellow flowers.

> "... the chieftain of the clan, a splendid hearty thing which, flinging out red-bronze arms of a yard in length, will float them on the water and adorn them with a succession of golden goggles until summer is nigh."—ATJ

CAMASSIA, Liliaceae. Bulbous plants which are admirable for naturalizing in the wild garden, in grass if necessary, but they produce the best spikes in cultivated ground, well nurtured, in sun or part shade. They should be planted in autumn 23 cm (9 in) deep. They die down by July.

leichtlinii

90 cm—1.2 m	[4–10]	Various	E.Summer	P DS
× 23 cm				
3 − 4 ft × 9 in				

W. North America. 1853. Without doubt this is the finest garden species; the lax bent leaves are scarcely an asset but the long slender spires of starry blooms are unlike anything else. It is naturalized at Hidcote, Gloucestershire, and the flowers vary from whitish to washed-out blue, to deep blue, sometimes light yellow. The deep blue forms are sometimes called *C.l. suksdorfii*, and from this are derived no doubt the old 'Atroviolacea', 'Orion' and the newer 'Eve Price';

the latter is established at Wakehurst, Sussex. 'Plena' has well-filled starry rosettes of creamy yellow and increases slowly. 'Electra' was raised by Eric Smith around 1960 and is a superb, tall, large-flowered light lavender-blue variety. Probably a tetraploid.

quamash
90 × 23 cm   *[4–10]*   *Various*   *E.Summer*   P DS
3 ft × 9 in

W. North America. 1837. The Common Camass varies similarly to *C. leichtlinii*, but does not reach the same depth of colouring and is a less valued plant. There has been much confusion over this plant, *C. esculenta* [4–10] and narrow-petalled *C. cusickii* [3–10].

CAMPANULA, Campanulaceae. The majority of these most beautiful plants are invaluable for grouping with pink, crimson, purple and white shrub roses, flowering as they mostly do at the end of June and into July with the Hybrid Musks and old shrub roses, and providing just the right contrasting colours. They will thrive in shade as well as in sun, in any fertile soil that is well drained.

alliariifolia ★
46 × 46 cm   *[4–8]*   *White*   *Summer*   P S
18 × 18 in

Caucasus, Asia Minor. 1803. A clump-forming plant with attractive, heart-shaped, green leaves forming a base, as it were, to the erect wiry stems from which shapely cream bells nod, along their entire length. Each plant can be a picture of poise and beauty.

bononiensis
90 × 30 cm   *[6–8]*   *Lilac*   *Summer*   PF DS
3 × 1 ft

Middle East. 1773. A refined plant with narrow pointed grey-green leaves and graceful spires of narrow, rich lilac, starry bells, borne almost horizontally. *C. rapunculoides*, a bad but beautiful weed, is apt to masquerade under this name and that of *C. trachelium*. *C.b. ruthenica* has wide leaves. There are white forms.

'Burghaltii' ● ★
60 × 30 cm   *[4–8]*   *Grey*   *Summer*   P D
2 × 1 ft

A rare hybrid, producing many erect stems hung with large tubular bells of strange, palest grey-lilac. The bells are some 7.5 cm (3 in) long and it is no doubt related to *C. punctata*; *C.* 'Van Houttei' is a similar hybrid of darker colouring. They need support. *C.* 'Burghaltii', if cut down after flowering and watered and fed, will usually produce a second crop of flowers.

carpatica ★
30 × 30 cm   *[4–7]*   *Blue/White*   *Summer*   P DS
1 × 1 ft

Carpathian Mts. 1774. Named clones do duty for the species, but a variety of tints and good-quality flowers can be raised easily from seed; they make neat tufts of bright green leaves and are covered, like a pincushion, with masses of stalks bearing large cup-shaped flowers from white to darkest violet-blue. It is best to select named clones when in flower or from a reliable list. The whole set can hardly be beaten for frontal positions, or the larger rock garden.

glomerata

30 – 90 × 60 cm	*[3–8]*	*Purple*	*Summer*	P	D
1 – 3 × 2 ft					

Europe, Britain, Asia. It is not worth growing the wild type, which is excessively invasive and about 46 cm (18 in) high. 'Superba' (1910) is a gorgeous plant, rather invasive it is true, but the intensive violet-purple flowers massed in rounded heads at the top of the 60 cm (2 ft) leafy stems give a warmth of colouring not usually seen at the time of the early roses and red peonies. There are paler and dwarfer forms; among the latter are 'Joan Elliott', early-flowering, and 'Purple Pixie', late-flowering, apart from *C.g. dahurica*, with good wide flowers and flower-heads of dark purple. 'Schneekrone' is a new white variety, achieving 50 cm (20 in). The strongest growers have smaller flower-heads in the leaf axils, which prolong the display after the terminal head has faded.

lactiflora

1.2 – 1.5 m	*[4–8]*	*Lilac-blue*	*E.Summer/*	DS
× 60 cm			*L.Autumn*	
4 – 5 × 2 ft				

Caucasus. 1814. One of the finest of hardy perennials, needing stakes in windy districts. The stout stems, set all the way up with pointed leaves, carry great branching heads full of pale or deep lilac bell-flowers. A magnificent plant for associating with shrub roses, it thrives anywhere, even in unkempt grassy areas. Lovely with *Lilium candidum* and *testaceum*. Rather uncertain as a cut flower.

★ —**'Loddon Anna'** (Raised by T. Carlile prior to 1952). A delightful counterpart in soft pink.   D

★ —**'Pouffe'**. A valuable, dense, dwarf plant raised by Alan Bloom for the foreground. The hummocks are smothered for weeks in pale blue flowers; it is well named. 46 × 46 cm (18 × 18 in).   D

★ —**'Prichard's Variety'**. A good form, violet-blue.   D

★ —**'Superba'**. Large violet-blue flowers.   D

latifolia

1.2 m × 60 cm	*[4–8]*	*Various*	*Summer*	PF	DS
4 × 2 ft					

Europe to Kashmir; Britain. A good clump-forming plant with handsome, rounded, basal leaves. These decrease in size up the stems, which are topped with many tubular flowers of fine quality and size. It spreads freely by seed and as a consequence I prefer to remove the seed-pods as soon as the flowers are over. In wild parts of the garden—as at Hidcote, Gloucestershire—its prolificity can be condoned. Both the violet-blue and also the white forms are first class; *C.l. macrantha* (1820) and 'Brantwood' are much the same but of rich violet-purple; 'Gloaming' is palest lilac. They all thrive in any soil in sun or part shade, and the white is superb with some of the orange lilies, of the *L. × hollandicum* type, as a contrast in colour and shape. Brantwood was the home of John Ruskin.

latiloba

90 × 46 cm	*[4–8]*	*Lavender*	*Summer*	P	D
3 ft × 18 in					

Siberia. 1828. *C. grandis*. This plant makes a mass of handsome green rosettes on the ground, the strongest of which throw up stiff, erect stems, studded for almost their entire length with stalkless, wide, cup-shaped, rich lavender-blue flowers. It is content with ordinary conditions, in sun or part shade. A good ground-cover.

● ★ 'Highcliffe' is a noted variety; 'Percy Piper' is very similar; it is supposed to be a hybrid with *C. persicifolia*, but there is little evidence. The corolla is slightly darker, the central button slightly whiter, and well-grown spikes have several branches at the base. At Hidcote *C. latiloba* has sported to a pleasing light lilac-pink which has been named 'Hidcote Amethyst'. All evergreen. Sometimes called *C. persicifolia sessiliflora*.

● ★ —'Alba'. 1839. Rare and beautiful white counterpart of scintillating quality.

"It is far more beautiful for picking if grown under the shade of bushes and trees ... and looks cool and beautiful when picked ... its rosette-like leaf-growth is also attractive and ornamental, especially in the autumn."— CWE

persicifolia ● ★
| *90 × 30 cm* | *[4–8]* | *Lilac-blue* | *Summer* | P | DS |
| *3 × 1 ft* | | | | | |

Europe, North Africa, Asia. Sixteenth century. Evergreen basal rosettes of narrow leaves produce slender wiry stems with pretty, stalked, nodding, cup-shaped flowers. It is in flower for a long time, and is excellent for cutting. A good companion for *Alchemilla mollis* and old roses. There is a lovely white form, 'Alba', and both can be raised easily from seeds, though they vary from pure white to the typical deep Spode-blue. They are reasonably good perennials, unlike some of the more capricious fancy-named kinds which can be chosen from lists. The ordinary species is acceptable to me, unless I yearn for double-flowered forms, such as 'Fleur de Neige', or 'Moerheimii', or the very large flowers of 'Telham Beauty' or 'Blue Belle'. A pleasing double white with bluish edge is 'Frances'. Evergreen.

punctata
| *30 × 46 cm* | *[4–8]* | *Pinkish* | *Summer* | DS |
| *1 ft × 18 in* | | | | |

Japan, Siberia. 1813. *C. nobilis*. A low, invasive plant but in spite of this it has large tubular bells of creamy white or mauve, variously flushed with pink and more or less heavily dotted inside with red. It needs a good sandy soil and a sunny position. Probably a parent of *C.* 'Burghaltii', and perhaps of 'Van Houttei'. Rare and unusual.

pyramidalis
| *1.5 m × 60 cm* | *[7–8]* | *Blue/White* | *Summer* | P | S |
| *5 × 2 ft* | | | | | |

Europe. 1596. The Chimney Bellflower or Steeple Bells is one of the most striking of herbaceous plants; when well grown it can achieve 1.8–2.1 m (6–7 ft). It is best treated as a biennial though the woody roots persist for some years in well-drained soil in full sun. The heart-shaped basal leaves make a good pyramid, a base for the erect stems with erect side branches, which produce quantities of stemless starry cups for many weeks in dry weather. Often grown to perfection in pots for standing in patios or indoors. Typical cool campanula-blue, or white.

rapunculoides

90 × 60 cm	*[3–8]*	*Violet*	*Summer*	PF	DS
3 × 2 ft					

Europe, Britain. A plant whose nettle-like leaves and gracefully ascending stems, bearing a long succession of starry bells of rich colouring, have always enchanted the unwary. It is one of the most prolific of ineradicable weeds, spreading freely by fleshy roots and by seed. For all that it is beautiful when naturalized in thin grass. But take care ...

sarmatica ● ★

46 × 30 cm	*[5–8]*	*Blue*	*Summer*	S
18 in × 1 ft				

Caucasus. 1803. The large lavender-blue bells are velvety-hairy without and borne on grey stems over a basal tuft of hairy leaves. It is a great beauty and a good sound perennial for a sunny foreground.

takesimana ●

60 × 46 cm	*[5–8]*	*Lilac*	*Summer*	DS
2 ft × 18 in				

Korea. This rare plant should be popular when distributed. Fine basal rosettes of large leaves. The large tubular-bell flowers are of great beauty, of rich lilac-white, densely spotted with maroon inside. The roots colonize freely. Closely related to *C. punctata*.

trachelium

60 × 30 cm	*[4–8]*	*Lilac/White*	*Summer*	P	DS
2 × 1 ft					

Europe. 1561. *C. urticifolia*. The Nettle-leafed Bellflower, or Coventry Bells, is described in part by its synonym. The wide bells are carried up the stems, which are thickly set with leaves below. (The usual lilac form has an unforunate resemblance to *C. rapunculoides*, q.v.) There is a double lilac form, 'Bernice', also a single white and—perhaps the choicest—a double white: 'Alba' and 'Albo Plena' respectively. All kinds increase slowly. The double white has long been treasured at Blickling Hall, Norfolk.

"... especially about Coventry, where they grow very plentifully abroad in the fields, and they are called Coventry bells."—GH

versicolor

90 × 30 cm	*[7–8]*	*Blue*	*Summer*	P	DS
3 × 1 ft					

Greece. 1788. Stout stems grow up from the basal clump of heart-shaped leaves studded with starry, open, yet cup-shaped, flowers of light or dark lavender-blue, with a darker eye. It bears some resemblance to *C. pyramidalis* but is less tall.

CANNA, Cannaceae. Luxuriant plants with magnificent greenery, needing rich cultivation in full sun in our warmest counties. The fleshy roots are easily divided. Snails are apt to bite through the young foliage while it is rolled up in late spring, with disastrous if amusing results.

indica

1.2 m × 90 cm	[9–10]	Reddish	L.Summer	P W	D
4 × 3 ft					

South America, West Indies. 1570. Indian Shot. This tender plant will add interest to the late summer border. Though usually grown in a greenhouse it may be tried outside in our very warmest counties. The erect, small, narrow flowers are red with yellow throats, emerging from grey-brown calyces. Some forms have deep coppery foliage, and one of these with orange flowers thrives at Sissinghurst, Kent, but is usually wintered under cover.

iridiflora ●

1.5 m × 90 cm	[9–10]	Pink	L.Summer/	P W	D
5 × 3 ft			Autumn		

1816. This rare Peruvian plant is hardy in very warm, sheltered gardens, in the south and west, but should be covered in winter with branches and dead flower-stems, such as those of border flowers, straw or bracken. The huge, smooth, handsome leaves are blue-green, 60 cm (2 ft) long and half as broad, and rather like those of a banana. Handsome great butterfly blooms of warm, deep pink appear late in the season at the tops of the leafy stems, like graceful gladioli; they assort well with late Monkshoods. This nonpareil avoids the ugly stiffness of most garden hybrid cannas. It has become known in gardens as *C.i.* 'Ehemannii'. It thrives at Trengwainton, Cornwall, and at Clevedon Court, Somerset.

lutea

1.2 m × 46 cm	[9–10]	Yellow	L.Summer	P W	D
4 ft × 18 in					

S. and Central America. 1824. One of the smallest, with small fresh green leaves and erect spikes of small clear yellow blooms with reddish spot. There are darker and lighter colour forms.

GARDEN HYBRIDS

1.2 m × 60 cm	[9–10]	Various	L.Summer/	W	D
4 × 2 ft			Autumn		

The cannas, popular in our public parks and other places where summer bedding is practised, form a complex race, derived from several species. Modern varieties are mostly compact plants producing great broad smooth leaves and bearing above them stiff spikes of broad-petalled flowers, in both colour and form somewhat resembling a gigantic wallflower. They achieve some 1.2 m (4 ft) or more by the autumn. Their tuberous roots will not stand frost but in extra warm gardens in our warmest counties, with a good winter mulch, they can be established, and produce flowers from July onwards. They are available in red, orange, yellow and pink, or variously speckled or edged. Some have rich green leaves, and of these I prefer the yellows, such as 'R. Wallace'. There are many with dark coppery purple leaves; several of these have orange or red flowers and are arresting. 'America', 'Feuerzauber' and 'Liebesglut' are some notables, while 'Le Roi Humbert' is used annually in the Red Borders at Hidcote, Gloucestershire, with great effect, and at Trelissick, Cornwall. 'Wyoming' combines apricot-orange flowers with purplish leaves.

"Purple-leaved Cannas are simply irresistible to group behind the Yuccas and the great ferny grey-green leaves of *Melianthus major*."—EAB

CARDAMINE, Cruciferae. The Cuckoo Flower or Lady's Smock, *C. pratensis*, and its pretty double form, are rather small for this list. The following species prefers damp ground and is easily grown. For some related plants, see *Dentaria*.

latifolia

46 × 60 m	*[3–9]*	*Purple*	*Spring*	D
18 in × 2 ft				

Pyrenees. 1710. The copious leafage makes a spreading rich green mat and the flower-stems carry many blooms something of the size and colouring of Honesty, but in smaller heads. *C. macrophylla* [3–9] is closely related. Also known as *C. raphanifolia*.

CARDIOCRINUM, Liliaceae. A small genus differing from *Lilium* in its large heart-shaped leaves. They need deep, very rich, humus-laden soil—which, though moist, should remain well drained—in broken shade. The bulbs take several years to flower, but by planting a group of different ages a yearly display can be ensured. The best spikes occur on bulbs raised from seed but it is a slow job. The bulbs should be planted so that their apex is level with the soil surface; they perish after flowering but usually produce offsets. The seed pods are as spectacular as the flowers. See RHS *Journal*, Vol LX, December, p. 551.

giganteum ●

1.8–3 m × 90 cm	*[7–9]*	*White*	*Summer*	F	DS
6–10 × 3 ft					

W. China. 1841. *Lilium giganteum*. This is perhaps the most imposing of all hardy flowering plants. Immense leaves lose size the higher they are disposed up the immensely stout stalk, from the top of which hang many long, narrow trumpet-flowers, pointed downwards, of greenish white, with maroon red in the throat. A numinous sight at Crathes Castle, Kincardineshire, at the Savill Gardens, Windsor, and at Wakehurst Place, Sussex.

—yunnanense

1.5–2.1 m × 90 cm	*[7–9]*	*White*	*Summer*	F	DS
5–7 × 3 ft					

W. China. This differs in being not so tall, having brown stems, rich bronze-tinted young foliage, and the flowers, opening at the top of the spike first, are held more or less horizontally, and are rich red within the throat. An established favourite at Rowallane, Northern Ireland.

cathayanum [7–9] and **cordatum** [7–9], from China and Japan respectively, lack the majesty of the above two, but are occasionally seen in the gardens of curiosos, and all are growing at the Savill Garden.

CATANANCHE, Compositae. Easily grown in full sun, with good drainage, but somewhat short lived. Best planted in spring or very early autumn.

caerulea

60 × 30 cm	*[4–8]*	*Blue*	*Summer*	PF	RS
2 × 1 ft					

S. Europe. 1596. Blue Cupidone. A clump of grassy short leaves puts up sheaves of branching wiry stalks, each ending in a lavender-blue, dark-eyed daisy enclosed in a papery "everlasting" calyx. Selected forms, raised by Perry of Enfield, Middlesex, are 'Major' (1935), a good lavender-blue; 'Perry's White'; 'Bicolor', white with a dark centre. Mingled with some grey foliage to give them rather better furnishing—*Artemisia stelleriana*, for instance—they give a long-lasting summer picture. The forms reproduce easily from root-cuttings; seeds will produce mixed tints.

CAULOPHYLLUM, Berberidaceae. A plant for a cool semi-shady place in woodland soil.

thalictroides

75 × 46 cm	*[3–9]*	*White*	*Summer*	F	DS
2½ ft × 18 in					

North America. Blue Cohosh. The erect stem bears one very large-lobed leaf. The flowers are of no account but the marble-sized berries are deep blue, maturing in autumn. Quite out of the ordinary.

CAUTLEYA, Zingiberaceae. Related to *Canna* and *Roscoea*, in many ways they are intermediate between the two genera. Their botanical status is confused. The plant grown as *Cautleya* 'Robusta' (*C. lutea* 'Robusta') in gardens is closely related to *C. spicata* and is a splendid hardy plant.

gracilis

46 × 23 cm	*[7–9]*	*Yellow*	*Summer*	PF	DS
18 × 9 in					

Himalaya. 1887. *C. lutea*. A slight, slim plant with narrow stalkless leaves and two or three small yellow flowers in a small spike. Not exciting.

robusta

60 cm	*[7–9]*	*Yellow*	*Summer*	PF	DS
2 ft					

Sikkim. Probably not in cultivation. I include it to differentiate from 'Robusta' of gardens. The long spikes of flowers develop into *drooping* sprays of seeds.

spicata

60 × 46 cm	*[7–9]*	*Yellow*	*L.Summer*	PF	DS
2 ft × 18 in					

Himalaya. An upstanding plant with good spikes of dark yellow flowers held in bracts and calyces, which may be green or maroon. The garden plant known as ★ 'Robusta' ('Autumn Beauty') undoubtedly belongs here, and may be just a good dark form of the species. It is very striking when in flower, the dark yellow contrasting well with the maroon bracts; the spikes are held just above the handsome, broad, long, rich green leaves; the black seeds are enclosed in almost white cases, on erect stems. A great sight at Lanhydrock, Cornwall.

CELMISIA, Compositae. Beautiful New Zealand daisies. They do not take kindly to the south-east of England, but thrive in the west and north and Scotland in mild districts or where true winter conditions keep them snug with snow. They thrive at Rowallane, Northern Ireland, and at Edinburgh Botanic Garden. All require well-drained soil with grit and humus, and full exposure. There are many smaller species for the rock garden; the following is large enough to be listed here. Evergreen.

coriacea ●

30 × 30 cm	*[9]*	*White*	*E.Summer*	P	DS
1 × 1 ft					

New Zealand. Leathery long-pointed leaves, glaucous white above, white-woolly below. Silvery-woolly stems, large daisies, pure white with handsome yellow centre. *C.c.* 'Stricta' varies in foliage from silvery to bronzy-yellow. These are very handsome plants. *C. hookeri, C. mackaui, C. spectabilis, C. monroi,* and *C. rigida* [all 9], among others, are rather less impressive than the above but all are worth growing.

CENTAUREA, Compositae. The Knapweed of our chalk hills belongs to this genus, and indicates the type of flower: large, with thistle-like centre surrounded by a ring of starry, trumpet-shaped petals. They all appreciate full sun and rough, limy soil, though they are easily satisfied as long as there is good drainage.

atropurpurea ● ★

1.2 m × 60 cm	*[4–8]*	*Purple*	*Summer*	PF	DS
4 × 2 ft					

Hungary. 1802. A rare plant in gardens. It may be likened to a superlative version of our native Greater Knapweed (*Centaurea scabiosa*), but with larger flowers of intense crimson-purple on stout stems and narrowly cut, dainty leaves on long stalks. Beautiful with *C. ruthenica.* There is a white form of great beauty, *C.a.* 'Alba'. They grow well at Powis Castle, Powys.

cynaroides

60 × 60 cm	*[5–8]*	*Lilac*	*Summer*	PF	DRS
2 × 2 ft					

Europe, Canary Isles. *Cnicus centauroides, Rhaponticum cynaroides.* Both this and *C. rhaponticum* have handsome foliage, rich green above, grey-white beneath and grey stems supporting very large round flower-heads of deep lilac-pink. In this the leaves are deeply cut into many pointed lobes, and the papery brown bracts around the flower-heads are very narrow and pointed. Also known as *Leuzea cynaroides.*

dealbata

90 × 60 cm	*[4–8]*	*Pink*	*Summer*	PF	DRS
3 × 2 ft					

Caucasus. 1804. The Perennial Cornflower is a free-flowering and easy plant to grow, but usually its stems flop over if it is not staked. (*C. hypoleuca* does not have this disadvantage.) The finely divided light green leaves are attractive; greyish beneath. Each stem bears one or more lilac-pink beautiful flowers of Sweet Sultan charm.

—**steenbergii.** 1939. The flowers are a rich dark carmine-lilac. It is lower-growing, with similar foliage, but has a very invasive root system. Possibly a hybrid.

glastifolia

1.5 m × 60 cm	*[3–8]*	*Yellow*	*L. Summer*	PF	DS
5 × 2 ft					

Central Europe. 1731. This might be described as a more elegant *C. macrocephala.* Good branching stems, winged with leaf-flanges, support round knobs of light yellow, emerging from silvery calyces.

hypoleuca ★

60 × 46 cm	*[4–8]*	*Pink*	*E. Summer*	PF	DRS
2 ft × 18 in					

N. Iran. *c.* 1939. Introduced by Miss Nancy Lindsay. From seeds raised at Regent's Park plants were sent to Kew. Admiring these plants, which were in a bed of *C. dealbata,* I gave one the name of ●★ 'John Coutts', the late Curator of the Garden, believing him to have selected it from *C. dealbata.* This is the reason for this superlative plant having appeared in lists for some years recently under this specific name; it is illustrated in colour in my book *Plants for Ground-Cover*. It has a running root—not unduly invasive—and long broad leaves, deeply lobed, soft green above and grey-white underneath. The flowers are borne singly on stout stalks and are of a rich deep rose; a second crop is produced in early autumn; in fact, with good cultivation it is seldom out of flower. The seed-heads are like silvery daisies. Beautiful with *Campanula latiloba*.

jankae

90 × 60 cm	[4–8]	Purple	Summer/	PF	DS
3 × 2 ft			E.Autumn		

S.E. Romania. A pleasing Knapweed with typical rich purple flowers over distinctive, much divided, greyish leaves. Prior to 1910.

macrocephala

90 × 60 cm	[3–8]	Yellow	Summer	PF	DS
3 × 2 ft					

Caucasus. 1805. A coarse leafy plant bearing large Knapwood flowers of rich yellow enclosed in brown papery bracts. Included for the sake of its value when dried.

"The Great Golden Knapweed ... this robust plant deserves a place."—WR

montana

46 × 60 cm	[3–8]	Various	E.Summer	PF	D
18 in × 2 ft					

Europe. 1596. The Mountain Knapweed, grown for centuries in gardens, is useful because it flowers before the main mass of herbaceous plants, assorting well with Lupins, Catmint, and other plant of the June border. It is an easily satisfied plant in any open sunny spot making a dense mass of roots and narrow leaves—of no particular merit; flopping stems bear one or more large, elegant cornflower blooms. The normal is a deep blue with reddish centre; there is a white ('Alba') and a pink ('Carnea'), 'Parham Variety' of deep amethyst, and other tints. They are all good plants for chalky gardens.

"The Great Blew-Bottle or Corne-Floure."—GH

rhaponticum

90 × 90 cm	[4–8]	Lilac	Summer	PF	DRS
3 × 3 ft					

Europe. 1640. *Rhaponticum cynaroides scariosum*. Larger than *C. cynaroides*, with leaves almost entire or occasionally cut or lobed, and fine large flower-heads enclosed in broad, brown, papery bracts. It may be considered a coarse weed by some, but it forms a handsome clump. The plant known as ● ★ *C. pulchra major* (of gardens) [7–8] is less coarse and equally handsome; the leaves have distinctly rounded lobes (*cf. C. cynaroides*) and rounded brown, papery bracts. It has a reputation of not being so hardy as the others, and as a precaution it should be planted only in spring in a well-drained, sunny, warm spot. Good for drying. (The true *C. pulchra* from Kashmir is an annual, cornflower blue, with papery calyces.)

ruthenica

90 × 46 cm	[5–8]	Citron	Summer	P	DRS
3 ft × 18 in					

E. Europe. 1783. Over ferny, dark green leaves, greyish beneath, the green stems hold fluffy heads of pale citron-yellow flowers. A pretty plant with flowers of an uncommon tint, invaluable for colour-grouping with *Centranthus ruber* 'Atrococcineus'.

". . . a border flower of the highest merit for suitable soils."—WR

". . . the most graceful of the tall yellow ones, is of a pleasant shade, and the leaves are beautifully cut and a rich green."—EAB

salonitana

1.2 m × 60 cm	[6–8]	Yellow	Summer	PF	DRS
4 × 2 ft					

S.E. Europe, Asia. The Yellow Knapweed is very beautiful but rarely seen in gardens. The leaves are deeply cut and pinnatisect, the reverses greyish like the stems, which branch towards the top, carrying several lovely knobs of soft butter-yellow flowers enclosed in papery brown calyces. A slender and elegant plant with an uncommon colour, but with a terribly invasive root.

simplicicaulis

23 × 23 cm	[3–8]	Pink	E. Summer	DS
9 × 9 in				

Armenia. Although usually grown on rock gardens it is quite at home in any well-drained soil in full sun; for foreground planting. Dense masses of deeply divided small leaves over which are held the silvery rose cornflowers.

stricta

30 × 60 cm	[3–8]	Blue	E. Summer	D
1 × 2 ft				

Hungary. (*C. triumphettii stricta.*) A close relative of *C. montana*. The freely running root-stock sends up masses of erect shoots, well clothed in greyish green leaves. The flowers are poised above all this, good though rather starry cornflowers of clear blue with mauve centres. Another crop is produced in late summer, after rain.

CENTRANTHUS, Valerianaceae. *Kentranthus*, Red Valerian.

ruber

60–90 × 46 cm	[5–9]	Pink/White	Summer	P	CS
2–3 ft × 18 in					

Europe. The fleshy glaucous leaves and large, long heads of minute deep pink flowers appear on many an old wall or rubble slope, particularly on limestone. The white form or the deep coppery red 'Atrococcineus' should be sought.

"It is often naturalized on walls, ruins, and on rocky or stony banks."
—WR

CEPHALARIA, Dipsacaceae.

gigantea

1.8 × 1.2 m	*[3–8]*	*Yellow*	*E.Summer*	PF	DR
6 × 4 ft					

Siberia. 1759. *C. tatarica* of gardens. This grand scabious-relative forms a magnificent clump of leaves, dark green and divided, and wiry stems branch freely, each ending in a large flower-head of primrose yellow on stalks of some 60 cm (2 ft). Ordinary soil, sun. A splendid garden plant where room can be found for it. The pale yellow of this and *Centaurea ruthenica* is all too rare among hardy plants. *C. flava* [3–8] is a much smaller plant, pretty in leaf and bud but disappointing in its small buff-yellow flowers.

CERATOSTIGMA, Plumbaginaceae. Most of the hardy Plumbagos are really shrubs but, since I have included *Fuchsia* and a few other shrubby genera, on the grounds that in Surrey they usually die to soil level in winter, I think I may be pardoned for including these. They are all ardent sun-lovers, and need a fertile, well-drained soil. Humming-bird hawkmoths sometimes deign to sip nectar from them.

griffithii

60 × 60 cm	*[9–10]*	*Blue*	*L.Summer*	W	CS
2 × 2 ft					

India, China. A tender shrubby plant for our warmest counties. It has a mass of twiggy stems with small somewhat greyish leaves. The knobs of bristly buds produce clear bright blue flowers daily for a long time. Autumn-tinted foliage.

minus

60 × 60 cm	*[8–10]*	*Indigo*	*L.Summer*	W	CS
2 × 2 ft					

W. China. *C. polhillii.* Similar to *C. willmottianum,* but smaller, and with dull blue flowers. Needs the warmest of positions.

plumbaginoides

30 × 46 cm	*[5–8]*	*Indigo*	*Autumn*	CD
1 ft × 18 in				

China. 1846. *Plumbago larpentae.* Almost too small for inclusion, but it is a valuable plant for frontal positions; it has an invasive root-habit. Every erect leafy shoot terminates in a bristly head with dark blue flowers daily in September and October, at which time the leaves are usually red or maroon. It thrives at Knightshayes Court, Devon.

willmottianum ★

90 × 90 cm	*[7–10]*	*Blue*	*L.Summer/*	CS
3 × 3 ft			*Autumn*	

W. China. 1908. This is the most reliable and showy species—a wiry bushy plant whose stems die to the ground in cold districts. They are rough and set with small leaves, branching into several bristly bud-heads. The flowers come daily for many weeks and are of clear cobalt blue. A most useful plant for associating with fuchsias and other autumnals, and silverlings.

CESTRUM, Solanaceae.

parqui

1.5 m × 60 cm	*[7–10]*	*Yellow*	*L.Summer*	P	CD
5 × 2 ft					

Chile. 1787. Although a shrubby plant, in this area it is best cut down to the ground (if the frost does not achieve this), when the resulting flower spikes will be larger, though later. Narrow leaves, and willowy stems bearing plumes of small lemon-yellow flowers from August onwards. A useful colour at that time. A good fertile soil not too abundant in nitrogen is required. Far-reaching fragrance in the evening. A success at Lanhydrock, Cornwall.

"... when fully out they are so unlike anything else that the plant always attracts attention."—EAB

CHAEROPHYLLUM, Umbelliferae.

hirsutum

60 × 30 cm	*[5–8]*	*Pink*	*Spring*	P	D
2 × 1 ft					

Europe. This is in effect a Cow Parsley with hairy stems and leaves. The lilac-pink form 'Roseum' or 'Rubriflorum' is to be sought, and few herbaceous plants can hold a candle to it in early May. It will often produce a good second crop of flowers in late summer and is easily grown in sun or part shade.

CHAMAELIRIUM, Liliaceae.

luteum

46 × 30 cm	*[6–8]*	*White*	*E.Summer*	DS
18 in × 1 ft				

North America. *C. carolinianum*. Narrow, rich green leaves spring from a tuberous root-stock. The wiry erect stems are studded with small white flowers with yellow stamens. Choice, rare, but scarcely exciting; for cool peaty soil. Deciduous, otherwise bears some resemblance to *Galax urceolata* when in flower.

CHASMANTHE, Iridaceae.

These plants used to be listed under *Antholyza*. They are rather tender South African corms and are closely related to *Curtonus*, but the flower spikes do not branch. In our warmer counties they may be expected to thrive in sunny places in well-drained soils.

aethiopica

90 × 30 cm	*[8–10]*	*Orange*	*Summer*	P	W	DS
3 × 1 ft						

South Africa. 1759. Tall, broad, grassy leaves above which the slender well-flowered spikes are held, set with montbretia-like flowers of narow outline in vivid orange, red-flushed. The top segment is long and projecting. *C. vittigera* is similar, with broader leaves.

caffra

60 × 23 cm	*[8–10]*	*Orange*	*Summer*	P	W	DS
2 ft × 9 in						

South Africa. 1928. A brilliant plant with elegant, long flowers of orange-red, set in level array on each side of the stems. Leaves grassy, narrow. *C. intermedia* is confused with this species.

115

CHELIDONIUM, Papaveraceae. These grow anywhere except in a bog, and will colonize waste places and thin woodland quickly. Orange-red sap.

majus

60 × 46 cm	*[5–8]*	*Yellow*	*E.Summer*	S
2 ft × 18 in				

Europe, Asia. Greater Celandine, Swallow Wort. Pretty, divided leaves and many small yellow flowers. 'Flore Pleno' (1771) is the double form; alas! far from being sterile it is as prolific with seedlings as the type. Not for the choice garden. There is also another double form, with leaves cut into narrow segments, equally prolific, *C. m. laciniatum.*

CHELONE, Scrophulariaceae.

lyonii

90 × 46 cm	*[3–8]*	*Pink*	*Autumn*	P	D
3 × 1 ft					

S.E. United States. 1812. The next species is better known. This has flowers in denser spikes, both terminal and axillary, and will perform similarly.

obliqua

90 × 46 cm	*[4–9]*	*Pink*	*Autumn*	P	D
3 ft × 18 in					

United States. 1752. A stiff but handsome plant, with stiff spikes of strangely shaped flowers, each somewhat resembling a "Turtle's Head", from which it derives this nickname. It is a reliable weather-resistant flower, as it has to be—flowering in September and October—and is of a deep warm lilac-pink. Copious basal leaves, extending up the stems. It increases readily at the root and is easy to grow. A dwarf, early-flowering clone has been named 'Praecox Nana'. There is also a white form.

"forms a dense mass of stems ... from July to September bearing clusters of showy pink blossoms."—WR

CHLOROPHYTUM, Liliaceae. A good sound perennial related to *Asphodelus* which will thrive only in a sunny place in our warmest counties. It grew out of doors for many years at Cambridge Botanic Garden in normal fertile soil.

bowkeri

1.5 m × 60 cm	*[9–10]*	*White*	*Summer*	PF	W	DS
5 × 2 ft						

Natal. Long narrow leaves cluster round the base of the stout ribbed stems. The starry, white and highly effective flowers are in a long slender spike.

CHRYSANTHEMUM, Compositae. A large genus containing several garden favourites of divergent characters: *C. coccineum,* the popular pyrethrum of the florists (its earlier name was *Pyrethrum roseum*); *C. parthenium* (*Pyrethrum parthenium*), the "Feverfue" whose yellow-leafed variant is often used in summer bedding; *C. maximum,* the big white Shasta Daisy, and several others, including of course some obvious "chrysanthemums". In addition, the botanists now segregate the tansy-flowered species in *Tanacetum* while the true daisy-flowers are variously assigned to *Argyranthemum, Dendranthemum, Leucanthemum* and *Nipponanthemum,* but I have not followed this revision of the genus because the reverse may yet be recommended!

coccineum ★

| 60 × 46 cm | [5–9] | Various | E.Summer | P | D |
| 2 ft × 18 in | | | | | |

Middle East. 1804. *Pyrethrum roseum*. The hardy named variants of this species, beloved by the florists, are sound garden plants. In the open field they usually stand up well, but in the garden often need some support. They thrive in good fertile soil, in sun, and are best planted or divided in July or August for good flower production the following season, but can also be moved in autumn or spring. James Kelway of Langport did much towards raising larger and brighter varieties in the early years of this century, following initial selection on the Continent, and his firm still lists many varieties. Numerous good colour forms have been named, single and double, white, pink and crimson, and they are best chosen when in flower, or from reliable lists. 'Eileen May Robinson' and 'Kelway's Glorious' remain the two best single varieties, in pink and crimson respectively; 'Evenglow' is a rich salmon-scarlet raised by Alan Bloom; 'Jubilee Gem' and 'Brenda' are magenta-pink. Excellent with Bearded Irises, Lupins and Catmint.

corymbosum

| 90 × 30 cm | [6–9] | White | Summer | P | DS |
| 3 × 1 ft | | | | | |

Caucasus. 1596. Deeply cut leaves, pyrethrum-like, make a dense clump. The single white daisies are carried in a cluster at the top of the stem; this, despite its description, is a thoroughly useful plant for summer.

frutescens

| 90 × 90 cm | [9–10] | Various | Summer | P | W | CD |
| 3 × 3 ft | | | | | | |

Canary Islands. 1699. The Paris Daisy or French Marguerite is a shrubby plant with neatly divided leaves, and makes a bush in our warmest maritime counties. The unending succession of yellow-centred daisies has made it popular for summer bedding. White, pink and yellow forms are available in singles or doubles, under many names, 'Coronation', 'Mary Wootton', 'Jamaica Primrose' and others.

leucanthemum

| 60 × 30 cm | [4–9] | White | E.Summer | P | DS |
| 2 × 1 ft | | | | | |

Europe, Britain, North America. The native Ox Eye Daisy is a well-known wild flower whose flowers are welcome for cutting. Single, white daisies with yellow centres. It is strange that this plant has no selected garden forms in this country; 'Maistern' is a noted selection in Germany.

macrophyllum

| 1.2 m × 60 cm | [5–8] | Whitish | Summer | PF | DS |
| 4 × 2 ft | | | | | |

Hungary. A most handsome plant for a monochrome photograph, but its flowers are of a dirty white unfortunately. It is not without beauty, with large flat heads of short-rayed small flowers and feathery basal and stem-leaves. It is tough and resilient and will grow anywhere in sun or shade. To a gardener's eye it resembles *Achillea* rather than *Chrysanthemum*. This is a plant for the breeders to improve; a good white-flowered form or hybrid would be valuable.

maximum ★

90 × 46 cm	[4–8]	White	Summer		P	D
3 ft × 18 in						

Pyrenees. 1816. The Shasta Daisy is one of summer's indispensables if you are looking for a hearty plant wih large white daisies suitable for picking or garden display. They are sound perennials in most soils, but in some refuse to stay. Most cultivars need some support. The original single-flowered types are seldom seen, having given way to kinds with pretty fringed petals: 'Phyllis Smith' is rather superseded by 'Bishopstone'; 'Aglaia' is a good short semi-double, which shows less of the yellow centre. A double which has yellowish centre florets is 'Cobham Gold', while 'Wirral Supreme' and 'T.E. Killin' have short white central petals, and there are full doubles, 'Fiona Coghill', tall, and 'Esther Read', short. Thus some blend best with pink and mauve flowers and others assort with yellow. 'September Snow' is reputed to give a second crop of its double white flowers in early autumn. A dwarf grower has been named 'Powis Castle' (1973) and another 'Snow Cap', both about 30 cm (1 ft).

nipponicum

60 × 60 cm	[5–9]	White	Autumn		P	D
2 × 2 ft						

Japan. One of the latest flowers to open and a lovely plant in a good season. It is semi-shrubby, with good dark leaves, and the purity of the big single white flowers in November needs to be seen to be believed. Best against a warm wall to hasten its blooms, in extra well-drained soil. It thrives at Oxford Botanic Garden.

pacificum

30 × 90 cm	[5–9]	Yellow	Autumn		PF	CD
1 × 3 ft						

Japan. *Pyrethrum marginatum, Chrysanthemum marginatum.* For the whole of the summer this low, stoloniferous plant delights with its lobed leaves edged with white, and, when practically all else is over, covers itself with branching heads of bright yellow, small buttons, like those of Tansy.

parthenium

60 × 30 cm	[4–9]	White	Summer		P	D
2 × 1 ft			and Autumn			

Caucasus, Britain. Feverfue. *Pyrethrum parthenium, Parthenium matricaria.* A free-seeding plant with single white daisy-flowers. 'Aureum' is also single but with yellowish leaves. *C.p. plenum* has ragged double flowers. 'White Bonnet' is an excellent fully-double form with neat button-flowers, with broad ray-petals surrounding them, all pure white. I found this lovely variety in a Reading garden and christened it. A similar cultivar with dark-brown stems grows at Rowallane, in Northern Ireland. They are all lush, leafy, aromatic plants for sun and ordinary soil; they sow themselves true to type.

rubellum of gardens

60 × 60 cm	[5–9]	Various	L.Summer		P	D
2 × 2 ft						

Hybrid? *C. erubescens.* A plant which occurred at the Happy Valley Gardens, Llandudno, about 1929. There is no record of its origin, but it has given rise to a number of extremely free-flowering named clones, each making bushy twiggy plants, covered with flowers for many weeks. 'Clara Curtis' (1938) in clear pink is one of the best; others range from yellow to apricot and 'Duchess of Edinburgh' in coppery red. Possibly *C. zawadskii* is one of its parents. Division in spring every few years keeps them in good health, and they thrive in any fertile, drained soil in sun.

uliginosum

1.8 m × 60 cm	*[4–9]*	*White*	*Autumn*		P	D
6 × 2 ft						

Hungary. 1771. *Chrysanthemum serotinum*. Hungarian Daisy. With *Aconitum carmichaelii* 'Kelmscott' and *Eupatorium purpureum* this cannot be beaten for a tall late display in a big border. Sprays of big white daisies at the top of the leafy stems. In placing, remember that the flowers always turn to the sun. It is a satisfactory perennial in almost any soil and will establish in grass.

yezoense

30 × 46 cm	*[5–9]*	*White/Pink*	*Autumn*		P	CD
1 ft × 18 in						

Japan. *C. arcticum* of gardens. A pretty, small plant for the verges of well-drained borders, or larger rock garden, in full sun. Single white daisies, weather-resistant, starry but of good size, are poised in branching sprays over tiny, hand-like foliage. A good pink form is labelled 'Roseum', and 'Schwefelglanz' is a sulphur yellow form or hybrid.

zawadskii

46 × 46 cm	*[5–9]*	*Pink*	*Summer/*		P	CD
18 × 18 in			*Autumn*			

Galicia. An obscure little plant with much divided foliage and a lengthy display of pale pink daisies. See also under *C. rubellum*.

HYBRID CHRYSANTHEMUMS, autumn-flowering. A complex strain which has been crossed and recrossed and selected by European breeders ever since the originals safely reached France in 1789 and England in 1795 from China, where they had already been grown and raised in quantity from ancient times, perhaps 500 B.C. It is believed they were originally derived from *Chrysanthemum morifolium* and *C. indicum*, and possibly some other, perhaps Japanese, species. In 1846 plants were obtained of the Chusan Chrysanthemum, a parent of the pompon varieties of today, and extravagantly shaped cultivars from Japan reached us in 1861. The Chinese incurved types, the pompons and the reflexing Japanese have become fused and developed into modern varieties of almost every colour (except blue), double or single, and in a great variety of shapes.

Unfortunately the highly bred strains of today, particularly those with the largest flowers, are not satisfactory perennial garden plants. They are a prey to slugs, usually need staking and tend to die out; the hardier kinds will grow in any good fertile soil, but are most permanent in well-drained ground in full sun, preferably harsh and limy rather than soft and acid. Most of the modern varieties that have any pretence of being garden plants flower too early—long before we are ready for the delicious autumnal tang of the flowers. As one goes about the country in October and November one sees certain good, old, clump-forming hardy varieties in brown and yellow, pink and purple, which need to take their rightful place in the autumn garden, but I have never been able to discover their names. The same few sorts occur in every town and village and they are remarkably frost resistant. Together with *Aconitum, Vernonia, Eupatorium,* Pampas Grass and other late-flowering grasses, a magnificent planting of perennials could be made for autumn.

I am not suggesting that the following very few varieties are the only ones which will prove perennials in good conditions; careful choice will reveal others among modern kinds, of which there are many. But these few are old-tried favourites with special merits.

'Anastasia'

60 × 30 cm	[5–9]	Pink	Autumn	P	D
2 × 1 ft					

A little "button" variety which is a sturdy plant and flowers freely every October and into November. Soft heather-pink. There is a soft madder-brown form also called 'Dr Tom Parr'. Will Ingwersen's little treasure from Japan, 'Mei-Kyo' [5–9] is similar to 'Anastasia' but a little later and darker and rather smaller leaves and flowers and thinner stems. This has sported to a soft brownish copper, named 'Bronze Elegance', and I suspect they may all be related.

'Emperor of China' ★ ●

1.2 m × 46 cm	[5–9]	Pink	L.Autumn	P	D
4 ft × 18 in					

'Old Cottage Pink'. An invaluable, soundly perennial, hardy chrysanthemum, flowering in November. Apart from the beauty of the clusters of silvery old-rose-pink flowers, deepening to crimson in the centre when in bud, and with somewhat quilled petals, the foliage at flowering time become richly suffused and veined with crimson. It needs support, but it is a great luxury to pick sheaves of blossom in November—with little or no trouble for the rest of the year. It is possible this may be an original Chinese garden form; its flowers closely resemble those on old Chinese paintings. It is depicted in William Robinson's *The English Flower Garden* of 1893 and in Gertrude Jekyll's *Flower Decoration*, p. 4.

> "After the first frost the foliage of this kind turns to a splendid colour, the green of the leaves giving place to a rich crimson that sometimes clouds the outer portions of the leaf and often covers its whole expanse."—GJ

'Innocence'

60 × 60 cm	[5–9]	Pink	E.Autumn	P	D
2 × 2 ft					

A very pale pink, single-flowered, old garden plant picked out by Margery Fish. Valuable, self-reliant.

Korean Hybrids

60–90 × 46 cm	[5–9]	Various	Autumn	P	D
2–3 ft × 18 in					

1937. By crossing *C. coreanum* with 'Ruth Hatton', a Pompon variety, Alexander Cumming of Bristol, Connecticut (the raiser of *Gypsophila paniculata* 'Bristol Fairy' and the *Weigela* called 'Bristol Ruby'), succeeded in raising a number of delightful hardy perennials of various tints. The selections were named after the planets, such as 'Apollo', a dark red which is still seen in gardens; 'Venus', a semi-double rich coral-pink, and others which flowered rather late for our climate. 'Nancy Perry', warm clear pink, single. Good and reliable. Of later raising is 'Wedding Day', a fine single white whose flowers have the merit of green centres instead of the yellow of most daisies. They are all excellent for cutting, producing sprays of lovely blooms. They have been merged with other strains of late years and the result is less of the carefree perennial habit.

CICHORIUM, Compositae. The culinary Chicory is also an ornamental plant for full sun on well-drained soils, particularly those which are limy.

intybus

1.2 m × 60 cm   [4–8[Blue, etc   Summer   DRS
4 × 2 ft

Europe, Britain. Good basal leaves and willowy rather bare stems. The azure-blue daisy-flowers stud the upper part of the stems for many weeks. These are white and clear pink forms. In the mornings they are exquisitely beautiful, but the flowers close by midday.

CIMICIFUGA, Ranunculaceae. Bugbane. The name *Cimicifuga* refers to the peculiarly scented leaves of some kinds, which are used to drive away bugs—in Siberia. Elegant, broad or ferny leaves are borne here and there up a wiry stalk carrying branching bottle-brushes of white or cream. Often the leaves turn to cream or pale yellow in autumn. Pretty and unusual plants for cool, moist places. In spite of their height they need no support.

"All the cimicifugas are well worth growing, and being tall and slender and not overweening in foliage, they take up little room."—ATJ

acerina

90 cm–1.2 m   [4–8]   White   L.Summer   F   DS
× 60 cm
3–4 × 2 ft

Japan. 1925. *C. japonica acerina. C. japonica* was introduced in 1879 but has never become popular because of its rather dirty white flowers in few-branched spikes. *C. acerina* is similar. Handsome maple-like, jagged leaves.

americana

90 cm–1.2 m   [3–8]   Cream   Summer   DS
× 90 cm
3–4 × 3 ft

Eastern N. America. 1812. This is also known as *C. cordifolia.* Doubly compound leaves. The flowers are in dense spikes, usually branched.

dahurica

1.8 m × 90 cm   [4–8]   White   L.Summer   F   DS
6 × 3 ft

Far East. 1835. This rare species has a much more widely balanced paniculate inflorescence than the others. The usual fluffy flowers are more widely spaced on the sprays. The foliage is much divided and toothed. An elegant plant, flowering in the mid-cimicifuga season, after *C. racemosa* and *C. rubifolia,* but before *C. foetida* and *C. simplex.*

europaea

90 × 60 cm   [4–8]   White   Summer   DS
3 × 2 ft

Czechoslovakia, Bulgaria. 1937. This species is for the collector. It does not hold a candle to others. Handsome pinnate or lobed leaves and spikes of greenish white flowers.

foetida

1.8 m × 60 cm	*[5–8]*	*Yellow*	*L.Summer*	F	DS
6 × 2 ft					

N.E. Asia. 1777. A very rare plant in cultivation, and the only one which can be called yellow, on account of the yellow sepals around each white tassel of stamens. The stems branch and the centre spike arches gracefully, like a shepherd's crook. The leaves are dark green, deeply veined and much divided. The flowers have the same fragrance as the yellow water-lily or Brandy Bottle. The arching sprays of green pods are extremely handsome.

racemosa ● ★

90 × 60 cm	*[3–8]*	*White*	*Summer*	F	DS
6 × 2 ft					

E. North America. 1732. Beautiful, divided, fresh green leaves make a pleasing clump. The flowers are produced earlier in the season than those of other species. They are pure white branching bottle-brushes; later flowering stems are frequently produced. Though it will grow in rather dry soil, it is better where moisture is not far away. A feature at Crathes Castle, Kincardineshire.

rubifolia

1.5 m × 60 cm	*[4–8]*	*Creamy*	*L.Summer*	F	DS
5 × 2 ft					

North America. 1812. *C. cordifolia* and *C. racemosa* var. *cordifolia*. The handsome, dark, broad leaves are much like those of a Japanese Anemone. The stiffly ascending spires of brown buds open to flowers of a sallow white or creamy green. A highly effective plant but it lacks the appeal of the white-flowered sorts. Its colouring is enhanced by neighbouring yellow flowers. Sometimes labelled *C. americana*, which is a distinct species.

simplex ● ★

1.2 m × 60 cm	*[4–8]*	*White*	*Autumn*	F	DS
4 × 2 ft					

Russia to Japan. 1879. Sometimes listed as *C. foetida intermedia*, but it bears little resemblance to *C. foetida*. Regularly the last to flower, with arching wands with one or two subsidiary wands branching from below, but these frequently arch over the terminal wand. Smooth, green, rather small, divided foliage. A lesser plant than all the others, flowering in October. A noted garden cultivar is 'White Pearl' ('Armleuchter') 1923, and 'Braunlaub' is a German variety with brownish leaves. In ● ★ 'Elstead Variety' the buds are purplish opening to pure white; it grows well at Wisley, Surrey, and at Trengwainton, Cornwall, and is a plant of exceeding grace and a great treasure.

The plant known in gardens as *C. ramosa* is a superb September-flowering plant, and the ideal contrast to *Aconitum carmichaelii*. The very large, much divided, leaves form an imposing but open pile above which tower the long slender stems, each branching into several shoots, the secondary ones prolonging the display. They are pure white narrow bottle-brushes 30 cm (1 ft) or more long. The rapidity with which they ripen their seeds is remarkable.

"... stately stems of 6–7 ft, deploying a great foaming spout of cream-white blossom in a broken panicle."—RF

It has given rise to dark purplish, leafed forms in Germany known as 'Brunette' ('Atropurpurea'). Stems and buds are also dark. They vary in colour when raised from seeds and only the best should be retained.

CIRSIUM, Compositae.

rivulare

1.2 m × 60 cm	*[4–8]*	*Crimson*	*Summer*	P	DR
4 × 2 ft					

A thistle of easy culture—spreading at the root—and which, because of its colour, merits inclusion in these pages. It is an erect, self-reliant plant with narrow rather prickly leaves and bears in its best *atropurpureum* variety dense pincushion heads of glowing vinous crimson. The pink forms are less attractive. It is also known as *Cnicus atropurpureus* in gardens.

CLEMATIS, Ranunculaceae. The following are reliable plants, more or less herbaceous, thriving in any fertile soil, well drained and in sun, preferably limy, but they are not particular.

douglasii

60 × 60 cm	*[5–7]*	*Purplish*	*Summer*	F	CDS
2 × 2 ft					

Rocky Mountains, USA. 1881. This rare species is allied to *C. integrifolia*; the variety *C.d. scottii* has glaucous leaves and makes a bushy plant with woody base. The flowers are nodding, variously tinted, purplish, bell-shaped, scarcely open. It grows well at Sissinghurst Castle, Kent. Very attractive seed heads.

× durandii ● ★

1.8 m × 90 cm	*[6–9]*	*Violet*	*L.Summer*	PF	CDL
6 × 3 ft					

Hybrid. *C. integrifolia × C. × jackmanii*. It retains the herbaceous character and rather nodding flowers of the former and the large-sized leaves and flowers of the latter parent. It is a superlative plant with wide handsome blooms of intense indigo-violet lit by cream stamens, and produced for some six weeks or more, from early July. The leafy plant needs the support of a shrub, pea-sticks or wire frame, or can be trained on a wall, or allowed to flop over ground-covering plants such as bergenias or heathers. Superb with yellow crocosmias.

'Edward Prichard'

90 × 60 cm	*[4–9]*	*Lilac*	*L.Summer*	P	CDL
3 × 2 ft					

c. 1950. (*C. heracleifolia × C. recta*). Panicles of small, sweetly scented flowers of white suffused with lilac. It forms a good clump but needs support. The leaves are similar to those of *C. heracleifolia*. A hybrid from Australia.

× eriostemon

1.8 m × 60 cm	*[4–9]*	*Blue*	*Summer*	P	CDL
6 × 4 ft					

Hybrid. *C. integrifolia × C. viticella*. 'Hendersonii (*c.* 1830) is a beautiful plant showing most influence from the first parent. Soft indigo-tinted blue flowers, nodding, with twisted somewhat recurving segments, singly borne on long stalks. Dark green leaves. Like *C. integrifolia* it needs support.

heracleifolia

    90 cm × 1.2 m   *[4–9]*   *Blue*   *L.Summer*   PF   CDL
    3 × 5 ft

China. 1837. This species has little in common with the climbing, large-flowered *Clematis* hybrids, and always puzzles visitors. It forms a woody base, creating a good clump of broad, divided leaves and ascending leafy stems which bear clusters, along their upper reaches, of small flowers like hyacinths—and sweetly scented too. Silvery, fluffy seedheads provide later beauty.

● ★ —**davidiana** [4–9] A form collected in China in 1867, with rich blue flowers with segments less reflexed and more spreading, creating a more worthy bloom. There are several garden clones, perhaps hybrids with the closely related *C. stans*; in this case they are classed under *C. × bonstedtii*. 'Côte d'Azur', 'Crépuscule' and 'Campanile' originated in France *c.* 1900, while 'Wyevale' came recently from Mr Williamson of Hereford. It is perhaps the most colourful, but none is to be despised.

integrifolia

    60 cm × 1.5 m   *[3–9]*   *Violet*   *Summer*   F   DS
    2 × 5 ft

S. Europe. 1573. This parent of *C. × durandii* is a comparatively dull plant with nodding small flowers usually of indigo-violet; a white form is recorded, which I should like to see. The whole plant is downy. It flops on the ground or can be supported on sticks. A variety or subspecies with elegant strongly recurved segments—just like a Turk's Cap Lily—is grown by Mr Treasure of Tenbury Wells, Worcestershire, under the name of *C. olgae*. *C. fremontii* is an allied species with rather closed flowers.

× jouiniana

    1.5–9 × 1.2–6 m   *[5–9]*   *Opal*   *L.Summer/*   CL
    5–30 × 4–20 ft   *E.Autumn*

Hybrid. *C. heracleifolia × C. vitalba. C. grata* of gardens. In cold districts it makes a woody base, achieving 2.1 m (7 ft), scrambling through shrubs or over fences and hedges, or on slopes. At Mount Stewart, Northern Ireland, it has made a huge woody climber. The display of small milky blue flowers in copious trusses, fragrant and with cream stamens, is one of the lovely finales of the season. 'Praecox' is earlier-flowering. 'Mrs Robert Brydon' (1935) is a selection from the United States rather nearer to the herbaceous parent.

recta

    1.2 m × 60 cm   *[3–9]*   *White*   *Summer*   PF   CDS
    5 × 2 ft

Europe. 1597. The general appearance resembles a herbaceous version of Old Man's Beard or Traveller's Joy but the flowers are larger and create a mass of white scented blossom. There is a rare double form, 'Plena' (1860), for still whiter effect. *C.r.* 'Foliis Purpureis' or 'Purpurea' has coppery purple foliage and this is the plant I should choose, but there are forms about with only slightly purplish foliage, and a good dark form should be sought. The purplish-leafed form was first recorded in 1772. Apart from the double, they all have clouds of silvery seed-heads, all need some support, and may achieve even 1.8 m (6 ft) in rich soil. It gives good effect at Blickling Hall, Norfolk.

"... the foam-white *Clematis recta*, a delightful foil to *Delphinium bella-donna*."—GJ

CLINTONIA, Liliaceae. Choice woodland plants needing cool, peaty, lime-free soil. They are of subdued charm. The foliage is of rich green, smooth, rather like that of Lily-of-the-Valley, but they are less invasive.

andrewsiana

60 × 30 cm	*[4–8]*	*Carmine*	*E.Summer*	DS
2 × 1 ft				

California. The small bell-like flowers are poised in a cluster at the top of the stem. The three outer segments are broad, of rich carmine-rose, the inner ones paler and narrower with a creamy central vein. They are followed by violet-blue berries. A highly desirable plant which thrives at Branklyn, Perth. It increases slowly.

borealis

30 × 30 cm	*[4–8]*	*Yellow*	*E.Summer*	DS
1 × 1 ft				

North America. 1778. This has clusters of yellowish-green flowers with protruding stamens in a cluster, followed by blue berries. *C. umbellata* is of similar stature, with umbels of fragrant white flowers. There are several smaller species. None is so handsome as *C. andrewsiana*.

COCHLEARIA, Cruciferae. Sun, deep well-drained soil.

armoracia

90 × 60 cm	*[5–8]*	*White*	*Summer*	DR
3 × 2 ft				

Europe. *Armoracia rusticana, A. lapathifolia.* The culinary Horse Radish has the disadvantage of smell, and an ineradicable root, so beware. While nobody could eat roast beef without its splendid flavour, a garden *could* go without its vast leafage. On the other hand the culinary and aesthetic values are combined in 'Variegata', whose leaves are handsomely splashed with cream, almost ready, as it were, for the sauce!

CODONOPSIS, Campanulaceae.

clematidea ● ★

60 × 60 cm	*[6–8]*	*Blue*	*L.Summer*	P S
2 × 2 ft			*onwards*	

Asia. A nodding flower always charms me, and these pale china-blue bells have a most wonderful surprise when lifted up—the centre of orange and maroon exceeds all imagination. A sound perennial on well-drained soil, making a good clump of greyish-green rounded leaves. In sheltered shrubby conditions it will scramble up to 90 cm or 1.2 m (3 or 4 ft). For many years this was known erroneously in gardens as *C. ovata*. This species is also charming but none is so colourful inside as *C. clematidea*. *C. ovata* and *C. mollis* and *C. cardiophylla* are all about 60 cm (2 ft) in height, whereas there are two exquisite twiners: *C. convolvulacea* and *C. vinciflora* (1936); these all hail from W. Asia [6–8]. Both of these will twine through shrubs or up pea-sticks, displaying periwinkle blue bells, the former wide open, the latter more tubular. They all thrive in a variety of positions but prefer part shade, with some humus, and grow best in the cooler north. The foliage of some has an objectionable smell.

"... placed on a high bank of the garden ... their pale pendent bells nod down at the passer-by, who can thus appreciate the full daintiness of their internal decorations."—RF

COMMELINA, Commelinaceae.

coelestis

| 90 × 60 cm | [8–10] | Blue | All Summer | P | W | D |

3 × 2 ft

Mexico. Prior to 1700. This is much like *Tradescantia × andersoniana*, but its stem grows from a tuberous, running rootstock. For the sake of the vivid, almost peacock-blue of its flowers it is worth growing in our warmest, sunniest counties in a sheltered position in full sun, where it can ramble underground at will. The flowers close up in the afternoon. (*C. tuberosa.*)

CONVALLARIA, Liliaceae. Their long, thong-like roots should be laid about 2.5 cm (1 in) deep, horizontally, and made as firm as possible. Alternatively, when transplanting, square sods can be dug out and planted elsewhere.

majalis

| 23 × 30 cm | [4–9] | White | L.Spring | P | D |

9 in × 1 ft

Northern Hemisphere. Lily-of-the-Valley. Now a comparatively rare British plant, this favourite flower is an admirable and rampant ground-cover. And who would not give up many square yards of his garden to the beauty of the long-lasting leaves and exquisitely scented flowers? It grows where it likes but not always where it is planted, and so my advice is to try it in many places. It usually seems to prefer semi-shade, but may often be found luxuriating in full sun, thriving in a variety of soils other than pure clay or bog. In some districts its flowers are followed by small scarlet berries.

"The Lily of the valley is the worst of all delicious weeds when it thrives."— RF

"One of the borders, on the sunless side, had been invaded by lilies of the valley, deep toned green foliage, out of which in Maytime the waxen little cups spilled their perfume." Richard Church, *The Golden Sovereign,* 1957.

● ★ —**'Fortin's Giant'.** An extremely fine form with large, tubby bells, broader foliage, equally delicious scent, and the invaluable character of flowering ten days later. By planting both kinds, some in sun and some in shade, a long succession of bloom can be ensured.

"Fortin's variety preserves in the open garden . . . its special size and nobility of bell."—RF

—**'Hardwick Hall'.** This is a fine form with large flowers, for long grown at Hardwick Hall, Derbyshire, and I think deserves notice. The leaves are extra broad, and very narrowly margined with pale green.

—**'Prolificans',** a double-flowered form, scarcely a thing of beauty.

—**'Rosea'.** Dainty sprays of mauve pink, very pretty when opening. It is possible that this belongs to a different species, because its flowers are of quite a different shape.

—**'Variegata'.** *C.m.* 'Lineata' or 'Albistriata'. Single white flowers; leaves longitudinally striped with creamy yellow; it is best in sunny places, where it will not so readily revert to the usual green-leafed type. Known since 1835.

CONVOLVULUS, Convolvulaceae. The silvery-leafed shrubby *C. cneorum* [8–10] assorts well with herbaceous plants in well-drained, warm gardens but scarcely comes within the scope of this book. *C. althaeoides* [6–8] and *C. mauritanicus* (*C. sabatius*) [8–9], the latter by no means hardy, have beautiful pink and lavender-blue flowers respectively; about 30 cm (1 ft) in height. The former has invasive roots.

COREOPSIS, Compositae. Easily grown plants in any reasonable soil, in sunny gardens.

verticillata

60 × 46 cm	*[4–9]*	*Yellow*	*Summer/*	P	D
2 ft × 18 in			*Autumn*		

E. United States. 1759. *C. tenuifolia.* If you are looking for a dense, upright, bushy plant with hair-fine leaves, covered all over for months with bright brassy yellow daisies, this is it. 'Grandiflora' ('Golden Shower'), raised by Hesse of Germany, is the best form to date and of a warmer yellow. They increase readily at the root and do not require support. 'Goldfink' is a useful dwarf about 30 cm (1 ft) high. 'Moonbeam' (1987) is a delightful form of light tint, primrose-yellow. 'Zagreb' [3–9] is a short-growing, bright yellow variant. Those who adore yellow daisies for cutting will not be able to resist *C. auriculata* 'Superba' [4–9]—with a central maroon blotch—*C. grandiflora* [4–9] 'Sunburst', 'Mayfield Giant' or 'Badengold' and *C. lanceolata* [4–9] forms. They are easily raised from seeds but are not truly perennial. They achieve 90 cm (3 ft) and flower for months.

CORIARIA, Coriariaceae.

terminalis

60 × 90 cm	*[9–10]*	*Berries*	*Autumn*	F	DS
2 × 3 ft					

Far East. A shrubby plant, which usually dies to the ground during winter. The species itself is seldom seen and has black fruits, but the variety *C.t. xanthocarpa* (1897) is a plant of great beauty, with long, arching sprays of juicy, amber-coloured "fruits". The petals thicken to produce the "berries" and ripen successively from August onwards in a sunny sheltered place, in any good soil, where its elegant clear green foliage is a further asset. Try it near *Gentiana asclepiadea.* The roots are apt to wander. It grows well at Sizergh Castle, Westmorland. *C. japonica* [9–10] is a more upright plant with red "fruits" turning to black.

CORTUSA, Primulaceae. *C. matthioli* is the species usually seen in cool woodland gardens where humus and some moisture are at hand.

matthioli

30 × 30 cm	*[5–8]*	*Purple*	*L.Spring*	DS
1 × 1 ft				

Europe. Asia. 1596. Might well be taken for a primula, with its hairy, rounded, lobed leaves and stems carrying a little shower of nodding starry bells of warm magenta-crimson. There is a white variety.

CORYDALIS, Papaveraceae. *C. lutea* and *C. ochroleuca* are two pretty, self-sowing, dainty plants for part shade—where their flowering season is far longer than in the sun. Sometimes called "common", "weeds", or trivial plants, they are undoubtedly garden toys of great charm.

bulbosa

23 × 30 cm	*[6–8]*	*Mauve*	*E.Spring*	P	DS
9 in × 1 ft					

Europe, Britain. *C. cava*. One of the most regular of spring blooms, considerably frost-resistant, suitable for any partly shaded position. It has died down by midsummer but its lush mounds of blue-green filigree leaves, overtopped by dense short spikes of small tubular flowers from creamy grey to rich lilac, are valuable. There is nothing like it. *C. solida* is similar, but smaller. While the tubers of *C. bulbosa* are hollow on the upper surface, those of *C. solida* are rounded. Pleasant companions for *Uvularia*.

chaerophylla

90 × 60 cm	*[5–8]*	*Yellow*	*L.Summer*	DS
3 × 2 ft				

W. China. A plant of great promise with its compact rootstock and elegant tall mass of very finely divided, lacy foliage, only to disappoint when its stiff short spikes of tiny yellow flowers open.

lutea

30 × 30 cm	*[5–8]*	*Yellow*	*Spring/*	P	S
1 × 1 ft			*Autumn*		

Europe, Britain, 1596. The lacy filigree clump of cool green, tiny leaves is scattered all over with pretty little heads of tiny snapdragon-shaped flowers. Ethereal cutting material for small vases.

"Graceful masses of delicate pale green leaves dotted with spurred yellow flowers."—WR

nobilis

46 × 30 cm	*[5–8]*	*Yellow*	*Spring*	DS
18 in × 1 ft				

Siberia. 1783. A rarity of stiff habit, with the usual deeply cut and fringed fresh green leaves. The flowers are in a dense bunch at the top of the stems, opening bright yellow from green buds; the lip has a brown spot. They fade to deep orange.

ochroleuca

30 × 30 cm	*[6–8]*	*White*	*Spring/*	P	S
1 × 1 ft			*Autumn*		

Italy, 1594. This is exactly like *C. lutea* but in greenish white; the leaves are greyish in spring. So far these closely allied plants do not seem to have hybridized, though they seed freely and are enjoyed where this type of small ground-cover is allowed. They are charming when hanging out of a cool north-facing wall behind blue *Meconopsis* and *Gentiana*, at Hidcote, Gloucestershire.

scouleri

50 × 46 cm	*[5–7]*	*Purplish*	*Spring*	P	DR
20 × 18 in					

N.W. America. *c.* 1895. A deep questing and spreading rootstock makes this plant inappropriate for small areas. It produces erect stems and a table-like mass of extremely finely divided, lacy leaves, over which are held the spikes of purplish-rose, small blooms. Best in cool conditions in retentive soil.

thalictrifolia

46 × 46 cm	*[7–8]*	*Yellow*	*E.Summer*	P	W	DS
18 × 18 in						

China. Not so hardy as the others, but like them it prefers a cool position. Lacy spreading yellowish green leaves overtopped by branching racemes of yellow flowers, large for the genus. Rootstock woody and spreading. It makes good ground-cover in moist warm valleys.

COSMOS, Compositae.

atrosanguineus

75 × 46 cm	*[7–9]*	*Maroon*	*L.Summer*	P	W	DS
2½ ft × 18 in						

Mexico. 1835. *Bidens atrosanguinea*. A unique plant like a miniature single-flowered *Dahlia*. The darkling, velvety maroon-crimson of the many flowers is capped by their delicious rich scent of chocolate. The blooms are produced continually until autumn. It needs full sun and a retentive soil, and may be left out of doors in our warmer counties, protected by a good winter mulch. Plant the tubers 15 cm (6 in) deep. Growth does not start before the end of May.

CRAMBE, Cruciferae. These are deep-rooting plants for rough, well-drained soil in full sun.

cordifolia

1.8 × 1.2 m	*[6–9]*	*White*	*E.Summer*	PF	DR
6 × 4 ft					

Caucasus. 1822. The enormous, limp, deeply-lobed hispid leaves create a large mound of dark greenery, above which arise stout stems branching into a huge gypsophila-cloud of small white stars, rather strongly scented. A noble plant for the larger garden. *C. tatarica* (*C. pinnatifida*) [6–9] is similar but with deeply divided leaves.

> "... one huge cloud every June is about five feet square (only like other clouds it is round), of myriads of white flowers."—EAB

maritima ★

60 × 60 cm	*[6–9]*	*White*	*E.Summer*	PF	DR
2 × 2 ft					

Europe, Britain. It is seldom that the Seakale is grown outside the vegetable patch, or used otherwise than for eating, but it has perhaps the most beautiful of all large glaucous leaves; the wide blades are exquisitely curved and lobed. It is superb in the border and ideal for cutting. The knobs of purple growth emerging from the soil are a joy to see and to eat in spring; large heads of white flowers expand in June.

> "In front is the grand glaucous foliage of seakale."—GJ

orientalis

1.2 m × 90 cm	*[6–9]*	*White*	*E.Summer*	P	DRS
4 × 3 ft					

Middle East. 1820. This is seldom seen but is another good perennial, throwing up large leaves, divided pinnately, and stout stems freely branching and carrying multitudes of palest lavender, almost white, flowers like those of a cabbage. Closely related is *C. koktebelica* [6–9].

CRINUM, Amaryllidaceae. Large plants springing from football-size bulbs which delve deeply into the soil. The tops of their long necks should be above ground. While their flowers are of great beauty, the leaves are limp and long and lie around untidily. Stout stems support a cluster of beautiful trumpet-flowers which open successively for several weeks. They are all sweetly scented. *C × powellii* seems perfectly hardy in our sunnier counties, in the open, but is usually seen against a sunny wall where the reflected warmth will increase the freedom of flowering. They all like rich deep soil and adequate moisture and repay a good mulch of manure every year or two. For bigeneric hybrids see under *Amaryllis*.

bulbispermum

1.2 m × 60 cm	*[9–10]*	*Pinkish*	*Summer*	P	W	DS
4 × 2 ft						

South Africa. 1752. *C. longifolium, C. capense.* Hardy in all but the coldest districts. Its main characters from a garden point of view are that it is earliest in flower—mid June—and has glaucous leaves, rather more upstanding than most. The flowers are of good quality, usually blush-white with a crimson or deep pink central stripe on the outer segments. It is perhaps the least ornamental and conspicuous in flower of the kinds listed here.

moorei ●

1.2 m × 90 cm	*[8–10]*	*Pink*	*Summer*	P	W	DS
4 × 3 ft						

Natal. 1874. *C. mackenii, C. makoyanum.* This parent of *C. × powelli* is not often seen but appears to be reasonably hardy in our warmer counties and thrives against walls in full sun. The leaves are very broad and have waved margins; they are arranged almost in a rosette on the tall necks. The beautiful pale pink flowers open widely and have broad segments. Good at Nymans, Sussex. There is also a fine white variety known as *C.m.* 'Album' or 'Schmidtii'. Neither of the above two species is usually so free-flowering as *C. × powellii.* A superb clear rose-pink form named 'H. N. B. Bradley' grows at Kew. There is a form with yellow variegated leaves, *C.m.* 'Variegata'.

× powellii ● ★

1.2 m × 90 cm	*[7–10]*	*Pink or White*	*Summer*	P	D
4 × 3 ft					

Hybrid. *C. bulbispermum × C. moorei.* Inheriting the hardiness of *C. longifolium,* the clones common in gardens are free-flowering and worthy garden plants. I find the ordinary pink form to be of rather poor quality and pinched shape; it is a rich rose-pink. The white, *C.p.* 'Album', is an exquisite flower of good quality and shape. They thrive at Nymans, Sussex. 'Haarlemense' in light pink and 'Krelagei' in deep pink are two superlative cultivars. They are all deliciously fragrant. 'Ellen Bosanquet' may be of the same parentage, and is of a rich deep rose tint, a highly desirable cultivar.

"The boldest and largest species I can keep alive in the ground here."— EAB

CROCOSMIA, Iridaceae. Montbretia. (Including *Curtonus.*) It is strange that these delightsome perennials are so little appreciated, apart from the ubiquitous *C. × crocosmiiflora,* which is sometimes classed as a weed in warm and damp climates. They are all hearty, good plants, increasing their bulbous roots freely, and bearing abundant blossoms unless overcrowded by their own exuberant growth, in which case division, preferably in early spring, is simple. The poise of their dainty flowers leaves nothing to be desired; they provide a welcome change from the usual daisy-flowers of August and September and are ideal for cutting. They are content in all soils apart from excessive clay or bog, but appreciate moisture and will thrive in sun or part shade. Plant 7.5 cm (3 in) deep.

aurea

90 × 30 cm	*[6–9]*	*Light*	*L.Summer*	P	W	DS
3 × 1 ft		*Orange*				

South Africa. 1846. *Tritonia aurea*. It gives the clear light colouring and the wide nodding flowers to the finest of the hybrids below. The stamens are long-projecting and arise deep in the tubular throat. Apricot yellow, flushed orange. It has grown for many years at Mount Stewart, Northern Ireland.

masonorum ● ★

90 × 23 cm	*[7–9]*	*[Red]*	*L.Summer*	P	DS
3 ft × 9 in					

South Africa. Prior to 1954. This species has flowers which, like those of *C. paniculata*, look up from the top of the arching stems, instead of being poised forward under the stems. It is a most brilliant plant of vermilion-orange, a plant for the most uninhibited colour schemes. It is charming when cooled by *Ceanothus* 'Gloire de Versailles', a silverling or two, and a pale yellow Day Lily; but is also effective with any coppery purple foliage. The leaves are much broader than others, approaching half way to the size and width of *C. paniculata*. An extra good selection from Bressingham is ★ 'Firebird'. (See also below.) Two paler forms have been named: 'Rowallane Yellow' [6–9], which originated in the garden of that name in Northern Ireland about 1970. It is a warm amber-yellow with orange overtones. Closely allied, but paler, is 'Jenny Bloom' [6–9], raised about 1980 by Alan Bloom. Both are strong growers.

paniculata

1.2 m × 23 cm	*[6–9]*	*Orange*	*L.Summer*	P	D
4 ft × 9 in					

South Africa. *Curtonus paniculatus* or *Antholyza paniculata*. One of those striking plants that are so necessary for variety of line in the garden. Broad, grooved, sword-like green leaves to 90 cm (3 ft) and large branching sprays of small orange-red trumpet-flowers, and like a giant *C. crocosmiiflora*. Full sun and ordinary soil; plant 8 cm (3 in) deep. A good form with large colourful flowers should be sought; there are some poor yellowish ones about.

pottsii

90 × 30 cm	*[6–9]*	*Red*	*L.Summer*	P	DS
3 × 1 ft					

South Africa. This hardy parent of *C. × crocosmiiflora* has flowers of uniform vivid vermilion-red with a yellow throat; they are smaller than any of the above and are borne erect and in less arching spikes than *C. × crocosmiiflora*. The stamens do not project, and arise halfway up the throat. A vigorous and showy plant. Prior to 1877.

HYBRIDS

In 1882 Messrs Lemoine, noted nurserymen of Nancy, France, put on the market a hybrid between *C. aurea* and *C. pottsii*, which they confusingly called *C. crocosmiaeflora*. It crept into Britain with a minimum of trumpeting, but by 1898 was "grown in hundreds of gardens". Since then it has become one of the commonest garden plants throughout these islands. This original hybrid is fertile and they raised and named two or three dozen other varieties, of which few remain, apart from 'Solfatare', 'Aurore' and 'Carmin Brilliant'. It is amusing to note that they considered by 1900 that 'Solfatare' was not worth keeping. It was not until 'Prometheus' arrived (c. 1906) that real strides were made in hybridizing, being taken in hand by George Davison, head gardener at Westwick Hall, near Norwich, Norfolk. Further hybridizing was carried on using Davison's best as a foundation, by Sydney Morris at Earlham Hall, also near Norwich, and from 1914 onwards by Hayward at Clacton-on-Sea, Essex. The Earlham Hybrids became very famous and numerous, growing up to 1.2 m (4 ft) and with flowers 10 cm (4 in) across, when well cultivated. By 1924 articles about them had almost ceased and today they are rarely seen, most being extinct. This is strange since they were highly decorative, prolific and brilliant, and are first-class plants. However, the fact that many are tender and need to be stored under cover for the winter no doubt went against them, but in the milder, damper west they are sound perennials. The few I have been able to rescue from old gardens and whose names I have been able to authenticate are growing well at Lanhydrock, Cornwall. Those with the largest and most nodding flowers, indicating a preponderance of C. aurea parentage, are usually the most tender. Two small-flowered yellow varieties, not far removed from C. pottsii, with erect blooms, were found at Gunby Hall, Lincolnshire, and Knightshayes Court, Devon, but I have been unable to name them from earliest lists. These have become known erroneously as 'George Davison' and 'Citronella' respectively; the latter should have a dark eye. The former plant is sometimes labelled 'Honey Angels'.

× crocosmiiflora ● ★

60 × 30 cm   [5–9]   Orange-red   L.Summer   P   D
2 × 1 ft

Hybrid. 1880. The common Montbretia is a cross by Lemoine in France between C. aurea (tender, nodding, orange-yellow) and C. pottsii (hardy, erect, red). It is a very common plant, hardy throughout the country, and may be taken as a type for comparing all the others. It produces sheaves of fresh green, arching, grassy leaves and graceful, branching stems, carrying nodding, small, lily-like flowers, flaming vermilion or orange-red outside, yellow within, and beautifully marked in the throat with red-brown. A weed-proof colonizer for sun or shade.

—'A. E. Amos'

60 × 23 cm   [6–9]   Orange-red   L.Summer   P   D
2 ft × 9 in

Orange-red, somewhat blotchy, fading towards a wide pale yellow throat with brown markings on the five lowest segments.

—'Aurore'

90 × 23 cm   [6–9]   Orange   E.Autumn   P   D
3 ft × 9 in

1890. Large flowers of pure orange on a tall branching stem. The three lower segments each have a maroon spot.

'Bressingham Blaze', 'Emberglow', 'Spitfire' and 'Vulcan' are good hybrids raised by Alan Bloom about 1970 between Crocosmia masonorum and C. (Curtonus) paniculatus, all with upward arching flowers (like the parents') of vivid orange-red. [All 5–9].

75 × 23 cm   *[5–9]*   *Orange-red*   *L.Summer*   P   D
2½ft × 9 in

—'Carmin Brilliant ★

60 × 23 cm   *[6–9]*   *Orange-red*   *L.Summer*   P   D
2 ft × 9 in

Late nineteenth century. Rich tomato-red buds, resulting in the flowers being flushed with red outside. Pale tomato-red inside, with yellow throat. Each segment has two reddish spots and is flaked with a deeper tint. The flowers fade to carmine-red. It creates a display as good as the common Montbretia, later and with far richer colouring. Found at Trelissick, Cornwall.

'Citronella'

60 × 23 cm   *[6–9]*   *Yellow*   *L.Summer*   P   D
2 ft × 9 in

The true 'Citronella' has soft yellow flowers with red-brown central markings. There is a painting of it by E.A. Bowles at Cambridge Botanic Garden. I am unable to suggest what name should be given to the prolific hardy plant which has become known, erroneously, during recent years, as 'Citronella'.

—'Emily McKenzie'

60 × 23 cm   *[6–9]*   *Orange*   *L.Autumn*   P   D
2 ft × 9 in

1954. Raised in Northumberland, it is vigorous, hardy, and free-flowering, with large, long-lasting, dark orange flowers, the segments well expanded to reveal wallflower-red splashes, contributing to a six-sided central star. Paler throat. Though the flowers nod, it is a spectacular garden plant, because the colour outside the segments is as good as within.

—'Firebird'

90 × 23 cm   *[6–9]*   *Orange-red*   *L.Summer*   P   D
3 ft × 9 in

Fiery orange-red outside; inside there is a large yellow circle with slight edge of darker colour and veining towards a small greenish throat.

—'Golden Glory'

90 × 23 cm   *[6–9]*   *Yellow*   *L.Summer*   P   D
3 ft × 9 in

Pure apricot-yellow, flushed with a darker tint inside towards the red-brown ring around the yellow throat.

—'His Majesty'

90 × 23 cm   *[6–9]*   *Orange-red*   *L.Summer*   P   D
3 ft × 9 in

c. 1919. Very vigorous. The outer three segments are wallflower-red outside, the inner ones flushed at the tip with the same colour. Inside the segments are soft orange flushed with red towards the tips but fade to a paler throat. A spectacular plant with a long flowering period but spoiled by wet weather.

—**'Jackanapes'** ★

$60 \times 23\,cm$ *[6–9]*   *Red/Yellow*   *L.Summer*   P   D
$2\,ft \times 9\,in$

A two-toned, deep red-and-yellow flower of startling effect.

—**'James Coey'**

$60 \times 23\,cm$ *[6–9]*   *Red*   *L.Summer*   P   D
$2\,ft \times 9\,in$

c. 1921. Donard Nursery. Very dark orange-red, somewhat paler inside. Large nodding blooms. Pronounced brown splashes on the two lowest segments, yellow throat.

—**'Lady Hamilton'** ★

$90 \times 23\,cm$ *[6–9]*   *Apricot*   *E.Autumn*   P   D
$3\,ft \times 9\,in$

c. 1907. This is the softest in colour of the large-flowered hybrids that I have found. The flowers are of good size, of soft orange-yellow with an apricot zone in the centre and two small maroon dots on each of the three lower segments; the upper two have flushed spots. The buds and the fading flowers are apricot, contributing to the picture. Found at Powis Castle, Montgomeryshire. If only we could find the variety 'Lord Nelson' again, to grow next to this!

—**'Lady Wilson'**

$90 \times 23\,cm$ *[6–9]*   *Orange*   *L.Summer*   P   D
$3\,ft \times 9\,in$

c. 1939. Pure orange with a faint flush of orange-brown towards the throat.

—**'Lucifer'** ★ ●

$1.2\,m \times 30\,cm$ *[5–9]*   *Red*   *L.Summer*   P   D
$4 \times 1\,ft$

c. 1979. Magnificent hybrid uniting the large flower of brilliant red of *C. masonorum* with the stalwart vigour of *C. paniculata* (*Curtonus*). A plant which is likely to become very popular in large gardens leaving 'Bressingham Blaze' and its relatives to smaller gardens. Broad, sword-like foliage in beauty all summer. One of Alan Bloom's best efforts.

—**'Mrs Geoffrey Howard'**

$90 \times 23\,cm$ *[6–9]*   *Red*   *L.Summer*   P   D
$3\,ft \times 9\,in$

Rounded segments of rich tomato-red outside, darker on the tube. Inside a uniform orange-red giving way to brownish yellow, with red-brown marks and narrow yellow throat. Superior to 'Sir Matthew Wilson'.

—**'Nimbus'** ●

$90 \times 23\,cm$ *[7–9]*   *Orange*   *L.Summer*   P   W   D
$3\,ft \times 9\,in$

c. 1918. One of the most spectacular. The large flowers are orange-red in bud, opening to orange. The throat is reddish, the centre around it orange and around this there is a nimbus or halo of orange-red. Rather tender but remarkable and worth a lot of trouble. Portrait in my *Complete Flower Paintings and Drawings*, 1987.

—'Queen Alexandra'

| 60 × 23 cm | [6–9] | Orange | L.Summer | P | D |
| 2 ft × 9 in | | | | | |

Orange outside, flushed maroon on the tube; inside the segments are light orange with small maroon blotches towards the throat on the three lowest segments. The fading flowers have a pinkish tint.

—'Queen of Spain' ●

| 90 × 23 cm | [6–9] | Orange-red | L.Summer | P | D |
| 3 ft × 9 in | | | | | |

1916. Judging by old photographs I believe this is the name of a plant found at Wakehurst, Sussex. It is vigorous and showy, with splendid large open flowers, dark orange-red in bud opening to clear orange with paler throat; small basal blotches decorate the inner segments.

—'Sir Matthew Wilson'

| 90 × 23 cm | [6–9] | Red | L.Summer | P | D |
| 3 ft × 9 in | | | | | |

c. 1928. Pure tomato-red outside, the colour inside giving way to a yellow area bounded by a heavy red-brown zone, with yellow throat.

—'Solfatare'

| 60 × 23 cm | [7–9] | Yellow | L.Summer | P | W | D |
| 2 ft × 9 in | | | | | | |

Prior to 1897. This is not reliably hardy in Surrey, but is admirable for those who garden in warmer areas, on account of the subtle contrast of the pale apricot-yellow against the smoky bronze of the grassy leaves. Highly attractive at Trengwainton and Trelissick, Cornwall.

—'Sprowston Glory'

| 60 × 23 cm | [6–9] | Orange | L.Summer | P | D |
| 2 ft × 9 in | | | | | |

1936. Broad segments, dark orange-red outside; inside they are orange-brown, fading to a pinkish tinge, with a wide ring of red-brown around the wide yellow throat. Raised by C. R. A. Hammond, Norwich.

—'Star of the East' ●

| 90 × 23 cm | [6–9] | Apricot | E.Autumn | P | W | D |
| 3 ft × 9 in | | | | | | |

c. 1912. The largest of all, with broad segments of soft apricot-yellow with paler throat and deeper flushes at the tips. The buds and outer segments are red-tinted. Found at Hidcote, Gloucestershire.

—'Tigridie'

| 60 × 23 cm | [6–9] | Apricot | L.Summer | P | D |
| 2 ft × 9 in | | | | | |

Prior to 1906. Small flowers of apricot tint, with a large red-brown splash around the centre, particularly on the lower segments, the two lowest having small crimson dots.

135

—'Vesuvius'

60 × 23 cm	*[6–9]*	*Red*	*E.Autumn*	P	D
2 ft × 9 in					

1907. Vivid rich orange-red, or vermilion, both in bud and when open. The two lowest segments each have two spots of a darker tint.

—'Walberton Red' and —'Walberton Yellow' ● ★

90 × 30 cm	*[6–9]*	*Red/Yellow*	*L.Summer*	P	D
3 × 1 ft					

Two extremely fine hybrids, the results of crossing and selecting over a number of years by Mr D. R. Tristram of Arundel, West Sussex, using *C. masonorum, C. pottsii*, 'Solfatare' and 'His Majesty'. Their special characters are the uplifted flowers (inherited from *C. masonorum*), which are large and of fine quality and have large corms which do not split into a choking mass of small corms. The former is pure tomato-red; the latter, deep warm yellow with three heavy brown marks in the throat on the three lowest segments. New.

"During recent years the *Montbretia* has been much improved, both as regards the size of the flowers and their colour."—WR

CYNARA, Compositae. This genus includes the Cardoon and Globe Artichoke. The young leaves of the cardoon are delicious when blanched as for celery, but this of course can only be done in the vegetable garden. Not so the Globe Artichoke, whose succulent flower-heads can be enjoyed without spoiling the effect of the leaves, though it may provoke a tussle between one's aesthetic and gastronomic tastes. Plant in spring in warm, sunny, well-drained positions.

cardunculus

1.8 m × 90 cm	*[7–9]*	*Violet*	*Summer*	PF	DRS
6 × 3 ft					

Europe. 1658. Cardoon. One of the most magnificent of all herbaceous plants. The leaves alone would warrant its inclusion in any large garden. They are 90 cm–1.2 m (3–4 ft) long, silvery grey, pointed and deeply divided, recurving and extremely elegant, lasting well in water. Stout grey stems bear further leaves and immense purple thistle-heads. A most striking plant; a near relative of the Globe Artichoke, *Cynara scolymus* (1548), whose leaves are not so grey and whose flowers are not prickly. When picked just before opening the flowers will open fully in water and remain expanded for drying for the winter.

"They commit great error who cut away the side or superfluous leaves that grow by the sides ... which would nourish it to the feeding of the fruit."—GH

So beware, you flower-arrangers! On the other hand few borders or groups of plants are large enough to take 2.4-m (8-ft) flower-stems, and I often remove these and just enjoy the great clump of incredible impressive foliage, the grandest of all silverlings.

hystrix

1.2 m × 60 cm	*[8–9]*	*Violet-blue*	*L.Summer*	PF	S
4 × 2 ft					

Morocco. Late 19th century. This is a much lesser plant, but it needs the same good drainage in our drier counties, and full sun. The foliage is greyish, divided and elegant, but dies away by midsummer, leaving the stems which bear several remarkable flower heads, each being a tuft of vivid bluish thistle-flowers surrounded by long, sharp, amethyst-crimson calyces. Introduced by Captain Collingwood Ingram.

CYNOGLOSSUM, Boraginaceae.

nervosum

60 × 60 cm	*[5–8]*	*Blue*	*E.Summer*	S
2 × 2 ft				

Himalaya. Hound's Tongue. Large, intense blue, Forget-me-not-like flowers open in profusion over the clumps of narrow green leaves. A gay plant and lovely in contrast to *Origanum vulgare* 'Aureum'. Any normal soil, in sun, suits it; the stems are apt to flop if over-nourished.

CYPRIPEDIUM, Orchidaceae. The Lady's Slipper Orchids or Moccasin Flowers are long-lived and hardy if only one can obtain established plants and give them what they need—a cool, peaty, open soil, well drained, in partial shade. Unfortunately up to the present they have defied us gardeners who wish to raise them from seeds; despite every care they will not germinate. As a consequence they have for many years been rooted up in the wild, despatched to the markets and have proved difficult to establish. *C. calceolus* is practically extinct in Britain; supplies are sent from Europe. American and Far Eastern species will become scarce in the wild if this wasteful rifling is continued. Wasteful because probably not more than 1 per cent of collected plants lives for more than a year or two in cultivation. Why then include them in this book? Because I think and hope that the difficulties of raising them from seeds will be overcome and we shall in due course be offered strong, young, established pot-grown stock which will have every chance. The leaves are soft and hairy, ribbed and folded, and the flowers have four outer segments surrounding a pouch or "slipper", usually of a different colour. When planting, the centre crown should be placed just under the surface; the soil should be made as firm as possible. Plant in autumn and see the frost does not lift the roots during winter, by means of placing some stones around the crown over the roots.

calceolus

30 × 23 cm	*[5–8]*	*Yellow*	*Spring*	D
1 ft × 9 in				

Europe. The native Lady's Slipper. Clear yellow pouch, rich red-brown segments. This thrives in a peaty mixture with broken mortar rubble or limy soil added.

"Touching the faculties of our Ladies' Shoo we have nothing to write, it being not sufficiently known to the old writers, nor to the new."—GH

californicum

46–60 × 30 cm	*[5–8]*	*Yellow*	*Spring*	D
18 in–2 ft × 1 ft				

California. 1888. Warm pale yellow segments, small blush white pouch; several flowers are borne on leafy stems.

parviflorum

46 × 30 cm	*[4–8]*	*Brown*	*Spring*	D
18 in × 1 ft				

North America. 1759. Small flowers of twisted, maroon segments and yellow pouch, more than one per stem.

pubescens

60 × 23 cm	*[4–8]*	*Yellow*	*Spring*	D
2 ft × 9 in				

North America. 1790. Sepals twisted, yellowish or brownish with dark veins, pouch large, light yellow with purplish veins inside. This and some others grow well at the Savill Gardens, Windsor.

reginae ●

30 × 23 cm	*[5–8]*	*Pink*	*Spring*	D
1 ft × 9 in				

United States. 1731. *C. spectabile.* Large flowers, white outer segments, soft pink pouch. A wonderful plant, worth all one's pocket money. Other species to be tried when available: *C. acaule*, difficult and short-growing; *C. arietinum* [6–8], *candidum* [6–8], *guttatum* [6–8], *japonicum* [6–8], *montanum* [6–8], *tibeticum* [6–8], *ventricosum* (*C. macranthum*) [5–8], etc. They are all nonpareils and almost need galoshes—in the shape of small ground-cover—to guard their "shoos" from splashes.

DACTYLORRHIZA, Orchidaceae. By this name are now known the following hardy terrestrial species of orchid, while others remain in *Orchis*. They are stately plants and sound perennials when their few needs are studied. Pure sand and heaviest clay, also pure chalky soil, should be avoided; in ordinary fertile soil all they need is some added humus. They like sun. Each hand-like tuber lasts for one year; the new is attached to the old at the base of every stem and should never be separated. They increase freely by duplication of new tubers and these fall apart readily when lifted in late summer or early autumn. Plant 20 cm (9 in) apart, or more; about 7.5 cm (3 in) deep; the bigger the tuber, the deeper. While the various clones which are grown in gardens are distinct enough at sight, botanically they are a confusing lot and I should not like to be dogmatic about them. Usually the Glasnevin plant is first to flower, followed closely by *D. majalis*, the latest being *D. braunii*. Their dominant shape and decisive colouring need a gentle foil such as *Dicentra formosa* or *Viola cornuta* 'Lilacina' and *V.c.* 'Alba'.

"If the plants are allowed to remain until August or September, when the tubers are matured, the risk of transplanting is lessened."—WR

× braunii ★

75 × 30 cm	*[5–8]*	*Purple*	*E.Summer*	D
2½ × 1 ft				

D. majalis × D. fuchsii. The spotted, sharply pointed leaves are highly attractive in spring and the almost pyramid-shaped flower spikes appear later than the others described. They are of a good, rich crimson-purple. Rapid increase.

elata

75 × 30 cm	*[6–8]*	*Lilac*	*E.Summer*	D
2½ × 1 ft				

S.W. Europe, N. Africa. Usually represented in gardens by the plant known as 'Glasnevin', which is of obscure origin. It is so far unsurpassed for height and magnificence. It has hollow stems and plain green leaves, and flowers of rich rosy lilac in long spikes. *D. foliosa* (*D. maderensis*) is a close relative endemic to Madeira. It usually has paler flowers with a broader, flatter, lower lip.

foliosa

46–60 cm	*[7–8]*	*Purple*	*E.Summer*	D
× 30 cm				
18 in–2 × 1 ft				

Madeira. 1833. *Orchis foliosa*. The Madeira orchid is closely allied to *O. elata* but is rather less tall, with grooved, shining leaves. The colour is less clear, deeper in the throat in some forms, but of gorgeous richness in others. In cool retentive soils it increases freely, as at Pitmedden, Aberdeenshire.

fuchsii

60 × 30 cm	*[5–8]*	*Lilac*	*E.Summer*	D
2 × 1 ft				

Europe, Asia, Britain. Common Spotted Orchid. Frequently found on chalk downland or limy meadows. It has solid stems bearing narrow, spotted leaves. The flowers are lilac, pale or dark; occasionally white, but all have a pattern of darker lines.

latifolia

60 × 30 cm	*[5–8]*	*Purple*	*E.Summer*	D
2 × 1 ft				

Europe, Britain. Our well-known native Marsh Orchis. Its narrow leaves often have maroon spots, and the spikes of lilac and rosy lilac flowers are paler in the throat. Good forms sometimes approach the magnificence of *D. elata*. It grows best in moist ground and is worth cultivating well, as in the Savill Gardens, Windsor.

majalis

46 × 30 cm or more	*[5–8]*	*Purple*	*E.Summer*	D
18 in × 1 ft or more				

Europe, Asia, Britain. *Orchis latifolia*. Marsh Orchid. The form I grow which is so resplendent at Sissinghurst, has been identified as *D. majalis* subspecies *majalis*. The stems are hollow, the flowers are produced early in the season, of a wonderful dark crimson-purple.

DAHLIA, Compositae. In our mildest counties many dahlias may be treated as hardy perennials. They need good cultivation in full sun. As we know them today they present a vast complex of hybrid strains, believed to be descended from *D. coccinea* and *D. juarezii*. But when discovered by Europeans in the sixteenth century double-flowered hybrids were already being cultivated by the Aztecs. The numerous hybrids are best selected in flower or from reliable lists. They all have a sharp bright fragrance which carries well on the air. Plant in fertile soil 12.5 cm (5 in) deep.

coccinea

1.2 m × 60 cm	*[9–10]*	*Scarlet*	*Summer/*	P	W	CDS
4 × 2 ft			*E.Autumn*			

Mexico. 1798. Single scarlet flowers are produced over a free-branching lush green plant with dark brown stems. Some kinds such as 'Laciniata Purpurea' and 'Bishop of Landaff' have their fierce red flowers augmented by metallic dark coppery purple foliage. The former thrives at Mount Stewart, Co. Down.

merckii

| 90 × 60 cm | [9–10] | Lilac | Summer/ | P W CDS |
| 3 × 2 ft | | | Autumn | |

Mexico. Prior to 1839. In warmer districts this has proved a hardy perennial. A typical yet slender and refined species with single, small, pure lilac blooms produced continuously until autumn. In complete and striking contrast the central cone is maroon with yellow stamens.

DARLINGTONIA, Sarraceniaceae.

californica

| 30–60 × 30 cm | [8–9] | Yellow | Summer | W D |
| 1–2 × 1 ft | | | | |

California. 1861. A curious plant which attract insects into its extraordinary cobra-like leaves, tubular and hooded, and then digests them. The flowers are yellowish green. It needs a prepared bed of sphagnum moss and peat, constantly moist, in the open. Evergreen.

DATISCA, Datiscaceae. Fine foliage plant for sunny positions in our warmer counties.

cannabina

| 1.8 × 1.8 m | [8–9] | Green | L.Summer | DS |
| 6 × 6 ft | | | | |

Middle East. 1739. Might be described as a herbaceous substitute for a bamboo, because of its graceful arching stems, clad in luxuriant pinnate leaves. The flowers are minute, yellowish, and male and female plants are needed to ensure the ripening of the green seed-heads on the female. Essentially, though, it is a foliage plant, suitable for isolated planting in large gardens.

DECODON, Lythraceae. Close relative of *Lythrum*, for swampy places, margins of ponds and streams, where it will colonize.

verticillatus

| 1.5 m × 60 cm | [5–8] | Purplish | Summer | DS |
| 5 × 2 ft | | | | |

E. United States. *Nesaea verticillata*. Erect willowy plant with mauve-purple small flowers in clusters on the upper part of the stems. An asset on account of its autumn colour.

DEINANTHE, Saxifragaceae. Choice clump-forming plants for cool shady spots in retentive soil with humus, sheltered from wind (which bruises the leaves). They are perfectly hardy and their flowers are highly intriguing in a quiet way.

bifida

| 60 × 46 cm | [5–9] | White | Summer | DS |
| 2 ft × 18 in | | | | |

Japan. Leaves opposite, in pairs, broad and somewhat hairy, each with a deep notch instead of a point. The flowers are fleshy, white, nodding, in small clusters. Seldom seen and not as remarkable as the next.

caerulea

| $46 \times 46\,cm$ | [5–9] | Blue | Summer | DS |
| $18 \times 18\,in$ | | | | |

China. Forms a fine clump of rounded bristly-hairy leaves immediately over which nod the fleshy, begonia-like, rounded flowers of a curious slate-blue, with stamens to match, borne on reddish stalks. This choice plant always excites interest, though full of wanhope. There is a rare variety, *D.c.* 'Alba'.

"... a curious and lovely tone of sad pale violet ... specially attractive in so weird a blossom as this, like that of some monstrous waxier *Pyrola* that has known sorrow both wisely and well."—RF

DELPHINIUM, Ranunculaceae. The popular image of a delphinium is of a great tall plant producing long spikes of blue flowers but, as in many other genera, the hybridists have concentrated on intermarrying one or two species only, and there are species in the genus with widely differing characters. In colour alone this genus is nearly unique (*cf. Anemone, Gentiana, Lobelia*) with all three primary colours represented in the different species. In height they vary from 30 cm–1.8 m (1–6 ft), but they all have beautifully fingered leaves, and the individual flowers somewhat resemble an elfin bonnet, with a tail or spur at the back, often with short, dark petaloids in the centre resembling a bee.

brachycentron

| $90 \times 90\,cm$ | [3–7] | Blue | Summer | PF DS |
| $3 \times 3\,ft$ | | | | |

Kamchatka. *D. cheilanthum brachycentron, D. stenosepalum.* This rare and beautiful plant should be better known. It can of course be staked to keep it erect but when grown without support its lax stems make a wide mound. It is a softly hairy plant with the usual divided leaves and spikes and sprays of widely spaced flowers. They give the effect of light, bright blue, but the sepals are darker than the petals and have a dark spot.

brunonianum

| $46 \times 30\,cm$ | [3–9] | Purplish | Summer | DS |
| $18\,in \times 1\,ft$ | | | | |

Asia. 1864. For its height this is a large-flowered plant, with rather coarse hairy leaves. The few flowers are of light lilac-blue with black and yellow central "bee". *D. cashmiriana* is similar, usually with darker flowers. In both species the flowers are carried in branching heads rather than in spikes.

cardinale

| $1.2\,m \times 60\,cm$ | [8–9] | Red/Yellow | Summer | PF S |
| $4 \times 2\,ft$ | | | | |

California. Rarely grown, and not easy, requiring a rich somewhat moist soil in full sun in our warmer counties, It is quick to flower from seed. Long spikes of flowers in tones of lustred red, with yellowish inner petals.

cheilanthum ★

| $90 \times 46\,cm$ | [3–7] | Blue | Summer | PF DS |
| $3\,ft \times 18\,in$ | | | | |

Caucasus, Asia Minor. *D. formosum* of gardens. This variable plant is a good perennial and a parent of many garden hybrids. A good form should be sought, or one can choose one's own after raising seedlings. It is a comparatively dainty plant, useful for cutting, and from wiry stems produces a spike of varying tints, from light blue ('Caelestinum') to dark blue or white.

elatum

1.8 m × 60 cm   *[2–9]*   *Blue*   *Summer*   PF DS
6 × 2 ft

W. Europe to E. Asia. 1578. The tall blue species which has been the main parent of the garden hybrids, for which see below.

grandiflorum

60 × 30 cm   *[4–9]*   *Blue*   *Summer*   PF S
2 × 1 ft

Siberia. W. North America. 1741. *D. sinense*. Although this is a true perennial, its long life is suspect particularly because of the numerous overbred seed strains: 'Blue Butterfly', 'Azure Fairy', etc. There is also a white form. Pretty, small plants with neat dark green leaves and airy spires of well-shaped flowers. Young plants are best.

nudicaule

30 × 23 cm   *[5–7]*   *Red*   *Summer/*   P S
1 ft × 9 in   *Autumn*

California. 1869. I include this dwarf species because of its influence in breeding. Soft orange-red blooms are produced on successive spikes; they do not open widely. The plant is a surprise, but unfortunately is not a good perennial.

requienii

60 × 60 cm   *[7–8]*   *Blue*   *Summer*   P DS
2 × 2 ft

S. France. 1824. Seldom seen, but a charming plant, more or less perennial in suitable soil and sunny position. Normal divided leaves of glossy dark green and woolly stems with singly disposed flowers for 30 cm (1 ft) or more at the top. The upper segments are often pale yellow and the lower of grey-blue, but they vary in tint considerably. Many subsidiary spikes continue the display.

tatsienense

60 × 30 cm   *[7–9]*   *Blue*   *Summer*   P S
2 × 1 ft

Szechuan. Daintily cut, deep green basal leaves and wiry stems; the flowers are of rich deep blue brightened by a cream and purple centre. A rather short-lived perennial for well-drained soils in sun.

trolliifolium

1.5 m × 60 cm   *[4–8]*   *Blue*   *Summer*   P CS
5 × 2 ft

Western N. America. 1872. Deeply cut leaves, smooth stems. The flowers are widely spaced, pale, with good spurs.

wellbyi ●

90 × 46 cm   *[8–9]*   *Blue*   *Summer*   P W S
3 ft × 18 in

Abyssinia. 1898. *D. leroyi*. Usually grown under cover, along with the still more tender *D. macrocentron* from Africa, this species will succeed in favoured districts. Elegant and open-growing, the flowers are a light greenish blue and sweetly fragrant; long erect spurs. Forms from high altitude in Abyssinia may well prove hardier than those earlier in cultivation. A nonpareil.

zalil

60 × 30 cm	*[8–9]*	*Yellow*	*Summer*	PF	S
2 × 1 ft					

Persia. 1892. *D. sulphureum* (of gardens). A tricky plant needing perfect drainage and a warm sunny spot. Deeply cut leaves. The clear pale yellow flowers are a great delight and are slowly making themselves felt in breeding delphiniums of startling colours. Wiry wind-resistant stems. (*D.semibarbatum.*)

Having disposed of the true species we can now consider the several hybrid races.

GARDEN HYBRIDS

The popular delphinium hybrids are sun-lovers, delighting in good, well-nurtured, retentive soils, particularly if limy. Almost all of the taller clones need most securely staking, individually, but their splendour is worth a lot of effort. Nothing else can take their unrivalled place in the July border, and they are among the most flamboyant of all garden plants. Elegant fingered leaves of soft green. The flowers of the hardy kinds for all their beauty—some even displaying a home-made bee in the centre!—unfortunately lack fragrance.

"... may be cut down bravely after flowering; it does them no harm, and they often break again and have stray flowering sprays in the autumn."—CWE

"... the flowers, and especially before they be perfected, have a certain shew and likenesse of those Dolphins ... with a crooked and bending shape ..."—GH

LARGE-
FLOWERED
HYBRIDS ★

1.2–2.4 m	*[2–8]*	*Various*	*Summer*	PF	DS
× 90 cm					
4–8 × 3 ft					

Descended in part from *D. elatum*, these were first hybridized by the firm of Kelway at Langport, Somerset, about 1875. Early in this century much more work of hybridizing was done by Blackmore & Langdon of Bath. Later hybridizers in this country and the United States have contributed, so that today these hybrids are available in doubles and singles, tall or short, from primrose yellow through cream and white to pale and dark blue, violet-mauve, dark purple and amethyst to almost pink, some with dark eyes and some with light: there are also some extra early and some extra late. There is a stately delphinium for every soft colour scheme, and the vivid true blues assort well with sharper schemes. But most of them need staking and all are like caviare to slugs. They need really good cultivation in well-enriched soil, preferably with some lime, and may be seen in some splendour at Anglesey Abbey, Cambridgeshire, and also at Mount Stewart, Northern Ireland. Needless to say, all this breeding for size and colour has opened the way to disease, sometimes resulting in stunted growth and distorted blooms; any such plants should be burnt at once. There are many named varieties of great excellence, and also seed strains which will produce many first-rate plants. For the strong blue varieties there is no companion so good as *Thalictrum speciosissimum*.

BELLADONNA
HYBRIDS ★

90 cm–1.5 m	[3–8]	Blue	Summer/	PF DS
× 60 cm			Autumn	
3–5 × 2 ft				

Hybridizing and selection have been going on since about 1900, using *D. elatum* forms crossed with *D. grandiflorum* and perhaps *D. cheilanthum* (*D. formosum* of gardens). The result is smaller plants which produce successive spikes from midsummer to autumn, particularly when young and well nurtured, and provided that the early spent spikes are removed after flowering. They are attractive garden plants, needing a little support, and available in a number of named varieties, white, pale blue, royal blue and navy, for which personal selection is best.

× **ruysii**

90 cm–1.2 m	[3–8]	Pink	Summer/	P D
× 60 cm			Autumn	
3–4 × 2 ft				

1935. A sensational hybrid by the firm of Ruys in Holland—long famed for herbaceous plants—the result of a cross between *D. nudicaule* with *D. elatum* hybrids. 'Pink Sensation' is a delightful plant, reminiscent of the Belladonna Hybrids in stance and size, but with clear pink flowers. It needs good cultivation if it is to be grown as a perennial.

NEW HYBRIDS [3–8]
Much as I admire a true-blue delphinium I eagerly await the arrival in nurseries of the new hybrids from Holland. Dr R. A. Legro is developing amazing colours embracing scarlet, orange, yellow and other tints, by using *D. zalil, D. nudicaule, D. cardinale* and hybrids of *D. elatum*, and endeavouring to include fragrance from *D. wellbyi*. Some have large spikes, others have the spaced, butterfly-elegance of *D. belladonna*. Unfortunately, so far, vegetative propagation on commercial lines has proved difficult. Superb red strains have also been raised at the Dupont garden, Longwood Gardens, Kennett Square, Pa., USA.

DENTARIA, Cruciferae. The following is the largest of several species of Toothwort. By some authorities they are all classed under *Cardamine*.

pinnata ★

| 50 × 30 cm | [5–9] | White | E.Spring | P D |
| 20 in × 1 ft | | | | |

Switzerland, etc. 1683. *Cardamine heptaphylla*. Forms a clump of light green, divided leaves which are surmounted by clusters of pure white cuckoo-flowers of good size and substance, long before we have begun to think about herbaceous plants. A cool spot is preferred in any reasonable soil; curious, white, tuberous roots, earning the name of Toothwort.

"One of the handsomest ... well-filled heads of 12–15 flowers, and palmate leaves of freshest green."—GJ

There are several lesser species of considerable spring charm needing the same cultivation. Among the better-known ones are the soft lilac *D. digitata* (*Cardamine pentaphyllos*) [6–8], introduced from S. Europe by 1659, and *D. enneaphylla* (*Cardamine enneaphyllos*) [5–8], also from S. Europe, whose creamy flowers are often accentuated by bronzed young foliage. They grow well at Nymans, Sussex, and at Hidcote, Gloucestershire.

Fig. 1   **Aconitum carmichaelii** Debx. var. **wilsonii 'Barker's Variety'.** The lowest flowers on a towering spike, whose formation is shewn on the left. Light Wedgwood blue. Top right, a single flower of **A. paniculatum** Lam., shewing the forward-pointing hood.

Fig. 2 **Ornithogalum nutans** L. Those who love all strange greenish flowers should try to naturalize this European to follow the daffodils in grass.

Fig. 3   **Anemone hupehensis** var. **japonica** (Thunb.) Bowles & Stearn ('Prince Henry' of gardens), deep old rose pink, and **'Honorine Jobert',** pure white; two of the most reliable plants for late summer and early autumn. (See text.)

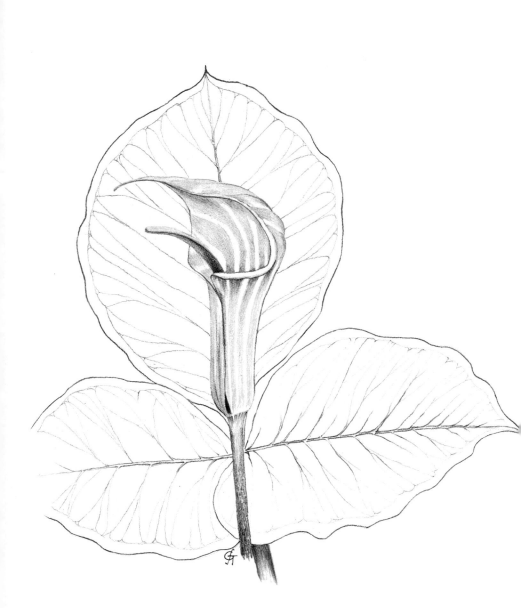

Fig. 4   **Arisaema candidissimum** W. W. Smith. The sudden appearance of spectacular blooms of white striped with pink and green, just before the leaves, is one of the highlights of the June garden.

Fig. 5   **Campanula 'Burghaltii'.** Hybrid. One of the largest flowers among campanulas, of palest grey-lilac.

Fig. 6   **Clematis heracleifolia** DC. var. **davidiana** Hemsl. **'Wyevale'.** Soft Wedgwood-blue
flowers, sweetly scented, are borne on a large sprawling plant for many weeks in late
summer.

Fig. 7   (1) **Crocosmia masonorum** (L. Bolus) N.E. Brown; (2) **C. pottsii** Bentham; (3) **Tritonia rosea** Klatt. The first is flaming vermilion-orange, the second vermilion-red (it is a parent of *C. × crocosmiiflora,* figure 8), the third is of light coppery pink. All flower in late summer.

Fig. 8   **Crocosmia** × **crocosmiiflora 'Queen of Spain'** sketched at Wakehurst; a flower of the common Montbretia, **C.** × **crocosmiiflora** (Lemne ex Morr.) N.E. Brown, is added for comparison.

Fig. 9   **Deinanthe caerulea** Stapf. A late summer flower from China for a cool spot. The slate-blue flowers are waxy and firm.

Fig. 10 (1) **Dicentra macrantha** Oliv., a rare species with flowers of light yellow. The flowers of (2) **D. formosa** Walp. and (3) **D. eximia** Torr. are soft mauve-pink, borne for many weeks. (4) **D. spectabilis** Lem. for comparison; the rosy red flowers are known as Bleeding Heart, Dutchman's Breeches, Lady-in-the-Bath, etc.

Fig. 11 **Geranium lambertii** Knuth. Often labelled *G. candicans* in gardens. The bright green of the sepals shews between the pure white, crimson-veined petals. The flowers are nodding, borne on trailing stems from summer to autumn.

Fig. 12   **Houttuynia cordata** Thunb. **'Flore Pleno',** whose cone-like flowers are more effective than those of the wild type, which is shewn for comparison. The flowers are pure white, appearing for three months. The foliage is strongly redolent of Seville oranges.

Fig. 13   **Kirengeshoma palmata** Yatabe. A distinguished Japanese autumnal with large handsome leaves and pale yellow flowers whose segments are thick and soft.

Fig. 14 **Lavatera cachemiriana** Cambess. This tall (but wind-resisting), sound perennial of the Mallow Family carries light rose-pink flowers for many weeks.

Fig. 15   **Meconopsis chelidoniifolia** Bur. & Franch. An airy-fairy perennial for woodland conditions. The flowers are of clear light yellow.

Fig. 16 **Salvia involucrata** Cav. **'Bethellii'.** As the spike of cerise-crimson, white-bearded flowers elongates the large pink bracts drop off. A useful autumnal.

DESMODIUM, Leguminosae. Mostly shrubs, closely related to *Lespedeza*, several of value for late flowering. *D. tiliifolium* [9–10] can be cut down each spring, to flower on new wood, as for *Indigofera*. The following is herbaceous.

canadense

90 × 60 cm *3 × 2 ft*	*[3–8]*	*Purple*	*Summer*	S

N. America. 1640. The lilac-purple racemes of pea-flowers are produced freely in sunny positions on branching stems furnished thinly with three-lobed leaves.

DIANELLA, Liliaceae. For lime-free soil in warm gardens.

caerulea

60 × 30 cm *2 × 1 ft*	*[9–10]*	*Blue*	*E.Summer*	PF	W	DS

Australia. Grassy leaves and white or light blue, nodding, tiny lily-like flowers in summer, giving way to shining, royal blue berries later. *D. revoluta* from Tasmania is a richer blue. Evergreen.

tasmanica

1.2 m × 46 cm *4 ft × 18 in*	*[9–10]*	*Blue*	*E.Summer*	PF	W	DS

Tasmania. 1866. A far larger plant. The flowers are plentiful in branching sprays, light blue, starry, followed by long-lasting, oblong, dark blue berries. Worthy of a sheltered corner in the south and west; thriving at Mount Stewart, Northern Ireland, and Trengwainton, Cornwall. Evergreen.

★ **DIANTHUS,** Caryophyllaceae. From the early days of history these have been much loved garden plants; their enemies are soggy soil, rabbits, pigeons, and long periods of drying spring winds, which sap the strength of old plants. To retain a collection it is necessary to keep propagating them, and fortunately all one has to do is to put heeled cuttings, torn off the old plants, into the open ground in September, with some sand. In fact they all grow best in well-drained friable soil, sandy or gritty. They are all barely tall enough—except the Clove Carnations—for inclusion in this book, but who could have a garden without enjoying their fragrant flowers and greyish tumps of leaves? They are ideal for the verges of beds and borders, where they will flop onto the path, softening the hard line, together with thrifts, alpine phloxes, aubrietas and other clump-forming dwarf plants. They prefer full sun but will grow where the ground is shaded by buildings though not with overhead shade. Evergreen. The Carnations are mainly derived from *D. caryophyllus*, the Pinks from *D. plumarius*, but undoubtedly over the centuries the parentage has become mixed.

● ★ CLOVE CARNATIONS [All 4–8] The Old Crimson Clove (sixteenth century), a dark crimson-red, was powerfully fragrant. Chaucer called it the Clove Gilofre. It was richly scented and was recorded in the sixteenth century; in the late nineteenth century it was still grown commercially. If, as was claimed, the petals had smooth edges, I have never seen it, though I have been given at least three distinct "old red cloves" with serrated petals, all richly scented. The Old Salmon Clove is in reality 'Lord Chatham' ● a famous variety of *c.* 1780; also known as 'Raby Castle'. It has a wonderful perfume, and flowers of bright salmon-coral. In Ireland a friend found a salmon-and-white-striped form, which has since sported back to 'Lord Chatham'; it is named 'Phyllis Marshall' (1990). The term "salmon" refers to uncooked fish; a strong colour. I have come across a bright scarlet-red, an old double white and a splendid full magenta-purple (perhaps 'Purple Emperor'), and a good striped one. It is worth having a look round cottage gardens in search of these treasures (which are seldom to be bought), in late July and August, as they flower well after the June display of the pinks. They require the same culture as pinks and are as easy to propagate. "Giloflour", "Gilliflower", "Gilliver" are variants of the old name for a clove-scented flower, or clove-shaped, and have been used for pinks and also for wallflowers.

"The old red Clove always holds its own for hardiness, beauty, and perfume."—GJ

"A familiar type is the old Crimson Clove, a sweet and lovely thing, which may be had in several different shades of self-colour. They combine hardiness and vigour with free blooming and great effect."—WR

"The Clove Gillofloure differeth not from the Carnation but in greatnesse as well of the flowres as leaves ... endureth better the cold, and therefore is planted in gardens."—GH

GARDEN PINKS [all 4–8] mostly double-flowered. The old double white 'Mrs Sinkins' (1868) is much beloved, but 'White Ladies' is a purer white, equally fragrant, less blowsy, and has more glaucous foliage. It is a better garden plant. 'Musgrave's Pink', c. 1730, is single, white, with a green centre; it was also known as 'Washfield', 'Tiverton' or 'Green Eyes'; today it sometimes masquerades under such names as 'C. T. Musgrave' or 'Charles Musgrave', the name of a former Treasurer of the Royal Horticultural Society. A double variant has been raised. 'Fragrans Plenus' is an exquisitely fragrant old double, small and much fringed. 'Bat's Double Red', dating from 1707, commemorating Mr Thomas Bat of London, has excellent glaucous blue-green foliage and is vigorous and free (though so old a variety); warm crimson-pink colour with red central zone, double. This is also known as 'Emperor', a name given to it erroneously by Ernest Ladhams in the 1930s. 'Thomas', 'Cockenzie' (1720) and 'Enid Anderson' are richly coloured, coppery crimson. 'Cockenzie' is also known as the Montrose Pink, from Montrose House. 'Inchmery' (eighteenth century) is an excellent, bland, pale pink. 'Dad's Favourite' and 'Coronation' have white flowers marked with maroon. A tall, single, very vigorous form is known as 'Brympton Red'; it is crimson-marbled with a deeper shade. It was found at Brympton d'Evercy by Margery Fish. But there are many more, and all pinks are to be treasured; foraging expeditions to old gardens in June frequently bring forth unexpected joys. All are very fragrant and excellent for cutting.

HIGHLAND HYBRIDS★

25 × 46 cm	[All 4–8] Varied	Summer	P S
10 × 18 in			

These should be raised from seed: all are beautiful. They form tussocks of grey foliage 30 cm (1 ft) or more across, and are covered in June with single flowers varying in tint from white to deep pink, with maroon centres. Care-free plants which thrive in any sunny, well-drained soil. Splendid for under-planting the old roses. One of the good original named hybrids was 'Highland Queen', deep pink with red eye; 'Highland Fraser' is much shorter, with flowers beautifully marked and eyed in similar tints—a great treasure.

knappii

17.5 × 25 cm	[3–8]	Yellow	Summer	P S
15 × 10 in				

Hungary etc. Inclined to be biennial or monocarpic. It forms tufts of grey-green leaves. The flower stems are stately carrying a cluster of lemon-yellow flowers at the top. For well drained soil in sun.

DIASCIA, Scrophulariaceae. From various parts of South and Eastern Africa these plants are not reliably hardy, but are so easy to grow from cuttings, so long in flower and, in general, of an unusual and appealing shade of soft salmon-pink with coralline and coppery overtones, that they have suddenly become popular, mainly thanks to the introduction of *D. rigescens* [7–9] by O.M. Hilliard and B.L. Burtt in 1978. They require full sun but do not thrive in dry soils. The flowers resemble those of *Nemesia* in shape.

barberae

30 × 46 cm	[7–9]	Pink	Summer/	W CD
12 × 18 in			Autumn	

South Africa. 1870 and 1980. Usually represented in gardens by the form or close hybrid 'Ruby Field'. A flopping, floriferous plant, barely tall enough to be included in these pages. Has survived winters at Hidcote. *D. anastrepta* (1981) has similar appeal.

fetcaniensis

46 × 60 cm	[7–9]	Pink	Summer/	W CD
18 in × 2 ft			Autumn	

South Africa. 1904 and 1979. Wholly herbaceous—as opposed to the other species which are more or less shrubby at the base — this may prove to be the hardiest. In good conditions—sunny but moist—it makes a splendid low clump covered with typical flowers of warm pink tints.

rigescens

46 × 46 cm	[7–9]	Pink	E./L.Summer	W CDS
18 × 18 in				

South Africa, eastern Cape. 1836. Collected afresh by Mr B. Burtt of Edinburgh. A spectacular plant, of low, somewhat shrubby growth, massed with narrow, toothed leaves. The dense spikes of warm coppery pink flowers catch the eye from afar.

vigilis

46 × 46 cm	[7–9]	Pink	Summer/	W CD
18 × 18 in			Autumn	

South Africa. 1981. Slender upright plant with much smaller narrower leaves than the others which I have included. Ascending spires of pink.

"Though mostly treated as half-hardy annuals, the roots are perennial ... spreading by stolons into handsome tufts."—WR

DICENTRA, Papaveraceae. The synonym *Dielytra* was a spelling mistake for *Dicentra*. These all prefer the cooler side of the garden in the south-east of the British Isles; their flowering period will thereby be longer and the foliage more lush.

147

chrysantha

90 × 60 cm	*[6–8]*	*Yellow*	*L.Summer*	W	S
3 × 2 ft					

California. 1852. This is well worthy of trial in hot sun with perfect drainage. The spires of small yellow flowers give a remarkable effect over the clump of extra glaucous, finely divided leaves. Successful at Kew through many less cold winters in the past.

eximia

30 × 46 cm	*[4–8]*	*Mauve-pink*	*L.Spring/*	P	D
1 ft × 18 in			*E.Summer*		

United States. *c.* 1810. Very uncommon in gardens, and a somewhat lesser plant than *D. formosa*. Apart from the leaf shape, the spurs of the outer segments are distinctive. A white form has exceptional charm, variously known as 'Alba', 'Purity' or 'Snowflake'. 'Snowdrift' [3–9] is reputed to have an extra long flowering period. Pale grey-green leaves.

formosa

46 × 60 cm	*[4–8]*	*Mauve-pink*	*L.Spring/*	P	D
18 in × 2 ft			*E.Summer*		

W. North America. 1796. A juicy, hairless plant, with beautiful deeply divided leaves, which make a ferny hummock, above which dangle the strangely shaped little flowers, like lockets, in branching, drooping sprays, of warm rosy mauve. It prefers a cool spot but is not difficult to grow. *D. formosa oregona* [4–8] has produced several garden forms or hybrids; 'Bountiful' (a prolific seeder), 'Débutante', 'Paramount' and 'Silversmith' are some pink and mauve-tinted cultivars named in the United States, all with the greyish leaves of *D.f. oregona*, while 'Adrian Bloom' and 'Luxuriant' are progressively richer in colouring, the latter a glowing dark pink—almost crimson. Soft pink 'Boothman's Variety' is a selection with glaucous and very narrowly divided foliage. A particularly glaucous-leafed, pale-flowered plant which commemorates Dr Rogerson's garden in Devon is 'Langtrees'.

—'**Alba**'. A dainty counterpart with pale green leaves and white flowers. Exquisite in small bunches of flowers. 'Silver Smith', a new American clone, may prove superior; it has glaucous foliage.

macrantha ●

46 × 30 cm	*[4–8]*	*Yellow*	*Spring*	P	D
18 in × 1 ft					

China. 1890. A great rarity. Leaves with jagged edges, but similar to those of *D. spectabilis*. The flowers are of pale amber yellow, dangling, about 7.5 cm (3 in) long. Cool conditions are necessary as its leaves tend to burn in dry winds and weather, but it is a sound and easy perennial and it is high time it reached the gardens of connoisseurs. Thrives at Wakehurst Place, Sussex, and at Wisley, Surrey.

scandens

2 × 1 m	*[6–8]*	*Yellow*	*L.Summer*	W?	S
6 × 3 ft					

Himalaya. A succulent plant, climbing by means of tendrils. The measurements given above are tentative. The dainty, divided leaves are matched by the beauty of the bunches of dangling yellow lockets, borne for several weeks from late summer till early autumn. Perhaps best when climbing through an open, wiry bush, or pea-sticks.

spectabilis ● ★

60 × 46 cm	*[3–8]*	*Rosy Red*	*L.Spring/*	P	DS
2 ft × 18 in			*E.Summer*		

Siberia, Japan. 1810. Bleeding Heart, Dutchman's Breeches, Lady's Locket, Lyre Flower—all fanciful names describing the beautiful rosy red flowers which dangle like a heart (in bud), from the arching stems. An open flower, turned the other way up, shows a Lady-in-the-Bath or Our-Lady-in-a-Boat, if the petals are pulled apart! This exquisite old plant is beloved by all who see it; not only its flowers but also its divided leaves are well above the average in beauty. A plant in full flower is one of the best sights of spring and it is content in most gardens in partial shade or sun. Good for cutting. A white form, 'Alba', is a noteworthy addition, and a form is claimed to be superior, called 'Pantaloons', has been selected in the United States by J. Schultz of Ohio. I understand that it is this selected form which has become common of recent years; the white form known earlier had lacked vigour.

"... resembling rosy hearts ... in strings of a dozen or more gracefully borne on slender stalks ... remarkable beauty."—WR

DICTAMNUS, Rutaceae. Easily grown in any fertile well-drained soil in sun. At one time these were very popular plants and are known as Burning Bush because on still hot days when the seed-pods are ripening a lighted match held at the base of the spike will ignite the volatile oil without harming the plant. If the seed-pods are brought indoors for drying first they will explode and shoot out the seeds, and then the lining of the pods will crackle.

albus ● ★

90 × 60 cm	*[3–8]*	*White*	*E.Summer*	PF	S
3 × 2 ft					

Europe, Asia. *Dictamnus fraxinella albus.* Fraxinella, or Dittany. Cultivated since Roman times. Erect stems bear lemony-aromatic leaves, deeply divided, and erect spikes of elegant white blooms with long stamens.

purpureus ● ★ [3–8] *D. fraxinella ruber.* The flowers are of soft mauve-purple, prettily veined. These two plants are long-lived perennials and awaken the early summer border with other old favourites like *Iris pallida dalmatica* and *Geranium psilostemon. D.a.* 'Giganteus' (*caucasicus*) is recorded as a fine form.

"... a very long-lived plant when it likes the soil."—WR

DIERAMA, Iridaceae. Bulbous plants, hardy in the warmer districts. They prefer a retentive soil which does not dry out, and full sun; best planted in spring, 12.5 cm (5 in) deep. Readily raised from seeds, which germinate freely around the parent plants.

dracomontanum

60 × 30 cm	*[8–9]*	*Various*	*Summer*	PF	DS
2 × 1 ft					

South Africa. *D. pumilum.* Also known as 'Hermia', this dwarf, grassy, evergreen plant is very vigorous, increasing freely and flowering freely, but for a short season. Satiny rose-pink flowers. Some hybrids raised by Mr Slinger at Slieve Donard Nursery, Northern Ireland, between this and *D. pulcherrimum* are midway between the two heights and very free-growing. Some distinct kinds are 'Ceres', pale cobalt-violet; 'Oberon', carmine-purple; 'Puck', soft rose-madder;

'Titania', light pink. These are all reasonably upright in growth, instead of having the wide-arching grace of *D. pulcherrimum*, and are therefore more suited to the smaller garden.

pulcherrimum ●

1.5 m × 30 cm	*[7–9]*	*Pink*	*L.Summer*	PF	W	DS
5 × 1 ft						

South Africa. *Sparaxis pulcherrima*. Wand Flower or Venus' Fishing Rod. Long, grassy, evergreen leaves. The wiry stems, of unparalleled grace, branch at the apex, sending forth showers of blossoms, like a rocket. Emerging from silvery calyces, the bells are beautifully shaped, opening from the end of the stems first, and varying from pale to deep "old rose" and lilac. Lovely with *Thalictrum dipterocarpum* at Bodnant, Denbighshire. Evergreen.

The Slieve Donard Nursery, Northern Ireland, specialized in these plants and selected several excellent forms named after birds, which fill the need when separate colours are wanted; such as 'Windhover', deep lilac-rose, 'Blackbird', violet-mauve, 'Jay', mallow-pink.

"... wavering and swaying this way and that beneath a long drooping shower of ... bells on pedicels so fine that they hardly seem to be attached at all to the tough wiry stems."—RF

DIGITALIS, Scrophulariaceae. Foxglove. These perennial sorts appreciate some humus, but are easy to grow in any fertile soil.

grandiflora ● ★

60 × 30 cm	*[4–8]*	*Yellow*	*Summer*	P	DS
2 × 1 ft					

Greece. 1596. *D. ambigua*. A pleasing, short, clump-forming, perennial Foxglove with typical foxglove-flowers in a soft creamy yellow; need I say more? For sun or part shade. Evergreen.

lanata

60 × 30 cm	*[5–9]*	*Yellow*	*E.Summer*	P	DS
2 × 1 ft					

E. Europe. 1798. Both this and the next are small-flowered, compared with the common foxglove, but are more or less perennial, and have very slender erect spires of little tubular flowers. The creamy yellow, purplish grey-tinted flowers have a large lip of white or pale grey. Evergreen.

lutea

60 × 30 cm	*[4–8]*	*Yellow*	*E.Summer*	P	DS
2 × 1 ft					

S. Europe, North Africa. Small creamy yellow flowers in slender spires and smooth green leaves. It is more or less perennial. The Grecian form is superior to the Italian form, which is called *D.l. australis*.

× mertonensis

60 × 30 cm	*[5–9]*	*Coppery*	*Summer*	P	D
2 × 1 ft					

Hybrid. 1925. *D. purpurea × D. grandiflora*. A rather coarse plant with bunches of soft basal foliage and spikes of large foxglove flowers of a strange tint of rosy mauve, shot with coppery-buff. Fairly perennial if it is kept on the move, dividing it after flowering, and it breeds true from seed. Part shade. Raised at the John Innes Horticultural Institution, Surrey, 1926. 'Dropmore Yellow' is a name which fits here. Evergreen.

parviflora

90 × 30 cm	*[5–8]*	*Brown*	*E.Summer*	P	DS
3 × 1 ft					

S. Europe. Narrow tubular flowers on a slender spike; of unusual colouring, brownish purple. Neat green leaves. Full sun. Prior to 1808.

DIPHYLLEIA, Podophyllaceae.

cymosa

60 × 30 cm	*[7–9]*	*White*	*Summer*	F	DS
2 × 1 ft					

United States. 1812. The Umbrella Leaf is so called because of its immense two-lobed, rounded leaves, 30 cm (2 ft) across. The flowers are in rounded heads and are inconspicuous; the berries that follow are striking, indigo blue, enhanced by their stalks turning red, borne well above the stalwart leafy plant. It needs a retentive soil and cool woodland conditions. Most unusual and dignified.

DIPLARRHENA, Iridaceae. For our warmest counties in well-drained sunny positions.

moraea ●

60 × 23 cm	*[9–10]*	*Mainly*	*E.Summer*	PF	DS
2 ft × 9 in		*White*			

Tasmania, S. Australia. 1873. Long grassy leaves 46 cm (18 in). The flowers, borne in a head of several on wiry stems, have three broad white segments; in the centres are three small erect segments, one yellow and two purple. A plant of true iris dignity and charm.

DISPORUM, Liliaceae. Woodland plants, related to *Polygonatum,* and delighting in cool conditions with ample humus. *D. hookeri* and *D. menziesii* are worth seeking also [4–9].

flavum

60 × 30 cm	*[4–9]*	*Yellow*	*Spring*	F	DS
2 × 1 ft					

Korea. The clear yellow bell-flowers, nodding amongst the topmost leaves, are an appealing sight. The leaves themselves are glossy and carried up stout stems, lasting attractively into late summer at which time the small black berries develop. An easily grown plant.

pullum

90 × 30 cm	*[4–9]*	*Various*	*E.Summer*	PF	DS
3 × 1 ft					

Far East. 1801. Dark stems with a few branches spring from a fairly tight clump, bearing pointed green leaves. The form usually seen in cultivation has purplish-green flowers; they are tubular with reflexed mouth. (*D. cantoniensis.*)

sessile

60 × 60 cm	*[4–9]*	*White*	*Spring*	PF	DS
2 × 2 ft					

Japan. Though it is normally green leafed, I have included this modest plant for the sake of its form 'Variegatum' (*Oakesiella variegata* of gardens). The erect stems arise from a far-questing rootstock, bear lance-shaped leaves cleanly striped with white, and creamy white bell-flowers, resembling those of *Uvularia.*

smithii

30 × 30 cm	[4–9]	Cream	Spring	PF DS
1 × 1 ft				

W. North America. Much confused with *D. oreganum* (*Prosartes oregana*) in gardens. They both form pretty clumps covered with fresh green leaves among which coyly hang the ivory bells turning later into conspicuous orange berries. They will seed themselves mildly in shady places. *D. smithii* has a three-lobed stigma and protruding stamens, while *D. oreganum* has an unbranched stigma and hidden stamens. *D. trachycarpum* [4–9], a close relative, has also a three-lobed stigma but is distinguished by rough fruits. It has a flowering season extending into full summer.

"... drooping ivory bugles an inch or so in length in the way of a Solomon's Seal."—ATJ

DODECATHEON, Primulaceae. The Shooting Stars resemble the cowslip in habit, but have smooth, often brownish green leaves, with stout stems up to 60 cm (2 ft) in height, from the top of which spring arching stalks each with a nodding pinky mauve flower. The petals are reflexed like those of a *Cyclamen*, and around the central purple pointel is a ring of yellow. Most beautiful plants, just like a bursting rocket. The species closely resemble each other; two of the most satisfactory and tall are *D. meadia* (1744) [5–7] and *D. jeffreyi* (1887) [5–7], the first from Eastern and the second from Western United States. Other species are mostly of shorter stature. Plant in damp soil containing humus, about 30 cm (1 ft) apart in shade. You may pick them for the house if you have the heart.

DORONICUM, Compositae. Leopard's Bane. Excellent for cutting and easy to grow. Bright yellow daisies, so welcome in spring, helping to fill the gap caused by the fading daffodils. A lovely contrast to *Lunaria rediviva*, euphorbias and *Chaenomeles japonica* (*maulei*). They are best transplanted, when necessary, in early autumn and thrive in any fertile soil.

austriacum

46 × 30 cm	[5–8]	Yellow	Spring	P DS
18 in × 1 ft				

Europe. A tuberous-rooted colonizer, shorter and earlier than *D. pardalianches*. The leaves are nearly smooth beneath, slightly hairy above, undulate-edged, decidedly heart-shaped, with flanges clasping the stems. Pure yellow daisies on slender stems.

carpetanum

90 × 60 cm	[4–8]	Yellow	Spring	P DS
3 × 2 ft				

Spain. A stout, leafy, rather hairy plant, spreading quickly into a good clump. The bright yellow daisies open after most of the others, and thanks to the freely branching stems, the plant lasts for many weeks in flower. A star-performer at Wallington, Northumberland.

'Miss Mason' ★

46 × 60 cm	[4–8]	Yellow	Spring	P D
18 in × 2 ft				

Hybrid. An invaluable old garden plant, forming an excellent clump of heart-shaped rather smooth leaves with scalloped edges. For some weeks the bright yellow daisies are held well aloft, in April and early May. Probably a hybrid of *D. caucasicum* or *D. austriacum*. Full sun or part shade.

pardalianches
90 × 60 cm	*[4–8]*	*Yellow*	*Spring*	P	D
3 × 2 ft					

Europe, Britain. The Great Leopard's Bane has somewhat invasive tuberous roots and will colonize thin woodland, or areas under small trees, in thin grass, or can of course be grown in the border. Slender branching stems with clear yellow daisies, smaller than *D. plantagineum*. Large areas of it may be seen just north of Jedburgh, on the Edinburgh road.

plantagineum
75 × 30 cm	*[4–8]*	*Yellow*	*Spring*	P	D
2½ × 1 ft					

Europe, Britain. The selection ● ★ 'Excelsum' or 'Harpur Crewe' (1876) is a tall hairy plant, making a less solid clump than 'Miss Mason', but the flowers are large, three to four per stem, and very handsome. It will grow in sun but part shade is better in drier areas. A magnificent, elegant spring flower, first recorded in 1570.

"by far the best."—WR

'Spring Beauty'
46 × 46 cm	*[4–8]*	*Yellow*	*Spring*	P	D
18 × 18 in					

Hybrid. 1962. 'Frühlingspracht'. For those who like double yellow daisies, this is just the sort of thing they like, and a gay spring plant it is!

DRACOCEPHALUM, Labiatae. The Dragon's Heads are not greatly exciting plants and now that *D. sibiricum* is classed under *Nepeta, q.v.*, we are left with a few *Salvia*-like herbs, with the usual hooded flowers of the family. *D. ruyschianum* [4–8], a European species introduced in 1699, is fairly well known, and has flower spikes of violet-blue, 46–60 cm (18 in–2 ft). Well-drained soil, in sun. From the Chinese hinterland are several good closely related species such as *D. forrestii, D. tanguticum, D. isabellae* [all 4–8], all of which make dense clumps of fragrant leaves which vanish under many short spikes of sage-like flowers of purplish blue. *D. grandiflorum* [3–8], from Siberia, is a showy plant with Spode-blue or violet-blue flowers held in purple calyces in good heads. 30 cm (1 ft).

DRACUNCULUS, Araceae.

vulgaris
90 × 46 cm	*[8–10]*	*Brown*	*Summer*	F	D
3 ft × 18 in					

Mediterranean Region. *c.* 1300. Dragon Plant. *Arum dracunculus*. A curiosity and monstrosity whose immense and handsome velvety, plum-crimson spathe with maroon spadix gives off a frightful odour of decaying flesh. The mottled snakelike stems bear rather coarse, divided leaves. It increases freely at its tuberous root and needs separating every few years so that the tuber can gather enough strength to flower. Heavy heads of scarlet berries usually mature. Full sun, good drainage; plant 15 cm (6 in) deep.

ECCREMOCARPUS, Bignoniaceae. Usually treated as an annual, it is truly a perennial in our warmest counties and quickly climbs a sunny wall, on wires or netting, during the summer months. It is not particular about soil; it usually dies to the ground each winter.

scaber
Climber   *[9–10]*   *Orange, etc*   *Summer*   W   S

Chile. 1824. The quick-climbing stems are set with elegantly cut leaves. It flowers continuously from June onwards, producing sprays of tubular flowers; the usual form is orange, but there are also yellow and red forms. They are established at Powis Castle, Montgomeryshire.

ECHINACEA, Compositae.

angustifolia
1.2 m × 46 cm   *[4–9]*   *Purplish*   *Summer*   P   DRS
4 ft × 18 in

1861. W. United States. Leaves narrow, sometimes linear. The large flowers are composed of long, drooping, very narrow ray-florets and the usual prominent brown centre. Warm pinky-mauve. It requires similar conditions to *E. purpurea* and is of similar value and appearance.

purpurea
1.2 m × 46 cm   *[4–9]*   *Purplish*   *Summer*   P   DRS
4 ft × 18 in

United States. 1699. *Rudbeckia purpurea*. Stout-stemmed, stately, leafy plants: foliage dark green. The branching stems display several exceptionally handsome large daisy-flowers, wide-rayed, of rich mauve-crimson, flushed with cerise, of varying intensity, the tips of the petals often being pale grey. An extraordinary touch is the large central boss of orange-brown. Sun; rich, well-drained soil with leaf-mould. Plant in spring. A good contrast for light pink sidalceas. 'The King' was the best variety for many years, with 'Abendsonne' of more cerise tint, and smaller. They have both been superseded by Alan Bloom's splendid variety ● 'Robert Bloom' of intense rich cerise-mauve-crimson with prominent central boss. The true variety is to be treasured and propagated, but a surprising number of well-coloured plants can be raised from its seed, surpassing the species as usually grown in quality and colour. 90 cm (3 ft). 'White Lustre' is best described as a warm white, a remarkable contrast to the orange-brown, central cone. It is an American cultivar, as is 'White Star' which is reputed to come true from seed.

ECHINOPS, Compositae. Globe Thistle. Statuesque plants with elegant, divided, prickly foliage arranged up the stout wiry stems, at the top of which are one or more spherical, prickly heads, like drumsticks. Full sun; they will thrive in poor as well as good soils, on chalk or sand. Unless cut immediately the actual flowers fade, the seed-heads are apt to disintegrate quickly.

> "Echinops ... I have often recommended them for entomologists' gardens where plants are wished for that can be visited after dark with a lantern, to surprise a supper party of noctuid moths."—EAB

nivalis or **niveus**
of gardens
    1.8 m × 60 cm   *[3–8]*   *White*   *L.Summer*   PF   DR
    6 × 2 ft
The leaves are extra grey and spiny, on grey stems which hold aloft grey-white drumsticks. A remarkable contrast for a purple clematis and a beautiful plant for foliage effect throughout the growing season. Slender and elegant. See also under *E. tournefortii.*

ritro ★
    1.2 m × 60 cm   *[3–9]*   *Blue*   *L.Summer*   PF   DR
    4 × 2 ft
Europe. W. Asia. 1570. Green leaves, jagged, and grey beneath. The deep steel-blue heads are borne on grey stems. A useful compact plant whose flower-heads provide good colour long before the actual flowers open, thereby prolonging the season. 'Veitch's Blue' is a trifle richer in colour. These are the usual types seen in gardens, but do not compare with *E. ruthenicus.* There are white forms of all. *E. humilis* is similar. If a much bigger grey-blue plant is required, I should choose *E. exaltatus* or 'Taplow Blue'; 1.5–1.8 m (5–6 ft) and very vigorous.

ruthenicus ● ★
of gardens
    1.2 m × 60 cm   *[3–9]*   *Blue*   *L.Summer*   PF   DRS
    4 × 2 ft
1820. *E. ritro tenuifolius.* This is undoubtedly the gem of the genus. The leaves are of dark shining green above, neatly and narrowly divided, and their under-sides and the stems are covered in a white sheen. The flowers are of bright blue. Unaccountably rare, but hardy and as easy as the others. A beautiful contrast to pink or white ploxes. It thrives at Polesden Lacey, Surrey.

"This is the most ornamental of its distinct family ... we have never seen any kind so good."—WR

sphaerocephalus
    1.8 m × 90 cm   *[3–8]*   *White*   *L.Summer*   PF   DR
    6 × 3 ft
Europe, W. Asia. 1542. A big coarse plant of considerable magnificence. Far more bulky than the refined *E. nivalis.* Green leaves, grey stems, and big grey-white heads of flowers. *E. commutatus* is similar.

tournefortii ●
    1.5 m × 60 cm   *[3–8]*   *White*   *L.Summer*   PF   DRS
    5 × 2 ft
E. Mediterranean Region. 1833. An extremely prickly plant; the whole thing is a symphony of white and grey-green. The leaves are pinnate with white thorns, the lower ones doubly pinnate; all are grey-white beneath. Stout white stems with one to four large handsome knobs of white flowers. Possibly a parent of *E. nivalis, q.v.* Spring planting in well-drained, even dry, soil is safest.

ELSHOLTZIA, Labiatae. A Mint-like sub-shrub, with Mint-like fragrant leaves, which is best cut down to ground level after the winter. Any reasonable, drained soil in sun suits it.

stauntonii

    1.2 m × 60 cm   *[5–7]*   *Mauve*   *Autumn*   P   CD
    4 × 2 ft

N. China. 1909. It forms a thicket of upright stems bearing at the top tiny flowers in dense, branched spikes. As it flowers in September it is a useful plant for associating with *Agastache foeniculum*, Japanese Anemones and grey-foliaged plants.

EOMECON, Papaveraceae.

chionanthum

    46 × 46 cm   *[7–9]*   *White*   *Spring*   P   DR
    18 × 18 in

E. China. Poppy of the Dawn. A rare relative of the Bloodroot (*Sanguinaria canadensis*), with orange-red sap. It is a beautiful glabrous plant, with large rounded leaves and nodding, white, crystalline flowers with yellow stamens. For cool, moist soil in shady positions; the running rootstock can be a nuisance, thus it should be grown under the large shrubs, as at Nymans, Sussex. Plant 7.5 cm (3 in) deep.

EPILOBIUM, Onagraceae. Sun-loving plants for well-drained soils, whose spires of blooms, enhanced by richly tinted calyces, give long display and are followed by fluffy seeds. These species, excluding *E. canum*, are sometimes assigned to the genus *Chamaenerion*.

angustifolium

    1.5 m × 60 cm   *[3–7]*   *Pink*   *L.Summer*   DS
    5 × 2 ft

Northern Hemisphere, Britain. French or Rose-bay Willow Herb. A plant of marvellous beauty but of impossibly invasive habit for the garden, however glorious it may be on waste ground. Narrow dark green leaves and tall spires of beautiful blooms. The pale pink form 'Isobel', enhanced by crimson calyces, is sometimes grown but is invasive. Some white forms, *E.a.* 'Album', are less invasive; they have green calyces usually.

canum

    46 × 46 cm   *[8–10]*   *Scarlet*   *L.Summer/*   C
    18 × 18 in   *E.Autumn*

S. and W. United States. 1847. Californian Fuchsia. *Zauschneria cana, Z. californica microphylla*. The various kinds are usually grown on the rock garden for the sake of better drainage; they need full sun and are reliable perennials in our warmer counties when once established. All of them have beautiful, scarlet, trumpet-shaped flowers carried in slender erect sprays well above the foliage. In the type species the leaves are very narrow and of a marked silvery grey, in striking contrast to the flowers.

—**angustifolium** (*Zauschneria californica*) has dark green leaves. Two variants have appeared: one was grown in Lady Moore's garden in Ireland and is known as 'Dublin' (or, incorrectly, as 'Glasnevin') and has extra good flowers of blazing colour. The other, 'Solidarity Pink', has flowers of clear pink, *c.* 1985. It was found by Daniel Campbell in Oregon Creek, USA, in 1980. There is also a good white, 'Alba'.

—mexicanum (*Zauschneria mexicana*) is short, bushy with light green leaves, but is not free flowering.

dodonaei

75 × 60 cm	*[3–7]*	*Mauve-pink*	*Summer*	DS
2½ × 2 ft				

Central France to W. Russia. 1800. *E. rosmarinifolium, Chamaenerion angustissimum*. When in full flower this is a beautiful plant in subdued colours. Greyish narrow leaves and long spires of small flowers with purplish calyces.

fleischeri

30 × 30 cm	*[4–7]*	*Mauve-pink*	*Summer*	DS
1 × 1 ft				

S. Europe, Britain. Confused with *E. dodonaei*, but it is smaller with very narrow small greyish leaves and small rosy blooms. Forms a graceful small clump.

latifolium

46 × 46 cm	*[2–6]*	*Pink*	*Summer*	DS
18 × 18 in				

Northern Hemisphere. The beautifully glaucous foliage is just the right tint for contrasting with the large rose-pink flowers with their crimson calyces. This grows well in the cooler north and is the most garden-worthy species, but its roots wander.

EPIMEDIUM, Berberidaceae. As ground-cover plants these are fully treated in my *Plants for Ground-Cover*; here we will consider them as ornamental plants, though only a few are tall enough for inclusion in these pages. I have accordingly omitted the very small *E. × youngianum* and its varieties. They will grow and slowly increase in shade or sun, in any reasonable soil, preferring a cool shady position. The value of their leaves—so prettily tinted in spring in *E. × versicolor, E. × rubrum* and *E. grandiflorum*—cannot be stressed too highly. Those of *E. perralderianum* are truly evergreen and of great beauty all the year; all the others exhibit pretty tints at some time in the autumn or winter. The flowers are borne in spring on wiry stems, each stem supporting an airy flight of tiny blooms variously coloured; some are like miniature columbines. It is a good plan to trim off all the foliage in winter (except of *E. perralderianum* and its hybrid) so that the flowers can more readily be enjoyed. The plants are perfectly hardy—though the flowers can be damaged by spring frosts—and the pretty, long-stalked leaves, divided into several sections, are ideal for cutting.

> "Delightful at all times for many of them are evergreen, their spring leaf tints which follow the flowers are delicious, and in autumn they fall into tone with the season with rich tints of brown, russet and gold."—ATJ

acuminatum

46 × 46 cm	*[5–9]*	*Various*	*L.Spring*	DS
18 × 18 in				

Western China. 1886. Although known for so many years, this highly desirable species has only recently appeared in gardens. The somewhat leathery, even prickly leaves have three narrow lobes and in late summer can be distinguished by the short bristles which develop on the undersides of the leaves—as in *E. sagittatum*. The only form I have seen has beautiful flowers of chocolate and cream, but yellow and pink forms have been recorded. Elegant and distinct. Semi-evergreen.

grandiflorum ●

30 × 30 cm	*[5–8]*	*Crimson*	*E.Spring*	D
1 × 1 ft				

Japan, Manchuria. 1830. 'Rose Queen' is the loveliest form of this species, also known as *E. macranthum* 'Rose Queen'. Deep pink or light crimson, extra large flowers with long, white-tipped spurs, held above the small leaves. 'White Queen' is a good counterpart; 'Violaceum' is a sulky dark lilac.

× **perralchicum** ★

46 × 30 cm	*[5–9]*	*Yellow*	*E.Spring*	D
18 in × 1 ft				

Hybrid. A handsome hybrid raised at Wisley, Surrey, between *E. perralderianum* and *E. pinnatum colchicum*; good evergreen leaves resembling those of *E. perralderianum*, with the large yellow flowers of *E. pinnatum colchicum*. Evergreen.

perralderianum ★

30 × 46 cm	*[5–9]*	*Yellow*	*E.Spring*	D
1 ft × 18 in				

Algeria. 1867. Large, glossy, toothed leaves. Bright yellow flowers with insignificant spurs. This is the most handsome species; the shining array of fresh green would be an asset to any garden, even without the flowers. Evergreen.

pinnatum colchicum

30 × 38 cm	*[5–9]*	*Yellow*	*E.Spring*	D
1 ft × 15 in				

Transcaucasia, Georgia. *c.* 1840. *E. colchicum*. Almost evergreen, turning to bright tints in autumn and winter. Wide yellow flowers, no spurs.

pubigerum

46 × 46 cm	*[5–9]*	*Creamy*	*E.Spring*	D
18 × 18 in				

Asia Minor, S.E. Europe, 1887. The least ornamental in flower, though the tiny creamy white or pink flowers are borne in tall elegant sprays. The usual excellent foliage, smooth and green. Evergreen.

× **rubrum**

23 × 23 cm	*[4–9]*	*Crimson*	*E.Spring*	D
9 × 9 in				

c. 1854. *E. grandiflorum × E. alpinum*. An extremely pretty hybrid with small crimson flowers, white spurs and compact growth. Foliage beautifully tinted while young, turning to pale green, over which hover the flowers.

× **versicolor**

30 × 30 cm	*[5–9]*	*Various*	*E.Spring*	D
1 × 1 ft				

1854. *E. grandiflorum × E. pinnatum colchicum*. Several very dainty clones have been separately named. 'Sulphureum' and 'Neo-sulphureum' are pale yellow, the first with up to nine leaflets, the latter up to five. 'Versicolor' has inner sepals pink-tinted and 'Cupreum' is more coppery. They make a charming quartet with beautiful tinting of the young leaves, and again in autumn. As might be expected the yellow forms are the more vigorous.

× warleyense
  30 × 30 cm   *[5–9]* *Orange*   *E.Spring*   D
  1 × 1 ft

1909. A hybrid, probably *E. alpinum × E. pinnatum colchicum*, raised in Miss Willmott's garden. It does not make such a dense mass as the other kinds but its flowers bring a new tone: they are orange. Light green leaves.

EPIPACTIS, Orchidaceae. Helleborine. Of subdued charm, but easy to grow in any reasonably drained, open soil with humus in part shade. The roots are rhizomes creeping very slowly and should be planted only 2.5 cm. (1 in) or so below soil level. They appreciate neutral or limy soils. They all have fine basal leaves, diminishing in size up the stems, which bear many small flowers, greenish brown in *E. gigantea* from N. America, and purplish in the Europeans *E. helleborine* (*E. latifolia*) and the paler *E. palustris*. Both of these are natives of Britain and the latter appreciates a moist position. *E. atrorubens* is still darker in tint but they all vary somewhat and are variations on the same theme, achieving 30–60 cm (1–2 ft) in good conditions. [4–8]. June–July. Some species thrive at Benthall Hall, Shropshire, and Lyme Park, Cheshire. *E.Summer* D

EREMOSTACHYS, Labiatae. Sun-loving plants for drained soil, which die down to a sort of bud for the winter.

laciniata
  1.2 m × 60 cm *[6–8]* *Creamy* *E.Summer*   PF S
  4 × 2 ft

Levant. 1731. Stout stems arise from the deeply divided basal leaves, and terminate in a spike of woolly buds. It is then full of promise, but the creamy brown sage-like flowers are a disappointment. *E. superba* is similar, and there are other species.

EREMURUS, Liliaceae. Foxtail Lilies. Without doubt these are some of the most magnificent of all perennials and among the tallest. All species and hybrids bear a strong resemblance to each other; all make rather lax clumps of strap-shaped, folded, bent leaves which die away in summer, and produce straight stems thickly set along their upper parts with small starry lily-flowers with long stamens, the whole making a striking column of blossom, followed by small pods of seeds. They need well-drained soil and full sun and succeed in our warmer and drier countries. As they increase the crowns tend to grow out of the ground, and they may be lifted as soon as the leaves have died away in summer and until early autumn. Large forks are needed for the biggest species; the fleshy roots radiate from the crown like the spokes of a wheel; the crowns can be gently prized apart, each with its own roots. When planting, set the crown just below the surface of the ground, enveloping it with sand, and see that the roots are laid horizontally around. It is advisable to put a stout peg just behind each crown so that one does not pierce the roots subsequently when putting in supports, which the taller kinds usually need. As some of the roots may take up a square yard of ground, and the leaves die away so early, it is a good plan to put behind them a plant which will flop forward and fill the gap in August, such as *Gypsophila paniculata* or *Clematis heracleifolia*.

159

elwesii

1.8 m × 90 cm   *[5–8]*   *White/Pink*   *E.Summer*   PF   DS
6 × 3 ft

Hybrid? 1884. *E. elwesianus*; *E. himalaicus* or *E. robustus elwesii*; *E. aitchisonii*. Of scintillating beauty, whether of white or pink. Its origin is obscure, and it may well be a hybrid between *E. himalaicus* and *E. robustus*, or a variety of one or the other. In those of richer colouring the flowers have a dark pink keel, giving an overall clear salmon tint. The centres are green. The leaf-margins are smooth, and they remain green until after flowering. A white form is called 'Albus'.

himalaicus

30 × 90 cm   *[5–8]*   *White*   *E.Summer*   PF   DS
1 × 3 ft

Himalaya. 1881. Usually the first to flower, with immense, cylindrical spikes of flower. Pure white.

olgae

2.1 m × 90 cm   *[6–8]*   *Pink*   *Summer*   PF   DS
7 × 3 ft

S.W. Asia. 1881. *E. angustifolius*. The flowers are usually pink, but white forms occur. It is variable in height, and as a rule even the shorter spikes need support. It flowers late in the *Eremurus* season.

robustus ●★

2.4 m × 90 cm   *[5–8]*   *Pink*   *Summer*   PF   DS
8 × 3 ft

Turkestan. 1874. *E. elwesianus grandis* (of gardens). The leaves are long and broad with rough margins and have usually shrivelled by flowering time. The numerous flowers often cover 1.2 m (4 ft) of the stem, and are of clear pink, with a brownish blotch at the base and a green keel. They last several weeks in bloom and the annual display is arresting. An even more vigorous form, much later-flowering, used to be grown as *E.r. tardiflorus*, named by Elwes; Sir Frederick Stern recorded growth up to 3 m (10 ft).

spectabilis

1.2 m × 60 cm   *[7–9]*   *Yellow*   *E.Summer*   PF   DS
4 × 2 ft

Asia Minor, etc. 1800. *E. tauricus, E. caucasicus, E. altaicus*. Rare species, seldom seen. A good sulphur yellow in its best forms, flowering before *E. stenophyllus*.

stenophyllus ★

1.5 m × 60 cm   *[6–9]*   *Yellow*   *Summer*   PF   DS
5 × 2 ft

S.W. Asia, etc. 1885. The slender spikes are well set with clear yellow flowers which fade to orange-brown, giving a lovely two-toned effect. *E. bungei* (of gardens) appears to be a form of this. The subspecies *E.s. aurantiacus* is close to the species. Many other species are recorded and it remains to be seen how they will compare with the established favourites.

★ HYBRIDS

Many good hybrids other than *E. elwesii* (if indeed it is a hybrid) were raised by W. E. Gumbleton in Ireland, Sir Michael Foster, Great Shelford, Cambridge, H. J. Elwes and Sir Frederick Stern. The Shelford Hybrids [6–9] were reputedly *E. olgae × E. bungei*, and are highly desirable garden plants and, like *E. stenophyllus*, are of a reasonable stature. Later Sir Frederick's 'Highdown' varieties carried on in the same style, bearing the same mark of quality and rich colours; they throve in the sharply drained chalky ground in his Sussex garden. Botanically many of these hybrids should be classed as *E. × isabellinus* [6–9], but since many may well have been influenced by bees, only controlled hybrids between *E. stenophyllus* and *E. olgae* should bear this group name. *E. warei* is another name for this hybrid. 'Himrob' (*E. robustus superbus*) [5–8] is a splendid pink hybrid of note, reputedly *E. himalaicus × E. robustus*; it is late-flowering. The pale yellow *E. × tubergenii* [6–9] is *E. himalaicus × E. stenophyllus* and has characters of both parents. They all flower freely when suited and inter-hybridize regularly. Flowering as they do, one and all, with the early and maincrop of Bearded Irises, and liking the same conditions, it is easy to make a glorious contrast of colours and shapes. No foil is so beautiful as the grey-white buds of *Senecio laxifolius*, or the flowers of *Nepeta × faassenii*.

"The spikes of early Eremuruses are now covered with seed pods like minute Greengages ... but the yellow foxes' brushes of *E. bungei* are beginning to light up from below."—EAB

ERIGERON, Compositae. Sun-loving daisy flowers for the open garden, in any fertile reasonably drained soil. They are successful in maritime districts, particularly *E. glaucus*, which will grow well within reach of sea spray.

glaucus

30 × 46 cm	*[5–8]*	*Mauve*	*E. to L.*	P	W	DS
1 ft × 18 in			*Summer*			

W. North America. 1812. This has settled down almost as a native on some southern maritime cliffs, making dense clumps of clammy, greyish green leaves on which for months appear the short-rayed daisies, usually of pale mauve, or darker, with large yellow centres. 'Elstead Pink', raised by Ernest Ladhams, has clear lilac-pink flowers. Successful in our warmest counties. Evergreen.

macranthus

60 × 60 cm	*[4–8]*	*Purple*	*Summer*	P	DS
2 × 2 ft					

Rocky Mountains. *E. mesa-grande* (of gardens). It makes a mat of narrow hairy leaves above which the stems are prolifically produced, each bearing several violet-blue daisies with numerous very narrow rays; centre orange-yellow. An old garden favourite. Excellent for cutting.

multiradiatus

30 × 30 cm	*[5–8]*	*Lilac*	*L.Summer*	P	DS
1 × 1 ft					

Himalaya. Prior to 1830. This excellent clump-former has long been neglected. The prolific display of flowers is accentuated by the multitudes of narrow rayflorets, creating a mass of colour.

philadelphicus

60 × 30 cm	*[4–8]*	*Lilac*	*Summer*	P	DS
2 × 1 ft					

North America. 1778. A meek plant whose erect stems, clad in hairy clasping leaves, just get the few flower heads up high enough to be noticed: small daisies of rosy lilac. A prolific seeder.

speciosus

60 × 60 cm	*[2–8]*	*Lilac*	*Summer*	P	DS
2 × 2 ft					

W. North America. Again an easily grown hardy dense clump with numerous stems, and flowers of cool pale lilac. A form *E.s.* 'Superbus' was often grown.

HYBRIDS ★

[5–8]	*Various*	*Summer*	P	D

The above species are seldom planted today, but their progeny are numbered among the most popular, prolific and easy of hardy perennials. Like *Anthemis*, they usually need some support such as short twiggy branches placed around them. 'Quakeress' was for many years the most popular of all, with well-formed flowers of a delicate and useful pale lilac-pink; with 'White Quakeress' it charmed us all. Selection and breeding—bringing in orange buds from *E. aurantiacus* in the old 'B. Ladhams', and dwarf habit from *E. glaucus* through 'Elstead Variety'—have resulted in a considerable range of tints and heights and seasons. Alan Bloom has several good ones of pink tint, such as 'Charity'. 'Foerster's Liebling' is another excellent pink, semi-double, of Continental origin. Bloom has also named the purple 'Darkest of All' and 'Prosperity' to take the place of *E. macranthus*, while 'Dimity' is one of his very dwarf pinks, with orange-tinted buds. But it is best to select your heights, colours and seasons from a reliable list or a visit to a grower—there are many varieties to choose from.

ERIOPHYLLUM, Compositae. A sun-loving plant for well-drained soil, sunny banks, rock gardens and border fronts. Wandering roots. Plant in spring.

lanatum

30 × 30 cm	*[5–8]*	*Yellow*	*Summer*	DS
1 × 1 ft				

North America. *E. caespitosum, Bahia lanata.* The combination of yellow daisies over silvery, divided leaves is not uncommon. A useful and gay plant, very free-flowering for many weeks.

ERODIUM, Geraniaceae. The Heron's Bills are mostly rock plants but the second is a good, tufty plant for the foreground. It prefers full sun in any reasonably drained fertile soil.

carvifolium

50 × 60 cm	*[6–8]*	*Purple*	*Summer*	S
20 in × 2 ft				

Central Spain. This is similar to the better known *E. manescavii*, and a more attractive plant. Leaves of carrot-like featheriness, almost glabrous, and a long succession of rich magenta-purplish flowers with maroon blotch. It needs good drainage and full sun.

manescavii

50 × 60 cm	*[6–8]*	*Pink*	*Summer*	S
20 in × 2 ft				

Pyrenees. The dense foliage clump is composed of much divided, feathery, hairy leaves; over them, held on straight stalks, are the clusters of rich deep lilac-pink flowers, five-petalled, with a deeper blotch on the upper two. It flowers for several months, starting in June. It seeds itself mildly and a good form should be selected.

ERYNGIUM, Umbelliferae. Sea Holly. Their long-lasting prickly flower-heads are most useful for winter drying. In every species the terminal flower on the stem opens first, being succeeded by the terminal flower on each of the side branches; since they each last a long time in flower, the whole branching stem is eventually covered with mature flowers. They thrive in open, sunny gardens in any well-drained, fertile soil, putting up with excessive lime, gravel, and poor soils remarkably well. Many of the American species contribute to a botanical tangle of great difficulty, and until the Floras of the different countries are revised and compared we cannot be certain of nomenclature. I have, however, attempted to solve the puzzle. The American species have evergreen, long narrow leaves, as opposed to the rounded or lobed Europeans.

agavifolium

1.5 m × 60 cm	*[9–10]*	*Green*	*L.Summer*	PF	DS
5 × 2 ft					

Argentine. A statuesque plant forming a loose rosette of broad, sword-like, rich green leaves about 46 cm (18 in) high. They are sharply toothed, likewise the few stem leaves which occur below each flower branch. The flower-heads are bulky, without pronounced calyces, like big green thimbles on short stalks. An arresting but rather coarse plant, closely related to *E. serra, q.v.* Evergreen.

alpinum ● ★

75 × 46 cm	*[5–8]*	*Blue*	*Summer*	PF	DRS
2½ ft × 18 in					

Europe. 1597. The largest in flower of the Sea Hollies. Good, rounded basal foliage and stout blue stems each with several great blue cones surrounded by the typical prickly blue calyx-frills. *E. spinalbum* is a similar European with deeply five-parted leaves. See also under *E × oliverianum.*

"... when well grown is not surpassed in beauty by any plant."—WR

amethystinum

60 × 60 cm	*[3–8]*	*Blue*	*Summer*	PF	DRS
2 × 2 ft					

Europe. 1648. It is like chasing a will o' the wisp to find the true plant as there are so many hybrids about, *E. tripartitum* (of gardens) probably being one of them. It is on the same scale as *E. tripartitum* and *E. planum* (though shorter than the latter); leaves pinnatisect and stalks winged. The small blue flowers are no improvement on those of *E. tripartitum.*

bourgatii ● ★

60 × 30 cm	*[5–9]*	*Green*	*Summer*	PF	DRS
2 × 1 ft					

Pyrenees. 1731. Deeply cut foliage at the base, crisp-curly, grey-green with white veins, and wiry stems branching into several medium-sized blue-green thistle flowers, like a more compact and grey-green version of the well-known *E. tripartitum* (of gardens). A beautiful plant at all times.

bromeliifolium

90 × 60 cm *3 × 2 ft*	*[9–10]*	*White*	*Summer*	PF	DS

South America. The graceful plant usually grown under this name is *E. eburneum, q.v. E. bromeliifolium* is a synonym of *E. monocephalum*, which is a stiff plant with white flower-heads. Evergreen.

campestre

60 × 46 cm *2 ft × 18 in*	*[5–8]*	*Greeny-blue*	*Summer*	PF	DRS

Europe, Britain. A very prickly plant for the collector. It has small flowers in branching heads borne on stems with green flanges. The glaucous green leaves are so dissected that they are little more than white veins with grey-green flanges.

decaisneana

2.4 × 1.2 m *8 × 4 ft*	*[9–10]*	*Purplish*	*Autumn*	PF W	DS

Uruguay, Argentina, etc. *E. pandanifolium.* An astonishing plant whose graceful rapier-like leaves with spiny edges are 1.2–1.8 m (4–6 ft) high and about 2.5 cm (1 in) wide, light green, creating an elegant effect. The stout, smooth green stems with their greyish sheathing leaves develop into a huge head of multitudes of tiny chocolate-purple flower-heads the size of peas. It likes moist soil and is only suitable for our warmer counties. Evergreen. *E. lassauxii,* closely related, is recorded to have pale green flowers.

eburneum ★

1.5 m × 60 cm *5 × 2 ft*	*[9–10]*	*Green*	*L.Summer*	PF	DS

Colombia, Argentina, etc. *E. paniculatum, E. balansae.* Probably the commonest of the S. American species in our gardens, and found under a variety of labels. I have grown it for many years as *E. bromeliifolium.* It provides good ground-covering clumps of 30–60 cm (1–2 ft) arching, grassy leaves, armed with numerous thin spines. The pale green stems have similar but shorter leaves; they gracefully arch and have several branches near the top; the flowers are green with white stamens. It is a beautiful, graceful plant, and quite hardy. Evergreen.

floribundum

1.2 m × 46 cm *4 ft × 18 in*	*[5–8]*	*Green*	*Summer*	PF	DS

1826. Very broad, doubly serrate basal leaves. Many small heads of flowers.

horridum

1.2 m × 46 cm *4 ft × 18 in*	*[5–8]*	*Green*	*Summer*	PF	DS

E. schwackeanum. Leaves serrate, similar to those of *E. floribundum.* The stem does not branch much; the flowers are of good size.

164

maritimum

30 × 30 cm	[5–8]	Pale blue	Summer	PF DRS
1 × 1 ft				

Europe, Britain. Sea Holly. It is strange that this beautiful native is not more often grown. The flowers are blue, while the calyces and glaucous leaves, lobed and spiny, are among the greyest things in the garden. It prefers hot, dry, sandy or gravelly soil.

"The wild Sea-holly of our coasts, with leaves almost blue, and a handsome tuft of flower nearly matching them in colour."—GJ

× oliverianum

60 × 46 cm	[5–8]	Blue	Summer	PF DR
2 ft × 18 in				

1731. A hybrid believed to have originated from seed of *E. alpinum*, collected in the wild, but variously attributed to *E. giganteum* or *E. planum*. *E. alpinum* and *E. × oliverianum*, and the hybrids mentioned under *E. × zabelii*, form the cream of the large-flowered garden kinds with good blue flowers.

"The stems are so singularly beautiful with their vivid steel-blue tints ... with the involucre even more brilliant, that the effect is hardly excelled."—WR

planum

90 × 46 cm	[5–9]	Blue	Summer	PF DRS
3 ft × 18 in				

E. Europe. 1596. More valuable for cutting than for its garden effect. Good basal leaves and erect stems resulting in an erect sheaf of small light blue flower-heads with blue-green spiky bracts. Inferior as a garden plant to *E. tripartitum*. 'Blue Dwarf' is a short-growing form. 'Blue Ribbon' is a richly coloured hybrid. 'Calypso' has beautiful creamy-white edges to the leaves.

proteiflorum

90 × 60 cm	[9–10]	Grey	Summer	PF DS
3 × 2 ft				

Mexico. The botanical authority for this name is Delaroux, and under this it may sometimes be found in seed lists. It is in the same class as the South American species, with its long, narrow, pointed leaves with distinct white midrib, armed with long sometimes tripartite prickles. When well grown in a warm position in fertile soil it is a remarkable plant, the big head of flowers being enclosed in many rather forward-pointing, leafy bracts, the whole a steely white tint. Ideal for drying. Evergreen. *E. involucratum* [9–10] is smaller.

serra

1.2 m × 46 cm	[9–10]	Green	L.Summer	PF DS
4 ft × 18 in				

Brazil. 1872. Bears a close resemblance to *E. agavifolium* but the broad, long leaves are doubly serrate. The bracts are small. The flower-heads are small, carried in often dense array. Less striking than *E. agavifolium*. Evergreen.

tripartitum ★
of gardens

75 × 60 cm	[5–8]	Blue	Summer	PF DR
2½ × 2 ft				

Probably a hybrid. Wiry stems arise from a good basal rosette of leaves, producing many widespread branches, each ending in a blue head with dark blue spiky bracts. An extremely effective garden plant, achieving best colour in full sun. Superb when grown behind *Crambe maritima*.

variifolium

46 × 25 cm	*[5–9]*	*Green*	*L.Summer*	PF	DRS
18 × 10 in					

Morocco. Beautiful, evergreen, small rounded leaves form a handsome rosette; they are toothed and spiny with conspicuous white veins. The flowers are not striking; they are grey-blue with wide, white spiny collars, carried stiffly aloft on erect stems. Sometimes considered a form of *E. dichotomum*. Evergreen.

yuccifolium

1.2 m × 60 cm	*[4–8]*	*Green*	*L.Summer*	PF	DS
4 × 2 ft					

North America. 1699. Long, rather limp, blue-grey leaves, narrow like those of the other Americans, 60–90 cm (2–3 ft) high, with finely spiny margins. Tiny bracts. The few small heads of bloom at the top of the stems are white and attractive, but not spectacular. Evergreen.

× zabelii ● ★

60–75 × 46 cm	*[5–8]*	*Blue*	*L.Summer*	PF	DR
2–2½ ft × 18 in					

Many of the best garden eryngiums are hybrids, though it is not certain always which species are involved. This name covers hybrids between *E. alpinum* and *E. bourgatii*, but for the sake of convenience we can group under it such beautiful large blue-flowered plants as 'Jewel' (1913), 'James Ivory', 'Donard Variety' and 'Violetta' (1913). They are all highly desirable, with exquisitely fashioned piccadills. Beautiful with *Hemerocallis* hybrids of lemon-yellow colouring.

ERYTHRINA, Leguminosae.

crista-galli ●

1.2 m × 60 cm	*[9–10]*	*Red*	*Summer/*	W	CS
4 × 2 ft			*Autumn*		

Brazil. 1771. One would not expect the Coral Tree to be hardy but with protection in winter, against a hot sunny wall in our warmest counties, it can be a spectacular success. Leafy plants throw up great sprays of large dark coral-red pea flowers, late in the summer. The large outer petal is held below the rolled inner petals, giving each flower the appearance of an arum. A form known as 'Compacta' is reported to flower more freely than the type. A success at Sissinghurst Castle, Kent, and at Oxford.

EUCOMIS, Liliaceae. Bulbous plants only suitable for a sunny, cosy corner in our warmer counties. Their soil requirements are not special. Plant 12.5 cm (5 in) or so deep and divide when necessary in spring. They flower in three or four years from seed. Though the long, lax leaves lie around rather untidily, they attract much attention when in flower, each great spike of densely packed stars being surmounted by an astonishing pineapple-like tuft of leaves at the apex. They are of equal beauty when the seed capsules are ripening; these are purplish-maroon and show up well against the pale flower segments, which last long.

"... tall cylindrical spikes of blossoms surmounted by a crown of leaves."

—WR

bicolor

| 46 × 30 cm | [8–10] | Greenish | L.Summer | PF | W | DS |

18 in × 1 ft

Natal. 1878. Substantial spikes densely packed with nodding starry pale green flowers; they are edged with maroon and overtopped by a big pale green rosette of bracts, strongly contrasting with the broad dark green leaves. Brown-spotted stem. There is a form *E.b.* 'Alba' whose flowers lack the maroon margins.

pole-evansii ●

| 1.5 m × 30 cm | [8–10] | Green | Summer | P | W | DS |

5 × 1 ft

Transvaal. Far finer—sometimes exceeding 1.5 m (5 ft)—but more tender; it will only thrive against warm walls in our warmest counties. The leaves, 15 cm (6 in) wide, have wavy edges and the spikes of wide-open pale greenish flowers with their pineapple tops, 25 cm (10 in) across, are astonishing. The true plant is rare, and the garden examples I have seen are possibly *E. pallidiflora*; in this the leaves are broad and long, the flowers are borne rather upright on the spikes, but it is more of the size of *E. punctata*, with short apical bracts.

punctata ● ★

| 75 × 30 cm | [8–10] | Greenish | L.Summer | PF | W | DS |

2½ × 1 ft

South Africa. 1783. *E. comosa*. The flowers are held outwards; pale creamy green to pale creamy lilac when fully open, at which time their violet centres and anthers are conspicuous. Elegant elongated spikes, with flowers separately disposed, crowned with a small green tuft of bracts at the apex. Leaves long, limp and narrower than those of *E. bicolor*. In *E.p striata* the spotting on the leaves develops into stripes; there are also forms with coppery purple leaves. A success at Overbecks, Devon. Some forms or hybrids of astonishing colouring, pink and red included, have been bred in New Zealand.

zambesiaca

| 46 × 46 cm | [8–10] | Green | | W | DS |

18 × 18 in

E. Africa. 1886. The leaves are large and long. The starry, palest green flowers are carried in a dense spike. Though from so warm a provenance it appears to be hardy. Plant 6 in deep.

EUPATORIUM, Compositae. Easily grown plants.

ageratoides

| 90 × 46 cm | [4–9] | White | E.Autumn | P | D |

3 ft × 18 in

North America. 1640. White Snakeroot. A very useful late-flowering plant producing stiff stems set with opposite green nettle-like leaves and flat heads of fuzzy white flowers which last a long time. Ordinary soil; can be grown in shade. Also known as *E. urticifolium*. A similar plant sometimes seen is *E. rugosum*, 1.5 m (5 ft).

cannabinum

| 1.2 m × 60 cm | [3–9] | Purplish | Summer | D |

4 × 2 ft

Asia, Europe. The Hemp Agrimony is a weed in Britain. The double-flowered form, 'Plenum', is sometimes grown for its soft *bois du rose* colouring, and it does not seed itself.

purpureum

1.8–2.4 m ×	*[3–9]*	*Purplish*	*E.Autumn*	D
90 cm				
6–8 × 3 ft				

North America. 1640. Joe Pye Weed. One of the most imposing of herbaceous plants. Pointed leaves in whorls punctuate the purplish stems, which bear at their apex wide, flat heads of fuzzy purplish rose flowers on dark purple stalks. It can be a striking plant in rich soil, but is only in scale at the back of a very wide border; it will outshine most flowers in September and October, and is a superb companion for the Hybrid Musk rose 'Vanity' and *Hydrangea paniculata* 'Grandiflora'. There is a white form and 'Atropurpureum' of rich colour.

EUPHORBIA, Euphorbiaceae. Spurge or Milkweed; the stems exude a milky juice when cut, which can injure the skin on hot days. These are most accommodating plants and are happy in any reasonably drained fertile soil, and all thrive in full sun or can be grown in part shade. They all bear a strong family likeness: the narrow leaves crowd the stems to where the flowers begin. The flowers themselves are insignificant but are surrounded by conspicuous, usually yellowish bracts, which last for weeks in beauty. Often called Euphorias or Euphobias by those striving to impress with their Latin names.

"... the floures are yellowish, and grow out of little dishes or Saucers."— GH

altissima

1.8 m × 60 cm	*[9–10]*	*Green*	*L.Summer*	P DS
6 × 2 ft				

Middle East. A greyish leafy plant with branching heads of dark greenish yellow flowers in a tall raceme after most others are over. *E. orientalis* is similar, but shorter.

amygdaloides

30 × 30 cm	*[7–9]*	*Yellowish*	*Spring*	DS
1 × 1 ft				

Britain, Europe, S.W. Asia. The Wood Spurge is a poor relative of *E. robbiae*, but has the merit of giving rise to two horticultural forms of unusual quality, that is 'Rubra' ('Purpurea'), whose leaves and stems are purplish-mahogany contrasting well with the yellowish flower-heads, and 'Variegata', whose leaves are cream-margined and the "collar" around the flowers is almost wholly cream. I have not found the latter such a good garden plant as might be expected. Spreading roots. Also see *E. robbiae*.

characias ★

1.2 m × 90 cm	*[7–10]*	*Green*	*E.Spring*	PF S
4 × 3 ft				

W. Mediterranean. Handsome winter foliage. While a great range of types of this species and its relatives may be found in the wild, in gardens the plant has rather narrow spikes of green flowers with dark brown centres. The subspecies *E.c. wulfenii* has broader spikes with yellowish green flowers with yellowish centres.

● ★ 'Lambrook Gold', selected by Margery Fish, 'John Tomlinson' and *E. sibthorpii* are fine yellowish types. All of them make imposing clumps of erect stems clothed in their first year with a bottle-brush array of narrow grey-green leaves, which become surmounted by the flower-heads the following spring, after which each stem dies to the base. They will thrive in sun or shade. There is a form, 'Variegata', with creamy leaf-edges. × *martinii* [7–9] is a hybrid between *E. characias* and *E. amygdaloides*. The green flowers with dark eyes may recommend it. Compact growth.

'Burrow's Silver' is the name of a very pleasing form with creamy edges to the leaves. This is likely to prove popular.

"... curious dull green heads of flowers with their conspicuous black spots ... and I like to call it a name I learnt [in Dublin] the Frog Spawn bush."— EAB

"Herbaceous plants of rather larger growth and with fine foliage in April and May are not many. The best ... are *Veratrum nigrum* ... and the newer *Euphorbia wulfenii*."—GJ

dulcis

30 × 30 cm	[4–9]	Yellowish	E.Summer	PF	DS
1 × 1 ft					

Europe. A small-growing species with small leaves and heads of greeny-yellow. Its chief attraction is that it develops rich autumn colouring. It seeds itself everywhere and can be a nuisance with its little tuberous root, but nothing like such a dangerous plant as the feathery *E. cyparissias*, which runs freely in the soil.

griffithii ●★

90 × 60 cm	[4–9]	Reddish	E.Summer	P	D
3 × 2 ft					

W. Asia. 1949. A select form, 'Fireglow', is usually grown; it has heads of vivid brick-red flowers over a mass of good foliage. The spreading roots enjoy good soil, in sun or partial shade. A striking plant, useful for "hot" colour schemes and with yellow azaleas. 'Dixter', selected by Christopher Lloyd from seedlings from Washfield Nursery. The orange flowers are accompanied by foliage of marked reddish colouring, lighter beneath.

hyberna

46 × 46 cm	[6–9]	Yellowish	Summer	P	DS
18 × 18 in					

W. Europe, Ireland. Irish Spurge. Seldom cultivated, but a handsome plant with broad dark green leaves. The usual heads of tiny flowers are held aloft as in *E. polychroma*, enhanced by yellow bracts.

longifolia

60 × 60 cm	[6–9]	Yellowish	L.Summer	P	DS
2 × 2 ft					

Himalaya. 1825. Useful and beautiful species in the class of *E. sikkimensis* and *E. schillingii* with good foliage; the leaves are in beauty throughout the growing season, with pinkish edges and white central vein. Conspicuous flowers. Thanks to A. D. Schilling for re-introduction.

myrsinites ●

15 × 30 cm	[5–8]	Yellowish	E.Summer	PF	S
6 in × 1 ft					

S. Europe. 1570. A strange plant producing during the summer foot-long trails clothed in glaucous grey leaves, which next spring have a head of greeny-yellow starry flowers in a collar of the same colour, turning pink as they fade. This is a "must" for the border front, and for sunny banks, dry walls, etc. Evergreen.

nicaeensis

60 × 46 cm	[5–8]	Yellow	Summer/	P	S
2 ft × 18 in			Autumn		

Mediterranean Region. This handsome plant, producing the usual "greenery-yallery" heads of flowers over a long period, is clad with copious, substantial greyish-green, fleshy leaves. A very close relative, with rather fewer rays, is *E. glareosa*.

palustris ★

90 × 90 cm	[5–8]	Yellow	L.Spring	P	DS
3 × 3 ft					

Europe. 1570. One of the most spectacular of spring-flowering plants. Great heads of brilliant gamboge yellow from the rounded bracts and waving plumes of greenery all summer, turning to yellow and orange in autumn. A much larger and later edition of *E. polychroma*. Superb with purple irises. A success at Nymans, Sussex.

pilosa

60 × 30 cm	[5–8]	Yellowish	Spring	P	DS
2 × 1 ft					

Europe, N. Asia. *E. villosa*. Comparing it with *E. palustris*, which is a more handsome plant, it has more pointed bracts and a less brilliant yellow tint in its flowers. 'Major' is a rather better type, resembling a stalwart *E. polychroma*.

polychroma ● ★

46 × 46 cm	[4–9]	Yellow	Spring	P	DS
18 × 18 in					

Europe. 1805. *E. epithymoides*. After the daffodils are over, bright yellow tinted with green is provided for many weeks by this clump-forming plant. It forms a rounded dome of stems with round, flat heads of greeny-yellow bracts setting off the inconspicuous flowers. Extra bright forms have been named.

rigida

46 × 46 cm	[7–10]	Yellow	E.Spring	P W	S
18 × 18 in					

Greece. 1808. *E. biglandulosa*. This superior plant may be likened to an erect-growing *E. myrsinites*. The pointed glaucous leaves are copiously set up the glaucous stems and are crowned by the usual vivid greenery-yallery starry heads, long-lasting and effective. For warm positions only. Evergreen.

robbiae ★

60 × 60 cm	[8–9]	Green	Spring	PF	D
2 × 2 ft					

Asia Minor. A useful evergreen ground-cover for shade, with spreading roots. Rosettes of darkest green on 23-cm (9-in) stems, above which stand the open spires of flat green flowers, 2.5 cm (1 in) across. Invaluable cover for shady places, even in poor, rooty soil.

schillingii ★ ●

90 × 60 cm	[7–9]	Yellowish	L.Summer	P	DS
3 × 2 ft					

Nepal, etc. *c.* 1977. A notable addition; the flowers have the size and impressiveness of *E. wallichii*, but the plant is stronger and increases more freely. A. D. Schilling has blessed our gardens with this plant.

seguierana

46 × 46 cm	[8–10]	Yellow	L.Spring/	P	S
18 × 18 in			L.Summer		

S.E. Europe. *E.s. niciciana* is a plant whose slender stems are well set with narrow glaucous leaves. As the large terminal heads of small sulphur-green flowers are produced for weeks on end it cannot fail to become popular. A good perennial, liking sunshine. It has settled down well in the heavy soil at Sissinghurst, Kent, and in my sand in Surrey.

sikkimensis

1.2 m × 46 cm	[6–9]	Yellowish	E.Summer	P	D
4 ft × 18 in					

E. Himalaya. The stems are like bright red glass in early spring, with tinted leaves, white-veined and beautiful later in their soft green. The flower-heads are compact, flat, greenish yellow with red bracts. A root-spreader. Prefers damp soil.

wallichii ●

46 × 30 cm	[6–9]	Yellow	E.Summer	P	DS
18 in × 1 ft					

Himalaya. Spurge-lovers should not miss this one, for its bracts are of large size, three circling each jade-tasselled flower, with further leafy bracts around, all of a splendid full-toned greeny yellow. The dark green leaves have purplish edges and white central vein. A plant of great quality, lasting in green beauty till autumn.

wulfenii or **E. veneta,** see under *E. characias.*

FASCICULARIA, Bromeliaceae. Stemless plants making a rosette of narrow prickly leaves, in the centre of which appear the flowers. They are hardy in our warmest counties, particularly in maritime districts, thriving in poor stony soil in sun or shade. Also known as *Rhodostachys.*

bicolor

46 × 60 cm	[10]	Blue	Summer/	W	DS
18 in × 2 ft			Autumn		

Chile. 1851. The small pale blue flowers are in a stemless cluster, and during the period in which they appear in bud and until they have faded away the base of the leaves turns to bright pink, making a zone of remarkable colour in the centre of the rosette. Grows well at Trengwainton, Cornwall, in retaining walls. Evergreen.

pitcairniifolia

46 cm × 1.5 m	[9–10]	Blue	Summer/	W	DS
18 in × 5 ft			Autumn		

Chile. 1866. The leaves are grey beneath and considerably longer than those of *F. bicolor,* which are brown beneath. The central blue flowers are surrounded by a brilliant red zone. Evergreen. It thrives at Wakehurst, Sussex.

FERULA, Umbelliferae. Fennel.

tingitana

2.1 m × 90 cm	*[7–9]*	*Yellow*	*Summer*	PF S
7 × 3 ft				

North Africa. 1680. The giant medicinal fennel is one of the most striking plants of the year. The leaves are finely dissected, like shining green lace, and every now and then a whole leaf will turn yellow. The mound of leaves, in good soil, may be 90 cm–1.2 m (3–4 ft) across and 60 cm (2 ft) high. After several years of gathering strength, a great glaucous stem will soar aloft, bearing heads of yellow cow-parsley flowers 30 cm (1 ft) or more across. Full sun, drained soil, into which its long tap-roots can descend; it does not recover well from transplanting except while quite young. *F. communis* [6–9] is similar.

FILIPENDULA, Rosaceae. These used to be called *Spiraea*. See also *Astilbe*. The Meadow Sweets all bear flat feathery heads of minute flowers. All like moist conditions except the first, and are not particular about soil.

hexapetala

60 × 46 cm	*[4–9]*	*White*	*Summer*	DR
2 ft × 18 in				

Europe, Asia. 1561. *F. vulgaris. Spiraea filipendula*. The Dropwort occurs on dry chalky uplands, usually, and thus is not a moisture-lover like other species. It has finely divided carrot-like foliage forming a mat. The stems branch into heads of bloom like the Meadow Sweet. 'Grandiflora' is a selected, larger form. I prefer the double form, 'Flore Pleno', but they suffer from mildew in some gardens.

palmata ★

1.2 m × 60 cm	*[3–9]*	*Pink*	*Summer*	D
4 × 2 ft				

Kamchatka. 1823. *Spiraea camtschatica, S. gigantea* (of gardens). The nomenclature is confusing because plants of *F. purpurea* have for many years been labelled *Spiraea palmata* in gardens, incorrectly. This plant usually flowers a fortnight later than *F. purpurea*, to which it is markedly similar, with handsome leaves and broad heads of lighter pink. 'Elegantissima' and 'Rosea' are named clones. It is also called *Spiraea digitata* and there is a pretty dwarf form, no more than 46 cm (18 in) high, 'Digitata Nana'. I used to have a distinctive purplish-leafed form of the last-named but lost it years ago and have not seen it since; it was, in those days, called *Spiraea digitata nana purpurea*.

purpurea ★

1.2 m × 60 cm	*[4–9]*	*Cerise*	*Summer*	D
4 × 2 ft				

Japan. 1765. *Spiraea palmata*. An extraordinarily handsome plant for moist borders or the waterside. Fine large leaves form big clumps from which arise leafy stems crowned by flat heads of hundreds of tiny, brilliant, cerise-crimson flowers. Partial shade and rich, deep soil suit it best. A superb companion to *Hosta sieboldiana* and *Rhododendron indicum* 'Crispiflorum', one of the latest flowering azaleas. For those who cannot stand cerise, 'Alba' is a good white form.

rubra

1.2–2.4 × 1.2 m	[3–9]	Pinkish	Summer	F	D
6–8 × 4 ft					

E. United States. 1765. *F. lobata, Ulmaria rubra*. The Queen of the Prairies can indeed queen it over any herbaceous plant of her season, and from her great height can look down on other filipendulas. It is a fairly rampageous spreader, forming large clumps in damp soil, in sun or part shade, and may be likened to a Meadow Sweet increased in size fourfold. The great jagged leaves grow up the stems to the huge flower-heads, 30 cm (1 ft) across. For many years the Old Garden at Hidcote, Gloucestershire, has been graced by this fine plant. 'Venusta' (1853) is usually considered the most pink of the many forms. It seldom needs staking, and is a grand plant for large boggy woodland gardens, adding lightness to the heavy greenery of rhododendrons. Also known as 'Magnifica'.

ulmaria

90 × 30 cm	[3–9]	White	Summer	D
3 × 1 ft				

Asia, Europe, Britain. **'Aurea'**. *Spiraea ulmaria aurea*. A form of Meadow Sweet or Queen of the Meadows. One of the most attractive of foliage plants in spring, producing its beautifully divided and veined leaves in a basal clump and also up the flowering stems. They are vivid golden green, in some lights pure yellow, becoming creamy yellow in summer where the sun strikes them. The flowers are insignificant; they should be removed before seeding, otherwise green-leafed seedlings will take over, being more vigorous. Deep, moist soil or bog; partial shade in hot districts. *F.u.* 'Variegata' has leaves striped with yellow and is a bizarre and inferior plant. *F.u.* 'Flore Pleno' might be desirable if it were not so prone to mildew—a fungus which will attack the species and all varieties if they become dry at the root or are ill nourished in any way.

"It groweth in the brinkes of waterie ditches and rivers sides, and also in meadowes.... it hath leaves ... on the upper side crumpled or wrinkled like unto those of the Elme tree; whereof it took the name Ulmaria."—GH

FOENICULUM, Umbelliferae. Sun, in any poor or good soil, well drained.

vulgare

1.8 m × 60 cm	[4–9]	Yellowish	Summer	PF	S
6 × 2 ft					

Europe. The common, fragrant green-leafed Fennel. The leaves are exceedingly finely divided, like hair, produced at every joint of the smooth, branching stems. The flowers are like yellowish-green cow-parsley, followed by green seeds which drop soon after turning yellow. It seeds itself very freely.

In *F.v. purpureum* the young foliage in sunny places is a deep purplish mahogany, an effective contrast to yellow buds. When the flowers appear in late summer the foliage is still bronzed. Both the species and this form sow themselves prolifically, and it is wise to remove the seed-heads.

FRANCOA, Saxifragaceae. Hairy-leafed plants something like an enlarged *Heuchera*, preferring full sun, on any good fertile soil.

sonchifolia

60–90 × 46 cm	[7–9]	White/Pink	Summer	P	DS
2–3 ft × 18 in					

Chile. 1830. Bridal Wreath. This is the main type-species, to which *F. ramosa, F. appendiculata, F. glabrata* and *F. rupestris* are closely allied. The long, erect, but gracefully leaning wands of small flowers may be white or deep pink, or between the two, and each petal is more or less spotted with red at the base. The stems are held well above the clump of deeply lobed dark green leaves. It does well at Overbecks, Devon, and also (grown in pots and wintered under cover) graces the pool at Tintinhull, Somerset. 'Bridal Wreath' is a good term since the flowers last long, resulting in the whole coronal being in beauty at once.

FRITILLARIA, Liliaceae. There are many smaller species of great charm and beauty, including our native Snake's Head Lily, *F. meleagris*, but I have selected just four species, three of them quite overpowered by the majesty of *F. imperialis*. These three require well-drained soil of good quality otherwise they are apt to dwindle.

imperialis ● ★

1.2 m × 46 cm	*[5–9]*	*Red/Yellow*	*Spring*	PF	DR
4 ft × 18 in					

W. Himalaya. Prior to 1590. The Crown Imperial, well known for many years, and a sound perennial, flowers freely in good soils—avoiding pure chalk, clay and bogs—in full sun. Its stout stems shoot up with great rapidity in early spring, clothed in a ruff of fresh green for their first 46 cm (18 in), then a bare, erect stalk from which the big bell-shaped flowers hang in a cluster at the top, surmounted by a tuft of green leaves. Depicted in many an old Dutch Flower Piece. Those with yellow bells are borne on green stems, while the red ones have purplish stems. Each bell has five "tear-drops" inside. I have never seen an ugly one, but there are specially good forms about, with fancy names such as 'Rubra Maxima', 'Aurora' and 'Orange Brilliant'. The plants and the bulbs give off a strong "foxy" odour but there is one, 'Inodora', which is reputedly free of this; there are also a rare double and a rare variegated-leafed form. They are easily increased by breaking off portions of the large bulb-scales, which root well in a frame. Old clumps, being congested, need thinning and replanting from time to time, and the moment for this is as soon as they have died down in summer, which is also the right moment for buying fresh bulbs. Plant with 15 cm (6 in) of soil over the bulbs. They are undoubtedly the most imposing and magnificent of spring flowers, and have been grown in our gardens since the sixteenth century. *F. raddeana* (*F. askhabadensis*) [5–8] is similarly beautiful, flowering even earlier; greenish yellow beautifully shaped bells. A form known as *F. eduardii* [5–8] has more open bells.

> "How that when Our Saviour entered the Garden of Gethsemane all the flowers bowed their heads save the Crown Imperial, which was too proud of its green crown and upright circle of milk-white blossoms to show humility ... when gently reproved by its Creator, it saw its error and bowed its head, flushing red with shame and has ever since ... carried tears in its eyes."—EAB

persica ●

90 × 30 cm	*[7–8]*	*Purple*	*Spring*	F DS
3 × 1 ft				

Persia. 1594. An erect leafy stem with a slender campanile of remarkable flowers, little hanging bells of deep livid colour outside, clouded with glaucous bloom, maroon within. *F. libanotica* is considered to be synonymous. It grows very early in the season and is liable to frost damage. A form 'Adiyaman' promises to be more reliable in cultivation.

"... little bels, of an overworn purple colour, hanging down their heads, every one having his own foot-stalke of two inches long, as also his pestell or clapper from the middle part of the floure ..."—GH

pyrenaica ●

46 × 23 cm	*[6–8]*	*Brownish*	*Spring*	P	DS
18 × 9 in					

Pyrenees. 1596. A few narrow leaves clothe the glaucous stems, which sport one or two maudlin purplish brown bells, variously spotted and tinted, and in contrast to the shining yellow or green inside. It usually settles down and seeds itself freely in well-drained but retentive soils in sun. *F. acmopetala* is of similar unusual beauty and may sometimes achieve 90 cm (3 ft).

verticillata ●

60 × 30 cm	*[6–8]*	*Green*	*E.Summer*	PF	DS
2 × 1 ft					

Central Asia to Japan. 1830. Apart from the beauty of the well-poised, wide, pale creamy green bells, slightly chequered within, this elegant species has upper leaves which curl in a prehensile way at the ends. It is a delicate symphony of pale colour accentuated by the glaucous tint of the leaves. This species seems to enjoy fairly moist soil with humus and part shade. The Japanese form *F.v. thunbergii* is most usually found in cultivation, with narrower bells. *F. roylei* [6–8], Himalaya, is similar, of more dusky colouring inside and lacks the tendril-like appendages to the leaves. *F. pallidiflora* [5–8] is of similar pale green and creamy colouring, but shorter and less elegant.

FUCHSIA, Onagraceae. Almost all the following fuchsias have proved hardy in Surrey but are usually cut to the ground by winter frosts. They are therefore here treated as herbaceous plants, and provide colour from July until the autumn frosts arrive. They thrive in any soil that is not too dry, and seem to flower equally well in sun or shade, but preferably not from overhanging trees. In the garden they are admirable for mixed planting with shrubs, herbaceous plants, and also with roses; their colours are predominantly purple and crimson and thus light foliage such as Jackman's Blue Rue, or white variegated hostas, show them to advantage. As they do not grow up from their woody bases until late spring, interplanting with spring bulbs is a good plan. In warmer coastal districts splendid hedges can be made with the stronger, hardier hybrids of *F. magellanica*, such as 'Riccartonii'. Though they root readily from quite short cuttings in a frame, some of the stronger growers can be divided in spring. Each flower is composed of four sepals, held more or less horizontally, while the petals form a bell or "skirt" usually of different tint. Many thrive in Cornish gardens.

"Fuchsias seems to belong to white walls which look to the setting sun and there are few shrubs which are less trouble than the old hardy sorts, few so generous in their ... yield of colour."—ATJ

cordifolia

90 × 90 cm	*[9]*	*Red*	*Autumn*	W	CD
3 × 3 ft					

Mexico. A late-flowering plant for our warmest counties. Copious green leaves. The flowers are of scarlet, with small green skirt. For the curious. It does well at Trelissick, Cornwall.

magellanica

1.2 m × 46 cm	*[7–9]*	*Crimson*	*Summer/*	CD
4 ft × 18 in			*Autumn*	

South America. 1788. The following forms and hybrids have small flowers but are very hardy and graceful. The heights given are for Surrey; in the warmer south and west where frost does not destroy the stems they will grow at least twice as tall.

—'Globosa'

60 × 60 cm	*[7–9]*	*Crimson*	*Summer/*	CD
2 × 2 ft			*Autumn*	

1832. Compact growth with flowers of more rounded outline than any, emerging from globular buds.

—'Gracilis'

1.2 m × 90 cm	*[8–9]*	*Crimson*	*Summer/*	CD
4 × 3 ft			*Autumn*	

1823. Apart from the hybrid 'Riccartonii', this is the best known of the hardy small-flowered kinds. Strong arching growth carrying narrow, dainty flowers with crimson sepals and purple skirt. A more vigorous but similar clone is known as 'Americana'. These clones and 'Thompsonii' are attributable to *F.m. macrostemma*.

—molinae

1.2 m × 60 cm	*[7–9]*	*Blush*	*Summer/*	CD
4 × 2 ft			*Autumn*	

F.m. 'Alba' of gardens. Not a true albino, but the light green leafy sprays are charming when hung with dainty, glimmering flowers, the almost white sepals enclosing a palest lavender skirt and pink stamens. Introduced by Clarence Elliott in 1931 from Chile, where it was growing in gardens. See also 'Sharpitor'.

—'Variegata'

60 × 60 cm	*[8–9]*	*Crimson*	*Summer/*	CD
2 × 2 ft			*Autumn*	

In this less vigorous form of 'Gracilis' green leaves are edged with creamy yellow.

—'Versicolor' ● ★

1.2 m × 90 cm	*[8–9]*	*Crimson*	*Summer/*	CD
4 × 3 ft			*Autumn*	

F.m. gracilis tricolor. The only shortcoming of the majority of fuchsias is that the crimson and purple colouring of the flowers is in such poor contrast to the dark green foliage. In the early year the leaves of this variety are of coppery pink, becoming grey-green as the season advances. An exquisite symphony of colour, which is unsurpassed in the floral world for its charming complement of shape, poise and tint. Beautiful with *Agapanthus*. It thrives at Wallington, Northumberland.

—'Thompsonii'

1.2 m × 60 cm	*[7–9]*	*Crimson*	*Summer/*	CD
4 × 2 ft			*Autumn*	

Similar to 'Gracilis' but erect, not arching. It is even more prolific of flower and is the best of these very hardy kinds with slender flowers for smaller gardens.

triphylla

90 × 90 cm	*[10]*	*Red*	*Autumn*	W	CD
3 × 3 ft					

West Indies. Vigorous stems of reddish colouring, with leaves in whorls of three. The flowers are long; small bright red petals with small, luminous, orange-red splayed skirt and cream stamens. For warmest counties.

HYBRIDS, mostly between *F. magellanica, F. coccinea* and other species. Several of these are only one stage larger in flower than *F. magellanica*: 'Chequerboard', 'Chillerton Beauty', 'Margaret Brown', 'Mrs W.P. Wood', 'Madame Cornelisen', 'Prodigy', 'Riccartonii' and 'Sharpitor'. The others have the larger, rounder flowers of the numerous tender hybrids.

Apart from the small-flowered kinds mentioned above, 'Mrs Popple' remains the criterion by which large-flowered hybrids are judged. There are times when the combination of crimson and purple becomes tiresome and some of the following add to the repertoire. In the warmer west they will exceed the heights given.

● **'Chequerboard'** 1948. 90 × 60 cm (3 × 2 ft). [9]. Long narrow flowers with white sepals and cerise-red skirt. It is free flowering and conspicuous at a distance. Erect growth. 　　　　　　　　　　　　　　　　　　　　　　　　　　W

● **'Chillerton Beauty'** 1.2 m × 90 cm (4 × 3 ft) [8–9]. A splendid addition to the hardy groups, vigorous and arching. The flower is light pink with a rich lilac skirt. Discovered in the Isle of Wight *c*.1954 and named by Rowland Jackman; I have been unable to find its original name.

'Corallina' 1843. 'Exoniensis' *F. cordifolia* × *F. magellanica* 'Globosa'. Vigorous, nearly prostrate with comparatively large dark leaves and long flowers with crimson calyx and purple skirt. Useful for banks, hanging over rocks, etc. Spreading to 90 cm (3 ft) or more. [9].

'Dr Foster' 60 × 60 cm (2 × 2 ft). [9]. Very large flowers of crimson with purple skirt. This is larger than 'Mrs Popple' but is less vigorous and less hardy.

● **'Eva Boerg'** 46 × 46 cm (18 × 18 in). [9]. This and 'Lena' (1862) are very similar. They are of low, arching growth and seen to best advantage in a vase or pot or on raised ground. Broad leaves and broad blush-pink sepals enclose a double bulky crinoline of rich lilac-pink. 'Eva Boerg' has a greenish white tube; 'Lena', flesh pink.

'Madame Cornelisen' 1860. 60 × 60 cm (2 × 2 ft). [9]. Bright crimson sepals, almost white skirt, with red veins. Foliage and stalks shaded with red. A very bright person.

'Margaret Brown' 1949. 75 × 60 cm (2½ × 2 ft). [9]. A compact bushy plant with fairly light green foliage, giving contrast to compact small blooms of deep rose-pink. Very free.

★ **'Mrs Popple'** 90 × 90 cm (3 × 3 ft). [8–9]. A splendid variety giving us some of the size of the greenhouse varieties with complete hardiness and abundant crimson and purple flowers of rounded outline. Discovered in a neighbour's garden by Clarence Elliott, and named after her—appropriately; the buds "pop" well. *c.* 1930.

'Mrs W. P. Wood' 60 × 60 cm (2 × 2 ft). [9]. A bushy plant with light green foliage. The sepals are flesh pink and the skirt pale lilac—a refreshing sight among fuchsias.

'Overbecks Ruby' ★

1.2 m × 90 cm	*[8–9]]*	*Crimson*	*Summer/*	CD
4 × 3 ft			*Autumn*	

We believe this was a self-sown seedling in the National Trust garden at Salcombe, Devon. It is a densely branched, erect grower, smothered in small flowers for weeks on end, crimson with purple skirt. A manavilin not to be missed. Occurred *c.* 1960.

'Paula Bayliss' 1974. 90 × 90 cm (3 × 3 ft). [9]. Slender arching growth. Large flowers with upturned sepals of bright scarlet-crimson and wide single skirt of lilac, veined red. Good with grey-foliaged plants.

★ **'Pee Wee Rose'** 1939. 1.2 m × 90 cm (4 × 3 ft). [9]. One of the smaller-flowered types. Extra bushy and free flowering. Vivid scarlet-pink sepals with small skirt of cerise-magenta.

● ★ **'Prodigy'** or **'Enfant Prodigue'** 1887. 1.5 m × 90 cm (5 × 3 ft). [9]. Brilliant crimson sepals, glowing purple, semi-double skirt. Splendid, vigorous, upright, free-flowering. It should be in every garden. One of the few fuchsias which last reasonably well in water.

'Riccartonii' ★

1.2 m × 90 cm	*[8–9]*	*Crimson*	*Summer/*	CD
4 × 3 ft			*Autumn*	

1830. An ancient hybrid; the commonest hardy fuchsia, frequently used for hedging in warmest counties and maritime districts. A vigorous branching plant. The flowers are the usual crimson and purple, with more rounded outline than those of typical *F. magellanica* varieties, except *F.m.* 'Globosa', of which it is a seedling, raised near Edinburgh about 1830.

● ★ **'Rufus'** 1951. 90 × 90 cm (3 × 3 ft). [9]. Simple flowers of uniform scarlet-red—a welcome change and very telling in the garden.

● ★ **'Sealand Prince'** 90 × 90 cm (3 × 3 ft). [8–9]. A most brilliant fuchsia with sepals of vivid dark pink and skirt of light violet. A fine contrast to white colchicums. Raised by Bees Ltd of Chester.

'Sharpitor'
[9]. A sport from *F.m. molinae*. Less vigorous than the type. The palest green leaves are edged with creamy white. It makes a pleasing symphony of pale tints. First noticed at Overbecks (Sharpitor), a garden of the National Trust at Salcombe, Devon, by C. D. Brickell in 1973. Lovely with colchicums.

There are many more good, reasonably hardy kinds which came through the trials at Wisley unprotected such as 'Monsieur Thibaud', 'Abbé Farges', 'Phenomenal', 'Brutus', etc. [all 9] but the above are distinct and cover most of the colour combinations satisfactorily. Farther west in sheltered gardens many of the large-flowered tender greenhouse varieties will of course thrive, together with other species.

GAILLARDIA, Compositae.

× grandiflora ●

| 60–90 × 46 cm | [3–8] | Red/Yellow | Summer | P | DRS |
| 2–3 ft × 18 in | | | | | |

This name applies to most garden clones and strains and is the result of hybrids principally between *G. pulchella*, an annual plant with mainly reddish flowers, and *G. aristata*, a perennial with yellow flowers, both natives of the United States; *G. pulchella* from Eastern and *G. aristata* [3–8] mainly Western areas. Introduced in 1787 and 1811 respectively. The large daisies are among the most flamboyant of garden flowers, varying from deep yellow to maroon red, set around a large dark reddish-brown centre. This, and the whole plant, is sticky and aromatic; the leaves are soft in colour and texture. The flowers are admirable for cutting and give "point" to many a vase of flowers. They are inclined to be short-lived except in rubbly, sharply drained soil; their stems usually need support. Easily raised from seed, there are several distinctive strains available. On the other hand there are good distinct named hybrids which are increased by root cuttings, such as 'Croftway Yellow', pure yellow all over; 'Ipswich Beauty', a typical old type with deep red petals, yellow-tipped; 'Mandarin' is a uniform deep flame-orange, and 'Wirral Flame' a dark brownish-red, lightly tipped with yellow.

GALAX, Diapensiaceae.

urceolata

| 46 × 30 cm | [5–8] | White | L.Summer | P | D |
| 18 in × 1 ft | | | | | |

E. North America. 1812. Well known by its other name, *G. aphylla*. One of the best things in winter is its tuft of evergreen, rounded leaves some 7.5 cm (3 in) across of shining dark green, which assume burnished tints; they are excellent for cutting. The slender spire of tiny white flowers appear at midsummer. A lovely plant for cool, woodland conditions on lime-free soils. It thrives at Knightshayes Court, Devon.

> "... develops wonderful crimson and bronze tints in autumn, more especially in those leaves which have the fullest exposure to light".—ATJ

GALEGA, Leguminosae. Goat's Rue. Stalwart plants, thriving in any sunny place in poor or fertile soil and producing sheaves of small pea-flowers in branched spikes over masses of pinnate leaves. They are like a giant vetch and usually need supporting.

officinalis

| 1.5 m × 90 cm | [4–8] | Various | Summer | P | D |
| 5 × 3 ft | | | | | |

S. Europe, Asia Minor. 1568. There are pale lavender-blue and also white types; one white has been called 'Candida' since 1771. Most of the garden forms are listed under *G × hartlandii* (*G. officinalis × G. patula*), 1904, and are of various lilac, lavender, pink or rosy mauve, such as 'His Majesty', 'Lady Wilson',

'Duchess of Bedford', and 'Carnea'. These appeared from 1904 onwards and were one of the mainstays of the herbaceous border.

orientalis

1.2 m × 60 cm	*[5–8]*	*Blue*	*E.Summer*	P D
4 × 2 ft				

Caucasus. 1810. It is unfortunate that this plant has an invasive root because its flowers are of a beautiful clear blue, violet-tinted. The general appearance is similar to *G. officinalis*, but it is a lesser plant, with hairy stems, and the flowers are borne erect in good spikes. Highly effective behind pink pyrethrums.

GALTONIA, Liliaceae. Summer Hyacinth, Spire Lily or Cape Hyacinth. Bulbous plants of great merit for the garden, thriving in sunny positions in any soil, but if they are to be continuously good, for years, they need a rich, well-nurtured, friable soil. They are apt to deteriorate in poor sandy soils. Plant in early spring about 23 cm (9 in) deep. They sow themselves freely when suited and can be a nuisance.

candicans

1.2 m × 30 cm	*[7–10]*	*White*	*L.Summer*	PF DS
4 × 1 ft				

South Africa. *c.* 1860. *Hyacinthus candicans.* The lax, long, rather glaucous leaves are not of great importance, which is fortunate in a way because these bulbs can be interplanted between, say, Bearded Irises, peonies, or other early crops and thus give a second display in the same place later; or among *Agapanthus campanulatus* which flowers at the same time. The stately stems are set with drooping, big white bells with dark stamens. Fragrant. The seed-pods are ornamental, but the plant seeds itself freely.

"Of easy culture and valuable for bold groups ... between choice shrubs and among hardy Fuchsias."—WR

princeps

90 × 30 cm	*[7–10]*	*Green*	*L.Summer*	PF DS
3 × 1 ft				

South Africa. A lesser plant with very pale green bells, fragrant. Equally adaptable even in dry sunny gardens.

viridiflora

90 × 30 cm	*[7–10]*	*Green*	*L.Summer*	PF DS
3 × 1 ft				

South Africa. 1955. The basal leaves are broad and handsome and the spire of pale green bells is most welcome in late summer and early autumn. Plant 6 in deep.

GAURA, Onagraceae.

lindheimeri

1.2 m × 90 cm	*[6–9]*	*White*	*Summer/*	S
4 × 3 ft			*Autumn*	

S.E. United States. 1850. It is not in the first flight of herbaceous plants but its long flowering period does much to recommend it. It is an open, bushy, graceful, willowy plant with pinky-white small flowers. Best planted in full sun in well-drained soil while quite young, and left alone. The foliage sometimes develops dark spots.

GENTIANA, Gentianaceae. The popular conception of a gentian—a dwarf rock plant covered in almost stemless blue trumpets—receives a jolt when considering the stature and deportment of even these few tall species.

andrewsii

46 × 30 cm	*[4–9]*	*Blue*		P	S
18 in × 1 ft					

N. America. 1776. Probably because its tubular flowers remain closed, this plant has never been widely grown. It is an easily satisfied plant in fertile soil and the flowers, borne in clusters at the top of the stem, are effective and colourful.

"*G. andrewsii* is the Gentian that never wakes up."—RF

asclepiadea ● ★

90 × 60 cm	*[6–9]*	*Blue*	*E.Autumn*	PF	S
3 × 2 ft					

Europe. 1629. The Willow Gentian is so called on account of its willow-like leaves and slender graceful growth. The arching stems boast many pairs of rich, pure blue flowers arranged in a coronal in the axils of the upper leaves. The greatest beauty and satisfaction will be obtained when they are grown in deep moist soil, with humus, and in part or full shade, though they will grow almost anywhere, even on chalky soils. First rate, long-lived and thoroughly reliable, improving yearly if left alone. Some seedlings flower before or after others and are worth selecting; there are dark blue forms with or without white throats, and there are also named varieties and forms: *G.a. alba*, for those with white flowers usually with greenish-cream throats; 'Knightshayes', a deep blue with conspicuous whitish throat, an erect grower; and 'Phaeina', a name given by Farrer to a very pale Cambridge blue form, now extinct.

"... with flowers like a summer sky at dawn".—RF

The names 'Caelestina' and 'Phyllis' have appeared in print also. Pale blues have grown for many years at Sizergh Castle, Westmorland, and at Wallington Hall, Northumberland, and a percentage breed true from seeds. Short basal cuttings may be struck in spring.

"... the glory of the sub-alpine woods, where its long bending sheaves of graceful blossom make a famous loveliness in late summer ... the same amiability in the garden ... swathes of flower 3 ft high ... inclining this way and that beneath the burden of its beautiful sapphire trumpets."—RF

lutea

1.2 m × 60 cm	*[7–8]*	*Yellow*	*Summer*	F	S
4 × 2 ft					

Europe. Felwort or Bitterwort, the Gentian-root of commerce. This noble plant is far from the usual conception of a gentian. The great tufts of aspidistra-like leaves give rise to stout unbranched stems, set towards their apices with whorls of dense clusters of short, pale yellow tubular flowers; each cluster is partially enclosed by a large, cupped, green bract. It grows best in sunny places in deep rich soil. Very handsome seed-heads. For lovers of the unusual are two related European species: *G. punctata* [6–8], yellow-spotted purple, and *G. purpurea* [6–8], reddish purple. Both achieve about 60 cm (2 ft). *G. burseri* [6–8], with yellowish flowers, belongs to the same group. 1596 or earlier.

makinoi

30 × 30 cm	[6–8]	Blue	L.Summer	S
1 × 1 ft				

Japan. 1894. One of the more tractable species of value late in the season, when its erect stems are crowned with good, richly coloured flowers. For semi-shade.

triflora ●

46 × 30 cm	[6–8]	Blue	L.Summer	P	S
18 in × 1 ft					

Japan. Little known as yet, *G. triflora* and its larger variant *G. triflora japonica* or *G. axillariflora* are good upstanding plants with good-sized bright blue flowers carried in the upper leaf axils. They need a moist and peaty soil in sun. Our native *G. pneumonanthe* [5–7] is rather smaller. I have found it difficult to exclude *G. septemfida* [4–8] and its relatives from these pages, but their flopping habit makes them more suited to the rock garden.

GERANIUM, Geraniaceae. The Crane's Bills, as a race, are easy and extremely valuable plants for the furnishing of borders, both as ground-covers (most of them) and producers of beautiful flowers, and are very amenable to cultivation, thriving in any reasonable soil that is not boggy, in sun or part shade; some, like *G. punctatum, G. phaeum* and *G. nodosum,* actually prefer shade. They have had full mention in my book *Plants for Ground-Cover,* but the following warrant equal mention here as they are beautiful plants in their own right, particularly the tallest, *G. pratense, G. psilostemon* and *G. sylvaticum.* I have omitted several small species, as their low stature does not warrant their inclusion. For those that garden in maritime or otherwise very warm climates there is *G. maderense* [9–10], a giant monocarpic plant up to 4 ft, with a huge mound of deeply cut leaves and a cloud of evil-smelling purplish pink flowers. *G. palmatum* is closely related.

"I found ... many of them invaluable for filling half-shaded positions with at least ten, if not the full twelve, months of beauty and interest. The leaves of many are good throughout the winter, whether last season's turning russet or even scarlet at times, or next season's newly appeared."—EAB

"It has always been a matter of astonishment to me that such splendid subjects as the hardier geraniums are so rarely grown in the average garden.... They fit into their surroundings with that subtle sympathy which weds the harebell to the heaths."—ATJ

'Ann Folkard' ★

46 × 46 cm	[5–8]	Purplish	E.Summer	D
18 × 18 in				

Named in 1974 by Mr O. G. Folkard, a natural hybrid which cropped up in his garden at Sleaford, Lincs., between *G. psilostemon* and *G. procurrens.* It forms a large spreading plant but does not root from the prostrate stems. It seems to be intermediate in leaf (yellowish early in the year) and flower colour—rich magenta-purple, with the expected black centre and radiating veins. A worthy addition.

candicans (of gardens). See *G. lambertii.*

× cantabrigiense ★

23 × 30 cm	*[5–8]*	*Mauve*	*E.Summer*	D
9 in × 1 ft				

Named in 1985 by Dr P. F. Yeo. *G. macrorrhizum × G. dalmaticum*. An invaluable, dense ground-covering plant producing masses of rounded leaves which are almost obscured by the masses of dull mauve-pink flowers. This was raised at Cambridge and is called 'Cambridge'. Another hybrid with white, faintly blushing flowers was found in Yugoslavia and is named 'Biokovo'. It is less vigorous in growth.

clarkei

30 × 30 cm	*[4–8]*	*Various*	*E.Summer*	D
1 × 1 ft				

Kashmir. *c.* 1968. A plant of good ornamental quality but with a rhizomatous root, spreading rapidly, which makes it a nuisance in smaller gardens, especially as the plant is not a dense ground-cover. Elegant deeply cut leaves. Two forms are grown, which were included erroneously under *G. pratense* in my earlier editions.

—**'Kashmir Purple'.** Rich lilac-purple. Sometimes labelled *G. bergianum*.

—**'Kashmir White'.** White, with lilac veins. Sometimes labelled *G.* 'Rectum Album'.

endressii

46 × 60 cm	*[4–8]*	*Pink*	*Summer/*	DS
18 in × 2 ft			*Autumn*	

Pyrenees. 1812. Always in flower, this pretty, evergreen, leafy ground-cover and colonizer shows its bright chalky-pink flowers well above its elegantly divided, light green leaves. The form known as 'A. T. Johnson' is of a light silvery-pink, while 'Rose Clair' approaches the next.

—**'Wargrave Pink'**

60 × 90 cm	*[4–8]*	*Pink*	*Summer/*	D
2 × 3 ft			*Autumn*	

The brightest form of this Pyrenean plant. Dense tuffets of dainty foliage and countless bright, salmon-pink, small blooms in June and onwards. A very vigorous useful plant for massing, completely weed-proof. Lovely with purple irises.

"... they are such vigorous colonizers and possessed of such admirable courage that with us they grow anywhere, in sun or shade, in grass or border, or bed of nettles ... scarcely a week when there will not be a pink bloom showing somewhere."—ATJ

grevilleanum

60 × 60 cm	*[4–8]*	*Lilac*	*E./L.Summer*	DS
2 × 2 ft				

Himalaya. A beautiful sprawling plant, copiously leafed. The nodding flowers have somewhat reflexed petals, of cool lilac, giving them a cyclamen-like poise. The anthers are almost black. This same charming poise is found in *G. lambertii*, *G. sinense* and *G. yunnanense*, apart from the better-known *G. phaeum* and *G. punctatum* (of gardens).

183

gymnocaulon

46 × 46 cm	*[4–8]*	*Violet*	*E.Summer*	DS
18 × 18 in				

Caucasus. *G. ibericum brachytrichon.* Closely related to *G. ibericum,* with leaves cut to the base, and finely toothed. The hybrid *G. magnificum* is the best of the group.

himalayense ★

30 × 60 cm	*[4–8]*	*Blue*	*E.Summer*	D
1 × 2 ft				

Sikkim. *G. grandiflorum, G. meeboldii.* Daintily cut leaves (which often turn to brilliant colours in autumn) over which hover the intense violet-blue blooms, like butterflies, beautifully veined. A most lovely plant; ideal companion for *Iris × flavescens.* It spreads freely by underground runners. *G.h.* 'Alpinum' or 'Gravetye' (prior to 1903) is similar but has a more marked reddish centre which detracts from the campanula-blue of the flowers. Ideal under Rose 'Frühlingsgold'. 'Irish Blue' is a name I gave to a form I found at St Catherine's Park, Leixlip, Ireland (*c.* 1947); it has flowers of a somewhat lighter tint with little of the reddish centre colouring. There is a form with double flowers of lilac-purple tint, 'Plenum', also known as 'Birch Double' (*c.* 1928). They all have invasive roots.

"Much the handsomest sort is the foot-high *G. grandiflorum* [4–8], which everybody should grow."—WR

ibericum

60 × 60 cm	*[5–8]*	*Violet-blue*	*E.Summer*	DS
2 × 2 ft				

S.E. Europe, S.W. Asia. 1802. For garden value it is slightly inferior to its hybrid *G. × magnificum.*

incisum

30 × 30 cm	*[5–8]*	*Purple*	*Summer*	DS
1 × 1 ft				

Doubtful garden name. A clump of silky hairy, greyish leaves, deeply incised, over which are poised mauve-purple flowers in clusters. Each petal is distinctly veined from the centre with darker purple.

'Johnson's Blue'

30 × 60 cm	*[4–8]*	*Violet-blue*	*E.Summer*	D
1 × 2 ft				

c. 1950. A really good plant with copious, elegant, divided leaves making a dense cover to 30 cm (1 ft); over them appear in a long succession ample lavender-blue flowers, with darker veins. Probably a hybrid between *G. himalayense* and *G. pratense,* which originated from seed of *G. pratense* sent by A. T. Johnson to Mr B. Ruys of Dedemsvaart. A worthy plant to commemorate a great gardener. Ideal with Rose 'Golden Wings' and other pale yellows.

kishtvariense

46 × 60 cm	*[5–8]*	*Pink*	*Summer*	DS
18 in × 2 ft				

Srinagar. 1980. Collected by Roy Lancaster. The invasive roots are the only blotch on the escutcheon of this beautiful plant. Elegant deeply cut leaves and flowers with broad, somewhat recurving petals of clear cerise-pink. Long flowering season.

lambertii ●

46 × 90 cm	*[5–8]*	*White*	*Summer/*	DS
18 in × 3 ft			*Autumn*	

Closely related to *G. candicans* under which name it is to be found in a number of British nurseries and gardens. The differences between the two species are more to be found in the eye of the botanist than that of the gardener, apart from the conspicuous crimson marks on the petals of *G. lambertii*. It is a useful late-flowering plant and is seldom out of flower before October. It has handsome leaves on long, trailing stems; from each axil is poised a nodding white bloom most beautifully crimson-veined in the centre, round which, between the petals, shows the vivid green of the calyx. This form has been called 'Swansdown'; there are also forms of very pale pink, without the crimson centre. Maroon pointel. It increases slowly at the root. Sometimes confused with *G. grevilleanum*.

macrorrhizum ★

30 × 60 cm	*[4–8]*	*Pink*	*L.Spring*	D
1 × 2 ft				

S. Europe. 1576. A splendid dense weed-proof ground-cover which can be relied upon absolutely. Divided, rounded, light green, clammy aromatic leaves. They develop bright autumn colour, but are semi-evergreen. Admirable for sun or shade in almost any soil; though a vigorous spreader above ground it is never a weed. The old type had undistinguished dark magenta blooms; two forms found by Walter Ingwersen are invaluable: 'Ingwersen's Variety', soft rose-pink, and 'Album', warm white with reddish calyces. 'Bevan's Variety' is the best of the crimson-purple tints. There is an ugly variegated form.

maculatum ●★

60 × 46 cm	*[4–8]*	*Blush-lilac*	*Spring*	DS
2 ft × 18 in				

North America. 1732. Usually in flower in May at which time there are few herbaceous plants to rival it, but it would be acclaimed at any time. Handsome, smooth or softly hairy, fingered leaves from a sound, increasing clump, producing a cloud of clear, lilac-rose, pale or dark, flowers for several weeks. A first-class plant. Beautiful with dicentras. The root is tuberous, even woody.

× magnificum

60 × 60 cm	*[4–8]*	*Violet-blue*	*E.Summer*	D
2 × 2 ft				

This is often labelled *G. ibericum* or *G. platypetalum* in gardens but is in reality a sterile hybrid of these two species and has been known for nearly a hundred years. It inherits the sticky-hairy flower stalks of the second species. Handsome, deeply cut, hairy, rounded leaves, often richly tinted in autumn. Copious flowers, darkly veined, ideal with Rose 'Nevada'.

malviflorum

46 × 46 cm	*[6–8]*	*Lilac*	*L.Spring*	D
18 × 18 in				

W. Mediterranean Region. Often labelled *G. atlanticum*. The tuberous roots produce their finely cut fresh green leaves in autumn. It is not surprising therefore that the whole plant dies away in summer after the wiry stems have held aloft the broad, deep lilac, beautifully veined flowers.

185

× monacense

46 × 60 cm	*[4–8]*	*Mauve*	*Spring*	D
18 in × 2 ft				

This new name, by Dr. P. F. Yeo, covers hybrids between *G. phaeum* and *G. reflexum,* known in gardens as *G. punctatum.*

nodosum

46 × 46 cm	*[5–8]*	*Lilac*	*Spring/*	DS
18 × 18 in			*Autumn*	

Europe, naturalized in Britain. This is not a spectacular plant, but is one of the few which will thrive even in the dark shade of evergreen oaks, cedars, etc. Glossy green, lobed leaves make fine hummocks, decorated continuously with small lilac flowers with paler centres. Pink forms occur in Europe.

× oxonianum (*G. endressii × G. striatum*) [5–8].

—'A. T. Johnson'. [5–8]. Usually considered to be a light silvery pink form of *G. endressii.* Dr Peter Yeo considers it to be a hybrid of the above parentage.

—'Claridge Druce'

60–90 × 90 cm	*[4–8]*	*Pink*	*Summer*	D
2–3 × 3 ft				

Named in memory of the noted botanist who discovered it, this splendid hybrid of *G. endressii* is extremely vigorous—even rampageous—and a successful weed-smotherer, suitable for large areas under trees or in sun. Handsomely divided foliage of greyish-green and masses of bright magenta-pink flowers over a long period. It seems to breed true from seed and will colonize ground on its own. Evergreen.

—'Rose Clair'. [5–8]. Named by A. T. Johnson: usually described as a form of *G. endressii;* flowers clear rosy salmon.

phaeum

60 × 46 cm	*[4–8]*	*Various*	*L.Spring*	DS
2 ft × 18 in				

Europe. The Mourning Widow is so-called on account of its very dark maroon-coloured flowers, nodding and with reflexed petals. It may very to a slate-colour (*G.p. lividum*) or to white (*G.p.* 'Album') when it reaches a high state of beauty. Like *G. punctatum* (of gardens) to which it is closely related, it is a most useful plant for deep shade. Soft green leaves. Seeds itself mildly, and is naturalized at Powis Castle, Montgomeryshire, and elsewhere. *G. aristatum* is similar.

platypetalum

46 × 46 cm	*[3–8]*	*Violet-blue*	*E.Summer*	DS
18 × 18 in				

Caucasus, Turkey. A name often given to the best-known and most worthy of this group, *G × magnificum*, but in reality a much inferior plant. The leaves, and in fact the whole plant, are smaller, only cut to half of their radius, and the flowers are a dull blue-violet, deeply veined. The flower stalks are sticky-hairy.

pratense
> *60 × 60 cm* *[4–8]* *Violet-blue* *Summer*   D
> *2 × 2 ft*

N. Europe, Britain, Asia. Most handsome, deeply divided leaves making a fine clump and developing good autumn tints. A sheaf of branching stems bears numerous clear flowers for several weeks. One of the most attractive of geraniums in the choice, old, double forms, which are to be preferred in the garden borders to the singles, because these seed themselves with such abandon as to become weeds—lovely though they are when naturalized in thin woodland. A particoloured or striped form is known as *G.p.* 'Striatum' ('Bicolor'). 'Mrs Kendall Clark' has flowers of pearl-grey, flushed rose. They all need some support.

—**'Plenum Album'** [4–8]. A double white form which has rather small flowers; I should like to see a better one, and am waiting for a double pink!—since single pinks have already appeared. This and the other doubles last in water when cut.

—**'Plenum Caeruleum'** [4–8]. Light lavender-blue flowers tinged with lilac, loosely petalled. The flowers lack the form of the next, but it is a useful plant because it flowers earlier.

● ★ —**'Plenum Violaceum'** [4–8]. Rich deep violet-blue, tinged with purple in the centre; the petals are arranged in cup-formation and each flower is an exquisite rosette. It flowers in July and is a wonderful contrast to orange-red lilies of the *L. davidii* breed, particularly 'Red Max'. It reaches its noblest proportions and colour in the cooler north and is magnificently used at Crathes Castle, Kincardineshire.

psilostemon ● ★
> *1.2 × 1.2 m* *[4–8]* *Magenta* *Summer*   D
> *4 × 4 ft*

Armenia. 1874. Until recently known as *G. armenum*, it is a foliage plant of excellence, forming a great clump of elegant broad leaves, deeply cut, and assuming fine autumn colour. When in flower in June it is a wonderful sight; the intense magenta-crimson flowers, borne in dozens, have black centres. A wonderful contrast for orange alstroemerias, *Lilium croceum*, etc., and for grey and cool-tinted groupings, especially with thalictrums and the Rose 'William Lobb'. Sun or partial shade, any deep soil. It usually needs some support. A great sight in the Purple Border at Sissinghurst Castle, Kent. 'Bressingham Flair' is of cooler colouring and a useful plant; a rich lilac-pink.

punctatum
of gardens
> *46 × 60 cm* *[4–8]* *Mauve* *Spring*   DS
> *18 in × 2 ft*

Related to *G. phaeum*. A good ground-cover, thriving in shade; the angular leaves are often primrose-yellow in the spring, on which the five maroon spots show up wonderfully; later they are always present but not so strikingly noticeable against the green of the leaves. Flowers of intriguing shape, dull mauve-purple, nodding, with maroon pointel. Woody rootstock.

reflexum
> *60 × 60 cm* *[5–8]* *Mauve* *E.Summer*   DS
> *2 × 2 ft*

Italy, France. 1758. Another of the pretty cyclamen-flowered kinds, with mauve-pink reflexed petals and red pointel, borne well above the fresh green deeply cut leaves. Prefers part shade.

renardii

30 × 30 cm	[6–8]	Whitish	E.Summer	D
1 × 1 ft				

Caucasus. 1935. A first-class foliage plant forming a solid dome of sage-green, prettily lobed, deeply veined, circular leaves. Over these are displayed the starry opal-white flowers veined with violet. An attractive plant through the growing season. A good form is named 'Walter Ingwersen', after its introducer.

× **riversleaianum.** *G. traversii* × *G. endressii.* [6–8].

—'Mavis Simpson'

46 × 90 cm	[7–8]	Pink	E./L.Summer	D
18 in × 3 ft				

1980. A clump of greyish, divided leaves wide-spreading annually form a compact rootstock. The trailing stems produce multitudes of clear pink flowers for about three months. It originated at Kew from self-sown seed of *G. traversii*.

—'Russell Prichard' ★

23 × 90 cm	[6–8]	Pink	Summer/	D
9 in × 3 ft			Autumn	

c. 1915. Considered to be a hybrid between *G. traversii* and *G. endressii*. With *G. wallichianum* this is one of the longest-flowering plants in cultivation. It makes a continuous display from June onwards. Chalky pink blooms are held over a mat of greyish green leaves—the perfect complement. It inherits a little tenderness from *G. traversii*, but is hardy in our warmer counties in sun in any fertile soil. Plant in spring. The tufts send out long carpeting branches each summer, dying back to the rootstock in autumn. Raised by Maurice Prichard. Sometimes called *G.* × *prichardii*. Lovely with white or blue *Agapanthus*.

sanguineum ★

30 × 46 cm	[4–8]	Magenta	E.Summer	DRS
12 × 18 in				

Europe, W. Asia. The Bloody Cranesbill makes wide hummocks of deeply divided dark green leaves, and for many weeks it daily produces scores of blooms of deep magenta or mallow-pink. The leaves often assume good autumn tints. Seeds itself mildly. European forms, of which 'Album' is one, are taller and more lanky than the British forms, to which the plants usually sold as *G. sanguineaum* belong; also, of course, 'Glenluce' and *G.s. lancastriense*.

—**'Album'** 1900. [4–8]. Pure white. An open-growing plant, achieving 60 cm (2 ft).

—**'Glenluce'** Found in Glenluce by A. T. Johnson, *c.* 1935. [4–8]. Clear pink flowers of cool tone. Good foliage, vigorous grower.

● ★ —**lancastriense** Prior to 1732. [4–8]. *G.s.* 'Striatum'. This form is variable from seed, but always produces light pink flowers with crimson veins. It only grows wild on the Isle of Walney, Lancs. All of these forms are ideal complements to plantings of old roses.

shikokianum

| *60 × 60 cm* | *[4–8]* | *Mauve* | *E.Summer* | DS |

2 × 2 ft

Japan. A clump-former. Elegant divided leaves, soft and hairy. In general appearance it resembles *G. wallichianum* closely, but the flowers are of rosy-mauve.

sinense

| *60 × 90 cm* | *[5–8]* | *Maroon* | *L.Summer* | DS |

2 × 3 ft

W. China. Usually wrongly labelled *G. delavayi* in gardens, this increases slowly from the root, producing annually a mass of good foliage and stems. Towards the end of summer the flowers appear, rather like those of *G. phaeum*, having reflexed petals of maroon-red with a projecting pointel of orange and red. The flowers are elegant and well poised and wasps are fascinated by them, thus contributing to the colour scheme! Seeds itself sparingly. Long-flowering period.

sylvaticum ★

| *90 × 60 cm* | *[4–8]* | *Various* | *Spring* | DS |

3 × 2 ft

Europe, W. to E. Asia, Britain. A most valuable May-flowering plant, with a lovely basal clump of fingered leaves. Branching stems bear violet-blue white-eyed blooms for weeks. There are also plum-coloured, pink ('Wanneri') and white ('Album') forms, and 'Mayflower' is a specially good rich violet-blue. Beautiful with *Cytisus × praecox*, and it wakes up the summer borders at Blickling Hall, Norfolk. 'Albiflorum' is a garden clone which breeds true from seeds.

traversii

| *15 × 46 cm* | *[8–9]* | *White/Pink* | *Summer* | W DS |

6 × 18 in

New Zealand. A tender prostrate species with white flowers. *G.t. elegans* from the Chatham Isles has grey leaves and pink flowers and has given rise to 'Mavis Simpson', *q.v.* under *G. × riversleaianum*.

versicolor

| *46 × 46 cm* | *[4–8]* | *Pink* | *Summer* | DS |

18 × 18 in

Europe. 1629. *G. striatum*. A weedy plant with small blush flowers with darker stripes. It seeds itself freely and is apt to hybridize with *G. endressii*, and should be left in the wild.

wallichianum ★

| *30 × 90 cm* | *[4–8]* | *Blue* | *July–Autumn* | DS |

1 × 3 ft

Himalaya. 1820. The oldest known garden form is ● ★ 'Buxton's Variety', selected by E. C. Buxton at Betws-y-Coed, N. Wales *c.* 1900, and it breeds true from seeds. It is a pearl beyond price, producing a non-stop display from the end of June onwards of lovely Spode-blue flowers with large white centres and dark stamens over a luxuriantly leafed plant. It makes a sound clump and enjoys any fertile drained soil in sun or shade. More recently Messrs Stainton, Sykes and Williams introduced a mauve-coloured variant which is an equally good plant but lacking the clear and rare blue of the early introduction. Beautiful with *Fuchsia magellanica* forms and the shrubby *Potentilla* 'Elizabeth'.

"The typical plant has a broad band of bluish lilac outside the large white eye, a poor colour which is totally eclipsed in ... Buxton's Variety, in which the coloured portion of the corolla is a lovely nemophila blue. Indeed the blossom as a whole bears no little resemblance to that popular Californian annual."—ATJ

wlassovianum

60 × 60 cm	[5–8]	Purple	E.Summer	DS
2 × 2 ft				

Siberia, Manchuria. Velvety stems and velvety dark leaves. The dark violet flowers have dark purple veins. A plant of dusky charm, to be linked with coppery and grey foliage.

yunnanense

60 × 90 cm	[5–8]	Pink	Summer	DS
2 × 3 ft				

Yunnan, Burma. 1956. A distinguished charmer of Kingdon Ward's. Rarely seen but well established at Edinburgh, where it grows in part shade. The rather lax stems make a large clump with lime-green mottled divided leaves, somewhat reminiscent of *G. wallichianum*, but the flowers, borne aloft freely on branching stems, are in the cyclamen-flowered class, nodding, with reflexed petals. Mallow pink, with crimson filaments projecting with yellow anthers.

GERBERA, Compositae. Beautiful daisies with large refined flowers suitable for growing at the foot of hot sunny walls in our warmest, sunniest counties, in any fertile and drained soil.

jamesonii ★

46 × 46 cm	[8–10]	Various	L.Spring/	P S
18 × 18 in			Summer	

South Africa. 1887. Barberton Daisy. Clumps of dark hairy leaves. Each stem carries one long-rayed daisy, orange-red in the normal wild type. The popular strains of today are hybrids with *G. viridifolia*, a crimson-purple species with small flowers; their status is *G. × cantabrigiensis* since they were first raised at the University Botanic Garden, Cambridge, by R. I. Lynch. The result is flowers of red, orange, pink, yellow, or white, some being semi-double. It is a very gorgeous race, which is being spoiled by excessive in-breeding and the development of doubles.

GEUM, Rosaceae. These plants all provide dense clumps of broad, hairy, fresh green leaves, over which stand the hairy stalks bearing single or double rosette flowers. They are among the gayest of early summer plants and are excellent for the front of borders and beds where their strong colours require some forethought. To keep them in health they should be divided every few years, and they thrive in any normal fertile soil in sun or part shade.

'Borisii'
of gardens

30 × 30 cm	[5–8]	Orange	E.Summer	D
1 × 1 ft				

Hybrid. The dense hummock of bright green, hairy, rounded leaves is useful as ground-cover. Few plants have the warm, pure orange tint of this plant; its single flowers cover a tenpenny piece. 'Georgenberg', another hybrid, has paler flowers.

chiloense

| 60 × 46 cm | [5–9] | Red/Yellow | E.Summer | P | DS |
| 2 ft × 18 in | | | | | |

Chile. 1826. *G. coccineum* of gardens. Two popular strains, easily raised from seed, are 'Lady Stratheden', pure warm yellow, and 'Mrs Bradshaw', flaming brick-red. They both have good foliage and double flowers. Intermediate between them in colour are some hybrids: 'Princess Juliana' (1923), 'Fire Opal' (1928) and 'Dolly North'. These should be raised by division of the clumps in early spring, and all of them when young and in good fertile soil will flower continuously until autumn after their first June crop. These and others are all gorgeous colours for associating with coppery-foliaged plants and vivid yellow-green leaves.

rivale

| 30 × 30 cm | [3–8] | Pinkish | E.Summer | | DS |
| 1 × 1 ft | | | | | |

Northern Hemisphere, Britain. It will be well to call attention to 'Leonard's Variety' (1923) of this pretty plant, whose flowers are somewhat bell-shaped and of soft, coppery, creamy pink, flushed with orange. They nod on reddish stalks over hairy, divided, dark green basal leaves. For a cool moist spot. 'Lionel Cox' is similar, but the flowers are primrose-yellow, of good size, and held in brown calyces.

GILLENIA, Rosaceae.

trifoliata

| 1.2 m × 60 cm | [4–8] | White | Summer | PF | DS |
| 4 × 2 ft | | | | | |

United States. 1713. *Spiraea trifoliata*. A tough, wiry plant whose reddish stems are sparsely leaved, but branch freely into flights of small white flowers. The red calyces persist in beauty after the petals have dropped. Dainty and refined. Almost any position and soil seem to suit it. *G. stipulata* is reputed to be smaller in bloom and later-flowering.

"Distinct and graceful."—WR

GLADIOLUS, Iridaceae. The European species are known as Corn Flag. The size and vulgarity of the large-flowered hybrids, evolved from tender South African species, reputedly *G. psittacinus* and *G. oppositiflorus*, are only surpassed by the very large dahlias and chrysanthemums. In mild gardens of the south-west, these big hybrid gladioli are true perennials and useful for cutting for the very largest of arrangements. Somewhat smaller and infinitely more decorative are the Primulinus hybrids, but I will leave these all to intending planters to choose from modern lists as varieties come and go pretty freely. Their corms must be treated as tender over most of Britain, lifting in autumn and planting again in spring. On the other hand the following few kinds are dainty and charming and more or less hardy in Surrey. They need a well-nourished soil—otherwise the size of the corm deteriorates with a consequent lack of flower—well drained, and in full sun. Plant 15 cm (6 in) deep. Unlike the big ones, none needs staking.

"The root consists of two bulbes one set upon the other; the uppermost in the spring is lesser . . .; the lower greater . . . which shortly after perisheth."—GH

191

byzantinus ● ★

90 × 30 cm	[7–10]	Purplish	E.Summer	P DS
3 × 1 ft				

Europe. 1629. This is quite hardy in Surrey and also in most of our sunnier counties, and in light soil spreads alarmingly by seed and stolon. (In heavier soils it "stays put".) But we can forgive it this habit for the sake of its warm-coloured flowers in which are tints of purple, magenta-crimson and coppery brown, with three cream flashes on the lowest segments. They are beautifully shaped and appear in June; a lovely companion to *Baptisia australis*. There is a less easy white variety. *G. illyricus*, which occurs wild in Britain, *G. communis* and *G. segetum*, both introduced prior to 1596, all grow in S. Europe and the Mediterranean region. They are hardy, similar, but no more beautiful, and are shorter in growth.

callianthus ●

90 × 30 cm	[8–10]	White	Autumn	P W D
3 × 1 ft				

Ethiopia, Tanzania, Malawi. Since 1896. For long known as *Acidanthera bicolor* and *A. murielae*, this is a refined and gracious plant with long grassy leaves and several large flowers poised archingly from the tall spike. They are white with dark blotches in the throat and sweetly scented. Always a spectacle with *Nerine bowdenii* at Tintinhull, Somerset. The corms should be planted in sunny borders in late spring, 15 cm (6 in) deep, and need lifting in late autumn in all but the warmest of gardens. The strains in cultivation are apparently superior to most wild plants and a specially good one has been named ● *Acidanthera tubergenii* 'Zwanenburg', commemorating the famous Dutch firm. Correctly, this should be *G. callianthus* 'Zwanenburg'; it has large corms and it flowers well before frosts occur, with large handsome dark eyes. A cloche in the spring will encourage the corms to make a good start for early autumn-flowering.

cardinalis

60 × 23 cm	[9–10]	Crimson	L.Summer	P W DS
2 ft × 9 in				

South Africa. 1789. The Waterfall Gladiolus. A parent of *G. × colvillei* and also of the big hybrids. A hybrid plant known under this name in gardens makes its leaves in autumn, and therefore like the *Watsonia* needs a mild climate without severe frost in winter. It is a spectacular success at Rowallane in Northern Ireland, its rich crimson hooded flowers on their curving stems having distant effect; each has three flashes of lighter tint.

× colvillei ●

46 × 23 cm	[5–10]	Various	E.Summer	P W D
18 × 9 in				

Hybrid. 1823. *G. nanus* (of gardens). *G. tristis × G. cardinalis*. In our warmer counties if planted in sheltered spots, these are true perennials and give much pleasure with their often charmingly marked flowers. They produce six or so flowers of good size on each stem, wide open and of good shape. The catalogues list a number of clones for our selection, but of all I think I prefer 'The Bride', a beautiful pure white. 'Blushing Bride' is white with carmine marks; there are pleasing pinks such as 'Apple Blossom', 'Peach Blossom', 'Impressive', 'Amanda Mahy' and 'Charm', and glowing salmon-orange-red forms: 'Mauve Charm', describes itself. Corms should be planted in autumn; the leaves push up in winter and this is one reason for its need of a warm climate. A related species, *G. melleri*, has also proved remarkably hardy in chosen spots in Surrey.

papilio ●
> 1.2 m × 30 cm   *[9–10]*   *Curious*   *Autumn*   P   D
> 4 × 1 ft

Natal. 1872. *G. purpureo-auratus*. Narrow grassy leaves and tall wiry stems hold strange, hooded flowers; the large outer segments are of soft slaty lilac, and the throat is a soft slightly greenish-yellow, with cream and mauve markings. Blue anthers. A forlorn, sad-looking charmer but quite hardy in Surrey. It increases freely at the root and can be a nuisance with its long leaves. Probably the main influence which has produced modern mauve-tinted hybrids.

primulinus ●
> 60 × 23 cm   *[8–10]*   *Yellow*   *Summer*   P   W   DS
> 2 ft × 9 in

1879. *G. nebulicola*. No doubt many of the species would be hardy at the foot of a wall heated from inside. I can think of no more beautiful plant than this species for such a use, and thus it thrives at Kew. The hooded flowers are dainty in shape and in colour a bland light yellow. The hooded shape has been carried on into many of its hybrids and has given a distinctive style to them. *G. natalensis*.

tristis
> 46 × 23 cm   *[9–10]*   *Cream*   *E.Summer*   P   W   DS
> 18 × 9 in

Natal. 1745. A dainty species whose fragrant flowers are cream, flushed green and subdued purple. This needs a warm spot. Some delicately beautiful fragrant hybrids, raised by Mr T. Barnard, such as 'Christabel', should be sought and tried in really warm and sheltered gardens.

GLAUCIDIUM, Glaucidiaceae.

palmatum ●
> 60 × 60 cm   *[6–9]*   *Lavender*   *L.Spring*   DS
> 2 × 2 ft

Japan. Like *Podophyllum* and *Diphylleia*, this plant has characterful, big, lobed leaves. If your garden can provide cool woodland conditions these leaves will be of fresh green, a worthy setting for the large, delicate, four-petalled flowers, like poppies, of cool pale lavender or, rarely, white in *G.p.* 'Leucanthum'. A great treasure, deserving a spot sheltered from wind, in a retentive soil, with humus.

GLYCYRRHIZA, Leguminosae. The following species is of easy cultivation in deep, sandy, fertile and somewhat moist soil in full sun. It is a plant of considerable economic importance, its roots being the source of liquorice; this name is derived from the Latin. Cultivated around Pontefract, Yorkshire, and in S. Europe.

glabra
> 1.2 m × 90 cm   *[9–10]*   *Blue*   *L.Summer*   DS
> 4 × 3 ft

Mediterranean Region. 1562. By no means a showy plant. The leaves, though pinnate, have alternate leaflets; they are borne with flower spikes in their axils up the erect stems. The flowers are pale blue.

GRINDELIA, Compositae.

chiloensis

90 × 90 cm	*[9–10]*	*Yellow*	*L.Summer*	P	W	DS
3 × 3 ft						

Argentine. 1852. *G. speciosa*. In a sunny, sheltered, well-drained corner this will make a mass of dark green, narrow, toothed leaves and sprawling branching stems. Each branch bears a flower or two of brilliant orange-yellow, with orange centre. They are semi-double daisies, opening from buds covered with a white glutinous substance. *G. squarrosa* has less conspicuous flowers.

GUNNERA, Haloragidaceae.

manicata

1.8 × 2.4 m	*[7–10]*	*Green*	*E.Summer*	D
6 × 8 ft				

S. Brazil. 1867. *G. braziliensis*. This enormous plant is usually seen at the waterside or in marshy ground. The coarse root-crowns are covered with light brown fur, and prickly leaf stalks bear vast leaves over 1.8 m (6 ft) across, harsh, bristly and deeply lobed. The flowers are in great besom-like spikes of dull green, the side-branches are long and flexuous. As a landscape plant it is unequalled. The crowns should have the old leaves bent over them in winter, and a further covering of bracken or herbaceous tops should be given in cold areas. Spring planting is best. *G. chilensis* (*G. scabra, G. tinctoria*) (1840) [7–10] is similar but somewhat smaller in flower and leaf; flowers borne on shorter rigid side-branches. One would hardly need to pick these—either the leaf or the flower—unless one were decorating the Royal Albert Hall.

"I believe the great secret for ensuring its reaching gigantic proportions . . . is to 'feed the brute'."—EAB

GYPSOPHILA, Caryophyllaceae.
These grow best in full sun in our warmer counties, preferably in well-drained, rubbly, limy soils. They prove short-lived in cold damp areas. They need deep soil for their questing roots and are best left alone when established. They may be regarded solely for the value of their flowers, the leaves being slight. All are ideal for cutting.

altissima

1.2 × 1.2 m	*[3–9]*	*White*	*Summer*	P	S
4 × 4 ft					

S.E. Russia, etc. 1759. A little-known species, for any sunny open place. Unlike *G. paniculata* its stems are somewhat sticky to the touch. The whole forms a large open mass with pure white flowers, later than *G. paniculata*. Lax habit.

oldhamiana

90 cm × 1.2 m	*[4–9]*	*Pink*	*L.Summer*	P	GS
3 × 4 ft					

N.E. Asia. 1911. Resembles *G. paniculata*, but the extra glaucous leaves assort well with the pink flowers and it is much later in flower. A valuable garden plant.

paniculata

90 cm–1.2 m × 1.2 m 3–4 × 4 ft	[4–9]	White	Summer	P	S

E. Europe, Siberia. 1759. Produces the well-known froth of tiny grey-white stars, a huge mound from which it is so difficult to extract stems for indoors. Fifty years ago it was much sought for putting with sweet peas and carnations in vases; today we should heed Gertrude Jekyll's tip and plant it behind spring bulbs, Oriental Poppies, etc., so that its mass can fill a bare space in late summer.

"... masses of the pretty mist-like bloom four feet across and as much high.... As the grey changes ... to a brownish tone, some of the taller Nasturtiums are allowed to grow over the bushes of Gypsophila." GJ

—'**Bristol Fairy'** 1928. Pure white, double. somewhat short-lived; the shorter-growing 'Bodgeri' or 'Compacta Plena' usually proves more reliable. Cuttings or grafts.

—'**Flamingo'** 1938. Pale pink, double. Somewhat delicate. The dwarfer 'Pink Star' seems more reliable. Cuttings or grafts.

'Rosy Veil' ★

30 × 46 cm 1 ft × 18 in	[4–9]	Pink	Summer	P	C

'Rosenschleier'. A hybrid between *G. paniculata* and *G. repens* 'Rosea'. 1933. Particularly merits the name of Baby's Breath. A low cloud of clear pink flowers, for rock garden or border-front. A newer variety is 'Rosa Schoenheit', rather taller and of good colour.

HEDYCHIUM, Zingiberaceae. Ginger Lily. Tuberous-rooted plants of great majesty, appreciating full sun in our warmest counties, in a rich moist soil. They die down in autumn. The rhizomes should only just be covered with soil. Plant in spring for the first time and cover with a good mulch at the approach of cold weather subsequently. The strong stems carry broad handsome leaves at intervals and terminate in a spike or bottle-brush of flowers with long stamens, sweetly scented. Several species thrive at Trengwainton, Cornwall, including *H. ellipticum* [9–10] and *H. greenei* [8–10]

coccineum

1.5 m × 90 cm 5 × 3 ft	[9–10]	Red	L. Summer	P W D

India, Burma. 1815. This is the richest in colour of these tender plants. Like all the others the flowers are in a big spike, held well above narrow clear green leaves, the whole array being carried on a stout stalk. Here the flowers are in varying tints of pink or coral-red with flesh-coloured lobes, and with long-projecting red stamens. It is fortunate that a form raised from seeds collected by A. D. Schilling high up near Kathmandu in 1972 has proved hardy in many districts in England; it is a bold plant named ● ★ 'Stephen', with handsome spikes of orange-red flowers in early autumn.

densiflorum

90 × 60 cm 3 × 2 ft	[7–9]	Coral	Summer	P W D

E. Himalaya. Leaves 30 cm (1 ft) long and 7.5 cm (3 in) or so wide, are borne up the stout stems, which are surmounted by dense spikes of tiny orange-red or coral-red flowers, enriched by coral-red stamens. A collection from Bhutan by

Ludlow & Sherriff, No. 17393, is proving hardy out of doors in our warmer counties. 'Assam Orange' is a little taller, later-flowering, with narrower leaves and larger flower spikes but may not prove so hardy. They thrive at Wakehurst, Sussex. A considerably finer form was collected from Eastern Nepal by A. D. Schilling in 1966 and named 'Tara' in 1982. It has fine large spikes of light orange. This has proved hardy in Surrey.

gardnerianum ●
1.5 m × 90 cm	*[9–10]*	*Yellow*	*L. Summer/*	P	W	D
5 × 3 ft			*E. Autumn*			

N. India. 1819. This giant of a plant needs a warm corner in our warmest counties. The stems have fine broad foliage 30 cm (1 ft) or more long, of glaucous colouring when young, turning to deep blue-green. The flower spikes, 38 cm (15 in) long are of clear yellow ornamented by projecting red stamens.

× raffillii ●
1.5 m × 90 cm	*[9–10]*	*Orange*	*L. Summer*	P	W	D
5 × 3 ft						

Hybrid. *H. coccineum × H. gardnerianum,* raised by C. P. Raffill at Kew, *c.* 1940. 'C. P. Raffill' is again a most handsome plant with broad, long, glaucous green leaves, and fine spikes of brilliant orange with dark red projecting stamens. It would need a very warm and sheltered corner.

spicatum
1.2 m × 60 cm	*[8–10]*	*Yellow*	*E. Autumn*	P	W	D
4 × 2 ft						

India. 1810. The big leaves are hairy beneath, and the bright yellow flowers have paler, even white, but red-flushed lip, and the whole is charmed to fuller elegance by the projecting reddish filaments and yellow anthers. *H.s. acuminatum* is a form with leaves having distinct stalks and distinct hairiness below; the flowers are rather smaller, with purplish filaments. Both kinds produce showy fruits. Naturalized in some gardens in western Ireland.

HEDYSARUM, Leguminosae. These are really shrubs, but if cut down annually in spring, as I recommend for *Indigofera heterantha,* they add very much to the garden. They need full sunshine and well-drained fertile soil for this treatment, though they will grow as shrubs in poor stony ground.

microcalyx
1.5 m × 60 cm	*[5–9]*	*Magenta*	*L. Summer*	DS
5 × 2 ft				

Himalaya. An uncommon plant which is an asset to the garden at Crathes Castle, Kincardineshire, on account of its graceful stems, well clad in dainty pinnate leaves and long terminal sprays of small magenta pea-flowers.

multijugum ★
1.5 m × 60 cm	*[3–8]*	*Purple*	*Summer*	CS
4 × 2 ft				

Mongolia. 1883. This is much larger in all its characters; the leaves are rounded and greyish beneath, markedly pinnate. The flowers appear in the racemes in the axils of the leaves, as the shoots develop, and thus it may continue flowering until autumn. A vivid and gorgeous crimson-purple, ideal for planting with grey-leafed plants and *Buddleja fallowiana* 'Alba'.

HELENIUM, Compositae. Sneezeweed. These provide the backbone, among yellow, orange and brown shades, of the garden from July to September. Their daisy flowers are attractive, covering the branching sprays, each flower with a velvety yellow or brown knob in the centre, and with broad, fringed, silky petals. The leaves are of no account. The stems are stout and erect but as a rule the weight of the many flowers makes staking necessary. Easily grown in almost any soil short of a bog. They soon get congested and need dividing. These plants all assort well with other yellow flowers and coppery-foliage plants, and need the big green leaves of bergenias to give solidity in the foreground and to act as a foil for the masses of strong colour. When mixed with the warring colours of phloxes, monardas, sidalceas and lythrums they appear blatant, vulgar and offensive, but if grouped with good greenery, creamy white flowers and the magnificent macleayas, with perhaps *Cornus alba* 'Elegantissima', they will come into their own. Reputedly *Helenium* sprang from ground watered by Helen of Troy's tears; dare we suggest that Sneezeweed is connected with this legend? The race has become mixed with numerous hybrids and it is impossible to indicate which species is involved, but generally the tallest cultivars owe their height to *H. autumnale*; the remainder—mainly *H. bigelovii, H. hoopesii, H. nudiflorum*—are shorter. They are sometimes grouped under *H.* Hybrids or *H.* × *haagei.*

autumnale

1.5 m × 46 cm	[4–8]	Yellow/	E. Autumn	P D
5 ft × 18 in		Brown		

E. North America. 1729. This species and *H. bigelovii* are the parents of a big range of hybrids which are constantly being made bigger and better. There are short varieties like *H. bigelovii* 'Aurantiacum' in vivid yellow with yellow centres, and the old 'Crimson Beauty' (really a soft mahogany brown, and nowhere near to crimson—a trap for the unwary!); these flower in July and early August. At the other end of the scale are the September-flowering, 1.5-m (5-ft) tall, old forms of *H. autumnale,* the invaluable 'Riverton Beauty', yellow with maroon eye, and its counterpart in reddish-brown 'Riverton Gem'. In between, both in height and season, is a range of varieties and hybrids of excellence, from deepest mahogany to brightest yellow, 'self' coloured or variegated. Some noteworthy sorts are 'Bressingham Gold', 'Bruno', 'Butterpat', 'Coppelia', 'Moerheim Beauty' (1930), 'Spätrot', 'The Bishop' (1937), and 'Wyndley'—but it is best to make a personal selection from growing plants or from catalogues.

bigelovii

60 × 46 cm	[7–8]	Yellow	Summer	P D
2 ft × 18 in				

California. This old species has scarcely been surpassed in its warm deep orange-tinted yellow. See above. Shining green leaves.

hoopesii

90 × 46 cm	[3–7]	Yellow	E. Summer	P D
3 ft × 18 in				

Rocky Mountains. 1865. Similar to the above in general appearance, but it has the merit of flowering earlier, from early June. Large broad grey-green leaves making a good rosette like that of a big primula.

HELIANTHUS, Compositae. I cannot write about these with any enthusiasm. Their large daisy flowers are of brilliant yellow, their leaves coarse and rough, the taller varieties have running roots and need staking. They prefer a rather stiff soil in full sun, well drained.

197

atrorubens ●

| 1.8 m × 60 cm | [5–9] | Yellow | L. Summer | P D |

6 × 2 ft

S.E. United States. 1732. *H. sparsifolius*. It has invasive roots and is a weed in some places. 'Monarch' is a noted selection, with large, gorgeous, semi-double daisy flowers with petals recalling a cactus dahlia, of vivid deep yellow with black centre. It is only reliably hardy in our warmer counties. 'Gullick's Variety' is smaller-flowered but more vigorous.

decapetalus

| 90 cm–1.5 m | [5–8] | Yellow | L. Summer | P D |

× 60 cm

3–5 × 2 ft

North America. 1749. For our purpose this name can cover not only the species but its probable hybrids *H. × multiflorus* and *H. × laetiflorus*. *H. rigidus, H. annuus, H. tuberosus* and others are suspected of the parentage. These are erect, showy plants with large flowers, whose double centres are surrounded by larger segments. Take your choice in flower from the old 'Miss Mellish' (1893) or 'Soleil d'Or' (1889), or newer 'Loddon Gold'; all are vivid deep yellow. 'Capenoch Star' (1938) is a cooler, lighter yellow and more easy to use with most other flowers.

doronicoides

| 1.5 m × 60 cm | [4–8] | Yellow | L. Summer | C D |

5 × 2 ft

E. United States. This is one of the few pale yellow flowers of summer and as such has been treasured for many years at West Green House, Hampshire. Running roots. Rough, pointed leaves and airy flights of small sunflowers. Prior to 1929.

salicifolius

| 2.1 m × 60 cm | [6–9] | Yellow | E. Autumn | D |

7 × 2 ft

United States. 1879. *H. orgyalis*. During the summer this can easily be mistaken for a magnificently healthy clump of lilies, the stout stems being thickly set with many narrow, somewhat drooping, deep green leaves. It gets taller and taller and eventually erupts with a few rather small yellow daisies at the top. It looks well in summer as a background to shorter plants.

"... though a small-flowered plant, is yet one of the best for the picturesque garden."—WR

scaberrimus

| 1.5 m × 60 cm | [3–9] | Yellow | L. Summer/ | P D |

5 × 2 ft   E. Autumn

United States. 1732. *H. rigidus, H. laetiflorus*. Vigorous, running roots make this a good plant for naturalizing in rough places. It has highly decorative bright yellow flowers of good size with dark brown centres.

tomentosus

| 1.5 m × 60 cm | [6–9] | Yellow | L. Summer/ | P D |

5 × 2 ft   E. Autumn

S.E. United States. Like most of the Sunflowers, this has running roots; the rough oval leaves are greyish. Large branching heads of bright clear yellow flowers for a long period.

HELICHRYSUM, Compositae. The following plant has recently crept into cultivation and will undoubtedly prove popular. It may be a hybrid, perhaps of *H. graveolens* or *H. arenarium*, natives of Europe and Asia Minor.

'Sulphur Light'

46 × 46 cm	*[5–9]*	*Yellow*	*L. Summer*	PF	D
18 × 18 in					

'Schwefellicht'. If we gave brilliant sulphur yellow colouring to the everlasting flowers of *Anaphalis margaritacea* this would be the effect. The narrow leaves are white-woolly and the whole plant is long-lasting in beauty. Aromatic.

HELIOPSIS, Compositae. Here again we are concerned with some of the most blatant, long-lasting and satisfactory of perennials; as a rule they do not require support, except the tallest, and are good hearty plants for any fertile soil. But to me they lack charm.

helianthoides

1.5 m × 60 cm	*[4–9]*	*Yellow*	*Autumn*	P	CDS
5 × 2 ft					

North America. 1714. *H. laevis.* Tarred with the same yellow brush as the better known *H. scabra,* but a useful late-flowering daisy with large semi-double flowers with yellow centres. Leaves serrated, pointed. Seldom seen.

scabra ★

1.2 m × 60 cm	*[4–9]*	*Yellow*	*L. Summer*	P	CD
4 × 2 ft					

North America. 1824. The flowers range from single to fully double and are mostly of a warm deep tint, verging on orange. There are several to choose from display gardens and lists, such as 'Incomparabilis' (1932) and 'Patula', 'Golden Plume' and 'Light of Loddon'. All give the same effect in the garden but some flowers may appeal and others may not. Sometimes classed as *H. helianthoides scabra.* Comparatively new is 'Sonnenglut'.

HELLEBORUS, Ranunculaceae. The Christmas Roses and the Lenten Roses provide us with certainly the most sumptuous hardy flowers of winter and early spring, and are also the possessors of large, handsome, ground-covering, handlike leaves. They are easy to grow in any ordinary, reasonably well-drained, fertile garden soil, preferably retentive. They are splendid plants for growing under deciduous trees and shrubs or in the shade of north walls, but will also thrive in sun. All the flowers have a thick sculptured quality and rounded gracious outline, unsurpassed in the floral world. There are many named varieties and these and all other hellebores are worth acquiring if offered!

They are of two types: most are genuine herbaceous plants, but a few others— *H. corsicus, H. lividus, H. foetidus,* and their hybrids—produce a leafy stem one year which bears flowers at its apex the next, and then dies to make room for succeeding shoots. Evergreen.

The hellebores are tricky subjects for cutting for indoors. Little stalks of *H. foetidus* and *H. corsicus* flowers are easy and long-lasting. *H. niger* and *H. atrorubens* are reasonably satisfactory. Many of the others and all the *H. orientalis* types are temperamental but are most lasting when well open and mature. They resent centrally heated rooms and are best put into the larder at night. The stems should be slit on one side for several inches.

atrorubens ★
of gardens

30 × 46 cm	*[5–9]*	Purplish	Winter	P	D
1 ft × 18 in					

1853. In effect a dark-coloured plant similar to some of the *H. orientalis* hybrids, of which it is a parent, but it is deciduous and the flowers, of rich plum-purple, are usually produced with *H. niger* in January. No more care is needed than with the Lenten Roses. It does not appear to set seeds in cultivation. The above description applies to the well-known garden clone. The true species, from Yugoslavia, has smaller, darker flowers and is rare in cultivation. It is evergreen.

corsicus ● ★

60 × 90 cm	*[7–9]*	Green	Winter/	PF	S
2 × 3 ft			Spring		

Corsica, Sardinia, Balearic Islands. *H. argutifolius, H. lividus corsicus.* A bushy plant with stout stems having only leaves in their first year. The leaves are among the most beautiful of all, tripartite, with prickly edges, greyish-green and veined. They make a handsome clump, and the stems in their second year produce an upstanding cluster of palest green pendant cups with pale green nectaries and stamens; the whole plant is a symphony of beauty in the early year. Quite hardy, but should be protected from icy winds. Evergreen. Lovely with *Iris reticulata.*

"... almost shrub-like, with highly ornamental pale emerald bells."—ATJ

cyclophyllus

46 × 60 cm	*[6–9]*	Yellow/green	Winter	F	DS
18 in × 2 ft					

S.E. Europe. A valuable plant which in my garden produces its vivid, light greenish yellow flowers soon after Christmas, with those of *H. atrorubens* and 'Bowles's Yellow'. On a warm day a distinct scent can be detected, of elder flower or black-currant leaves. As good a grower as any *H. orientalis* type into whose later season the flowering extends.

foetidus ★

46 × 46 cm	*[6–9]*	Green	Winter/	PF	S
18 × 18 in			Spring		

S. Europe, Britain. This strange poisonous native plant has very handsome, deeply divided, black-green leaves making a clump in the same way as *H. corsicus.* In winter or earliest spring the flowers are borne in airy clusters at the end of the stems, each one a perfect bell of pale green, edged with maroon. Evergreen. An invaluable plant for sun or shade and a marvellous foil for silver-foliage plants, also for *Erica carnea* and *Lathyrus vernus.* The Italian form as grown by Mr Bowles is usually judged to be finer than our native type. 'Wester Fliske' is a selection with reddish stems and pedicels. Scottish origin.

"It has the darkest green leaves of any low growing plant ... their interlacing mass is a wonderfully telling object, especially among such plants as Megasea and Funkias whose large, entire leaves make a striking contrast."—EAB

lividus

46 × 30 cm	*[8–9]*	Green	E. Spring	P W	S
18 in × 1 ft					

Majorca. 1710. This is only for our warmest counties, and is established at Overbecks, S. Devon. Most beautiful tripartite evergreen leaves, overlaced with grey, recalling the markings on those of *Cyclamen hederifolium.* The flowers appear, like those of *H. corsicus,* at the ends of the leafy stems in the second year; they are pinkish green and delicately scented, which is most noticeable when growing under cover.

niger ● ★

30 × 46 cm	*[4–8]*	*White*	*Winter*	P	DS
1 ft × 18 in					

Europe, W. Asia. Cultivated since Roman days, the dark green broad leathery leaves of this well-known plant are less noticeable than those of the *H. orientalis* group, but form an equally beautiful setting for the sumptuous nodding white blooms, often faintly tinged with pink on the outside, and having a crown of golden stamens. They stand up well above the leaves. It is not always easy to establish; it usually grows best in a "tacky" soil that does not dry out, in shade. It appreciates old manure and leaf-mould in spring. Evergreen.

GARDEN FORMS Special seedlings have been named from time to time. Mrs Lawrenson of Kildare raised 'St Brigid', which may still be growing in Ireland. Ernest Ladhams produced 'Ladhams' Variety' during the 'thirties. The most recent is Miss Davenport-Jones's 'Potter's Wheel' (1958). They all were selected for their sumptuous large white flowers. Unless propagated from division they are not entitled to their clonal names, though from seed forms nearly as good may continue to appear. 'Louis Cobbett', raised by its namesake at Cambridge prior to 1962, is a superb new clone; deep rose-pink outside, with brown flush around the calyx and stalk, and clear blush inside with a star-like green flush around the nectaries—a nonpareil if ever there was one.

—**macranthus.** *H. altifolius.* [4–8]. In this botanical variant the leaves are somewhat narrower, and the segments of the flower also narrower. On the other hand, several flowers of large size, often pink-tinted outside, or flushed with pink all over, are borne on each stem. The leaves are borne above the flowers.

"*H. altifolius,* though sometimes considered a variety of *H. niger,* is a distinct kind ... much larger ... each stem bearing two to seven flowers which have a stronger tendency to assume a rosy hue than the ordinary kind."—WR

● **nigericors** [6–9]. Hybrids between the Christmas Rose and the Corsican Hellebore. The cross has been made on several occasions and a few plants are being distributed among keen gardeners, but it is not likely to reach catalogues very freely for some years as it is slow from division. It is usually midway between the parents in all particulars, bearing wide-open flowers in large clusters at the ends of the stout short stems, well set with good dark foliage. The colour is greenish white in marked contrast. First raised by J. E. H. Stooke, *c.* 1938. The cross has been made subsequently several times and some of the results are better, even excellent, garden plants, but vary in the tint of the flower and the type of foliage, and should be chosen while growing; 'Beatrix' was named and raised by E. B. Anderson. Other raisers have been Miss Strangman and Eric Smith; the latter, using *H.* × *sternii* [6–9], has developed a strain labelled Nigristern. Miss Strangman's clone is called 'Alabaster'.

● **nigriliv** Hybrids have also been raised between *H. niger* and *H. lividus.* The results I have seen are very beautiful with wide, pale green flowers suffused with clear rosy mauve. Those nearest to *H. lividus* have marbled leaves but will probably prove to be tender.

201

orientalis ● ★

46 × 60 cm	[4–9]	White	Winter/	F DS
18 in × 2 ft			Spring	

Bithynian Olympus, Asia Minor. 1839. It is very difficult to know what to list under this name, as the botanists do not all agree. As, however, it is a name which is well known, and in gardens covers a mixed lot of hybrids, I think it best to persist in this grouping. The plants vary in colour from blush-white to plum colour, often—in fact, usually—with wide-open nodding flowers, more or less beautifully spotted inside with crimson and maroon, and with subtle green flushes both inside and out. The flowers are very hardy outdoors, but not patient of warm rooms. The splendid evergreen foliage makes a sort of prostrate platform for the sheaf of flowering stems; the plants grow happily in almost any soil except bog, and are best in partial or full shade. They form the ideal groundcover for deciduous shrubs. In flower from December to April; always a great sight at Knightshayes Court, Devon, and at Sissinghurst Castle, Kent. Beautiful with Snowdrops.

"... easy to grow, long-lived, weed destroying, and they scorn cultural help."—ATJ

Many authorities separate certain forms:

—**abschasicus**   *H. colchicus*. Purplish-ruby colour, more or less densely covered with minute maroon dots inside; nearly evergreen.

—**antiquorum**   Creamy, rose-tinted, green at base, nearly evergreen.

—**atrorubens**   See above. Deciduous.

–**guttatus**   Flowers white or greenish-pink, usually heavily spotted with maroon inside. Strains or plants inheriting the conspicuous spotting are sometimes labelled 'Prince Rupert', but this name strictly applies to one clone only.

—**kochii**   of gardens. By some botanists this is considered the true *H. orientalis* and is a very rare plant. It blooms regularly when the Christmas Rose and *H. atrorubens* bloom, and is thus a month or so earlier, usually, than the *H. orientalis* hybrid strains. Slightly shorter in growth, but with very large coarsely toothed leaves, the nodding flowers are yellow-green in bud, opening wide to a delicate primrose-yellow, in which colouring it is unique in this genus. Just as easy to grow as *H. orientalis* strain. I have had my plant for over fifty years and call it 'Bowles' Yellow' after the donor.

—**olympicus**   This breeds reasonably true from seed. Large white flowers open from pale green buds. Good at Hidcote, Gloucestershire.

It is easily understood how over many years fine forms have cropped up and have received names, and old lists used to contain numerous clones, including the very dark 'Ballard's Black', raised at Colwall, Hereford. However, I am told on the best authority that the original 'Ballard's Black' died, and all plants found under this name are merely seedlings and not entitled to the name. Mrs Helen Ballard of Mathon, Worcestershire, has raised an astonishing array of hybrids, using *H. cyclophyllus* to achieve true lemon-yellow and *H. purpurascens* or *H. serbicus* to develop the darkest, almost navy-blue tints. One of the first raisers was Archer Hind of Coombe Fishacre, Devon. Seedlings crop up in great quantity in gardens on retentive soil and practically all of them are good, many of superlative quality, so that it seems almost unnecessary to go to the slow process of division. It is an operation not appreciated by Hellebores, because they take at least two years to settle down again. It is best done immediately after flowering, separating individual crowns, each with roots of its own, with a knife, after washing all soil off the lifted clump.

purpurascens ●

30 × 30 cm	*[5–8]*	*Purplish*	*Spring*	DS
1 × 1 ft				

E. Europe, Ukraine, etc. 1817. The leaves are very deeply cut, narrowly fingered. The small flowers are nodding, elegiac, glaucous maroon outside and a surprising light green inside. This choice and unusual plant intrigues the uninitiated; it is neat and well chiselled. The best forms of these two plants are worth seeking. Eric Smith has raised a good new hybrid 'Pluto'. The plant known as *H. torquatus* [5–8] in gardens is related to *H. purpurascens* and may be a hybrid of this species. Its flowers are of the same dark tint outside but the insides may be similarly dark instead of green. Later findings attribute *H. torquatus* to a large area in central and southern Yugoslavia. It is sometimes classed as *H. serbicus* or *H. multifidus* subsp. *serbicus*.

× sternii

46 × 46 cm	*[6–9]*	*Green*	*Winter/*	PF	DS
18 × 18 in			*Spring*		

H. × baueri. H. corsicus × H. lividus. These hybrids have the shrubby growth of the parents and leaves and flowers intermediate between them. The greater hardiness and vigour of *H. corsicus* have been linked with the strange rosy green of *H. lividus*. Ordinary soil, sunny; shelter from icy winds. The strain varies somewhat when raised from seed and is apt to revert to *H. corsicus*.

vesicarius

46 × 60 cm	*[7–9]*	*Green*	*E. Spring*	F	W S
18 in × 2 ft					

Asia Minor. A rarity with coarsely toothed, deciduous leaves of considerable size; small green flowers with brownish edges, followed by remarkable bladder-like seed-capsules. For sheltered corners in warm gardens.

viridis

30 × 46 cm	*[6–8]*	*Green*	*Winter/*	F	DS
1 ft × 18 in			*Spring*		

Europe, Britain. Of the *H. orientalis* group, slightly smaller. The flowers are of pure and brilliant green. Deciduous leaves, *H.v. occidentalis* is a native of Britain and is smaller-flowered and larger-leafed, but no less attractive. The flowers of both kinds last pure and green until well into summer. Other green-flowered species worth growing when obtainable are *H. multifidus* [5–9], whose leaves are truly multifid, cut into many very long narrow lobes, and *H. dumetorum* [5–8], which is not fragrant and, confusingly, has a subspecies *H.d. atrorubens,* with flowers less good than our *H. atrorubens* (of gardens). Its leaves stand erect.

HEMEROCALLIS, Liliaceae. The Day Lilies have many assets recommending them to gardeners and all who love flowers. They are almost indestructible and can be transplanted at any time, although the autumn or early spring should be chosen. Their leaves are arching, grassy, bright green, reaching 60 cm (2 ft) or more and are one of the loveliest foils for early spring flowers, for they are of light colouring after piercing the soil; the leaves of many turn to bright yellow in autumn. The flower stems are stout, not usually leafy, bearing a branching cluster of exquisitely shaped lily-like flowers, deliciously scented in most yellow and some other varieties. Though each flower lasts only a day there is a long succession of them, and different varieties prolong the season. They thrive in sun or partial shade, in any soil, preferring not to be too dry. When the clumps begin to flower less freely they should be divided. Excellent ground-cover. These normally very accommodating plants are sometimes a failure in the colder north, where they should be given warm conditions and good drainage. They all form compact dense root-clumps except *H. lilio-asphodelus* and *H. fulva,* which increase freely by rhizomes and can be a nuisance in smaller gardens, but are of course admirable for densely colonizing large areas. The name *H. esculenta,* indicating that the plant has some edible quality, has little botanical standing. The Chinese consider the buds and the dried flowers a table delicacy, and indeed fresh or withered flowers are pleasant in salads. It was this culinary asset that caused the Day Lily to be grown thousands of years ago in the Far East. One of the distinguishing characters of the various species is found in the roots, some of which have tuberous swellings.

aurantiaca

90 × 60 cm	*[5–10]*	*Orange*	*Summer*	P	D
3 × 2 ft					

Japan. Prior to 1890. Probably a garden form or hybrid, since it is self-incompatible. Like the next variety its foliage remains evergreen in warm districts. The firm shapely flowers are of intense orange with some fulvous tinting in the segments. A parent of many old hybrids. The roots of this species have tuberous swellings.

'Aurantiaca Major'
of gardens

90 × 60 cm	*[8–10]*	*Orange*	*Summer*	P	D
3 × 2 ft					

c. 1890. An old clone perhaps introduced from Japan, related to *H. aurantiaca,* but with larger, very fine flowers of pure rich orange. It is reputedly not so hardy as others, or the parent species, and has a compact rootstock and rather coarse foliage. The flowers are wide and starry.

citrina

90 × 60 cm	*[3–9]*	*Citron*	*L. Summer*	P	D
3 × 2 ft					

China. 1902. *H. citrina* 'Baroni' (of gardens). Rather broad, dark green leaves, glaucous on reverse side. This is for the commuter because its flowers open in the evening. They are fragrant, of light citron-yellow but not of so lovely a shape as the others, the segments being narrow and stiff, and they tend to close in the morning. It forms a compact clump with the flowers borne well aloft. *H. thunbergii* [3–9] is related, of similar colouring, but lasting until the afternoon. Some of the roots of this species have tuberous swellings. To confuse matters there is also *H.* 'Baronii' which is a hybrid between this species and *H. thunbergii.*

dumortieri

60 × 46 cm	*[3–9]*	*Yellow*	*L. Spring*	P	D
2 ft × 18 in					

Japan, Siberia. 1832. Noted for its early display. The rich deep yellow of the flowers is enhanced by the dark brown buds, all held together in a dense cluster by an attenuated bract. Fragrant. It forms a dense clump, with roots mostly swollen.

exaltata

1.2 m × 46 cm	*[3–9]*	*Yellow*	*Summer*		D
4 ft × 18 in					

Japan. 1934. A satisfactory plant, but the soft orange flowers are borne in a tight cluster at the top of the high stem so that the plant lacks charm. It is scarcely scented. Forms a compact clump.

fulva

1.2 m × 90 cm	*[3–9]*	*Orange-buff*	*Summer*	P	D
4 × 3 ft					

Japan. 1576. *H. disticha.* An old plant, very free and vigorous, with erect stems and broad foliage. The flowers have a zone of brown tint around the throat and an apricot central line on each segment; the whole gives a soft brick-red effect. This, the normal form, is a sterile plant known as 'Europa'. All forms increase freely at the root. It is established at Cliveden, Buckinghamshire.

> "These Lillies do grow in my garden, as also in the gardens of Herbarists, and lovers of fine and rare plants; but not wild in England as in other countries. They do floure somewhat before the other Lillies."—GH

—'Kwanso Flore Pleno' ★ ●

90 × 90 cm	*[3–9]*	*Orange-buff*	*Summer*	P	D
3 × 3 ft					

1860. The most beautiful and well-known of the original old double orange varieties; it was imported from Japan. This variety has the most perfectly double flowers with broad, regular, overlapping segments. Another double orange variety with white edged or striped leaves was introduced prior to 1864 also from Japan and was originally called 'Kwanso foliis variegatis' and is now called 'Variegated Kwanso'. It has rather poorly shaped flowers compared with 'Kwanso Flore Pleno' and is apt to revert to a green type. This is sometimes called 'Green Kwanso'. The name 'Kwanso' is the Japanese equivalent to Day Lily. 'Kwanso Flore Pleno' is every year a great feature in the Red Borders at Hidcote, Gloucestershire. *H. disticha* Donn 'Flore Pleno' was a name originally attached to one of these old forms. There are new double hybrids, 'Gay Music' and 'King Alfred'. While I should be the last to claim that the doubling of petals improves or enhances the flowers, the fact that they do not shrivel so quickly makes them the more valuable for landscape effect.

—'Maculata' ● ★

1.2 m × 60 cm	*[3–9]*	*Buff*	*Summer*	P	D
4 × 2 ft					

1897. Particularly graceful stems with elegantly poised flowers, the top segments being decisively reflexed, the lower curved up and forwards. The colour is a soft coppery buff with a dark zone in the centre. Of very large proportions; a gracious, prolific and lovely plant which, like most of these species, is scorned by today's hybridists. A good contrast for blue-flowered echinops and eryngiums.

—rosea

90 × 60 cm	*[3–9]*	*Pink*	*Summer*	P	D
3 × 2 ft					

China. *c.* 1930. A natural variant from Kuling, China, and the forerunner of the pink varieties. Pretty flowers with narrow, recurving segments emerging from a long throat, half the size of *H.f.* 'Maculata', of soft coppery rose. It is a graceful plant, with narrow foliage, and a beautiful companion to *Eryngium tripartitum* and *Buddleja davidii* 'Royal Red'. It increases freely at the root.

lilio-asphodelus ● ★

75 × 46 cm	[3–9]	Yellow	Spring	P	D
2½ ft × 18 in					

E. Asia, S.E. Europe, etc. 1596. *H. flava.* This old garden plant, grown since the sixteenth century, flowers after *H. dumortieri* and *H. middendorfii.* It spreads freely at the root and the roots are mostly swollen. The flowers are a beautiful lily-shape, with recurving petals, of clear and lovely yellow, and have an unforgettable fragrance. This beautiful plant ushers in the lily season with great quality and charm. Try it with *Geranium* 'Johnson's Blue', and with lupins. Lovely at Oxburgh Hall, Norfolk, and Hardwick Hall, Derbyshire.

"Few plants can be grown with so little trouble . . . and give such a valuable return."—WR

littorea

90 cm–1.2 m	[3–9]	Orange	L. Summer/	P	DS
× 60 cm			E. Autumn		
3–4 × 2 ft					

Japan. *H. aurantiaca littorea.* Seldom seen in gardens but valuable for display—and for hybridizing—on account of its flowering time, late August and September, with *H. multiflora.* Small, soft, reddish orange flowers with dark yellow throat in a wide-branching head. *H. fulva littorea.*

middendorfii

60 × 46 cm	[3–9]	Orange	E. Summer	P	D
2 ft × 18 in					

Siberia, etc. 1866. Another useful early-flowering plant, following *H. dumortieri.* It forms a compact root (without tuberous swellings) and has bright orange-yellow, broad-segmented, fragrant flowers, the dense clusters held together by cup-shaped, blunt bracts. Brown-tipped buds. Beautiful for blending with azaleas of the Mollis group. Fragrant.

minor

46 × 46 cm	[3–9]	Yellow	L. Spring	P	D
18 × 18 in					

E. Asia. 1759. A pleasing small species, forming a compact clump of lax leaves. The scented flowers are of clear yellow, tinted brown outside, and are borne well above the leaves. This species and others have been used to create dwarf hybrids for small gardens. *H. forrestii* [3–9] and *H. nana* [3–9] are two small species, with orange flowers. Their leaves are more rigid; in *H. nana* the flower stems are scarcely as long as the leaves. The roots of *H. minor* are not conspicuously enlarged at the ends as in *H. nana* and *H. forrestii.*

multiflora

1.2 m × 60 cm	[5–9]	Yellow	L. Summer	P	D
4 × 2 ft					

China. 1934. The last species to flower, usually when all other species are over and also after nearly all the large-flowered hybrids—to which it comes as a refreshing surprise. It has a much branched head of small fragrant flowers, like butterflies, of soft orange-yellow. 'Isis', 'Corky' and 'Golden Chimes' are small-flowered day lilies perhaps descended in part from this. Compact root and narrow leaves, considerably shorter than the flower stems. This and *H. littorea* may well be potential parents of a late-flowering race.

thunbergii

46 × 46 cm	*[3–9]*	*Yellow*	*Summer*	P	D
18 × 18 in					

China, Korea, Japan. 1890. *H. serotina*. A good lemon-yellow species, flowering after *H. lilio-asphodelus*; the flowers are carried in branching heads over the leaves which do not succumb to the first frosts. It is a useful and refined species for garden use; the roots are seldom swollen and are compact.

GARDEN HYBRIDS

90 cm–1.5 m	*[4–9]*	*Various*	*Summer*	P	D
× 60–90 cm					
3–5 × 2–3 ft					

During this century the Day Lilies have become popular with breeders, and the vigour of the plants, the number of flowers per stem, the size of bloom and thickness of petals, have been increased—inevitably to the loss of charm and poise. However, they are valuable garden plants. George Yeld and Amos Perry led the way, and some of their varieties, like 'J. S. Gayner', 'Thelma Perry' and 'Radiant', are still found in gardens, a tribute to their beauty and longevity. Breeding has proceeded apace both in this country and the United States since their day but along rather stereotyped lines. Little use has been made of the divergent beauties and seasons of the species.

From the above list of species—which are by no means common in gardens—it will be seen that many characters are of importance and we should look for these when making our selection of the hybrids. Apart from beauty, colour and fragrance, I should look for those cultivars whose flowers are held well above the foliage, a point which is not always borne in mind by breeders. A plant whose flowers sit among the leaves is far less ornamental than one whose flowers are held well aloft. The foliage should not be over-luxuriant, and the modern tendency towards broader, stiffer leaves, often twisted, is to be deplored. The flowers should be of pure, open lily-shape, not with twisted and frilled segments, which destroy the outline. Flowers of one tint are more telling in the garden than bicolors. The lighter colours are very much more telling in the garden than the dark pinkish or reddish varieties and particularly is this true of the light yellows; they can be seen from afar, blend well with the foliage and are usually fragrant. Running roots can be a nuisance at times; these are inherited from *H. flava* and *H. fulva*.

Though I have as a rule in this book not permitted myself the luxury of indicating cultivars which appeal to me, I will call attention to a few, because day lilies, like astilbes and peonies, are good permanent garden plants and do not quickly go out of fashion. 'Alan' and 'Stafford' are two superlative glowing mahogany reds, very colourful in the garden landscape, which cannot be said of the maroon-red varieties, which are too dark. 'Missenden' (1966) is a glowing mahogany red and bids fair to outclass both 'Alan' and 'Stafford' with its upright growth and fine flowers. 'Marion Vaughn' is the outstanding clear lemon yellow, of great vigour, with 'Lark Song' and 'Dorothy McDade' excellent runners-up, but rather shorter. 'Jake Russell' is a soft warm yellow; 'White Jade' is of palest Isabelline tint. There are many of soft peachy apricot such as 'Dream Waltz', 'Duke of Windsor', 'Salmon Sheen', and brilliant oranges among 'Cartwheels', 'Doubloons' and 'Spanish Gold' and their kindred. Everyone should make his or her choice from the many available. For particular comment is 'Golden Chimes' whose deep yellow small flowers, borne in branching sprays, are mahogany on the reverse—characters inherited perhaps from *H. dumortieri* and *H. multiflora*.

Attention is also being given, particularly in the United States, to breeding with dwarf species such as *H. minor,* and a strain of plants with small flowers, leaves, and of small stature is evolving. One of the most important is 'Eenie Weenie' raised by Paul Aden in the United States, but, likely to eclipse it is 'Stella d'Oro' (Jablonski, USA) which is similarly dwarf but repeats its flower crops in September and October. Neither exceeds 45 cm (1½ ft). Slightly larger is 'Happy Returns' whose shapely yellow flowers last for two days, being produced in summer and again from late summer until autumn. There is no doubt that these two varieties will be followed by more; the class is known as "Dwarf" in the United States. Another class is known as "Miniature"; these embrace such small-flowered kinds as mentioned under *H. multiflora.* Their small flowers are not necessarily coupled with small stature. But Day Lilies are perhaps the most popular of summer flowering perennials in the States and breeding new cultivars is carried on apace everywhere with hundreds, even thousands, of new names every year. There is no doubt that the new tetraploid seedlings are setting new standards in form and colour.

HERACLEUM, Umbelliferae.

mantegazzianum

3 × 2.8 m	*[3–9]*	*White*	*Summer*	F	S
10 × 6 ft					

Caucasus. 1893. An immense plant like a gigantic Cow Parsley, and more or less biennial or monocarpic. The huge basal divided leaves are 90 cm (3 ft) wide, and a stout, cylindrical, polished coppery stem produces more leaves and several wheel-like heads of white flowers. As it sows itself freely after flowering and can become a nuisance, the heads should be removed before the bulk of the seed falls. Splendid for wild gardens, park planting, and wherever a tropical effect is required. Deep, moist soil, sun or shade. Fine seed-heads. This is another plant to use when decorating the Royal Albert Hall! Very rarely one hears of a person whose skin is allergic to the sap in the stem. Established at Blicking Hall, Norfolk, and Hinton Ampner, Hampshire.

HESPERIS, Cruciferae.

matronalis

1.2 m × 60 cm	*[4–9]*	*White/Lilac*	*Summer*	P	DS
4 × 2 ft					

S. Europe, Siberia. 1350. Sweet Rocket or Dame's Violet. Though a perennial, it is best to raise young plants every few years because the roots become woody and less productive with age. From seed it may vary from white to deep lilac; tall branching stems hold many very fragrant, single, stock-like flowers for many weeks. There are also double-flowered varieties, to be propagated from cuttings; they are unfortunately highly temperamental and difficult even in the retentive but well-drained limy soil which suits the species best. The single-flowered type will seed itself freely and can put up with hungry ground. The scent is most pronounced in the evening.

HEUCHERA, Saxifragaceae. All of these plants have woody roots which slowly spread into large clumps copiously bearing rounded hairy leaves, sometimes beautifully tinted or marbled with grey, and creating good ground-cover. Above these dense mats their wiry stems arise, holding numerous tiny bell-shaped flowers. They are happy in reasonably well-drained fertile soils in full sun or part shade, and need pulling to pieces and replanting every few years. They transplant best in August or early September rather than in the drying winds of spring; it is important at whichever period is chosen to sink the woody roots well into the soil so that only the crown of foliage is above ground. Well-fed plants flower through May and June and often continue with a few stems until autumn. A good contrast for 'Mrs Sinkins' pinks. Evergreen.

americana

46 × 30 cm   *[4–8]*   *Greenish*   *E. Summer*   PF   D
18 in × 1 ft

North America. 1656. Alum Root. The dainty spires of tiny greenish flowers followed by green seed-pods are not the main features of this beautiful ground-covering, clump-forming plant. The leaves broad and somewhat like an ivy's in outline are, when young, of glistening quality, dark green, flushed and veined with coppery brown. They become dark green with age, but are still glistening or of satiny sheen. If grown well, young leaves are in constant production. Sometimes called *H. rubescens*.

"The Satin-leaf ... the beauty of the plant is in the colour and texture of the foliage."—GJ

× brizoides ● ★

60 × 30 cm   *[3–8]*   *Red/Pink*   *E. Summer*   P   D
2 × 1 ft

Hybrid. *H. sanguinea* perhaps crossed with *H. micrantha*. This covers a race of very pretty plants, the colour of *H. sanguinea* having been given to the larger flower sprays of the other species. 'Gracillima' in pale pink, 'Blooms' Variety' and 'Splendour' of a richer tone, are typical clones bearing multitudes of tiny flowers on their long feathery sprays. Alan Bloom has made many hybrids with larger flowers in a variety of brilliant tints, such as 'Coral Cloud', 'Pearl Drops', 'Sparkler', and 'Oakington Jewel'.

cylindrica

60 × 30 cm   *[4–8]*   *Cream*   *Summer*   P   DS
2 × 1 ft

W. North America. 1830. This is neither graceful nor dainty, but is unique and worth cultivating if only for its excellent clumps of heart-shaped, lobed, dark green leaves. The stiff stem carries a spike of small brownish flowers. *H.c.* 'Alba' is a good creamy white form of considerable value. Two selections by Alan Bloom are 'Greenfinch', 90 cm (3 ft) creamy green in large spikes, and 'Hyperion', rather shorter in soft rosy red. Useful to create a bold erect line in frontal plantings.

micrantha

90 × 46 cm   *[4–8]*   *Blush*   *E. Summer*   P   D
3 ft × 18 in

W. United States. 1827. The grey-marbled leaves are conspicuously beautiful and the waving mass of feathery stems set with innumerable minute blush-white flowers has charm for those who like the refinement of species.

★ —**diversifolia 'Palace Purple'**   [4–8] Raised from wild-collected seeds at Kew (since 1980) by Brian Halliwell, this produces plants which have quickly become popular. The colour of the leaves is a metallic coppery purple and the flowers and seed pods have caught some of the colour also. Though it breeds reasonably uniformly from seeds, good coloured ones are worth preserving. They all go under the name of 'Palace Purple', to commemorate Kew Palace, 1631, built before the species was introduced.

pilosissima

46 × 46 cm *18 × 18 in*	*[8–9]*	*White*	*E. Summer*	P	D

California. The whole plant, leaves, stems and flowers, is covered in velvety hairs. The mats of soft green foliage show up the sprays of grey-white tiny blooms, which have a pinkish tinge.

sanguinea

46 × 46 cm *1 × 1 ft*	*[3–8]*	*White*	*E. Summer*	P	D

S.W. United States. 1882. Coral Bells. The short stems bear large bells of brilliant colouring over the usual dark leaves, somewhat marbled. 'Bressingham Blaze', 'Red Spangles' and 'Shere Variety' are all excellent, brilliant seedlings, and Alan Bloom usually has a new one "up his sleeve" to keep our appetites whetted in this pretty genus.

"One of the most precious of the American flowers."—CWE

villosa

60 × 30 cm *2 × 1 ft*	*[6–9]*	*White*	*L. Summer*		D

S.E. United States. 1812. Clear green, large, lobed leaves. Though the tiny deep-creamy flowers are small they are borne in large airy sprays from August onwards and therefore this plant has value. It is a good companion for *Gentiana asclepiadea,* and conspicuous when flowering well.

× **HEUCHERELLA,** Saxifragaceae. Hybrids between *Heuchera* and *Tiarella*; those listed below bear a marked resemblance to *Heuchera,* having similar foliage densely covering the ground and similar pretty wands of tiny flowers, which are produced rather earlier than in *Heuchera.* They are both clump-forming. Evergreen.

alba

46 × 30 cm *18 in × 1 ft*	*[4–8]*	*Pink*	*E. Summer*	P	D

1925. *Heuchera brizoides × Tiarelli wherryi.* 'Bridget Bloom' is a charming plant by Alan Bloom which makes good basal greenery and throws up many clear pink flower spikes. Fortunately they appear not only in May and June but in later summer as well. It grows well in ordinary soil that will not dry out in summer, in part shade.

tiarelloides ● ★

46 × 46 cm *18 × 18 in*	*[4–8]*	*Pink*	*E. Summer*	P	D

1912. *Heuchera brizoides × Tiarella cordifolia.* A pretty hybrid from Nancy, France, making a beautiful ground-cover, slowly spreading, with its dense clusters of short leaves; well above these are the spires of tiny salmon-pink bells appearing mainly in May but with some later. It will grow well in any fertile soil which is not too dry, and thrives in partial shade. Evergreen.

HIBISCUS, Malvaceae. Mallow.

moscheutos ●

90 × 60 cm	*[5–9]*	*Various*	*Summer*	W	DS
3 × 2 ft					

E. United States. 1574. Swamp Rose-Mallow. Seldom seen, but it is easy to raise from seed and it will grow in any good soil that does not dry out, in full sun. (Having written this I must mention that my great success was in rather dry soil.) Most handsome plants with good foliage, borne up the erect stems from clumps which increase slowly. Huge, satiny, rounded mallow flowers 15 cm (6 in) across, crimson, pink or white; an eye-opener in many ways. It needs a warm garden in our warmer counties. Hybrids with *H. coccineus* have been raised in the United States which may be hardy in our warmest counties. 'Lord Baltimore' crimson; 'Lady Baltimore', pink with crimson eye, 'Ann Arundel', dark pink are noted selections bred in Iowa by Robert Darby. [5–9]

HIERACIUM, Compositae. Hawkweed—a name which is hardly complimentary to this beautiful plant.

lanatum

60 × 30 cm	*[5–8]*	*Yellow*	*Summer*	DS
2 × 1 ft				

Europe. *H. waldsteinii*. The silvery-grey, downy, broad leaves form a lovely bold rosette about 30 cm (1 ft) high, and last in beauty the whole season; it is perhaps best to remove the branching sprays of yellow daisies, unless the plant is required to seed itself, which it will do sometimes. The flowers add little to the beauty of the leaves. Sun, poor well-drained soil.

villosum

30 × 30 cm	*[4–8]*	*Yellow*	*Summer*	DS
1 × 1 ft				

Central Europe. 1739. This forms a mat of woolly, grey-green leaves, and produces large bright yellow dandelions for a long period. The only other species sometimes grown is the invasive *H. brunneocroceum* (*H. aurantiacum*), 1616, with bright reddish-orange daisies. 46 cm (18 in). Sun, drained soil.

HIPPEASTRUM, Amaryllidaceae. Bulbous plants with strap-shaped dark green leaves and stout stems carrying a head of several lily-like blooms. They need a hot sunny spot against a wall in our warmest counties, and should be planted about 7.5 cm (3 in) deep.

× acramanii

60 × 30 cm	*[9–10]*	*Red*	*Summer*	P	W	D
2 × 1 ft						

Hybrid. Prior to 1870. *H. ackermannii*. *H. aulicum × H. psittacinum*. A rare plant which will thrive in warm conditions outdoors and gladden us with rich red trumpet blooms, held above the foliage, with narrow segments. Plant in spring.

pratense ● ★

38 × 23 cm	*[9–10]*	*Vermilion*	*E. Summer*	P	W	D
15 × 9 in						

Chile. 1840. *Habranthus pratensis*, and better known under this name. It has for many years flowered freely along an east-facing wall, without protection, and also in the open ground in sheltered places, at Blickling Hall, Norfolk. The flowers appear in May and are of brilliant vermilion red lightened by yellow filaments. Plant in autumn.

HOSTA, Liliaceae. Funkia; Plantain Lily or Giboshi. A group of noble, soundly perennial plants thriving in damp or fairly dry soil, in dense or partial shade or full sun. In the sunnier positions they will be more compact and flower freely; whereas in the denser shade fewer flowers will be produced but the stems will be taller and generally the foliage is larger. The sunnier the position, the moister should be the soil. They do best in ordinary garden soil to which old manure and humus is occasionally given, and thrive under a north wall; ample humus should be applied on limy soils.

They are easy to divide and replant at almost any time of the year, but preferably in autumn or spring. Young plants can be lifted and pulled or cut apart. It is a pity to disturb grand old-established clumps, and an easy way of increasing them without disturbance is to cut pieces out of them with a spade— as one would cut a slice out of a round cake. If the hole is filled with soil no harm will result. Their enemies are slugs and snails, and suitable poison should be spread well around the whole area just before the leaves start to appear and later, in gardens where these pests abound.

They form slowly increasing clumps, usually of broad, striking foliage in a variety of tints. In summer the stately stems of lily-like flowers appear but beautiful though these are, their foliage is more valuable in the garden, in fact they are unequalled for creating interest and contrast through the growing season. As a contrast to sword-like foliage or the filigree of ferns they cannot be surpassed. They make excellent ground-cover; several kinds are illustrated in my book *Plants for Ground-Cover*. Many are good again briefly in autumn, the leaves of *H. sieboldiana, H. fortunei* and their forms turning to creamy or amber yellow.

Their nomenclature has for long been in a confused state. Many of them have been named from Japanese garden clones and hybrids, not from wild species, which makes more confusion. A few, such as *H. sieboldiana, H.s. elegans* and *H. ventricosa,* do not vary greatly from seed, but others do and with the present craze for producing yet more garden forms, it is natural that many hybrids of unknown origin are occurring; many have been named in the United States. In addition, apart from the well-established garden clones with broad leaves, some obscure, small-leafed species are arriving from Japan; though interesting and charming, they mostly lack the nobility and garden value of the larger kinds.

The main kinds can be roughly divided into several groups, headed by the glaucous-leafed *H. sieboldiana* and *H. tokudama.* Also glaucous are some forms of *H. fortunei.* Then there are the green-leafed *H. fortunei* forms, *H. plantaginea, H. ventricosa* and *H. undulata erromena,* all of rich green colouring. Those with white edges to the leaves will be found among *H. fortunei* 'Marginato Alba', *H. crispula, H.* 'Thomas Hogg', and *H. albomarginata* in a descending scale of magnificence. *H. undulata* forms give us creamy-white leaf-blades with green edges, while yellow leaf-blades are found in *H. fortunei* 'Albopicta' and *H. ventricosa* 'Aureomaculata'. For those with yellow edges to the leaves we should choose *H. sieboldiana* 'Frances Williams', *H. fortunei* 'Obscura Marginata' and *H. ventricosa* 'Variegata'. Some narrow-leafed small hostas with variegation recently from Japan are *H. rhodeifolia, H. helonioides* 'Albopicta', *H. lancifolia thunbergiana* ('Kabitan').

The flowers vary from pure white (*H. plantaginea*) to lilac-white (*H. sieboldiana*), pale lilac (*H. crispula*), to rich purple (*H. ventricosa*). Most kinds have graceful outward-reaching stems with flowers borne almost horizontally; others, like *H. ventricosa, H. albomarginata* and *H. albomarginata* 'Alba' have erect stems with acutely nodding flowers.

In the drier parts of the country, when they are grown under trees, the puckered leaf surfaces of *H. sieboldiana, H. tokudama* and *H. fortunei* are apt to get shabby from tree-drip. In such conditions *H.* 'Thomas Hogg' and *H. ventricosa* with their shiny surfaces do not suffer in this way. The whole genus is susceptible to spring frosts, and frost-pockets should therefore be avoided especially since one crop of leaves only is put up, in spring and early summer. *H. sieboldiana* contributes yellow autumn colour and its seed-bearing stems stand aloft through the winter and are highly ornamental.

"Admirable plants for picturesque groups, very hardy, easy of increase by division, thriving in any soil, but the foliage effect is finer on deep rich soil."—WR

albomarginata

50 × 38 cm	*[3 9]*	*Violet*	*Summer*	P	D
20 × 15 in					

Japan. 1830. *H. lancifolia albomarginata, Funkia ovata albomarginata.* Having been introduced before its green-leafed type, this plant bears the specific name. It is a lowly plant with elliptical leaves (glossy beneath) which have a narrow white margin, and the creeping rootstock quickly enables it to make a wide clump, forming a good foreground to taller plants. The flowers are of good size, rounded, of rich violet and beautifully marked inside. To be correct botanically one should call this *H. sieboldii,* but I have decided against using this in the hope of avoiding the inevitable confusion with *H. sieboldiana.*

—alba

50 × 38 cm	*[3–9]*	*White*	*Summer*	P	D
20 × 15 in					

H. minor alba, H. caerulea minor albiflora, Funkia lancifolia alba. In this the leaves are bright green and the flowers are white. It is a highly ornamental and effective plant. There is a form with variegated leaves, named 'Louisa', in the United States. I have also a green-leafed form with violet flowers. The white has a flowering season extending into autumn.

caput-avis

46 × 46 cm	*[4–9]*	*Lilac*	*L. Summer*	P	D
18 × 18 in					

Japan. *H. tosana caput-avis.* Lance-shaped fresh green leaves of no particular distinction, but the flower-heads are remarkable. When in bud they are enclosed in broad bracts and the whole head resembles that of a bird, the bracts' long points uniting to form the beak. The bracts are pale green; there is a white-flowered form whose bracts are nearly white, *H.c. leucantha.* The flower stems of both are nodding. Sometimes considered to be a variety of *H. kikutii, q.v.*

clausa

60 × 30 cm	*[3–9]*	*Lilac*	*L. Summer*	P	D
2 × 1 ft					

Japan. The normal green form—*normalis*—has dark purplish stems bearing rich red-lilac flowers, carried horizontally, over narrow green leaves. Stoloniferous.

crispula

75 × 46 cm	*[3–9]*	*Lilac*	*E. Summer*	P	D
2½ ft × 18 in					

1829. *H. fortunei marginato-alba, H. latifolia albomarginata.* This, when well grown, is the most striking of the white-margined cultivars; it has large, long and broad, dark green leaves, long-pointed, with undulate margins which are broadly edged with white. In a good season in a sheltered garden it is no less than sumptuous, but in windy gardens the white edge is apt to turn brown by mid-July. The flowers are trumpet-shaped, pale lilac in elegant spires. It flowers before most kinds.

decorata
60 × 46 cm   *[3–9]*   *Purple*   *E. Summer*   P D
2 ft × 18 in

Japan. 1930. *H. decorata marginata.* As with *H. albomarginata,* the variegated form reached Europe before the green-leafed type (which is known as *H.d. normalis).* Good, rounded, blunt leaves of dark green, of mat yet almost glistening appearance; there is a broad white margin, carried right down the wide and deeply cleft stalk—a characteristic of all these hostas with variegated margins but most pronounced in this. The rich deep lilac bells are beautifully marked within. The roots spread freely on rhizomes of 5–7.5 cm (2–3 in) in length. *H.d. normalis* (1931) denotes the green-leafed type.

elata
75 × 75 cm   *[3–9]*   *Lilac*   *E. Summer*   P D
2½ × 2½ ft

Japan. Characterized by its pale green mat leaves, long-pointed and with markedly undulate edges, and by its pale lilac flowers produced early in the season; each flower has strongly recurved bracts. One of the first to flower. Closely related to *H. montana* and *H. fortunei, q.v.*

fortunei
75 × 60 cm   *[3–9]*   *Lilac*   *Summer*   P D
2½ × 2 ft

Japan. 1876. A good form has long-pointed and wavy-edged leaves of soft sage-green, quickly making a handsome clump. It is one of the most common in British gardens, a bold plant whose flowers of pale lilac are carried well aloft. It should be regarded as one of a group of hybrids; though nothing definite is known, probably it has been cultivated in Japanese gardens for centuries and may well show affinity to *H. sieboldiana* at the glaucous extreme of its variation, while possibly approaching *H. undulata erromena* at its green-leafed extreme. In between are several listed below, and probably *H. elata* and *H. montana* fit into the complex. Used as a carpet under tall shrub roses at Montacute, Somerset.

—'Aoki'. [3–9] A Japanese garden form with the usual flowers and good greyish green foliage.

—'Albopicta'
75 × 60 cm   *[3–9]*   *Lilac*   *Summer*   P D
2½ × 2 ft

Funkia ovata aurea; F. ovata albopicta; Hosta fortunei viridi-marginata. One of the most spectacular of spring foliage plants. By the middle of May the 30 cm (1 ft) high sheaves of scrolled leaves open out to display their remarkable colouring. Bright butter-yellow blades are edged with pale green; later the yellow fades to primrose, and the green darkens; by midsummer two tones of soft green obtain over the whole of the surfaces. The flowers are trumpet-shaped, of light lavender on graceful stalks.

—'Aurea' [3–9]. A beautiful form whose leaves are entirely of the yellow colouring of 'Albopicta', fading gradually to green. It is rather less vigorous. A great sight at Wakehurst, Sussex. 60 × 38 cm (2 ft × 15 in)   P D

—hyacinthina ★

75 × 60 cm	*[3–9]*	*Lilac*	*Summer*	P	D
2½ × 2 ft					

A good, hearty plant with bold grey-green leaves edged with a very thin line of glaucous grey. The flowers are held well aloft and are of good size and quality, of cool lilac. In many ways this is the best grey-leafed hosta; though it is slightly less grey and large in leaf than *H. sieboldiana elegans,* its flowers are markedly superior. Superb with pink-flowered filipendulas.

—'Marginato-Alba' ★

75 × 60 cm	*[3–9]*	*Lilac*	*Summer*	P	D
2½ × 2 ft					

A development of *H. fortunei* whose sage-green leaves are broadly edged with white, and grey beneath. This is perhaps the most sumptuous of all white-edged kinds and less prone to wind bruising than *H. crispula.* Leaves glaucous beneath. Also known as 'Shogun'.

—'Obscura'

75 × 60 cm	*[3–9]*	*Lilac*	*Summer*	P	D
2½ × 2 ft					

Broad dark green leaves and the usual flowers.

★ **—'Obscura Marginata'** [3–9]. For some years this was known as 'Yellow Edge'—which was a good name for it, aptly describing the band of creamy-yellow surrounding the broad leaves. The colouring lasts well through until autumn. This is an excellent contrast for *Heuchera americana.* Great garden value. It is sometimes labelled 'Sprengeri'.

—rugosa [3–9]. A form with leaves only slightly glaucous, but distinctly corrugated (rugose) between the veins.

—stenantha [3–9]. A form with green leaves, but corrugated between the veins.

glauca, see *H. sieboldiana,* also *H. tokudama.*

gracillima

60 × 46 cm	*[3–9]*	*Lilac*	*L. Summer/*	P	D
2 ft × 18 in			*Autumn*		

Japan. 1936. The narrow, erect, dark green leaves make a dense clump. Wiry, erect, dark purplish stems bear a showy array of horizontally carried, rich amethyst-lilac, trumpet-shaped flowers, with protruding white style and filaments.

helonioides

30 × 46 cm	*[3–9]*	*Lilac*	*L. Summer*	P	D
1 ft × 18 in					

Japan. 1937. The form 'Albopicta' is extremely pretty. Narrow leaves broadly edged with yellow; this colouring is carried well down the stalks, which have wide flanges.

'Honeybells' ● ★

90 × 60 cm	*[3–9]*	*Lilac*	*L. Summer*	P	D
3 × 2 ft					

A hybrid from Bristol Nurseries, Connecticut, one parent being *H. plantaginea,* and it inherits its fragrant blooms. These are of palest blushing-lilac produced on good stems late in the season over blunt-pointed light green leaves with wavy edges—again inherited from *H. plantaginea.* This is a notable addition.

hypoleuca
46 × 46 cm	[4–9]	White	Summer	P	DS
18 × 18 in					

Japan. Unique species which in its native haunts inhabits rocky, sunny hillsides, hot and dry. The very broad long leaves with undulate edges are pale green above and markedly glaucous beneath.

kikutii
46 × 46 cm	[3–9]	White	L. Summer	P	D
18 × 18 in					

Japan. Closely related to *H. caput-avis* with its leaf shape and bird-head-like bract-covered flower sprays; the flower stems are carried erect.

'Krossa Regal' ★
1.5 × 1 m	[3–9]	Lilac	L. Summer	P	D
5 × 3 ft					

Sometimes labelled *H. nigrescens elatior,* this is a handsome and outstanding Japanese seedling. It is one of the largest, producing a dome of glaucous, pointed leaves which is overtopped by the graceful spires of lilac flowers. This has no doubt a great future.

lancifolia ★
60 × 30 cm	[3–9]	Lilac	L. Summer	P	D
2 × 1 ft					

Japan. 1829. *H. japonica, Saussurea japonica, Funkia lancifolia.* Beautiful shining dark green leaves, small and long-pointed, provide a covering mantle to the ground, over which rise the deep-lilac trumpet-flowers on graceful stalks. A most useful late-flowering plant with a long-flowering display, usually in September; the flowers are borne nearly horizontally on the stems. A lovely companion for *Polygonum amplexicaule* 'Atrosanguineum'. It seldom produces seeds and may well be a Japanese garden clone. It is in evidence along the stream at Hidcote, Gloucestershire. A form known as 'Viridis Marginata' is a lesser plant, whose blades are of brilliant, lasting yellow, edged with a narrow green band. *H.l. thunbergi* has rather broad upright leaves and erect stems with wide-open bell-shaped flowers.

longipes
60 × 46 cm	[3–9]	Lilac	L. Summer	P	D
2 ft × 18 in					

Japan. 1894. *Funkia longipes.* Leaves of a subdued mat-green, usually heart-shaped with an abrupt point and with wavy edges. A note of distinction is the heavy brown spotting on the stalks and central veins. A handsome but dwarf plant; the flowers are borne on dark-spotted stems well above the leaves; pale lilac, profuse, carried horizontally in a bunch at the top of the stems.

longissima
46 × 46 cm	[3–9]	Lilac	L. Summer	P	D
18 × 18 in					

Japan. 1935. *H. japonica longifolia* or *angustifolia, H. lancifolia longifolia.* Notably narrow, small leaves of rich green. Small flowers on wiry stems; one of the latest to open. *H.l. brevifolia* is scarcely different. There is a form with leaves broadly edged with cream, 'Variegata'. The species resembles *H. lancifolia.*

minor

23 × 38 cm	*[3–9]*	*Violet*	*L. Summer*	P	DS
9 × 15 in					

Korea. 1911. One of the smallest species with small twisted leaves, broad at the base, long-pointed, of matt green. A few rich violet, narrowly trumpet-shaped flowers per stem. Figured in colour in my book *Complete Flower Paintings and Drawings*. An appealing plant of refinement.

montana

90 × 60 cm	*[3–9]*	*Blue*	*Autumn*	P	D
3 × 2 ft					

Japan. *H. fortunei gigantea*. See also under *H. fortunei*. Rich green leaves, narrowly heart-shaped, deeply veined, making a large clump. The flowers are in a large heavy spike, Spode-blue, borne horizontally for a long time on very long brownish stems. Very variable. There is a wonderful form with broad yellow margins to the leaves, *H.m.* 'Aureo-marginata'. By some authorities *H. montana* is considered synonymous with *H. elata*.

nakaiana

46 × 46 cm	*[3–9]*	*Violet*	*L. Summer*	P	D
18 × 18 in					

Japan and Korea. *H. capitata*. Fresh green, mat, wavy-edged, heart-shaped leaves. The rich violet flowers are held on dark-spotted stems and occur in a bunch at the top.

plantaginea

60 × 60 cm	*[3–9]*	*White*	*Autumn*	P	D
2 × 2 ft					

China. *c.* 1780. *H. plantaginea stenantha; H.* or *F. japonica, F. subcordata, Saussurea plantaginea*. After having enjoyed for the whole summer the clear bright green, glossy, beautiful, arching, heart-shaped leaves, which form as noble a clump as any of the others, it is something of a surprise to find very late in the season a head of long, marble-white trumpet flowers, developing in the evening and having a delicious lily-like fragrance. It needs moist soil and a warm position to hasten its flowering. 'Aphrodite' is a form with double white flowers recorded in China.

● ★ —**grandiflora** 1841. *H. plantaginea japonica*. [3–9]. While the Chinese species sets fertile seeds (in suitable autumn weather) this is a Japanese cultivated form which is usually sterile, and was introduced much later. It has similar flowers but the foliage is longer and narrower and makes a looser clump. They are equally good garden plants and are sometimes grown as conservatory plants, where the added shelter and warmth encourage them to flower in good time. Gertrude Jekyll used funkias mainly for pots and tubs, particularly *H. plantaginea* 'Grandiflora' and *H. sieboldiana*, but records the value of the first in the border:

"... fresh-looking pale-green leaves are delightful with ... brilliant light yellow, and pale blue of Delphinium, Mullein and sulphur Sunflower."— GJ

rectifolia

75 × 46 cm	[3–9]	Lilac	Summer	P	DS
2½ ft × 18 in					

Japan, Sakhalin, etc. 1897. *H. longipes* of gardens. In spite of its tall stems and good flowers, this is a poor plant, with undistinguished plain green leaves held so erect that they do not make a luxuriant overlapping mass.

—'Tall Boy' [3–9]. A superior hybrid with much better foliage than the above species. Leaves heart-shaped, long-pointed, fresh green, making a good clump. The flowering stems sometimes achieve more than 1.5 m (5 ft) and are well hung with rich lilac bells. It is certainly the most spectacular in flower of all the hostas. This was named at the Savill Garden, Windsor, having been imported from the United States under an erroneous name. It grows well at Lanhydrock, Cornwall.

rhodeifolia

60 × 46 cm	[3–9]	Lilac	L. Summer	P	D
2 ft × 18 in					

Japan. A little-known plant; I have only seen the yellow-edged form. Erect stems with flowers of wide-splayed segments.

'Royal Standard'

90 × 60 cm	[3–9]	Lilac/White	L. Summer	P	D
3 × 2 ft					

1964. A hybrid from Wayside Gardens, South Carolina. Certainly a valuable late-flowering plant, slightly fragrant. Broad, heart-shaped, rich green leaves, somewhat puckered and deeply veined, and with wavy edges. The flowers are carried well above the foliage and inherit much of the beauty of *H. plantaginea*, being almost white and fragrant. 'Wayside Perfection' is a similar clone. They are similar to 'Honeybells'.

rupifraga

60 × 30 cm	[3–9]	Lavender/	L. Summer	P	D
2 × 1 ft		Violet			

Japan. *H. pycnophylla*. A rare plant whose rather dull green leaves are rounded but acutely pointed. The leaf stalks and flower stalks are dotted with purple and the flowers are of lavender or violet in a dense raceme.

sieboldiana

75 × 60 cm	[3–9]	Lilac/White	Summer	P	DS
2½ × 2 ft					

Japan. 1930. *H. glauca, Funkia sieboldii, F. glauca, Hosta* or *Funkia fortunei robusta*. The leaves are the largest and most sumptuous of all the hostas. They are very broad, sometimes 30 cm (1 ft) wide and more than 30 cm long, of deep grey-green, bluish or glaucous, distinctly pointed. The resulting magnificent clump is let down by the dumpy flower-heads which only just stand up above the leaves; they are held in a dense head and are white with a faint lilac flush, borne early in the season, immediately after those of *H. elata* and *H. crispula*. For *H. sieboldii* see under *H. albomarginata*.

★ —elegans [3–9]. The finest development of this species. The leaves, large, rounded, and up to 30 cm (1 ft) wide are blue-grey, crinkled and deeply veined, and always attract attention whether growing or when cut. It is difficult to name a more striking herbaceous plant. The dense heads of lilac-white trumpet flowers just overtop the leaves. Superb with *Hypericum patulum*, also with purple phloxes.

—'Frances Williams' ★

75 × 46 cm	*[3–9]*	*Lilac/White*	*Summer*	P	D
2½ft × 18 in					

'Gold Edge'. Noticed at the Bristol Nurseries, Connecticut, by Frances Williams, of Massachusetts; it was named after her, but had previously reached British gardens under the name of 'Gold Edge'. It is in effect *H. sieboldiana elegans* with a striking yellow margin, deepening as the season advances. 'Gold Circles' and 'Aurora Borealis' are other similar clones.

★ **—'Great Expectations'** [3–9]. A recent and extremely handsome sport which occurred in John Bond's garden, Windsor. The large, broad leaves are centrally splashed and veined with creamy yellow. It is likely to become very popular.

'Snowden'

1.2 × 1 m	*[3–9]*	*White*	*L. Summer*	P	D
4 × 3 ft					

c. 1971. A hybrid between *H. sieboldiana* and *H. fortunei* 'Aurea' raised by Eric Smith at The Plantsmen nursery. Long pointed grey-green leaves make a mound about 90 cm (3 ft) high. The white flowers have a hint of lilac. Similar to *H.* 'Krossa Regal'.

tardiflora

23–30 × 23 cm	*[3–9]*	*Mauve*	*Autumn*	P	D
9–12 × 9 in					

Japan. 1903. *Funkia* or *Hosta lancifolia tardiflora, H. sparsa*. A diminutive species with narrow, shining, dark green leaves of thick texture and short spires of surprisingly large deep-mauve lily-like bells, borne on maroon stems. It is scarcely large enough for inclusion but it forms a pleasing little clump and is lovely with white colchicums.

'Thomas Hogg' ★

60 × 50 cm	*[3–9]*	*Lilac*	*E. Summer*	P	D
2 ft × 20 in					

Frequently confused with *H. albomarginata* and *H. crispula,* this probable hybrid may be distinguished by the smooth dark green pointed leaves and tall spires of light lilac, trumpet-shaped flowers. The leaves have a broad creamy margin and are glossy beneath. This is perhaps the most satisfactory of all the white- or cream-edged cultivars for general garden use, and owing to the smooth upper surface of the leaf it does not collect sediment from dripping trees. One of the earliest to flower.

tokudama

46 × 46 cm	*[3–9]*	*Lilac/White*	*Summer*	P	DS
18 × 18 in					

Japan. *Funkia sieboldiana condensata, H. sieboldiana glauca*. Closely allied to *H. sieboldiana,* it may best be described as a smaller version, with very corrugated leaves, cup-shaped in poise, of a markedly glaucous tint, good forms in some lights appearing really blue. The flowers are lilac-white opening from rounded buds, carried in the short heads peculiar to *H. sieboldiana*. It is slow of increase. A remarkable sight at Rowallane, Northern Ireland. There are two variegated forms, *H.t.* 'Aurea Nebulosa' ('Variegata') in which the blue-green leaves are variously marked and striped with yellowish green. In *H.t.* 'Flavo-circinalis' the variegation is at the edge of the leaf. This variety has been treasured for many years at Crathes Castle, Kincardineshire. In both the yellowish colouring darkens with age. The leaf-form of this species makes it very prone to collect sediment and rubbish from dripping trees.

undulata

| 46 × 30 cm | [3–9] | Lilac | Summer | P | D |
| 18 in × 1 ft | | | | | |

Japan. 1834. *H. undulata undulata, H. japonica undulata, H. lancifolia* 'Medio-Variegata', *Funkia lancifolia undulata*. This is a smaller plant than the cream-edged hostas, with very undulate, or even spirally twisted, pointed leaves of shining rich green, with a large central area of the blade creamy white, varying in width and shape, with dark green edges. The trumpet flowers appear in early summer, of rich lilac, on graceful stems. A form of Japanese origin. Beautiful with *Smilacina racemosa*.

"Its waved leaves are so beautifully rich in cream ... that they lighten the general effect."—EAB

—erromena ● ★

| 1.2 m × 60 cm | [3–9] | Lilac | Summer | P | D |
| 4 × 2 ft | | | | | |

H. japonica fortis, H. lancifolia fortis. One of the tallest hostas and a plant of luxuriant beauty. The flowers give a splendid effect; the rich-lilac trumpets dangle from the 90-cm (3-ft) stems over the shining mound of lovely, rich green broad leaves. A form of Japanese origin, only less tall than 'Tall Boy'.

—univittata

| 60 × 46 cm | [3–9] | Lilac | Summer | P | D |
| 2 ft × 18 in | | | | | |

Japan. Very similar to *H. undulata*, but more vigorous and taller; the deep cream markings are more in the form of a broad central stripe of varying shape and width.

ventricosa ● ★

| 1.2 m × 60 cm | [3–9] | Violet | L. Summer | P | DS |
| 4 × 2 ft | | | | | |

E. Asia. 1790. *H. caerulea, Funkia latifolia*. A noble plant with broad heart-shaped leaves of rich, dark, shining green with wavy edges, making a handsome clump; the undersurfaces of the leaves appear to be varnished. The flowers are bell-shaped, more richly coloured than any of the others, and beautifully veined. A splendid plant for grouping with *Anemone × hybrida* 'Prince Henry' and fuchsias.

—'Aureo-maculata'

| 75 × 50 cm | [3–9] | Lilac | L. Summer | P | D |
| 2½ ft × 20 in | | | | | |

The dark green of the leaves is striped and splashed with yellowish white in spring, but this becomes less noticeable as the season advances. A good contrast for *Lilium × hollandicum*.

—'Aureo-marginata' ('Variegata') ● ★

| 1.2 m × 60 cm | [3–9] | Lilac | L. Summer | P | D |
| 4 × 2 ft | | | | | |

Broad dark green leaves handsomely margined with deep cream. Most striking when in flower, the deep-violet blooms contrasting with the cream-edged leaves, which retain their colouring until autumn. This is one of the most handsome of hostas, and looks well with *Echinacea purpurea*.

venusta   [3–9] is a small species for rock garden use, similar to *H. minor* but smaller and the leaves are not long-pointed.

'Wogon'

46 × 46 cm	*[3–9]*	*Lilac*	*Summer*	P	D
18 × 18 in					

'Wogon Giboshi', 'Wogon Gold'. The smallish lanceolate leaves are pure yellow and remain so throughout the summer if grown in shade. The flowers are undistinguished.

NEW HYBRIDS [3–9]. In dealing with hostas we are confronted at the outset, as I intimated earlier, with a race of plants that have been hybridized, or have hybridized, in Japan and also in Europe. This accounts for the fact that about a score of the plants described above are already hybrids. They are however accepted and recognized as distinct plants today. But during the last two decades or so innumerable (literally) new hybrids, sports and seedlings have cropped up, particularly in the United States. Names galore are beginning to crowd the list in bewildering array. No book of today can expect to be up to date. Far too many have been named, but time will thin their ranks. Over here particularly Eric Smith led the way with a lot of hybrids between *H. tardiflora* and *H. tokudama*; as a result the progeny are on the small side. These have become known as *H. × tardiana* hybrids but the new name has yet to be registered botanically. Likewise in the United States not only large hybrids, ringing the changes on shape and colour, but also small, spreading, almost carpeting, dense growers have been selected. A number have come my way but I am not fully up to date with them. They need to be assessed over the years. Meanwhile I list the following arranged fairly accurately in their colour ranges, listing the larger growers first in each group. Paul Aden of New York has been very active, as was Eric Smith in England until his death.

BLUE-GREEN (GLAUCOUS):
'Blue Umbrellas' (Aden, USA)
'Love Pat' (Aden)
'Krossa Regal' (Japan) (*see main list*)
'Snowden' (Smith, England) (*see main list*)
'Halcyon' (Smith)
'Hadspen Blue' (Smith)
'Blue Wedgwood' (Smith)
'Blue Moon' (Smith)

DARK GREEN OR GLAUCOUS, WHITE OR CREAM EDGE:
'Wide Brim' (Aden)
'Northern Halo' (Walters Gardens, USA)
'Antioch' (C. Tompkins, USA)
'Francee' (Klopping, USA)
'Bunchoku' (Japan)

LIGHT GREEN, CREAMY EDGE:
'Shade Fanfare' (Aden)
'Golden Tiara' (Savory, USA)

WHITE OR YELLOW CENTRES:
'White Magic' (Aden)
'White Colossus' (Aden)
'Gold Standard' (Japan)

SELF-YELLOW OR YELLOWISH GREEN:
'Sum and Substance' (Aden)
'Sun Power' (Aden)
'Zounds' (Aden)
'Piedmont Gold' (Payne, USA)
'Midas Touch' (Aden)
'Hydon Sunset' (Hydon Nurseries, England)
'Gold Edger' (Aden)

All of the above have conventional broad handsome leaves, though some are quite small. The following have long narrow leaves with quite different appeal.

NARROW, GREEN, PALE EDGE:
'Ginko Craig' (Craig-Summers, USA)
'Louisa' (F. Williams, USA)
'Celebration' (Aden)

NARROW, YELLOW, GREEN EDGE:
'Sea Sprite' (Seaver, USA)
'Kabitan' (Japan)

There are also among the narrow-leafed kinds some with undulate edges, such as 'Chartreuse Wiggles' (Aden).
The very smallest make dense ground-cover and are valuable, on this account, bringing something fresh into our gardens, but they do not of course compete with the larger hostas in general which are noted for the majesty of their leafage. The plain yellow, the yellow variegated and the glaucous blue ones can put up with more sunshine than those with white or cream in the leaves.

HOUTTUYNIA, Saururaceae.

cordata

46 × 46 cm *18 × 18 in*	*[5–9]*	*White*	*Summer*	P	D

Far East. 1820. A marsh plant which will also succeed in any cool, fairly moist border, where it will creep freely underground. It is very invasive. Plant 7.5 cm (3 in) deep. The stems bear elegant, heart-shaped, dark metallic-green leaves, and several small white flowers with cone-like green centres. The leaves have the smell of Seville oranges, refreshing and pungent. In sunny places it takes on rich autumn tints.

—**'Chamaeleon'** ('Variegata'). [5–9]. The usual single flowers, but the foliage is as bright as it could be—dark green variegated with red, yellow and bronze.

—**'Flore Pleno'** [5–9]. A rare and more showy plant than the type species in which centres of the flowers develop into cones of white petals; it has grown at Hidcote, Gloucestershire, for many years.

HUMULUS, Urticaceae. The Common Hop is a rampageous herbaceous climber whose fragrant green—turning to brown—seed-heads are highly attractive in autumn on the female plant.

lupulus

Climbing	*[5–9]*	*Greenish*	*L. Summer*	P	DR

Europe, Britain, Asia, America.

"The floures are used to season Beere or Ale with, and too many do cause bitternesse thereof, and are ill for the head."—GH

—'Aureus' 1889. This form is not nearly so rampageous, and unfortunately does not flower freely, but it makes up for this by its clear yellow-green leaves, prettily divided, and will twine up sticks or wires. It turns to green in late summer. The male form is more common than the female.

HYACINTHOIDES, Liliaceae. At last our two Bluebells, native and Spanish, seem to have settled down to this new generic name. *H. non-scripta* prefers rich woodland soil and conditions: *H. hispanica* is thrifty almost anywhere. They hybridize freely, and are apt to seed about and increase too freely, particularly at the expense of daffodils. It is wise to pick off all seed-pods except in wild areas. The perfect companions for the late white *Narcissus poeticus recurvus*.

hispanica ★

60 × 23 cm	[4–9]	Various	L. Spring	PF	DS
2 ft × 9 in					

Spain. 1683. *Scilla campanulata, Endymion hispanicus.* The Spanish Bluebell has erect stems, with bell-shaped Spode-blue bells. There are white and pink forms. A giant form, perhaps a tetraploid, has cropped up in several gardens, and one has been named ● ★ 'Chevithorn' after Mrs Ludovic Amory's garden in Devon. This is of the typical colour. Dark blue, white and pink large-flowered forms are also grown.

non-scripta

60 × 23 cm	[6–9]	Various	L. Spring	PF	DS
2 ft × 9 in					

W. Europe, Britain. *Scilla nutans, Endymion non-scriptus.* Noted for its usually darker, more tubular blooms on a nodding stem. The pure white 'Grandiflora Alba' is a thing of great beauty, but I have yet to admire a pink form of this species.

HYDROPHYLLUM, Hydrophyllaceae.

virginianum

60 × 30 cm	[5–8]	White	E. Summer	P	DS
2 × 1 ft					

Eastern N. America. 1739. A pretty moisture-lover with elegant leafage, neatly cut, and sprays of small drooping white bells with long-protruding stamens. One of those plants which brings charm without flamboyance to a garden. There are also handsome variants with purplish flowers.

HYLOMECON, Papaveraceae.

japonicum

30 × 23 cm	[5–8]	Yellow	Spring	D
1 ft × 9 in				

Japan. 1870. A pretty woodlander for cool retentive soils. Slowly spreading clumps of fresh green leaves have clear yellow poppies hovering over them in the spring. A charming manavilin for April.

"... dainty as a wood anemone with its fine-leafletted leaves and rich butter-yellow flowers."—ATJ

HYMENOCALLIS, Amaryllidaceae. [All 9–10]. Like their close relatives, *Elisene* and *Pancratium,* these are bulbs for the foot of a sunny wall in our warmest counties. Many species are only suitable for a warm greenhouse but the following may be tried out of doors: *H. calathina, H. littoralis; H. festalis,* the name usually given to a hybrid between *Elisene longipetala* and *H. calathina.* 'Zwanenburg' is an excellent clone raised by Van Tubergren. All species and hybrids have strap-shaped leaves and stout stems with a cluster of flowers at the top. They are fragrant, beautifully shaped, with a central cup and long twisting outer segments, like attenuated white daffodils. 'Sulphur Queen' is light yellow, touched with green. They are all exceedingly elegant and worthy of every care. Plant about 15 cm (6 in) deep in spring. They will not tolerate frozen ground. Natives mainly of South America. The ultimate is found in *H. macrostephana,* a beautiful plant with very broad leaves 1.2–1.5 m (4–5 ft). The immense white blooms are yellow in the throat, turning reddish after pollination. Origin unknown. It thrives on a sunny border at Kew, against a greenhouse.

IMPATIENS, Balsaminaceae.

tinctoria

1.5 × 1.5 m	*[9–10]*	*White*	*Autumn*	W	DS
5 × 5 ft					

Ethiopia. Very large, clump-forming, with stout stems and copious lance-shaped leaves. The flowers are large, pure white with violet eye, and borne in the upper leaf axils. It needs a very warm corner in our milder counties, and thrives against a greenhouse wall at the Savill Garden, Windsor.

INCARVILLEA, Bignoniaceae.

delavayi ●

60 × 30 cm	*[6–8]*	*Rose-red*	*E. Summer*	PF	S
2 × 1 ft					

W. China, Tibet. 1893. Deeply divided foliage forms a clump from which arise the stout stems, each supporting several large trumpet-flowers of rich rosy red. The trumpets open out into large attractive flowers with wide, rounded petals. A plant of rich appearance. It needs a good but well-drained soil in a sunny position, and should be covered with bracken or other dead foliage in winter. It would be worth a lot of trouble, but does not usually need it. Plant 20 cm (8 in) deep. Handsome seed-pods with fascinating tongues.

> "... that splendid find of Abbé Delavay's, which, in itself, is almost enough to reconcile oneself to the existence of missionaries."—RF

emodi

46 × 46 cm	*[6–8]*	*Pink*	*Summer*	DS
18 × 18 in				

Himalaya. *I. arguta. c.* 1854. This and *I. olgae* are slighter plants than the other two. The usual elegant pinnate leaves and the flowers are of good colour with wide lobes to the trumpet, orange in the throat. These three names are often considered under the generic name of *Amphicome.*

mairei ●

30 × 30 cm	*[7–8]*	*Rose-red*	*E. Summer*	PF	S
1 × 1 ft					

W. China, etc. 1909. *I. grandiflora brevipes.* A much shorter plant than *I. delavayi,* with leaves as deeply pinnate but with rounder segments. Sumptuous flowers, with short stems in 'Bees' Pink', 'Nyoto Sama' and 'Frank Ludlow': the last two are only about 15 cm (6 in) high, but warrant inclusion since they are hardly rock garden plants. A lovely contrast for *Iris kerneriana.*

olgae

90 × 60 cm	*[7–8]*	*Pink*	*Summer*	CDS
3 × 2 ft				

Turkestan. 1880. *I. koopmannii*. Totally distinct from the purely herbaceous species here listed, this is a sub-shrubby plant with short woody stems. It produces a mass of deeply divided, narrow leaves and airy sprays of pink, penstemon-like flowers. Full sun.

INDIGOFERA, Leguminosae. Sun-loving shrubs which thrive in the milder parts of the country; my purpose in including them in this book is that, like fuchsias, some die to the ground in the winter and others, like *Phygelius,* give most abundant flower when pruned down to the ground every March. They are happy in any well-drained soil. The foliage is pretty, pinnate and fern-like.

decora

46 × 46 cm	*[7–9]*	*Pink/White*	*L. Summer*	CDS
18 × 18 in				

China, Japan. 1845. A dainty front-line plant whose ferny mound of foliage is bespangled with clusters of pea-flowers for many weeks; they have both pink and white petals. There is also a white variety *I.d.* 'Alba'. This species needs a sheltered position in our warmer counties.

heterantha ★ (*I. gerardiana***)**

Shrub	*[6–9]*	*Rosy-lilac*	*E. Summer/*	CDS
			Autumn	

Himalaya. 1840. There are several other shrubby species, such as *I. amblyantha* [6–9], clear shrimp-pink; *I. potaninii* [6–9], clear rose-pink. *I. heterantha* has soft lilac-pink flowers; all are borne in small sprays among the ferny pinnate foliage. All of them are shrubs, but if cut down to the ground each spring they make a most lovely mass of erect stems and remain in flower for at least two months. A good complement for fuchsias and Japanese Anemones.

INULA, Compositae. Sun-loving yellow-flowered daisies of very varied qualities. They thrive in any reasonable soil.

ensifolia

30 × 30 cm	*[4–9]*	*Yellow*	*L. Summer*	P D
1 × 1 ft				

Caucasus. 1791. For frontal positions, where its dense growth and narrow small leaves create a good base for the numerous deep yellow daisies, borne singly on wiry stalks. This might be likened to a smaller edition of *Buphthalmum salicifolium,* which has been called *Inula* 'Golden Beauty'.

glandulosa

46 × 46 cm	*[4–8]*	*Yellow*	*Summer*	P D
18 × 18 in				

Caucasus. 1804. *I. orientalis*. A first-rate short, compact plant with the usual hairy leaves and stout stalks each carrying usually one fine, large, orange-yellow daisy from woolly buds.

hookeri

    75 × 60 cm   *[4–8]*   *Yellow*   *Summer*   P   D
    2½ × 2 ft

Himalaya. 1849. A fairly rapid colonizer; the spreading clumps throw up a mass of stems, somewhat branched, with small oval hairy leaves. As in *I. royleana* the rays of the flower are very narrow; they are of a light greenish yellow. Those who value this unusual tint prize the plant in spite of its coarse growth. It prefers damper rather than drier places and looks well with *Lobelia vedrariensis*.

magnifica ● ★

    1.8 m × 90 cm   *[4–8]*   *Yellow*   *L. Summer*   P   DS
    6 × 3 ft

Caucasus. 1925. *I. afghanica* of gardens. A superb and dignified plant but it needs a lot of space, not only to grow it well, but to show to best advantage the great pile of broad rough foliage, ascending the stout brownish stems to the heads of brown buds opening to large vivid deep-yellow daisies, 12.5–15 cm (5–6 in) across, at the top. This is a gorgeous plant for growing against shrubs with coppery foliage, purple-leaf fennel, and modern orange-red roses. It is also suitable for growing as a great clump in rough grass, bog garden or waterside. *I. helenium,* the 'Elecampane', is a smaller-flowered edition of *I. magnifica*.

"The Elecampane ... groweth plentifully in the fields on the left hand as you go from Dunstable to Puddlehill ... and ... neere to Dover by the sea side."—GH

oculis-christi

    40 × 60 cm   *[4–8]*   *Yellow*   *Summer*   P   D
    18 in × 2 ft

E. Europe. 1759. A highly desirable dense clump, with downy leaves and large flowers of a glowing orange-yellow borne singly on stout stems.

racemosa

    2.7 × 1.5 m   *[4–8]*   *Yellow*   *L. Summer*   D
    9 × 5 ft

W. Himalaya. A huge coarse plant for the wildest spots. Basal leaves broad, wavy, rough, arching, 1.2 m (4 ft) long; those on the stems decrease in size until quite small approaching the apex. Light yellow narrow-rayed daisies are borne among them in a long spike. It thrives at Wisley, Surrey.

royleana ●

    60 × 46 cm   *[4–8]*   *Orange*   *Summer*   P   DS
    2 ft × 18 in

Himalaya. 1897. *I. macrocephala* of gardens. The immense fine-rayed flower found in *I. magnifica* is here reproduced in orange-yellow, borne singly on stout stems with clasping, almost perfoliate leaves. Basal leaves broad, on long stalks. This very fine plant thrives in cool air, and needs some years to become fully established.

IRIS, Iridaceae. We have here a genus abounding in the characters which qualify for inclusion in this book. The species are almost all easy to keep in good fettle if their simple wants are studied; they usually require no staking; only a few need division to keep them in good health, and their flowers are of exquisite beauty, mostly fragrant, and many are followed by good seed-pods. They resolve themselves into several distinct groups, both cultural and descriptive.

    They all grow best in full sun except *I. foetidissima,* which is truly evergreen.

They will all thrive in limy soil except *I. kaempferi.* The next great division is between those which prefer a really wet soil and those which prefer it successively drier: *I. laevigata* enjoys the most moisture with *I. pseudacorus* a close second, while *I. kaempferi* needs also abundant moisture and lime-free soil with lots of humus. These all have fairly broad rich green leaves which are wholly deciduous, and medium to large flowers, and it should be noted here that all iris species which require a really damp soil show tiny dark dots in the leaves if held against a bright light.

I.I. chrysographes, fulva, ×*fulvala, kerneriana, setosa, sibirica, versicolor*— and to these we may add some less important species, *I.I. clarkei, delavayi, wilsonii* and *forrestii*—prefer moist soil but will also flourish in any well-nourished border that does not dry out in summer. These are all narrow-leafed, deciduous, with comparatively small neat flowers. *I. chrysographes* and the last four above are markedly similar, with small standards.

Closely allied to the above are the much larger plants with tall deciduous greyish leaves and usually very tall, 1.2–1.5 m (4–5 ft), flower stems, headed by *I. spuria,* with *I.I. monnieri,* 'Monspur', *orientalis* (*I. ochroleuca*), 'Ochraurea' and *aurea* (their hybrid names will denote the hybridity of some). These have highly decorative large flowers, with good ascending "standards" (the upper segments) and recurving "falls" (the lower segments) and they thrive in any reasonable soil, moist or dry.

The rest need really well-drained soil, dry rather than damp. *I.I. innominata, douglasiana, longipetala, sintenisii, graminea,* and *ensata* are all small-flowered, with grassy leaves. The first two, together with *I.I. tenax, hartwegii, purdyi* and *bracteata,* are known collectively, with some others, as Pacific Coast Irises.

Here follows the big group of Bearded Irises (so called because of the plush-like surface of the narrowest part—the "haft"—of the falls) whose standards are usually nearly as large or larger than the falls, derived in great part from the original parents of *I. germanica.*

The remainder require the sharpest drainage on porous soils in the hottest positions and are only suitable for our warmer, drier counties. They succeed on a bank or against a sunny wall: *I.I. confusa, wattii, milesii, japonica, tectorum* and *unguicularis.* For similar positions, with the soil heavily mixed with broken brick, mortar rubble, old cinders, broken pots, etc., there are the Regelia and Regeliocyclus varieties; to keep them in good health, protect them from rain from July to the end of September, so that the sun (what there is of it) can shine through the glass or polythene suspended above them and thoroughly bake them. All of the above have flat, woody rootstocks (rhizomes) which creep *on* the soil.

Although most irises are long-suffering plants, so long as their minimal needs are studied, and all the kinds described (apart from those in the above paragraph) can be transplanted at any time, the general rule is to do this immediately after flowering. This is to enable them to make fresh roots promptly, to gather up nourishment for the following year. The general rule too is to keep the rhizomes—the horizontal woody part of the root—on, or level with, the surface of the soil.

We are left with the tuberous-rooted *I. bucharica* and its relatives, which require sharp drainage and sunshine, and some purely bulbous groups—the Dutch, Spanish and English Irises, derived variously from *I. xiphium, I. xiphioides* and *I. tingitana.* These usually thrive in the same sunny well-drained ground that suits the Bearded Irises.

Iris foetidissima, I. germanica and others sometimes suffer from leaf-spot disease. See Chapter 14.

aurea

| 1.2 m × 30 cm | [5–9] | Yellow | Summer | P | DS |

4 × 1 ft

Kashmir. 1847. *I. crocea.* The first alphabetically of the great Spuria group. Tall elegant leaves and stalwart stems bearing vivid rich yellow flowers, with alert splaying standards and beautifully recurved falls. The parent of *I.* 'Ochraurea', an even better garden plant, since *I. aurea* does not thrive and flower well everywhere. See also under *I. spuria.* (It should be noted here that an ancient, diploid Bearded Iris was called *I.* 'Aurea'.)

bucharica ●

| 46 × 30 cm | [4–9] | Yellow | Spring | DS |

18 in × 1 ft

Bokhara. 1902. A tuberous root gives rise to arching, folded leaves produced, fan-like, in one plane, and the yellow-and-white flowers are small, highly attractive, and curiously shaped in that the inner three segments (standards) hang down below the outer ones. Alphabetically the first of its group, to which belongs also *I. orchioides* (1870) yellow; *I. magnifica* (1880) pale lilac and yellow, 60 cm (2 ft). *I. graeberiana,* pale bluish mauve; *I. aucheri* (*I. sindjarensis*), lilac-blue; and *I. warleyensis,* violet and white, etc. Since they are scarcely large enough for our specification, and bear a very marked resemblance to each other, I will excuse myself from going into further details. There are several other exquisite shorter species in this Juno Iris group. They all require really good drainage and hot sunny positions in our warmer counties, when they are likely to prove sound perennials, delighting the eye for a short time in spring. Plant about 10 cm (4 in) deep in autumn.

chrysographes

| 46 × 30 cm | [4–9] | Various | E. Summer | PF | DS |

18 in × 1 ft

W. China. 1911. The darkest velvety indigo-violet or nearly black forms such as 'Black Knight' are highly desirable, though this is not meant in disparagement of the numerous paler forms of varying tones of yellow and violet. They are all delicately marked with gold, like true samite. A striking and beautiful plant, very free-flowering, with narrow, grassy, lax leaves of clear green. A hybrid with *I. pseudacorus* is 'Holden Clough', whose yellow flowers are heavily netted with brown. *I. clarkei* is a similar species with a solid stem, not hollow as in *I. sibirica;* its flowers are purplish with white patch on the falls. *I. delavayi* is again similar, taller, with hollow stems. Neither of these has marked garden value though, like *I. chrysographes,* they are beautiful in their short flowering period. *I. delavayi* may well be a hybrid of *I. chrysographes;* the flowers are purplish, much of the falls' area is yellow.

—'Margot Holmes'

| 60 × 30 cm | [4–9] | Claret | E. Summer | P | D |

2 × 1 ft

1927. This hybrid has the attraction of very richly coloured claret-crimson flowers, beautifully marked with lemon stripes towards the throat. It is a hybrid probably with *I. douglasiana,* raised by Perry.

confusa

| 90 × 90 cm | [9] | White | Spring | P | W | D |

3 × 3 ft

W. China. This is sometimes erroneously called *I. wattii,* which is a more tender and larger version of it. A luxuriant plant with stems supporting great fans of rich green leaves, giving a palm-like effect. In warm districts it reaches 1.2 or 1.5 m (4 or 5 ft) in height. The small flowers are borne in airy branching sprays: they are lilac-white with dark lavender dots and orange markings, exquisitely shaped and frilled. Only hardy in very mild districts. Evergreen.

douglasiana ●
    30 × 60 cm   *[7–9]*   Lilac   *L. Spring*   PF   DS
    1 × 2 ft

California. 1873. The wide-spreading, arching leaves are rich green and arise from bright rose-coloured rhizomes. Few flowers are more exquisitely shaped and marked than these dainty orchid-like blooms. The six crinkled segments are of various tints of rosy lilac—or white or yellow—marked with white, warm yellow and violet. Beautiful related species are *I. tenax, I. purdyi, I. hartwegii* and *I. bracteata,* but they are all dwarf for our purpose. These and *I. fulva* have produced innumerable hybrids, *I. innominata* participating, and an endless colour range is available. Beautiful with dicentras. Evergreen.

ensata
of gardens
    30 × 30 cm   *[5–9]*   Purplish   *E. Summer*   PF   DS
    1 × 1 ft

Temperate Asia. *I. pallasii.* Narrow glaucous leaves forming a dense tuft, but flopping down towards the end of summer. Small flowers of variable tint, violet, slaty blue or white. *I. ensata* 'Major' is a taller form or hybrid, achieving 46 cm (18 in) with deeper-coloured flowers. *I. ensata* (of Thunberg) is in reality the correct name for the plant we know as *I. kaempferi.*

florentina
    60 × 30 cm   *[4–9]*   White   *E. Summer*   P   D
    2 × 1 ft

Much treasured by the ancients, considered to be one of the selected forms which are often grouped under *I. germanica, q.v.* One reason for its remaining for so long in cultivation is because its rhizomes, when dried, yield the fragrant Orris Root, used in toilet preparations and in pot-pourri. The grey-white of the sweetly scented flowers, borne well above the broad greyish leaves, is one of the sights of May; throughout south-east England, this and others of the *I. germanica* group flower freely—as they did at Myddelton House, Enfield, Middlesex:

> "When this bed is in full glory in the middle of May, it is as beautiful as anything in the garden."—EAB

—**albicans.** [4–9]. A form said to have flowers of a clearer white, but either I have never seen the true plant or they are indistinguishable. There is much confusion over this plant. Some authorities consider it to be a white form of a purple-flowered type, 'Madonna', which has a pale blue beard. The main trouble is that it has been spread far and wide for centuries by the Muslims, who prize it for planting in their cemeteries, so that its natural habitat is not known; it may be a hybrid or selected clone. It is difficult to intimate the differences between these two plants, but according to Dykes (and at Kew) *I. albicans* has a greenish yellow haft to the falls, whereas in *I. florentina* they are tinted with lilac; moreover the spathes in *I. albicans* are green, in *I. florentina* scarious.

foetidissima

46 × 60 cm	*[5–9]*	*Lilac-green*	*E. Summer*	PF	DS
18 in × 2 ft					

W. Europe, Britain. The native Gladwin or Stinking Gladdon is an invaluable plant with handsome, rich dark green leaves, thriving in any soil, including pure chalk, under trees and in any untoward conditions, also to a lesser degree in sun; a splendid foil to other foliage, particularly grey foliage. The leaves smell vaguely of roast beef when bruised. The flowers are insignificant but delicately tinted and veined. The splendour comes in autumn, when the big pods burst, displaying orange seeds, which are excellent for cutting for winter. Forms with white or yellow seeds have been recorded. Evergreen.

—'Citrina'

60 × 46 cm	*[5–9]*	*Citron*	*E. Summer*	PF	DS
2 ft × 18 in					

This was known erroneously as the 'Chinese Form' at Hidcote, Gloucestershire, for many years. It is an altogether superior plant to the species; of greater stature, with broad, better leaves, large and freer flowers of citron and pale mauve and far larger seed-pods. It makes a superb late autumn picture when planted with *Mahonia* 'Charity'. Evergreen. Division.

—'Variegata' 1772. All the attributes of the type species coupled with the attraction of distinctively cream-striped leaves. Again a true evergreen and very beautiful in winter when used as a contrast for the brown heads of Hortensis hydrangeas. It seldom flowers. Division.

forrestii

60 × 30 cm	*[4–9]*	*Yellow*	*E. Summer*	PF	DS
2 × 1 ft					

Yunnan. 1909. A pleasing small plant of the *I. chrysographes* persuasion. Very bright, rich green, narrow leaves toning well with the sprightly lemon (usually) yellow flowers, pencilled brown on the haft. Erect standards and arching styles. A good companion for the hardy species of orchid (*Dactylorrhiza*).

fulva

60 × 46 cm	*[5–9]*	*Red*	*Summer*	PF	DS
2 ft × 18 in					

United States. Early nineteenth century. *I. cuprea*. This gorgeous beauty is one of the last irises to flower, in July. It prefers a reasonably moist soil and does not object to lime. The leaves are broad, arching, of rich green, and the narrow lax segments of the flower are of an unusual tint—a rich, velvety, embrowned terracotta. It is not free-flowering unless suited. *I. × fulvala* [5–9] is a hybrid of this species with *I. foliosa* [6–9], a species from S.E. United States; it is a more reliable garden plant and equally late-flowering, but the colouring has lost the red-brown tint and assumed a rich crimson-purple, murrey-tinted, with a bright yellow centre. The flowers have gained in size. The "*la*" added to the name of *fulva* indicates its parentage with the other species which was at one time called *lamencei*.

germanica

60–90 × 46 cm	*[4–9]*	*Purplish*	*E. Summer*	P	D
2–3 ft × 18 in					

An anciently cultivated, fragrant, sterile clone, whose origin is lost in the mists of time. It was in every garden before the hybridists got to work and flooded the lists with new combinations of colour. The old type we know well—it is still seen in old gardens in every street and village—a stately thrifty plant whose standards are lavender-purple, coupled with dark violet-purple falls. Slightly dwarfer is 'Kochii', wholly of rich dark glowing purple. For colour variety with them we used to grow *I. florentina, q.v.,* a white flower with faintest lavender-grey tinting, and the light lavender *I. pallida* and palest yellow *I. × flavescens.*

It might seem that *I. germanica* was the obvious parent of our modern irises, and it is well to point to the broad outline of development under this name. However, like *I. florentina,* it is sterile and it is believed that many other old hybrid clones, such as those known as *I.I. trojana, amoena* and *plicata,* and species such as *I.I. pallida, variegata* and *cengialtii,* are the real basic parents, together with *I. chamaeiris.* From the early years of this century in this country and in France, and later in the United States, these have been interbred with remarkable results, so that today there are varieties for all tastes, in colour varying from white to darkest indigo-purple, from palest pink to deepest claret, and from cream through yellow to salmon and coral to richest brown, and every combination of these colours is available. From somewhat dowdy and small flowers the transformation is almost unbelievable. Unfortunately, in order to raise ever brighter and bigger flowers certain disadvantages have cropped up— the new kinds are often unduly tall and therefore unstable and require support; they are too long in the rhizome or root and therefore require weeding or the use of weedkiller. Further, the flowers of many today are of tetraploid grossness so that the petals are ruffled and gophered to such a degree that the classic *fleur de lys** outline has gone. Yet another disaster has occurred: taste has decreed that falls shall be "flaring", that is, raised nearly to the horizontal. This may be all very well on the show bench or when one is looking down on the flowers, but through this character half the total effect of the bloom is lost when seen at a distance. But for those interested in them—and there are many—I suggest a visit to a specialist nursery or flower show, or resorting to a reliable catalogue, for personal selection. A book which listed recommended varieties would soon become out of date, because the varieties come and go quickly.

In addition to the Tall Bearded Irises there are nowadays many short or Intermediate Bearded Irises. These started life by hybridizing the taller sorts with the small *I. chamaeiris.* For a long time the mere two flowers per stem and very early flowering of this species resulted in poor effect. Of recent years careful selection has resulted in some first-class plants up to about 60 cm (2 ft) in height, covered with good-sized blooms in an ever increasing range of colour. Kelways of Langport have been to the fore with these. There is no doubt that such as 'Arctic Fancy' will become very popular.

I. germanica itself has some points that make it worthy still of being grown: it flowers freely and is indestructible; it is very fragrant, and its blue-purple coincides exactly with the light yellow Rose 'Frühlingsgold', a charming accompaniment. In addition both it and *I. pallida, I. albicans* and the hybrid *I. × flavescens, I. cengialtii, I. variegata, I. squalens* and others of the ancestral kinds, have dense-growing rhizomes, which colonize the soil to the exclusion of weeds. The early successes in the breeding of irises were diploids, and some of the earliest are preserved in the University Botanic Garden at Oxford, and also at Polesden Lacey, Surrey, and every year they flower with such freedom that one wonders why they should be so neglected today. They are some of the most foolproof and satisfactory of garden plants. Among them are 'Fro', 'Gracchus', 'Aurea' and 'Lorelei'. It is pleasant to think that the new Intermediate Irises embody all that is good in these old varieties. These types, near to the original species, have much to commend them for labour-saving gardens, in the same

---

*Derived from *fleur de Louis* (VII), *fleur de luce* or *lys.*

way that the narcissi which are near to the species score over the highly bred daffodils of today.

graminea

46 × 23 cm	[5–9]	Purple	Summer	P	DS
18 × 9 in					

Europe, 1597. The Plum Tart Iris. This species forms dense tufts of dark green, arching leaves, narrow and glossy, among which nestle the flowers; the rosy-purple styles and violet-blue falls make together a small flower of great beauty. But it is the fragrance that is outstanding, a rich and satisfying odour of hot stewed plums or apricots. It needs to be smelled to be believed! Happy in any sunny position, in ordinary soil. *I.g. pseudocyperus* is, I believe, synonymous with 'Hort's Variety'. It has broader leaves and larger flowers, but lacks the entrancing fragrance.

hoogiana ●

60 × 30 cm	[7–9]	Lavender	E. Summer	P	D
2 × 1 ft					

Turkestan. 1913. One of the most beautiful of all irises, of the Regelia Section, and needing cultivation as outlined in the introductory remarks to the genus. Above bluish green foliage stand refined flowers of clear uniform lavender-blue with yellow beard. Fragrant. A nearly white form from Tadjikistan is called 'Alba'; a rich purple 'Purpurea'. 'Bronze Beauty' is a very vigorous and bold plant, the standards light violet, the falls darker, both tinged with brown at the edges. *I. hoogiana* is named after the proprietor of the Dutch bulb firm Van Tubergen, who have done so much for bulbous plants generally.

innominata ●

15 × 30 cm	[4–9]	Various	Spring	PF	DS
6 in × 1 ft					

Oregon. 1935. The original species in gardens had yellow flowers and was rather tricky in cultivation, but in nature varies to orange, magenta and purple. A good varied strain, raised from seed, partly hybridized with *I. douglasiana* and other species, has flowers of many tints and a bunch is one of the most exquisite sights of the year. Prettily shaped, daintily marked and veined. They embrace many colours, white, yellow, lilac, rosy amethyst, violet and all intermediate shades and combinations of tints. They are easy to grow in any sunny, well-drained place, in lime-free soil, and, if division is required to reproduce specially beautiful seedings, this is best done immediately after flowering. The leaves are narrow, copiously produced, making a good cover and background to the flowers poised above them. Evergreen.

japonica

46 × 46 cm	[8–9]	Lilac	Summer	P	D
18 × 18 in					

Japan, China. 1800. 'Ledger's Variety' is the form usually grown, with white flowers very prettily marked with purple and with orange crest, crinkled and crisped at the edges of the segments. The leaves are broad and dark green. This requires a hot, sunny, well-drained position. (Named after Walter E. Ledger who brought it from Tokyo in 1912.)

—'Variegata' [8–9]. Leaves beautifully striped with creamy white.
I. japonica × *I. confusa* is intermediate between the parents, but not an improvement on either.

232

kaempferi ●

90 × 46 cm	*[5–9]*	*Various*	*Summer*	PF	DS
3 ft × 18 in					

Japan, E. Asia. 1839. It is now considered that the correct name for this plant is *I. ensata,* Thunb.

The wild species is a pretty, stately plant, with ribbed, bright green, deciduous leaves, increasing freely in any moist or very moist spot, or in a good retentive garden border, in rich soil, well mixed with humus, lime-free, and in full sun. The flowers have three short standards and three large drooping falls, and are usually of a rich red-purple, sometimes varying towards lilac or white. A garden name for a red-purple type is 'Regel', probably erroneous. The variety known as 'Rose Queen', and usually considered to be a hybrid with *I. laevigata,* is from a garden point of view very similar except for its colour. Selection from seed in Japan, where this plant was, and is, greatly admired and treasured along with the peony and chrysanthemum, started during or before the seventeenth century in Tokyo. Gradually developed in the Edo, or Tokyo, group of varieties, the dainty flower of the species became enlarged, with three or six big and nearly horizontal segments. Later the Higo group of varieties with even more sumptuous blooms developed; in many of these the six segments were not enough; the doubling was continued into enlarged stigmata until an untidy mop of segments destroyed all the original shape. Meanwhile from 1800 in Honshu the Ise group was developed; in these the original shape was fostered, and the normal three drooping falls remained the model of perfection. During this century further hybridizing has been carried on and also in the United States. Every possible combination of size and shape has been achieved, coupled with the great range of colouring from white through palest lavender to dark blue-purple and from red-purple to palest pink, of one or more of these colours in a flower, plain or exquisitely veined. The Slieve Donard Nursery, Northern Ireland, long held stocks of several reliable and distinct kinds; 'Gei-sho-Ui' and 'Tsuru no Kegoromo' date from 1856; 'Warei Hotei', 'Aoigata' and 'Koki-no-Iro' from early in this century, but it is best to make a selection from varieties in flower. Newer Higo and American varieties arrive from one decade to the next.

Of all irises these are the most sumptuous, the most velvety and the largest in flower. The size of the largest has not resulted in top-heavy stalks. They make fine leafy clumps and should be divided in early September, before they finish growth.

"... those miracles of beauty and infinite grace which leave all who behold them agasp in silent awe."—ATJ

—variegata A pleasing form whose dark red-purple flowers are offset by leaves variously striped with grey and grey-green. This is probably a form of the clone alluded to above as 'Regel'.

kerneriana ● ★

46 × 23 cm	*[6–9]*	*Yellow*	*E. Summer*	PF	DS
18 × 9 in					

Turkey and Armenia. Narrow green leaves and flowers of exquisite shape, with strongly recurved falls, in tones of soft yellow. It is a real gem for June, enjoying open spots, ideal with species of orchid. In effect a miniature *I.* 'Ochraurea'.

korolkowii ●

46 × 30 cm	*[8–9]*	*Brownish-white E. Summer*	P DS
18 in × 1 ft			

Turkestan. 1874. For cultivation see introductory remarks to this genus, under Regelia Irises. The narrow, angular and very beautiful flowers are of creamy white so heavily veined with brown that the exact tint is difficult to describe. There is a pronounced chocolate blotch below the yellow beard. *I.k.* 'Concolor' is a uniform rich violet purple; *I.k.* 'Violacea' has white flowers heavily veined and blotched with purple. They are all gems worth studying, and worth growing.

laevigata ● ★

46 × 30 cm	*[5–9]*	*Lavender-* *Summer*	P D
18 in × 1 ft		*blue*	

Japan. 1856. This plant needs moist soil, and will even grow in a few inches of water. It is most happy at the sides of ponds and streams or in peat bogs, but does not object to lime. The masses of broad, soft green, smooth leaves provide a good background for the hosts of broad-petalled flowers, of a particularly soft yet clear lavender-blue. It is closely allied to *I. kaempferi*. 'Alba' is a most beautiful white form and should be planted with the former for contrast. 'Albo Purpurea' is a remarkable form with white standards; the falls are purple mottled with white around the edges. In 'Variegata' the usual lavender-blue flowers contrast well with the clearly variegated leaves, cream and green striped. 'Dorothy Robinson', 1978, has violet-blue falls with white central streak. 'Rose Queen' is a hybrid with *I. kaempferi*, as shown by its ribbed leaves. It is rather taller than *I. laevigata*, and more upright, and is not so tolerant of wetness. The broad-petalled flowers with handsome drooping falls are of soft old-rose, very telling in the garden. It is annually a great joy at Mount Stewart, Northern Ireland.

lazica

30 × 30 cm	*[8–9]*	*Violet* *E.Spring*	P DS
1 × 1 ft			

N. Turkey. 1895. This might best be described as a broad-leafed form of *I. unguicularis*. The flowers appear in late winter or earliest spring, of rich violet blue.

longipetala

60 × 30 cm	*[7–9]*	*Lavender* *L.Spring*	PF DS
2 × 1 ft			

California. 1862. Flaccid grey-green leaves, which are inclined to be evergreen. The flowers appear, severally, from conspicuous green spathes and are of rather poor quality. The falls are of creamy white heavily netted with violet veining; the standards narrow, lavender, notched at the apex. It is one of a confusing group and not the best. *I. missouriensis* (1880), from the Rocky Mountains, differs in having deciduous leaves of glaucous green, flowers of a more decisive lavender colouring with standards equally notched at the apex; it is an excellent garden plant. *I. montana* has pointed, not notched, standards. A hybrid raised by Sir Michael Foster is called 'Tol-long' [6–9]; it has pointed standards. Its strange name indicates that it is a hybrid between *I. tolmeiana* (*I. missouriensis*)— under which name the raiser mistakenly grew *I. montana*—and *I. longipetala*. All of these are ideal with *Rhododendron luteum* (*Azalea pontica*). Their foliage is good for several months. 1982: *I. longipetala* has a ridge to the falls and a crest to the styles.

milesii

90 × 30 cm	*[8–9]*	*Mauve*	*E.Summer*	PF	W	D
3 × 1 ft						

Himalaya. 1881. This slender dainty species with light green leaves has wiry glaucous stems. The small crinkly flowers are of light mauve marked with darker tints on the falls and lit by a yellow crest. It requires a warm sunny position.

monnieri

90 × 30 cm	*[8–9]*	*Yellow*	*Summer*	P	DS
3 × 1 ft					

Crete. The second alphabetically of the great Spuria group. This species, or form, is less often seen than the others, and it will suffice to say here that the flowers are of clear light yellow, that otherwise it resembles *I. spuria* and *I. orientalis*, and it may well be of hybrid origin connected with the latter and *I. aurea*.

'Monspur' ● ★

1.2 m × 46 cm	*[4–9]*	*Blue*	*Summer*	PF	D
4 ft × 18 in					

1882. *I. monnieri × I. spuria*, raised by Sir Michael Foster early in this century. Similar in growth and stature to *I.* 'Ochraurea', but having flowers of soft Spode blue. *I. orientalis* has contributed most of the vigour to this excellent hybrid. It is a plant of great beauty. 'Cambridge Blue', 'Dorothy Foster' and 'A. J. Balfour' are three notable old cultivars. This far-away cross has of late years proved productive in the United States, and several new hybrids with large flowers and varied colouring have appeared; over here 'Norton Sunlight' has been bred, with bicolor flowers of brown and blue, likewise 'Academus'.

'Ochraurea' ● ★

1.2 m × 38 cm	*[5–9]*	*Yellow*	*Summer*	PF	D
4 ft × 15 in					

I. ochroleuca (*I. orientalis*) × *I. aurea*. A splendid early hybrid of greater vigour than *I. orientalis, q.v.,* and with more handsome seed-heads. The flowers are of soft daffodil yellow with deeper markings on the falls, and several are borne on each stem. Easily grown in ordinary soil, in sun. A really tiptop garden plant, lovely with Hybrid Peonies and ideal with *Rosa rugosa*.

● **Oncocyclus Group.** Exquisite flowers from the Middle East, demanding raised beds of the most perfect drainage, with brick rubble and also with good nourishment (bonemeal, hoof-and-horn meal) below; protection from summer rains and requiring a glass light and a dry covering of bracken, straw, etc. in severe winter weather. If you can cope with all this your efforts with *I. susiana, I. lortetii, I. atropurpurea*, etc., may reward you. Their flowers are beautifully shaped and veined. For our warmest, driest counties.

orientalis

1.2 m × 38 cm	*[4–9]*	*White*	*Summer*	PF	DS
4 ft × 15 in					

Asia Minor. 1790. *I. ochroleuca*. This iris is represented in gardens by a stalwart plant making striking clumps of stiff sword-like foliage up to 1.2 m (4 ft) high. Few leaves give such a splendid contrast to the prevailing garden greenery and especially to the shrub roses, which flower at the same time. The large beautifully formed flowers are weather-resistant, of pure white with a broad yellow mark on the decisively recurving falls. Possibly an ancient hybrid or form of *I. spuria*, it varies in height and quality in the wild. It flowers excellently at Peckover House, Cambridgeshire, with Rose 'Sarah Van Fleet'.

"*Iris ochroleuca* is one of the well known old garden favourites whose origin and history are somewhat mysterious."—EAB

pallida dalmatica ★

90 × 30 cm	*[4–8]*	*Lavender*	*E.Summer*	P	D
3 × 1ft					

Europe. 'Princess Beatrice'. A well-known anciently cultivated plant with typical flowers of the Bearded Iris class, silky, crinkled and of clear, light lavender-blue with golden imperials, and deliciously fragrant. The buds are lapped in sere papery calyces, as opposed to the living green of most others. From a garden point of view it is almost the only iris of this Germanica type that retains the beauty of its exceptionally grey foliage until the autumn, and it is therefore a valuable landscape plant. It is happy anywhere in sun, in drained soil, and flowers well at Polesden Lacey, Surrey. (*I. pallida pallida*).

"*Iris pallida dalmatica* has the quality rare amongst its kind of maintaining its great leaves in beauty to near the end of the year."—GJ

"The great Floure de-luce of Dalmatia . . . riseth up a stalke of foure foot high . . . whereupon doth grow faire large floures of a light blew, or as we term it a watchet colour. The floures do smell exceeding sweet, much like Orenge floure."—GH

—'**Variegata**'. [4–8]. Yellow-striped leaves and flowers almost as good as those of *I.p. dalmatica*.

—'**Argentea**'. [4–8]. Most beautiful white and grey striped leaves, but rather poor flowers.

pseudacorus

1.2 m × 30 cm	*[5–9]*	*Yellow*	*E.Summer*	PF	DS
4 × 1ft					

Britain, Europe, Asia. The common Yellow Flag of our streams and ponds and the Fleur de Lys of heraldry. A coarse and luxuriant species for colonizing marshy ground, banks of streams and very shallow water; it will also grow in the open border in not too dry positions. Though it has scarcely been used in hybridizing, good forms can be selected in which the fuscous markings on the falls are absent; one such is called 'Golden Fleece', while 'Bastardii' is of clear creamy yellow, a useful colour with blue poppies (*Meconopsis*). Both this form and that with variegated leaves should be propagated by division. While their seed-pods are as ornamental as those of the normal species, their progeny will usually result in the normal kind and thus their pods should be picked before they split open, to avoid a deterioration of the stock. 'Holden Clough', see under *I. chrysographes*.

"Although it be a watery plant of nature, yet being planted in gardens it prospereth well."—GH

—'**Variegata**' 1903. [5–9]. This extraordinarily handsome form has all the attributes of the species, coupled with beautiful yellow stripes on the leaves in spring; they turn green in late summer. A most striking plant for foliage effect. The falls of the flowers have distinct brown marks.

purpureobractea

46 × 30 cm	*[5–9]*	*Lavender/*	*E.Summer*	P	DS
18 in × 1 ft		*yellow*			

Turkey. *c.* 1980. The large purplish red spathes and bracts are a special character of the species which otherwise resembles the *I. germanica* group. Introduced by C. D. Brickell.

● **Regeliocyclus Group.** ('Aril Irises'.) Evolved by the Zwanenburg firm of Van Tubergen, 1900 onwards, these need careful cultivation as outlined in the opening remarks to this genus. They are hybrids between various Oncocyclus and Regelia species. They all demand best care but are more amenable to cultivation than their parents. There is nothing like them. The outline of the flower is trim, acute and dashing, with mostly pointed segments, and they may be of white through lilac to darkest purple, grey, bronze or brownish variously toned and mixed, veined or with central blotch. They are named after classical personages and since, in spite of being hybrids, they are of classical shape, all is well. They fascinate and impel, and are garden toys of the greatest interest.

Although I have indicated in the introductory paragraphs to Iris that these are by no means easy to grow, I would emphasize that given the right conditions, namely, a good limy loam, well drained, baking hot sunshine, and shelter from heavy rains after flowering until late September, they can be cultivated successfully and are easier to grow than the species from which they are descended. Some modern bungalows have widely projecting eaves; a raised bed under them facing south or west would be ideal for these and indeed many of the Cape bulbs. They all flower in late spring.

setosa

60 × 30 cm	*[4–9]*	*Purple*	*E.Summer*	PF	DS
2 × 1 ft					

Siberia, Japan, North America. 1864. Light green leaves which make a fine thicket in any damp ground; the flowers are particularly rich in the depth of their purple colouring. The rounded falls have white centres and are daintily veined with yellow. Happy in ordinary soil that is not too dry, it is a good companion for yellow primulas.

sibirica ★

90 × 46 cm	*[4–9]*	*Various*	*E.Summer*	PF	DS
3 ft × 18 in					

Europe, N. Asia. Sixteenth century. Tufted roots produce sheaves of grassy leaves in almost any position and in any ordinary soil, moist or dry. The best results are from plants in moist soil in sunny places. They are exquisite as a foil for azaleas, and the purples are a pleasing contrast to *Hemerocallis lilio-asphodelus*. Neat, shapely seed-heads.

> "What we like about *I. sibirica* apart from its slender grace and lovely blues and whites ... is its willingness to do anywhere and to continue doing for years without asking for division."—ATJ

Although plants raised from seeds might do well for very large areas and for naturalizing—for if planted 30 cm (1 ft) apart they will speedily make their own ground-cover—most gardeners will desire separate colours. As with other genera, I recommend personal selection when in flower, or recourse to reliable lists. The points to look for are not over-large flowers with flopping standards, but those of medium size, and the flowers should be held well above the foliage. An old and pretty blue, 'Heavenly Blue', will please many of us and is good for comparison. 'Caesar' and 'Emperor' are reliable very rich purples, and 'Wisley

White' or 'White Swirl' are good in their own field. There are two reddish varieties: 'Helen Astor', a dark, plum-tinted rosy red, with conspicuous white veins towards the throat, and 'Eric the Red', rather paler with the addition of brownish yellow tinting on the haft. Neither is particularly vigorous and needs moving on to fresh soil every few years. Newer varieties of excellence are 'Anniversary', white; 'Cambridge', Cambridge or turquoise blue; 'Sea Shadows', mid-blue—all raised by Majorie Brummitt, a leading hybridist in these delights— and 'Caesar's Brother'. 'Navy Brass' (1933)—dark violet blue, yellow reticulations and edge—and 'Show Bounty', white with yellow "eyes"—are two good new ones from the United States. Other outstanding new varieties are 'Silver Edge' (1973), 'Fourfold White' (1969) and 'Fourfold Lavender' (1987). *I. sanguinea* (1760) (*I. orientalis* of Thunberg), which differs markedly in having shorter stems and rich reddish spathes enclosing the flower buds, has had considerable influence in many of these hybrids, particularly in size and deep colouring. Throughout the race the falls are marked in the centre with a zone of yellow or white veining, which adds greatly to their decorativeness. *I. prismatica* is closely related.

sintenisii

30 × 30 cm	*[6–8]*	*Purple*	*E.Summer*	PF	DS
1 × 1 ft					

S.E. Europe, Asia Minor. A gem whose flowers resemble those of *Iris reticulata*, being of the same size, violet-purple with prettily marked falls. It forms a tuffet of narrow leaves over which are poised the flowers.

spuria ● ★

90 cm–1.5 m	*[5–9]*	*Various*	*E.Summer*	PF	DS
× 30 cm					
3–5 × 1 ft					

Algeria to W. Asia. 1573. A variable species, some being quite short, even less than 90 cm (3 ft), others achieving 1.5 m (5 ft). Some large-flowered garden types are often given specific rank in gardens and will be found alphabetically under *I.I. aurea, monnieri* and *orientalis* (*I. ochroleuca*). If we exclude these we can visualize *I. spuria* as being a neat and refined species with elegant flowers with strongly reflexed falls in shades of lilac and lavender. 'A. W. Tait' is a charming and noted garden clone in pale blue-lavender with yellow throat. *I.s. halophila* (*I.s. notha*) is perhaps the most refined and delicately tinted form, but is variable. In all these the foliage is of blue-green, or glaucous, erect and swordlike, foetid when bruised. They are all easy to cultivate, and the two last mentioned achieve 75 × 90 cm (2½–3 ft). Reputedly a native of Britain.

stolonifera

46 × 30 cm	*[6–8]*	*Lilac*	*E.Summer*	P	D
18 in × 1 ft					

Bokhara, Turkestan. 1884. Regelia Section; for cultivation see introductory remarks to the genus. A creamy white beard lights the subdued colouring of this exquisite flower. Lilac-white standards, deeper falls, both veined and flushed at the margins with light chocolate. For ease of cultivation the species is surpassed by 'Zwanenburg Beauty', of richer colouring and frilly outline.

tectorum

30 × 30 cm	*[5–9]*	*Lilac*	*E.Summer*	P	D
1 × 1 ft					

China. 1872. The "iris of the roofs" indicates that it will grow in very dry conditions. The broad glossy dark green leaves reach a high-light in 'Variegata' in which they are striped with cream. Evergreen. The standards are of clear lilac, the falls prettily crinkled and with darker veining and white crest. There is also a green-leafed form with pure white flowers, 'Alba', and 'Lilacina' with heavily blotched falls. Two rare hybrids are grown occasionally: 'Tol-tec', a hybrid with *I. tolmeiana* (now *I. missouriensis*), and 'Dorothea'. They both bear light lavender-blue flowers (the second is larger and paler) flecked with a deeper tone.

tingitana

60 × 23 cm	*[8–9]*	*Blue*	*E.Summer*	P	DS
2 ft × 9 in					

N.W. Africa. Late nineteenth century. Rather tender, but it is grown successfully in warm gardens, displaying its splendid lavender-blue flowers with yellow markings well above the narrow, rush-like green leaves, silvery on the upper surfaces. ● *I.t. fontanesii* is a richer colour and is to be preferred; intense navy-purple with smart yellow blotch. These plants make their foliage very early and thus should be given a sheltered corner even in our warmest counties, in full sun. The bulbs should be planted in autumn about 15 cm (6 in) deep.

trojana

90 × 30 cm	*[8–9]*	*Purple*	*L.Spring*	P	D
3 × 1 ft					

Greece. 1888. It is a pity that this, one of the parents of modern bearded irises, has been so neglected. Its beautiful, well-spaced flowers are in light and dark lavender-purple, emerging from purplish spathes. Sun and good drainage.

unguicularis ●

60 × 30 cm	*[8–9]*	*Lavender*	*Autumn/*	P	D
2 × 1 ft			*Spring*		

Algeria. 1845. *I. stylosa*. This forms a dense grassy tuft up to 60 cm (2 ft) high among which, in mild spells between September and April, the exquisite, rich lilac-lavender flowers nestle, beautifully marked and veined, and of a quivering delicacy and deliciously scented. An ideal plant for cutting for winter decoration, it is free-flowering when planted hard against a hot, sunny wall in poor, dry soil and left undisturbed. There is a good white ('Bowles's White'); the dark purple *I.u. speciosa* forms ('Ellis' Variety', 'Lindsayae', 'Mary Barnard') are difficult to obtain, and seldom flower before the spring. 'Walter Butt' is a very free-growing and free-flowering form in palest lilac, but it has rather weak standards. The last three were collected in the wild, in Algeria. See also *I. lazica*.

"Patience seems to be the only manure these Irises need, poor soil inducing flowering instead of production of leaf, and the older a clump grows the better it flowers."—EAB

versicolor

60 × 30 cm	*[4–9]*	*Purple-red*	*E.Summer*	P	D
2 × 1 ft					

North America. 1732. In contrast to the normal purplish colouring of the species, the highly desirable form *kermesina* has flowers of a particularly rich claret colour, daintily reticulated with white. A free-flowering plant for moist soil in sun. Narrow grey-green leaves. (*I. virginica*.)

wattii

90 × 90 cm	*[8–9]*	*Lilac*	*Spring*	P W	D
3 × 3 ft					

Assam, W. China. Allied to *I. confusa*. It is less hardy than that species, but has larger flowers of a pale lilac-blue with darker spotting on the falls, and prominent orange crests. There is a hybrid between the two which seems no improvement on either. For a warm spot in our warmest counties. Evergreen.

wilsonii

60 × 30 cm	*[4–9]*	*Yellow*	*E.Summer*	PF	DS
2 × 1 ft					

W. China. 1909. In effect a shorter *Iris sibirica* with light yellow flowers veined with brown; the standards stand widely apart, which is its main difference from *I. forrestii*.

xiphioides ● ★

60 × 23 cm	*[6–9]*	*Blue*	*Summer*	P	DS
2 ft × 9 in					

N. Spain. 1568. *I. anglica* of gardens, *I. latifolia*. The so-called English Iris is normally a glorious violet-blue in the wild, but many named colour-forms and hybrids are available, from white through pale to dark violet-blue and reddish violet, all with a fine yellow zone on the rounded falls. These are good garden plants in well-nourished soil, moist rather than dry, in sun. Rush-like, blue-green leaves. Plant 10 cm (4 in) deep.

xiphium

46 × 23 cm	*[6–9]*	*Various*	*E.Summer*	P	DS
18 × 9 in					

S. France to N. Africa. 1564. *I. hispanica* of gardens. The Spanish Iris flowers a good fortnight before the English Iris, and has equally shapely flowers but with less handsome falls. They are compensated for by the more prominent yellow marks on them, and by the greater range of colours available in the named forms and hybrids—from white through yellow and bronze to tones of violet-blue. *I. tingitana* and *I. xiphioides* have probably played a part in these hybrids and also in the Dutch Irises, which are of similar quality, with coarser flowers earlier in the season. Any good fertile soil, well drained, in full sun, suits them. Plant 10 cm (4 in) deep.

JABOROSA, Solanaceae. The real reason for including this invasive underground spreader is that it is the sole representative of the letter J for this book—though some may complain of the omission of *Jasione perenne*. *Jaborosa* needs a sunny warm spot against a wall where it can run without hurting other low plants.

integrifolia

15 × 90 cm	*[8–10]*	*White*	*Summer*		D
6 in × 3 ft					

Buenos Aires. The broad dark green stemless leaves make a good background for the white flowers, so like those of the Tobacco Flower.

KIRENGESHOMA, Saxifragaceae.

1. *Crinum bulbispermum* (Burm.) Milne-R. ex Schweick (*C. longifolium* Thunb.), at Edinburgh. A parent of *C.× powellii* Baker.

2. **Crinum moorei** Hook. F., at Talbot Manor.

3. **Wachendorfia thyrsiflora** L. at Trengwainton. Photo: Paul Miles.

4. **Watsonia beatriçis** Math. & Bolus, at the Hillier Arboretum, sheltered and well baked at the foot of a hedge.

5. **Cautleya spicata** Baker, the form known in gardens as **'Robusta'** or 'Autumn Beauty', at Hidcote.

6. **Hedychium densiflorum** Wall. The spike on the right is **'Assam Orange'.** At Wakehurst.

I.

II. 1. **Incarvillea delavayi** Bur. &
       Franch.,   at   Keillour
       Castle.

    2. **Incarvillea mairei** (Levl.)
       Griers. (*I. grandiflora* Bur.
       & Franch.), at Keillour
       Castle.

    3. **Bletilla striata** (Thunb.)
       Reichb. (*Bletia hyacin-
       thina*), at Kew in a sunny
       border against a green-
       house.

    4. **Dactylorrhiza elata** (Poir.)
       Soó (*Orchis elata* Hartm.),
       at Edinburgh.

    5. **Lobelia tupa** L., at Edin-
       burgh.

    6. **Lobelia laxiflora** HBK.
       var. **angustifolia** DC. (*L.
       cavanillesii* of gardens), at
       Hidcote.

1. **Nepeta govaniana** Benth., at Kew.

2. **Kniphofia triangularis** Kunth subsp. **triangularis** Codd (*K. galpinii* of gardens), at Wisley.

3. **Kniphofia 'Wrexham Buttercup'** with **Solidago 'Goldenmosa'**.

4. **Iris kerneriana** Baker, at Threave.

5. **Crocosmia × crocosmiiflora** (Lemne ex Morr.) N.E. Br. **'Solfatare'** at Sissinghurst. The brownish leaves enhance the flower colour. Photo: Pamela Schwerdt.

6. **Crocosmia × crocosmiiflora** (Lemne ex Morr.) N.E. Br., **'Emily McKenzie'**, at Kew. One of the largest-flowered hardy kinds.

1. **Actaea alba** Mill., at Knightshayes Court.

2. **Actaea rubra** Ait. (W.) with red fruits and the white **A.r.** var.**neglecta** (Gillm.) Robinson, at Sissinghurst.

3. **Trillium grandiflorum** Salisb. **'Roseum'**, at Edinburgh.

4. **Trillium chloropetalum** Howell, at Hidcote. A good dark form.

5. **Hosta sieboldiana** (Hook.) Eng. **'Frances Williams'**.

6. A group of hostas: at back the white-edged **H. 'Thomas Hogg'**; a yellow-edged form of **H. montana** Maek. **'Aureo-marginata'**; the blue-leafed green-edged **H. tokudama** Maek. 'Flavo-circinalis' ('Variegata') and a variegated form of **H. fortunei** (Bak.) L. H. Bailey.

IV.

1. **Euphorbia wallichii** Hook.f. Each flower head lasts in beauty for months.

2. **Euphorbia griffithii** Hook.f. **'Fireglow'**, at Sissinghurst.

3. **Papaver lateritium** C. Koch, at Edinburgh. A good perennial.

4. **Paeonia obovata** Max. var. **alba** Saund., at Knightshayes.

5. **Paeonia wittmanniana** Hartw. **'Avant Garde'** at Hidcote.

6. **Paeonia mlokosewitschii** Lomak (yellow) and **P. cambessedesii** Willk. at Oxford.

V.

1. **Geranium wallichianum** D. Don **'Buxton's Variety'** at Wallington.

2. **Aconitum vulparia** Reichb. (*A. lycoctonum* of gardens).

3. **Gillenia trifoliata** Moench. at Bodnant.

1. **Nomocharis mairei** × **N. pardanthina** hybrids at Edinburgh.

2. **Meconopsis** × **sarsonsii** Sarsons.

3. **Meconopsis** × **sheldonii** G. Taylor, **'Slieve Donard'** at Rowallane, with **Hosta fortunei 'Picta'**.

4. **Meconopsis** × **sheldonii** G. Taylor, at Edinburgh.

1. **Tropaeolum polyphyllum** Cav., at Hidcote.   2. **Scabiosa ochroleuca** L., at Kew.

3. **Salvia haematodes** L., at Bressingham.

4. **Hemerocallis liliohyacinthina L.** (H. flava L.), at Hardwick Hall. One of the earliest-flowering species and deliciously fragrant.

1. **Fuchsia 'Prodigy'** ('Enfant Prodige'). The tallest and brightest of the hardy fuchsias.

2. **Parahebe perfoliata** R.Br. (*Veronica perfoliata* R.Br.) at Edinburgh.

3. **Reynoutria japonica** Sieb. & Zucc. (*Polygonum cuspidatum*) 'Compactum' of gardens, in autumn.

4. **Penstemon hartwegii** Benth., at Hidcote.

X.

1. **Trollius yunannensis**
Franch., at Rowallane.

2. **Ligularia macrophylla** DC., at Kew.

3. **Veratrum nigrum** L.

4. **Rodgersia pinnata**
Franch., **'Superba'**. Photo:
Valerie Finnis.

1. **Eucomis punctata** L'Hér. (*E. comosa* (Houtt.) Hort. ex Wehrh.) at Overbecks.

2. **Eucomis bicolor** Baker, at Kew.

3. **Veronicastrum virginicum** (L.) Farwell **'Album'** at Bressingham.

4. **Beschorneria yuccoides** Hook.f., at Mount Stewart.

5. **Salvia argentea** L., at Kew.

6. **Artemisia ludoviciana** Nutt., at Wisley.

1. **Phormium tenax** Forst. **'Variegatum'**, at Glendurgan.

2. **Rheum palmatum** L. **'Atrosanguineum'**.

3. **Paeonia × smouthii,** a splendid early-flowering hybrid.

4. **Iris aurea** Lindl., at Oxford.

2. **Geranium pratense** L. **'Plenum Violaceum'**, at Crathes Castle.

Polemonium foliosissimum ray, at Bressingham.

3. **Dicentra oregona** Eastw. 'Boothman's Variety'.

Iris kaempferi Sieb., a garden form. This species is attributable to *I. ensata* Thunb.

XIII.

1. **Geranium maculatum** L., a useful early-flowering species.

2. **Centaurea pulchra major,** a handsome plant whose leaves are white beneath.

3. **Galega orientalis** Lam. is shorter and earlier flowering than the usual garden hybrids.

4. **Astilbe × arendsii** Arends **'Ostrich Plume'** with the paler **'Betsy Cuperus'** behind, in the Trials at Wisley. These cultivars with drooping panicles make a pleasant change from the usual erect kinds.

1. The pink **Cortaderia selloana** (Schult.) Aschers. & Graebn. **'Rendatleri'** with the **'Pumila'** form of **C. selloana** in the Trials at Wisley.

2. **Pennisetum orientale** Rich. in foreground with the brown flowers of an early form of **Miscanthus sinensis** Anderss. and **M. sacchariflorus** (Maxim.) Hack., at Cambridge.

3. **Carex stricta** Good. **'Bowles' Golden'** at Kew.

4. **Stipa pennata** L. at Wisley.

1. **Adiantum pedatum** L. **japonicum** of gardens. The fronds become green when fully developed.

2. **Dryopteris erythro-sora** (Eaton) O. Kuntze. The fronds become greener when mature and have scarlet sori on the reverse.

3. **Dryopteris walli-chiana** (Spreng.) Hyl. with **Tellima grandi-flora.**

4. **Dryopteris pseudomas** (Wollaston) Holub & Pouzar (*D. borreri* Newm.). The brilliant yellow-green fronds are here contrasted with **Hosta sieboldiana** var. **elegans.**

5. **Osmunda regalis** L. The Royal Fern in autumn.

6. **Athyrium niponicum** (*A. goeringianum* Moore) **'Pictum'.** The Painted Fern.

XVI.

palmata ● ★

| 90 × 60 cm | [5–8] | Yellow | E.Autumn | P | DS |

3 × 2 ft

Japan, 1891. A unique plant of great beauty, thriving in deep soil where moisture is not far away, and free from lime, as at Rowallane, Northern Ireland. Leaves of clear green, broad and angled like a plane's, placed oppositely up the arching stems. In September the sprays of cool yellow, crystalline-textured, shuttlecock flowers are produced. There is nothing like it. An ideal companion for *Aconitum carmichaelii*. Some forms have more or less erect flowers, and thereby lack charm, though they may be considered better garden plants. From the fact that a distinct plant with dull green leaves and erect flowers is known in gardens as *K. koreana* it would appear that there may be two species.

> "A Japanese dignitary with ebony stems and vine-like leaves in a hearty green ... loose, airy flights of ivory shuttlecocks about 2 inches long ... in harmony with that line and deportment which pervade the entire plant."—ATJ

KITAIBELIA, Malvaceae.

vitifolia

| 1.8 m × 90 cm | [6–8] | White/pink | L.Summer | CS |

6 × 3 ft

With its tall stems clad in pointed vine-like leaves, this is a statuesque plant. It flowers over a long period but its small, mallow-like flowers make little effect, and look up to the sky for inspiration.

KNAUTIA, Dipsacaceae.

macedonica

| 60 × 60 cm | [5–9] | Crimson | Summer | P | DS |

2 × 2 ft

Macedonia. *Scabiosa rumelica*. Pure crimson is not a common colour in border flowers; this throws up many curving stems from the basal clump, each one branching into several stalks and each has a lovely, pure dark crimson, very double, dense "pin cushion" 5 cm (2 in) across. Sun, well-drained ordinary soil. Good with Rose 'Buff Beauty'. It varies to pink but is usually seen as above in gardens.

KNIPHOFIA, Liliaceae. Red Hot Poker, Torch Lily. *Tritoma*. The common conception of a Red Hot Poker is of a rather coarse plant with long leaves and autumn spikes of flower. This is *K. uvaria*, and a useful plant it is for shrubberies and rough places, the seashore, etc. There is, however, an untidiness of leaf and flower that spoils it for the choicer gardens. I do not propose here to do more than briefly mention the many hybrid glories that are available for those who garden in our warmest counties—such as the resplendent 'Samuel's Sensation', 'Star of Baden-Baden', etc., as these are seldom able to support their huge spikes unaided. Though initial hybridizing took place in the Botanic Garden at Baden-Baden by Max Leichtlin, and the older, bigger varieties met with much favour originally in some warmer districts of the British Isles, they have never become universally popular; no doubt because they are on the tender side. Rather would I call attention to a few unique species that are hardy and stalwart, and to a number of hybrids that have mostly appeared of late years, and which are hardy in our sunnier counties, self-supporting, and of a neatness and charm which are not met with in the big and flamboyant ones. Many set abundant seeds and these can be raised with very varied results if one does not necessarily require named clones. Those which are slow of increase can be made to hurry up by cutting off the top of the crown, when side-shoots will appear which can be turned into cuttings. Both this and division are best done in spring. Although they all demand full sun, they do best in soil which does not dry out in summer. There is one Poker named 'Erecta' whose flowers are brilliant orange-red which, as they open, turn upwards on the spike. It is not only a curiosity, but an ugly one. Its colour is its only recommendation. All broad-leafed kinds are more or less evergreen.

'Brimstone' ● ★

| 90 × 46 cm | [5–9] | Yellow | E.Autumn | P | D |
| 3 ft × 18 in | | | | | |

A slender brilliant yellow miniature poker for October, of imperturbable hardiness.

caulescens ★

| 1.2 m × 60 cm | [6–9] | Varied | E.Autumn | D |
| 4 × 2 ft | | | | |

South Africa. 1862. A very valuable and hardy plant and almost unique on account of its stems, which are like elephants' trunks, and which lie on, and root in, the ground, and also because of its beautiful grey leaves, very broad at the base, arising in grassy tufts from the ends of the stems. When the old dying leaves are pulled off in autumn, the bases reveal a lovely amethyst colouring. Stout flower-stems appear in September in Surrey; in other areas they may appear as early as June. At first the flowers are of soft coral-red, turning to greenish lemon-white. Sun, and ordinary drained soil. Often erroneously labelled *K. northiae*, *q.v.* In dry counties like Surrey, unless growing luxuriantly in good soil, the leaves tend to wither at the end, but in cooler counties, and particularly at Crathes Castle, Kincardineshire, the foliage is a valuable jade-green all the summer. This is the only truly hardy large Poker that I have met. Naturalized on the coast of the Firth of Forth, at the very water's edge. Evergreen.

gracilis (*K. sparsa*) [6–9]. I have not seen this plant but it is as well to state here that one or the other name may be the correct identification of the species *K. modesta*, as distinct from *K.* 'Modesta' (of gardens), *q.v.* under Dwarf Hybrids.

northiae

| 1.2 m × 90 cm | [6–9] | Yellowish | E.Summer | DS |
| 4 × 3 ft | | | | |

South Africa. 1889. A very rare plant whose leaves reach up to 1.8 m (6 ft) in length, and may be 15 cm. (6 in) wide at the base; they are smooth and grey-green (the type in cultivation in England is without the usual keel on the reverse) and create a fascinating, if untidy, rosette. It needs a sunny but moist position to encourage it to flower, but the coral-red buds opening to greeny-yellow are not among the brightest and are borne in dense spikes. In the wild it grows on stony mountainous slopes and also at stream-sides. It does well at Lanhydrock, Cornwall. Evergreen.

"...one of the most tropical-looking of plants that are hardy enough to be left out."—EAB

praecox ● ★

| 1.8 m × 90 cm | [6–9] | Scarlet | L.Summer/ | DS |
| 6 × 3 ft | | | E.Autumn | |

Cape Province. Prior to 1870. Known in gardens as *K. uvaria* 'Nobilis', *K.u.* 'Grandiflora', *K. alooides* 'Maxima', this is a tremendous plant; in spite of its height it seldom needs staking. The fiery red spikes are large and long and imposing, and are seen to best advantage against dark coppery foliage.

rooperi

| 1.2 m × 60 cm | [6–9] | Orange | E.Autumn | W DS |
| 4 × 2 ft | | | | |

1854. This flowers well at Trelissick and Trengwainton, Cornwall. and brightens the garden in September and October with its ovoid heads of bloom, orange-red opening to greenish yellow. The usual lax green leaves. At one time known as *K. uvaria* 'C. M. Prichard'. The last to flower.

rufa
of gardens

| 90 × 30 cm | [6–9] | Red/Yellow | Summer | P W D |
| 3 × 1 ft | | | | |

This is probably a hybrid, possibly with *K. triangularis*, and is sterile. It is a charming plant of subdued colouring with dainty spikes of widely spaced flowers, soft terracotta in bud opening to straw-yellow. Grassy foliage. The true species has curved, well-spaced spikes of yellowish white flowers.

snowdenii ●

| 90 × 30 cm | [7–9] | Coral | Summer | P W DS |
| 3 × 1 ft | | | | |

Uganda. 1918. *K. thomsonii snowdenii*. A rare and tender species only suitable for mild districts. The flower-stems bear comparatively few, widely spaced, curved flowers, of varied tones between pale coral and scarlet. It grows well at Mount Stewart, Northern Ireland. *K. rogersii* is closely related.

triangularis ● ★

| 60–90 × 46 cm | [6–9] | Flame | E.Autumn | P D |
| 2–3 ft × 18 in | | | | |

South Africa. This name covers several garden plants of great value, in part parents of many of the small Pokers. One of the brightest things for the late September and October garden, this species is perfectly hardy in all but our very coldest counties. Two almost identical garden plants, known as *K. nelsonii* (1892) and *K. macowanii*, both with flowers of vivid orange-red, are seen in gardens; the former flowers first, usually. The plant grown in gardens as *K. galpinii* is again almost identical, but of more orange tint; it usually flowers even later. All three have green, grass-like leaves, and wiry thin stems bearing dainty little flower-spikes. The tubular flowers have splayed lobes. *K. galpinii* (of gardens) was made popular in the 1930s by a Cranleigh nursery, owned by Gibson & Amos. It appears that these three garden clones are in reality *K. triangularis triangularis*. The colouring of the flowers of all of the above is uniform from bud to open bloom. In the true *K. galpinii*, which I have not seen, the flower-buds and open flowers are of different tints and the flower-lobes are not splayed.

> "... this perfectly hardy species seems to wait for that magic moment when its scarlet flowers will give an intenser glow in response to the influence of October's golden days."—ATJ

tuckii
of gardens

1.2 m × 60 cm	[6–9]	Red	Summer	P	D
4 × 2 ft					

Well-known old plant, resembling *K. uvaria* but it is less red-hot in colour and flowers in early summer. The flowers are in dense spikes, pale straw-yellow opening from coral-red buds. Long leaves, with finely toothed margins. This old garden plant is a reddish type of *K. ensifolia ensifolia*, which is often much paler. See also 'Atlanta', page 245.

uvaria ★

1.5 m × 60 cm	[5–9]	Red	Autumn	P	D
5 × 2 ft					

Cape Peninsula. 1705. *Tritoma uvaria, Kniphofia alooides; K. linearifolia* is closely allied. The well-known Red Hot Poker. It makes a wonderful splash in the late summer and autumn garden and is invaluable in the landscape. The foliage is lax and untidy, evergreen. Hardy in all but our coldest winters. For *K. uvaria* 'Grandiflora' or *K. alooides* 'Maxima' see under *K. praecox*.

THE DWARF HYBRIDS ● ★ [All 5–9 unless otherwise listed] P D
Since the nomenclature of Red Hot Poker is so involved and since most of the plants grown under specific names in Britain may well be hybrids, it is difficult to say more than that the following are closely related and probably mostly derived from the dwarf species described above, and a few others. Leslie Slinger of the Slieve Donard Nursery, Beth Chatto, and Alan Bloom have been to the fore of late years in producing these treasures. They are all plants with reasonably tidy grassy leaves, and mostly bear dainty slender spikes of bright colouring, some flowering as early as June. Very cold and wet winters have sometimes caused losses with 'Maid of Orleans' [6–9] and 'Goldelse' [6–9] but the remainder seem perfectly hardy in Surrey. They all need well-drained soil; this cannot be too much stressed, and in colder districts should be given a heavy mulch in late autumn.

All achieve about 90 cm (3 ft) and should be planted about 46 cm (18 in) apart. They flower during different weeks in June, July and early August, and sometimes young plants produce blooms later as well. The palest, an ivory- or primrose-white, is 'Maid of Orleans', raised by Amos Perry of Enfield, *c.* 1950; somewhat darker is 'Tubergeniana', a soft old-parchment tint, raised by Tubergen of Holland. The older light yellows, 'Goldelse' (1906) [6–9], and 'Buttercup' have been joined by 'Candlelight' (Bloom) and 'Sunningdale Yellow'—raised from *K. galpinii* (of gardens) seed by A. Bryce Wilson—and darker yellows are 'Canary Bird', 'Goldfinch' and 'Yellow Hammer' from the Slieve Donard Nursery. Yet darker are 'Amberlight' and 'Ada' also from Ireland. Next we might choose the old *K. rufa*, referred to among the species; a larger edition of this soft tint is found in Alan Bloom's 'Bressingham Glow' [6–9]. Six charmers in cream and coral are 'Snow Maiden', 'Jenny Bloom' (Bloom), 'Enchantress' (Slieve Donard Nursery), 'Modesta' (of gardens), 'Percy's Pride' (an excellent seedling of Alan Bloom's) and 'Strawberries and Cream' (Chatto). Red Start' (Slieve Donard), 'Timothy' (Carlile) and two of Bloom's, 'Bressingham Flame' and 'Bressingham Torch', bring us to the threshold of the dwarf autumn-flowering species listed above, the last being 'Brimstone'. Altogether they form a chain of brilliant 'events' in the garden and they are almost indispensable for display or cutting.

'Little Maid' is of similar colouring to 'Maid of Orleans' but short. It is excellent for associating with colchicums. Raised about 1966 by Beth Chatto. Autumn.

TALL HYBRIDS

As intimated earlier many hybrids have been named in the past, but many have not stood the test of time, being similar and none too hardy, and often needing staking. The following hybrids have proved hardy and satisfactory in Surrey.

'Atlanta' ★

1.2 m × 60 cm	[6–9]	Red	E.Summer	P	D
4 × 2 ft					

A remarkable hardy hybrid Torch Lily which from a Sussex garden had been planted in the garden of the Atlanta Hotel, Tintagel, Cornwall, and there found, named and distributed by Neil G. Treseder of the Truro Nurseries. It grows as an escape from gardens in many places around the coast, up to Scotland. It forms a dense evergreen clump, even within spray of the sea—or anywhere else inland—and produces a lavish crop of orange-red pokers in May. Thus it is the first of the Torch Lilies to flower. Its early-flowering habit may indicate that another plant (equally early), *K. ensifolia* [6–9], is in its parentage, or it may be synonymous with it. Evergreen.

'Corallina' (*K. pfitzeri*) [5–9]. A name which repeatedly crops up but it is best to beware, because it simply indicates hybrids between *K. macowanii* and *K. uvaria*. It is obvious that anything might happen!

'Green Jade'

1.2 m × 60 cm	[5–9]	Green	L.Summer	P	D
4 × 2 ft					

c. 1968. This was raised by Beth Chatto from seeds from the garden of Sir Cedric Morris Bt, Suffolk. It has most pleasing slender spires of pale green, with a hint of cream.

'Royal Standard' ● ★

1.2 m × 60 cm	[5–9]	Red/Yellow	Summer	P	D
4 × 2 ft					

1921. An old favourite and rightly so for it is reliably hardy in warmer counties, and its scarlet buds opening to bright yellow flowers recall the colours of the well-known flag.

'Underway' ★

1.2 m × 46 cm	[6–9]	Apricot-	Autumn	P	D
4 ft × 18 in		orange			

A beautiful very late-flowering hardy hybrid raised from seed of *K. galpinii* (of gardens) by Norman Hadden of West Porlock, Somerset. Fairly stout dark foliage and good spikes of flowers in dense array; they have the late-flowering habit and orange colouring of *K. galpinii* contrasted by long protruding cream stamens—wedded to a more substantial plant. It has proved quite hardy. Ideal with *Aster novi-belgii* 'Climax'.

'Wrexham Buttercup' ● ★
   1.2 m × 60 cm   *[6–9]*   *Yellow*   *Summer*   P   D
   4 × 2 ft
A splendid pure yellow poker, bright and clear; substantial large spikes. Lovely with flame and orange roses. A success at Mount Stewart, Northern Ireland. 'Bees' Lemon' [6–9] is similar. *K. primulinus* (of gardens) [6–9] is a smaller yellow variety.

LACTUCA, Compositae. Lettuce. There are several species of ornament for big gardens, but they are somewhat invasive, a few being terrible, ineradicable weeds (*L. bourgaei*) [6–9]. All the garden kinds have blue-lilac or purplish lilac daisies on branching stems. *L. plumieri* [2–9] is a useful high plant in the big beds at Blickling Hall, Norfolk. *L. alpina* [2–9] is shorter and more acceptable in smaller gardens, likewise *L. perennis* [2–9]. Also known as *Mulgedium* or *Cicerbita*.

LAMIUM, Labiatae. Deadnettle. The ground-covering species are dealt with in my *Plants for Ground-Cover*.

orvala
   30 × 30 cm   *[4–8]*   *Pink*   *Spring*   DS
   1 × 1 ft
Europe. 1596. Very much like a white Deadnettle, and liable to get pulled up, but it is non-invasive and makes a beautiful clump of leaves. The flowers are a subtle shade of coppery pink. At home in shade anywhere. There is also a rare and very beautiful white variety, 'Album', which

    "... first saw light in ... E. C. Buxton's garden."—ATJ

LATHYRUS, Leguminosae. The annual Sweet Pea belongs to this genus but the following are sound perennials for sunny positions in well-drained soils. The climbing kinds are attractive when trained up pea-sticks or growing over a spring-flowering shrub, hedge or wall, or just allowed to flop down a bank. They climb by means of tendrils.

aureus
   46 × 60 cm   *[6–9]*   *Yellow*   *Spring*   DS
   18 in × 2 ft
S.E. Europe, S.W. Asia. 1883. *Orobus aurantiacus* (of gardens). The fresh yellowish green leaves make a dense clump, and every shoot is tipped with erect heads of pea-flowers of a strange subdued brownish amber. It needs coppery foliage nearby to bring it to life. *L. luteus* (*L. gmelinii*) [6–9] is a poor relative.

grandiflorus ●
   Climber   *[6–9]*   *Rose*   *Summer*   P   D
S. Europe. 1814. Everlasting Pea. A splendid old garden climber, spreading freely by means of its tuberous roots. Sparse blue-green leaves. The large flowers (not fragrant) are produced in twos and threes for many weeks, of classic form, deep magenta-pink with maroon-red keel. 1.8 m (6 ft).

latifolius ● ★
   Climber   *[5–9]*   *Pink*   *Summer/*   P DS
                                   E.Autumn
Europe. 1596. The Perennial Pea to give it its proper name—it is often erroneously called Everlasting Pea, which rightly belongs to *L. grandiflorus*—

has long been grown in our gardens and can be trained on sticks or fence or encouraged to ramble over a hedge. Better still it can be planted on a bank and allowed to sprawl downwards, as at Nymans, Sussex, and The Weir, Herefordshire. It is naturalized on many a railway embankment and waste ground. The strong magenta-pink of the normal form is far surpassed by the pure white form variously known as *albus, albiflorus,* or 'White Pearl'; although scentless it is a flower of great quality. This white form can often be raised from seed, and sometimes pale, clear pinks also appear, such as 'Rose Queen', pink with white eye. The white was often used by Gertrude Jekyll for draping foward over some plant whose flowering was over. 1.8 m (6 ft).

"Delphiniums ... we plant behind them the white Everlasting Pea, and again behind that Clematis Jackmanii ... the white Peas are trained over the Delphinium stems (shortened); when the Peas go out of bloom, the Clematis is brought over."—GJ

maritimus

| *Sprawler* | *[3–9]* | *Purple* | *E. to L.* | P | DS |
| | | | *Summer* | | |

Northern Hemisphere. *L. japonicus maritimus.* Sea Pea. An uncommon native of British sand dunes, and thus of use in very sandy gardens, hot sunny banks, etc. Invasive rootstock. The good-sized flowers occur severally on the stalks, magenta buds opening to lavender-blue, over masses of glaucous leaves, with tendrils to help the plant to climb. 90 cm (3 ft).

nervosus ●

| *Climber* | *[3–10]* | *Blue* | *Summer* | P | DS |

Patagonia. 1744. Lord Anson's Blue Pea. A rare plant originally discovered by the creator of Shugborough Hall, Staffordshire. Clear periwinkle blue flowers, small, but several in a spray, are produced over a long period among grey-green leaves. Distinctive fragrance. 1.5 m (5 ft). I had been searching for this for many years and eventually was given it by the Director of Wisley for the garden at Shugborough. Distinct from *L. magellanicus.*

rotundifolius

| *Climber* | *[5–10]* | *Pink* | *Summer* | P | DS |

Tauria. 1822. Persian Everlasting Pea. Easily grown in any friable soil, ascending to some 1.8 m (6 ft) annually from a creeping rootstock. Copious fresh green leafage. Flowers are in clusters, the standards of light pink, the keel coppery red. Of similar character and uses to *L. tuberosus*; a good hybrid between the two grows at Kew. Some forms are invasive; others have compact roots.

tuberosus

| *Climber* | *[5–9]* | *Pink* | *Summer* | P | DS |

Europe. 1568. A creeping tuberous root throws up many shoots which will clamber through a shrub, ascending to some 1.5 m (5 ft), or on pea-sticks, or will sprawl on a bank or over a stump. Like a smaller version of the Perennial Pea (*L. latifolius*), with elegant flowers of a good clear pink, not scented. Easily grown in any friable soil.

undulatus

| *Climber* | *[7–9]* | *Red-purple* | *E.Summer* | P | W | DS |

Turkey. 1889. *L. sibthorpii.* Another climbing perennial, for sunny well-drained places in our warmer counties; it grows well in the open at Kew. Typical pea-foliage and several pea-flowers in magenta-crimson, of good size and on stout stalks are borne for many weeks. 1.5 m (5 ft).

vernus

38 × 30 cm	~ *[5–9]*	*Purple*	*Spring*	DS
15 in × 1 ft				

Europe. 1629. This forms clumps of much-divided, almost ferny, foliage over which are sprinkled the heads of tiny purple pea-flowers, like those of a giant vetch, and having crimson, magenta and maroon in their tones. A happy little plant in most soils that are not waterlogged, it thrives in poor gravelly soils. Sun. Lovely with daffodils and red tulips. There are some charming colour forms: *L. v. variegatus,* pink and white; *L. v. roseus,* pink; *L. v. albiflorus,* white, and *L. v. cyaneus* (of gardens), pale blue. They are of less stature than the type and only creep into this book, so to speak, by proxy.

LAVATERA, Malvaceae. Tree Mallow. I have included two shrubby species because they assort so well with summer and autumn flowers. Certain botanists are claiming that all species mentioned below (except *Lavatera maritima*) are geographical forms of *L. olbia*. Be this as it may, they are quite distinct from a garden point of view so I have retained the established nomenclature.

cachemiriana ★

1.8 m × 90 cm	*[6–8]*	*Pink*	*Summer*	PF	S
6 × 3 ft					

Kashmir. A remarkable, stately plant with a long flowering season, whose wiry branches sway in the wind but seldom need staking. The big, clear pink mallow-blooms, blanched towards the centre, are silky and elegant and are carried in a branching panicle above the downy ivy-shaped leaves. Ordinary soil, sun. Good seed-heads, downy capsules.

maritima ●

1.5 m × 90 cm	*[6–8]*	*White*	*Autumn*	W	CS
5 × 3 ft					

Mediterranean Region. *L. bicolor.* This is like the much better known *L. olbia* 'Rosea', but smaller and later-flowering. The shrubby growth is well covered in velvety grey-green leaves, of jagged outline. The flowers are of good size, of palest lilac-pink, nearly white, contrasted by magenta-crimson veins which converge at the base of the petals into a handsome blotch. Between the bases of the petals are revealed the emerald green calyces. Provides a good autumn picture at Sissinghurst, Kent, but is not hardy there.

olbia

1.8 × 1.2 m	*[8–10]*	*Pink*	*Summer/*	PF	CS
6 × 4 ft			*Autumn*		

S. France. 1570. The Tree Mallow is an erect, self-reliant plant with downy lobed leaves of sage green. The stiff upright stems have old-rose pink small hollyhock flowers in fairly dense spikes. It is an excellent tall, woody plant, more of a shrub than a herbaceous plant. It is seldom seen in gardens, its place being taken by the less hardy:

● 'Rosea' [8–10]. The name originated from Ladhams' Nursery, Southampton, prior to 1920. It is perhaps a hybrid with *L. thuringiaca* or *L. cachemiriana*. It is a more lush, widely branched and more graceful plant than the species, with larger flowers of clearer colouring. It suffers in cold winters and is apt to revert to an inferior type. It should be raised from cuttings. It is one of the most prolific of summer-flowering plants for our warmer counties, in full sun. Lovely with *Campanula lactiflora* and *Agapanthus*. Non-stop display. 'Barnsley' [6–10] is a sport of 'Rosea' with flowers of clear light pink with crimson centres. It was found prior to 1985 by Rosemary Verey in the village of Barnsley, Gloucestershire. A brilliant pink, 'Kew Rose', was raised at Kew, and the rich, dark 'Burgundy Wine' was raised by Peter Catt.

"The most notable being the bushy pink-flowered *Lavatera olbia*, all the more valuable because there are not many flowers of pink colouring for the time of year." August—GJ

thuringiaca
1.5 m × 90 cm	*[7–9]*	*Pink*	*Summer*	PF	CS
5 × 3 ft					

S.E. Europe, etc. 1731. Woody at the base, this is a herbaceous plant, and comes somewhere between *L. cachemiriana* and *L. olbia*. Soft hairy foliage of sage green and soft pink flowers in a branching spike. The leaves are rounded, somewhat lobed and the seed-capsules are not downy; the petals overlap more than in *L. cachemiriana*. A good pure white form has been selected.

LEONTOPODIUM, Compositae. *L. alpinum* is the well-known Edelweiss, and the species are usually found on rock gardens. The following, with good cultivation and drainage in full sun, is a lovely plant in many ways.

haplophylloides
30 × 30 cm	*[4–9]*	*White*	*E.Summer*	PF	DS
1 × 1 ft					

W. China. 1915. *L. aloysiodorum* (of gardens). A dense clump or mat throwing up unbranched stems clad in narrow leaves and grey-felted leafy heads of white flowers. The whole plant is deliciously redolent of lemon.

LEPACHIS, Compositae.

pinnata
1.2 m × 60 cm	*[5–9]*	*Yellow*	*Summer*	P	D
4 × 2 ft					

E. United States. 1803. *Rudbeckia pinnata, Ratibida pinnata.* One of the few late summer daisies that appeal to me, on account of the soft clear colouring. It is an erect, wiry plant with narrowly lobed leaves, and bears for a long time the wide flowers with drooping petals around a small brown central cone. Easy to satisfy in a sunny position in any fertile reasonably drained soil; beautiful with strong purple phloxes.

LESPEDEZA, Leguminosae.

thunbergii
1.8 × 1.2 m	*[5–9]*	*Purple*	*E.Autumn*	D
6 × 4 ft				

China, Japan. 1837. *L. sieboldii, Desmodium penduliflorum.* For one of the last gorgeous splashes of colour of the year this can hardly be beaten. Though semi-shrubby, the stems usually die to the ground each year and develop into a feathery arching mass during summer. In late September or October the graceful, branching, silky sprays become covered with rich crimson-purple pea-flowers. In a sunny position on a bank or raised ground, with good drainage, near to silvery foliage this can be a great sight in a sunny autumn, when the dew has dried. *L. bicolor* [5–9] is far less showy in flower but is an elegant upright plant.

> "The general effect may be described as that of a rich purple Laburnum
> … if grown on an upper portion of rocky bank and allowed to wave out
> … a really magnificent sight."—EAB

LEUCOJUM, Liliaceae. Snowflake.

aestivum
60 × 23 cm	*[4–9]*	*White*	*Spring*	P	D
2 ft × 9 in					

Europe, Britain. The Summer Snowflake or Loddon Lily—it grows near the River Loddon and elsewhere in England—flowers well before summer, at daffodil time. While the wild species is a rather second-rate, flopping plant, 'Gravetye Giant' is a very superior form, evolved or selected by William Robinson. This upstanding plant has daffodil-like leaves of richest green, and stout stalks of the same colour bearing six-segmented white bells, like snowdrops, but with green tips. It enjoys deep rich soil, moist rather than dry, in sun or shade. *L.a. pulchellum* (*L. pulchellum, L. hernandezii*) [6–9] hails from Majorca and is a floriferous and pleasing smaller version of the type. *L. vernum* [4–8] flowers in earliest spring and *L. autumnale* [5–9] flowers in late summer but both are rather small for this book.

LIATRIS, Compositae. One of the few genera in which the flowers at the top of the spikes open first. They are striking plants, with tufts of grassy leaves from which arise leafy stems bearing at the apex stiff bottle-brushes of dense flowerheads. They succeed best in full sun on well-drained soils.

aspera
90 × 30 cm	*[4–9]*	*Mauve*	*Summer*	P	DS
3 × 1 ft					

E. United States. 1805. In this the flower-heads are placed well apart on the spike, revealing the conspicuous, incurved papery bracts. There is a white variety, 'Alba'; both are plants of refinement and far more elegant than the others mentioned below.

pycnostachya
1.2 m × 30 cm	*[4–9]*	*Mauve*	*Summer*	P	DS
4 × 1 ft					

United States. 1732. The Kansas Gay Feather is the tallest of the three listed, with flower spikes of a strong mauve-pink. *L. scariosa* also has dense tall spikes, and white forms are listed.

spicata
60 × 30 cm	*[4–9]*	*Mauve*	*Summer*	P	DS
2 × 1 ft					

United States. 1732. *L. callilepis* of gardens. Both the white variety, *alba*, and 'Kobold' ('Gnome') (1946), brilliant mauve-pink, are spectacular plants. These forms are sometimes attributed to *L. callilepis*. Both species are hardy and reliable. 'Floristan' [4–9] is a good, pure white.

LIBERTIA, Iridaceae. Clump-forming plants with good, dark green, grassy leaves, tending to brown at the tip. They need good drainage and grow well in sun or part shade in our warmer counties. The orange seed-pods are decorative in autumn. Evergreen.

formosa

90 × 60 cm *3 × 2 ft*	*[9–10]*	*White*	*E.Summer*	PF	W	DS

Chile. 1837. Sprays of pure white saucer-shaped flowers top the foliage. Each has a cluster of yellow stamens. It loves the moist air of western coastal gardens.

"... beautiful at all seasons ... owing to the colour of its foliage, which is as green as the Holly."—WR

ixioides

60 × 60 cm *2 × 2 ft*	*[9–10]*	*White*	*Summer*	PF	W	DS

New Zealand. 1865. Like the above it is a desirable and elegant plant but of less size. By late winter the leaves have often turned to bright orange-brown. *L. peregrinans* [9–10], also from New Zealand, has similarly coloured leaves and similar flowers, but its rootstock is stoloniferous. A form is known as 'Goldleaf'.

LIGULARIA, (*Senecio*) Compositae. All species need moist or even boggy conditions. They are very prone to slug and snail damage in spring.

dentata

1.2 m × 60 cm *4 × 2 ft*	*[4–8]*	*Orange*	*Summer*	F	D

China. 1900. *L.* or *Senecio clivorum*. One of the most handsome of plants, producing large leathery heart-shaped leaves on 30-cm-high stalks, of rich dark green, and stout stems supporting branching heads of large vivid orange daisies in July and August. A selection has been named 'Orange Queen'. It needs rich, moist soil and sunshine, and usually thrives steadily, increasing and making good ground-cover. It contrasts strongly with *Lobelia* × *vedrariensis*.

"A very fine plant for a moist place or, failing that, the north side of a wall or line of shrubs, where the sun will not scorch it."—EAB

★ —'**Desdemona**' 1940. [4–8]. A more compact and refined plant than *L. dentata* with equally good flowers and requiring the same cultivation. Its leaves are among the most striking, of rich dark brownish green above, fading to metallic green, while beneath they are of gorgeous mahogany-red. 'Othello' (1915) is almost identical, and both produce similar coloured forms from seeds. 'Moorblut' is from Germany, with still darker leaves, a contrast for *Scrophularia aquatica* 'Variegata'.

'Gregynog Gold' ★

1.8 m × 60 cm *6 × 2 ft*	*[4–8]*	*Orange*	*Summer*	D	

1950. *L. dentata* × *L. veitchiana*. A superb hybrid raised in Wales, suitable for rich, moist soil in sunshine. Grand, handsome, heart-shaped leaves and the vivid orange flowers of *L. dentata* arranged in a great conical spike. It has few peers at flowering time and looks quite sumptuous with rich purple phloxes. *L.* × *hessei* (1934) (*L. dentata* × *L. wilsoniana* × *L. veitchiana*) is similar and 'Gregynog Gold' is sometimes classed under this name.

"This noble plant ... eclipses all others of its family in size of blooms."—ATJ

hodgsonii

90 × 60 cm	[4–8]	Yellow/	Summer	DS
3 × 2 ft		Orange		

Japan. A useful small species for small gardens. The large kidney-shaped leaves are sharply toothed. The flowers are broad daisies in a cluster at the top of the stem. Some forms apparently have green leaves, stems and calyces, with yellow flowers, others have orange flowers with purplish brown calyces; this tint is also on stems and reverse of leaves.

japonica

1.5 m × 90 cm	[4–8]	Orange	E.Summer	DS
5 × 3 ft				

Japan. *Senecio japonicus, Erythrochaete palmatifida.* The deeply cut leaves, divided into many long segments, give great promise but the flowers are rather few. See also *L. × palmatiloba.*

macrophylla ★

1.5 m × 60 cm	[4–8]	Yellow	L.Summer	F DS
5 × 2 ft				

Orient. 1896. *Senecio ledebourii.* This revels in good deep soil and is a striking, rare plant. The large tall horseradish-like leaves are of grey-green, and the dense spikes of yellow daisies stand aloft like paint-brushes in the August landscape.

× palmatiloba ★

1.5 m × 90 cm	[4–8]	Orange	L.Summer	D
5 × 3 ft				

Prior to 1939. A hybrid raised by Herm. A. Hesse of Germany, between *L. dentata* and *L. japonica.* The deeply cut leaves of the latter species give this hybrid great elegance, and the big clusters of orange flowers derive more from *L. dentata.* Although the two parents are handsome, I place the hybrid top.

przewalskii ★

1.8 m × 90 cm	[4–8]	Yellow	Summer	F DS
6 × 3 ft				

N. China. 1866. *Senecio przewalskii.* Elegant, decorative, deeply fingered, dark green leaves of otherwise triangular outline extend up the nearly black stems, ending in a narrow spire of small clear yellow flowers. 'The Rocket' is a particularly good form of this species.

sibirica

1.2 m × 60 cm	[4–8]	Clear	Summer	PF DS
4 × 2 ft		Yellow		

Far East, Himalaya. *Senecio ligularia.* Closely allied to the other species grown in gardens, this is noted for the black or very dark brown anthers which contrast strongly with the strap-shaped petals. The flowers are borne in close erect spikes over large, rounded leaves, neatly toothed. Not too strong a yellow to associate with *Lythrum.* Prior to 1849.

stenocephala

1.2 m × 60 cm	[4–8]	Yellow	E.Summer	F DS
4 × 2 ft				

Japan, N. China. *Senecio stenocephalus.* Big rounded leaves with jagged teething. The flower-stems may be purplish, bearing big heads of orange-yellow daisies.

veitchiana ★

1.5 m × 60 cm	[4–8]	Yellow	Summer	F DS
5 × 2 ft				

China. 1901. *Senecio veitchianus*. Almost circular, large, basal leaves, often 30 cm (1 ft) across, in complete contrast to the slender stiff spike of golden yellow daisies set among broad bracts. *L. wilsoniana* (1905) [4–8] resembles it from a garden point of view, differing mainly in having hollow leaf-stalks and very narrow bracts. The leaves of both species make handsome clumps 60 cm (2 ft) high and wide. They are striking plants, as conspicuous in their fluffy seeds as in flower.

LILIUM, Liliaceae. Lily. The numerous species and multitudes of hybrids of Lilium deserve a whole book to themselves—and in fact they have had several. It would not be right, however, to exclude all mention of them from this book on this account, particularly since they contribute much to the garden and because there are some excellent, easily grown perennials among them. Accordingly I will just throw out a few general hints about their cultivation and indicate some of the more reliable long-established species and cultivars, leaving you to find out more about them from detailed publications. As a rule all the kinds listed here can be considered as healthy, long-lived perennials if their simple needs are studied. See also *Cardiocrinum*.

One group prefers damp soil; it is headed by the well-known perennial *L. pardalinum* [5–9], a gorgeous orange-red fellow with boldly recurved flowers "spotted like the pard". It seems to thrive almost anywhere. Its *L. superbum* [4–9] can take more moisture, even in a sopping peaty bog. The Bellingham Hybrids (between *L. humboltii ocellatum*, *L. pardalinum* and *L. parryi*) [4–9] are splendid tall plants, and are also good perennials if they are moved to a fresh site every few years. Other reliable cultivars of this type are 'Shuksan' (1924), 'Afterglow' (1954) and 'Eric Mayell' [all 4–9].

For all the rest that I am going to mention *drainage* is the prerequisite—repeat, drainage. It is the one factor on which they all insist. More failures are due to inadequate drainage than to anything else. If your ground is inclined to be poorly drained in winter while the bulbs are dormant, plant them on raised mounds or beds or on banks. The next point is that they are sun-lovers, though they will grow in part shade and are often recommended for it. Their soil should be well mixed with humus and a fertilizer rich in potash and phosphate—such as bonemeal, or a suitable general fertilizer of similar analysis; strongly nitrogenous fertilizers and dung should not be used. Fresh bulbs are best planted in late summer or very early autumn, or in spring; when once they are in the garden, division is best done soon after flowering, and in fact they are better moved while in growth than when dormant in winter, when the soil is cold and damp. On heavy soils, or in slug-ridden gardens, it is advisable to envelop each bulb in sharp sand. They may be increased by division, or by means of stem-bulbils (where they occur), or by separating the fleshy scales of the bulbs, or by seeds. Plant 7.5–15 cm (3–6 in) deep according to the size of the bulb.

My own soil is an acid sand and I have grown the same bulbs in it for twenty-five years of *Lilium martagon* [4–8], the soft pink Turk's Cap and its white and maroon forms, its yellow counterpart *L. hansonii* [4–8] and some hybrids therefrom like 'Marhan'; the small erect orange-red *L. tsingtauense* [5–8], and larger Orange Lily, *L. bulbiferum croceum* [5–8], together with several of the hybrid groups, *L. × hollandicum* [5–8] and *L. × maculatum* [5–8], also 'Enchantment' (1944) [5–8]; the tall orange-red Turk's Cap *L. davidii* [5–8] and hybrids 'Maxwill' and 'Red Max', all of extreme value when used with some of the yellow perennials of summer; the large white trumpet-flowered *L. centifolium*

[5–8]; the soft buff-yellow *L. henryi* [4–9] and the overpoweringly fragrant *L. pyrenaicum* [5–8], yellow, and its vermilion-red form 'Rubrum'; I should expect the newer *L. ciliatum* [5–8] to thrive with them. *L.* × *testaceum* [5–8] is also successful. Were I on heavier soil, but still acid, I would expect *L. martagon, L. hansonii, L. henryi* and *L. davidii* to do better [all 4–8]. 'Thunderbolt' (1954) [4–8] is a good strong *L. henryi* derivation and thrives at Wisley. If the heavier soil were limy all of the above would be expected to thrive, together with *L. candidum* [4–9], the peerless white Madonna Lily; *L. monadelphum* [4–8] and *L. szovitzianum* [4–8]; *L. regale* [4–9] likewise, but this last is susceptible to spring frosts. None of these four thrives for me. In acid soil it is well worth trying the imperial *L. auratum* [5–8], the Golden Rayed Lily of Japan, so beautiful in its unadulterated state, or *L.a. platyphyllum*, and *L. tigrinum* [3–8] (*L. lancifolium*) *fortunei* (infinitely superior to *L.t.* 'Splendens'), the coral-red Tiger Lily, though they may be short-lived—perhaps from nostalgia but more likely from virus.

L. speciosum [5–8] is superb at Nymans, Sussex, on heavy acid soil. *L. lankongense* and *L. duchartrei,* pink and white respectively, run about with their stoloniferous roots in acid sandy peaty soil at the Savill Garden, Windsor [5–8]; *L. szovitzianum* [5–8] seeds itself in the paths of several Cotswold gardens. One could go on citing successes—the white Martagons at Killerton and *L. pardalinum* [5–8] at Peckover House, Cambridgeshire, both in full sun, for instance; one could also cite many failures. I do not pretend that the above are all that one should try, but they would provide a good base for further exploration.

The many lists of today abound in hybrids enough to whet all appetites. Some which have stood the test for many years at Wisley, Surrey, are those splendid reds and orange-reds of *L. davidii* [5–8] derivation such as 'Lady Bowes Lyon' (1956), 'Joseph Fletcher' (1957), 'George Soper' (1958) and 'Walter Bentley' (1965). New hybrids are coming thick and fast still from De Graaf in the United States, a pioneer hybridist on a big scale; Rosewarne Experimental Station, Cornwall, is producing *L.* × *hollandicum* [4–8] types, and lately Dr G. North of the Scottish Horticultural Research Institution near Dundee has brought forth some beautiful hybrids [all 5–8] between *L. lankongense, L. duchartrei, L. cernuum* and *L. davidii,* which are not only unusual but seem likely to prove good perennials.

There are named varieties in the lists of every colour and shape, height and season, but unfortunately they are seldom perennial, and die out after a few years. But who, having delighted in such exquisite blooms for just one summer, would grudge their cost? Their enemy, apart from slugs and mice (which eat the leaves and buds), is virus, and since this is often spread by aphides, it behoves us to have the insect sprayer at hand. The Lily disease, caused by Botrytis, is particularly apt to be troublesome in damp weather in early summer; many lily specialists spray their plants weekly with Bordeaux mixture or other copper-containing preparation, as a preventive.

Many Lilies will grow happily among herbaceous plants or shrubs. It is a good idea to plant some among peonies—avoiding early orange-red kinds like *L.* × *hollandicum*—for they contribute a second crop of flower on the same spot, and like the same cultivation. *L.* × *testaceum* is a lovely companion to *Campanula lactiflora; L. candidum* for delphiniums and pink and purple roses; *L. henryi* for mauve and purple phloxes; *L. davidii* or 'Maxwill' for *Philadelphus incanus. L. bulbiferum croceum* and *L.* × *hollandicum* hybrids are suitable for the strongest colour schemes and contrast well with *Hypericum* 'Hidcote'. *L. martagon* in all its forms is unobtrusive and is best in an open woodland setting. *L. pardalinum* makes a gorgeous contrast for *Primula florindae. L. speciosum* and *L. auratum* look well with late hydrangeas. I seldom have to stake any of them, or only after a severe gale, but *L. henryi*'s arching stems usually require support.

LIMONIUM, Plumbaginaceae. Statice or Sea Lavender.

latifolium

30 × 46 cm	*[4–9]*	*Blue*	*L.Summer*	PF	DRS
1 ft × 18 in					

Bulgaria, S. Russia. 1791. *L. platyphyllum. Statice latifolia.* A well-known plant with large dark green leathery leaves. The wiry branching stems burst into a cloud of tiny lavender-blue flowers, beautiful for many weeks, and attractive when dried. Full sun, well-drained soil. 'Blue Cloud' and 'Violetta' (1933) are two fine selected forms, to be increased by division or root cuttings. A tall lacy, open-growing selection is named 'St Pierre'. Evergreen.

mouretii

90 × 90 cm	*[8–9]*	*White*	*E.Autumn*	P	DRS
3 × 3 ft					

Morocco. 1928. The woody rootstock produces long, lobed and crinkled leaves, and flopping wiry sprays of tiny whitish flowers in brown calyces. Not in the first flight by any means but useful in a maritime garden.

LINARIA, Scrophulariaceae. Toadflax.

dalmatica ●

90 × 60 cm	*[5–8]*	*Yellow*	*All*	P	DS
3 × 2 ft			*Summer*		

S.E. Europe. 1731. *L. grandiflora.* Apart from a somewhat running rootstock this plant has no faults and yet it is seldom seen. Graceful, sometimes bent, stems bear glaucous blue, small leaves and branch freely, one or more branches being continuously in flower from June onwards. The flowers are snapdragons of clear bright yellow. Full sun; poor gravelly soil suits it well. *L. genistifolia* [5–8] is similar, with narrower leaves.

purpurea

90 × 46 cm	*[5–8]*	*Lilac*	*All*	P	S
3 ft × 18 in			*Summer*		

E. Europe. 1648. Slender spikes of tiny antirrhinum-like flowers over the thin array of narrow greyish leaves light up many an old garden, or retaining wall or waste ground. 'Canon Went' is a pleasing light pink variant. All forms are lit by an orange spot on the lip of the flower. Sun, light soil. *L. purpurea* seeds itself freely. There is a white variety. 'Yuppee Surprise' is a hybrid with *L. repens*; it is a compact bushy plant continuously in flower, light lavender blue.

triornithophora ●

90 × 60 cm	*[7–10]*	*Purple/*	*All*	P	W	CS
3 × 2 ft		*Yellow*	*Summer*			

S.W Europe. 1710. A sun-loving tender plant for hot positions in our warmest counties in any reasonably drained soil. The ascending stems, branching and flowering successively from June onwards, bear glaucous leaves and snapdragons of deep lilac with yellow markings on the lip and brown tails. A fine sight at Trengwainton, Cornwall.

LINDELOFIA, Boraginaceae. Less coarse than many of the Borage plants and a wonderful colour. Of easy culture in any fertile soil, in sun.

longiflora

46 × 46 cm	*[6–9]*	*Blue*	*E./L.Summer*	RS
18 × 18 in				

W. Himalaya. 1839. *Lindelofia spectabilis, Cynoglossum longiflorum.* Long narrow hairy leaves. The flower-stems are leafy, bearing side-shoots, and are produced from late spring to early autumn. The flowers are small, anchusa-like, of a splendid gentian-blue. A plant that one cannot pass by without admiring its flower colour. It bears some resemblance to *Cynoglossum nervosum.*

LINUM, Linaceae. Flax provides linen thread and is made from *L. usitatissimum,* an annual; *L. perenne* is a useful blue plant but short-lived. The following is the finest and largest-flowered of hardy blue flaxes, requiring well-drained soil and full sun, sheltered from severe cold.

narbonense

46 × 46 cm	*[5–8]*	*Blue*	*Summer*	CS
18 × 18 in				

S. Europe. 1759. I include this not for its ease of growth or longevity but because of the glorious deep azure blue of its flowers, which for many weeks cover the small twiggy plant. They are silky, of open funnel shape. It can be raised from seed, which is variable, but fine forms such as 'Six Hills' or 'June Perfield' (1934), propagated from cuttings, should be sought. *L. hirsutum* [5–8] is a plant of similar size with lilac-blue flowers and hairy stems, and *L. viscosum* [5–8], again similar, with lilac-pink flowers.

LIRIOPE, Liliaceae. Sunny or shady places suit these plants so long as they are in reasonably drained, fertile soil. They flower most freely in the sun. Many species are of rapid colonizing habit, such as *L. gigantea* [6–10], *L. graminifolia* [6–10], *L. spicata* [4–10] and *L. exiliflora* [6–10]; an introduction to them, together with the closely related *Ophiopogon,* occurs in my *Plants for Ground-Cover.* In the United States they have earned the name Lily Turf. The following species is a first-class flowering plant in its own right.

muscari ★

30 × 46 cm	*[6–10]*	*Violet*	*Autumn*	P D
1 ft × 18 in				

E. Asia. *L. platyphylla, L. graminifolia densiflora, Ophiopogon muscari.* Dense tufts of dark shining leaves, arching and grassy, above which are thrust the dense spikes of tiny bright violet flowers, making columns of colour. Ideal for associating with *Nerine bowdenii.* The normal form has been christened 'Big Blue' in the United States; 'Munro White' denotes a good white. Others have been named. There is a pretty variegated form whose leaves are striped with cream; it seems hardy in Surrey, but is not a strong grower. Perhaps the newer American variegated form 'Silvery Sunproof' will prove more vigorous; this and 'Majestic' are popular in that country. Evergreen.

> "Well worth growing in every garden because its pretty foliage is in its prime about December and January."—CWE

LOBELIA, Campanulaceae. These are mostly rather inclined to be tender and are about as far removed from the blue bedding lobelia as could be imagined.

cardinalis

90 × 30 cm	*[3–9]*	*Red*	*L.Summer*	P	CDS
3 × 1 ft					

North America. 1626. Cardinal Flower. This has a basal rosette of green leaves with toothed margins and glabrous green leafy stems topped by a great spike of brilliant scarlet, lipped flowers. Hardy.

fulgens

90 × 30 cm	*[8–9]*	*Red*	*L.Summer*	P	CDS
3 × 1 ft					

Mexico. 1809. Apart from other characteristics this has downy reddish stems and often reddish leaves, otherwise it resembles the above but is not so hardy. Both need rich moist soil.

HYBRIDS ●

90 cm–1.2 m	*Various*	*L.Summer*	P	CD
× 30 cm				
3–4 × 1 ft				

Included in this convenient name are the results of crossing *L. cardinalis, L. fulgens, L. splendens* and *L. syphilitica;* sometimes these are more scientifically segregated into *L. × gerardii* [4–8] and *L. × speciosa* [4–8]. There is also *L. × vedrariensis, q.v.* The well-known 'Queen Victoria' and 'Bees' Flame' are two hybrids with blazing red flowers in long spikes over beetroot-coloured foliage. The former is used successfully at Lyme Park, Cheshire. 'Mrs Humbert' is rose-pink and 'Eulalia Berridge' a brilliant cerise-mauve seedling, raised at Annesgrove, Ireland, and given to Miss Berridge prior to 1943 and there are many others. Of recent years some new crosses have been made mainly with *L. cardinalis* and *L. syphilitica* and the results are from purple to scarlet, with mainly green, but coppery tinted leaves; they have been on trial at Wisley, Surrey, from Ontario, Canada, where they were raised by W. M. Bowden and it is believed they will prove more hardy than the old hybrids. 'Will Scarlett', bright red; and 'Dark Crusader', dark red; 'Cherry Ripe', cerise-scarlet, are some examples. They all need rich damp soil and full sun, and in cold districts 'Queen Victoria' and others need a heavy mulch for protection since they do not take kindly to the alternating coldness and mildness of an English winter. Immediately after flowering the stems can be cut into lengths with two or more nodes, to make cuttings which should be over-wintered in a frame or cold house.

laxiflora

60 × 30 cm	*[8–9]*	*Orange*	*Summer*	W	D
2 × 1 ft					

Mexico. 1825. *L.l. angustifolia,* also known as *Lobelia cavanillesii,* grew for many years without protection at Hidcote, Gloucestershire, but was killed by an extra cold spell. It should prove perfectly hardy in the south and west in any fertile soil in sun. Many ascending stems produce lots of narrow dark green leaves and lots of narrow, tubular red-and-yellow flowers, creating a unique display for weeks.

sessilifolia

90 × 30 cm	*[4–8]*	*Violet-blue*	*L.Summer*	P	CDS
3 × 1 ft					

Kamchatka. 1882. Stately, narrow-leafed plant, supporting unbranched spikes of lavender-blue flowers with purple throats.

syphilitica

90 × 30 cm	*[5–9]*	*Blue*	*Summer*	P	CDS
3 × 1 ft					

E. United States. Prior to 1665. Of the same style as the unreliable *L. fulgens* and *L. cardinalis*, and the hybrids 'Queen Victoria', 'Huntsman', etc. which need frame culture for the winter, this is a true perennial in damp, heavy soils, producing leafy rosettes and erect stems well set with clear blue flowers for many weeks. It looks well with *L. × vedrariensis* and also with *Primula florindae*. There is a white variety. They are all inclined to be short-lived unless divided and moved into fresh soil every few years, in spring. A selection by Alan Bloom is 'Blue Peter', 60 × 90 cm (2–3 ft); it is a reliable perennial.

tupa ●

1.5 m × 90 cm	*[8–9]*	*Red*	*Summer*	W	CDS
5 × 3 ft					

Chile. 1824. Anything less like the conventional bedding lobelia could not be imagined. A magnificent plant with long, downy, light green leaves; the stout erect darkling stems have at their apices tapering spikes of strangely shaped flowers. They have a red-brown tube dividing into claw-like segments, with a pale grey projecting tuft. For sunny sheltered gardens in deep moist soils. It may achieve 1.8 m (6 ft) in ideal conditions, and usually needs supporting.

× vedrariensis ★

90 × 30 cm	*[5–8]*	*Purple*	*L.Summer*	P	DS
3 × 1 ft					

Hybrid. *L. × gerardii*. Another hybrid owing some of its colour to *L. syphilitica*, and strictly should be listed under *L. × hybrida*, but this is a true perennial in any good, rich, damp soil. Stout stems bear starry flowers for 46 cm (18 in) or more of their length, in varying tones of rich dark crimson-violet. Though a hybrid this breeds fairly true from seeds. A gorgeous contrast for *Ligularia dentata* or *Hemerocallis*. A similar hybrid, 'Tania', raised recently at Myddelton House, Enfield, Middlesex, is impressive with better spikes of flowers of a fulminating crimson-purple, of petunia-like richness. Brown stems and green leaves, orange-tinted when young.

LUNARIA, Cruciferae. Honesty.

rediviva ★

60 × 30 cm	*[6–9]*	*White*	*Spring*	PF	DS
2 × 1 ft					

Europe. 1596. Related to the well-known biennial Honesty, this plant is a true perennial and has been grown since the sixteenth century but is little known, in spite of its excellent qualities. The flowers are four-petalled, lilac-white, held in sprays high over the basal rosettes of leaves. The white papery seed-pods are elliptical, and are useful for winter decoration. One of the few early-flowering herbaceous plants. It is very beautiful when contrasted with the pale orange *Kerria japonica* in April. It thrives at Cliveden, Buckinghamshire.

LUPINUS, Leguminosae. Sun-lovers for well-drained soils.

albifrons
> 1.2 m × 90 cm   [9]   *Bluish*   *Summer*   W   CS
> 4 × 3 ft

California. 1833. Both this and the next are really shrubs, but assort so well with perennial plants that I crave indulgence for their inclusion. The leaves are of silvery silky quality and thus it is beautiful till the autumn. The short spikes of flowers are creamy, yellowish or lavender, becoming violet blue. *L.a. douglasii* is similar. It needs sharp drainage and full sun in our warmest counties.

arboreus ★
> 1.5 × 1.2 m   [8–9]   *Yellow*   *Summer*   CS
> 5 × 4 ft

California. 1793. The Tree Lupin is really a shrub, of sprawling and quick growth, not only suitable for borders and beds but for temporary use among young shrubs. Full sun, well-drained soil, in our warmer counties. The deliciously fragrant flowers of clear yellow are borne very freely in short spikes over copious leafage. For naturalizing on rough banks in poor soil it is a great delight. White forms occur.

> "*lupinus arboreus* ... a precious plant for dry ... rough banks the scent of a single bush reminding one of a field of Beans."—WR

ornatus
> 60 × 60 cm   [8–9]   *Blue*   *E.Summer*   CS
> 2 × 2 ft

W. North America. 1827. I have always had a special *penchant* for this plant. It is, I regret to say, short-lived, and needs a bed of gravel in full sun—such as some of us have to put up with—and with perfect drainage. Its neat, fingered leaves are like silver silk, and when a three-year-old plant is covered with spires of blue and white it is one of the loveliest sights in the garden. Definitely a connoisseur's plant.

polyphyllus ★
> 1.2 m × 60 cm   [3–6]   *Blue*   *E.Summer*   P   CDS
> 4 × 2 ft

W. North America. 1826. The popular, multicoloured race of large-flowered lupins is mostly descended from this blue species, but may have derived some of the more brilliant tints from annual species and *L. arboreus*. The first "break" of note was the strawberry-red 'Downer's Delight', followed by 'Pink Pearls', both of which were raised prior to 1920. In these varieties the size of flower resulted in a dense spike, as opposed to the interrupted whorls of the species. In rapid steps the strains became larger and brighter and more varied in colour; George Russell, of York, spent years on selection of colours and broadening the upper petals, and today the best are the late results of his efforts. There are named clones either in self-colours, or multicolours, embracing all tones from the original blue, white, palest pink, deep pink to crimson, lilac and purple; and from pale yellow through stronger tints to dark orange-red. I think it best to pursue my policy of leaving you to make a selection from the lists; or alternatively to purchase seeds. Strains are tall or short, and the best plants are those which stand up on their own, with their fine clump of basal, deeply fingered, rich green leaves. The flower spikes should be cut off before they set seeds; seedlings are apt to crop up everywhere; moreover by saving the plant from the effort of seed-setting more strength is available for secondary spikes. They are not reliable when cut; the best results are obtained when the hollow stem is filled with water prior to placing it in the receptacle. They are all sweetly scented. Young plants give the best effect. They are not as a rule long-lived.

Of late years seedsmen have developed strains which will breed more or less true to height and colour, and thus we may not be faced in the future with laborious propagation by basal cuttings. Moreover raising from seed tends to add vigour to the strain of plants, and the virus which attacks old, over-propagated clones is thus combated.

Lupins are among the brightest of the garden's June flowers. Since they do not as a rule flower much later, it is a good plan to plant them behind other plants which will obscure them in the summer.

LYCHNIS, Caryophyllaceae. See also *Viscaria*. Sun-loving plants for any fertile soil.

chalcedonica

90 cm–1.2 m	*[4–8]*	*Red*	*Summer*	PF	DS
× 30 cm					
3–4 × 1 ft					

E. Russia. 1593. The sun-loving Maltese Cross or Jerusalem Cross (on account of the shape of the flowers) dates from Crusade times; it needs a well-nourished, drained soil away from buffeting winds. The leaves are undistinguished and I value it because it is one of the really red flowers—startling vermilion—of early summer. The flat heads of blossom provide a harsh note sometimes needed to enhance yellow flowers and coppery foliage. There are some washed-out salmon-pink forms, a rare double red, and a rare white. A double white was grown in 1772.

coronaria

90 × 46 cm	*[4–8]*	*Various*	*Summer*	PF	DS
3 ft × 18 in					

S. Europe. 1596. *Agrostemma coronaria*. Dusty Miller. Grey flannelly leaves make good basal clumps, and are borne in pairs up the stems, also grey and woolly. The rounded flowers are like good Pinks and may be red-purple, or white (*L.c.* 'Alba') or white with cerise eye (*L.c.* 'Oculata'). Dry soils will support these plants well.

flos-jovis

46 × 46 cm	*[5–9]*	*Reddish*	*E.Summer*	DS
18 × 18 in				

Europe. 1726. *Agrostemma flos-jovis*. Flower of Jove. Dense tufts of grey woolly leaves overtopped by many heads of reddish purple flowers of variable tint. 'Hort's Variety' is a clear rose-pink and a most effective frontal plant. It does not require a rich soil.

× haageana

46 × 30 cm	*[4–8]*	*Various*	*Summer*	S
18 in × 1 ft				

Hybrid. 1858. *L. fulgens × L. coronata*. Originally spelt *L. × haagena*. These cannot be called good perennials; they are short-lived and loved by slugs. The weak stems have brilliant flowers of white, orange or red. A further cross, *L. chalcedonica × L. × haageana*, has better flowers usually of vivid orange-red; they are called *L. × arkwrightii* (1912) [6–8], and 'Vesuvius' is a splendid form and seemingly more perennial. Orange-red flowers contrast with dark brownish foliage.

× **walkeri**
    60 × 46 cm   *[4–8]*   *Cerise*   *E.Summer*   P   D
    2 ft × 18 in
L. coronaria × L. flos-jovis.★ 'Abbotswood Rose'. The clumps of silvery-grey leaves form a good setting for the long display of dazzling cerise-crimson flowers, borne on branching stems which are the same colour as the leaves.

LYSICHITUM, Araceae. Erroneously called, of late years, Skunk Cabbage, which refers to *Symplocarpus, q.v.* Bog plants, slow to establish, but increasing freely later by seeds.

americanum
    1.2 × 1.8 m   *[7–9]*   *Yellow*   *E.Spring*   F   S
    4 × 6 ft
1901. Bog Arum. It is fascinating to watch the yellow arum-flowers 30 cm (1 ft) high, with green spadices, arise from the soil in earliest spring. They are extraordinarily handsome and form a striking picture, and are followed by enormous paddle-shaped rich green leaves 1.2 m (4 ft) long and 30 cm (1 ft) wide or larger, which remain in beauty till the autumn. The ideal plant for smothering weeds in wet, boggy soil and at the sides of streams, ponds, etc. The flowers give off a heavy, unpleasant scent. It is well established at Powis Castle, Montgomeryshire, and at Bodnant, Denbighshire, Wisley and Windsor. It may well become a common ditch-weed in Britain before long. Western N. America.

camtschatcense ●
    90 × 90 cm   *[7–9]*   *White*   *E.Spring*   F   S
    3 × 3 ft
Kamchatka 1886. This counterpart of the above has slightly smaller but more open flowers of pure white with pale green spadices, and leaves slightly smaller and less glossy. Cultivation as for the above. The flowers are sweetly scented. Hybrids between the two often have pale creamy yellow spathes and can be very beautiful.

> "... enormous, banana-like leaves of imposing proportion in cool, pea-green, which are invaluable for creating a strong note among the foliage plants of summer."—ATJ

LYSIMACHIA, Primulaceae. Loosestrife—not to be confused with the next genus.

atropurpurea
    90 × 30 cm   *[7–9]*   *Red*   *Summer*   P   DS
    3 × 1 ft
1783. Eastern Mediterranean Region, in stony moist plates. This brings a rich colouring to the garden kinds. Slender stems with slender greyish leaves; long spikes of violet-red buds opening to light crimson flowers.

ciliata
    1.2 m × 60 cm   *[3–9]*   *Yellow*   *Summer*   P   DS
    4 × 2 ft
North America. 1732. *Steironema ciliata.* Though introduced so long ago it is seldom seen, which is a pity; at first sight it might be taken for *L. punctata* but is a far prettier plant, with pleasant foliage on upright stems, and plentiful somewhat nodding flowers of clear light yellow. It needs a retentive soil. Ideal for grouping with the magenta astilbes. Invasive roots. Autumn colour.

clethroides

| 90 × 60 cm | [4–9] | White | L.Summer | P | DS |

3 × 2 ft

China, Japan. 1869. This is a running plant for fairly moist places. The leafy erect stems develop dense spikes of grey-white tiny flowers in pretty arching spikes. Unique and late-flowering. *L. fortunei* [4–9], is similar but less effective, with erect flower-spikes.

ephemerum

| 90 × 30 cm | [7–9] | Grey | Summer | PF | DS |

3 × 1 ft

S.W. Europe. 1730. Those who love grey plants should grow this; it is happy in sun or shade in any soil, preferably moist but not sandy and dry. The leaves are leathery and grey, rather like those of a phlox, borne up the stems to the base of the flowers. These are grey-white in slender, erect, dense spikes, and are long-lasting. The seed-heads are also attractive. It makes a neat clump, non-spreading.

"A refreshing coolth in its glaucous foliage and tall spires of pale flowers in the hot, summer days."—ATJ

leschenaultii

| 60 × 30 cm | [8–9] | Reddish | Summer | P | DS |

2 × 1 ft

N. India. 1854. A slight, rather tender plant, for our warmer counties in moist peaty soil. It makes a slender plant with narrow leaves and spires of rosy red flowers over a long period.

punctata

| 90 × 60 cm | [4–8] | Yellow | Summer | P | D |

3 × 2 ft

Asia Minor. 1820. This has become a ditch-weed in places in this country. It is of invasive habit, producing spires of brassy yellow flowers, and is suitable for broad sweeps of self-maintained colour in the wilder parts of larger gardens.

LYTHRUM, Lythraceae. Purple Loosestrife. While preferring boggy soil, they will grow happily in any reasonably moist border and last many weeks in beauty. Apart from their lasting floral beauty they often produce startling autumn colour.

"The only precaution we exercise with these consists of the prompt removal of the spent flower heads lest they sow the parish with their spurious offspring."—ATJ

salicaria ★

| 1.2 m × 46 cm | [4–9] | Pink | Summer | PF | CD |

4 ft × 18 in

Britain. N. Temperate Regions. The Purple Loosestrife is a most satisfying plant for late summer, when it acts as a relief from the all-pervading yellow flowers, from which they should be widely separated. Slender spikes of flaming magenta-pink sway in the wind on wiry stems. The old pink 'Brightness' has given way to 'Robert', 'Morden's Pink' and intense rosy red varieties such as 'Firecandle' ('Feuerkerze') and 'The Beacon'.

virgatum

90 × 46 cm	*[4–9]*	*Pink*	*Summer*	PF	CD
3 ft × 18 in					

Asia Minor. 1775. A more dainty plant with more slender spikes of flower. In the type its colour is deep violet-pink; in 'Rose Queen' it is clearer. 'The Rocket' is another highly desirable plant. These plants blend and associate well with the greyish lysimachias listed above.

MACLEAYA, Papaveraceae. Plume Poppy. *Bocconia.* In spite of their height these seldom need staking. The foliage is beautiful from the ground upwards and therefore they should not have tall plants in front of them.

cordata ★

2.1 m × 60 cm	*[4–9]*	*White*	*Summer*	P	DR
7 × 2 ft					

China, Japan. 1795. This is often confused with the ubiquitous *M. microcarpa,* but has a compact scarcely running root; the same lovely foliage is topped by white flowers of better quality. Cultivation as for *M. microcarpa.*

kewensis (or *M. × kewensis*) [4–9]. A hybrid named at Kew, which may have arisen there, or may have been raised from seed collected in the wild. It is more or less intermediate between the two species here mentioned.

microcarpa

2.1 m × 90 cm	*[4–9]*	*Flesh*	*Summer*	P	DR
7 × 3 ft					

China. 1896. For long known erroneously as *Bocconia cordata*, the Plume Poppy is a most imposing perennial with a running rootstock, quickly colonizing the ground, and throwing up leafy stems. The leaves are rounded and large, beautifully lobed, grey-green above and grey-white beneath, making a fitting complement to the branching plume of numerous small buff- or flesh-tinted fluffy flowers. Give it plenty of room in any drained soil, in sun. It is grand in a clump of its own among shrubs and will cool down and yet blend with the hottest colour schemes.

—**'Coral Plume'** raised by Kelways of Langport prior to 1930. A richly coloured variety. Lovely with soft-toned phloxes.

MALVA, Malvaceae. Lovers of sunshine and reasonably drained, fertile soil, in which conditions these hardy plants will put up a long display of blossom. Closely allied to *Lavatera* and *Sidalcea.* Though perennials they are not notably long-lived, and young stock always gives the best display.

alcea

1.2 m × 60 cm	*[4–8]*	*Pink*	*Summer*	PF	CS
4 × 2 ft					

Europe. 1797. Soft green, fingered leaves. The good-sized bowl-shaped flowers profusely stud the branching stems. *M.a.* 'Fastigiata' (1820) is the erect form usually seen and is seldom out of flower until October.

moschata

90 × 60 cm	*[4–8]*	*Pink/White*	*Summer*	PF	CS
3 × 2 ft					

Europe, Britain. The Musk Mallow is one of our most beautiful natives. Much like the above, but shorter. The white form *M.m. alba* is a pure white and highly desirable.

MARRUBIUM, Labiatae. For sunny, drained places.

incanum

90 × 90 cm	*[3–9]*	*White*	*Summer*	F	CDS
3 × 3 ft					

S. Europe, Asia Minor. 1789. *M. candidissimum.* One of the best silvery, silky plants, but little known. The entire plant is silky grey, with nettle-like leaves, and terminal spikes of white flowers set densely in grey woolly calyces. Shrubby at the base. Evergreen.

MECONOPSIS, Papaveraceae. The Blue Poppies of the Far East—and others. The blue poppies are tantalizing to those who garden in areas subject to drying winds and drought. They require moist, not wet, lime-free soil with a good stint of humus; their crowns should be level with the surface of the soil; they need sheltered woodland conditions in the south-east of England and are happier in the cooler north and west. The European Welsh Poppy is not nearly so demanding and seems to flourish everywhere. The following few are my choice among the many, as these alone are good perennials if given reasonable conditions, and are unique in the floral world.

betonicifolia ●

1.2 m × 46 cm	*[7–8]*	*Blue*	*E.Summer*	DS
4 ft × 18 in				

W. China. 1924. The popular Himalayan Blue Poppy was known as *M. baileyi* for many years after its discovery in 1886. It was a wonderful experience having this plant in flower in my Cambridge garden in 1927. It leapt into popularity on account of its colour and the fact that it is more or less perennial in gardens on lime-free, moist soil in a cool atmosphere, where its blue is extra good. In drier counties it is frequently a washy mauve. It is reported that seed from the topmost pod breeds the best plants. It can be divided as recommended for *M. grandis.* Until the later introductions of *M. grandis* become known it was the supreme blue perennial poppy, and a well-grown plant can be superb, especially as it flowers when *M. grandis* is fading. The betony-shaped leaves are borne in diminishing size up the stems, which bear one topmost flower, with flowers lower down the stems, borne in the leaf axils. The petals reflex away from the yellow stamens in elegant fashion. There is a good white form, *M.b. alba.* A form known as *M.b. pratensis* (KW. 6062), which had good blue flowers, has since been transferred to *M. grandis,* and it may well be that this plant is the parent of several listed under *M. × sheldonii.* It had long flower-stalks which is one of the characters distinguishing *M. grandis* from *M. betonicifolia.*

cambrica

46 × 30 cm	*[6–8]*	*Yellow/*	*L.Spring*	S
18 in × 1 ft		*Orange*		

Europe, Britain. The Welsh Poppy is an ardent colonizer by seed, but for all that I enjoy its vivid beauty. Ferny, fresh green foliage above which are poised single poppy flowers of clear vivid lemon or rich orange. Though they grow together they do not seem to hybridize. The paler form is lovely with early flowering mauve rhododendrons. Those who cannot tolerate colonizers by seed should seek for the double forms, available occasionally in each colour, increased slowly by division. Will naturalize under dense shade.

chelidoniifolia ●

1.2 m × 60 cm   *[6–8]*   *Yellow*   *Summer*   DS
4 × 2 ft

Szechuan. 1904. Beautiful, lobed, hairy leaves and waving stems, branching into a sheaf of pale yellow bells. A plant of exquisite charm for cool sheltered woodland, where it will ramble through dwarf shrubs; it does not tolerate the drying winds in the south-east.

"... hanging out delicate egg-shaped buds that expand into flat four-petalled flowers of crumpled pale yellow silk on stems as fine as wire."— RF

grandis

90 cm–1.5 m   *[7–8]*   *Blue*   *E.Summer*   DS
  × 60 cm
3–5 × 2 ft

Nepal to China. 1895. In its best form it is a great improvement on *M. simplicifolia*, with which it is allied by its large blooms borne singly on stems. It is truly perennial when suited. The blooms are usually four-petalled, the first and biggest flower sometimes having more; they are carried like lampshades at the top of long stout stalks, which usually spring from a ring of leaves on the stem about 30 cm (1 ft) from the ground; sometimes the stalks appear to grow up from the ground. The basal leaves are hairy, erect, pointed and more or less toothed; and make a handsome clump. The filaments are nearly white and the stamens dark yellow. They need a cool part-shaded position in lime-free soil that remains moist with humus; division in September is advised; some growers prefer to do this after flowering or in the spring. It is necessary to replant them every three years or so to prevent them from deteriorating. The best blue kinds are superb with yellow primulas and cool-coloured azaleas such as 'Daviesii'. This species has been introduced on several occasions, the first (1895) being a form from Nepal with large purplish flowers known as 'Prain's Variety'. (Subsequently a seedling was named 'Keillour Purple'.) This introduction was from cultivated plants. From Sikkim came a vivid blue form collected from wild plants. From Tibet came ★ 'Sherriff No. 600' (G.S. 600) form which is a splendid large plant of vivid blue, though sometimes the flowers on first opening are purplish. The leaves are only slightly toothed and the beautiful very nodding flowers are "neckit like a swan"; it is a plant of very great refinement and beauty. Stainton, Sykes & Williams No. 5506 has deeply toothed leaves, and flowers of a purplish blue. Ludlow & Sherriff No. 21069 has leaves also deeply toothed and flowers of good blue. A diaphanous white has been named 'Miss Dickson' ('Puritan'). Though often sterile, they hybridize freely with *M. betonicifolia* and only in gardens such as the Royal Botanic Garden at Edinburgh, where seed pods are carefully removed to prevent self-sown hybrids occurring, are they to be found true to name. See also under *M. × sheldonii*.

quintuplinervia ★

46 × 30 cm   *[7–8]*   *Lavender*   *Spring*   D
18 in × 1 ft

W. China. 1877. The exquisite Harebell Poppy slowly makes a dense mat of leaves up to 10–12.5 cm (4–5 in). Above this on arching hairy stalks wave the lavender-blue bells, stained with purple at the base of the petals, and with cream stamens. One beauty per stem. Some forms increase more quickly than others and soon increase by division in early spring or September. Lovely in association with *Rhododendron sargentianum*.

"... so beautiful that the senses ache at the multitudinous loveliness of its myriad dancing lavender butterflies over the rolling upper Alps of the Da-Tung chain (N. Kansu-Tibet)."—RF

An exceedingly rare and difficult plant, except in favoured districts of Scotland, is its counterpart in red, *Meconopsis punicea* [7–8]. The hybrid between the two, *M. × cookei*, raised by R.B. Cooke, 1946, with dangling flowers of soft coppery pink, seems to be more amenable.

× sarsonsii ●

1.2 m × 60 cm	*[7–8]*	*Ivory*	*E.Summer*	D
4 × 2 ft				

1930. *M. betonicifolia × M integrifolia.* A great treasure; though it is not of the prevailing blue, it has great beauty in its ivory-cream flowers. It is a good perennial in cool favoured gardens and requires cultivation as for *M. betonicifolia.*

× sheldonii ● ★

1.2–1.5 m	*[7–8]*	*Blue*	*E.Summer*	D
× 60 cm				
4–5 × 2 ft				

1937. *M. grandis × M. betonicifolia.* Raised at Oxted, Surrey, and named after the raiser. A magnificent plant. Very leafy clumps of neatly toothed leaves and splendid flowers of clear blue. Though the plant known as 'Branklyn' is usually ascribed to *M. grandis* Sherriff No. 600, it is almost certain that this is in reality a hybrid with *M. betonicifolia* and should be grouped here. While *M. grandis* Sherriff No. 600 is the most refined all-blue *Meconopsis* species, the fine hybrid *M. × sheldonii* 'Branklyn' is undoubtedly the ultimate in size and magnificence, with flowers as much as 20 cm (8 in) across. At times it is overpowering. The leaves are coarsely toothed and the colour is inclined towards purple. The plant known as ● 'Slieve Donard' was originally distributed by that famous nursery as 'Prain's Variety' erroneously. It was raised by Dr A. Curle in Scotland, crossing *M. grandis* with *M. betonicifolia* and was acquired by Mrs. M. Dickie of Omagh in County Tyrone, and thence came to the Slieve Donard Nursery. A sister seedling was named 'Ormswell' and it, like many of these treasures, is cultivated by Edrom Nurseries of Eyemouth, Berwickshire. It is a diaphanous, light, clear blue. 'Slieve Donard' is a sound perennial; though a lesser plant than 'Branklyn' it is no less beautiful; the leaves are almost without teeth and the flowers have a butterfly elegance and brilliant colour. 'Quarriston' is a name given to a similar Irish hybrid. Two other vivid blues grown by Jack Drake at Aviemore, Invernessshire, are Mrs Crewdson's Crewdson Hybrids, *c.* 1940, and a stunner called 'Archie Campbell. Equally beautiful is 'Springhill' at Logan, Wigtownshire. A hybrid with distinct and beautiful lilac flowers grows at Edinburgh, but unlike all the others it usually needs staking. All of these hybrids have more or less the leafy stems and inflorescence of *M. betonicifolia.* All should be divided as advised for *M. grandis.*

simplicifolia

60 × 30 cm	*[7–8]*	*Bluish*	*E.Summer*	DS
2 × 1 ft				

Nepal, Tibet. 1848. Rarely seen, but in some gardens it is more or less perennial. Hairy basal leaves, with large nodding blooms of purple-blue poised singly on stout stalks. *M.s. baileyi* is usually of clearer blue, but less perennial.

villosa ●
    60 × 30 cm   *[7–8]*   *Yellow*   *Spring*   DS
    2 × 1 ft
Nepal, Bhutan. 1851. *Cathcartia villosa*. A superbly beautiful plant, rather neglected because it has been known for so long, and because it is not blue. Lovely hairy rosettes of leaves and hairy stems bearing beautiful wide nodding globes of clear yellow in the upper leaf axils. Stamens dark yellow. Apt to die out; easily raised from seeds; needs the same conditions as all the others, but its golden-tawny hairy winter rosettes are impatient of excess wet, and it should be kept away from tree-drip in damp climates.

MEGACARPAEA, Cruciferae. A sun-lover for well-drained fertile soil.

polyandra
    1.8 m × 90 cm   *[6–8]*   *White*   *Summer*   F   S
    6 × 3 ft
Kumaon. 1849. A large plant with enormous pinnate leaves. The flower-heads are well branched and covered with hundreds of tiny yellowish-white flowers, followed by numerous seed-pods. Not in the first flight of flowering plants but with notable foliage.

MELANDRIUM, Caryophyllacear. See *Silene*.

MELIANTHUS, Melianthaceae. A tender shrubby plant, only for the warmest counties and maritime districts. It is often cut down by frost but will sprout again from the base. The flowers are borne usually on strong shoots which have survived the winter, but they are not the plant's major attraction. The foliage has a fetid smell when bruised.

major
    2.4 × 1.8 m   *[9–10]*   *Maroon*   *L.Summer*   F   W   DS
    8 × 6 ft
South Africa. 1688. This has probably the most beautiful large foliage of any plant that can be grown out of doors in these islands. Grey-green, deeply fingered, deeply serrated, beautifully poised, curved, with handsome grey-green stipules on a grey-green stem. Flower sprays made attractive by chocolate-maroon bracts and green stamens; they exude a nectarous liquid. To encourage flowers, grow on poor soil.

MELISSA, Labiatae. Balm or Lemon Balm. An easily grown plant in almost any soil, in sun or shade.

officinalis
    60 × 46 cm   *[4–9]*   *Insignificant*   *Summer*   DS
    2 ft × 18 in
Europe, Britain. A hairy-leafed, dense erect herb, whose leaves are deliciously scented of lemon when crushed. It seeds itself freely and can be a nuisance. There is a form 'Variegata' whose leaves are prettily speckled with yellow, but this seeds itself freely too, reverting to the green form. 'Allgold' is the name given to a form with leaves entirely yellow. They fade to white—or burn—in hot sun. It is a most valuable addition for gardens and breeds true from seeds. Yellow effect in broken sunshine, lime-green in shade. It has also been known as 'Aurea'.

"it is profitably planted in Gardens ... about places where Bees are kept ... when they are straied away they doe finde their way home againe by it."—GH

MELITTIS, Labiatae. Bastard Balm.

melissophyllum ★

| 46 × 46 cm | [6–9] | White/Pink | E.Summer | DS |
| 18 × 18 in | | | | |

Europe, Britain. This engaging Dead-Nettle relative is ideal in the shade of shrubs or in thin woodland in any reasonable soil. The leafy stems bear clusters of white tubular flowers marked with a pinky-mauve stripe. A pure white form, *M.m. album*, is native to the Dolomites and is occasionally seen.

MENTHA, Labiatae. Mint. Invasive plants, preferring moist rather than dry soil, but easily pleased in sun or shade. Most of them are just weedy, culinary herbs, but the two variegated forms noted below are frequently cultivated for ornament—and they are just as good for culinary purposes as well.

× gentilis

| 46 × 60 cm | [4–9] | Mauve | Summer | D |
| 18 in × 2 ft | | | | |

M. arvensis × M. spicata. 'Variegata' had dark green leaves speckled and striped with yellow. Best in sun.

longifolia

| 1.2 m × 60 cm | [6–9] | Mauve | Summer | P D |
| 4 × 2 ft | | | | |

Europe. This may merit a place in the grey or white border; the whole plant is grey-green with downy hairs; the flower spikes are effective.

× rotundifolia

| 60 × 60 cm | [5–9] | Mauve | Summer | D |
| 2 × 2 ft | | | | |

M. longifolia × M. suaveolens. Round, hairy pale green leaves, particoloured with creamy white in 'Variegata'. A beautiful piece of variegation for part shade.

MERTENSIA, Boraginaceae. A few species are grown in gardens, preferring well-drained fertile soil; their chief attribute is their blue colouring, so often a prerequisite of the Borage Family.

asiatica

| 30 × 30 cm | [6–8] | Blue | E.Summer | DS |
| 1 × 1 ft | | | | |

Japan. A procumbent plant with greyish leaves, consorting well with the bunches of drooping pale blue tubular flowers. This is a useful species for maritime gardens in drained soil, full sun. *M. simplicissima.*

ciliata

| 60 × 30 cm | [4–8] | Blue | Spring | DRS |
| 2 × 1 ft | | | | |

Rocky Mountains. A close relative of *M. sibirica*, which is usually rather shorter and darker in colour. The fringed calyx of *M. ciliata* is a distinguishing mark. Pink buds open to light blue tubular flowers over glaucous leaves; a charming picture. A selection by Alan Bloom is 'Blue Drop'; a worthy plant.

maritima

30 × 90 cm	*[3–7]*	*Blue*	*Summer*	DRS
1 × 3 ft				

N. Europe. Britain. *Pulmonaria maritima*. The Oyster Plant provides beautiful glaucous leaves and clusters of light blue narrow bell-flowers. It needs gravelly or sandy soil in full sun. A sprawling plant with a pretty colour scheme.

paniculata ★

60–90 × 60 cm	*[4–8]*	*Blue*	*E.Summer*	P	DRS
2–3 × 2 ft					

North America. Though the narrow bell flowers are small, their profusion—in branching nodding sprays—and cool Delft blue makes a delightful picture amongst the profuse grey-green leaves. A bushy sprawler, which if cut over at midsummer will produce more flowering stems.

virginica ●

46 × 23 cm	*[4–9]*	*Blue*	*Spring*	P	DRS
18 × 9 in					

Virginia. 1799. Virginian Cowslip. *M. pulmonarioides*. One of the most charming of spring plants. The smooth, greyish leaves make a soft blend with the arching sprays of flowers which overtop them. The flowers are tubular, hanging in branches of cool violet-blue. The plant dies down in the middle of summer. Cool woodland conditions. There is a pink variety, 'Rubra'.

"The very embodiment of the freshness of early spring."—GJ

MEUM, Umbelliferae. A dense-growing plant of the cow-parsley type.

athamanticum

46 × 46 cm	*[5–8]*	*White*	*Summer*	DS
18 × 18 in				

Europe. 1574. Like *Athamantica* itself, the Bald-money or Spignel provides a dense mass of fennel-like leaves, which are fragrant, and conspicuous heads of white flowers. A useful mass of greenery for frontal placing in any fertile soil in sun.

MILLIGANIA, Liliaceae. Sun-loving plants for a warm garden in humus-laden soil.

longifolia

46 × 46 cm	*[8–9]*	*White*	*E.Summer*	DS
18 × 18 in				

Tasmania. Green narrow leaves make a handsome *Kniphofia*-like clump. The numerous creamy white starry flowers are arranged in panicles on branching silvery-hairy stems.

MIMULUS, Scrophulariaceae. The Monkey Musks are rather rampant plants for full sun in permanently damp soil, except *M. aurantiacus*, which will thrive with less moisture; those descended from *M. guttatus* and its relatives like really wet places. *M. guttatus, M. cupreus* and *M. variegatus* are hardy anywhere in Britain, though many of their offspring are apt to die out and a plant or two raised from cuttings should be reserved.

aurantiacus

1.2 m × 60 cm	*[7–10]*	*Various*	*Summer*	W	CDS
4 × 2 ft					

California. *Diplacus glutinosus*. The sticky leaves are narrow, carried up the shrubby stems, which branch and successively produce crops of flowers from June onwards. They have less of the snapdragon shape than the others listed here, and are of any colour from pale orange to bright orange-red and scarlet. For our warmest counties, best against a sunny wall; they thrive in dry positions.

cardinalis

90 × 60 cm	*[7–10]*	*Red*	*Summer*	CDS
3 × 2 ft				

S. and W. North America. 1835. An erect-growing plant with downy foliage. The lipped, snapdragon-like flowers are narrow and pinched in shape but are borne on successive sprays from June onwards and are red or yellow or both in graded tinting, sometimes pink, such as 'Rose Queen'. Hardy in all but our coldest counties. The red form is the most common and is of a striking appearance with its purplish calyx and dark throat; a lovely contrast for *Filipendula ulmaria* 'Aurea'. It gets untidy by August and should be cut over to stimulate fresh growth.

guttatus

60 × 60 cm	*[8–10]*	*Yellow*	*Summer*	CDS
2 × 2 ft				

North America. 1826. *M. luteus* (of gardens), *M. langsdorfii*. The Monkey Musk is naturalized in Britain and loves a sopping wet place; prolific, lush in growth, it produces a succession of bloom from June onwards of lax monkey flowers, bright yellow usually dappled with red-brown, particularly on the lower lobes. The form known as 'A. T. Johnson' was found by its namesake prior to 1937 in a Welsh brook, and is so heavily blotched with wallflower-red that the flowers appear to be of this colour, but outlined with yellow. It is more compact than some forms.

"A very charming thing massed along the water when the stately *Iris sibirica* is belting the banks with blue."—ATJ

M. guttatus, together with two Chilean species, *M. cupreus* and *M. variegatus*, are the parents of the many Monkey Musks in a variety of colours. The more reliably perennial are descended from the first two; all are rather dwarf for our purpose.

lewisii

60 × 46 cm	*[6–9]*	*Pink*	*Summer*	W	CDS
2 ft × 18 in					

W. North America. *M. bartonianus* (of gardens). Sticky, downy, greyish leaves, a good setting for the handsome glowing deep rose flowers with yellow throat, of the usual monkey-flower shape. There is also a beautiful white, *M.l.* 'Albus'; 'Sunset' is a sport which occurred at Daisy Hill Nurseries, Northern Ireland, in rich tones of fiery red. Hardy in our warmest counties. They flower from June onwards and are not dependent on moisture for their wellbeing.

ringens

90 × 30 cm	*[4–9]*	*Mauve*	*Summer*	CDS
3 × 1 ft				

E. North America. A self-reliant plant, with narrow snapdragon-like flowers usually of mauve-purple, or white, on erect stems. Moist ground. 1759.

MIRABILIS, Nyctaginaceae.

jalapa

60 cm–1.2 m	*[10]*	*Various*	*Summer*	W DS
× 60 cm				
2–4 × 2 ft				

Tropical America. 1596. The Marvel of Peru should suit commuters who spend only the evening at home, because the fragrant flowers do not open until late afternoon. Shaped like a pink bellvine, they may be crimson, pink, white or yellow, variously marked, and cover the dense bushy plants for many weeks. The tubers are tender and may only be left in the ground for the winter in our warmest climates. It is easy to grow in any reasonable soil and has been cultivated since the Spaniards brought it from Peru in the sixteenth century. A dwarf strain is known as 'Nana' and embraces all colours.

"... one is not like another in colour though you shall compare one hundred which floure one day, and another hundred ... from day to day."—GH

MOLOPOSPERMUM, Umbelliferae.

peloponnesiacum

1.8 m × 90 cm	*[5–8]*	*Yellow*	*Summer*	PF S
6 × 3 ft				

South and Central Europe. 1596. *M. circutarium.* Striped Hemlock. Seldom seen, this is a most handsome plant for any fertile soil in a sunny spot. The leaves alone are distinct in their many long, narrow segments. The stout branching stems carry typical rounded heads of creamy yellow, tiny flowers, developing into useful kecksies.

MOLTKIA, Boraginaceae. For any fertile soil in sun.

doerfleri

46 × 46 cm	*[6–9]*	*Purple*	*Summer*	DS
18 × 18 in				

Also known as *Lithospermum doerfleri.* The somewhat invasive roots produce wiry stems bearing narrow hairy leaves and drooping heads of tubular violet bells. An unusual plant, attractive with the shorter achilleas.

MONARDA, Labiatae. Sun-loving plants with erect square stems clad in pointed, fragrant, mint-like leaves. The basal leaves make a dense spreading clump when suited. *M. didyma* needs a moist soil, while *M. fistulosa* will thrive in dry soil; therefore as a rule the purplish cultivars will stand drought better than the red. The hooded, sage-like flowers are borne in successive heads at the top of the stems, and are highly effective.

didyma ★

90 × 46 cm	[4–8]	Red	Summer		P	D
3 ft × 18 in						

North America. 1744. Bee Balm or Oswego Tea; the leaves if steeped in boiling water make a refreshing drink and were used in Oswego, U.S.A. 'Cambridge Scarlet', prior to 1913, is the cultivar usually grown. The flowers are rich red held in plum-crimson calyces. 'Adam' is a newer variety of perhaps better habit, 'Croftway Pink' (c. 1932), a beautiful clear rose-pink, and 'Prairie Glow' a warm salmon-red; 'Beauty of Cobham', pale pink with purplish calyces.

"Now the colour strengthens with the Scarlet Balm or Bergamot".—GJ

fistulosa ★

1.2 m × 46 cm	[3–8]	Purple	Summer		P	D
4 ft × 18 in						

Virginia. 1637. Of similar appearance to *M. didyma*, but with hairy calyces, less sharply angled stems, and the flowers are dull lilac-purple in smaller heads. It will tolerate drier conditions than *M. didyma*. Many hybrids have been raised, such as 'Dark Ponticum' and 'Prairie Night' (1955), of purplish tone. While 'Cambridge Scarlet' and 'Prairie Glow' are strong enough to blend with bright yellows, these hybrids are on the other side of the spectrum and assort well with *Lythrum* and *Phlox* of the more subdued tones. 'Snow Maiden' ('Schnee-wittchen') is a good white. Wild Bergamot.

MORAEA, Iridaceae. The Butterfly Irises hail from the Southern Hemisphere, and the yellow species has proved perfectly hardy in Surrey, delighting in well-drained soil in full sun. Plant 10 cm (4 in) deep.

iridoides ●

60 × 23 cm	[9–10]	White	E.Summer	PF	W	DS
2 ft × 9 in						

South Africa. 1758. *Dietes iridoides*. Beautiful, white, iris-flowers, with lilac-blue crests. The flowering stems branch into more flowers when the terminal bloom fades. Short, stiff, grassy leaf-blades. For warmest gardens.

spathulata ● ★

60 × 30 cm	[8–10]	Yellow	L.Spring	PF	DS
2 × 1 ft					

South Africa. 1875. *Dietes huttonii*. This is our old friend *M. spathacea*, which is having a shuttlecock affair with *M. galpinii* and those two charming names *M. moggii* and *M. muddii*. I must say my mind was as clear as mud after reading the botanical differences founded in part on the presence or absence of fibrous-coated corms. It remains to say that this lovely plant produces one very long leaf, which lies untidily around, while the erect stem produces flower after flower of iris-style in clear, brilliant yellow. A wonderful contrast to "black" Darwin Tulips.

MORINA, Dipsacaceae.

longifolia ●

90 × 30 cm	[5–8]	Pink	Summer	PF	DS
3 × 1 ft					

Nepal. 1839. An elegant plant. The basal leaves are fragrant, slightly prickly and thistle-like, and form a rich green rosette. Stout stems bear whorls of hooded tubular flowers, white turning to clear rose and later to crimson after fertilization, set in thorny collars. The dried stems are particularly useful for winter decoration. It likes good soil, in fairly drained yet moist conditions. Does well in softer climates of the west and in Ireland, but sometimes succumbs to cold in the south-east. Good with *Geranium* × *himalayense*. Evergreen.

"... a handsome and singular perennial with large spiny leaves."—WR

M. persica has a narrower, more dense and more spiny spike of flowers.

MUSA, Musaceae. Banana. This one species is successful in our warmest counties and will even produce fruiting sprays. It may be seen at Overbecks, South Devon. The stems should be wrapped against winter cold, and a place sheltered from wind is best because of the large leaves. Good rich soil in full sun.

basjoo

1.8 × 1.5 m	*[9–10]*	*Brownish*	*L.Summer*	W	D
6 × 5 ft					

Japan. 1890. *M. japonica* (of gardens). This is mainly grown for its magnificent paddle-shaped, arching, smooth, blue-green leaves. With cordylines, Tree ferns, gunneras and phormiums it is a marvellous plant for tropical effect in the largest gardens.

MYOSOTIDIUM, Boraginaceae.

hortensia ●

46 × 46 cm	*[9]*	*Blue*	*E.Summer*	P	W	DS
18 × 18 in						

Chatham Islands. 1859. *M. nobile.* Imagine a *Bergenia* with leaves deeply veined like those of *Hosta sieboldiana* or *Viburnum davidii*, and flowers of forget-me-not blue, and I need say no more, except to apologize for tantalizing you: it is only hardy in salubrious southern maritime gardens and needs to be fed on seaweed. It thrives at Trengwainton, Cornwall, Knightshayes Court, Devon, and at Inverewe, Ross and Cromarty, but is covered for the winter. Evergreen.

MYOSOTIS, Boraginaceae. Forget-me-not.

scorpioides

23 × 60 cm	*[4–10]*	*Blue*	*Summer*	P	D
9 in × 2 ft					

Europe, Asia, Britain. Water Forget-me-not. The species is frequently found rampaging in marshy ground. The form known as 'Mermaid' is more compact and thrives in any cool soil, producing its bland pure blue flowers all summer; also known as 'Semperflorens'. Evergreen.

"... one is called *semperflorens*, from its long season of flowering."—WR

MYRRHIS, Umbelliferae. A charming self-sowing plant for any reasonable soil in shade or sun.

odorata

60 × 60 cm	*[4–8]*	*White*	*E.Summer*	PF	S
2 × 2 ft					

Europe, Britain. Sweet Cicely must have been very attractive, a fair woodland nymph, to have given her name to this refined and fragrant Cow Parsley. The flowers are of a startling creamy white and light up any dark corner.

"the handsome fern-like Sweet Cicely of old English gardens."—GJ

NECTAROSCORDUM, Liliaceae.

siculum ●

| 90 × 30 cm | [4–10] | Mauve and | L.Spring | PF | DS |
| 3 × 1 ft | | green | | | |

Balkans. *Allium siculum, A. dioscoridis. N. siculum* itself occurs in other southern Mediterranean countries; its flowers are plum-coloured while those of *N.s. bulgaricum* are creamy green with purple flush. The flowers of all are large, bell-shaped, hung from drooping stalks at the top of the stout stems, and after fertilization stand erect. These plants have stoloniferous bulbs which quickly increase; they can become a nuisance, but the flowers are of great beauty, also the seed-heads. Try it with *Paeonia broteroi* or *P. arietina.*

"... I enjoy breaking a leaf in half and getting my friends to help in deciding whether it most resembles an escape of gas or a new mackintosh."—EAB

NEPETA, Labiatae. Catmint. Lovers of sunshine and well-drained soil. The first two are excellent ground-covering plants, and all of them have a subdued colouring which blends well with all soft colour schemes. Their dead tops should not be cut down until winter is past, and division is best in spring.

× faassenii

| 46 × 46 cm | [4–8] | Lavender | E./L.Summer | P | CD |
| 18 × 18 in | | | | | |

Hybrid. 1784. *N. mussinii* (of gardens). (*N. mussinii* × *N. nepetella.*) The popular Catmint needs little description, save to call attention to the weeks and weeks of sprays of lavender blooms held over bushy, greyish, small-leafed plants. It is at its best in June, but continues until autumn. It is a good plan to cut all spent flower-stems severely back after the main flush is over, to encourage later crops. Cats love to roll in it, but are soon cured if a few prickly twigs of rose or berberis are inserted. Lovely with roses of all kinds and particularly good for bringing out the best in pink-tinted flowers. 'Blue Dwarf' ('Blauknirps') is a compact German selection. There is a form with leaves variagated or flushed with creamy yellow, 'Variegata'. It is apt to revert to green. 'Dropmore' [3–9] is a good, rich coloured variant or hybrid from Manitoba, Canada.

"Its normal flowering time is June, but it is cut half back, removing the first bloom, by the middle of the month, when it at once makes new flowering shoots."—GJ

gigantea ★
of gardens

| 90 × 90 cm | [4–8] | Lavender | E./L.Summer | P | CD |
| 3 × 3 ft | | | | | |

The plant variously known under this name or 'Six Hills Giant'—after the famous Clarence Elliott nursery—is probably a hybrid. It is at least twice as large as *N. × faassenii* and has similar uses. It is also valuable in the colder damper districts where *N. × faassenii* does not prove hardy.

govaniana ●

| 90 × 60 cm | [5–9] | Yellow | Summer | P | CDS |
| 3 × 2 ft | | | | | |

Kashmir, etc. *Dracocephalum govanianum*. One of the strange facts of horticulture is that this beautiful plant is not well known. It has been growing in the open bed at Kew for many years. An erect, well-branched plant with pointed leaves and effective open spikes of long-tubed flowers of clear light yellow, produced for many weeks. Charming and graceful. Best in cool, moist conditions.

mussinii [3–8] and **N. nepetella** [3–8] are plants inferior in garden value to *N. × faassenii*.

'Porcelain' [3–8]. A hybrid between the above two species from Holland, flowering over many weeks, light lavender-blue. 23 cm (9 in) × 46 cm (18 in)

nuda

| 1.5 m × 60 cm | [5–9] | Lilac-white | L. Summer | P | CDS |
| 5 × 2 ft | | | | | |

S. Europe, Orient. 1715. This upstanding plant is also seldom seen. Easy in any sunny place, its greyish basal leaves are small but plentiful and the tall stems branch freely into a candelabra of spires of tiny lilac-white flowers. In port it is not unlike *Verbascum chaixii*, but taller. There are white forms. The calyces of all forms add colour by being soft bronzy lilac. *N. latifolia* is similarly beautiful.

sibirica ★

| 90 × 46 cm | [4–8] | Blue | Summer | P | CD |
| 3 ft × 18 in | | | | | |

Far East. 1760. Also known as *Nepeta macrantha, N. tatarica* and *Dracocephalum sibiricum*. The refreshing Spode blue of the flowers is welcome during the summer months. They are borne on erect leafy stems, and it is a plant of great charm, long in flower; it needs a well-drained soil and spreads freely.

'Souvenir d'André Chaudron'

| 46 × 46 cm | [5–9] | Blue | Summer | | CD |
| 18 × 18 in | | | | | |

Also called 'Blue Beauty'. This may be described as a shorter version of *N. sibirica*, and a useful front-of-the-border plant it is too. Long-flowering season; invasive roots. Probably a hybrid.

NEPHROPHYLLIDIUM, Gentianaceae. A dense clump-forming plant for cooler positions and districts.

crista-galli

| 46 × 46 cm | [5–7] | White | Summer | | DS |
| 18 × 18 in | | | | | |

Japan, North America. *Fauria, Menyanthes* or *Villarsia crista-galli*. The few, fringed, small white flowers closely resemble those of the Bog Bean (*Menyanthes*) but the plant's real beauty lies in the clump of shining, rich green, rounded leaves, 30 cm (1 ft) high. It thrives at Rowallane, Northern Ireland.

NERINE, Amaryllidaceae. Ardent sun-lovers for any well-drained soil. In the warm south-west they can be grown in the open ground, but in Surrey they appreciate the shelter and baking that follow from a sunny wall. The bulbs should be planted with their "noses" showing above the soil. Plant in late summer or after flowering. The leaves, strap-shaped and rich green, are produced after the flowers, and on most kinds tend to die away in late summer. The heads of lily-like flowers are extremely elegant, carried on stout stems, and appear in September, October and November. Their beauty is enhanced by *Zephyranthes candida* and *Liriope muscari*.

bowdenii ● ★

| 60 × 23 cm | [8–10] | Pink | Autumn | P | W | DS |
| 2 ft × 9 in | | | | | | |

South Africa. 1889. An indispensable plant for our warmer counties, producing freely its lovely flowers at a time when they are most welcome. Several lily-like flowers are held at the top of a stout stem, with glistening frilled segments and long stamens. Of extreme elegance. The form to be sought is 'Fenwick's Variety', raised at Abbotswood, with larger flowers and greater vigour. Other good selected forms are 'Pink Triumph' and 'Blush Beauty'; the latter adds to the colour range in a light tone, while the hybrid 'Hera' is much richer. These splendid plants bridge the autumn gap until *Mahonia* 'Charity' opens. 'Quinton Wells', obtained by Dr A. Q. Wells from the wild in South Africa, is a richly coloured form, possibly a hybrid, of dark colouring and crinkled segments. There is also a good white form 'Alba'.

flexuosa

| 60 × 15 cm | [8–10] | Pink | Autumn | P | W | DS |
| 2 ft × 6 in | | | | | | |

South Africa. 1795. A related species for the connoisseur, with smaller flowers and leaves. There is a pretty white variety 'Alba'. *N.f.* var. *sandersonii* is a reliable summer-leafing variant, which should be sought.

humilis

| 46 × 15 cm | [9–10] | Pink | Autumn | P | W | DS |
| 18 × 6 in | | | | | | |

South Africa. 1795. A species which seems to be as hardy as *N. bowdenii*. The leaves are narrow. The extremely dainty flowers are of soft pink, pale or white in the throat with narrow, crinkled segments; the upper segments are gathered together, producing a cockade effect reminiscent of *Lycoris*.

'Paula Knight' ●

| 60 × 23 cm | [8–10] | Pink | Autumn | P | W | D |
| 2 ft × 9 in | | | | | | |

A hybrid of unknown origin introduced by Mr H. J. Joel of St Albans, England, in 1959. It is a strong grower, producing brownish stems above the dark leaves. The segments of the flower are mainly smooth, slightly crinkled, of rich rose-pink with a silvery mauve zone or stripe up the centre of each. Buds rich carmine. Anthers maroon. A valuable plant owing its colour perhaps to *N. sarniensis* [9–10] and its hardiness to *N. bowdenii*. It thrives at the Savill Gardens, Windsor.

undulata

46 × 15 cm	*[9–10]*	*Pink*	*Autumn*	P	W	DS
18 × 6 in						

South Africa. 1767. A beautiful plant, a lesser *N. bowdenii*.

NIEREMBERGIA, Solanaceae. This shrubby plant will thrive in warm sunny positions.

frutescens

46 × 46 cm	*[8–10]*	*White/*	*E./L.Summer*	W	CS
18 × 18 in		*Purple*			

Chile. 1867. Wiry stems clad in inconspicuous leaves put up a very long succession of saucer-shaped flowers, about the size of a 2p piece. Normally pale lavender, but purple and white forms have been named: *atroviolacea* and 'White Queen'.

NOMOCHARIS ●, Liliaceae. Close relatives of the true lilies, these have if possible even more charm; their exquisite, nodding butterfly-blooms are in tones of pink and mauve variously spotted, borne on wiry erect stems. But unless you garden in the cooler north and west and have well-drained lime-free soil, well laced with humus, or can provide cool woodland conditions and shelter from srrong winds, you should omit them. They are so supremely beautiful that an ill-grown specimen offends. They are easily raised from seeds; mature bulbs should be planted about 10 cm (4 in) deep. When suited they are sound perennials, flowering in early summer. All were introduced from Western China and neighbouring areas in the early part of this century. *N. pardanthina* [7–9] and its form or subspecies *N. farreri* [7–9] achieve 90 cm (3 ft) and are the most vigorous and beautiful, with wide-open starry lily-flowers, several on a stem, in varying shades of pink, more or less spotted in the centre with maroon. The inner segments of *N. pardanthina* have fringed edges. *N. mairei* [7–9] is of similar beauty to these two, but the spotting often extends over the whole of the flower. *N. aperta* [7–9] and *N. saluenensis* [7–9] are less tall and flamboyant. There are several smaller species.

"... their wide bells of delicatest shell-pink trembling in translucent loveliness."—ATJ

NOTHOLIRION ●, Liliaceae. The pride and despair of lily lovers. The several species continue hesitantly in British gardens and seem to thrive best in the milder damp counties and in Scotland. They have an unfortunate habit of leafing in late autumn or winter and of producing numerous tiny bulblets around the bulbs; the main bulb dies after flowering. They appreciate plenty of humus in the soil, with perfect drainage. The species bear narrow or wide bells of pale to deep lilac or purplish red, and beyond suggesting that *N. thomsonianum* [7–9] and *N. bulbiferum* (*N. hyacinthinum*) [7–9] may in ideal conditions produce their 1.2–1.5 m (4–5 ft) stems and corresponding glory of blossom, I will leave it to you to try whichever you can obtain. *N. campanulatum* [7–9] and *N. macrophyllum* [7–9] have also been grown; they all hail from Western China, Burma, Himalaya, etc. Their colours are lilac to crimson. After flowering the bulb dies but leaves offspring, which should be separated and nursed.

OENOTHERA, Onagraceae. Evening Primrose. Sun-loving plants for well-drained soils.

missouriensis ● ★

23 × 60 cm	*[5–8]*	*Yellow*	*Summer/*	F S
9 in × 2 ft			*Autumn*	

Central United States. 1811. *Megapterium missouriensis, O. macrocarpa.* For the front line this can hardly be excelled if yellow is wanted. Great flowers, some 10 cm (4 in) across, are produced for weeks from reddish calyces, followed by immense seed-pods. The stems lie prostrate, well clothed in dark green narrow leaves with silver midribs. Full sun; any fertile soil. A first-rate front-line plant. *O. fremontii* is similar, with neater habit and narrower leaves, which are glaucous beneath.

odorata

90 × 30 cm	*[5–8]*	*Yellow*	*Summer*	S
3 × 1 ft				

South America. 1790. *O. stricta.* The plant known in gardens as *sulphurea* is an evening-flowering plant of great beauty, producing several slender stems from a basal rosette of narrow crinkled leaves. The stems and buds are tinted with red, making a pleasing contrast to the wide pale yellow blooms, to which the fading flowers of coral contribute also.

tetragona ★

46 × 30 cm	*[5–9]*	*Yellow*	*Summer*	D
18 in × 1 ft				

E. North America. 1737. *O. fruticosa; O. youngii* (of gardens). A gay plant making dwarf clumps of dark foliage, over which stiff stems sport silky, wide-cupped blooms of clear and brilliant yellow from reddish buds. *O. tetragona fraseri* (sometimes labelled *O. cinaeus*) is one of the most ornamental variants, with not only good flowers but richly tinted foliage in spring. Many garden seedlings have been named, such as 'Yellow River', 60 cm (2 ft), 'Fyrverkeri' ('Fireworks') and the large and brilliant 'Lady Brookborough'. A related garden plant known for many years as *O. glaber* (of gardens) has leaves richly mahogany tinted, a lovely contrast to the bright flowers. Gorgeous with *Eryngium tripartitum*.

ORCHIS, Orchidaceae. See also under *Dactylorrhiza*. From a garden point of view the two genera are hardly distinct and descriptions of the several species should be read together. For cultivation see *Dactylorrhiza*.

militaris

46 × 30 cm	*[6–8]*	*Purple*	*E. Summer*	D
18 in × 1 ft				

Europe, England. Military Orchid would be a good name for the other species too; they all have an upright carriage! In this the pervading colour is magenta-purple with heavily spotted lip. Good broad green leaves.

purpurea

46 × 30 cm	*[6–8]*	*Purple*	*E. Summer*	D
18 in × 1 ft				

Britain. *Orchis fusca.* Another handsome native. Broad basal foliage and typical stout maroon stems with a thick spike of flowers at the apex. Calyx and flowers purple, lip white densely spotted with purple. As easy to grow as the others, they both thrive at the Savill Garden, Windsor.

ORIGANUM, Labiatae. The Marjorams form a group of culinary herbs, justifiably beautiful for the ornamental garden. They appreciate light or medium heavy soil and full sun, limy or acid. *O. marjorana* and *O. vulgare* are the herby types usually seen, and good forms may be picked out. Aromatic foliage.

laevigatum ★

46 × 46 cm	*[5–9]*	*Purplish*	*L.Summer*	DS
18 × 18 in				

Turkey, Syria. Prior to 1960. The hairy leaves are scarcely aromatic. A useful late-flowering plant producing sheaves of little bunches of purplish pink flowers in darker calyces. Good with grey-leafed plants, and highly effective on its own.

vulgare

46 × 46 cm	*[4–8]*	*Mauve*	*Summer*	DS
18 × 18 in				

Europe, Britain. The Common or Wild Marjoram is a culinary, aromatic herb, also an ornamental plant. The turf of small dark leaves disappears under many-branched wiry stalks bearing clusters of tiny thyme-like mauve flowers. 'Hopley's' is a good selected form. *O.v.* 'Aureum' is also a turf-former, but its flowers are not much in evidence, its garden value being raised by the bright golden yellow of the leaves from spring until midsummer, when they begin to turn green. A brilliant complement to the brighter heucheras and as useful for the pot as the green type.

ORNITHOGALUM, Liliaceae. There are many species, some dreadful, though pretty, weeds and all have white or whitish flowers. *O. thyrsoides* is the South African Chinckerinchee, a tender plant.

nutans

46 × 23 cm	*[6–10]*	*Green*	*E.Summer*	P	DS
18 × 9 in					

Europe. *O. chloranthum.* Those who love all strange greenish flowers should try to naturalize this to follow the daffodils in grass. The hyacinth-like flowers are silvery grey-green within, green and white outside. One should never pass this by without contemplating its form and colouring; both are exquisite.

pyramidale

60 × 23 cm	*[7–10]*	*White*	*Summer*	PF	DS
2 ft × 9 in					

Mediterranean Region. 1752. This has proved a satisfactory perennial in reasonably drained soil in sun. Plant 10 cm (4 in) deep. The leaves are of little account, but the neat pyramid-shaped heads of starry white flowers have distinctiveness and charm. A less imposing relative is *O. narbonense* [7–10], which has a narrower, almost cylindrical, head of flowers; *O. sphaerocarpum* [7–10] is usually considered a variant of *O. pyramidale.*

pyrenaicum

60 × 23 cm	*[6–9]*	*Greenish*	*E.Summer*	PF	DS
2 × 9 in					

Europe. Known as French Asparagus because of the flavour of the young fleshy leaves and stems. The slender spikes of creamy green starry flowers are of considerable appeal in a quiet way, followed by seed-pods. They are held well above the bent grassy leaves.

OSTEOSPERMUM. Compositae. Rather tender, sub-shrubby plants suitable for sunny gardens in our warmer counties, where they make dense tufts of growth.

jucundum

30 × 30 cm	[9–10]	Mauve	Summer/	P	CDS
1 × 1 ft			Autumn		

Eastern Cape, Natal, etc. *Dimorphotheca jucunda*; *D. barberae* (of gardens). There are many clones and hybrids in gardens with flowers from nearly white to soft pink, some with dark eyes. 'Compactum' is a soft pink of note. Their daisy-flowers are borne with great freedom for months over the narrow light green leaves. Particularly useful for sunny places in mild and maritime districts. *O. ecklonis* [9–10] is taller, usually white with dark blue centres, and no doubt contributes to the hybrid race. Evergreen. Purplish varieties are derived from other species.

OSTROWSKIA, Campanulaceae.

magnifica ●

90 × 46 cm	[7–8]	Lilac	E.Summer	RS
3 ft × 18 in				

Turkestan. 1887. An unbelievable plant until seen. It is the most magnificent of campanula-types, having whorls of rather glaucous leaves and a few-flowered head of great bell-shaped blooms of white, heavily suffused and veined with lilac; yellow stigma. It can only be grown satisfactorily in very deep well-drained soil in a baking hot position. Plant 15 cm (6 in) deep. Its glory is over by the end of July, when it retires to rest for another year.

"Unique among perennials it is worthy of any care to make it a success."—WR

OURISIA, Scrophulariaceae. The following species are among the largest and suitable for this list, revelling in moist peaty soil in cool conditions in our milder counties.

macrophylla

30 × 30 cm	[7–8]	White	E.Summer	DS
1 × 1 ft				

New Zealand. 1907. A spreading carpet of good leaves makes a green setting for the sprays of mimulus-like white flowers, borne in whorls up the stems. *O. macrocarpa* [7–8] is taller and similar and to be sought. 'Loch Ewe' [7–8] is a good and vigorous hybrid between the species and the red *O. coccinea*. The flowers are of a clear and lovely pink. Raised at Inverewe, Ross and Cromarty, during the 1970s.

PAEONIA, Ranunculaceae. The peonies provide both herbaceous plants and shrubs, but I feel it necessary to omit the latter. There is no doubt that herbaceous peonies are just the very type of plant we are all looking for. Apart from their large and lovely flowers, they have splendid foliage, often richly tinted in both spring and autumn, which makes a good ground-cover. The seeds in the opening seed-pods are highly coloured, with cerise and blue or scarlet and black, in many species and varieties. A few of the taller varieties need staking in windy places. They appreciate a rich, well-drained soil and should have a dressing of bonemeal lightly forked in every autumn, together with a mulch of humus; sunny positions suit them best, on chalk or other soils. They flower year after year in the same spot; if they cease to produce flowers after several years, it is usually due to lack of nourishment, and they should be lifted in October, divided and replanted (taking care that the crowns are not more deeply in the soil than they were), first preparing deeply the ground with bonemeal, or very old rotted manure well below the roots, and some humus. In some gardens they suffer from a fungus in damp chilly periods of early summer; a dusting with a copper dust and spraying with a similar compound will help. Liking the same conditions as many bulbs and enjoying the same rest period (when they can be transplanted) it is a good plan to interplant them with any small bulbs for early spring and narcissus and daffodils, which will contrast well with their often reddish young growths, or with later bulbs such as *Galtonia* and *Gladiolus*, which will flower above the peony foliage.

P.P. *arietina, mollis, officinalis, peregrina* and *tenuifolia* spread fairly freely by means of tuberous roots; the remainder "stay put" with slowly increasing rootstocks.

When cutting peonies care should be taken to cut only one or two stems per plant, thus leaving plenty of foliage to help the roots to develop.

Let us look first at some of the better-known species and old garden forms.

anomala

| 60 × 60 cm | [2–8] | Red | L.Spring | PF DS |
| 2 × 2 ft | | | | |

E. Russia, Central Asia. 1788. A flower of intense red is borne on each stout stem, and gives excellent effect. The leaves are much divided into long narrow segments, of dark green, rather like those of *P. veitchii*, but it is a more stalwart plant. At first sight it might be taken or *P. × smouthii*, by this hybrid has looser nodding flowers of less quality. *P.a. intermedia* is distinguished by its hairy carpels and is the form most usually seen. A lovely companion for *P. emodi*.

arietina

| 75 × 60 cm | [5–8] | Pink | L.Spring | PF DS |
| 2½ × 2 ft | | | | |

S. Europe, Asia Minor. 1824. A subspecies of *P. mascula*. A free-growing plant, spreading at the roots, with somewhat greyish but otherwise typical foliage. The flower can be of deep or light magenta-pink, but the most beautiful I have seen is a light cool rose-pink—apart from a white of great purity. Two of these light pink varieties have been named: ● ★ 'Mother of Pearl' and the more recent 'Hilda Milne' (1950). There is little to choose between them. 'Northern Glory' is of sumptuous, silky, deep magenta-carmine. All have beautiful creamy yellow stamens. *P. rhodia* [8–9] is a species related to the above and to *P. clusii*, from the island of Rhodes. It is none too hardy and requires a sheltered corner, because it starts growing very early in the year. The flowers are white and the leaves thin and narrow. Spicy fragrance.

cambessedesii ●

| 46 × 46 cm | [7–8] | Pink | L.Spring | PF DS |
| 18 × 18 in | | | | |

Balearic Islands. 1896. This rather tender plant needs well baking with sunshine. Beautiful though the deep rose-pink flowers are, with their red filaments and purple stigmas, the foliage is outstanding. The deep green is offset by the intense crimson-purple of the reverses and stalks. A gem for picksome people.

clusii ●

25 × 30 cm   [8–9]   White   E.Summer   PF   DS
10 in × 1 ft

Crete. *P. cretica*. A choice small species with dark green narrowly divided leaves, somewhat glaucous beneath. The flowers are held by reddish stems and are of startling white offset by pink filaments. For extra well-drained, sunny, sheltered corners. Reputedly short-lived. One of the earliest flowering peonies.

daurica

75 × 60 cm   [4–8]   Magenta   L.Spring   PF   DS
2½ × 2 ft

Asia Minor, S.E. Europe. 1790. Bold rounded leaves of greyish green provide the perfect setting for the large vivid cerise-magenta flowers with bright yellow stamens. It is well established at Hidcote, Gloucestershire. Often considered to be a subspecies (*tridentata*) of *P. mascula*. *P. broteroi* is a similar species from Spain and Portugal, with narrow, smooth leaflets.

emodi ● ★

90 × 90 cm   [5–8]   White   L.Spring   PF   DS
3 × 3 ft

N.W. India. 1862. A most gracious spring flower; graceful arching stems bear several pure white flowers, with golden stamens, of singular beauty and purity, and deliciously scented. The clump of fresh green luxuriant foliage remains in beauty for many months. It seems to appreciate some shade in gardens, as it does in its native habitat.

japonica

46 × 46 cm   [5–8]   White   E.Summer   DS
18 × 18 in

Japan. 1910. The leaves are grey beneath, the flowers comparatively small, pure white, with the usual yellow anthers. Will not set the Thames on fire.

lactiflora ● ★

90 × 60 cm   [3–9]   White   E.Summer   PF   D
3 × 2 ft

N.E. Asia. *c.* 1784. *P. albiflora*, 'Whitleyi Major', or 'The Bride'. This superlative plant is the forerunner of most of the large-flowered Chinese hybrids, none of which, however, quite capture its graceful freedom. The huge, white, single silky flowers have a mass of yellow stamens in the centre, and have the added beauty of dark reddish brown foliage and stems. A lovely plant in every way.

"... a plant adorned with the grace of a thousand years of adoration by the Chinese before it entered our shores."—ATJ

mlokosewitschii ● ★

60 × 60 cm   [5–8]   Yellow   Spring   PF   DS
2 × 2 ft

Caucasus. 1907. Few plants have such a direct appeal as this early-flowering species, presenting its large, cool lemon-yellow flowers with golden anthers over the clump of soft grey-green downy foliage. It is undoubtedly one of the most wonderful flowers of the early year and thrives in any sunny position, given good drainage. Affectionately known as "Mollie-the-Witch". It grows well at Sissinghurst, Kent.

"This pleasant little assortment of syllables should be practised daily by all who wish to talk familiarly of a sovereign among Paeonias."—RF

mollis

| 46 × 46 cm | [5–8] | Various | L.Spring | PF | DS |
| 18 × 18 in | | | | | |

1818. Perhaps a hybrid. Leaves of soft greyish colouring, lilac-tinted in some lights, and grey beneath. The flowers are single, of intense magenta, with pale yellow stamens.

obovata alba ●

| 46 × 46 cm | [5–8] | White | Spring | PF | DS |
| 18 × 18 in | | | | | |

Siberia, China. 1899. From a beautifully tinted stalk are spread leaves of soft grey-green flushed with copper, which continue to grow in size after the flowers have dropped; each stem supports one superb cup-shaped, pure white flower, transparent and crystalline, and offset by a circle of golden stamens around a crimson centre. Brilliant blue seeds. It is of ethereal beauty but is quite a happy garden plant for sheltered conditions, away from icy spring winds. Ordinary or semi-woodland soil. It thrives at Knightshayes Court, Devon. *P.o. willmottiae* is if anything even more beautiful in palest lemon-white.

officinalis ★

| 60 × 60 cm | [3–9] | Various | L.Spring/ | P | DS |
| 2 × 2 ft | | | E.Summer | | |

S. Europe. c. 900. A popular old garden plant, at home in any fertile soil; it will also grow, if in good soil, in grass. It loves peace and sunshine—as we all do. No doubt it started life as a single-flowered species, and some good single red forms or hybrids are labelled 'Splendens', 'Phyllis Prichard', 'J.C. Weguelin'. They are all worth seeking. In all kinds the dark green handsome leaves remain in beauty until late summer. *P.o. mascula* (usually labelled *P. mascula*) is a form which is naturalized on Steep Holm Island, in the Bristol Channel; another synonym is *P. corallina*. A white form of *P. officinalis* is occasionally seen, with single flowers.

—'Anemoniflora Rosea' ●

| 46 × 46 cm | | Deep Pink | L.Spring | P | D |
| 18 × 18 in | | | | | |

P. 'Paradoxa Rosea'. While all peonies are extremely beautiful, special marks should be given to those with "petaloid" centres. In these the stamens are turned into ribbon-like strips; here we have a cluster of these ribbons, crimson edged with yellow in a cup of rosy red petals.

—'China Rose' ● ★

| 46 × 46 cm | | Pink | L.Spring | P | D |
| 18 × 18 in | | | | | |

The most beautiful clear salmon-rose of this choice variety is very telling in the garden. Handsome, single, cupped flowers with orange-yellow stamens. Brilliant. A hybrid, no doubt, with *P. peregrina*. Successful at Hidcote, Gloucestershire.

—'Crimson Globe'

46 × 46 cm		*Red*	*L.Spring*	P D
18 × 18 in				

Intense garnet-red, incurved, single flowers with boss of crimson and golden petaloid stamens. A very vivid flower.

– **Double Varieties.** 'Rubra Plena' is the favourite old double red—and what a wonder it must have been considered when it was first introduced in the sixteenth century. It strikes the first really deep note from herbaceous plants in May. 'Albo Plena' is blush white, turning to white; 'Mutabilis Plena' opens rich pink and fades to blush and is beautiful the whole time; 'Rosea Superba Plena', extra large bright, light pink of great substance. There is also a sumptuous dark maroon-red, 'Red Ensign', which is probably a hybrid with the Chinese Garden Hybrid Peonies. Its colour is superb and it flowers between the two groups and is thus particularly valuable.

peregrina

60 × 60 cm	*[5–8]*	*Scarlet*	*L.Spring*	P D
2 × 2 ft				

Balkans. 1629. *P. lobata* 'Fire King', 'Sunbeam'. Smooth, glossy, fresh green leaves and resplendent large single blooms of intense fiery scarlet. A most impressive plant at Hidcote, Gloucestershire, whose flowers have no equal in their season.

● ★ —'Sunshine'. A lighter coloured form of intense salmon-scarlet, with orange sheen.

"Then glut thy sorrows on a morning rose, …
Or on the wealth of globed peonies."—Keats

potaninii

60 × 60 cm	*[5–8]*	*Various*	*E.Summer*	DS
2 × 2 ft				

W. China. 1904. While nowadays completely overshadowed by other shrubby peonies which are much too woody for our project, I must beg leave to include this pretty small shrubby plant. It suckers from the root, making a mass of twiggy stems, covered with a canopy of finely divided elegant leaves. The small nodding flowers are of rich maroon-red, or white in 'Alba', yellow in *P.p. trollioides*.

russii

46 × 46 cm	*[6–8]*	*Pink*	*L.Spring*	PF DS
18 × 18 in				

Corsica, etc. An unusual small species whose stems and leaves are of a glossy brown-green. The single flowers are glowing magenta pink with a boss of cream stamens. It needs a hot, well-drained spot. The form *P.r. reverchonii* has flowers of clearer pink and is to be preferred. Possibly these are subspecies of *P. mascula*.

tenuifolia

46 × 46 cm	*[4–8]*	*Red*	*E.Summer*	P D
18 × 18 in				

Caucasus. 1594. The leaves are so finely divided into narrow sections as to warrant the term "ferny". The single flowers have leaves immediately below them and are of intense, glistening, dark crimson with conspicuous yellow stamens; or pale pink in 'Rosea'. The rare double form is called 'Plena' (1765) but is scarcely an improvement on the type though the flowers last longer. This fine old plant has become difficult and rare. *P. × smouthii* (*P. laciniata*) (1843), a single-flowered hybrid with *P. lactiflora*, is of similar quality and colour, but taller. More recent is 'Early Bird' (1939) from Dr Saunders, a good and reliable garden plant of rich red, single. Both of these hybrids inherit some of the characteristic narrowly divided foliage of *P. tenuifolia*.

veitchii ★

| 30 × 30 cm | [5–8] | Magenta | L.Spring | PF | DS |
| 1 × 1 ft | | | | | |

China. 1907. Particularly good, fresh green leaves form the chief character of this species and its variety. The long-fingered foliage gives a luxuriant setting for the several gracious, nodding, single, open blooms of soft deep magenta, with pink filaments and cream anthers. *P.v. woodwardii* has flowers of a clear light pink. Both of these seed themselves freely, and good large-flowered forms should be sought or raised, as they vary considerably. They seem to prefer part shade but are easy to grow. There is also a creamy white variant. They all have bluish seeds.

wittmanniana ●

| 90 × 60 cm | [5–8] | Yellow | L.Spring | PF | DS |
| 3 × 2 ft | | | | | |

N.W. Caucasus. 1842. *P. tomentosa*. A magnificent plant with ample, bullate and shining, almost coarse, leaves, richly tinted in spring. Like all single peonies the flowers are fleeting but are of great beauty while they last. The large blooms are of white, tinted yellowish green when opening—much paler than those of *P. mlokosewitschii*—with reddish filaments and crimson stigmas in the centres. The synonym *P. tomentosa* refers to the downy carpels; another form with glabrous carpels has been named *P.w. nudicarpa*. Shelter from cold winds as it is so early-flowering. A form with immense leaves has been called *P.w. macrophylla*. The foliage has a box-like odour.

> "... flowers are more fugitive than those of *P. mlokosewitschii*, yet both excel in the brilliance of the scarlet and jet seeds of their gaping pods."
>
> —ATJ

There are several hybrids of *P. wittmanniana* (with *P. lactiflora* hybrids). 'Le Printemps' and 'Mai Fleuri' are of delicate colouring; the first pale creamy yellow, the second cream tinged with pink. 'Mai Fleuri' has darker, bronzy foliage. 'Avant Garde', like these two, has beautiful downy foliage of a rich coppery tone which provides a lovely setting for Narcissus 'Binkie'. The flowers are large, soft, peach-pink with yellow stamens. It is vigorous, and a superb late April bloom. All raised by Lemoine 1905–9.

GARDEN HYBRIDS OR CHINESE PEONIES ● [3–9]

Probably derivatives of *P. lactiflora* which came from Siberia about 1784 and again from China in 1805. In China and Japan peonies had been developed in gardens for hundreds of years into a many-coloured race. Earlier in this century European nurserymen listed many of these Eastern varieties. These were the main parents of our European and American modern hybrids. They were first evolved by Continental nurserymen, but in England principally by James Kelway of Langport. The wonderful, sumptuous, illustrated catalogues by the Kelway firm early in this century show to what a pitch their culture had risen. The genus is still a speciality with the firm.

In most of the big, highly bred families of garden varieties I have omitted recommending named kinds because they come and go so quickly from catalogues. But I have altered this treatment in favour of listing at least a range of all colours and seasons in astilbes and will do the same with the Chinese Peonies, as these plants, being slower of increase, are more static in nurserymen's lists. The hybrids range from white through pink to deep reddish crimson and maroon, both single and double, and have fine foliage, often assuming gay tints in autumn. As a rule their large and heavy flowers need staking; this is most simply and permanently done by fixing a hoop of thick, galvanized wire around each clump.

Double varieties in white include the pure whites—with creamy centres—like 'Duchesse de Nemours' (1856) and 'Kelway's Glorious' (1909); there is also 'Festiva Maxima' (1851), whose white is accentuated by a dark crimson fleck or two in the centre. The incomparable 'Marie Crousse' (1892) and 'Baroness Schroeder' are both blush. In pale pink we have a considerable range, such as 'Sarah Bernhardt' (1895), 'British Beauty', 'Auguste Dessert' and the less regularly double 'Lady Alexandra Duff' (1902); while rather deeper are 'Kelway's Lovely', 'Carmen' and 'Carnival'. 'Président Poincaré', 'Félix Crousse' (1881) and 'Inspector Lavergne' (1931) are light crimson or deep carmine, and still darker are 'Karl Rosenfeld' (1908), 'General MacMahon', and the darkest 'Monsieur Martin Cahusac'. Try this last with the variety which most nearly approaches yellow, 'Laura Dessert' (1913)—a good double white with pronounced lemon flush in the centre. 'Hidcote Purple' is the only kind I have met with flowers of maroon-purple.

The range is not quite so full in single varieties, but much as I like the doubles I prefer the singles. They do not last so long in flower as the doubles but they have all the refinement of the species in their great cups, lit by the big bunch of yellow stamens. For pure white we could not do better than 'Whitleyi Major' (see under *P. lactiflora*); 'Pink Delight' is blush, with the following gently and progressively darker: 'Dayspring', 'Beersheba', 'Poetic', with 'Lord Kitchener' and 'Sir Edward Elgar' magnificent dark crimsons.

Having run through these few representative varieties in doubles and singles we are still left with the most entrancing of all—single varieties whose stamens have turned into narrow petals and make a great colourful centre, sometimes yellow, sometimes the same colour as the petals. They are known as 'Imperial' varieties. Taking some blush and palest pink first we have 'Evening World' and 'Palamino', followed by the richer 'Bowl of Beauty' and 'Globe of Light' (both of these have a beauty quite stunning to those who have not met them before), 'Calypso' and 'Kelway's Majestic'; in dark crimson there is 'Kelway's Brilliant', 'Instituteur Doriat' and 'Colonel Heneage'. In the last the petaloid centre is the same colour as the petals.

The spring foliage tints of many of the above are of rich mahogany and provide a good setting for *Fritillaria imperialis*, with *Valeriana phu* 'Aurea' in front.

The entire race of hybrid peonies are worthy of the best that can be given them, and they start to flower when the varieties of *P. officinalis* and *P. peregrina* have dropped.

"June ... the peony is the month's crown, the focus, the highlight of all that is beautiful in the garden picture."—James Kelway

THE SAUNDERS HYBRIDS [3–9]
While the above hybrid strain might for want of a better name be called Edwardian Peonies, later work in hybridizing the many species has been done, notably by the late Dr A. P. Saunders of New York. Practically every species that would cross has been made to mate with one or more others, and there is a bewildering number of named hybrids on the American market as a result. After Dr Saunders's death his daughter, Miss Silvia Saunders, carried on the

good work and has recently passed her entire collection to Dr David Reath of Vulcan, Michigan. Some of the earlier hybrids are already growing in gardens over here, such as 'Rose Garland' (1943), 'Defender' (1932) and 'Legion of Honour' (1941), two splendid early reds. All three are early-flowering and descended from *P. peregrina* or *P. officinalis* and have single flowers. There are two superb single whites, 'Archangel' (1950) and 'Chalice' (1932) (*P. albiflora* × *P. wittmanniana macrophylla*) and the extra late and extra tall, 1.2–1.5 m. (4–5 ft) (needs staking) 'White Innocence' (1947), which has green centres (*P. lactiflora* × *P. emodi*). *P. emodi* has been used again with *P. veitchii* to produce two nodding charmers, 'Early Windflower' (1939) and 'Late Windflower' (1939) both white with narrow ferny foliage. 'Early Bird' (1939) has bright crimson flowers; to the already narrow leaflets of *P. veitchii* is added the still narrower *P. tenuifolia*. The yellow *P. mlokosewitschii* has been hybridized with *P. tenuifolia* and the result 'Daystar' (1949) is a very early flower with pointed leaves.

But it is from *P. officinalis, P. peregrina* and *P. lactiflora* that the bulk of this remarkable strain comes; Dr Reath likes particularly 'Victoria Lincoln' (1939), pink, semidouble; 'Cytherea' (1960), cherry rose, semidouble; 'Constance Spry' (1941), cherry, semidouble; 'Moonrise' (1949), ivory. Two short ones in salmon-red are 'Good Cheer' (1942) and 'Little Dorrit' (1949). There are dozens more, and they are slowly proving themselves and finding their way to Europe. 'Coral Sunset', 'Coral Supreme', 'Coral Charm', 'Pink Hawaian Coral' (Klehm), 'Raspberry Charm' and 'Scarlet O'Hara' are just a few to whet your appetites.

DWARF HYBRIDS [3–8]
Bred by Roy Klehm and William Krekler in the United States, a number of these, called 'Rock Garden Peonies'' have been put on the market. These are likely to prove popular since they are under 46 cm (18 in) in height. 'Dutch Dwarf', 'Little Emperor', 'Tinkerbell', 'Toy Delight' are all good.

THE KLEHM HYBRIDS
A great firm, Charles Klehm & Son of Illinois in the United States, has been specializing in peonies for three generations. The outcome is a range of upstanding, weather-proof superlatives which they call Estate Peonies—a tribute to their reliability and landscape value. Undoubtedly the peonies of the future if you are looking for the paler colours. There are some wonderful whites—'Bowl of Cream', 'Bridal Gown', 'Bridal Shower'; whites showing yellow stamens and petaloids—'Cheddar Gold' and 'Cheddar Supreme'. Palest pinks 'Dinner Plate', 'Petticoat Flounce', 'Pillow Talk', 'Pink Lemonade' and richer pinks 'First Lady', 'Raspberry Sundae' and 'Angel Cheeks'.

PANCRATIUM ● Amaryllidaceae. A bulbous genus, producing strap-shaped leaves and stout stems holding aloft deliciously fragrant, diaphanous, white flowers, rather like an upturned narcissus, with long narrow outer segments and a wide trumpet in the centre; protruding anthers. *P. illyricum* (1592) and *P. maritimum* (extra large trumpet), Southern Europeans, prove hardy in sunny well-drained corners in our warmer counties. June [8–10]. Plant 15 cm (6 in) deep.   P   W   D

PAPAVER, Papaveraceae. The Flower of Forgetfulness: opium is derived from *P. somniferum*, an annual. The poppies are flamboyant sun-loving plants for deep soil, poor and dry rather than rich, and certainly not moist. Poppies are often inclined to droop when picked, but much can be done to obviate this by dipping the tips of the stems into hot water when picked (in bud, in the evening) and keeping them cool through the night, arranging them in the morning, when they will be bursting open. The buds nod on the plant until mature, but those getting ready to open stand erect.

lateritium ●

46 × 46 cm	*[4–9]*	*Orange*	*E.Summer*	F	S
18 × 18 in					

Armenia. This is perhaps the most beautiful of the group of poppies listed below after *P. orientale*. It is similarly hairy, with good basal leaves, and produces nearly leafless stems each with a beautiful tangerine-orange flower of good size.

orientale ● ★

30 cm–1.2 m	*[4–9]*	*Various*	*E.Summer*	F	DR
1–4 ft					

Armenia. Prior to 1714. The Oriental Poppies form a race of sound perennials bearing enormous gorgeous flowers on stems which are rather apt to sprawl, and whose hairy foliage dies away by July, leaving what may be an unfortunate gap. Gertrude Jekyll had a remedy for this: see under *Gypsophila paniculata*. Their roots are difficult to get rid of when deeply established. The type species has flowers of brilliant vermilion set off by the maroon blotch and stamens and the velvety knob of the seed-capsule of the same tint. This dark capsule is found in all varieties, some of which were raised by Amos Perry of Enfield, Middlesex. A species or variety, *P. bracteatum* (1817) [4–9], from the Caucasus and Persia, is believed to have contributed to some of the colours of the garden clones. This plant has leafy stems whereas in the true *P. orientale* the stems only bear leaves at the base. A gorgeous red closely related to *P. bracteatum* is 'Goliath'. In the hybrid group 'Marcus Perry' (1942), and 'Stormtorch' ('Sturmfackel') are good tall reds; 'Mrs Stobart' is cherry pink; 'Mrs Perry' (1906), clear pink; 'Indian Chief' maroon-red. 'Peter Pan' is a useful dwarf of about 46 cm (18 in) in brilliant red, which alone of these varieties does not require support. 'May Queen' is an old fully double orange vermilion variety treasured for many years at Hidcote, Gloucestershire, and is always an eye-catcher but is of flopping growth; 'Olympia' is boldly upright and 'Salmon Glow' is a new, double, rich deep salmon-pink. Apart from those of vivid colouring, there are others to be considered: 'Perry's White' (1912); 'Black and White', huge flowers of white with large basal blotches of maroon-black; ★ ● 'Cedric Morris', which commemorates so well the noted artist-plantsman, has petals of subtle greyish pink with maroon-black blotches. 'Fire Ball'; sometimes labelled 'Nana Flore Pleno'. Probably a seedling between *P. lateritium* and *P. pseudo-orientale*. Raised by Mrs Webber, *c.* 1878, of County Kildare, named by H. den Ouden of Boskoop. Its invasive habit is partly excused by its brilliant vermilion very double flowers. 46 cm (18 in).

"The pink of the Oriental Poppy in the midst of all this silver foliage looks simply delicious, like a strawberry ice on a frosted glass plate."—EAB

★ *P. pilosum* from Asia Minor (1852) [5–9], *P. rupifragum* [8–9] from Spain, and *P. atlanticum* from Morocco (1889) [8–9] are three closely related species forming good clumps in well-drained positions. They have leafy bases and ascending branching stems, holding refined flowers of orange-red or tangerine, silky and butterfly-like. *P. atlanticum* and *P. rupifragum* are much alike; the former is practically glabrous, and has seed-capsules wrinkled at the sides. *P. pilosum* is a more substantial leafy plant. All of these have the flowers on long stalks. In *P. spicatum* (*P. feddei*) [4–9] the flowers are very short-stalked and form a close spike; the buds are white-hairy and very effective with the open flowers. The top flowers open first (*cf. Meconopsis betonicifolia*). PF S

In common with all poppies they are most enjoyed on sunny days. These are all reasonably perennial, and are easily raised from seeds. The same may be said of the Iceland Poppy (*P. nudicaule*) [4–8] available in many colours, but the plants are short-lived. The seed-strains of this species provide an excellent range of colours from white through yellow and pink tones to orange-red.

PARADISEA, Liliaceae. Closely allied to *Anthericum*, St Bruno's Lily is another good perennial for ordinary cultivation in sun.

liliastrum

| 30–60 × 30 cm | [5–9] | White | E.Summer | PF | DS |
| 1–2 × 1 ft | | | | | |

S. Europe. 1629. Grassy but broad and greyish flaccid leaves make a clump. The stout stems have pure white flowers larger and more lily-like than those of *Anthericum* species. A form 'Magnificum' is larger but less elegant.

lusitanica

| 1 m × 30 cm | [7–9] | White | E.Summer | P | W | DS |
| 3 × 1 ft | | | | | | |

1913. A tender, very tall relative of *P. liliastrum* for warm gardens, but moist soil. Widely spaced, outward-facing, small trumpet flowers on erect stems. Grassy foliage.

PARAHEBE, Scrophulariaceae.

perfoliata ●

| 60 × 46 cm | [8–10] | Blue | L.Summer | CS |
| 2 ft × 18 in | | | | |

Australia. 1834. *Veronica perfoliata*. Digger's Speedwell. A distinguished-looking plant with glaucous leaves that clasp right round the stem (perfoliate), of a leathery evergreen texture. It is in fact sub-shrubby. The sprays of Spode-blue flowers are long and branching and elegant, and have cream stamens. It needs a sheltered spot in full sun.

PARIS, Liliaceae. A woodland plant related to our native Herb Paris, delighting in sandy or heavier soil with humus, and part or full shade. Plant 12.5 cm (5 in) deep.

japonica ●

| 60–90 × 30 cm | [5–8] | White | E.Summer | DS |
| 2–3 × 1 ft | | | | |

Japan. 1889. *P.polyphylla* is better known than this superb species with conspicuous white flowers. Many of the other characters are the same for both species. The leaves are up to 30 cm (1 ft) long.

polyphylla ●

| 90 × 46 cm | [5–8] | Green | Summer | DS |
| 3 ft × 18 in | | | | |

Himalaya. 1826. This remarkable plant produces a smooth bare stem, bearing at the top a wide ruff of pointed green leaves. Above this is a further ruff, of green sepals, then a circle of thread-like yellow petals, yellow stamens and a violet-coloured, knob-like stigma. It lasts in flower for about three months and astonishes everyone. What would a flower arranger do to get hold of this!—it is exceedingly rare as yet. It appears to be self-infertile but when two clones are grown together the resulting pods of orange-red seeds are as conspicuous as those of *Iris foetidissima*.

PASITHEA, Liliaceae. May be tried in warm sunny spots in our warmer counties in rich soil with good drainage.

caerulea ●
90 × 46 cm	*[8–9]*	*Blue*	*L.Spring*		W P	DS
3 ft × 18 in						

Chile. 1889. This might be described as a splendid *Anthericum lilago* with flowers of *Agapanthus*-blue. It has the branching flower-stem and lax narrow leaves of the former. A worthy plant seldom seen.

PATRINIA, Valerianaceae.

gibbosa
46 × 30 cm	*[5–9]*	*Yellow*	*L.Summer*	F	DS
18 in × 1 ft					

Japan. A strange plant. The long-lasting flowers, beautiful still when faded, are small, but with one long petal of sharp greenish yellow. They appear in massed array over broad basal leaves. For part shade or at least a cool root-run. It gives the effect of a coarser *Alchemilla mollis* late in the season. The flowers give off a horrid whiff of dogs; dog-lovers please note.

PELTIPHYLLUM, Saxifragaceae.

peltatum
90 × 60 cm	*[5–9]*	*Pink*	*Spring*	F	D
3 × 2 ft					

California. 1873. *Saxifraga peltata*. Umbrella Plant is its other name on account of the shape of the great leaves, 30 cm (1 ft) or more across on single stems which arise after the flowers are over. The flowers are starry, pink, set in wide round heads at the top of a stalk, red-tinted, from the creeping rhizome like an elephant's trunk. It thrives in marshy ground, and is ideal at the side of a stream or pond, where it will bind the soil together and prevent erosion. Sun or shade. Also known as *Darmera peltata*.

"... the water of some long-awaited summer shower lying in glistening pools in the centre of its dew-pond leaves."—ATJ

P.p. 'Nana' is a useful dwarf, only 30 cm (1 ft) or so high, and brings the value of giant leaves to the lesser waterside.

PENSTEMON, Scrophulariaceae. Apart from *P. barbatus* and *P. ovatus*, the others listed here must be treated with some reserve regarding hardiness. As a general rule the larger the flower and leaf the more tender is the variety. They all prefer full sun in a fertile, drained soil, and are easily propagated from cuttings. As they have lovely colours and a long-flowering season, and there is nothing like them except *Phygelius*, they deserve care. Often they encouragingly survive the winter, only to succumb to drying winds in spring. All are evergreen in mild districts.

barbatus ● ★

90 × 30 cm	*[4–8]*	*Scarlet*	*Summer*	P	DS
3 × 1 ft					

Colorado, etc. 1784. *Chelone barbata*. *Penstemon coccineus* (of gardens). From a tuft of basal leaves spring branching stems with many tubular flowers, like small foxgloves, very gay and of bright scarlet touched with pink in the hairy throat. Long-flowering period. There is a light pink form called 'Carnea' and selected scarlet forms as well. *P.b. torreyi* also has scarlet flowers but is less hairy in the throat. Beautiful with erigerons. This is hardy in Surrey.

campanulatus

46 × 46 cm	*[8–9]*	*Various*	*Summer*	CD
18 × 18 in				

Mexico, Guatemala. 1794. The narrow leaves and small flowers are transmitted to two hybrids, probably with *P. hartwegii*, of great garden merit. Evergreen.

—'Evelyn'. [6–8]. Very bushy plants, 46 cm (18 in) high and wide, covered with small tubular rose-pink flowers from June onwards. This has proved hardy in Surrey. Ideal with *Polemonium foliosissimum*. 'Pink Endurance' is equally hardy and slightly larger; a desirable plant. 'Apple Blossom' is paler.

—'Garnet' ★

75 × 60 cm	*[4–9]*	*Wine*	*Summer/*	CD
2½ × 2 ft			*Autumn*	

'Andenken an Friedrich Hahn'. A splendid, hearty grower, very bushy, springing readily from the base if the tops are destroyed by frost. Narrow fresh green leaves. The tubular flowers appear continuously from June to October, of deep port wine colour with a flush of crimson. Valuable for its deep colour; lovely with *Phlomis russeliana*, with the Gallica Rose, 'Rosa Mundi', in June, and with hydrangeas later.

—'Hidcote Pink'

75 × 60 cm	*[4–8]*	*Pink*	*Summer/*	CD
2½ × 2 ft			*Autumn*	

A plant raised in the garden of that name which is of hybrid origin and possibly fits here. It has soft salmon-pink flowers, paler in the throat, with crimson streaks.

confertus

46 × 30 cm	*[7–9]*	*Cream*	*Summer*	CS
18 in × 1 ft				

Rocky Mountains. 1827. *P. attenuatus, P. micranthus*. The very small creamy yellow or pale sulphur flowers make dainty spikes over a clump-forming plant with long smooth leaves. It inhabits dry sandy pinewoods in the wild.

digitalis ●

90 × 46 cm	*[3–9]*	*White*	*Summer*	CS
3 ft × 18 in				

Arkansas. 1825. This splendid plant has remained in obscurity too long. Like others it is not fully hardy but is easy to strike from cuttings. The large panicles of tubular flowers are one of the best sights of midsummer.

gentianoides

1.2 m × 60 cm	*[9–10]*	*Purple*	*E.Summer*	W	CD
4 × 2 ft					

Mexico, etc. A refined but leafy plant, rich green, with long spikes of blooms, the whole plant downy. Tubular flowers of rich bluish purple with wide lips. Evergreen. The true species is rare, a larger-flowered pale lilac garden hybrid, of considerable merit, doing duty for it, known as 'Gentianoides' (of gardens) or 'Alice Hindley' [4–8].

gloxinioides (of gardens) [9–10]. A race, mainly of tender bedding plants, to which the following similar but hardier hybrids may be added.

● ★ 'Schoenholzeri' is a vigorous plant achieving 90 cm (3 ft) and nearly hardy. The flowers are larger than *P. hartwegii* and of really brilliant scarlet. A joy for months. It is synonymous with 'Firebird' and 'Ruby'. 'Schoenholzeri' more closely resembles the numerous, tender garden hybrids between *P. hartwegii* and *P. cobaea*. Both of these species were introduced around 1820 and there are good seed strains as well as named varieties. Among the favourites are 'Gentianoides' (of gardens) in cool lavender (a confusing name as it is a separate species, *q.v.*), 'Southgate Gem', brilliant scarlet, and 'Sour Grapes', a livid grape-purple. The raiser's description in 1948/9 was 'metallic blue and violet'. I am glad to say this has been found again. They all have large flowers but are only trustworthy perennials in our warmest counties and maritime districts.

'Stapleford Gem' is of the persuasion of *P. hirsutus*, *q.v.*, and has become confused in gardens with the true 'Sour Grapes'.

—'Rubicunda'

60 × 60 cm	*Crimson-*	*Summer/*	C
2 × 2 ft	*scarlet*	*Autumn*	

Depicted in colour in my *Gardens of the National Trust* and *Complete Paintings*. Long treasured at Lyme Park, Cheshire, where it was raised in 1906.

hartwegii

60 × 30 cm	*[8–10]*	*Scarlet*	*Summer/*	W	CD
2 × 1 ft			*Autumn*		

Mexico. *c.* 1825. In spite of its habitat this species is usually hardy in sheltered gardens in full sun. A bushy plant with rich green leaves and an unending succession of brilliant scarlet, tubular flowers. Evergreen.

hirsutus

60 × 46 cm	*[4–9]*	*Lavender*	*Summer*	CS
2 ft × 18 in				

North America. 1834. *P.pubescens* (of gardens), *P.mackayanus*. The gentle colour scheme of lilac-blue and cream of the tubular flowers is appealing. Narrow, clammy foliage. A short-lived plant, but worth raising.

isophyllus ● ★

90 × 30 cm	*[9–10]*	*Scarlet*	*Summer/*	W	C
3 × 1 ft			*Autumn*		

Mexico. 1908. Similar to *P.hartwegii*, but taller, with narrow tubular scarlet flowers. A startling but rather gawky plant, needing a warm position. There is a creamy white form.

292

ovatus

75 × 30 cm	*[4–9]*	*Blue*	*Summer*	F	S
2½ × 1 ft					

Central United States. Included for the value of its beautiful true blue flowers; though it is not long-lived it is easily raised from seed and thrives in any sunny reasonably drained soil. Basal leaves are bold and oval, and the erect stems bear clusters of narrow tubular blooms. Hardy in Surrey.

strictus

46 × 46 cm	*[5–8]*	*Violet*	*L.Summer*	CS
18 × 18 in				

W. United States. An excellent but little-known plant whose glaucous leaves assort well with the violet-blue or lilac tubular flowers, borne in a long spike.

PEROVSKIA, Labiatae. Ardent sun-lovers for well-drained soil. In shade they will flower but tend to sprawl. Though truly shrubs they are best cut to the ground every spring to encourage strong shoots and good flowers.

abrotanoides ★

1.2 m × 60 cm	*[6–9]*	*Lavender*	*L.Summer*	P	CDS
4 × 2 ft					

Afghanistan to Tibet. This rare species has very finely dissected leaves and is seldom seen, various hybrids presumably with *P. atriplicifolia* doing duty for it. They all resemble this better-known species but have more branching flower spikes; two have been named 'Blue Spire' (Bloom) and 'Blue Haze' (Notcutt). The former has dissected leaves; in the latter they are almost entire. In winter all species and cultivars are conspicuous for their grey stems. A good form thrives at Polesden Lacey, Surrey. All are aromatic.

atriplicifolia ★

1.2 m × 46 cm	*[6–9]*	*Lavender*	*L.Summer*	P	CDS
4 ft × 18 in					

Afghanistan to Tibet. 1904. A beautiful plant of the sage family and thus aromatic. The base sends up grey-white stems and aromatic coarsely-toothed leaves, grey-white beneath, supporting elegant bright lavender-blue flowers, like lavender, but in open spires. A lovely combination of colours and it is in flower for many weeks. The grey stems are attractive in winter. Full sun, good drainage, ordinary soil. This grows and flowers remarkably well at Wisley, Surrey, on top of a retaining wall. Beautiful with *Anemone tomentosa*.

> "... the plant is worth a place in the choicest garden for its graceful habit and long season of beauty."—WR

scrophulariaefolia

60 × 46 cm	*[6–9]*	*Lavender*	*L.Summer*	P	CDS
2 ft × 18 in					

Turkestan. 1851. Though so long in cultivation, this is little known. Its merits are a shorter habit, not requiring any support, and broad, deeply cut leaves. The usual open spires of flowers make as good a show as the other species. A good companion to *Anemone* 'September Charm'.

PETASITES, Compositae. Several species are of value for their vast leaves— *P. × hybridus, P. japonicus*—and for their sweetly scented flowers in winter— *P. fragrans*; also *P. albus*, but they have such dangerous far-questing roots that they can only be considered as ground-cover in very large areas. For this purpose they are considered in my *Plants for Ground-Cover*.

PHLOMIS, Labiatae.

russeliana ● ★

90 × 60 cm	*[4–9]*	*Yellow*	*Summer*	PF	DS
3 × 2 ft					

Syria. 1821. *P. samia* and *P. viscosa* (of gardens). A handsome plant whose rough large leaves make an excellent ground-cover up to 30 cm (1 ft). The flower-stems are stout and bear several whorls of soft butter-yellow hooded flowers, which make a pleasing contrast to the blue geraniums, such as *G. pratense*. The statuesque stems last in beauty through the winter; luxuriant at Cliveden, Buckinghamshire. Easily grown in ordinary soil. Evergreen.

tuberosa

1.2 m × 90 cm	*[4–9]*	*Purple*	*Summer*	DS
4 × 3 ft				

E. Europe to Siberia. 1759. Tuberous rootstock; this is a bushy perennial of rather prolific leafy growth and interrupted spikes of rosy-lilac sage-flowers in reddish calyces.

PHLOX, Polemoniaceae.

× arendsii

30 × 30 cm	*[4–8]*	*Various*	*E.Summer*	P	R
1 × 1 ft					

1910. *P. divaricata × P. paniculata*. A race of showy dwarf phloxes for frontal positions, needing the same cultivation as the others. Long-flowering season. There are mauve and white varieties; one of the most reliable is 'Lisbeth' (1913) in clear lavender-blue. *P. divaricata* also has a noted variety, 'Laphamii', which may well be a hybrid also. This generally grows best in a cool position with ample humus. New *P. × arendsii* hybrids from Germany are 'Anja', reddish purple, 'Hilda', lavender, pink eye, and 'Susanne', white with red centre.

glaberrima

60 × 60 cm	*[4–8]*	*Lilac-rose*	*E. to L.*	CRS
2 × 2 ft			*Summer*	

E. North America. 1705. A very beautiful and unusual species for moist, cool lime-free positions with plenty of humus. It is completely smooth, with good foliage, and a long succession of heads of good flowers appears, in deep or light lilac-rose. *P. pilosa* [4–8] may very briefly be described as shorter, hairy, and suitable for drier positions, and earlier-flowering. They both assort well with *P. arendsii* in style.

maculata ● ★

90 × 46 cm	*[4–8]*	*White/*	*Summer*	P	DR
3 ft × 18 in		*Mauve*			

E. North America. 1740. This plant has had far too little publicity, having been overshadowed by *P. paniculata* and all its brilliant cultivars. So far bright colours have not been bred from the mauve-pink *P. maculata*, but it is an erect plant, of slighter outline than *P. paniculata*; the flowers are borne in tall cylindrical heads, not pyramid-shaped, and the individual flowers are rather smaller. It does not need staking and is not usually subject to eelworm. After the main display is over later shoots arise. 'Alpha' is a good lilac-pink, and 'Miss Lingard' (prior to 1933), a pure white which is rather temperamental. I hear better reports of Alan Bloom's 'Omega', which is white with lilac eye. They are all fragrant and very elegant.

ovata

46 × 46 cm	[3–8]	Purplish	E.Summer	CDS
18 × 18 in				

E. North America. 1759. Smooth green leaves and multitudes of flowers often of warm carmine-pink with dark eye; some forms are more purplish. From a garden point of view it resembles *P. × arendsii* and others of like height, and is often considered as a large rock garden plant.

paniculata ● ★

1.2 m × 60 cm	[4–8]	Various	L.Summer	P R
4 × 2 ft				

E. North America. 1730. This is seldom seen today, its place having been taken by the many named varieties. This is a pity because it is a far more soundly perennial plant than these highly bred, brilliant clones. Forms in cultivation range from tall white and pale mauve to a fairly strong lilac of shorter growth. Their individual flowers are small compared with the highly bred varieties, but they are tough, healthy, of willowy growth and to be recommended for the more natural gardens—such as the Stream garden at Hidcote, Gloucestershire, where they have been used for very many years, and are still in a healthy condition. A superb tall white named *P.p.* 'Alba Grandiflora' grows at Kew; this is a selection rather than a wild form.

"... the wild type of *P. paniculata*, ... very tall and rosy lilac."—EAB

A hundred years or more ago selection of colour forms started in France and for most of this time the name *P. decussata* has been given to these supposed hybrids, which were in reality seedlings from different natural types of *P. paniculata*. Many forms were raised by H. J. Jones early in the present century and later Captain B. Symons-Jeune took up the task. Today there are tall cultivars available—also some quite short—from pure white through lilac to purple and wine-crimson; and fiery red, crimson, varying pinks to blush. Some have darker colour in the centre and others have a paler zone; some whites have crimson eyes. Their great season is August and their rich fragrance wafts through the garden. They are mostly on the soft side of the spectrum, but some of the brightest reds and strongest purples and wines will assort courageously with the bright yellow and orange flowers so prevalent at the time. 'Eva Callum', pink, and 'September Schnee', blush-white, flower after most others. There are two kinds with beautiful ivory-variegated leaves, the old 'Norah Leigh' and Alan Bloom's newer 'Harlequin'. 'Harlequin' is a sport from 'Border Gem'; the flowers are pale lilac and purple respectively. It is best to select varieties in bloom, personally, or from reliable lists.

These phloxes suffer from eelworm and to avoid this young stock propagated only from root-cuttings should be obtained, off clean ground. Stem-cuttings and divisions, particularly in ground where phloxes have long been grown, are liable to develop the swollen shoots and twisted wispy leaves which are a sure sign of the disease. There is no recourse but to burn them and to avoid growing phloxes in the same spot again. Where they are growing well in not-too-dry, well-nourished soil (avoiding chalk and clay) containing humus, and top-dressed with humus yearly, they are likely to thrive. It is a good plan to thin out weaker shoots on big clumps when they are about 15 cm (6 in) high; another tip, for smaller gardens, is to pinch out the tops of a few of the frontal shoots when a little taller; the resulting side-shoots will prolong the display and furnish the groups better. They seldom need staking except in very windy gardens, where their big pyramid-shaped heads of bloom are apt to prove over-heavy after rain.

There have always been many named forms of *P. paniculata*, but a splendid late flowering cultivar has recently found its way from the United States. It is 'Fujiyama'. It flowers after all but 'September Schnee' are over, achieves 1.5 m (5 ft) or more, has light green leaves and large heads of snow-white flowers. No staking is required. A plant with a great future and a mainstay of the September border.

PHORMIUM, Liliaceae. Sun-loving plants of striking outline for warmer counties.

cookianum ● ★

1.2 m × 30 cm   *[9–10]*   *Green-brown*   *Summer*   PF DS
4 × 1 ft

New Zealand. 1868. *P. colensoi, P. hookeri.* Similar to *P. tenax* but the form grown in this country is of modest height, more suitable for smaller gardens. The flowers are sallow-brown outside, pale green inside with red-brown filaments and orange anthers. It is still rare though hardy. There is also a variegated form; another, 'Tricolor', is gay with red, yellow and green leaf stripes. 'Cream Delight' describes itself. Evergreen.

tenax

3 m × 90 cm   *[9–10]*   *Red*   *Summer*   PF W DS
10 × 3 ft

New Zealand. 1789. New Zealand Flax. One of the most striking of plants for garden effect. The great, smooth, grey-green, sword-like leaves stand stiffly up to 1.5–2.1 m (5–7 ft) and are overtopped by several feet by the magnificent plum-blue flower stems which erupt for a yard or so of their apices into side brackets bearing dull red flowers 5 cm (2 in) long. The big seed-pods are held more or less erect in this species, while in *P. cookianum* they nod. The dead leaves are as tough as cord and useful for tying. A splendid contrast to the rounded contours of shrubs and plants. They thrive and flower best in sunny maritime districts in the mildest counties, but they are hardy in Surrey. It is wise to provide a deep mulch of decaying leaves, etc. around the clumps for winter protection in cold districts. 'Goliath' is an extra-vigorous clone selected in New Zealand.

—**'Purpureum'.** In this rare variety the grey-green of the leaves is overlaid with a red-purple sheen, producing in the best forms a rich dark coppery tone. It is usually increased by division, though a percentage of purplish forms can be raised from seed; a richly coloured form is worth seeking. 'Bronze Baby' is a short form with wine-dark foliage which I have not found hardy, while 'Purple Giant' is of vast dimensions in New Zealand; the foliage is bronze-purple where the sun warms it, glaucous behind. 'Rubrum' is another good one recorded in New Zealand and is reported to be a hybrid with *P. cookianum*.

—**'Variegatum'.** This is similar to the species in every respect except the colour of its leaves, which are most handsomely striped with yellow for their entire length. Wonderful for really big arrangements indoors. There are several forms with special names but all are good. This is perhaps the most handsome as a flowering plant because of the contrast of the plum-red flowering spikes among the yellow-striped leaves. It is worth a special visit to Glendurgan, or another Cornish garden, in late summer, to see this remarkable effect.

There are several variegated forms grown in New Zealand, and from what one hears the old cultivars are outclassed by the brilliant yellow variegation of 'Williamsii Variegatum', 'Radiance' and 'Yellow Queen'. Hybrids with *P. cookianum*, with amazing tones of yellow, salmon, orange, red and bronze, are such as 'Aurora', 'Dazzler' and 'Smiling Morn', raised by Mr W. B. Brockie around 1940 at the Christchurch Botanic Garden, New Zealand.

PHUOPSOS, Rubiaceae. Closely allied to *Crucianella* and *Galium* species, this is easily cultivated in any fertile soil in a sunny position.

stylosa

30 × 60 cm	*[5–8]*	*Pink*	*Summer*	D
1 × 2 ft				

Caucasus. 1836. *Crucianella stylosa*. For the verge of a border or bed this is a worthwhile plant in spite of the strong smell. Flopping stems are covered with narrow foliage, and the dense heads of tiny pink flowers are produced for a long period. A selected form has been called 'Brilliant' or 'Purpurea'.

PHYGELIUS, Scrophulariaceae. Although these are shrubs in warm climates, and assume shrubby proportions when trained on walls in the sunnier parts of this country, they are highly satisfactory when cut down in winter in common with other herbaceous plants. They thrive in sunshine but are also wonderful for giving brilliance to a north wall, so long as it is not too exposed. They are not particular about soil. They flower from July until the frosts stop activities. Stoloniferous roots.

aequalis ● ★

90 × 46 cm	*[7–9]*	*Coral*	*Summer/*	P CD
3 ft × 18 in			*Autumn*	

South Africa. Persistently flowering through the summer, this shrubby plant needs good drainage and thrives best against a sunny wall, where its numerous stems will give rise to the intriguing panicles of slender trumpets of soft rosy coral-red with lemon throat and mahogany lip. It grows well at Crathes Castle, Kincardineshire, but is not reliably hardy everywhere.

A new colour form should be added to the repertoire, from Eastern Cape Province. According to Mr L. Burtt of Edinburgh the species varies much in colour and he introduced in 1977 a creamy butter-yellow variant, which is already becoming well known. It is named 'Yellow Trumpet' ★ ● and grows as satisfactorily as the normal type in not-too-cold gardens.

capensis ● ★

1.2 m × 60 cm	*[8–9]*	*Red*	*Summer/*	P CD
4 × 2 ft			*Autumn*	

South Africa. 1855. Cape Figwort. A lovely plant for the sunny border, throwing up many stems carrying numerous tubular bright red flowers with yellow throats. When growing against a wall it becomes a shrub and will reach 1.8 to 2.4 m (6 to 8 ft) high; it is a wonderful sight from July till autumn. *P.c.* 'Coccineus' is doubtfully more brilliant, but has a slightly more pronounced yellow throat. It may be seen thriving at Stourhead, Wiltshire, in the North Court. *Phygelius aequalis* and *P. coccinea* both grow in damp places in the wild. They seem happy in ordinary conditions in our gardens, but need full sun. Many hybrids have been raised recently, most by Hillier's Nursery. They are called *P. × rectus* [8–9], and combine the bright colours and one-sided spike of *P. coccineus* with the broader leaves and softer flower-tones of *P. aequalis*, whose flowers hang on all sides of the spike. 'African Queen' is a dusky red; 'Moonraker' pale yellow; 'Devil's Tears', 'Salmon Leap', 'Winchester Fanfare' and 'Pink Elf' are in various tones of flame, red and salmon. They are all in the sharper tones of the spectrum.

PHYSALIS, Solanaceae. Winter Cherry, Chinese Lantern. The first named has been a popular plant for its edible and ornamental fruit all through history. Both will thrive in almost any soil in sun or shade, freely increasing by means of running roots, which should be planted about 7.5 cm (3 in) deep. Their stems are weak and are apt to flop; the plants look weedy in summer, and have inconspicuous, starry, creamy flowers.

alkekengii

46 × 60 cm *18 in × 2 ft*	*[5–8]*	*Autumn*	F D

Caucasus to China. 1549. The Bladder Cherry of the ancients has rounded 'lanterns' in autumn, of bright orange-red.

"The gorgeous orange-red chinese lanterns of the winter cherry."—EAB

franchetii

60 × 90 cm *2 × 3 ft*	*[5–8]*	*Autumn*	F D

Japan. 1894. This species is more luxuriant, with larger leaves, and larger more pointed "lanterns" of bright orange-red. 'Gigantea' is to be sought. Both are useful for drying for the winter and for using with *Iris foetidissima* berries and seed-heads of *Hosta sieboldiana*, Honesty, etc. The green pods in summer, defoliated, are also very beautiful. There are hybrids between the two, such as *P. × bunyardii* [5–8], and monstrous forms and a dwarf.

PHYSOCHLAINA, Solanaceae. Any fertile soil.

orientalis

46 × 30 cm *18 in × 1 ft*	*[6–9]*	*Lilac*	*Spring*	DS

Iberia. 1821. By no means a showy plant but its early-flowering habit recommends it, and though in a different family, it assorts with pulmonarias and early geraniums. Clump-forming; with large hairy leaves, and bell-shaped blooms in sprays.

PHYSOSTEGIA, Labiatae.

virginiana

90 × 60 cm *3 × 2 ft*	*[4–8]*	*Various*	*L.Summer*	P D

E. United States. 1683. The Obedient Plant—so called because its flowers have hinged stalks and will "stay put" when moved—has a running rootstock, but makes dense clumps. 'Alba' or 'Summer Snow' are attractive white varieties. 90 cm (3 ft). They thrive in any fertile soil, not too dry and preferably in sun. There is a neatly white-edged form, *P.v.* 'Variegata'.

—**speciosa.** A variety with rather more coarsely toothed and larger leaves, from which a form of pale lilac-pink has been named 'Rose Bouquet'. 90 × 60 cm (3 × 2 ft).

—**'Vivid'** ★

30 × 30 cm *1 × 1 ft*	*Pink*	*E.Autumn*	P D

1931. This variety is fairly compact, making a dense mass. Numerous flower-stems bear tubular dark lilac-pink flowers, very welcome in September, with white Japanese Anemones.

PHYTEUMA, Campanulaceae. A genus of beautiful plants, many of which are ideal for the rock garden. The following species are among the tallest, and thrive in any fertile well-drained soil in sun or part shade.

campanuloides
60 × 30 cm   *[5–8]*   *Violet*   *Summer*   S
2 × 1 ft
Caucasus. 1804. *Asyneuma campanuloides.* Narrow basal leaves. Stiff stems bear almost stalkless violet-blue stars in a long slender spike. Neither this nor the other species are in the first flight of plants.

spicatum
60 × 30 cm   *[5–8]*   *Various*   *Summer*   S
2 × 1 ft
Europe, Britain. 1597. The tiny flowers are crowded into a cylindrical spike, and may be creamy white or pale or deeper blue. The foliage is heart-shaped and toothed; the whole a pleasant plant without being striking.

PHYTOLACCA, Phytolaccaceae. Coarse but striking plants which will seed themselves—too freely sometimes—in retentive soil, in sun or shade. They are unpleasantly smelly and poisonous—but even so are sometimes grown and their autumn effect is considerable, especially against yellowing leaves of shrubs.

americana
1.2 m × 60 cm   *[4–9]*   *White*   *L.Summer*   F   DS
4 × 2 ft
Florida. 1768. *P. decandra.* Poke Weed or Red Ink Plant. A stalwart leafy plant. The flower spikes are white followed by spikes of shining maroon berries.

clavigera
1.2 m × 60 cm   *[6–9]*   *Pink*   *L.Summer*   F   DS
4 × 2 ft
China. 1913. A more handsome plant than *P. americana* and rather earlier-flowering. The stems are vivid crimson in autumn (brighter than the best rhubarb) showing up the yellowing foliage and jet-black shining berries.

PIMPINELLA, Umbelliferae.

major 'Rosea'
60 × 30 cm   *[5–9]*   *Pink*   *Summer*   P   D
2 × 1 ft
Europe. *P. magna rosea.* In effect a very refined pink-flowered Cow Parsley and thoroughly charming. The pale pink of the flowers is excellent and the divided leaves makes a good basal mat. Happy in ordinary soil, in a cool position.

PLANTAGO, Plantaginaceae. *P. major* is a troublesome weed in lawns, and the purple-leafed form below seeds itself equally freely, so beware. Easy plants in any sunny spot.

major
30 × 30 cm   *[3–10]*   *Green*   *Summer*   S
1 × 1 ft
Europe, Britain. Great Plantain. The variety *rubrifolia* is noteworthy for its wholly purplish colouring, especially in full sun. Bold rosettes of broad leaves below slender flower spikes. In the variety *rosularis* (Rose Plantain) the flower

spikes are reduced to a neat rosette of small green bracts. This produces no seed and must be increased by division. There is also 'Variegata' which is attributed to *P.m. asiatica*. More desirable is the cream-edged form of narrow-leafed *P. lanceolata*, 'Streaker'.

PLATYCODON, Campanulaceae. A long-lived plant for the foreground allied to *Campanula* and thriving in most fertile soils in sun.

grandiflorus ● ★

46 × 46 cm	*[4–9]*	*Blue/White*	*L.Summer*	PF	CS
18 × 18 in					

Far East. 1782. The Balloon Flower has blue-green neat leaves closely arranged up the stems, which make a compact clump, overtopped by the large round balloon-like buds opening into wide cup-flowers. Of soft texture and tint, they are from deep Wedgwood-blue to white, sometimes soft pink—'Perlmutter-schale' or 'Mother of Pearl' (1956). *P.g.* 'Mariesii' (1884) is equally fine in flower but shorter and earlier flowering, and is the form usually grown. There are also double-flowered forms. Lovely with fuchsias.

PODOPHYLLUM, Podophyllaceae. Lovers of moist, humus-laden soil in part shade, these plants have fleshy roots which slowly colonize. Though not related, they bear some resemblance to *Trillium*, but in contrast their leaves come through the ground folded like an umbrella from the top of the stem. They are deeply lobed, and the coy, sculptured flower is often succeeded by a large plum-like fruit. Though the plants are quite hardy the young leaves are frost-tender. Since the leaves are few it is better to resist cutting the flowering stems. The plants are poisonous but the fruits are edible.

hexandrum ● ★

46 × 30 cm	*[5–8]*	*White/*	*Spring*	F	DS
18 in × 1 ft		Pink			

India. 1820. *P. emodi*. Handsome pairs of brownish, deep-lobed leaves, which last well, as in all species. The flower is nodding, cupped, and of crystalline texture. Shining red fruit. ● ★ *P.h.* 'Majus' is a fine large form and *P.h. chinense* has flowers of rose-pink.

"... fruits of a brilliant red as large as a hen's egg, and edible, though of a mawkish flavour."—WR

peltatum ●

46 × 30 cm	*[4–9]*	*White*	*Spring*	F	DS
18 in × 1 ft					

North America. 1664. May Apple. Similarly handsome, with one great lobed leaf and good-sized creamy nodding flower; rosy-coloured fruit. A vigorous colonizer.

pleianthum

46 × 30 cm	*[5–8]*	*Purple*	*Spring*	F	DS
18 in × 1 ft					

China. 1889. The usual big broad leaves and nodding flowers of maroon in large bunches at the top of the stem. Sometimes labelled *Dysosma pleiantha*. *Podophyllum versipelle* [5–8] is a similar species.

POLEMONIUM, Polemoniaceae. Although these species are not all reliably long-lived, unless carefully divided in spring and given fresh soil, they can be easily raised from seeds. They all make basal clumps of finely divided foliage and produce sheaves of small silky flowers, cup-shaped, with deep yellow stamens. They are happy in any reasonably fertile soil, preferably in sun.

caeruleum

60 × 60 cm	*[4–8]*	*Blue*	*E.Summer*	P	DS
2 × 2 ft					

Northern Hemisphere, Britain. The old garden Jacob's Ladder—cultivated since Roman days—has masses of cool lavender-blue flowers, of open bell-shape, with orange stamens. There is a good white form. Among the varying blue kinds the richer coloured garden plant 'Richardsonii' should be sought; this is considered to be a hybrid with *P. reptans* and its botanical names is *P. × jacobaea*. 'Sapphire' is a good light blue. *P. reptans* (1758) is considerably shorter than all these.

—'Dawn Flight'

90 × 60 cm	*[4–8]*	*Lilac*	*E.Summer*	P	D
3 × 2 ft					

A pleasing variant—or possible hybrid of *P. carneum*—grown in Irish gardens, with flowers of cool pinkish-lilac. I have been unable to trace its origin.

carneum

46 × 46 cm	*[4–9]*	*Pink*	*E.Summer*	P	DS
18 × 18 in					

W. North America. The pale flesh pink of the silky cups is very appealing. A deeper form has been named 'Rose Queen'.

flavum

60 × 60 cm	*[4–8]*	*Yellow*	*Summer*	P	W	DS
2 × 2 ft						

S. North America. The downy stems carry many pale yellow cup-shaped silky blooms. Needs a well-drained soil in full sun in our warmer counties.

foliosissimum ★

75 × 60 cm	*[4–8]*	*Lilac*	*Summer*	P	DS
2½ × 2 ft					

W. North America. A long succession of rich lilac cups, lit by orange stamens. This is about the best of the bunch, and ideal with some of the shorter yellow achilleas. The terminal leaflets are adnate in this species.

POLYGONATUM, Liliaceae. Solomon's Seal, David's Harp. All of these species and hybrids like nothing so much as to be left alone to spread by their rhizomes, which are just below ground-level, and revel in cool positions in a humus-laden retentive soil. They will, however, grow almost anywhere that is not hot and dry. With their splendid foliage they give a woodland air to gardens, planted alongside ferns and hostas. The stems of most of them arch prettily when 30–60 cm (1–2 ft) in height, and display a series of horizontal, broad, clear green leaves for the rest of the length of stem, under which hang the little, white, green-tipped bells, faintly fragrant and sometimes followed by blue-black berries. Their leaves turn to buttery yellow in autumn. One sort or another has been cultivated for hundreds of years. A watch should be kept for sawfly caterpillars in June.

canaliculatum ★

| 1.5 m × 60 cm | [4–9] | White | L.Spring | P | D |
| 5 × 2 ft | | | | | |

United States. *P. commutatum*; *P. giganteum* of gardens. Imagine an ordinary good Solomon's Seal increased to at least twice its size, and yet with all its parts in proportion, and you have a fair image of this superb plant. Large rounded leaves. An excellent grower, achieving 1.2 m (4 ft) in poor sand, but in good soil it is said to reach 2.1 m (7 ft) in height. I doubt it. Flowers in large clusters.

falcatum

| 90 × 30 cm | [4–9] | White | L.Spring | P | DS |
| 3 × 1 ft | | | | | |

Japan. *P. japonicum* (of gardens) (not to be confused with the little plant known in gardens as *P. falcatum*, which is a different species). Somewhat pointed leaves and reddish stems mark this apart from others. Best known in its variegated form, 'Variegatum', in which the leaves are narrowly edged with white. A lovely harmony when grown with the pink Lily-of-the-Valley.

× hybridum ★

| 90 × 30 cm | [4–9] | White | L.Spring | P | D |
| 3 × 1 ft | | | | | |

P. multiforum (of gardens); *P. multiflorum* × *P. odoratum*. This is the usual Solomon's Seal or David's Harp. A gracious woodland plant which will thrive in any spot without sun, behind a wall or under trees. The stems bear along their arching length broad, horizontally poised leaves and little bells of greeny white in clusters. Being a hybrid, it is important to obtain a good form. The ideal companion is a lacy fern.

"The roots ... and applied, taketh away ... any bruise gotten by fals or womens wilfulnesse, in stumbling upon their hasty husbands fists, or such like."—GH

—'**Flore Pleno**'. The double flowers are like ballet dancers' skirts—or tiny seals to hang on one's watch-chain.

—'**Variegatum**'. Foliage striped with creamy white; less vigorous than the green type, and a less good garden plant than *P. falcatum* 'Variegatum', though it is far more heavily variegated.

latifolium

| 90 × 30 cm | [4–9] | White | L.Spring | P | D |
| 3 × 1 ft | | | | | |

S.E. Europe, Asia Minor, etc. *P. hirtum*. A rare species with extra broad leaves, hairy beneath, and minutely hairy stems and leaf-stalks; the usual flowers are in bunches of as many as five. Late-flowering compared with the others.

multiflorum

| 60 × 30 cm | [3–9] | White | L.Spring | P | DS |
| 2 × 1 ft | | | | | |

Britain, Europe, and N. Asia. Less good than *P. × hybridum*, but a charming native. The rounded stems are a noticeable character.

odoratum

60 × 30 cm	*[4–9]*	*White*	*L.Spring*	P	DS
2 × 1 ft					

Britain, Europe, and N. Asia. *P. officinale*. Again a connoisseur's plant, this time with distinctly angled stems. The flowers are carried one or two at a time, instead of two to five as in *P. multiflorum*, and almost as many in *P. × hybridum*. They are fragrant and there is an intriguing double form, *P.o* 'Flore Pleno'. *P. humile* [4–9] from the Far East is related.

verticillatum

1.2 m × 46 cm	*[4–9]*	*Greenish*	*E.Summer*	P	DS
4 ft × 18 in					

Asia Minor, etc. I do not place this plant very high in beauty or in garden value, but it makes an intriguing change when considered with the foregoing kinds, all of which resemble one another. This has narrow leaves borne in whorls at intervals up the erect stems, with clusters of small flowers hanging under each whorl, followed by some red berries. Two related species are *P. roseum* [5–8], with tinted flowers as its name suggests, and rather less in growth, and *P. sibiricum* [4–9], with cream flowers but distinguished by its leaves ending in a recurving tendril-like tip. *P. geminiflorum* [5–8], with cream flowers in pairs like the Gemini twins, has handsome, broad, shining leaves in whorls of three, or opposite, and often richly purple-tinted while young, and with a maroon spot at their base. It achieves about 60 cm (2 ft). The red-flowered *P. kingianum* [9] is related to this group but is very tender.

POLYGONUM, Polygonaceae. The Knotweeds are on the whole rather rampageous plants, from the dwarf carpeter *P. affine* (described in my *Plants for Ground-Cover*) to those terrible spreaders *P. cuspidatum* and *P. sachalinense*. The following selection brings forward some very good plants, mostly long in flower, and not particular about soil, except that, apart from *P. equisetiforme*, they prefer it good and moist. See also *Tovara*. Some botanists now class all the species mentioned below in the genus *Persicaria* or *Fallopia*.

affine

23 × 30 cm	*[3–9]*	*Pink*	*Summer/*	P	D
9 × 12 in			*Autumn*		

Nepal. I omitted this species from the first edition because it was covered in my *Plants for Ground-Cover*. Since then the form ★ 'Superbum' has burst upon us. I obtained it from H. Hagemann of Hanover. It has proved superior in vigour and colour to 'Donald Lowndes' and 'Darjeeling Red'. The flower spikes open blush-white and turn to crimson. Also known as 'Dimity'. A first-rate carpeter for long effect; rich brown in winter. A great sight at Wakehurst. Superb as a foreground to *Perovskia*.

alpinum

90 × 90 cm	*[3–7]*	*White*	*E.Summer*	P	D
3 × 3 ft					

Europe. 1816. Somewhat invasive but easy to control. It is a dense, bushy plant with narrow leaves and the whole thing is smothered with small branching spikes of tiny creamy white flowers for two months.

amplexicaule ★

| 1.2 × 1.2 m | [5–9] | Blush/ | Summer/ | P D |
| 4 × 4 ft | | Crimson | Autumn | |

Himalaya. *P. oxyphyllum*. An amazing plant, in beauty from the end of June until the frosts of autumn. It forms a big leafy clump, steadily increasing in size, with innumerable erect spikes of flowers, like the spikes of lavender, but in 'Atrosanguineum', of rich crimson; a brighter form with rather larger spikes is 'Firetail'. The white or blush-white form is often labelled *oxyphyllum* in gardens. They are all good companions for *Aster × frikartii*; all thrive in moderately moist soils, in sun or part-shade.

"... yard-long, branching arms crested in summer and autumn with heads of brilliant ruby blossoms."—ATJ

—'Arun Gem'

| 60 × 60 cm | [5–9] | Pink | Summer/ | P D |
| 2 × 2 ft | | | Autumn | |

Introduced by the Bangor University Expedition from Nepal in 1971, this is a charming variant with small, nodding spikes of "shocking" pink flowers, on freely branching stems. Its only fault is that the faded spikes turn to ginger-brown and remain on the plant.

—'Inverleith'

| 70 × 60 cm | | Crimson | Summer/ | P D |
| 2½ × 2 ft | | | Autumn | |

This has been growing for many years at the Royal Botanic Gardens, Edinburgh, but its origin is unknown. It is a useful extra, with short spikes of dark flowers and the usual masses of leaves.

bistorta

| 75 × 60 cm | [4–8] | Pink | E. Summer | P D |
| 2½ × 2 ft | | | | |

Europe, Asia. ★ 'Superbum' is a useful and beautiful, strong clump-forming plant with masses of broad, basal leaves derived from the Bistort, a native of Britain. During May and June these are overtopped by branching stems bearing bottle-brush flower-heads of cool pink. Subsequently more flowering stems appear. Its flowering period is lengthened in moist conditions. *P. bistorta* has a very wide distribution and, as might therefore be expected, is a variable plant. A close relative of some garden value is *P. regelianum* [4–8] or *P. ussuriense*, with a profusion of whitish spikes with a light mushroom tint. *P. carneum* [4–8] is a small light pink variant. Many others have been named.

campanulatum

| 90 × 90 cm | [5–9] | Pink | Summer/ | D |
| 3 × 3 ft | | | Autumn | |

Himalaya. 1909. A stout, colonizing plant, with attractive foliage and a never-ending display of pink flowers from midsummer onwards. They are tiny bells, set in branching elegant heads, and create a beautiful effect in moist or cool soil and part-shade, as at Nymans, Sussex. Lovely with *Aconitum carmichaelii*, and should always be planted well below the eye, and not above it. Since it likes a damp spot this is usually not difficult.

cuspidatum (Now classed in the genus *Reynoutria*, q.v.)

equisetiforme
>*46 × 60 cm*   *[7–10]*   *White*   *Autumn*   D
>*18 in × 2 ft*

Mediterranean Region. This strange plant closely resembles an *Ephedra*. The leafless grey-green wiry stems make a tangle and are studded with tiny white flowers when most are over. There is nothing like it among herbaceous plants, but it needs a warm sheltered corner in well-drained soil. (*P. scoparium.*)

milletii
>*60 × 60 cm*   *[5–9]*   *Crimson*   *Summer*   P D
>*2 × 2 ft*

W. China. A species comparatively new to cultivation, in the Bistort class, but with narrow leaves and spikes of rich crimson over a long period. A welcome colour on a very satisfactory garden plant which is of rather stiff habit. It has been known as *P. sphaerostachyum, q.v.,* and is dependent on good moist soil. Compact.

paniculatum ★
>*1.5 m × 90 cm*   *[4–9]*   *Creamy*   *Summer*   D
>*5 × 3 ft*

Himalaya. The stout woody rootstock, once established, will do good work every year. It is a bushy leafy plant with a great display in June of feathery sprays of creamy white tiny flowers, sometimes flesh-tinted. After the main display the plant is seldom out of flower. Sun or part shade, any reasonable soil. Clump-forming.

polystachyum
>*1.8 × 1.2 m*   *[4–9]*   *White*   *Autumn*   D
>*6 × 4 ft*

Himalaya. A tremendous spreader and only fit for landscape planting, in moist ground, where it will smother everything and provide a wonderful display of fragrant plumes in October, above copious pointed foliage which looks attractive during the whole summer.

rude
>*1.8 × 1.8 m*   *[4–9]*   *Cream*   *L.Summer*   D
>*6 × 6 ft*

Far East. This and *P. molle,* which is similar, and also *P. paniculatum,* which is horticulturally distinct, are now considered to be variants of one species. *P. rude* is a valuable, hearty, invasive plant making a great leafy clump of long pointed leaves on stout ascending stems. The pointed panicles of bloom are like those of a cream *Buddleja,* lasting long in beauty and succeeded by maroon seeds. A grand companion for *P. amplexicaule* 'Firetail'. *P. weyrichii* (1859) is similar.

sphaerostachyum ★
>*60 × 30 cm*   *[4–9]*   *Pink*   *Summer*   P D
>*2 × 1 ft*

Himalaya. *P. macrophyllum.* This comes midway between *P. milletii* and *P. bistorta* 'Superbum'; the flowers are produced considerably later than the latter, and are of rich deep old rose. A lovely colour to lead one into the phloxes. Compact and floriferous, with narrow, long leaves.

POTENTILLA, Rosaceae. Sun-loving plants creating a brilliant early summer effect—with some later flowers—in any fertile, drained soil.

argyrophylla ★

46 × 60 cm	*[6–9]*	*Yellow*	*E./L.Summer*	DS
18 in × 2 ft				

Kashmir, Nepal. 1829. *P. insignis.* Silvery, lobed, strawberry-leaves make an attractive low clump over which are displayed multitudes of clear yellow strawberry-flowers on branching stems. Lovely with *Linum narbonense.*

atrosanguinea ★

46 × 60 cm	*[5–8]*	*Red*	*E./L.Summer*	DS
18 in × 2 ft				

Himalaya. 1824. *P. argyrophylla atrosanguinea.* In effect like the previous species but the flowers are of dark red; a sumptuous plant.

GARDEN
HYBRIDS ● ★

46 × 60 cm	*[5–8]*	*Various*	*E./L.Summer*	D
18 in × 2 ft				

Bred from the above species and perhaps others are the dazzling single scarlet 'Gibson's Scarlet', 'Congo' and 'Flamenco'; single maroon 'Etna', dark red-brown 'Hamlet'; and several large-flowered doubles. Years ago there were many of these and they are well worth picking up and treasuring when found. Some of the more usual varieties grown today are 'Gloire de Nancy', orange-brown and deep coral-red; 'Yellow Queen', clear brassy yellow, reddish eye; 'Monsieur Rouillard', mahogany; 'Volcan', vermilion; and 'William Rollison', orange-red, yellow reverse. All of these are brilliant plants, needing care in placing, and are best used in the strongest colour schemes, with some coppery foliage.

" 'Gibson's Scarlet' . . . no member of the race has flowers of so dazzling a scarlet . . . profuse . . . indispensable."—WR

delavayi ★

60 × 60 cm	*[6–8]*	*Yellow*	*Summer*	DS
2 × 2 ft				

Yunnan. Prior to 1890. A little-known plant, but of considerable garden value. It is a far superior plant to *P. recta*, and is related to *P. argyrophylla*, having similar grey-hairy leaves, silvery beneath, and good branching stems with numerous single yellow flowers, fading to pale yellow. Vigorous.

nepalensis ★

46 × 60 cm	*[5–8]*	*Various*	*Summer*	DS
18 in × 2 ft				

W. Himalaya. 1820. This and its single-flowered forms or hybrids make a gay garden picture, and are good perennials for foreground planting, like the above and, in fact, all listed here. Good, lobed, green leaves and numerous branching stems which produce a surprising number of strawberry-flowers. *P. nepalensis* itself varies from carmine to a purplish tint; selected forms or hybrids of excellence are 'Roxana', a vivid rosy orange; 'Miss Willmott' (1920), warm cherry-pink; 'Master Floris', primrose and coral-red; × *hopwoodiana* (*P. nepalensis* × *P. recta*) 1829, creamy flesh with rosy centre. The first two breed fairly true from seeds; the others must be divided for increase. *P. thurberi* [5–8] is a geographical form from North America with flowers of dusky wine-red.

recta

60 × 30 cm	*[4–8]*	*Yellow*	*Summer*	PF	S
2 × 1 ft					

Europe to E. Asia. 1648. Hairy divided leaves and ascending stems bearing numerous yellow strawberry flowers in June. I have included this species for the sake of *P.r. sulphurea,* which has pale yellow flowers and thus adds to our very small list of plants of this colour. The brighter yellow type is often called *P. warrenii* (in gardens) or *P. recta macrantha.*

rupestris

46 × 46 cm	*[5–8]*	*White*	*E.Summer*	PF	DS
18 × 18 in					

Northern Old World. 1789. One of the best early flowers, pure white with yellow eyes. They are carried in branching heads over the dense tuft of good, green, pinnate leaves. The whole plant is hairy. Useful with June flowers in the border front.

PRIMULA, Primulaceae. The following species all thrive in moist or retentive soil, heavy rather than light, neutral rather than excessively acid. *P. helodoxa* and *P. florindae* thrive on lime, and the others are not resentful of it. In very acid soils it is sometimes necessary to apply some lime to bring the soil fertility up to a reasonable level. Some humus is beneficial. In the cooler north and west they are often garden weeds, as they seed themselves so freely. They can all be raised from seeds except where stated. The bigger hardy primulas mostly flower with rhododendrons and azaleas, and as much care should be taken over assorting the colours of the primulas as the shrubs. But it all depends on one's sensitivity to the red of the spectrum—whether it may verge towards blue as well as to yellow, in mixture, with impunuty.

denticulata ★

30 × 30 cm	*[6–8]*	*Various*	*Spring*	DRS
1 × 1 ft				

Himalaya, W. China. 1842. One of the most reliable of spring flowers, resistant to frost. In retentive soils the snug winter buds suddenly erupt into knobs of blooms, on stout stalks—like drumsticks—followed by long leaves. The original type introduced was clear pale lavender; this developed a range of colouring in the hands of Georg Arends, and today good white forms and breeders' selections, including rich carmine and purple, may be raised. A geographical form or hybrid with extra powdery leaves and stems is known as *P.d. cachemiriana.* While they may all be raised from seeds, root-cuttings are best for specially good forms. 'Karryann' has leaves handsomely edged with cream.

'Devon Cream'

30 × 30 cm	*[5–7]*	*Yellow*	*Spring*	P	D
1 × 1 ft					

This is undoubtedly a primrose hybrid, but curiously has no fragrance. It was found in the garden at Buckland Monachorum when Lionel Fortescue went to live there. Heads of creamy yellow nodding flowers over good clumps of foliage. While not as big as *P. florindae,* this is a good hearty plant for a cool border. Best divided in earliest spring; it sulks for a year if divided after flowering.

florindae ● ★

60 × 60 cm   [6–8]   Yellow   Summer   PS   S
2 × 2 ft

Tibet. 1924. A stalwart handsome plant for moist or wet ground, flowering later than the others. Forms a clump of big rounded leaves; several stems arise, when established, each having a drooping head of fragrant citron-yellow bells, powdered with white. A good perennial, in flower for weeks. Its health and vigour caused it to spread quickly in cultivation; I was growing it in 1928. Strains with orange-red flowers—presumed hybrids with *P. waltonii*—are often seen, but do not compare in garden value with the clear colour of the type. The vulgarly named 'Rasp Red' is rather better. The yellow type assorts well with *Lobelia × vedrariensis*.

"... goes its own way and subduing its own weeds—unchanging good temper under any conditions that have any pretence at wetness."—ATJ

CANDELABRA
PRIMULAS ● ★

60–90 × 46 cm   Various   E.Summer   D or S
2–3 ft × 18 in

There are many other good primulas from Japan and China, etc. but few so successfully perennial as the above species. However, those who desire to grow primulas, having retentive, moist soil in light shade or sun, could not do better than to start with the Candelabra Section—whose flowers are arranged in whorls up the stems. One of the most reliable is *P. japonica* (1871) [6–8] in some of its selected forms, such as 'Millar's Crimson', 'Etna' and 'Postford White'; these are closely followed by, but should be widely separated from, the more elegant *P. pulverulenta* (1905) [6–8], in rich crimson-purple on mealy stems, and Hew Dalrymple's pale pink Bartley strain. This strain, which many regard as the queen of the tribe, owes its inception to a pink self-sterile seedling found among plants grown by James Veitch at Combe Wood, Surrey, from collector's seed. The magenta-lilac *P. beesiana* [5–8] will assort well with the above, but it has a less elegant inflorescence. *P. burmanica* (1914) [5–8] is a similar colouring, but lacks the appealing dusting of white meal on the stems. Of sharper colouring are the orange-tinted *P. bulleyana* (1906) [6–8] and *P. chungensis* (1913) [6–8], and hybrids between these and *P. pulverulenta* and others have occurred many times. *P.* 'Bullesiana' [6–8] is a strangely mixed strain from orange-yellow to mauve; also known as 'Asthore Hybrids'. *P × chunglenta* [6–8] is first rate; 'Red Hugh' is a splendid vivid orange-red, breeding more or less true from seed, whereas there are several excellent ones whose names recall their gardens of origin: 'Rowallane Rose' and 'Ravenglass Vermilion' ('Inverewe'). These are sterile, but hearty growers, easily increased by division in September or early spring. *P. aurantiaca* [6–8] is again orange, seldom more than 46 cm (18 in), and has distinctive mahogany stems and leaf-midribs. *P. poissonii* [6–8] is one on its own, more closely related to the yellows following, but with flowers of intense crimson-purple. There are three fine yellow species: *P. helodoxa* (1912) [6–8], *P. smithiana* [6–8] and *P. prolifera*. They are strong colours and need careful placing. *P. prolifera* [6–8] has rich green leaves, green stems and orange buds and assorts best with the *P. pulverulenta × P. bulleyana* hybrids listed above; the green buds, paler leaves, and white-mealy stems of the other two—particularly *P. helodoxa*—render these suitable for assorting with *P. pulverulenta, P. beesiana* and *P. burmanica*. As intimated above *P. japonica* and its forms are best on their own; the type is naturalized at Arlington Court, North Devon. These primulas of the Candelabra Section are among the most striking and ornamental of moisture-loving plants for cool positions. *Hosta sieboldiana* provides a wonderful contrast.

SIKKIMENSIS
PRIMULAS

60 × 46 cm *2 ft × 18 in*	*Various*	*E.Summer*	D or S

The other group of great value is headed by *P. sikkimensis* [5–8]. *P. florindae* (above) is included here, but these other species are of considerably less stature and size, and not so perennial; they have the same deliciously fragrant bells, and narrower leaves. *P. sikkimensis* and *P. alpicola luna* [6–8] are pale yellow; *P. alpicola violacea* is in soft purplish shades; *P. secundiflora* [6–8] deep crimson-lilac. All have creamy white powder on stems, calyces and in the throats of the flowers. *P. waltonii* [5–8], of wine-dark colouring, has smaller flowers and is to be avoided because it hybridizes so freely with all these species and with *P. florindae*, usually to their detriment.

PTERIDOPHYLLUM, Papaveraceae. Anything less like a poppy could hardly be imagined. For cool positions in peaty soil.

racemosum

30 × 30 cm *1 × 1 ft*	*[5–8]*	*White*	*Spring*	DS

Japan. 1914. The neatly pinnate leaves form a small clump, overtopped by the spires of small white flowers. Intriguing and more attractive than it sounds.

PULMONARIA, Boraginaceae. The leaves of several bear grey spots of varying size, providing the reason for the Latin name and the term Lungwort. Rough-leafed herbs of considerable value for ground-cover, and early flowers; easily pleased in any fertile soil, preferably in part or full shade. Since they cross-fertilize freely, good forms are best increased by division; root-cuttings may be tried. All are more or less evergreen except *P. angustifolia*.

angustifolia

23 × 46 cm *9 × 18 in*	*[3–8]*	*Blue*	*Spring*	DS

Central Europe. 1731. Elliptic leaves, bristly and of plain dark green opening with the first flowers. These are carried in little sprays, pink in tight bud, opening a pure rich blue. Ideal as a ground-cover under forsythia. There are several named cultivars: 'Azurea', 'Mawson's Variety' and 'Munstead Variety' are very similar. There is also a white, *P.a.* 'Alba' recorded.

longifolia

30 × 46 cm *1 ft × 18 in*	*[5–8]*	*Blue*	*L.Spring/* *Summer*	DS

W. Europe. Narrow acutely pointed leaves, becoming narrower and smaller up the stems; dark green conspicuously spotted with white. Dense terminal heads of vivid blue flowers. 'Bertram Anderson' is a good violet-blue.

mollis

46 × 60 cm *18 in × 2 ft*	*[4–8]*	*Blue*	*Spring*	DS

E. Europe, N. Asia. 1816. The largest-growing species with velvety (not harshly hairy), long deep green leaves. The flowers are of rich deep blue, fading to purple and coral-red, though by far the most remain blue. Prolific and admirable, though seldom seen. The calyces are sticky. 'Royal Blue' (1977) originated at Hidcote. *P. vallarsae* [4–8] is a related species.

officinalis

| 25 × 46 cm | [4–8] | Pink/Blue | Spring | DS |
| 10 × 18 in | | | | |

Europe. Prior to 1597. *P. maculosa*. The old garden Spotted Dog, Lungwort or Soldiers and Sailors, is pretty enough with its bright pink flowers, which turn to light lilac-blue, but the flowers and spotted, heart-shaped leaves are less handsome than those of *P. saccharata*. Sometimes plants occur without spots and are then called *P.o. immaculata* (*P. obscura*). 'Sissinghurst White' is equally descriptive, like 'Barfield Pink' from Richard Nutt, *c*. 1980. Evergreen.

rubra

| 30 × 60 cm | [5–8] | Coral | E.Spring | DS |
| 1 × 2 ft | | | | |

Middle East. Prior to 1914. Velvety, long, rather light green leaves. The earliest to flower, the coral-red bells beginning to open by the end of January, but it is at its best in early March. Evergreen. There is a white variety recorded, *P.r.* 'Albocorollata'. A good red form, known as 'Bowles' Variety', has slightly spotted leaves. 'Redstart' is another. 'David Ward', which occurred *c*. 1986 in Beth Chatto's famous nursery, has leaves of pale green with a cream margin. A notable addition.

saccharata ★

| 30 × 60 cm | [4–8] | Pink/Blue | Spring | DRS |
| 1 × 2 ft | | | | |

Europe. Prior to 1863. *P. picta, P. grandiflora*. Handsome, long, elliptic leaves, more or less heavily spotted or almost wholly grey. The flowers are conspicuous, pink buds emerging from purplish velvety calyces, bright pink turning to blue. An extremely handsome plant in its best forms. Evergreen. The old 'Mrs Moon' is a good cultivar but is eclipsed by 'Margery Fish' (1974), named in honour of its originator. 'Boughton Blue' is a particularly good colour. 'Leopard' (1977) has regularly spotted leaves, flowers mainly pink; it occurred in the author's garden, *c*. 1970. 'Cambridge Blue' describes itself. 'Argentea' is a name given to forms with leaves wholly grey.

PULSATILLA, Ranunculaceae. These anemones are exquisite flowers of spring, enjoying full sunshine and a perfectly drained, fertile soil.

alpina ●

| 46 × 30 cm | [3–5] | White | Spring | PF S |
| 18 in × 1 ft | | | | |

Europe. The only form I have grown with any success in the open border is the yellow one, *P.a. apiifolia* or *Anemone sulfurea*. This for years produced above the ferny downy foliage great cups of clear sulphur yellow of sumptuous beauty, followed by silvery seed-heads. It thrived in my ordinary sandy soil with bone-meal and leafmould. This is a wonderful plant and worth some trouble.

vulgaris ● ★
   30 × 30 cm   *[5–7]*   *Various*   *Spring*   PF   S
   1 × 1 ft
Europe, Britain. *Anemone pulsatilla.* Pasque Flower. Reputed to grow wild in this country where the Danes shed their blood. A beautiful plant but barely tall enough for our purpose. The filigree-fern-like leaves make a lovely tuffet and the nodding flowers emerge from a veil of silky hairs. It is normally mauve, but varying to pink and purple. Many of the darker ones are in reality hybrids of *P. montana* [5–7] and *P. halleri* [5–7]. The original pink form, raised in 1904, was named 'Mrs Van der Elst', but is no longer in cultivation.

> "There is nothing extant in writing among Authors of any particular vertue, but they serve onely for the adorning of gardens and garlands, being floures of great beautie."—GH

There are some exciting, taller species and forms arriving from Eastern Europe in a variety of tints—one of almost forget-me-not blue named 'Budapest', attributable to *P. halleri*. *P. violacea* [5–7] from the Caucasus is a dull violet-blue.

PUYA, Bromeliaceae. One of the few plants in this Family which can be grown out of doors in Britain. It will thrive in maritime districts in our warmest counties, in hot sunny positions in well-drained soil, limy or acid.

alpestris ●
   90 × 60 cm   *[9–10]*   *Blue*   *E.Summer*   W   DS
   3 × 2 ft
Chile. Prior to 1869. It is well worth the cost and the effort to grow this rare plant, whose clump of prickly, long, narrow, greyish-green leaves forms a rosette; when it has gathered enough strength—after a few years—an astonishing yucca-like spike appears, with reddish stems and bracts; the flowers are three-petalled, of intense, satiny, sea-blue or "electric" blue. It is at once sumptuous and unusual, and grows happily at Clevedon Court, Somerset, and at Mount Stewart, Northern Ireland. Evergreen.

PYRETHRUM, see *Chrysanthemum coccineum.*

RANUNCULUS, Ranunculaceae. Most of the Buttercups prefer soil moist rather than dry and thrive in sun or part shade. *R. lingua*, a native, is a splendid bog plant, growing best in shallow water, and thus is outside the scope of this book. Its large buttercups are borne on 1.2 m (4 ft) stems in late summer.

aconitifolius
   90 × 90 cm   *[5–9]*   *White*   *Spring*   P   DS
   3 × 3 ft
Europe. 1596. A vigorous leafy plant, with deeply divided, dark green, buttercup-leaves. A galaxy of single white buttercups covers the branching stems for some weeks in April and early May. A good selection has been called *R.a. platanifolius* (*R.a.* 'Grandiflorus').

> "... pyramids of lucent handsome leafage, and its yard-high loose showers of lovely white stars."—RF

—'Flore Pleno' ● ★

60 × 46 cm	*White*	*L.Spring*	P D
2 ft × 18 in			

Sixteenth century. This exquisite double form, the Fair Maids of France–or of Kent—is a rare plant; over its clumps of deeply cut, dark green buttercup leaves, it disposes a branching mass of stalks, each ending in the most perfect, pure white, densely double buttons imaginable. It thrives in any fertile soil which does not dry out; sun or partial shade. Its French title is supposed to have connections with Huguenot refugees in the sixteenth century.

"... little double flowered form ... which sometimes dares to appear in lists even to the exclusion of that noble fairy, the type."—RF

acris

90 × 30 cm	*[4–8]*	*Yellow*	*L.Spring*	P D
3 × 1 ft				

Europe, N. Asia, Britain. I am not recommending the ordinary Buttercup for garden planting, but the large-flowered form, 'Stevenii', might be considered worthy of inclusion. It can be single or semi-double, and will achieve 1.2 m (4 ft). Hairy leaves.

—'Flore Pleno'

90 × 30 cm	*Yellow*	*L.Spring*	P D
3 × 1 ft			

1480. *R.a. multiplex.* This double yellow Batchelor's Buttons—found wild in Lancashire in the late sixteenth century— a variety of the tall Meadow Buttercup, has not much basal foliage and keeps quietly to its clump, not running or seeding. The wiry stems bear several branches, each poising a perfect rosette, dense and shining, of dazzling yellow. Ordinary soil, not too dry; sun.

bulbosus

30 × 30 cm	*[5–8]*	*Yellow*	*Spring*	D
1 × 1 ft				

The bulbous yellow buttercup has a double form, 'Pleniflorus', which is sometimes seen in gardens, and has been cultivated since the sixteenth century. There is also a pretty primrose-yellow form, 'F. M. Burton'.

cortusifolius ●

60 × 30 cm	*[8–9]*	*Yellow*	*E.Summer*	W S
2 × 1 ft				

Azores, etc. 1826. A somewhat tender species for sharply drained warm sunny positions. Bright green leaves, sometimes speckled with black, kidney-shaped at the base, but divided up the stem, which carries very large buttercups of brilliant yellow.

insignis ●

60 × 46 cm	*[8–9]*	*Yellow*	*E.Summer*	DS
2 ft × 18 in				

New Zealand. Like the celebrated white-flowered *R. lyallii* this is a difficult plant in the south of England, though it thrives in the north. They both have handsome, broad, rounded, toothed or crenate leaves, and splendid large blooms on branching stems. They are both sumptuous plants, worth a deal of trouble, and are perhaps best in a moist but well-drained soil with humus, in sun.

repens
   30 cm   *[4–9]*   *Yellow*   *Spring*   D
   1 ft
Europe. The Creeping Buttercup is a notorious weed.

—**'Flore Pleno'.** A rare old plant and a prolific spreader. Typical buttercup leaves. Double flowers tightly packed with shining bright yellow petals. A showy carpeter.

speciosus plenus ● ★
of gardens
   46 × 46 cm   *[4–8]*   *Yellow*   *E.Summer*   D
   18 in × 18 in
An old garden plant, sometimes labelled *R. gouanii,* and judging by the shape of the root, it may well be derived from this species. It makes typical buttercup-leaves of jagged outline and spotted with grey-white here and there, and the whole leafy clump is decorated with very large—5 cm (2 in) across—double rosette flowers of bright yellow for five or six weeks. A valuable plant for a moist patch, and inexplicably rare. If it is to be increased, divide the woody rhizomes after flowering, or in early autumn. Sometimes labelled *R. constantinopolitanus.*

RANZANIA, Podophyllaceae.

japonica
   46 × 30 cm   *[5–9]*   *Mauve*   *E.Summer*   DS
   18 in × 1 ft
Japan. A strange little woodlander for soil with humus. Two-lobed leaves appear at the top of the stem; above them are carried a flight of small rosy lilac blooms. A good companion to *Disporum, Prosartes* and the like.

REHMANNIA, Scrophulariaceae.

angulata ●
   60 × 46 cm   *[9–10]*   *Pink*   *E.Summer*   W   S
   2 × 1 ft
China. 1890. The handsome, lobed, hairy leaves create a good basal clump, from which arise the flowers on hairy stems; they are large, tubular, with large lobes, of a rich warm mauve-pink with yellow, spotted throat. Only for really warm gardens and perhaps best treated as a biennial. Tropical effect.

"The Rehmannias suggest in their flowers that a Foxglove has married a Salpiglossis."—RF

REINECKIA, Liliaceae. Close relative of *Speirantha* and *Convallaria;* for the same culture, with humus in part shade. Shy-flowering.

carnea
   30 × 30 cm   *[4–8]*   *Pink*   *E.Summer*   D
   1 × 1 ft
China, Japan. 1792. *Sansevieria sessiliflora.* Leaves like those of Lily-of-the-Valley, but narrower, and short sprays of starry light pink flowers with protruding stamens. A variegated form is recorded.

REYNOUTRIA, Polygonaceae.

japonica

2.4 × 1.2 m	[4–10]	White	Autumn	D
8 × 4 ft				

Japan. 1825. *Polygonum cuspidatum.* A vast, ineradicable weed of great beauty for the largest landscape. It is usually a pest wherever it occurs. It has rounded leaves. *R. sachalinense* is similar but has larger, longer leaves. There is a variegated form of the first, to trap the unwary, called 'Spectabilis', or sometimes *Polygonum sieboldii,* erroneously. It is less invasive; the leaves vary from being particoloured to wholly butter-yellow or deep cream; it is best in shade.

—compacta

1.2m × 90 cm	Pink	L.Summer	F D
4 × 3 ft			

Japan. 1935. This pretty plant was introduced under the name of *Polygonum* 'Reynoutria' and was said not to spread, but it shares some of its parents' propensity in this respect. *R.j. compacta,* of which a female form is in cultivation, is a gay, late-season plant, with leathery rounded leaves and multitudes of white flowers turning to deep rose and eventually to crimson seeds. Useful for making "rough places plain", and not unduly invasive.

RHAZYA, Apocynaceae.

orientalis ★

46 × 30 cm	[5–8]	Blue	Summer	P D
18 in × 1 ft				

Orient. 1889. This forms a slowly-increasing clump of wiry stems set with willowy leaves of grey-green tint. The flowers are small, starry, displayed in wide heads, of a soft grey-blue. Lovely in association with *Geranium* 'Russell Prichard', *Crambe maritima, Allium cernuum* and Rose 'Penelope'. Well-drained soil; sun. Closely allied to *Amsonia tabernaemontana,* which is a more leafy but less showy plant, with flowers of the same colour.

RHEUM, Polygonaceae. The common culinary rhubarb, *Rheum rhaponticum,* is by no means to be despised in flower, but one's visitors might look askance at its leaves in a bed or border! The following are all highly ornamental plants.

'Ace of Hearts'

90 cm × 1.2 m	[5–9]	Pink	E.Summer	D
3 × 4 ft				

Reputedly a hybrid between *R. kialense* and *R. palmatum.* It is a useful large-leafed plant for the smaller garden. The leaves are dark green, heart-shaped, and tinted with crimson on the reverse.

alexandrae ●

90 × 60 cm	[6–8]	Cream	E.Summer	DS
3 × 2 ft				

Szechuan. Smaller leaves than might be expected, of shining dark green. This rather tricky plant is noted for the large cream bracts which obscure the flowers; the tall spikes thus accentuated are different from anything else. The bracts become tinted with red as they age and act as a protection against rain for the flowers and ripening seeds. It grows best in cool moist climates. *R. nobile* [6–8] is from Nepal; it is similar but has not proved very amenable in cultivation. The bracts grow to 30 cm (1 ft) in width in nature.

australe
> *2.1 × 1.5 m*   *[5–9]*   *White/Red*   *E.Summer*   F   DS
> *7 × 5 ft*

Himalaya. *R. emodi*. Leaves broad and entire, with huge spikes of flowers in an erect plume. Seldom seen.

officinale
> *1.8 × 1.2 m*   *[5–9]*   *White*   *E.Summer*   F   D
> *6 × 4 ft*

Tibet. 1871. The medicinal rhubarb has magnificent green leaves, only slightly lobed, and spikes of creamy white flowers on arching branchlets.

palmatum
> *1.8 × 1.8 m*   *[5–9]*   *Crimson*   *E.Summer*   F   D
> *6 × 6 ft*

China. 1763. Though any form of this plant is worth growing, the following should be sought:

● ★ —'**Atrosanguineum**'. The leaves are large, very deeply cut. On emerging from the soil they are vivid red, and much of this colour is retained on the reverse of the leaves until flowering time. The flowers are of vivid cerise-crimson, in great fluffy panicles, and as with all rheums the seeds give later attraction. 'Bowles' Variety' and other clones are of similar quality. Apart from its own beauty it is one of the very few tall red-flowered plants for early summer, and is thus an asset at Hidcote, Gloucestershire, in the Red Borders.

—**tanguticum**. In this form, with leaves less deeply cut but often richly purplish tinted on both surfaces, the flowers are carried on erect side-shoots, making a less rewarding sight than in *R.p.* 'Atrosanguineum'. They may be white, pink or crimson on different clones.

RIGIDELLA, Iridaceae. Tender bulbous plants for warm sunny corners in our warmest counties.

flammea ●
> *60 × 30 cm*   *[9–10]*   *Red*   *E.Summer*   P   W   DS
> *2 × 1 ft*

Mexico. 1839. Most elegant pendulous flowers borne on a stout stem; they somewhat resemble three-petalled cyclamens, in bright orange-red with a long projecting stigma. The leaves are rich green, plaited, sword-like and elongate to about 1.2 m (4ft) after the flowers are over. *R. orthantha* [9–10] has larger, erect flowers. Plant about 7.5 cm (3 in) deep.

RODGERSIA, Saxifragaceae. A race of extremely noble plants, with grand foliage like large hands borne on stout stalks, 30 cm (1 ft) or more across, and imposing flower spikes. Suitable for moist soil, in sun or partial shade; they thrive in marshy ground and at the waterside. The flowers are carried on stout stems well above the foliage, and are of fluffy cream or pink effect, somewhat like those of *Filipendula* or *Astilbe*. The seed-heads of *R. aesculifolia* and *R. pinnata* develop reddish tints in autumn. While the several species are distinct and botanically separate, there seem to be many hybrids in gardens between *R. aesculifolia* and others.

aesculifolia ★

| 1.2 m × 60 cm | [5–8] | Cream/Pink | Summer | F | DS |
| 4 × 2 ft | | | | | |

China. 1902. Broad, crinkled, bronze-tinted leaves on hairy stalks, with the lobes extending down to the stalk. The flowers unfurl in crozier-fashion in clusters in a wide pyramid and vary from creamy white to creamy pink. Very decorative and extremely beautiful. *R. henrici* [5–8] from N. Burma is similar but has pink flowers turning to red as they age and is worth seeking.

"... enormous metallic foliage and foamy white blossom in crest over crest to the summit of the spumy pyramid."—RF

pinnata ★

| 90 × 60 cm | [5–8] | Pink | Summer | F | DS |
| 3 × 2 ft | | | | | |

China. 1902. As its name would suggest, the leaves are arranged in pairs, pinnately. The flowers are of cream-pink colouring—or white in 'Alba'—but the form to secure is ● ★ *R.p.* 'Superba', whose leaves are extra burnished and the flowers brilliant pink. Its origin is not recorded, and its leaves are not always pinnate. Superb at Rowallane, Northern Ireland, with blue-leafed hostas.

podophylla

| 90 × 90 cm | [5–8] | Cream | Summer | F | DS |
| 3 × 3 ft | | | | | |

Japan. 1880. Big jagged lobes distinguish these smooth leaves from the other species. They are bronzed when young turning to green, and taking on dark coppery tones as they mature in summer. The flowers are less fine than those of the other species. This plant is illustrated in colour in my book *Plants for Ground-Cover*.

sambucifolia

| 90 × 60 cm | [5–8] | White | Summer | F | DS |
| 3 × 2 ft | | | | | |

China. 1904. Having pinnate leaves, this is nearest to *R. pinnata*, but is a neater plant with elegant flower sprays in creamy white. The leaves are distinctly pinnate, with several inches of stalk between each pair of narrow leaflets.

ROMNEYA, Papaveraceae. The Californian Poppies are, as might be expected, ardent sun-lovers, for any deep and somewhat retentive soil. They are tricky to divide and best established by means of well-rooted pot plants. Their bold, branching stems may in mild areas remain alive above ground in the winter, but the effect is more satisfactory if all are cut away in the spring. The glaucous stems and deeply divided copious grey foliage make a lovely setting for the gracious flowers, which are markedly and sweetly fragrant. The roots spread freely and may travel some distance underground and come up through a paved path! For all that they are very valuable.

coulteri ●

| 2.1 m × 90 cm | [8–10] | White | Summer/ | P | DRS |
| 7 × 3 ft | | | Autumn | | |

S.W. California. 1875. The huge white poppies, with a great mass of dark yellow stamens, are silky and crinkled, gracious and lovely.

"The fairest plant that ever came to our land from that country of flowers, California."—WR

trichocalyx ●

| 2.1 m × 90 cm | [8–10] | White | Summer/ | P | DRS |
| 7 × 3 ft | | | Autumn | | |

S.W. California. This is a similar plant, distinguished by its habit of branching lower down—thus producing more flowers earlier—and by its bristly buds. ● ★ R. × hybrida [8–10] is the name given to hybrids between the two and though there is not a lot to choose between them all, the hybrid in commerce seems the most satisfactory; one has been named 'White Cloud' in the United States. It has sumptuous flowers and bold grey foliage with rounded lobes.

ROSCOEA, Zingiberaceae.

Fleshy rooted perennials which sometimes suffer frost-damage; it is best to plant them deeply and add a thick mulch in autumn. Though they are usually grown in peat beds, rock gardens and in shady places, and appreciate coolth and humus, they do not object to lime. R. auriculata and R. humeana are both natives of dry hillsides, the others frequent cooler positions. Other smaller species, such as R. alpina, are scarcely tall enough for inclusion in this book and are best grown on the rock garden. The genus is related to the Ginger, Zingiber, Cautleya and Hedychium, and always excite interest with their strange, orchid-like flowers, usually with hood aloft and labellum hanging. They can be safely divided when growth is just starting in spring.

auriculata ★ ●

| 46 × 46 cm | [7–9] | Purple | E./L.Summer | DS |
| 18 × 18 in | | | | |

Sikkim, Nepal, Tibet, etc. 1904. A fine leafy plant with long mid-green leaves with their bases clasping right round the stem, creating "ears" or auricles. The handsome flowers have drooping lower lobe or labellum; they are usually deep purple, but may be paler, particoloured or even white. Makes a handsome floriferous clump when established.

capitata

| 30 × 30 cm | [6–9] | Mauve | L.Summer | DS |
| 1 × 1 ft | | | | |

Nepal. 1822. R. purpurea var. purpurea of some authors. A narrow-leafed plant whose flowers may be of shades of purple or mauve, or pinkish to white. They emerge from hairy calyces.

cautleoides ★ ●

| 46 × 30 cm | [7–9] | Yellow | E.Summer | DS |
| 18 in × 1 ft | | | | |

China, Yunnan, etc. 1912. R. yunnanensis, R.y. purpurata, R. chamaeleon. Its synonyms call attention to the flowers which, though usually yellow in cultivation, may also be purple or occasionally white. The leaves are tall, narrow, upright. R. cautleoides 'Grandiflora' is a shorter, stocky plant with wide leaves and may be a hybrid with R. humeana. 'Beesiana' [7–9], a free-flowering yellow plant, has the leaf-characters of R. auriculata and may be a hybrid between it and R. cautleoides.

"... distinct from all else, and of a beauty quite apart."—WR

"... a plant of quite singular loveliness."—RF

humeana ★ ●

30 × 30 cm	[7–9]	Purple	E.Summer	DS
1 × 1 ft				

China, Yunnan. 1916. The broad almost horizontal leaves and the tall, hooded, upper segments of the flowers are distinguishing characters in this most handsome species. Though known in gardens mostly in its rich purple form, the colour in the wild varies to lilac, yellow and white. *R. forrestii* [7–9] has narrower segments.

purpurea ★

30 × 30 cm	[6–9]	Mauve	L.Summer	DS
1 × 1 ft				

India, Nepal etc. 1804. *R. procera, R. purpurea procera; R. purpurea* var. *purpurea* of some authors. Long, lance-shaped leaves of rich green. The flowers, with their protruding lower lobes, vary from purple to mauve, pink to white.

RUDBECKIA, Compositae. Coneflower. As in *Lepachis* and *Echinacea*, a character of *Rudbeckia* is the drooping circle of broad petals around the central cone of stigmas and stamens. Easily satisfied in sun in any fertile soil.

fulgida ★

60 × 30 cm	[4–9]	Yellow	Summer/	P D
2 × 1 ft			Autumn	

North America. 1760. *R. speciosa, R. newmanii.* This may be regarded as the type of several brilliant varieties or garden forms such as *R.f. sullivantii, deamii,* 'Goldsturm' (1937), etc., all prolifically bearing on erect stems over leafy clumps vivid yellow daisies with short, black, central cones, earning them the name of Black-eyed Susan. Happy in any fertile soil, moist rather than dry, in full sun. They are thrifty and satisfactory, being saved from the commonplace by their "fetching" black eyes.

laciniata

1.8–2.1 m	[3–9]	Yellow	Summer	P DS
× 60 cm				
6–7 × 2 ft				

North America. 1640. The species is not often seen in gardens. It is a wiry upstanding plant, with deeply laciniate leaves. Large single yellow flowers with greenish central knobs start to open at midsummer. 'Golden Glow' ('Hortensia') (1894) achieves 2.1 m (7 ft), a showy plant with brassy yellow double flowers. See also *R. nitida.*

maxima ●

1.2 m × 60 cm	[6–9]	Yellow	Summer	P D
4 × 2 ft				

Texas. *c.* 1818. There are many rudbeckias with yellow flowers and black centres, but there is nothing like this one. It has broad, upstanding, basal leaves of a distinctly glaucous hue, and the flowers with their characteristic drooping golden petals have great black cones in their centres. Sun; moist, good soil. Doubts have been expressed as to its hardiness but, in my experience in Surrey, without proof. It grows well at The Courts, Holt, Gloucestershire.

mollis

60 × 60 cm	*[6–9]*	*Yellow*	*Summer*	P	DS
2 × 2 ft					

Florida, Georgia. This bristly hairy plant adds one more good yellow daisy to the summer display. The centre is greenish brown, a contrast to many species. It grows best in sunny, rather dry, positions.

nitida

1.2 m × 60 cm	*[5–9]*	*Yellow*	*L.Summer*	P	D
4 × 2 ft					

S. USA. Closely related to *R. laciniata*, but the leaves are entire or only slightly lobed, and the flowers open for a lengthy display in late August. 'Herbstsonne' is a very tall plant achieving 2.1 m (7 ft), with very large single yellow flowers, with high green central knobs. 'Goldquelle' (1951) [3–9] is equally late; it has double flowers of brassy yellow, and is about 2.1 m (4 ft) high. Both these and *R. laciniata* need bright rich greenery around them to purify their colour, and assort well with *Artemisia lactiflora*.

subtomentosa

1.2 m × 60 cm	*[4–9]*	*Yellow*	*L.Summer*	P	D
4 × 2 ft					

North America. The downy, divided foliage at once distinguishes this from the others listed. The clear yellow flowers are freely produced over a long period and have black centres. A stalwart self-reliant plant at Wisley, Surrey.

SALVIA, Labiatae. Sage, *Salvia officinalis*, is a sub-shrub, and brief reference to its varieties is found in Cuttings from My Notebook, No. 2. Invariably sun-loving plants, they prefer well-drained soil; this particularly applies to the several tender species described below. Handsome foliage is found in *S. interrupta*, *S. argentea* (see Cuttings from My Notebook, No. 5), and *S. glutinosa*. The shrubby species, particularly *S. microphylla* and *S. greggii*, will in time build up to a good size but are apt to be spoiled by frost. As a rule the leaves and stems of all kinds are hairy, also the bracts, and the whole plant is often aromatic; the flowers are beautifully shaped, the upper petal arching forward in the shape of a hood, as in the White Dead Nettle.

argentea

90 × 60 cm	*[5–8]*	*White*	*Summer*	S
3 × 2 ft				

E. Mediterranean. 1594. A statuesque plant forming a great basal clump of large, woolly-white leaves the first year, to act as a plinth to the candelabra-like branching stems set with grey-white calyces and white hooded flowers. This needs full sun and a well-drained position, and both it and the similar *S. aethiopis* are best in our drier counties. They are excellent in dry walls.

aucheri

46 × 46 cm	*[6–8]*	*Purple*	*L.Summer*	CS
18 × 18 in				

Turkey etc. An unusual species in that the leaves are glabrous, sometimes glaucous, above, but purplish and pubescent below. Pairs of flowers are borne up the slender flower stems.

azurea

1.8 m × 60 cm	*[5–9]*	*Blue*	*L.Summer/*	W	CDS
6 × 2 ft			*Autumn*		

S.E. United States. 1806. For warm sunny gardens, where it will make a dense mass of ascending stems, clad in very narrow greyish green leaves. The flowers are clear blue (or white) in slender, dense spikes. A useful late-flowering plant. *S.a. pitcheri* is closely related, with hairy calyces and somewhat larger flowers in closer spikes.

bicolor

90 × 60 cm	*[7–9]*	*Purple*	*Summer*	S
3 × 2 ft				

Spain, North Africa. 1793. Spires of small violet blue—or mauve—flowers with pale lips and yellow dots, held well above large hairy basal leaves. *S. dichroa* (1871) from Morocco, is similar, but less hardy.

blepharophylla

46 × 46 cm	*[9–10]*	*Red*	*Summer*	W	CDS
18 × 18 in					

Mexico. 1930. Somewhat shrubby, and tender, needing a warm spot. The roots are fleshy and questing. Leaves small, shining dark green above, suitably contrasting with the slender spikes of vivid red flowers set in maroon calyces.

bulleyana

60 × 60 cm	*[5–9]*	*Yellow*	*L.Summer*	DS
2 × 2 ft				

China. *S. flava megalantha*. Rather coarse leaves form a good base to the spires of yellow flowers, with maroon lips. Not showy, but a handsome plant. Dark green deeply veined leaves.

candidissima

90 × 60 cm	*[6–9]*	*Yellow*	*Summer*	DS
3 × 2 ft				

S.E. Europe, Asia Minor. *S. odorata* is a synonym denoting the strong aromatic scent of all parts of the plant. Its white flowers held in yellow-green bracts up the long racemes are well suited with greyish basal leaves.

confertiflora

1.5 m × 60 cm	*[9–10]*	*Vermilion-*	*L.Summer/*	W	CDS
5 × 2 ft		*orange*	*Autumn*		

Brazil. An extra handsome plant with pointed bright green leaves, brownish below, and foetid when crushed. The long unbranched flower spikes are closely set with velvety red-brown calyces and vermilion-orange small flowers, with fine effect. It needs a warm position, in our warmer counties. A very useful late flower.

discolor

46 × 46 cm	*[9–10]*	*Violet*	*Summer*	W	S
18 × 18 in					

Peru. 1817. It is the "black and white" contrast which catches the eye. The calyces and underside of the leaves are densely white tomentose, the flowers darkest violet-blue, near black. Needs a particularly warm corner.

farinacea

    1.2 m × 60 cm   *[9–10]*   *Lavender*   *Summer/*   W   CS
    4 × 2 ft   *Autumn*

S. North America. 1848. This tender plant in its selected forms 'Blue Bedder' or 'Alba' is popular for summer bedding but is hardy in our warmest counties. The Mealy Sage is a handsome plant, the freely branching white stems being densely clothed with small flowers. Very long flowering period.

forskaohlei

    90 × 46 cm   *[8–10]*   *Purple*   *L.Summer*   S
    3 ft × 18 in

Asia Minor, etc. 1800. Quite hardy in a well-drained and sunny position. The leaves are very large, hairy and of varied shape, making a good base for the branching stems holding long spires of vivid blue-purple flowers, which have a reflexed upper lip and are marked with white or yellow in the throat.

fulgens ●

    90 × 60 cm   *[9–10]*   *Red*   *Summer*   W   CDS
    3 × 2 ft

Mexico. 1829. The Cardinal Sage is resplendent with vivid red flowers, large and hairy, set in purplish red calyces, in good spikes above a lush leafy plant. It is hardy in our warmest counties in sheltered corners. *S. gesneriiflora* [9–10], brought from Mexico in 1840, is similarly gorgeous.

glutinosa

    1.2 m × 90 cm   *[5–8]*   *Yellow*   *Summer*   DS
    4 × 3 ft

Europe, S.W. Asia. 1759. Jupiter's Distaff is a coarse, large-leafed, hairy plant. The flowers of pale yellow are of the usual hooded shape, in spikes. Useful for rough places.

greggii

    60 × 60 cm   *[9–10]*   *Crimson*   *Summer*   W   C
    2 × 2 ft

Texas, Mexico. 1885. Usually a conservatory plant, this is shrubby and grows well in our warmest counties against a sunny wall. Small neat leaves cover the twiggy growth; a long succession of small bright flowers in small clusters is produced from June onwards.

guaranitica ●

    1.5 m × 60 cm   *[9–10]*   *Blue*   *Autumn*   P W CD
    5 × 2 ft

South America. 1925. *S. ambigens, S. caerulea.* To see this plant in full flower in October, next perhaps to *Hypericum* 'Rowallane' or some silvery foliage, is to taste of the fullness of gardening—as at Knightshayes Court, Devon. The dark green leafy stems support numerous branching spikes of intense royal blue sage-flowers. Unfortunately it is not reliably hardy except in our warmest counties, and it usually needs some support. Some forms have almost black calyces, contributing considerably to the general effect.

haematodes ★

90 × 46 cm	*[6–9]*	*Lavender*	*E.Summer*	S
3 ft × 18 in				

Greece. 1938. Sometimes classed as a variant of *S. pratensis*. Large basal leaves form a rosette of dark green, above which arise branching, airy sprays, nearly leafless, of cool lavender-blue sage-flowers with a paler throat. A complete contrast in colour and form to peonies. Sun, well-drained soil; short-lived, but easy from seed. Exquisite when planted behind *Alchemilla mollis*. Compact forms or hybrids of richer colouring are 'Indigo' and 'Mittsommer'.

hians

60 × 60 cm	*[6–9]*	*Purple*	*E.Summer*	DS
2 × 2 ft				

Kashmir. 1830. Again a much-branched plant with plentiful spikes of purplish blue flowers over copious, large hairy leaves. The purplish brown hairy calyces add to the colour scheme.

"One of the best border salvias."—WR

hierosolymitana

60 × 60 cm	*[9–10]*	*Lavender*	*E.Summer*	DS
2 × 2 ft				

Lebanon, Palestine. Of similar character to *S. interrupta* and needing the same conditions, but far more compact and pleasing. Most beautiful, large, lavender-blue flowers on stems well above the clump of oval leaves.

indica

1.2 m × 60 cm	*[9–10]*	*Purple*	*E.Summer*	S
4 × 2 ft				

Middle East. *S. brachycalyx*. In a warm sunny place it will develop fine large lobed leaves, dark green and hairy, with much branched stems of large flowers; the pale lilac hood projects over dark purple lip. Striking.

interrupta

1.5 m × 90 cm	*[9–10]*	*Purple*	*Summer*	W	S
5 × 3 ft					

Morocco. 1867. The rather small violet-purple flowers marked white on the lip are a bit ineffective on the immense branching stems, standing elegantly over the big clump of large dark green hairy leaves, grey beneath. It is shrubby at the base and needs a warm corner in our warmer counties. *S. candelabrum* is similar.

involucrata

1.2 m × 90 cm	*[7–9]*	*Red*	*L.Summer/*	W	DS
4 × 3 ft			*Autumn*		

Mexico. 1824. A shrubby plant for sunny corners in our warmest counties. Smooth, long-pointed, rich green leaves. It is beautiful in bud, the flowers being protected by pink bracts. Large flowers of brilliant cerise-crimson are provided in 'Bethellii', a favourite form with long spikes.

jurisicii

46 × 46 cm	*[6–9]*	*Lilac*	*E.Summer*	DS
18 × 18 in				

Serbia. 1922. Attractive tufted perennial with spreading spikes of rich lilac flowers (occasionally white) which have the curious habit of growing upside-down. Much-divided leaves. A good plant for a sunny well-drained spot.

leucantha

90 × 60 cm	[9–10]	Violet/	Autumn	W CDS
3 × 2 ft		White		

Mexico. 1846. A tender sub-shrub which will thrive in the open only in our very warmest gardens, where it is useful and very beautiful, producing branching sprays of white flowers in woolly, violet-tinted calyces. The stems and the undersides of the pointed wrinkled leaves are grey-white.

microphylla

1.2 m × 90 cm	[9–10]	Crimson	E.Summer/	W C
4 × 3 ft			Autumn	

Mexico. 1829. *S. grahamii* is a synonym of the species but is often applied to *S.m. neurepia* in gardens. The species has very small leaves, dull green, nearly glabrous above and an endless display of small bright magenta-crimson flowers fading to a purplish tint. In very mild districts it makes a small shrub.

—**neurepia.** A well-known and gay shrubby plant, with bigger fresh green leaves. The flowers are brilliant scarlet. Highly effective from June onwards. Both kinds need a sunny wall in our warmest counties. It has made a large shrub against a wall at Knightshayes Court, Devon.

"... the large six-foot-high bush of *Salvia Grahamii* ... has begun its five months' display."—EAB

multicaulis

30 × 25 cm	[6–9]	Violet-purple	Summer	PF DS
1 ft × 10 in				

S.W. Asia. Often labelled *S. acetabulosa*. Greyish-green wrinkled leaves. The stems bear heads of flowers surrounded by conspicuous purplish calyces which expand later. Prior to 1930.

nemorosa ★

90 × 46 cm	[5–9]	Purple	Summer	D
3 ft × 18 in				

S.E. Europe. In its best-known hybrid clone 'Superba' (1900) (*S. virgata nemorosa*) (1913) it is a well-known bushy plant with many stems, each branching into many erect spikes of violet-blue flowers; the colouring is intense and enhanced by the crimson-purple bracts, which last in colour long after the flowers drop. Sun, any fertile soil. The ideal contrast for *Achillea filipendulina*. 'Lubeca' and 'East Friesland' (1955) are two good dwarf forms useful for the front of the border. They are equally rich in colour, achieving 46 cm and 75 cm (18 in and 2½ ft) respectively.

nutans

1.2 m × 60 cm	[5–9]	Lavender	Summer	DS
4 × 2 ft				

E. Europe. 1780. A good clump of dark, deeply veined leaves with waving, nodding, branching spires of small lavender-blue flowers.

patens ●

60 × 46 cm	[8–9]	Blue	Summer/	W CDS
2 ft × 18 in			Autumn	

Mexico. 1838. A half-hardy plant, but a true perennial in the warmest western counties. Large flowers on a compact leafy plant, of intense pure blue. 'Cambridge Blue' indicates its own colour; there is also a white, 'Alba'. Good at Powis Castle, Powys.

pratensis

1.2 m × 60 cm	[3–9]	Violet	Summer	DS
4 × 2 ft				

Europe, Britain. The Meadow Clary is a sturdy hardy plant forming a good basal clump of leaves with long spikes of rather dull flowers of violet-blue. White, pink and other forms of different tints have been named; *S.p. tenorii* is a richer blue colour and freer-flowering; 'Baumgartenii', rich violet. See also *S. haematodes* and *S. × sylvestris*.

przewalskii

1.2 × 90 cm	[5–9]	Violet	L.Summer	DS
4 × 3 ft				

China. A most handsome plant, with large, heart-shaped, pointed leaves, grey beneath, forming a big clump. Freely branching stems carry many rather disappointing purplish-rose flowers.

recognita

1.2 m × 60 cm	[6–9]	Lilac	Summer	S
4 × 2 ft				

Asia Minor. Broad basal foliage, distinctly crenate, gives rise to tall stems bearing widely spaced, large, lilac-blue, somewhat upturned, typical salvia-flowers. Close to *S. ringens*. Prior to 1929.

ringens

30 × 30 cm	[6–9]	Blue	E.Summer	S
1 × 1 ft				

Greece. A clumpy plant, woody at the base. Deeply divided leaves and short spikes of good violet-blue flowers.

rutilans

60 × 60 cm	[9–10]	Red	Winter	W CD
2 × 2 ft				

1873. This is not known in the wild but is close to *S. elegans* from Mexico. It starts to flower in autumn, and in very warm corners of gardens in our warmest counties will keep up a display till spring of spikes of rich red flowers. The leaves when crushed smell of pineapple. It thrives at Overbecks, Devon.

× **sylvestris**. [5–9]. The name covers hybrids between *S. nemorosa* and *S. pratensis*. The two following plants are believed to have these two parents, the first occurring in Miss R. B. Pole's garden near to *S. nemorosa* and *S. haematodes*, which is sometimes classed as a variant of *S. pratensis*.

—**'Lye End'** ★

1.5 m × 60 cm		Lavender	Summer	P D
5 × 2 ft				

1969. In growth like an enlarged *S. haematodes*, with fine upstanding candelabra-like open spikes. The numerous flowers are of lavender-blue held in purplish-brown calyces, and the whole makes good effect for many weeks. Dark green foliage of quality, deeply veined but smooth.

—'**Mainacht**'

| 60 × 30 cm | *Indigo* | *E.Summer* | D |

2 × 1 ft

'May Night'. Probably *S. pratensis* × with *S. nemorosa*, this is a useful plant to give deep colour in May and June. It is similar in growth to *S. nemorosa* 'Lubeca', but has larger hooded flowers of darkest indigo-velvet with purple bracts. Gorgeous with *Paeonia officinalis* or *Papaver orientale*. Of German origin, 'Indigo' is a noted hybrid of *S. haematodes*, and is of good rich violet-blue; 46–60 cm (1½–2 ft); summer-flowering over a long period.

uliginosa ●

| 1.5 m × 46 cm | *[8–9]* | *Blue* | *Autumn* | P W D |

5 ft × 18 in

South America. 1912. *S. azurea* (of gardens). A graceful tall plant, usually needing support. The foliage is broad and saw-edged; the waving sprays of clear azure blue flowers in stout branching spikes are unique in the garden, and last for many weeks. It needs a warm sheltered position in moist soil and is not hardy in cold districts. A graceful contrast to *Canna iridiflora*.

verticillata

| 1.2 m × 60 cm | *[5–9]* | *Blue* | *L.Summer* | DS |

4 × 2 ft

Europe, Caucasus. 1594. A stately species, well-leafed all the way up the stems. Long, arching spikes of purplish buds open into small violet-blue flowers. The white variety 'Alba' has green buds, and greyish foliage. Not showy. 'Purple Rain' is a richly coloured form with conspicuous purple calyces.

SAMBUCUS, Caprifoliaceae. A herbaceous representative of the common Elder, suitable for landscape grouping or the less sophisticated parts of the garden, in sun, in any soil.

ebulus

| 90 × 90 cm | *[3–9]* | *White* | *Summer* | F CDS |

3 × 3 ft

Europe, North Africa. Occasionally seen as a wild plant in Britain. It resembles the common Elder in foliage, flower, fragrance and berries, but dies to the ground each winter.

SANGUISORBA, Rosaceae. Burnet. Vigorous perennials, increasing fairly freely at the root, delighting in full sun and moist soil. They usually need support, but with their elegant pinnate foliage and long bottle-brush flowers they bring something fresh to the late summer borders.

canadensis

| 1.8 m × 60 cm | *[3–8]* | *White* | *L.Summer* | P D |

6 × 2 ft

E. North America. 1633. *Poterium canadense*. Green leaves and a copious supply of white flowers.

dodecandra

| 1.2 m × 60 cm | *[4–8]* | *White* | *Summer* | P DS |

4 × 2 ft

Alps. 1833. *S. vallistellinae*. Usually after midsummer, the nodding white "catkins" are conspicuously beautiful.

obtusa

| 1.2 m × 60 cm | [4–8] | Pink | Summer | P | D |
| 4 × 2 ft | | | | | |

Japan. 1860. The Japanese Burnet has a lovely colour scheme in its greyish, handsome leaves overtopped by sheaves of large bottle-brush flowers in rich rose-pink. There is also a white variety, *albiflora*.

officinalis

| 1.2 m × 60 cm | [4–8] | Reddish | L.Summer | P | D |
| 4 × 2 ft | | | | | |

Northern Hemisphere. A leafy, weedy plant whose variety 'Rubra' may be considered worth its space. The small red-brown heads create a good impression in the mass.

tenuifolia

| 1.2 × 60 cm | [4–8] | Pink/White | Summer | P | DS |
| 4 × 2 ft | | | | | |

China. 1874. The leaves being finely cut and narrow give a feathery appearance. I particularly like the white form; the flowers are borne well aloft, like a shower of rain. Small drooping "catkins".

SAPONARIA, Caryophyllaceae.

× lempergii

| 30 × 30 cm | [4–8] | Pink | L.Summer | | C |
| 1 × 1 ft | | | | | |

S. cypria × S. haussknechtii. Valuable hybrid for a long flowering season and frontal position. The only selected cross is 'Max Frei' which originated in Germany. Raised by Dr Fritz Lemperg. A mass of fragile stems, clear rose-pink flowers, resembling pinks.

officinalis

| 75 × 90 cm | [4–8] | White/ | Summer | | D |
| 2½ × 3 ft | | Crimson | | | |

Europe, Asia. Bouncing Bet; Soapwort (the lather from the leaves is a delicate cleanser for old tapestries, etc. and was used for this at Uppark, Sussex; it grows in the garden). Naturalized in Britain and well able to hold its own, with its invasive roots and procumbent stems. Campion-like flowers, in singles and doubles, white or pink, also a rich crimson-purple; 'Albo Plena', 'Roseo Plena', 'Rubra Plena'. Many forms have been in cultivation since the seventeenth century. Coarse and untidy.

SARRACENIA ●Sarraceniaceae.

purpurea

| 30 × 30 cm | [6–9] | Maroon | E.Summer | | DS |
| 1 × 1 ft | | | | | |

E. United States. 1640. An insectivorous plant, closely related to *Darlingtonia*, but the leaves are flagon-shaped, of greenish brown. Elegant nodding flowers carried singly on stout stalks. *S. rubra* [6–9] is similar with taller leaf-tubes. *S. flava* [7–9] has still narrower leaf-tubes and remarkably beautiful, nodding, clear yellow flowers with a strong odour. They require constant moisture in a mixture of growing sphagnum moss and peat and are occasionally cultivated in our milder counties, when they will reproduce the brightest green tints in envious plantsmen. It is naturalized in bogs in Central Ireland.

SAUROMATUM, Araceae. The Monarch of the East will produce flowers even if the dry corm is placed in the living-room, but however interesting or surprising this may be, it is as a foliage, rather than as a flowering, plant that it should be considered in the garden.

venosum

60 × 60 cm	*[9–10]*	*Brown*	*E.Summer*	**W**	**D**
2 × 2 ft					

Himalaya, etc. 1815. *S. guttatum.* The Lords and Ladies flowers are of purple and brown, with long protruding spadix. The brown-dappled, almost reptilian, leaf stalks arise later, branching into splendid, deeply lobed, umbrella-like leaves. It has proved hardy for many years in Surrey but needs a sheltered position in full sun.

SAXIFRAGA, Saxifragaceae. Most of the species are saxatile and will be found in books on alpine plants. *S. rotundifolia* is a rather undistinguished woodlander of easy culture; it has rounded leaves and airy sprays of white flowers speckled with pink. The London Pride group have been dealt with in my *Plants for Ground-Cover*; suffice it to say here that apart from the hybrid *S × umbrosa* (of gardens), with wedge-shaped leaf bases, the most spectacular in flower and leaf of the group is *S. geum* 'Dentata', with orbicular, distinctively toothed leaves and even more luxuriant flower sprays than London Pride.

fortunei

46 × 30 cm	*[4–7]*	*White*	*Autumn*	**P**	**DS**
18 in × 1 ft					

China, Japan. 1863. One of the last plants to flower. Airy sprays carry a galaxy of small white flowers above a rosette of broad, glistening green leaves with reddish reverses. A handsome plant, even if it did not flower; it is useful for picking with late nerines. It enjoys a cool shady place. *S. cortusifolia* [4–7] is smaller, but earlier.

"... for a well-sheltered corner, where autumn is not likely to hurt the foot-high star-showers of pure white blossoms ..."—RF

—**'Wada's Variety'** is a sumptuous form from Japan whose rather shorter flowering shoots contrast well with the mahogany-red stalks and leaves.

—**'Windsor'** is white and grows to 60 cm (2 ft) in the Savill Gardens, Windsor, and at Knightshayes Court, Devon.

mandschuriensis

46 × 30 cm	*[4–8]*	*White/*	*Summer*	**DS**
18 in × 1 ft		*Pink*		

N. China, Manchuria, Korea. 1917. Another very handsome plant, with rounded fleshy leaves and rounded heads of starry flowers of pink or white.

pensylvanica

90 × 46 cm	*[5–8]*	*Whitish*	*Summer*	**DS**
3 ft × 18 in				

North America .1732. With its handsome, large hairy leaves, and reddish flower stems branching into copious bud this plant is full of promise. Its flowers are, however, poor, of dirty greenish white. Cool woodland conditions.

SCABIOSA, Dipsacaceae. Sun-lovers for any fertile soil, well drained and preferably limy. On acid soils *S. caucasica* is apt to be short-lived.

'Butterfly Blue' ★ is reputedly a hybrid with the Field Scabious, *Knautia* or *Scabiosa arvensis*, a native of Europe including Britain. It was put into commerce in 1985 and combines the refinement of *S. columbaria* with the larger flowers of the *Knautia*. July–October. 46 × 46 cm (18 × 18 in) [5–8]. There is also 'Butterfly Pink' with flowers of lilac-pink.

caucasica ● ★

60 × 60 cm	*[4–9]*	*Blue*	*E./L.Summer*	P	D
2 × 2 ft					

Caucasus. 1803. This popular florists' cut-flower can be raised from seeds but there are many named varieties available to tint. 'Clive Greaves' (1929) has long been regarded as a prolific and lovely lavender-blue; there are darker clones like 'Moerheim Blue', also good creamy whites, 'Loddon White' (1958) and 'Miss Willmott' (1935). The flowers of all are wide and full of quality, and produced without stint for a long period on long stalks. The longest display is obtained from young plants and therefore they should be divided every few years in spring. The leaves are deeply incised on the stems, entire basally, and make an attractive clump of light green.

"The finest perennial in my garden, it flowers from early summer to late autumn."—WR

columbaria ★

90 × 90 cm	*[5–8]*	*Lilac-blue*	*L.Summer*	PF	DS
3 × 3 ft					

Europe. The Small Scabious, found on our chalky hills, is a worthy garden plant. It is an exact counterpart of *S. ochroleuca*, and the two grown side by side make a complementary colour scheme of rare beauty.

graminifolia ★

46 × 46 cm	*[7–9]*	*Lilac*	*Summer/*	PF	CDS
18 × 18 in			*Autumn*		

S. Europe. 1683. One of the prettiest short plants for a sunny well-drained border, where it will make dense mats of narrow silvery foliage. Over this, on stalks 30 cm (1 ft) high, appears a long succession of lilac daisies. 'Pinkushion' is a rosy variant by Alan Bloom.

minoana ★

60 × 60 cm	*[6–8]*	*Pink*	*Summer*	P	CDS
2 × 2 ft					

c. 1969. Crimea. The leaves are simple, greyish-hairy, and the pale lavender-pink flowers are on long stalks. Similar in general appearance to *S. graminifolia*, but larger in all parts with broader leaves. A pleasing grey-and-pink plant for colour schemes in warm dry conditions. A very good dwarf shrub.

ochroleuca ★

90 × 90 cm	*[4–7]*	*Lemon*	*L.Summer*	PF	DS
3 × 3 ft					

S.E. Europe. 1517. Since the crimson *S. rumelica* is now known as *Knautia*, and the giant lemon scabious is now *Cephalaria*, the genus is limited to these few species. The present makes a delightful wiry mass of stems with pretty cool yellow flowers, produced for many weeks. The whole plant is refined and the foliage dissected. See also under *S. columbaria*, of which it is sometimes considered to be a variety.

SCHIZOSTYLIS, Iridaceae. Though the Kaffir Lily hails from a warm part of the world, it is hardy at least in our warmer counties, but needs a lot of moisture during the summer to enable it to throw up good flower spikes in autumn. It is said to thrive best where the air is damp. It appears to grow well in almost any fertile soil, in full sun, and its freely-increasing roots quickly make a mat. To keep up the production of good flower stems the thick roots should be divided in spring every few years, and moved to a fresh place.

coccinea ● ★

60 × 23 cm	*[6–9]*	*Crimson*	*E.Autumn*	P	D
2 ft × 9 in					

South Africa. 1864. Kaffir Lily or Crimson Flag. A most useful grassy-leafed plant which in flower resembles a miniature *Gladiolus*. The silky, cup-shaped blooms of rich crimson with a coppery glint are held in slender spikes in September and October, just when such things are most welcome. It grows like a weed at Trengwainton, Cornwall. The following selected clones are preferable to the normal crimson species.

A quite new variety 'Tambara' (1970), collected by Lady Drewe in Rhodesia, opens the season in August with large flowers of warm rose-pink. After this *S. coccinea* and the preferable *S.c.* 'Major' or 'Gigantea', with superlative crimson flowers, are followed by the well-known pale pink 'Mrs Hegarty', an Irish variety named in 1921. Then there is The Plantsmen's 'Sunrise' with fine large pink flowers, newly on the market, 'Professor Barnard' in deep dusky pink, and two newer pinks, 'Rosalie', Orpington Nurseries, Surrey, and 'November Cheer', Alan Bloom's sport from 'Major'. Lastly 'Viscountess Byng', raised prior to 1933, which is a strong plant carrying on the flowering period well into November; it would not flower for its namesake in the dry air of Essex.

"... a great difficulty in a light dry soil ... they were watered until rain came."—CWE

SCILLA, Liliaceae. For Bluebells, see *Endymion*.

peruviana

46 × 30 cm	*[7–10]*	*Violet*	*E.Summer*	P	DS
18 in × 1 ft					

Mediterranean Region. 1607. This achieved its exotic name from the fact that it reached the port of Bristol in a ship named "Peru"! A freely increasing bulb for hot sunny positions, having green, flopping leaves. The broad dense heads of violet-blue—or white—stars are conspicuous, and gorgeous with scarlet tulips.

SCOPOLIA, Solanaceae. Coarse, leafy plants, useful for their early flowering, and tolerance of shade, in any dryish fertile soil

carniolica

60 × 60 cm	*[5–8]*	*Yellowish*	*E.Spring*	DS
2 × 2 ft				

C. and S.E. Europe, Russia. 1780. The orange, or reddish or yellowish flowers are mostly green outside and appear with the very early leaves, which become gross and overbearing later. *S.c. hladnikiana* is a better known plant, but a tongue twister.

SCORZONERA, Compositae.

purpurea

60 × 23 cm *2 ft × 9 in*	*[5–8]*	*Purple*	*E.Summer*	P	DRS

E.Europe. 1759. Salsify. Perhaps because its roots are so tasty when cooked—as are those of the Common Viper's Grass, *S. hispanica* (biennial)—this pretty plant is seldom grown in the flower garden. The long narrow leaves give no promise of the beauty of the daisy-rosette flowers, borne in succession; purplish or pinkish.

SCROPHULARIA, Scrophulariaceae.

aquatica
'Variegata'

60 × 30 cm *2 × 1 ft*	*[5–9]*	*Foliage*	*Summer*	CD

The water Figwort has minute brown flowers and is a British weed, but this variegated form must rank high among plants with leaves splashed and striped with cream. A statuesque evergreen plant forming a basal clump with ascending rigid stems, clothed at intervals with opposite leaves. It is best in semi-shade and makes a splendid contrast with *Ligularia* 'Desdemona'. Cut off the flower spikes to prevent seeding. The leafy stems last well in water. Evergreen, fibrous-rooted. This plant is often erroneously attributed to *S. nodosa* (Knotted Figwort), which is a deciduous plant with tuberous roots. It is also known as *S. auriculata*.

SCUTELLARIA, Labiatae. The native species is known as Skullcap on account of the curiously shaped seed-capsules, a character shared by all species. The following is an easily grown, sun-loving plant and is the only tall species of any merit that has come my way.

canescens

90 × 60 cm *3 × 2 ft*	*[4–9]*	*Lavender*	*L.Summer*	PF	DS

E. and Central USA. *S. incana.* An erect plant covered with sage-grey leaves. The flowers are in branching elegant spikes, quite small, lavender-blue, but make a good effect in the mass, for all cool colour schemes. A lovely plant when well grown.

SEDUM, Crassulaceae. Stonecrop flowers are beloved by butterflies. All the kinds thrive in full sun in well-drained fertile or even poor soils. They are of a "succulent" nature, with thick, fleshy leaves.

aizoon

46 × 46 cm *18 × 18 in*	*[4–9]*	*Yellow*	*Summer*	PF	CD

Far East. 1757. *S. maximowiczii.* A comparatively early-flowering plant making a stout root from which ascend stems with fleshy, toothed green leaves. At the top is a flat head of yellow stars. Its more noted development is 'Aurantiacum', a dusky beauty with reddish stems, dark green leaves and gorgeous dark yellow flowers followed by reddish seed capsules.

alboroseum

30 × 60 cm	*[4–9]*	*Pinkish*	*L.Summer*	P	CD
1 × 2 ft					

Far East. 1860. Clump-forming but with sprawling shoots. The fleshy grey-green leaves are a good foil for the flat heads of white stars with pink eyes. 'Medio-variegatum' has leaves heavily marked with creamy yellow; green reversions should be pulled out from the base of the plant as soon as they appear.

"One of the best patches of soft, creamy yellow in the whole garden is provided by a variegated form."—EAB

'Autumn Joy' ★

60 × 60 cm	*[3–10]*	*Pink*	*E.Autumn*	PF	CD
2 × 2 ft					

'Herbstfreude'. A hybrid, probably between *S. spectabile* and *S. telephium,* which avoids the puce of the former and is a remarkably good plant. The flowers are borne in large flat heads, of rich pink turning to salmon-bronze and later coppery red. The plants quickly make a handsome clump of toothed, grey-green, fleshy leaves which, like that of *S. spectabile,* is beautiful through the summer. Unless divided from time to time in the spring, the stems tend to overcrowd and flop away from the centre of the clump. Excellent for autumn effect with *Ceratostigma willmottianum* and *Caryopteris × clandonensis*; it does well in clay soil at Lytes Cary, Somerset, but is not particular

kirilowii

46 × 46 cm	*[4–9]*	*Yellow/Red*	*L.Summer*	D
18 × 18 in				

W. China, Tibet, etc. 1859. A good, late-flowering, erect plant with light green leaves with jagged edges. The flat flower heads are yellow, or dark brick-red in 'Rubrum'.

maximum

60 × 60 cm	*[4–9]*	*Yellow*	*L.Summer*	PF	CD
2 × 2 ft					

Europe. 1794. Succulent leaves like those of *S. spectabile* and flat flower-heads of palest yellow stars. In *S.m. atropurpureum* the foliage is of rich dark maroon, bloomy and smooth. The flat flower-heads of tiny reddish stars tone in well with the general scheme. Full sun; rich, drained soil. Sometimes considered a sub-species of *S. telephium.* Leaves opposite.

"... by far the most important is *atropurpureum,* so called from the vivid purple of the stems and large fleshy leaves."—WR

rosea

30 × 30 cm	*[2–8]*	*Yellow*	*Spring*	CDS
1 × 1 ft				

Northern Hemisphere. *S. rhodiola* or *Rhodiola rosea.* The Rose Root is a fascinating plant when the young shoots are growing up, clad in small, glaucous, toothed leaves, richly ornamented by the deep pink flower buds. They later develop into heads of small yellow stars.

spectabile ★

46 × 46 cm	*[4–9]*	*Pink*	*L.Summer*	PF	CD
18 × 18 in					

China. The fleshy, glaucous-grey clump of leaves is beautiful through the summer and each stem produces a large flat head of tiny starry flowers in September, in chalky mauve-pink, making a strange contrast to tortoiseshell and peacock butterflies that love to sip its nectar. 'Brilliant' and 'Meteor' are two selected clones of more vivid and decisive colouring; 'September Glow' is reputedly even darker. 'Iceberg' is a good white.

—**'Savill Burgundy'** is a richly coloured seedling (both leaf and flower), probably from this species, 30 cm (1 ft) [4–9].

'Sunset Cloud' ★

30 × 30 cm	*[4–9]*	*Wine-purple*	*L.Summer*	CD
1 × 1 ft				

Raised by Jim Archibald; has dark glaucous foliage and conspicuous heads of rich wine-purple flowers. This is one of two good short growing hybrids (the other is 'Vera Jameson'—see below) that have come to the fore lately, raised *c.* 1972; they are possibly both descended from 'Ruby Glow', which is rather short for inclusion though a worthy frontal plant, with glaucous foliage and ruby-pink flowers in late summer. The other parent may be *S. maximum atropurpureum.*

telephium

46 × 30 cm	*[4–9]*	*Purplish*	*L.Summer*	PF	CD
18 in × 1 ft					

Europe, Britain. Orpine. This British wild plant would scarcely find a place in our garden were it not for Gertrude Jekyll's selected clone 'Munstead Red'. The stems are inclined to flop, but bear toothed, fleshy, dark green leaves, purplish-tinted in this clone, and the flat heads are of dusky chocolate-red. Useful for giving a sombre touch to late colour schemes, or as a contrast to white colchicums. *S.t.* 'Roseo-Variegatum' has leaves of pinkish colouring in spring, turning green later. *S.t.* 'Borderi' has extra greyish leaves and pleasing heads of coppery rose. Leaves alternate.

'Vera Jameson'

23 × 23 cm	*[4–9]*	*Pinkish*	*L.Summer*	CD
9 × 9 in				

Introduced by Joe Elliott; has glaucous purple leaves and heads of dusky pink. One of two good short growing hybrids (the other is 'Sunset Cloud'—see above).

SELINUM, Umbelliferae.

tenuifolium ★

90 cm–1.5 m	*[6–9]*	*White*	*Summer*	P	DS
× 60 cm					
3–5 × 2 ft					

Himalaya. *Oreocome candollei*. In more spacious days this used to be grown as a "lawn specimen" (William Robinson). It is a very ornamental Cow-Parsley with very finely cut leaves and handsome flat heads of white flowers with black anthers. Sun, ordinary soil. *S. carvifolia* is similar, but seldom grown.

> "... the queen of umbellifers, with its almost transparent tender greenness and the marvellously lacy pattern of its large leaves ... the most beautiful of all fern-leafed plants."—EAB

SENECIO, Compositae. For other species of *Senecio*, see *Ligularia*.

cineraria

60 × 60 cm	*[8–10]*	*Silver*	*Summer/*	P	W	CDS
2 × 2 ft			*Autumn*			

S. Europe. 1633. *Cineraria maritima.* Often used as a bedding plant, this shrubby grey-leafed plant is quite at home as a perennial in maritime and other warm districts, in well-drained soils. The yellowish heads of small daisy flowers are no particular asset. Two specially silvery-grey forms, even silvery white, are 'White Diamond' and 'Hoar Frost'. Superb with blue Agapanthus. *S. leucostachys* has more finely divided leaves.

doronicum

30 × 30 cm	*[5–9]*	*Yellow*	*E.Summer*	DS
1 × 1 ft				

C. and S. Europe. 1705. Forms a good tuft or mat of tongue-like dark green leaves, over which are poised the upright, bright yellow, substantial daisies.

pulcher

46 × 46 cm	*[8–10]*	*Magenta*	*Autumn*	P	DS
18 × 18 in					

Uruguay. 1872. A hairy plant, unique on account of the colour and season of its flowers. The dark green, leathery, hairy leaves are surmounted by the stems, each carrying several good-sized dandelions of most brilliant cerise-magenta. It needs a well-drained but deep soil, in a sunny corner in our warmer counties. A good contrast for *Aster ericoides* and silverlings.

"... successful in breaking away from the household traditions, for its daisies flaunt a fierce crimson-magenta with an eye of gold."—ATJ

smithii

1.2 m × 60 cm	*[7–9]*	*White*	*Summer*	F	DS
4 × 2 ft					

S. Chile, Falkland Islands. 1895. A coarse plant with flaccid, shining, puckered large leaves of greyish green, a foot or more high, surmounted by large plumes of small lemon-white, yellow-eyed daisies followed by fluffy white seed-heads. A pleasant change from the green and yellow of the more usual *Ligularia* species, with which it shares a liking for rich moist soil.

tanguticus

1.5 m × 60 cm	*[6–9]*	*Yellow*	*E.Autumn*	P	D
5 × 2 ft					

China. 1902. An invasive-rooted plant, with pretty divided foliage up the erect stems. The flower-heads are pointed and filled with tiny bright yellow daisies, much like a *Solidago*. The plant's chief attraction is that the seed-heads are pale and fluffy and stand elegantly aloft until winter really arrives, and are beautiful against berried shrubs. Any reasonable soil will satisfy it.

SERICOCARPUS, Compositae. Close relative of *Aster* and giving no more trouble in cultivation.

conyzoides

60 × 60 cm *2 × 2 ft*	*[4–9]*	*White*	*Autumn*	P	DS

North America. 1778. *S. asteroides.* Closely resembles *Aster macrophyllus,* with neater growth and paler flowers. Not in the front rank of autumnals but it forms an attractive clump, long in flower.

SERRATULA, Compositae. Plants for any fertile soil in full sun. The several species bear small Knapweed flowers in dusky puplish tones on stiff stems over tumps of divided foliage. The species are seldom seen since they are scarcely ornamental; white forms are still more rare in gardens but have some appeal. Perhaps the most conspicuous species are *S. quinquefolia* [5–8] from the Caucasus, (1804), Summer, or *S. tinctoria seoanii* (*S. shawii*) [5–8].

SIDALCEA, Malvaceae.

malviflora ★

1.2 m × 46 cm *4 ft × 18 in*	*[5–8]*	*Various*	*Summer*	PF	D

California. 1838. The garden forms of this species make excellent basal clumps of ground-covering foliage. The flowers, carried in stately branching spikes, are silky and like small hollyhocks. Sun, ordinary soil. *S. candida* provides the only white, but its flowers are rather small. There are many named hybrids or clones which are preferable to the species, and I find the light pinks are by far the most telling in the garden; the dark ones are muddy and subdued. 'Sussex Beauty' remains the loveliest of the clear pinks; 'Reverend Page Roberts' and 'Mrs T. Anderson' (1964) are a tone darker, while 'Elsie Heugh' (1936) is the palest, with prettily fringed petals. These sometimes need some support, which is not required by 'Loveliness' nor by Alan Bloom's 'Oberon' and 'Puck' in clear pink, both 90 cm (3 ft) or so.

SILENE, Caryophyllaceae. Easily grown in sun in any fertile soil

asterias

30 × 23 cm *1 ft × 9 in*	*[5–8]*	*Crimson*	*E.Summer*	P	DS

S.E. Europe. 1895. The smooth leaves of the basal rosettes lead one to expect nothing special, but the tiny flowers form a flat head of refulgent crimson-maroon. For frontal positions in sun.

dioica

60 × 30 cm *2 × 1 ft*	*[5–8]*	*Pink*	*E.Summer*		D

Europe, etc. *S. diurna*; formerly classed as *Melandrium rubrum.* The Red Campion is seldom grown in gardens, but 'Flore Pleno' is an ancient cultivar which charms whenever seen. Blowsy rose-red flowers over dark hairy leaves. There are two forms in cultivation; the taller is to be preferred.

—'Richmond' ● ★

50 × 60 cm *20 in × 2 ft*		*Pink*	*Spring*	P	D

This occurred in the Royal Park at Richmond, *c.* 1978. From the usual dense clump of dark green hairy leaves is put up a display over many weeks of brilliant, "shocking" pink, semi-double flowers. Excellent with grey-leafed plants. 'Compacta' is only a few inches high.

fimbriata
> 60 × 60 cm   [5–8]   White   Summer   D
> 2 × 2 ft

Caucasus. 1803. A hairy, dark green-leafed plant, much like the White Campion of the hedgerow. The freely branching stems have white flowers with heavily fringed petals, in baggy calyces. A second crop can be induced by cutting back— if you really want them.

SILPHIUM, Compositae. Coarse yellow late-flowering daisies for any fertile soil in sun, *S. perfoliatum* (1766) is occasionally seen and reaches 1.8 m (6 ft) in height, but I should not want it in my garden.

laciniatum
> 1.8 m × 90 cm   [5–8]   Yellow   L.Summer   P   DS
> 6 × 3 ft

Central and S.E. USA. 1761. The beautiful much divided foliage is highly attractive, more so than the small yellow daisies. Has earned the name of Compass Plant because its leaves turn their faces to the east or west to minimize the heat of the sun; thus they point north and south.

terebinthinaceum
> 1.5 m × 90 cm   [4–8]   Yellow   Summer   S
> 5 × 3 ft

Central and S.E. USA. The Prairie Dock has undistinguished yellow flowers in a cluster at the top of a tall stem. Below, the giant leaves reach 90 cm (3 ft) in height; they are rough, flat, dark green and extremely handsome, borne on long stalks, lasting in water. Would serve as a punkah on a hot day. It is a very noble foliage plant.

SISYRINCHIUM, Iridaceae. A semi-perennial, especially if divided in late summer, and seeds itself abundantly in almost any reasonable soil.

striatum
> 60 × 23 cm   [7–8]   Straw   Summer   F   DS
> 2 ft × 9 in

Chile. 1788. Makes a good tuffet of grey-green iris-like leaves about 30 cm (1 ft) high. The slender spikes bear numerous pale straw-yellow flowers, beautifully striped with purple on the reverse of the petals. Since every flower-stem causes the death of the leaf-shoot producing it, the clump must be kept well nurtured. The flowers fade in the afternoon. Evergreen. There is a beautiful form, 'Aunt May', with leaves striped with creamy yellow. It originated at Chevithorn, Barton, Tiverton, Devon.

SMILACINA, Liliaceae. Closely related to *Maianthemum*, to which genus the species are sometimes referred.

racemosa ★
> 75 × 46 cm   [4–9]   White   Spring   P   DS
> 2½ ft × 18 in

North America. 1640. False Spikenard. Related to Solomon's Seal, and much like it in the arching growth and poise of the delightsome fresh green leaves, but having its flowers in a fluffy creamy white spike at the end of the stem. Deliciously scented. Occasional reddish berries. It is not difficult, so long as it is given shade and lime-free soil. Lovely with *Paeonia veitchii*. *S. stellata* (1633) is nothing like so good; it has far smaller flowers and is an errant, arrant colonizer in light soil, but more stay-at-home where the soil is heavier. *S. purpurea* [5–9] is similar to *S. racemosa*, but the flowers are of chocolate-maroon, not unlike the tint of *Veratrum nigrum*. Himalaya.

". . . especially handsome with its ample . . . leaves alternating up the stems, and then the . . . creamy plume in May or June followed by berries like vitrified drops of bright blood."—RF

SOLIDAGO, Compositae. Easily grown in sun or part shade in any reasonable soil and increasing readily at the root, these are very ancient garden plants. How rich America is in these yellow composites!—*Helenium, Heliopsis, Rudbeckia* and now *Solidago*—the mainstay of the summer border to many people. But I seem to have a satisfying garden without them. For those who want a really good clear yellow for July, on a neat plant growing to 90 cm (3 ft), and not requiring support, I recommend choosing one of the short varieties (bred from *S. virgaurea* and *S. brachystachys* and perhaps × *Solidaster* by a Mr Walkden of Cheshire) which have *yellow flower stalks*. These are far more effective, and lack the greenish tinting of those with green stalks in the fluffy-head of tiny flowers; 'Goldenmosa' (1949) is as good and descriptive as its name, and would be my choice. 'Citronella' [4–9] is a new, freely branching cultivar, from Holland, in clear light yellow. Long flowering period.

The taller kinds—notorious greedy colonizers and seeders—like 'Golden Wings' are first rate for establishing in poor weedy ground, with wild types of *Aster novi-belgii*; in fact thay may often be seen gracing railway embankments, and give gaiety to the sere touch of the waning year. [All 4–9].

". . . loden with small yellow floures; which when they ripen turn to downe which is carried away with the winde."—GH

× **SOLIDASTER** A name coined to cover a bigeneric hybrid between *Solidago* and *Aster*. The following hybrid is a good garden plant for any fertile soil, preferably in sun.

hybridus ★

60 × 30 cm	*[4–9]*	*Yellow*	*Summer*	P	D
2 × 1 ft					

1910. *Solidaster luteus, Asterago luteus, Aster hybridus luteus. A. missouriensis* (of gardens). It is believed to be a hybrid between a *Solidago* and *Aster ptarmicoides*. It is a pleasing and useful plant for garden display and for cutting. Narrow leaves on wiry stems carrying open heads of tiny light canary-yellow daisies, fading paler. A long-flowering season from July. 'Lemore', a name given to a *Solidago*, is apparently of the same parentage.

SOPHORA, Leguminosae.

flavescens

1.2 m × 60 cm	*[9–10]*	*Yellow*	*L.Summer*	S
4 × 2 ft				

China. This resembles *Lespedeza* and *Fuchsia* in that it is a shrub in warmth but may be treated as a herbaceous perennial since it usually dies to the ground in winter. Lush growths are clad in bright green neat pinnate leaves, and end in spires of small, pale yellow pea-flowers emerging from brownish calyces; long in production. A pleasant change from almost everything else.

A. **Nectaroscordum siculum** var. **bulgaricum** (Janka) Stearn. The creamy green bells have a purplish flush.

B. **Agapanthus inapertus** Beauv. emend Leighton **'Albus'** at Wisley. The stems of this species remain stiffly erect in contrast to most other species and hybrids.

. **Anemone vitifolia** Ham. at Kew. Note the undivided, vine-ke leaves. Pure white flowers. The name *A. vitifolia* is usually pplied in gardens to *A. tomentosa*.

D. **Clematis heracleifolia** DC. var. **davidiana** Hemsl. Sweetly scented light blue flowers. At Oxford.

A. **Anemonopsis macrophylla** Sieb. & Zucc. A charming wood-lander with soft lavender flowers.

B. **Anemone pavonina** Lam., at Hidcote. They seed them-selves in the heavy soil and vary from cream and salmon to scarlet, purple and blue.

C. **Aster tradescantii** of gardens. One of the last autumnal flowers. Pure white with yellow eyes. On the right is **Polygonum amplexicaule** Don **'Atrosanguineum'** whose crimson flowers make a good contrast.

A. **Aster×frikartii** Frik. **'Mönch'**. This, the finest hybrid yet raised between *A. thomsonii* and *A. amellus*, flowers for about three months. Lavender-blue.

B. **Dictamnus albus** L. The Burning Bush is an aromatic and beautiful perennial; *D. a.* var. **purpureus** is mauve-purple.

C. **Campanula trachelium** L. **'Albo Plena'**. Pure white flowers. At Blickling Hall.

D. **Campanula alliariifolia** Willd. at Edinburgh. Milk-white flowers.

4. **A.** **Artemisia canescens** of gardens. Extra silvery and very hardy.

B. **Digitalis grandiflora** Lam. (*D. ambigua* Murr.) A perennial Foxglove with flowers of creamy yellow.

C. **Asphodelus cerasiferus** J. Gay. White flowers with rich brown exterior. Photographed at Kew.

A. **Arum creticum** Boiss. & Heldr. The Cretan Arum is clear yellow and quite hardy at Hidcote. With it is growing a white fritillary.

B. **Arum italicum** Mill. **'Pictum'** of gardens. The beautiful leaves are of rich green marbled with creamy grey.

C. The flowers of **Arum italicum 'Pictum'** are rather insignificant, of pale green, but are followed by spikes of orange-red fruits. At Cambridge.

D. **Zantedeschia aethiopica** Spreng. (*Richardia africana* Kunth) **'Crowborough'.** A form of Arum which has proved hardy when well established in our warmer counties, in the open border.

6.

A. **Cimicifuga racemosa** (L.) Nutt. at Wisley. Pure white flower spikes in summer.

B. **Cimicifuga simplex** (Wormsk.) Ledeb. **'Elstead Variety'.** The purplish buds open to white flowers in autumn. At Wisley.

C. **Astelia nervosa** Hook.f. The silvery leaves of this New Zealand plant are its major attraction; the flowers are inconspicuous.

A. **Cimicifuga foetida** L. This differs from other species in cultivation by having yellowish flowers and a drooping leading shoot. At Kew, in late summer.

B. **Crambe maritima** L. Seakale is as good an ornamental plant as it is a culinary delicacy. Pure white flowers in early summer, followed by the most handsome of all large glaucous leaves.

C. **Crambe cordifolia** Stev. at Kew. A cloud of white, like a huge gypsophila.

D. **Crambe orientalis** L. Lavender-white flowers in early summer, at Oxford.

B. **Eryngium proteiflorum** Delar. Bracts of astonishing shining whiteness.

8. A. **Eryngium maritimum** L. The native Sea Holly is a very deserving garden plant and thrives at Oxford. Pale blue flowers surrounded by glaucous bracts.

C. **Eryngium agavifolium** Gris. at Edinburgh. The species from Mexico and South America have narrow leaves as opposed to the Europeans.

D. **Eryngium eburneum** Decne. Sometimes wrongly labelled *E. bromeliifolium* or *E. pandanifolium* in gardens. A study in cream and green.

9. A. **Chrysanthemum parthenium** Pers. **'White Bonnet'.** The best double form of the Feverfew.

B. **Echinops tournefortii** Ledeb. Pure white heads over spiny grey-white leaves.

C. **Eremurus 'Highdown',** a hybrid of *E. stenophyllus* (Boiss. & Buhse) Baker, growing at Highdown. Warm yellow. *Iris pallida dalmatica* foliage in foreground.

D. **Geranium malviflorum** Boiss. The leaves appear from tuberous roots in autumn, the deep lilac blooms in spring.

10.

A. Irises which flower like this, prolifically, and form a compact clump are being bred again today. **Iris 'Gracchus'** at Oxford; raised in 1884.

B. A garden strain of **Iris inno-minata** Hend. Some of the most desirable of them inherit the clear warm yellow of the species.

C. **Iris pseuda-corus** L. **'Varie-gatus'**, handsomely striped with yellow at flowering time.

A. **Cardiocrinum giganteum** (Wall.) Mak. (*Lilium giganteum* Wall.). One of the most imposing of all perennials. White flowers. At the Savill Gardens.

B. **Cardiocrinum giganteum** var. **yunnanense** (Elwes) Stearn, at Rowallane. Creamy white, reddish throats, brown stems.

C. **Lysichitum camtschatcense** (L.) Schott. A big bog plant with immense leaves whose large white arums appear in early spring. Sweetly scented; an improvement on the yellow *L. americanum* Hult & St. J.

12.   A. Iris confusa Sealy. The dark lavender and orange markings give point to pale flowers of exquisite shape.

B. Selinum tenuifolium Wall. (*Oreochome candollei* Edgw.). A white Cow Parlsey of special excellence.

C. **Gentiana asclepiadea** L. The Swiss Willow Gentian. A first-rate, rich blue September flower for cool shady positions.

13.

A. **Helleborus lividus** Ait. Greyish marbled leaves, fragrant pale green flowers, pinkish outside. For sheltered gardens, as at Overbecks, Devon.

B. **Hibiscus moscheutos** L. The Marsh Mallow needs good cultivation in a sheltered position. Crimson, pink or white.

C. **Silene dioica** L. (*Lychnis dioica* L.; *Melandrium rubrum* (Weigel) Garcke) **'Flore Pleno'**. An old double garden form of the Red Campion.

14. A. **Morina longifolia** Wall. whose intriguing white flowers turn to pink and crimson after fertilization.

B. **Francoa sonchifolia** Cav. The Bridal Wreath has in its various forms flowers of white to deep pink.

C. **Lysimachia ephemerum** L. The greyish leaves and grey-white flowers are useful for cooling down the many orange-flowered plants that bloom after midsummer.

D. **Hosta 'Tallboy'.** The tallest and most imposing of all hostas in flower. Lilac. Photographed at Bressingham.

5. A. **Kniphofia snowdenii** C. H. Wright (*K. thomsonii* Baker var. *snowdenii* (C. H. Wright) Marais) in soft coral tone, a plant for sheltered gardens.

B. **Moraea spathulata** Ker. An Iris relative from South Africa with brilliant yellow flowers.

C. **Ligularia 'Gregynog Gold'.** Sometimes attributed to *L.* × *hessei* Bergm. A splendid late summer bog plant in rich orange.

D. **Paeonia arietina** Anders. **'Mother of Pearl'.** The greyish green leaves are just right for this light pink form of a usually magenta species.

16.

A. Paeonia emodi Wall. One of the few peonies which appreciate part shade. The pure white flowers are lit with yellow stamens.

B. Galax urceo-lata (Poir.) Brummit (*G. aphylla* L.). A sturdy woodland plant whose ever-green burnished leaves are of more importance than the spires of white flowers.

C. Primula pul-verulenta Duthie **'Bartley strain'.** A queen among the candelabra primulas. The white mealy stems support whorls of light pink flowers.

17.

A. Meconopsis quintuplinervia Regel. The Harebell Poppy at Wisley. Light lavender blue.

B. Lupinus ornatus Dougl. ex Lindl. A three-year-old plant with over fifty spikes of blue flowers, borne above silvery foliage. For well-drained gravel.

C. Libertia formosa Graham. An evergreen whose white flower spikes last for several weeks.

18. A. **Lilium × testaceum** Lindl. It would be difficult to name another hybrid lily of greater elegance. Of Isabelline tint and sweet fragrance.

B. **Inula royleana** DC. The large flowers are of clear orange-yellow.

C. **Lamium orvala** L. The subtle coppery pink of the normal form of this spring-flowering Dead-nettle is matched by the beauty of the white form.

D. **Lunaria rediviva** L. At Sissinghurst. The perennial Honesty is a useful and beautiful plant whose spring flowers are followed by elliptical silvery pods. Lilac-white.

19.

A. **Peltiphyllum peltatum** (Torr.) Engler (*Saxifraga peltata* Torr.). The hairy stems crowned with pink flowers are followed by large handsome leaves. **(Darmera peltata)**

B. **Ranunculus aconitifolius** L. Pure white flowers in late spring.

C. **Ranunculus speciosus plenus** of gardens. The largest of the several double-flowered Butter-cups. At Bressingham. Bright yellow.

20

A. **Heuchera cylindrica** Doug. A more imposing plant than other heucheras. The flowers are of rich brown tint, or they may be creamy white in **'Album'**. At Bressingham.

B. **Veratrum album** L. Compare with Plate X 3. Palest green-white flowers. The False Helleborine.

C. **Veratrum viride** L. The whole plant, leaves, stems and flowers, is of uniform green.

A. **Podophyllum hexandrum** Royle (*P. emodi* Wall.). The leaves pierce the ground like a folded umbrella and are richly tinted. Flowers white or pink.

B. **Senecio pulcher** Hook. & Arn. Flowers of dazzling magenta in autumn, and through mild winters. At Wisley.

C. **Rheum alexandrae** Veitch at Bodnant. The immense cream bracts protect the flowers from rain.

D. **Yucca whipplei** Torr. at Bodnant, 2.4 m. (8 ft) high; it requires a very sheltered position.

22. **Astilboides tabularis** (Hemsl.) Engel (*Rodgersia tabularis* Kom.). When in good moist soil the leaves will achieve 900 mm. (3 ft) in width. Flowers white.

B. **Rudbeckia maxima** Nutt. Unusually for this genus the leaves are distinctly glaucous. The yellow daisies have conical black centres.

C. **Yucca flaccida** Haw. A free-flowering short-growing species of great garden value. Creamy white.

D. **Yucca filamentosa** L. var. **concava** Baker. Three-year-old plants flowering uniformly in nursery rows.

A. **Cortaderia fulvida** (Buchanan) Zotov. (Often confused with *C. conspicua*.). This extremely graceful flesh-pink New Zealand Pampas Grass has the great merit of flowering at midsummer.

B. **Cortaderia richardii** (Endl.) Zotov. The New Zealand Toe-toe is hardier than *C. selloana*, and may be seen in Scottish gardens. It flowers in late summer.

C. **Cortaderia selloana** (Schult.) Aschers. & Graebn. **'Pumila'.** This is the most compact cultivar of the South American Pampas Grass. It flowers in early autumn.

D. **Miscanthus sinensis** Anderss. **'Silver Feather'** ('Silberfeder'). Silky, shimmering, pale brownish pink flowers in September. A new free-flowering cultivar, at Bressingham.

24. A. **Osmunda claytoniana** L. (*O. interrupta* Michx.). This North American fern has the strange character of bearing all its fertile pinnae in the middle of the frond.

B. **Polystichum aculeatum** (L.) Roth. **'Pulcherrimum Druery'.** One of the most beautiful and glossy of semi-evergreen ferns.

C. **Polystichum setiferum** (Forsk.) Woynar **'Divisilobum'.** An exceptionally delicately lacy form of the species.

D. **Polystichum setiferum 'Densum'.** In addition to the finely cut tracery of the fronds, the pinnae are piled thickly over one another. It is growing in a harmless groundcover of *Oxalis acetosella* at Nymans.

SPEIRANTHA, Liliaceae.

convallarioides ★

30 × 30 cm	*[6–8]*	*White*	*Spring*	C
1 × 1 ft				

China. 1854. *S. gardenii.* Related to Lily-of-the-Valley, but though spreading at the root it is far less invasive, simply making a good clump of rich green leaves. Just above these are poised the sprays of pure white, fragrant, starry flowers. A desirable plant for cool woodland or a shady border; at home in limy or acid soil, with humus. Evergreen.

SPIGELIA, Loganiaceae.

marilandica

30–60 × 30 cm	*[6–9]*	*Red*	*Summer*	CDS
1–2 × 1 ft				

S.E. United States. 1694. Indian Pink, though it bears no resemblance to *Dianthus.* Opposite leaves are carried up the stems, each bearing a one-sided array of tubular crimson flowers, yellow inside the lobed mouth. For sun or part shade. Quite on its own.

"... a beautiful native of N. America, distinct from all other hardy plants."—WR

SPHAERALCEA, Malvaceae. Plants for warm sunny positions in well-drained soil in our warmer counties. They are sub-shrubby, like *Lavatera olbia,* and are frequently reduced in cold winters. They assort well with *Buddleja crispa* and *Ceratostigma willmottianum.*

fendleri

46 × 46 cm	*[8–10]*	*Orange*	*Summer/*	W	CS
18 × 18 in			*Autumn*		

S.W. USA. Softly hairy, lobed leaves on a branching shrubby plant. The flowers continue to be produced in the axils of the leaves until stopped by cold weather; they are round, silky, mallow-like, of soft orange-coral tint. *S. ambigua* is a similar plant; their long-flowering period recommends them.

munroana

46 × 46 cm	*[8–10]*	*Reddish*	*Summer/*	W	CDS
18 × 18 in			*Autumn*		

W. and N.W. America. Smoother leaves, and scarcely shrubby, dying to the ground each winter, but even so needing and deserving a warm corner. The flowers are similar but of brilliant coral-pink, tending to deteriorate in wet weather.

STACHYS, Labiatae. For well-drained soils in full sun; these specifications are needed by *S. byzantina,* but *S. macrantha* will put up with shade. None is particular about the quality of the soil provided the drainage is good.

alpina

1.5 m × 60 cm	*[5–8]*	*Mauve*	*Summer*	P	DS
5 × 2 ft					

S. Europe. 1597. A rather coarse plant but effective. Crinkled rough-hairy leaves are borne up stiff stems with whorls of mauve-pink flowers at the top. *S. germanica* is similar, with lighter flowers and greyish hairy leaves.

byzantina ★

46 × 30 cm *18 in × 1 ft*	*[4–9]*	*Grey foliage*	*Summer*	P	D

Caucasus to Persia. 1782. *S. olympica, S. lanata*. Lamb's Tongue, Lamb's Ears. A well-known silvery plant, whose nomenclature is somewhat confused. Long known in gardens as *S. lanata*, it is now called *S. byzantina*, with a synonym *S. olympica*. It is inevitable, as with other favourite garden plants, that garden forms are given special names. An excellent ground-cover, with its dense mats of woolly grey leaves. The small magenta flowers are densely swaddled in grey wool along the stem. A splendid carpeter and an admirable plant for association with the "old" roses. All forms of late years have been increasingly susceptible to spotting with mildew, a trouble not found in other silvery plants such as *Artemisia* species and *Tanacetum herderi*. Evergreen.

"Not the smallest and driest garden should be without *Stachys lanata* ... and most useful for picking. When cut, they go on growing in water, as Buttercups and Forget-me-nots do."—CWE

"The grey bordering is not merely an edging, but a general front ground-work, running here and there a yard deep into the border."—GJ

—**'Cotton Boll'**   Selected by Beth Chatto a few years ago, this produces flower spikes, like the parent plant, but they are abortive and content themselves with producing cottony bobbles up the stems. A somewhat similar form, showing tiny flowers in the cottony heads, has been selected by Sheila Macqueen. There is a much larger variant of *S. byzantina* in cultivation known as *S. olympica*, but these two names are synonymous; the dense, broad foliage clumps of this big form reach nearly 60 cm (2 ft) high and 90 cm (3 ft) across very quickly.

—**'Silver Carpet'**   A non-flowering form, raised by W. Cunningham & Son of Heacham, Norfolk, and the best silver carpet-plant I know, ideal for border verges. Excellent ground cover, used exclusively on the rose-beds at Cotehele, Cornwall, and at Powis Castle, Powys. Evergreen.

coccinea

60 × 46 cm *2 ft × 18 in*	*[9–10]*	*Scarlet*	*E. to L.* *Summer*	W	CDS

Mexico, Chile. 1798. A tender plant for fertile soil, well drained, in sunny spots in our warmest counties. It has small leaves and slender spires of long-tubed scarlet flowers protruding from purplish red calyces. It bears a resemblance to *Agastache mexicana*, but is larger and brighter.

macrantha ★

60 × 23 cm *2 ft × 9 in*	*[4–8]*	*Mauve*	*Summer*	PF	D

1800. *Betonica grandiflora, Stachys grandiflora*. A Caucasian plant making a mat of good, corrugated, dark green, downy leaves, and having erect stems set with three or four whorls of hooded blooms of rich rosy mauve. Pleasing with "old" roses. It is worth seeking a good form, such as ● ★ 'Superba', 'Robusta'.

officinalis

60 × 30 cm *2 × 1 ft*	*[4–9]*	*Pink, etc.*	*Summer*	PF	D

Europe, Britain. *S. betonica, Betonica officinalis*. Bishop's Wort, Wood Betony. In spite of its latter name it is quite happy in full sun. Its basal leaves make a thick mat and, like *S. macrantha*, it produces a lot of stiff stems supporting two or three tight heads of flowers. The clear pink and white forms are attractive, 'Rosea' and 'Alba' respectively.

STANLEYA, Cruciferae. Sun-lover for any fertile, drained soil.

pinnatifida

90 × 46 cm	*[4–9]*	*Yellow*	*Summer/*	DS
3 ft × 18 in			*E.Autumn*	

W. United States. 1812. This woody-based perennial has leaves narrow and entire, or pinnate, leathery and grey-green. The long spire of flowers, with later side-branches, has grey-green buds opening to lime-green flowers which turn to buff yellow on fading, immediately after which the styles develop into long thin pods, adding to the display.

STENANTHIUM, Liliaceae.

robustum

1.2 m × 60 cm	*[7–9]*	*Creamy*	*Summer*	P	DS
4 × 2 ft					

United States. 1813. Bent leaves like those of a Day Lily, and airy tall sprays of creamy green stars, closely resembling those of a *Veratrum* but more graceful and dainty. It appears to thrive in a sunny place in rich moist sandy soil, but is seldom a success though well worth a try. *S. gramineum* [7–9] is a smaller plant and more suitable for those who garden in somewhat drier conditions.

STEVIA, Compositae.

purpurea

46 × 46 cm	*[8–10]*	*Mauve*	*L.Summer*	DS
18 × 18 in				

Mexico. 1812. Velvety, branching stems bear flat heads of tiny flowers for many weeks. Narrow leaves.

STOKESIA, Compositae. Well-drained soil in full sun.

laevis ●

46 × 46 cm	*[5–8]*	*Blue*	*Summer*	PF	DRS
18 × 18 in					

North America. 1766. *S. cyanea.* The best form I have seen is 'Blue Star'. It is a plant for the border front, lovely with *Achillea* 'Moonshine', and gives a good basal rosette of strap-shaped, evergreen leaves. The handsome cornflower-like blooms with wide outer petals are 10 cm (4 in) across, borne in clusters over a long period, of clear Spode-blue with creamy white centre. There are also attractive purple, pink and white forms. 'Wyoming' is a good purple.

STREPTOPUS, Liliaceae. A small genus allied to *Polygonatum*, but the segments of the flowers are free to the base. Pleasing small woodlanders for cool positions in humus-laden soil, where their roots will travel.

amplexifolius

60 × 30 cm	*[4–8]*	*Pink*	*E.Summer*	PF	DS
2 × 1 ft					

Europe, North America. 1752. Similar to *S. roseus* but rather larger in all parts; the whitish flowers hang in pairs and are followed by red berries in early autumn.

roseus

| 46 × 30 cm | [4–8] | Pink | E.Summer | PF DS |
| 18 in × 1 ft | | | | |

E. United States. 1806. A charming small plant for a dimpsy corner, allied to Solomon's Seal, with alternate smooth green leaves on the twisting, branching, upright stems. From the leaf-axils hang small bells of old-rose tint, followed by red berries.

simplex

| 60 × 30 cm | [5–8] | Creamy | E.Summer | P DS |
| 2 × 1 ft | | | | |

Nepal. 1822. Equally branching, with narrow, clasping leaves; the bell-shaped flowers are mainly cream but with brownish-pink centre and outer segments; stamens cream.

STROBILANTHES, Acanthaceae.

atropurpureus

| 1.5 m × 60 cm | [7–9] | Violet | Autumn | C D |
| 5 × 2 ft | | | | |

Himalaya. A bushy-growing plant, resembling a *Salvia* more than an *Acanthus,* with nettle-like leaves. The violet-blue flowers which cover the plant for some weeks in September lose their beauty by midday, when they fade and turn to purple. Grows best in a sunny border out of the wind in any fertile soil. There is a dwarf form, 'Nanus'. 60 cm (2 ft).

STYLOPHORUM, Papaveraceae. For cool conditions with humus.

diphyllum ★

| 46 × 30 cm | [5–8] | Yellow | Spring/ | S |
| 18 in × 1 ft | | | Summer | |

E. North America. 1854. The Celandine Poppy is a charming plant, somewhat resembling the Greater Celandine, but only seeds itself occasionally. A downy, hairy, leafy plant in light green, the good-sized yellow poppies appear for many weeks, eventually turning into silvery pods.

"... handsome green leaves, finger-lobed to the base in veiny divisions each like an oak-leaf ..."—RF

SWERTIA, Gentianaceae. Modest, upright herbs with good basal leaves and small starry flowers of creamy green and other tints. "Poor relatives" of the gentians! but pleasant for cool moist spots in humus-laden soil.

petiolata

| 90 × 46 cm | [5–8] | Creamy | L.Summer | P S |
| 3 ft × 18 in | | | | |

Himalaya. The erect stems bear clusters of creamy greenish flowers, with deeper veins, the whole making a gentle symphony. There are many other species worth trying; *S. aucheri* [5–8] is similar.

SYMPHYANDRA, Campanulaceae. There are several species, all having somewhat hairy leaves forming a basal clump. Above these arise stems of a foot or so, carrying bell-like flowers of purple, lilac, pale yellow or white. My choice is *S. hofmannii* [5–9], white, from Bosnia. Recorded first in 1884, this has been a long time in "arriving". It prefers a cool position.

SYMPHYTUM, Boraginaceae. The ground-covering Comfrey, *S. grandiflorum* (*S. ibericum*) and its hybrids, are described in my book *Plants for Ground-Cover*; they range up to 46 cm (18 in). The following are easily-grown plants which like some shade.

caucasicum

60 × 60 cm	*[4–9]*	*Blue*	*Spring*	DRS
2 × 2 ft				

Caucasus. The usual hairy Boraginaceous leaves make a good clump and there is something very appealing in the clusters of azure-blue tubes hanging from the leafy stems.

grandiflorum 'Variegatum'. [5–9] A compact form recently raised by Eric Smith; the light green leaves are bordered with creamy green. Bluish flowers. This will lighten many a dark shady corner.

rubrum
of gardens

46 × 60 cm	*[4–9]*	*Crimson*	*E.Summer*	DR
18 in × 2 ft				

This may be a hybrid between *S. officinale* 'Coccineum' and *S. grandiflorum*. It spreads but not unduly, and is an admirable ground-cover for cool places. Deep crimson tubular flowers hang in little croziers above hairy green leaves.

× uplandicum

1.2 × 1.2 m	*[4–9]*	*Blue*	*L.Spring/*	DR
4 × 4 ft			*E.Summer*	

Hybrid. Probably a cross between *S. asperum* and *S. officinale,* and often labelled *S. peregrinum* or *S. asperrimum*. It is a coarse leafy plant with leafy, branching stems terminating in arching clusters of tubular flowers in spring. They are pinkish in the bud, and open to pure blue. Highly decorative when in flower, and superb with late yellow rhododendrons and yellow azaleas.

—**'Variegatum'.** The leaves are all that could be desired in variegation, greyish green, broadly margined with cream. It is best to cut the lanky stems down after flowering to encourage good basal foliage which lasts in beauty until the autumn, out-lasting indeed the hostas themselves. The flowers of this particular form are pale lilac-pink. Unfortunately too its variegation reverts to dark green, when it becomes a poor garden plant. 90 × 60 cm (3 × 2 ft)   D

SYMPLOCARPUS, Araceae. A deep fleshy rootstock for really moist ground, bog garden or waterside.

foetidus

46 × 46 cm	*[4–8]*	*Purplish*	*E. Spring*	D
18 × 18 in				

N.E. Asia, N.E. America. This, the true Skunk Cabbage (*cf. Lysichitum*), has insignificant purplish brown, stemless hooded flowers appearing like toads, squat upon the ground. Its beauty is provided by the large oval leaves, somewhat resembling those of *Hosta* 'Honeybells', sometimes 30 cm (1 ft) across; they last until late summer only. The flowers have a strong odour but are far from the nose. (*Spathyema foetida*.)

TANACETUM, Compositae.

herderi ★

23 × 23 cm	*[8–9]*	*Yellow*	*Summer*	CD
9 × 9 in				

Turkestan, etc. An imperturbable silvery plant for light or heavy soil. Dense masses of small filigree leaves and occasional small heads of ray-less yellow flowers. An ideal frontal plant.

TELLIMA, Saxifragaceae.

grandiflora, 1826, and *T.g.* 'Rubra'. [4–9]. Good evergreen ground-cover plants for shade or sun, with sprays of creamy bells. These plants are fully discussed in my book *Plants for Ground-Cover.*

TEUCRIUM, Labiatae. Sun-loving plants for any fertile soil. *T. chamaedrys* is a dwarf, shrubby, spreading ground-cover or small hedging plant with mauve-pink flowers.

hyrcanicum

60 × 90 cm	*[7–10]*	*Mauve*	*L. Summer*	CDS
2 × 3 ft				

Persia. 1763. This unusual plant forms a bushy mass of sage-like growth and aromatic leaves. For many weeks slender dense spikes of tiny dark lilac flowers decorate it. They are grey in bud and assort well with like colours and grey-leafed plants.

THALICTRUM, Ranunculaceae. Meadow Rue. Dainty yet stately plants.

aquilegiifolium ★

90 × 30 cm	*[5–9]*	*Lilac*	*E. Summer*	PF	DS
3 × 2 ft					

Europe, N. Asia. Early eighteenth century. Slowly forming a close clump, this plant has beautiful columbine-like smooth foliage in light green; the stems, with more lovely leaves, branch into a wide head of fluffy flowers of rich rosy lilac, which make a good combination with shrubs of coppery purple foliage. There are short and tall, dark, pale or white forms which can be increased by division, though they originate from seeds. The white, 'Album', is specially good at Sissinghurst, Kent. Ordinary fertile soil, sun. Good seed-heads.

> "... the misty red-grey-purple of *Thalictrum aquilegiifolium purpureum* with the warm white foam-colour of *Spiraea sylvester.*"—GJ

chelidonii ●

1.5 m × 60 cm	*[5–9]*	*Lilac*	*Summer*	PF	DS
5 × 2 ft					

Himalaya. This plant is similar in many ways to *T. delavayi* and is most at home in the cooler north, in rich peaty soil that will not dry out. *T. rochebrunianum* [5–9] is again of the same general effect but is no easier to grow in the south. *T. reniforme* [5–9], a similar plant, is sometimes seen.

delavayi ● ★

1.5 m × 60 cm	*[5–9]*	*Lilac*	*Summer*	PF	DS
5 × 2 ft					

W. China. 1890. Better known in gardens as *T. dipterocarpum,* it was discovered by the Abbé Delavay. (The true *T. dipterocarpum* is a different plant.) It is far more elegant than *T. aquilegiifolium*, with daintier foliage. Instead of being fluffy and borne in a dense head, the flowers are carried on wide branches making a great pyramidal airy-fairy display; when well grown the panicles can be over 30 cm (1 ft) wide and 60 cm (2 ft) high. Each flower is exquisite; a tuft of cream stamens hangs from a covering of four or five rich lilac sepals. There is also a white form, 'Album' (1920). It needs individually staking in windy districts and grows best in rich, deep soil in woodland clearings or sheltered borders, in sun or partial shade. Plant 23 cm (9 in) deep in a hollow and cover with rich soil as they grow the first season. If needed for cutting, plant at least 90 cm (3 ft) apart because the flower stalks get entangled and make one say *Cardamine!* or *Damnacanthus!*; they are impossible to separate, but of course help to hold each other in place in the garden. It makes a strong and beautiful contrast to crinums at Trelissick, Cornwall. Grouped with *Gypsophila* 'Bristol Fairy' a unique effect is obtained.

● —**'Hewitt's Double'.** Though this lacks the lovely contrast of the pale yellow stamens, the tiny rosettes of pure lilac are delightful. Increased by division or cuttings. Prior to 1937.

diffusiflorum ●
90 × 30 cm	*[5–9]*	*Lilac*	*Summer*	PF	S
3 × 1 ft					

Tibet. 1938. An exquisite beauty with very large flowers (for a *Thalictrum*). The foliage is dainty, of leaden green, much divided. The rich lilac blooms hang like bells from hair-fine stalks. Without doubt the queen of the tribe, but I have found it short-lived in the south; it thrives in the cooler north in well-drained peaty soil.

minus
30–90 × 30 cm	*[3–7]*	*Yellow*	*Summer*	PF	D
1–3 × 1 ft					

Europe, Britain. This varies from a tiny plant with minute maidenhair-fern-like leaves to a big vigorous plant with leaves the size of a 2p piece; it is then often known as *T. majus* or *T. adiantifolium*; also known as *T. foetidum*. The smaller forms are charming and usually make dense clumps; the more vigorous plants are more invasive, particularly in light soil, and can be a nuisance. The flower sprays mostly consist of yellowish stamens, and, with the leaves, are lovely in vases.

speciosissimum ★
1.5 m × 60 cm	*[6–9]*	*Yellow*	*Summer*	P	D
5 × 2 ft					

Spain, N.W. Africa. Early eighteenth century. *T. flavum glaucum, T. rugosum.* Glaucous blue-green divided foliage invaluable for cutting, remaining in beauty long after the fluffy heads of lemon-yellow have dropped. Ordinary soil, sun. An indispensable plant for blue-and-yellow planting schemes, as in Mrs Winthrop's garden at Hidcote, Gloucestershire, where the blue foliage makes such a contrast to *Alchemilla mollis*.

A similar plant is *T. flavum* [6–9]; but beware, both it and some named forms, such as 'Illuminator', have ordinary green foliage, which puts them into the second class. *T. lucidum* [6–9] has also these dark green leaves, narrowly lacini-ated, with pale yellow flowers (*T. angustifolium,* of gardens); the leaflets are reputedly broader in *T.l. laserpitiifolium.*

THERMOPSIS, Leguminosae. Well-drained soil in sun.

montana

90 × 60 cm	*[3–8]*	*Yellow*	*E. Summer*	P	DS
3 × 2 ft					

W. North America. 1818. *T. fabacea, T. lupinoides*. At first sight this lupin-like plant with bright straw-yellow flower spikes might be taken for a colour form of *Baptisia australis*. Unfortunately it has a rapidly running root. *T. lanceolata* [3–8], far less well known, has not this disadvantage, and is very similar, with the same needs, and is a valuable plant.

THLADIANTHA, Cucurbitaceae. Rampageous climbers for sunny walls and hedgerows or banks, concrete abortions and fences. They die to the ground each autumn but grow rapidly every summer. Full sun, any fertile soil. The tendrils need wires or twigs for support. Wandering roots. The sexes are on separate plants.

dubia

4.5 m Climber	*[7–10]*	*Yellow*	*Summer*	DRS
15 ft				

China. Closely related to marrows and cucumbers, the flowers are dark yellow like those of the latter. Profuse heart-shaped hairy green leaves.

oliveri

4.5 m Climber	*[7–10]*	*Yellow*	*Summer*	DRS
15 ft				

China. 1894. A similar plant with larger, smoother leaves. The flowers are more freely produced. They are both grown more for their interest than for ornament. It thrives at Berrington Court, Herefordshire.

TIGRIDIA, Iridaceae. Tender bulbous plants for well-drained sunny places in our warmest counties. Plant 7.5 cm (3 in) deep.

pavonia ●

46 × 23 cm	*[8–10]*	*Various*	*Summer*	P	W	DS
18 × 9 in						

Mexico. 1796. Peacock-Tiger Flower. Broad, ribbed green leaves in an iris-like fan. The flowers may be up to 15 cm (6 in) across, with three large outer segments. These may be white, yellow, orange, pink, red, purple, etc. The three smaller segments and the bases of the three outer ones form a central cup with extraordinary stripes and dots. *T. pringlei* [9–10] is perhaps less hardy, scarlet, with less marking.

TOVARA, Polygonaceae. The following are easy enough to grow, in any fertile soil that does not dry out, and are best when placed among shrubs out of the wind, which is apt to bruise the beautiful leaves. The species is sometimes ascribed to the genus *Persicaria*.

virginiana

60 × 60 cm	*[3–9]*	*Foliage*		CD
2 × 2 ft				

North America, Japan, etc. 1640. *Polygonum virginianum*. I have never seen the normal green-leafed type but the form *T.v.* 'Variegata' is a plant of considerable beauty. The clumps of broad leaves grow up rather late in the summer, developing their ivory-yellow stripes and splashes until the picture is complete in August. In my experience this produces no flowers. *T.v. filiformis* from the Himalaya produces very thin wisps of brownish tiny flowers above its leaves, and to this species I believe belongs another variegated form whose leaves have a handsome brown zone across their beautiful variegation, touched with pink. This has been christened 'Painter's Palette' (1975).

TRACHYSTEMON, Boraginaceae.

orientale

46 × 60 cm	*[5–9]*	*Blue*	*Spring*	D
18 in × 2 ft				

Asia Minor, Caucasus, etc. 1752. *Nordmannia cordifolia.* Immense, hairy, heart-shaped leaves, resembling those of a *Hosta,* grow up very quickly in late spring and create a handsome ground-cover. Branching heads of blue starry flowers appear before them, carried on hairy stems, with purplish calyces. It thrives in sun or shade, dry or moist soil, almost anywhere. Invasive; for large areas, where it will dominate handsomely.

TRADESCANTIA, Commelinaceae. Easily grown, preferably in sun, in any reasonable soil. Their long season of flowering, from July to autumn, commends them, but the presentation of their charming three-petalled blooms among the untidy and prolific greenery leaves much to be desired.

× andersoniana ★

60 × 60 cm	*[5–9]*	*Various*	*Summer/*	D
2 × 2 ft			*Autumn*	

Hybrids of *T. virginiana* and other species, dating from late seventeenth-century introductions. The Spiderworts are available from white through pale, medium and dark blue to purple and claret; they bear fancy names and should be chosen from lists or when in flower. They form dense clumps, stalwart and effective in the garden at a distance; somewhat disappointing at close range. Some established favourites are 'Osprey', white, blue eye; 'J. C. Weguelin', pale blue; 'Purewell Giant', red-purple; 'Purple Dome', purple.

virginiana

46 × 90 cm	*[5–9]*	*Lilac*	*Summer/*	DS
18 in × 3 ft			*Autumn*	

Eastern United States. 1629. A variable species, rather lanky compared with the above stocky garden hybrids, and of less garden value. The double forms in lavender or purple have some appeal.

TRAUTVETTERIA, Ranunculaceae. Easily satisfied in regard to soil and position. Rather undistinguished, with flowers like those of *Thalictrum.*

caroliniensis

90 × 46 cm	*[5–8]*	*White*	*Summer*	P	DS
3 ft × 18 in					

North America. *T. palmata.* Because it was also called *Cimicifuga palmata* it has acquired the name False Bugbane. Leaves rounded, deeply lobed and handsome; the flowers are mere white tassels of stamens in branched heads.

TRICYRTIS, Liliaceae. The Toad Lilies, so-called because of their spotted flowers, are sound perennials, preferring a soil that does not dry out, and containing a good stint of humus. They do well in the north, but the cooler the district the more sun should be available to them, to hasten their late flowers. In the south they appreciate part shade. They all form elegant clumps of ascending or arching stems, clad with oval, pointed leaves, and bear their flowers in a loose sheaf at the top. They are most intriguingly shaped, slightly cupped with splayed segments, and with a centre that deserves close examination. They are not showy but of considerable beauty.

"... wried by perversity into an almost Aubrey Beardsley freakishness of outline and heavy waxen texture, freckled and spotted ... till their name of Toad Lily is felt to be apt."—RF

formosana

60–90 × 46 cm	[5–9]	Mauve	E. Autumn	P	DS
2–3 ft × 18 in					

Formosa. *T.f. stolonifera.* Shining dark leaves and upstanding stems branching into fine open heads of mauve-brown effect, from brown buds; the petals are much spotted with mauve on lighter ground. They are yellow in the throat and some have red stigmata. Stoloniferous. The variety *amethystina* has white flowers spotted with purple and flushed with lilac towards the ends of the petals.

hirta ●

90 × 60 cm	[4–9]	Lilac	E. Autumn	P	DS
3 × 2 ft					

Japan. 1863. Hairy leaves. The flowers are borne in the axils of the leaves, unlike those of *T. formosana,* but are larger, nearly white but more or less heavily spotted with lilac, and with colourful stamens and stigma. Excellent with the white *Anemone vitifolia.* There is a pure white variety, 'Alba', which has pink stamens, as a good albino should. There is a form with yellow-edged leaves from Japan, known as 'Miyazaki Gold'. Two hybrids have been named at Kew: 'Jasmin' and 'Cumberland'.

latifolia

46–90 × 60 cm	[6–9]	Yellowish	Summer		DS
18 in–3 ft × 2 ft					

Japan. China. 1910. *T. bakeri.* A tall species bearing branching heads of erect yellow blooms, heavily spotted with red-brown, above broad, enclasping rich green leaves. *T. macrantha* (1888) [8–9] is very similar but with broader leaves. Both are seen at their best when planted on a peat ledge, to reveal the beauty of their nodding flowers. Shikoku, Japan.

macranthopsis

90 × 46 cm	[8–9]	Yellow	E. Autumn	P	DS
3 ft × 18 in					

Honshu, Japan. In this species the flowers nod from the leaf axils, of pale yellow with brown-purple dots. Unlike anything else. Leaf bases enclasp the stem. *T. ishiiana* is similar with the flowers mostly in terminal clusters.

macropoda ●

60 × 46 cm	[5–9]	Yellowish	E. Autumn	P	DS
2 ft × 18 in					

Far East. 1868. The flowers are of creamy white with heavy spotting of mauve or purple. An erect and beautifully poised plant.

ohsumiensis ●

    30 × 30 cm   *[7–9]*   *Yellow*   *E. Autumn*   DS
    1 × 1 ft

Kyushu, Japan. 1930. Another good species with large waxy open flowers held above broad, enclasping, rich green leaves. Pale yellow flowers, spotted brown.

TRIFOLIUM, Leguminosae. A beautiful plant for any fertile soil in sun.

pannonicum

    90 × 90 cm   *[6–9]*   *Yellow*   *Summer*   P   DS
    3 × 3 ft

Turkey, S.E. Europe. 1752. Lobed leaves at the base of the stems, which branch somewhat, each branch ending in a clover head of creamy white flowers. It adds to the short list of light yellow flowers. It is rather variable but *T.p. pannonicum* seems to be the best for gardens; it is from S.E. Europe, and is the Hungarian Clover.

TRILLIUM, Liliaceae. Moist cool woodland conditions in good soil suit them, when planted about 5 cm (2 in) deep. The very beautiful Wood Lilies flower in early spring, each stout stem bearing three leaves, three calyces and three petals—hence the name *Trillium*. They are usually too scarce to cut, but last well in water; unfortunately one cuts all the leaves at the same time, which is harmful to the plants. Long-lived, abiding joys of spring.

catesbaei ● ★

    30 × 30 cm   *[6–9]*   *Pink*   *Spring*   P   DS
    1 × 1 ft

Eastern N. America (Carolina). Named after Mark Catesby (1682–1749), one of the earliest botanist-naturalists to explore those regions. Confused with *T. stylosum* and *T. nervosum*. While the leaves are as beautiful as any other species', the thick, recurving, clear pink segments of the flowers mark it apart. A gem among gems. Illustrated in my book *The Rock Garden and its Plants.*

cernuum

    46 × 30 cm   *[4–9]*   *White*   *Spring*   P   DS
    18 in × 1 ft

E. North America. 1758. Truly named, with flowers that modestly nod and hide themselves under the luxuriant green leaves. Segments rather small, recurving, divided by green sepals, and with handsome maroon centre and anthers.

chloropetalum ● ★

    60 × 30 cm   *[5–9]*   *Various*   *Spring*   P   DS
    2 × 1 ft

W. United States. Stout reddish-green stems carry dark green leaves mottled and marbled with grey, forming a handsome collar for the stalkless upright lily-flower. I like the rich crimson-maroon forms best, but they vary to pink and white, usually with greenish brown stems. *T. sessile* (1635) [5–9] is a very similar species, perhaps rather shorter, with the same colour-range, but it is reported from the Eastern States. The anthers are considerably shorter than in the Western species. Heavy sweet scent in a warm room.

erectum ● ★

| 38 × 30 cm | [4–9] | Various | Spring | P | DS |
| 15 in × 1 ft | | | | | |

Central & E. North America. 1759. Birth Root, Lamb's Quarters. *T. foetidum*, *T. rhomboideum*. Another most handsome plant; the maroon flowers have recurving segments, indigo centre and paler anthers. The sepals are brownish and the leaves large, rich green. In *T.e.* 'Album' the segments are of palest greenish-white, offset by the striking indigo centre, yellow anthers and light green sepals. *T.e.* 'Ochroleucum' (*T.e.* 'Viridiflorum') is a name given to greenish-flowered forms.

grandiflorum ● ★

| 38 × 30 cm | [4–9] | White | Spring | P | DS |
| 15 in × 1 ft | | | | | |

E. North America. 1799. The Wake Robin is the best known species and a striking companion to *T. chloropetalum*. It is a hearty good garden plant. The pure white flowers in good forms have broad segments and arch over the broad green foliage. A gracious beauty. 'Roseum' has flowers of delicious clear rose-pink; there is also a still more rare, sumptuous, full-petalled double white form, 'Flore Pleno'. They flower in good contrast to the earlier Blue Poppies.

"A plant unsurpassable anywhere for heartiness of habit, charm of manner, and refulgent purity of bloom."—RF

The above may be considered among the best and largest species; for the connoisseur there are several smaller species such as *T. luteum* [4–9], yellowish; *T. kamschaticum* [4–9], *T. nervosum* [4–9], white, and *T. ovatum* [5–9], white or pinkish; and *T. undulatum* [4–9], white with veined pink centre, earning the sobriquet "Painted Lady"; and others, all natives of North America. *T. kamschaticum* has a yellow centre, and there is a rare, double, pale pink form of *T. ovatum* named 'Kenmore'.

TRIOSTEUM, Caprifoliaceae.

perfoliatum

| 90 × 60 cm | [5–8] | Brownish | | PF | DS |
| 3 × 2 ft | | | | | |

1730. The flowers are of little account but they result in clustered white berries at the tip of each leafy shoot. Its chief merit is for small autumn bouquets. *T. pinnatifidum*—apart from its leaves—is similar; *T. erythrocarpum* has red berries. All require semi-woodland conditions.

TRITONIA, Iridaceae. Closely allied to *Crocosmia*.

rosea

| 90 × 15 cm | [7–10] | Pink | L. Summer | P | D |
| 3 ft × 6 in | | | | | |

South Africa. A beautiful, dainty Montbretia for sunny gardens with grassy leaves and wiry branching stems carrying small, pink, lily-like flowers. Excellent for cutting and lovely with *Aster thomsonii* 'Nanus' in front of it, or blue *Echinops* behind it. This is one of the prettiest flowers of August and September, and has a particularly warm, clear colouring. It thrives in a sunny spot in any fertile soil; plant about 7.5 cm (3 in) deep in spring. (*T. disticha rubrolucens*.)

"... yields its long sprays of rosy shrimp-pink year after year without clamouring for division."—ATJ

TROLLIUS, Ranunculaceae. Globe Flower. In nature many frequent boggy areas but so long as the soil—about which they are not particular—in gardens does not dry out they are easy to grow. Slowly increasing clumps from masses of fibrous roots, they are best transplanted in early autumn. The leaves of all kinds are glabrous, deeply divided or lobed, mainly forming a basal clump but a few are carried on the stems. There are several small species such as *T. pumilus*, which do not come within the scope of this book.

asiaticus

60 × 30 cm	[4–8]	Orange	Spring	PF	DS
2 × 1 ft					

N.E. Asia. 1759. A smaller plant than *T. europaeus*, with darker yellow or orange flowers. *T.a. aurantiacus* is a rich colour.

× cultorum ● ★

90 × 46 cm	[4–8]	Yellow/	Spring	PF	D
3 ft × 18 in		Orange			

Hybrid. *T. europaeus* × *T. asiaticus* × *T. chinensis*. The popular race of garden Globe Flowers, gracious plants of good leafage with large, beautifully incurved, globe-shaped flowers—like big double buttercups. Though there are many named kinds they vary little and are either yellow or orange. 'Canary Bird' is a lovely lemon-yellow, assorting well with *Rhododendron* 'Susan', while the deeper cultivars like 'Orange Princess' and 'Prichard's Giant' blend with coppery-leafed astilbes and Mollis azaleas. There is a pretty ivory-tinted clone named 'Alabaster' (Arends, 1952) but it is not over vigorous. 'Byrne's Giant' is a good butter-yellow, late; while 'Earliest of All' opens the season in light yellow.

europaeus ★

60 × 46 cm	[4–8]	Yellow	Spring	PF	DS
2 ft × 18 in					

Europe, Britain. This British native inhabits squelchy ground in northern and western uplands and was growing in London gardens by 1581. A selected form *T.e.* 'Superbus' is to be sought. The cool lemon-yellow incurved blooms are a sheer delight.

"*Trollius europaeus* ... a plant of the alpine meadows ... whole acres shining with the bland and moony citron of its unbroken mass of bloom."—RF

ledebourii ● ★

of gardens

90 × 46 cm	[4–8]	Orange	Spring	PF	DS
3 ft × 18 in					

N.E. Asia. 1912. This garden plant (probably *T. chinensis*), distinct from the true species—which is apparently not in cultivation—is taller, later than, and equally beautiful as, the clones mentioned under *T. × cultorum*, but the formation of the flower is different. The outer petals preserve the globe-shape but the inside is filled with narrow petaloid-stamens. 'Golden Queen' is a well-known strain or hybrid but is likely to be superseded by 'Imperial Orange' from New Zealand, but any form is good. *T. riederianus* is closely related.

"... tongues of flame in bowls of burning orange."—ATJ

ranunculoides
30 × 30 cm	*[4–8]*	*Orange*	*Spring*	PF	DS
1 × 1 ft					

Caucasus, Asia Minor. 1800. *T. patulus.* The flowers are flat and buttercup-like, of light orange.

stenopetalus ● ★
75 × 46 cm	*[5–8]*	*Yellow*	*Summer*	PF	DS
2½ ft × 18 in					

China. This has the usual good divided foliage and stately stems holding aloft the large, single, light yellow flowers. A useful and unique species because it flowers at midsummer, needing the same generous moist soil as the others. Closely related to *T. yunnanensis.*

yunnanensis
60 × 30 cm	*[5–8]*	*Yellow*	*E. Summer*	PF	DS
2 × 1 ft					

W. China. 1903. Rather lighter green leaves than most species, elegantly lobed and making a good base for the wiry erect branching stems. Each branch ends in one or more wide, bright yellow, single flowers, often green-tipped. It is similar to *T. stenopetalus* but is earlier-flowering. Sometimes considered as a form of *T. pumilus,* which is a much smaller plant.

TROPAEOLUM, Tropaeolaceae. Perennial deciduous climbers of the garden "nasturtium" family. Both grow well at Hidcote, Gloucestershire, and at Mount Stewart, Northern Ireland.

polyphyllum ●
90 cm (3 ft) apart	*[7–9]*	*Yellow*	*E. Summer*	DR
Sprawler				

Chile. 1827. Long trails of blue-grey leaves lie on the ground, 90 cm–1.2 m (3–4 ft) long. An astonishing display of warm ochre-yellow "nasturtiums" occurs in June, each flower held above the foliage. Questing fleshy roots make this plant difficult to establish; it usually seems most at home in hot sunny positions in well-drained soils. Plant 23 cm (9 in) deep.

"... foaming billows of silver and cascades of gold toppling over some rocky bank with ... nepeta's lavender blue mist immediately below to give piquancy and tone to the effect."—ATJ

speciosum ●
60 cm (2 ft apart)	*[7–9]*	*Scarlet*	*Summer/*	DR
Climber			*Autumn*	

Chile. 1847. Scotch Flame Flower. Though from the same country this plant does best in the cooler north or, in the south, against a north-facing wall or hedge, in peaty retentive soil, which should always be cool and moist. Its quick-climbing, frail stems, set with lobed, rich green leaves, clamber up any support, and carry small scarlet "nasturtium" flowers for many weeks, followed by indigo berries. The fleshy roots are difficult to establish in unsuitable positions and should be planted about 7.5 cm (3 in) deep, laid horizontally.

"... soon after the azaleas are over the Tropaeolum appears, to wreathe the branches with ... garlands of scarlet."—ATJ

tuberosum

60 cm (2 ft) apart	*[8–10]*	*Orange-*	*Autumn*	W	D
Climber		*Scarlet*			

Bolivia, Peru. 1827. This is less hardy than the two above, and has tuberous roots like small potatoes. It climbs during the summer, with copious, lobed leaves, and in early autumn is covered with flowers prettily shaped and marked. For sunny walls and positions in our warmest counties. 'Ken Aslet' is the name given to an extra free-flowering form found by its namesake.

TULBAGHIA, Liliaceae. There are several species, of which the following is the only one usually seen in British gardens where little or no frost occurs. It is happy in any sun-baked position in well-drained soil.

violacea

60 × 23 cm	*[8–10]*	*Lilac*	*Spring/*	PF	W	DS
2 ft × 9 in			*Autumn*			

South Africa. 1838. Narrow basal grey-green leaves and stout stems carrying umbels of small, rich lilac-blue, narrowly bell-shaped flowers. A pretty enough plant for warm corners; it thrives at Mount Stewart, Northern Ireland. Plant 5 cm (2 in) deep. *T. natalensis* is a pleasing small white species, with little green central cups turning to yellow.

TULIPA, Liliaceae. Tulip. The bulbs should be planted 15 cm (6 in) deep in autumn.

sprengeri ● ★

50 × 15 cm	*[3–8]*	*Red*	*E. Summer*	PF	DS
20 × 6 in					

Asia Minor. 1894. Having proved this to be a true perennial over many years I include it as the sole representative of the genus. No doubt there are other species as long-lived and as free-flowering, but I have not found them among the taller ones. Pale outside, the dainty flowers are a glowing, deep orange-red, borne well aloft over shining green leaves. With me it thrives and seeds itself in a shady position in damp, acid, sandy soil. It needs the yellow-green of variegated hostas to enliven it.

TYPHONIUM, Araceae. For a well-drained sunny position.

giraldii

30 × 30 cm	*[8–10]*	*Maroon*	*Summer*	DS
1 × 1 ft				

China. Dark maroon-purple spathes on short stems appear among the fresh green leaves in summer; these are broad and shield-shaped, coming to an abrupt point, and very handsome.

UROSPERMUM, Compositae. A sun-loving plant for any fertile soil.

dalechampii
46 × 60 cm	*[6–9]*	*Yellow*	*Summer*	P	DS
18 in × 2 ft					

S. Europe. 1739. *Arnopogon dalechampii.* Large lemon-yellow Dandelion-flowers overtop a spreading clump of toothed grey-green leaves. Useful colour for mixing with blue- and violet-tinted plants in the border front or large rock garden.

UVULARÏA, Liliaceae. Dainty woodlanders for the peat garden.

grandiflora ● ★
60 × 23 cm	*[5–9]*	*Yellow*	*Spring*	P	D
2 ft × 9 in					

North America. 1802. A delightful relative of Solomon's Seal, whose fresh green perfoliate leaves are on an arching stem, under which hang the straw-yellow lily-like flowers. 'Pallida' has more handsome flowers of paler yellow.

"... abounding in the beauty of its creamy yellow bells in May."—RF

perfoliata
46 × 30 cm	*[5–9]*	*Yellow*	*Spring*	P	D
18 in × 1 ft					

E. North America. A rather smaller plant than *U. grandiflora,* with markedly perfoliate lower leaves. The flowers are of paler yellow, with rather twisted up-turned segments, and produced a fortnight or more later; they are carried conspicuously above the leaves.

sessilifolia
30 × 30 cm	*[5–9]*	*Flesh*	*Spring*	P	D
1 × 1 ft					

E. United States. A plant quickly spreading in cool peaty soil, making a mass of erect stems which are hung sparingly with narrow tubular creamy bells. The young leaves are often brownish, and do not clasp the stem. A pretty companion for *Dentaria pinnata.*

VALERIANA, Valerianaceae. See also *Centranthus.* Apart from the species listed below, *V. phu* 'Aurea' is also sometimes seen in use in spring bedding for the yellow colouring of its young leaves; it is undistinguished in summer. Full sun is required for its best colour. All kinds are easily satisfied in any reasonable soil; the others listed here will thrive in sun or part shade.

alliariifolia
90 × 90 cm	*[5–8]*	*Pink*	*Summer*	P	DS
3 × 3 ft					

E. Europe, W. Asia. Like all the following kinds this is a plant of handsome appearance with a good clump of heart-shaped leaves and stout stems carrying a great compound head of tiny flowers, more or less pink in tint. The fluffy seeds are also attractive. *V. pyrenaica* is similar.

officinalis
1.2 m × 90 cm	*[5–8]*	*Pink*	*Summer*	P	DS
4 × 3 ft					

Europe, Asia. 1561. Vervain. Common or Cat's Valerian—because they love it so much. Both this and the closely related *V. sambucifolia* have good pinnate leaves, deeply toothed. In all kinds the flowers can vary from white to pale pink.

"... among the more effective things for grouping in the mixed border."
—WR

VALLOTA, Amaryllidaceae.

speciosa ●
| 46 × 30 cm | [8–10] | Red | E. Autumn | P | W | DS |
| 18 in × 1 ft | | | | | | |

South Africa. 1774. *V. purpurea. Cyrtanthus purpureus.* The Scarborough Lily will grow and flower out of doors in our warmest counties, against a south wall in well-drained fertile soil. Dormant in early summer (for planting), it produces vivid orange-red lily-like flowers on stout stems above strap-shaped rich green leaves. Plant 15 cm (6 in) deep. Sometimes ascribed to the genus *Cyrtanthus.*

VANCOUVERIA. Close relations of *Epimedium,* but rather smaller. *V. hexandra* [5–8] and *V. planipetala* [5–8] are described in my book *Plants for GroundCover.*

VELTHEIMIA, Liliaceae. Tender bulbous plants needing the most sheltered sunny corners in our warmest counties. The nose of the bulb should be above the surface of the soil.

bracteata ●
| 46 × 46 cm | [9–10] | Pink | Spring | W | D |
| 18 × 18 in | | | | | |

South Africa. 1768. *V. viridifolia, V. capensis* (of gardens). The leaves form a beautiful rosette; they are of rich shining green, long and broad, with crisply undulating margins. Held in a spike like a small Red Hot Poker the flowers are pale green in bud opening to very soft pink. The stems are purplish, delicately spotted with yellow.

capensis
| 46 × 46 cm | [9–10] | Pink | Spring | W | D |
| 18 × 18 in | | | | | |

South Africa. 1781. *V. glauca.* Similar to the better-known *V. bracteata,* but with glaucous leaves and pink flowers tipped with green, borne on mottled purplish stems.

VERATRUM, Liliaceae. Stately plants needing deep rather moist soil and good cultivation. They will grow for years without attention, but when it is needed to transplant or divide them, it is best done in autumn because they start into growth early in the spring. They are very slow from seeds. To retain the foliage in good shape, grow in rich soil in shade.

album ★
| 1.8 m × 60 cm | [4–7] | Green | L. Summer | PF | D |
| 6 × 2 ft | | | | | |

Europe, Siberia. The False or White Helleborine was grown in gardens by 1548. Most species resemble each other closely, and this has leaves like those of *V. nigrum* and the same bare stem. The flowers are in large dense heads, of palest green—almost white—and each little bloom is like a miniature bowl. A great sight at Raby Castle, Co. Durham. Yellow forms exist.

californicum

1.5 m × 60 cm	*[4–8]*	*Green*	*L. Summer*	PF	D
5 × 2 ft					

W. North America. 1896. The big flower-head is composed of rather drooping spikes in a tousled mass; their tint is pale greenish white, or old ivory. The leaves, held cupped and upright, occur up the stem nearly to the flowers, thus it is quite distinct from and less beautiful than *V. album*. But if it were growing well in my garden I should be proud of it!

nigrum ★

1.8 m × 60 cm	*[4–8]*	*Maroon*	*Summer*	PF	D
6 × 2 ft					

Europe, Siberia. Late sixteenth century. One of the rarest and most striking of garden plants. The leaves alone would make it worthy of cultivation for in the early year they push up, folded like a fan, clear green, large as an *Aspidistra* leaf, and of extraordinary beauty, 30 cm (1 ft) high. When established the flower-stems arise from the clump almost leafless, but branching into a plume of maroon stars. Lovely with *Agapanthus* and lilies, particularly with *L. pardalinum*. Good seed-heads. There is an annual display of it at Newby Hall, Yorkshire. The leaves last best in shade.

viride

1.2 m × 60 cm	*[3–7]*	*Green*	*Summer*	PF	D
4 × 2 ft					

North America. Late eighteenth century. The Indian Poke is well named, for its tiny bell-flowers are in a dense spike, wholly green; the entire plant is a symphony of pure fresh green. It grows well at Oxford Botanic Garden.

"These plants all do best in moist half-shady places ... rarely attaining their full beauty in dry sun-scorched soils."—WR

"... the curse of the cows in all the high meadows of the Alps ... stars of blossom ... of unmitigated dinginess, greenish, yellowish, or of a grubby brownish-black ..."—RF

(He must have been out all day without sustenance ...)

V.V. stenophyllum, grandiflorum and *yunnanense* are all names of species from the Far East, which have smaller spikes than those of the above, composed of vivid green starry flowers. They average 60 cm–1.2 m (2–4 ft) in height, and have narrow leaves [all 4–7]. *V. wilsonii* [4–7] is similar, with creamy green flowers.

VERBASCUM, Scrophulariaceae. Mullein. Several of the most striking species are biennial, but the following are sound perennials. They all appreciate well-drained soil in sun.

chaixii ★

90 × 46 cm	*[5–9]*	*Yellow*	*Summer*	PF	DRS
3 ft × 18 in					

Europe. 1821. Slender spires of small yellow flowers with mauve eyes are borne on stout stems over large basal leaves. I prefer *V.c.* 'Album', whose flowers, on account of the mauve eyes, give a soft grey-white touch, blending well with most colour groups, and particularly with campanulas.

'Golden Bush' ★

60 × 46 cm	*[5–9]*	*Yellow*	*Summer/*	R
2 ft × 18 in			*E. Autumn*	

Hybrid. 1963. *V. nigrum* × *V. spinosum*. A chance seedling from Hillier's Nursery, Winchester, and its long-flowering period, compact bushy habit and clear yellow flowers have much to recommend it. Innumerable ascending stems making a dense mass. A useful and beautiful frontal plant.

phoeniceum

1.2 m × 46 cm	*[5–9]*	*Various*	*E. Summer*	S
4 ft × 18 in				

S. Europe, N. Asia. 1796. The Purple Mullein is a most beautiful plant, but not long-lived; it has a handsome basal rosette of dark green broad leaves. It is easily raised from seed and will seed itself freely—and varies from white to pink and purple. It is one of the parents of the taller, pretty Cotswold hybrids—'Cotswold Queen' (1935), also 'Pink Domino', 'Lilac Domino', 'Bridal Bouquet', 'Rose Bouquet', 'Gainsborough', etc.—which have flowers of varied tints, but are, likewise, not truly perennial and need to be propagated from root-cuttings. By cutting back the spent flower-spikes, secondary spikes can be induced.

vernale of gardens ★

1.8 m × 90 cm	*[5–9]*	*Yellow*	*Summer*	DR
6 × 3 ft				

1869. The name is without status and has at times been made synonymous with *V. chaixii* and *V. nigrum*; also *V. pyramidatum*; probably a hybrid between *V. densiflorum* and *V. nigrum*. It is well established horticulturally, however, and is a splendid plant with many attributes, forming as it does a soundly perennial clump; it has big basal leaves which act as a ground-cover, and statuesque spikes, freely branching, of vivid yellow flowers. Like a great paint-brush in the garden landscape, it is in flower for many weeks. In common with plants of similar quality, like *Macleaya*, the basal leaves should not be obscured by tall plants in front.

"... its branching stems bear innumerable flowers for a long period."—EAB

VERBENA, Verbenaceae. For the warmer counties.

bonariensis

1.5 m × 60 cm	*[7–10]*	*Lavender*	*Summer/*	P S
5 × 2 ft			*Autumn*	

South America. 1737. *V. patagonica*. Rough dark green leaves make a satisfactory base for the wiry, angular-branching stems, each branch topped by a dense tuft of tiny lavender-blue fragrant flowers. They appear from June onwards. A single plant is curious, three together are beautiful, and a large group is a splendid sight. Seeds itself freely at Killerton, Devon, and looks well with *Cornus alba* 'Spaethii'.

corymbosa

60 × 90 cm	*[7–9]*	*Heliotrope*	*E./L.*	P CDS
2 × 3 ft			*Summer*	

Southern S. America. Introduced by Clarence Elliott in 1928. The tiny flowers are borne in conspicuous heads and are sweetly scented. A lovely sight when grown near to *Primula florindae*. A rampageous plant for a sunny but moist position.

hastata

1.2 m × 60 cm	[4–8]	Purple	Summer		P	DS
4 × 2 ft						

North America. 1827. A stiffly erect plant with pointed leaves. The stems branch into a refined candelabra at the top, emitting tiny purple flowers from purple bracts. It lasts long in flower, and is happy in any fertile soil. There are several named forms, including a grey-white one. *V. stricta* is a similar type but hairy and coarser.

rigida

46 × 30 cm	[8–10]	Violet	Summer/	W	DS
18 in × 1 ft			Autumn		

Brazil to Argentina. 1830. *V. venosa.* This is often used as a bedding plant but its tuberous roots are perennial and it is hardy in warm gardens. Erect, leafy stems, branched at the top, with heads of small violet flowers. A useful late-flowering plant.

VERNONIA, Compositae.

crinita

1.8 m × 60 cm	[5–9]	Purple	Autumn	P	D
6 × 2 ft					

United States. *V. arkansana.* By no means a distinguished plant in flower or leaf, but those who love the last flowers, creating a group, say, with *Cimicifuga simplex, Aconitum carmichaelii, Chelone obliqua* and *Aster tradescantii,* will appreciate the stiff stems surmounted by flat heads of daisy-flowers, of a very rich crimson-purple. White forms are known. Sun, any soil. There are several closely related species; *V. noveboracensis* (1710) [5–9] is much the same but less effective.

fasciculata

1.5 m × 60 cm	[5–9]	Violet-blue	Autumn	P	D
5 × 2 ft					

Ohio to Texas. 1972. The same stance and small flowers as the others, but often of a more telling colour.

VERONICA, Scrophulariaceae. Sun-loving plants of easy culture for any well-drained soil.

exaltata ★

1.2 m × 30 cm	[4–8]	Blue	L. Summer	PF	D
4 × 1 ft					

Siberia. 1816. This most beautiful plant is far superior to *V. longifolia,* and as a rule stands well without staking. Jagged-edged leaves are arranged up the single stems, which each support a plume of clear and lovely light blue tiny flowers. Superb when grown near late astilbes, but in drier ground. Beautiful with *Hermerocallis* 'Marion Vaughn'.

gentianoides ★

46 × 46 cm	[5–8]	Blue	E. Summer	P	D
18 × 18 in					

Caucasus. 1784. A mat-forming plant with broad dark green leaves. The spires of palest washy blue flowers in May are lovely for cooling down *Geum* 'Borisii'. There is a white-flowered form. Somewhat less vigorous is 'Variegata', whose leaves are splashed with cream. They are good frontal plants.

incana ★

    30 × 30 cm   *[3–7]*   *Blue*   *Summer*   D
    1 × 1 ft

Russia. 1759. The matted silvery foliage is more or less evergreen and it is a very lovely plant, with its contrasting spikes of blue flowers. Sometimes considered a subspecies of *V. spicata,* from which it is distinguished by its very grey foliage. A good form should be sought. 'Wendy' is a hybrid of rather larger growth, showy in flower but less grey in leaf.

longifolia

    90 × 30 cm–1.2 m   *[4–8]*   *Blue*   *Summer*   PF   D
    3–4 × 1 ft

Europe, Asia. 1731. Though the species itself is a rather dull plant when compared with *V. exaltata,* the Japanese *V.l. subsessilis* (*V. hendersonii* (of gardens)) is most attractive. About 60 cm (2 ft) in height the spikes of flowers are large and of deep yet bright blue. A hybrid 'Romiley Purple' is also excellent. They often need some support. 'Sunny Border Blue' [4–8] is rated highly in the United States for its self-reliant growth, dark violet colour and long flowering period.

    "... should always have a position among the choicest hardy flowers in a good deep loamy soil and open situation."—WR

'Mrs Adamson'

    90 × 46 cm   *[4–8]*   *Violet*   *Summer*   P   D
    3 ft × 18 in

Raised by Dingle Hollow Nurseries, Romiley, Cheshire, c. 1960. The erect stems bear somewhat greyish leaves and branching spikes of violet-blue flowers. A useful contrast to pink phloxes.

spicata ★

    30–60 × 46 cm   *[4–8]*   *Blue/White*   *Summer*   P   D
    1–2 ft × 18 in

Europe, Britain. A compact tussock-forming plant for sunny frontal positions, in any reasonable soil. Numerous stems arise, with dense spikes of flowers. Alan Bloom has successfully combined this species with *V. incana,* resulting in some first-rate plants: 'Barcarolle' and 'Minuet' are two excellent pinkish varieties. 'Sarabande', violet-blue; they all have somewhat grey foliage inherited from *V. incana* to complete the symphony. 'Icicle' is a good white from the United States.

teucrium ★

    46 × 30 cm   *[5–8]*   *Blue*   *Summer*   D
    18 in × 1 ft

Europe, N. Asia. 1596. Sometimes considered a subspecies of *V. austriaca.* The tallest forms or hybrids of this species just qualify for inclusion in these pages, especially as they provide that rare colour, true blue. They form dense tussocks covered over with spikes of tiny flowers. 'Crater Lake Blue', 'Royal Blue' and 'Blue Fountain', 60 cm (2 ft), are all first class.

VERONICASTRUM, Scrophulariaceae.

virginicum ★

    1.2 m × 46 cm   *[4–8]*   *Various*   *L. Summer*   PF   D
    4 ft × 18 in

E. North America. 1714. *Veronica virginica, Leptandra virginica.* For the perpendicular and the horizontal in borders this is hard to beat. Erect stems, set at intervals with whorls of horizontal dark green leaves, are terminated by erect spikes of flowers. It is clean-cut and distinctive, and is available in several tints, pale blue, pale lilac-pink or, more telling in the landscape, white. Easy to grow in any fertile soil. A form with curved flower-spikes is known as 'Pointed Finger'.

VICIA, Leguminosae. For any fertile soil in sun. Pinnate leaves.

orobus

60 × 46 cm	[3–8]	Creamy	Summer	P	S
2 ft × 18 in					

Europe, Britain. A plant of dainty, feathery leaves on upright stems. The tiny pea flowers are borne in clusters in the upper leaf-axils.

unijuga

60 × 46 cm	[3–9]	Lavender	E. Summer	P	S
2 ft × 18 in					

N.E. Asia. 1758. *Orobus lathyroides*. Seldom seen, but it has a lot of good points. Wiry erect stems carry heads of lavender-blue vetch flowers; with the pretty pinnate foliage a dainty effect is created.

VINCA, Apocynaceae. The Periwinkles have been treated fully in my *Plants for Ground-Cover,* and for that reason I shall omit all here except one, included solely on account of its late autumn flowers—which go on appearing in mild areas until spring.

difformis ●

30 × 60 cm	[6–9]	Milky blue	Autumn	W	CD
1 × 2 ft					

W. Mediterranean Region. Not so hardy as *V. major* and *V. minor*, needing the shelter of a wall, but reliable in the south-west. The fresh green leaves would lead one to think it was *V. major* until October when it begins its display of palest milky blue large flowers. Very charming when grown near *Nerine bowdenii*. The Sardinian subspecies, recently named by Dr W. T. Stearn, *V.d. sardoa*, has larger and more richly coloured flowers.

VIOLA, Violaceae. Most of the violets and violas are too small for our purpose, charming though they may be for naturalizing under shrubs. The following are easy to grow in sun or part shade, in any fertile soil. These are scarcely scented.

canadensis

60 × 30 cm	[3–8]	White	Summer		DS
2 × 1 ft					

North America. Broad, glabrous, rich green leaves. Large violets of near-white, flushed violet, with yellow throat. It prefers a cool position and is very similar to *V. rugulosa*, but forms a neat clump.

cornuta ★

30 × 60 cm	[5–8]	Violet	E./L.	P	CDS
1 × 2 ft			Summer		

Pyrenees. 1776. A vigorous clump-forming plant with copious small rich green leaves; a complete ground-cover. The flowers are perky, of rich deep violet, produced in masses in early summer. If the clumps are then cut over, and rain falls, a second crop will appear. I like best the cool 'Lilacina' and the clean 'Alba'. The latter looks particularly well with *Hosta sieboldiana*, the former with *Alchemilla mollis*. Evergreen.

elatior
>46 × 30 cm   *[4–8]*   *Blue*   *Summer*   DS
>18 in × 1 ft

Europe, W. Asia. A strange plant with erect sparsely-leafed stems and small pale blue flowers borne in each leaf-axil. The "tree-violet", so called.

rugulosa
>60 × 30 cm   *[3–8]*   *White*   *Summer*   DS
>2 × 1 ft

North America. Particularly rich green, copious pointed leafage, hairy beneath, and a long succession of small blush-white flowers daintily veined with blue. It spreads by underground stolons.

VISCARIA, Caryophyllaceae. Catchfly, from the sticky stem. An easily grown plant requiring sun and any fertile and reasonably drained soil.

vulgaris
>46 × 30 cm   *[4–8]*   *Pink*   *E. Summer*   P   D
>18 in × 1 ft

Europe, Britain, Far East. *Lychnis viscaria.* The double form, 'Splendens Plena', is a very striking front-line plant whose vivid "shocking pink" flowers are like the pinks to which it is related. Narrow green leaves in tufts. Divide and give fresh soil from time to time. The species with single magenta-pink flowers has a white variety, 'Alba'.

WACHENDORFIA, Haemodoraceae. Leafy bulbous plants striking in flower. *W. thyrsiflora* is possibly the most ornamental. Plant 7.5 cm (3 in) deep.

thyrsiflora ●
>1.8 m × 46 cm   *[9–10]*   *Orange*   *E. Summer*   P   W   DS
>6 ft × 18 in

South Africa. 1759. This is a most handsome plant, thriving at Trengwainton, Cornwall. It has coarse leaves like those of *Curtonus*—or even a tall *Aspidistra*—which are frequently frayed and brown at the tip; the flower stems overtop them and branch into short side-shoots, each carrying several starry flowers of good size of rich yellow-orange. The yellow-flowered species, *W. paniculata,* should also be tried.

WATSONIA, Iridaceae. A genus of tender South African corms which make lovely groups in our warmest south-western counties in sunny places, if planted about 12.5 cm (5 in) deep, preferably in retentive soil. Elsewhere it will be necessary to lift *W. pyramidata* and store for the winter, as for the large-flowered *Gladiolus* hybrids. *W. beatricis* is more or less evergreen and does not take kindly to drying off.

beatricis ●
>90 × 30 cm   *[8–10]*   *Apricot*   *Summer/*   P   W   DS
>3 × 1 ft   *Autumn*

South Africa. Tall iris-like leaves, glaucous and prominently veined. The flowers are funnel-shaped, spreading at the mouth, and elegantly lined on opposite sides of the stem, in various tones of orange, red, coral, apricot. Excellent at Mount Stewart, Northern Ireland.

pyramidata ●

1.5 m × 30 cm	*[8–10]*	*Pink*	*L. Summer*	P	W	DS
5 × 1 ft						

South Africa. *W. rosea*. Small flowers in plenty on a one-sided spike, of clear pink, broadly funnel-shaped, borne well above the leaves. This most beautiful plant and its white form or hybrid 'Ardernei' are of great charm and easy to grow in the right conditions. It has lived for me in Surrey over many years and sometimes flowers, but does not thrive as it does in Cornwall. *W. densiflora* is an allied species with pink flowers in summer.

XEROPHYLLUM, Liliaceae.

60 × 30 cm	*Cream*	*E. Summer*	W	DS
2 × 1 ft				

Two species. *X. tenax* [7–9] and *X. asphodeloides* [7–9], hail from North America. Extremely elegant, with grassy basal leaves and tall stems covered with narrow, appressed leaves and crowned with a broad short spike of creamy starry flowers. They are not easy to cultivate. *X. tenax* grows best in damp peaty soil in our warmest counties; *X. asphodeloides* again prefers peaty soil but an open and drier situation in full sun. Summer-flowering and fragrant, desirable, but ...

YUCCA, Liliaceae. Palm Lily. Strictly speaking these are shrubs, but I feel they merit inclusion in this book as they resemble shrubs so little, and so little has been written about them. They are magnificent evergreens, with stout sword-like leaves of greyish green, slowly forming clumps of foliage. They are happy in any reasonably drained soil in full sun, and their giant plumes of creamy white bell-flowers are one of the highlights of late summer. *Y. filamentosa* and *Y. flaccida* are dwarf growing and are very free-flowering, suitable for general work, while *Y. gloriosa* and *Y. recurvifolia* make eventually huge shrub-like plants occasionally producing giant spikes of flowers. The flowers last for a few days in water. In all species when a crown produces a flower spike it dies, but side-shoots are always present to carry on; in *Y. filamentosa* and *Y. flaccida,* related short-growing species and their hybrids, a crown takes about four years to flower if in good soil. They can all be raised from imported seeds but do not set seeds in this country; on the other hand the root-knobs found below the soil, if detached, can be used as root-cuttings and soon produce leaves in a frame or greenhouse. Though most of the following are perfectly hardy in Surrey, they need all the sun they can get, and should be given sheltered positions in cooler, damper counties. There are several more species which might well be hardy in the south-west, such as *Y. aloifolia* [8–10]. Evergreen.

elata

1.5 m × 60 cm	*[5–10]*	*Creamy*	*L. Summer*	P	DR
5 × 2 ft					

S.W. United States. 1886. Set with filaments, the extremely narrow leaves distinguish this species from its nearest relatives, *Y. filamentosa* and *Y. flaccida*. It has similarly beautiful, wide, starry flowers.

filamentosa ● ★

1.5 m × 60 cm	*[5–10]*	*Cream*	*L. Summer*	P	DR
5 × 2 ft					

S.E. United States. 1675. Adam's Needle. The fairly stiff, 46-cm (18-in), greyish green leaves have thread-like hairs along their margins—representing the needle and thread. The glistening pale greenish cream flowers, often flushed red-brown in the bud, are exquisitely beautiful and deliciously fragrant in the evening; they are borne on fairly erect side-shoots on the stiff stems, well above the foliage. A succession of flower spikes each year can be attained by planting crowns of different ages in a group. *Y.f.* 'Variegata' has most ornamental leaves distinctly striped with creamy yellow, but is considered to be less hardy. Most of the plants of *Y. filamentosa* in this country are derived from a free-flowering clone imported from French nurseries; it has very broad leaves and I believe is correctly designated *Y.f. concava*. Several other clones are to be found in Continental lists, such as 'Elegantissima', 'Rosenglocke' and 'Schneefichte'. 'Golden Sword' (yellow-edged leaves) and other variegated forms exist.

flaccida ● ★

1.5 m × 60 cm	*[5–10]*	*Cream*	*L. Summer*	P	DR
5 × 2 ft					

S.E. United States. 1816. In this the leaf-threads are also present, but the leaves are narrower, and usually much greyer, limp and bent over at the apex. The downy flower-spike is even more elegant, the long side-shoots—appearing well above the foliage—being carried more horizontally than in *Y. filamentosa* and thus displaying to better advantage the more rounded flowers, usually green in the bud. It is equally free-flowering and a highly satisfactory plant. Excellent at Killerton, Devon. There is a form with variegated leaves. The clone 'Ivory' raised by Rowland Jackman of Woking, Surrey, is of proved merit and very free-flowering. The flowers are held prettily poised outwards.

"... one of the best of its family for flowering generously."—EAB

glauca

1.8 m × 60 cm	*[4–10]*	*White*	*Summer*	P	W	DR
6 × 2 ft						

Central United States. 1811. *Y. angustifolia.* A rare species whose leaves are very narrow indeed, and have a thin grey line and grey threads along their edges. The flowers are of greenish white; and are well above the foliage in a narrow almost unbranched slender spike. It is seldom seen and probably needs almost desert conditions in our warmest sunniest counties to make it flower. United with *Y. filamentosa* or *Y. flaccida,* it has produced a hybrid, *Y. × karlsruhensis;* the foliage is somewhat broader as might be expected, but it is more free-flowering than *Y. glauca.* The buds are tinted with soft violet. From the photograph in the *New Flora and Silva,* vol. 1, it would appear to be very near to *Y. flaccida,* but the accompanying article mentions that there is more than one clone in cultivation.

gloriosa

1.8–2.4 × 1.2 m	*[7–10]*	*Cream*	*Autumn*	DR
6–8 × 4 ft				

S.E. United States. 1596. The appearance every several years of the dense flower spikes is no doubt a great event, but the magnificence of the great rosettes of stiff pointed foliage is an asset to the design of the garden throughout the year. It is used with effect at Lanhydrock, Cornwall. The flowers have a habit of appearing in autumn and often getting spoiled by frost before they are properly open. *Y.g.* 'Variegata', whose leaves are striped with yellow, is a rare and conspicuous plant, but may not be as hardy as the type. A form or hybrid raised by Rowland Jackman at Woking has been named 'Nobilis'. This has rosy-tinted buds and the leaves are less dangerous than those of *Y. gloriosa,* probably indicating *Y. recurvifolia* as the other parent. It flowers safely in late summer before the autumn frosts, unlike the parent species. *Y.* 'Vomerensis' is a hybrid between *Y. gloriosa* and *Y. aloifolia,* which has fine spikes of flowers and is worth seeking.

● ★ 'Vittorio Emmanuele II' is a hybrid with *Y. aloifolia* 'Purpurea' which seems quite hardy and is a magnificent sight in flower. The buds are plum-red tinted, opening cream, borne in tall panicles. Good foliage, and it branches freely making a good clump. Raised in 1901. Good at Polesden Lacey, Surrey.

recurvifolia ● ★

1.8–2.4 m	[5–10]	Cream	Summer/	DR
× 90 cm			Autumn	
6–8 × 3 ft				

S.E. United States. 1794. Perhaps the most magnificent of all and it takes pride of place in a small part of the garden at Montacute, Somerset. The flower spikes, produced no more freely but earlier than those of *Y. gloriosa,* have a more open and elegant formation, and the leaves are longer and less stiff, making huge rosettes of bent swords, truly superb for contrast and exotic elegance. A form, *Y.r.* 'Marginata', has leaves with yellow edges, and there is also *Y.r.* 'Variegata', with a yellow central stripe.

smalliana

1.2–1.8 m × 90 cm	[6–10]	Cream	L. Summer	P	DR
4–6 × 3 ft					

S.E. United States. Closely related botanically to *Y. filamentosa,* but to a gardener it resembles *Y. glauca,* with stiff, narrow, very sharp leaves, with marginal threads. The flowers are numerous in a dense slender spike.

whipplei ●

2.4 × 1.8 m	[7–9]	Cream	Summer	W	DRS
8 × 6 ft					

W. United States. 1854. *Hesperoyucca whipplei.* An astonishing plant but only hardy in our warmest counties in maritime areas, where it should be given the benefit of a hot sunny position. The leaves are long, grey, narrow and sharp. When it has gathered enough strength it produces a vast panicle of hundreds of incurved cream bells, purplish without. This has flowered at Bodnant, Denbighshire. It is one of the most wonderful plants in the whole world.

ZANTEDESCHIA, Araceae.

aethiopica ●

1.2 m × 60 cm	[8–10]	White	Summer	PF	W	DRS
4 × 2 ft						

South Africa. 1731. *Richardia africana* is the old botanical name for the well-known Arum Lily, or Lily of the Nile, so much used in greenhouses. It is hardy in our warmer counties when established deep in the mud of lakes and streams. Apart from the beauty of the great white spathes with their deep yellow spadices, it is a noble foliage plant. The leaves are of dark glossy green, broadly spear-shaped.

> "By occasional reinforcements of old pot plants we have maintained a small group of the White Arum, *Richardia africana,* in the deeper end of the pond, where its roots are always below freezing line, and the white spathes are as effective as anything of their season."—EAB

● ★ —'Crowborough' I secured this in a Crowborough, Sussex, garden where it was thoroughly established in an open sunny border. It had been growing without protection for many years. It has proved hardy throughout our warmer counties *when established,* but needs protection for the first few years—and to be on the safe side, a thick mulch thereafter. The mature roots delve very deeply, but youngsters should only be put in about 10 cm (4 in) deep. It is almost identical with the type species, apart from its being content in dry conditions, as well as wet, and it thrives at Tintinhull, Somerset. 90 cm (3 ft).

—'Little Gem'

60 × 46 cm	*White*	*Summer*	P W D
2 ft × 18 in			

1890. 'Perle von Stuttgart'. Raised by a Mr Elliott of Jersey, C.I. I am simply including this to call attention to the several dwarf varieties that have been named: others are 'Compacta' and 'Childsiana'. I have found several in old gardens but time is needed to compare all together and sort out the nomenclature. Some of these dwarfs are hardy in Surrey.

—'White Sail' This has been grown out of doors at Evesham, Worcestershire, by Fibrex Nurseries for many decades. It is little shorter than 'Crowborough' and the spathe flanges do not overlap so much. It is equally prolific and hardy. I have also found Sir Cedric Morris's 'Green Goddess' perfectly hardy; the spathe is green with a white throat. It is a "must" for flower arrangers.

elliottiana ●

75 × 46 cm	*[9–10]*	*Yellow*	*Summer*	P W DS
2½ ft × 18 in				

Transvaal. 1896. *Richardia elliottiana.* Like a smaller edition of *Z. aethiopica,* with brilliant yellow spathes and dark green leaves speckled with white. Hardy in warm gardens if well mulched during the winter.

ZAUSCHNERIA, See *Epilobium canum.*

ZIGADENUS, Liliaceae.

elegans

60 × 23 cm	*[5–9]*	*Green*	*Summer*	P DS
2 ft × 9 in				

North America. 1828. The grassy leaves are of no real importance, but the open spire of creamy green stars on greyish stems is very appealing. A charming companion to *Rhazya* and *Allium cernuum.* Sun, in any well-drained soil. *Z. glaucus* is closely related. *Z. fremontii* [5–9] is rather more vigorous.

Chapter 11

Alphabetical List of Grasses, Sedges and Rushes

Grasses have hovered on the fringe of horticulture for a long time, but have never really made the grade, so to say, having been overshadowed by more flamboyant flowering plants. They are today as popular as ever they have been. They were little used in the heyday of the herbaceous border, the accent then being on flower colour, but with a greater awareness of the value of plants versus just flowers they have to a certain extent come into their own, and the more aesthetic of landscape designers use them freely. In our own smaller gardens they are often used as a foil to the rounded outline of other shrubs and plants; in this way they add lightness and a different line and texture to the general planting. Sometimes they are given a bed or border all to themselves, but when too closely placed or exclusively used they tend to lose value. In moist ground many of them make the sharpest possible contrast to the vast leaves of gunneras, rheums, rodgersias and peltiphyllums. Sometimes indeed, far from being just a foil, the greater kinds such as Pampas Grass and *Arundo donax* can be the dominant plant in an area.

A novel way of creating something completely different in large gardens and parks is to plant grasses of contrasting kinds together with yuccas, phormiums and the like very widely spaced apart, and to cover the ground with shingle. This prevents weeds growing; the grasses can each be appreciated on their own, and the whole gives an arid, dune effect which is a delightful surprise from the usual luxuriousness of our gardens, and assorts well not only with modern building schemes and garden masonry, but also as an adjunct to a large planting of heathers and other dwarf bushes. A further scheme, perhaps an original thought, would be to grow the stronger grasses in single or grouped clumps in large areas of rough-mown grass.

The effect they give is due in the main to a reiteration of line: the constant curving of every grassy blade. To this they add flowers of varying calibre—great heavy plumes which catch the eye, or a mass of smaller plumes which together contribute an infinite softness to the scene. It is this line and denseness which is so useful for giving contrast to the heavy rounded contours of shrubs, the horizontal touch of *Juniperus × media* or the solid colour from herbaceous plants. Any grouping of *Helenium, Heliopsis* and the like would be the better for some yellow variegated grasses, such as *Spartina* or *Glyceria,* while the mass of soft *Phlox* colour benefits from the white-striped or glaucous grasses. And one only has to go to Sheffield Park, Sussex, to realize what a clever stroke it was to punctuate the display of autumn colour with clumps of creamy silver Pampas Grasses, so well reflected with the stems of Silver Birches in the lakes.

There is no doubt that the grassy leaf is specially attractive around water. Not only is the contrast of line perfect, but the sibilance of reeds and grasses, stirred by the wind, and the rippling of the water, is a lovely summer combination. Bamboos, which are shrubby grasses and therefore outside the scope of this book, are likewise perfect, by nature and by contrast, against a sheet of water.

For greater landscape and park planting the species listed under *Arundo,*
Calamagrostis, Cortaderia, Miscanthus and *Stipa gigantea* are all admirable,
over 1.5 m (5 ft) tall. Rather less in height but of an invasive character and not
suitable for smaller gardens are *Cyperus longus, Elymus, Glyceria, Phalaris* and
Spartina as listed.

These paragraphs have been written with the larger garden in mind, but there
are plenty of grasses for the smaller areas and many of them are not invasive.
Keeping to my rule of excluding very dwarf plants I have regretfully omitted
from the list several quite small grasses. As, however, grasses are somewhat
neglected and misunderstood I will refer briefly to them here to keep the
collection together. I referred to several in my *Plants for Ground-Cover,* and
treated the invasive Woodrush, *Luzula maxima,* therein; *L. nivea* is a charming
small relative, densely clump-forming, with sprays of white flowers in June.
Alopecurus pratensis 'Aureus', *Holcus mollis* 'Variegata', are two gay but somewhat invasive variegated grasses. *Dactylis glomerata* 'Variegata' and *Festuca
glauca* are two clump-formers of pretty white-variegation, and blue-grey respectively. *Carex morrowii* 'Variegata' (*c.* 1865) brings creamy yellow striping to its
very dark green, narrow arching leaves, and *C. fraseri* has surprising tufts of
white flowers over very broad leaves, 2.5 cm (1 in) or more wide. Between these
dwarfs and the giants are many for general gardening, listed below. A good
collection is maintained at Kew, and the trials at Wisley, Surrey, brought some
interesting things to light.

While their summer growth and colour are invaluable as a complement
to planting schemes of all kinds, their winter effect is also good. I am not
referring to broken or bent plumes dragged by the wind into the mud;
these should be removed before the winter really starts. But *Molinia caerulea*
and *Pennisetum alopecuroides,* to name but two, hold their pale parchment-
coloured leaves and stems well until snow flattens them, and add very
much to the winter scene. They should be considered for enlivening in winter
heavy plantings of shrubs as well as giving relief to the herbaceous plant
areas.

If one plants according to the species' requirements, grasses are easy to grow,
but they are often intolerant of the winter when freshly planted. The spring is
best for planting, even late spring when a few new leaves are showing. *Pennisetum
orientale* and all the Pampas Grass breeds are notoriously difficult to establish;
there are many failures at planting time. The nurseries may gradually work up
a stock from division in spring for some years successfully, and then, treating
them in exactly the same way the next spring, the operation may result in
complete failure and unfortunate loss; it is like playing snakes and ladders, in
fact!

It is advisable to cut down *Miscanthus* in autumn or early winter if you do
not want the tedious job in the spring of gathering up the multitudes of leaves
that have fallen and blown about. On the other hand I believe in keeping the
tops on the smaller and more tender grasses until spring has really arrived, as
an autumn hair-cut sometimes results in losses. For drying, most grasses should
be cut when in flower; they lose much of their grace and bulk if allowed to dry
on the plant. Moreover some of the dense spikes shed the whole display if left
to ripen. I have endeavoured to indicate those kinds which may be suitable for
later picking.

There is no real reason why grasses should not have been included alphabetically with all other flowering plants, but it does make for easier reference to
list them all together. They are not the only plants which give a grassy effect;
for other plants please refer to *Acorus, Cautleya, Crocosmia, Curtonus, Dianella,
Dierama, Gladiolus, Hedychium, Hemerocallis, Iris, Libertia, Liriope, Phormium,*

365

Sisyrinchium, Watsonia and *Yucca*. There are many others in the foregoing pages with grassy leaves of lesser calibre.

"Many of our gorgeous summer flowers look all the better when they have clumps of grassy foliage or feathery flower-heads growing among them to soften their effect."—EAB

ARUNDO, Gramineae. For other species sometimes listed under *Arundo* see *Cortaderia.*

donax
  2.4 m × 90 cm   *[7–10]*   DC
  8 × 3 ft
S. Europe. 1305. Giant Reed. For the sake of its leaves alone this is well worth growing; it does not flower in England and I cannot trace flower colour. A noble plant whose stems grow up each season, bearing on alternate sides broad, long, drooping, blue-grey leaves. To get the tallest and best effect it is usual to cut out stems which are two years old in spring. It is quite hardy in the south and thrives at Oxford Botanic Garden. An excellent form is known as 'Macrophylla' and there is a most lovely variegated form ('Versicolor' or 'Variegata') [8–10] but this unhappily does not seem to be hardy in Surrey and needs a cool greenhouse. It grows out of doors at Trengwainton, Cornwall. Happy in moist or dry soil in sun. Plant in spring. Cuttings of the stems or, better, the side-shoots, root readily if inserted in wet sand in summer in frame or greenhouse.

"... the king of grasses for foliage effect."—EAB

"*Arundo donax* makes more noise in a moderate breeze than ... in a gale, for then the long ribbon-like leaves are blown straight out and play much less against each other; the Arabs say 'It whispers in the breeze and is silent in the storm'."—GJ

BOTHRIOCHLOA, Gramineae. Sun-loving grasses for well-drained fertile soil.

caucasica
  60 cm × 1.2 m   *[5–9]*   *Purplish*   *L. Summer*   P DS
  2 × 4 ft
W. Asia. This is rarely seen but is a useful, dense, spreading plant for open spaces, where it will make a complete cover, the narrow leaves purplish-tinted after exposure. Purplish, elegant, open panicles.

saccharoides
  90 × 90 cm   *[5–10]*   *Silvery*   *L. Summer*   P DS
  3 × 3 ft
North and South America. *Andropogon saccharoides*. The Silver Beard Grass has dense silvery white panicles which decorate clumps of narrow greyish leaves.

BOUTELOUA, Gramineae.

gracilis
  46 × 23 cm   *[5–9]*   *Brown*   *Summer*   P DS
  18 × 9 in
S. United States, Mexico. *B. oligostachya*. The Mosquito Grass is so called on account of its strange spikes of flowers being held horizontally. A pretty little plant with narrow leaves, of unassuming beauty; to be looked into, but not for landscape decoration. When in flower it achieves a soft brownish purple effect.

B. curtipendula has less conspicuous erect spikes. Confused with the genus *Chondrosum*.

BRIZA, Gramineae. This species is one of the few perennial hardy species of Quaking Grass.

media ●

30–60 × 30 cm	*[5–9]*	*Green*	*Summer*	PF	DS
1–2 × 1 ft					

Europe, S.W. Asia. 1687. Common Quaking Grass or Trembling Grass. Leaves of no particular account, but delicate stems bear locket-shaped, nodding heads of great beauty. Excellent for drying.

"The flowers do continually tremble and shake, in such sort that it is not possible with the most steadfast hand to hold it from shaking."—GH

CALAMAGROSTIS, Gramineae. Of easy culture.

× acutiflora

1.8 m × 60 cm	*[5–9]*	*Brown*	*L. Summer*	P	D
6 × 2 ft					

Europe, Russia. *C. arundinacea × C. epigeios*. This sterile natural hybrid crops up in northern Europe, and the plant seen in gardens usually leans towards the first parent. While the foliage might be taken for any undesirable grass, by mid-summer the stems have grown bolt upright. And so they remain, without support through the winter. The feathery brown flower-heads fade to grey. A useful upright line for garden planners. It is shorter and also earlier in flower. 'Stricta' is a name sometimes given to these erect grasses. A selection, 'Karl Foerster', is recommended in Germany. 'Overdam' is esteemed in Holland for its white variegated leaves.

CAREX, Cyperaceae. Sedge, whence Sedgemoor, where they abound and their roots help to create peat. The triangular stems and flowers, male and female in separate sections in the spike, are distinguishing features.

buchananii

46 × 46 cm	*[6–9]*	*Brown*	*Summer*	DS
18 × 18 in				

New Zealand, North Island. This curious plant pleases the curious. Its wispy tuffets of very slender leaves of soft brown are at least different from everything else.

morrowii

23 × 46 cm	*[7–9]*	*Creamy*	*Summer*	P	D
9 × 18 in					

Japan. 1900. Not conspicuous in floral beauty but there is a form 'Variegata' whose arching, slender, dark green leaves are neatly margined with creamy yellow. Part shade. A smaller, brighter form is known as 'Evergold'.

pendula

1.2 m × 90 cm	*[5–9]*	*Green*	*Summer*	P	DS
4 × 3 ft					

Europe, N. Africa, Britain. Great Drooping Sedge. A woodlander, delighting in cool damp soil. It is a rather coarse plant with long, lax, arching, rather broad green leaves and erect stems which bear long, drooping, green whips. Its lovely graceful lines place it in a class apart, for contrasting with rounded clumps of hostas and stiff plants like phormiums, even though it be a British woodland weed.

riparia

60 × 60 cm	[4–8]	Brown	Summer	P	D
2 × 2 ft					

Northern and Southern Hemispheres, Britain. Greater Pond Sedge. In ● 'Variegata' the long, arching, narrow leaves are distinctly striped or nearly all white, accompanied by spikes of brown flowers in June. It likes a moist position, and the root is invasive. One of the most dainty and elegant of grassy plants.

stricta ★

60 × 46 cm	[5–9]	Brownish	Summer	P	D
2 ft × 18 in					

Europe, etc., Britain. 'Bowles' Golden' is a most lovely plant for a sunny place, preferably moist. Rough arching leaves by the end of May turn to brilliant golden yellow with a hint of green, and gradually lose their colour by the end of the summer. Fluffy, creamy grey flowers overtopped by brownish spikes. It is slow to increase and not always easy to establish. (*C. elata.*)

"... a very beautiful Sedge, with golden-striped leaves, another of my finds in the Norfolk Broads."—EAB

trifida

60 × 60 cm	[4–8]	Brown	E. Summer	PF	DS
2 × 2 ft					

Antarctic, Falkland Islands, Chile, etc. A distinguished-looking sedge with broad arching evergreen leaves forming a handsome tuft. The heavy flower spikes, yellow turning to brown, appear among the leaves.

CHIONOCHLOA, Gramineae. New Zealand tussock-grasses of graceful clump-forming habit for sunny well-drained positions in our warmer counties.

conspicua

1.2 m × 90 cm	[7–10]	Creamy	Summer	PF	DS
4 × 3 ft					

New Zealand. Hunangamoho Grass. Confusing nomenclature, in that this is the botanical synonym for *Cortaderia conspicua* and *Arundo conspicua,* which names have been erroneously used for *Cortaderia fulvida (q.v.)* (in gardens) and *Danthonia cunninghamii.* A dense tuft of fine leaves, arching, over which loose, open panicles of creamy white flowers appear, after midsummer.

rigida

90 × 90 cm	[7–10]	Creamy	Summer	PF	DS
3 × 3 ft					

New Zealand. Equally densely tufted, a mass of narrow arching leaves and arching stems with long wispy creamy sprays of flowers, all contributing to and within the shape of the clump.

CORTADERIA, Gramineae. The Pampas Grass is a well-known autumnal flowering plant of considerable majesty. Less well known are the two summer-flowering species and the richly tinted Pink Pampas. They are at their best in dry sunny weather, when their plumes glisten. Their leaves have uncomfortably sharp edges and make great basal clumps. Division is tricky and is best done in late spring, taking care not to let the roots get dry; they can also be raised from seeds. Old clumps of the deciduous varieties can be burnt over in spring.

fulvida ●
2.1 × 1.2 m	*[8–10]*	*Flesh*	*Summer*	P	D
7 × 4 ft					

New Zealand. *Cortaderia* or *Arundo conspicua fulvida* (of gardens). A rare plant and somewhat tender; only suitable in the south and west. In effect this is a refined Pampas Grass which produces its graceful flower-heads in late June, and they continue in beauty till September. The evergreen leaves are comparatively short and tidy. The flowers are borne on erect stems in a one-sided, nodding head, shining and silky, creamy flushed with pink when young, turning to ivory later. Best to protect with a mulch and sacking in cold weather, but it is worth a deal of trouble. Lovely with shrub roses.

richardii
2.4 × 1.8 m	*[8–10]*	*Creamy*	*Summer*	P	D
8 × 6 ft					

New Zealand. *Arundo richardii*. The Toe-toe has also been known as *Cortaderia* or *Arundo conspicua,* erroneously. This species is the one often seen in milder parts of Scotland, with widespreading, long, narrow, very arching plumes of creamy white, often bedraggled in the rain but holding on till the next summer. The stems arch outwards to support the plumes, giving a totally different "line" from the other species. In the south it is at its best in July and August.

selloana
1.5–3.0 × 1.8 m	*[7–10]*	*White/Pink*	*E. Autumn*	P	D
5–10 × 6 ft					

Temperate South America. 1842. *Gynerium argenteum, Cortaderia argentea.* Pampas Grass. The foliage is very luxuriant, making immense clumps. The stems are erect and bear splendid symmetrical plumes. There are many forms, both good and bad, in British gardens; some of the best have been distinguished as follows, and it pays to get the form most suited to your needs rather than take pot luck with simply "Pampas Grass".

Forms with variegated leaves have also been named, 'Albo-lineata', white-striped, 'Aureo-lineata', yellow-striped, but are rare in gardens.

● —'Monstrosa'. Immense, creamy white plumes, very feathery and open, spaced well apart, slightly inclining outwards. 2.7 m (9 ft).

★ —'Pumila'. A compact plant with short leaves, achieving about 1.5 m (5 ft). Dense erect plumes of creamy-white. A dwarf-growing variety is named 'Silver Comet' in Australia. It occurred as a seedling and was named thus by N. B. Cleaves of Victoria, *c.* 1960. It appears to be as hardy as other varieties in our gardens, and is a most useful addition for smaller gardens.

● —'Rendatleri'. *Gynerium rendatleri, Cortaderia rijndatleri.* Prior to 1873. Imagine the tallest Pampas Grass, magnify its graceful arching plumes and colour them with rosy lilac and you have this species—or at least the usual garden form known as 'Rendatleri'. It is a giant of a plant. The plumes are one-sided, borne on erect stems. 3 × 2.4 m (10 × 8 ft). Other pinkish forms have been named such as 'Roi des Roses' (1867) and 'Kermesina' (prior to 1875), but they have not come my way. 'Rendatleri' is sometimes erroneously ascribed to *C. jubata* (*C. quila*) [9–10], which is a less hardy species.

369

—**'Sunningdale Silver'.** A medium-sized plant, with very feathery, creamy white, open plumes, borne erect and densely grouped. About 2.1 m (7 ft).

CYPERUS, Cyperaceae.

alternifolius
46 × 46 cm	*[9–10]*	*Greenish*	*Summer*	P	DS
18 × 18 in					

Madagascar. The Umbrella Plant is popular in conservatories or as a room plant, but can be grown out of doors in our warmer counties. Narrow, grassy, bright green basal leaves; triangular stems with heads of green leaves and brown flowers. There is a variegated form.

longus
1.2 m × 60 cm	*[4–8]*	*Green*	*Summer*	DS
4 × 2 ft				

Britain, Europe, etc. The Galingale is a beautiful grassy rush for somewhat moist or very wet soil—even in 2.5 cm (1 in) or so of water. Increasing quickly, it makes a dense mass of stems bearing arching narrow leaves of a shining dark Hooker's green, overtopped by brownish, branching flower-heads. An excellent contrast to *Peltiphyllum* and *Rodgersia*.

DESCHAMPSIA, Gramineae.

caespitosa
1.2 m × 60 cm	*[4–9]*	*Green*	*Summer*	P	DS
4 × 2 ft					

Northern and Southern Hemispheres, Britain. *Aira caespitosa*. Tufted Hair Grass. A neglected ornamental species, easily the most beautiful and one of the largest of native grasses. It forms a dense tussock of narrow, arching dark leaves, and has numerous erect stems adorned by large plumes of tiny green or purplish flowers, turning to straw yellow—the quintessence of dainty elegance. It is frequently found in damp, acid areas of the country. *D.c. parviflora* is somewhat smaller but equally dainty. The form 'Vivipara' is an ugly curiosity which spreads alarmingly. 'Golden Veil', ('Goldschleier') is of bright yellow colouring, in autumn and winter.

flexuosa
30–90 × 30–60 cm	*[4–9]*	*Green*	*Summer*	P	DS
1–3 × 1–2 ft					

Northern and Southern Hemispheres, Britain. *Aira flexuosa*. Wavy Hair Grass. A smaller edition of *D. caespitosa* but no less charming.

ELYMUS, Gramineae.

arenarius
1.2 m × 90 cm	*[4–9]*	*Grey*	*Summer*	P	D
4 × 3 ft					

Northern Hemisphere. Britain. *Leymus arenarius*. A graceful grass, whose 60-cm (2-ft)-long, blue-grey, broad leaves create a unique effect, and are overtopped by stiff wheat-like spikes of blue-grey flowers in summer. It is a rapid colonizer, as bad as couch grass of a giant type, and dense enough for a ground-cover in poor soils, but cannot be recommended except for large waste areas. As a landscape plant it is of exceptional beauty. The flower-heads are excellent for drying. Gertrude Jekyll was very trusting when she recommended it; in her light soil it would be highly invasive, but perhaps more easy of eradication. Her garden staff must have hated it.

"... the fine blue foliage of Lyme Grass, a plant of our sea-shores, but of much value for blue effects in the garden."—GJ

canadensis
1.2–1.8 m × 60 cm   *[4–9]*   *Greyish*   *L. Summer*   PF   DS
4–6 × 2 ft

Canada, United States. Canada Wild Rye. This is seldom seen in gardens, though it is an erect grass, graceful on account of its arching ryc-like plumes, which in *E.c. glaucifolius* are a pretty glaucous green. *E. interruptus* [4–9] is a similarly beautiful species of glaucous tint, also from the United States.

ERAGROSTIS, Gramineae. Many species of Love Grass are annuals; some of the perennials are hardy in southern England. They prefer well-drained soils in full sun.

trichodes
1.2 m × 60 cm   *[5–9]*   *Purplish*   *E. Autumn*   PF   DS
4 × 2 ft

United States. *Poa trichodes*. The very long plumes overtop the dense dark green, tall grassy tufts. Flowers purplish brown. A useful late-flowering grass.

ERIANTHUS, Gramineae. Sun-loving grasses for warm positions.

hostii
1.5 m × 90 cm   *[7–9]*   *Purplish*   *L. Summer*   P   DS
5 × 3 ft

S.E. Europe, Asia Minor. *Erianthus strictus* or *Saccharum strictum*. The broad green leaves, 60 cm (2 ft) long or so, have a neat white midrib. Purplish stems produce brownish purple flower-heads, handsome and silky.

ravennae ●
1.8 m × 90 cm   *[6–9]*   *Grey*   *L. Summer*   P   W   DS
6 × 3 ft

Mediterranean Region and East to India. *Saccharum ravennae*. 1816. Ravenna Grass. In hot summers this grass is a striking addition to the garden; it needs heat to encourage its tall purplish stems which hold aloft long spikes of purplish grey flowers. The big clump of grey leaves completes the colour scheme. Only for our warmer counties, and best in full sun on well-drained soils.

FESTUCA, Gramineae. Small tufted grasses in green or steel-blue. *F. eskia* (*F. crinum-ursi*) [4–8] and *F. glauca* [4–8] are described in my book *Plants for Ground-Cover,* and are ideal for frontal positions. ★ *F. amethystina,* Central Europe, is a size larger, making tufts up to 46 cm (18 in) [4–8]; the most ornamental forms are of bright glaucous violet, or lilac-grey.

371

GLYCERIA, Gramineae.

maxima

1.2 m × 60 cm	[5–9]	Creamy	Summer	P	D
4 × 2 ft					

Britain, Europe, Asia. *G. aquatica.* 'Variegata' (1895) is a most beautiful form, with smooth arching leaves neatly and distinctly striped with creamy yellow. In the spring, the young shoots are flushed with deep pink. The sprays of greenish cream flowers are held well above the 60 cm (2 ft) clump of leaves. It is fairly compact in dry soils, but to be grown at its best it should be in moist or wet places, with plenty of room for its invasive roots. A lovely contrast for astilbes.

HAKONECHLOA, Gramineae. In nature it grows in shade, in soil containing humus.

macra ★

30 × 46 cm	[4–9]	Green	L. Summer	D
1 ft × 18 in				

Japan. *Phragmites macer.* This is usually represented in our gardens by the brilliant yellow-striped form. ★ 'Aureola' [5–9]. It makes a dense mass of short arching leaves and spreads slowly below ground. The green-leafed form is richly attractive too, and both produced pretty sprays of flowers in autumn.

HELICTOTRICHON, Gramineae.

sempervirens ★

1.2 m × 30 cm	[4–9]	Grey	Summer	P	DS
4 × 1 ft					

S.W. Europe. 1820. *Avena sempervirens, A. candida* (of gardens). Dense clumps, of about 60 cm (2 ft), non-spreading, of brilliant, narrow, erect, blue-grey leaves, overtopped by slender waving flower stems of grey. A most effective, safe grass for sunny places. Ideal in combination with *Sedum maximum atropurpureum.* *H.s.* 'Pendula' is recorded as the most vigorous and gracefully arching, with particularly grey foliage.

IMPERATA, Gramineae.

cylindrica

60 × 30 cm	[6–9]	White	Summer	W	D
2 × 1 ft					

Mediterranean Region. 1812. The form 'Rubra', from Japan, has leaves which turn to crimson as summer proceeds, contrasting with silvery inflorescences.

MELICA, Gramineae. Dainty erect grasses particularly at home on limy soils and will also thrive in shade, where their colouring is less noticeable but their growth more open and elegant. They prefer an open soil.

altissima

1.2 m × 60 cm	[6–9]	Brownish	Summer	P	D
4 × 2 ft					

Europe, Britain. Very dainty branching heads carrying brownish flowers. The variety 'Atropurpurea' ('Rubra') is richly coloured, and there is a white-flowered variety, 'Alba'. *M. ciliata, M. nutans* and *M. uniflora* [all 5–8] are less ornamental but the last has a variegated form.

MILIUM, Gramineae.

effusum

60 × 30 cm	*[5–8]*	*Yellow*	*Summer*	DS
2 × 1 ft				

Northern Hemisphere, Britain. Wood Millet Grass. The variety ★ 'Aureum', 'Bowles' Golden Grass', is a famous form of a British native; it is spectacular in the spring, when it is ideal for picking with bunches of early flowers. Gamboge-yellow leaves, stems and flowers; the whole grace of spring time in colour and quality. It is best in partial shade and seeds itself mildly.

MISCANTHUS, Gramineae. The roots increase steadily but are not invasive. Moist or dry soils.

sacchariflorus

2.7 m × 90 cm	*[5–10]*	D
9 × 3 ft		

E. Asia. 1862. A grand landscape plant for the largest planting, with something of the effect of a bamboo. It will form an excellent windscreen for the late summer garden, the long arching leaves rustling in every breeze, but I have not seen flowers develop. In warmer climates they are effective, silvery mauve-brown. This is a well-known plant; it seldom flowers. It did, however, in 1983 and it was considered that it was none other than *M. floridulus* [5–10], a related species from much the same area. *M. sacchariflorus* is reported to be more invasive than *M. floridulus*. A variegated form, 'Aureus', is recorded; it has not come my way.

sinensis

1.8 m × 60 cm	*[5–10]*	*Brownish*	*Autumn*	P	D
6 × 2 ft					

China, Japan. 1875. *Eulalia japonica*. These grasses have wiry, erect stems and are clump-forming, giving a graceful effect in any border of plants or shrubs. They provide an excellent foil to flowers and leaves of all sorts, remaining in beauty until the autumn. Easy in any soil in sun or shade. The flowers are not regularly produced in England except on the varieties 'Silver Feather' and 'Zebrinus' *q.v.*; it is the flower sprays of this grass that were so often depicted by Japanese artists.

★ —**'Gracillimus'** 1888. The leaves are very narrow and the sheaf of stems reaches about 1.5 m (5 ft), giving a most graceful dainty effect, the perfect antidote to solid clumps of hydrangeas. A noted plant at Tintinhull, Somerset. Two free-flowering varieties of shorter growth are 'Flamingo' and 'Kleine Fontana', both with flowers of brownish pink over the narrow leaves. 'Morning Light' has the distinction of being free-flowering and having leaves edged with white.

● ★ —**'Silver Feather',** 'Silber Feder'. From a flowering point of view this is a superlative grass, regularly producing arching sprays of silky, shimmering pale brownish pink. One of the greatest delights of the September garden. The foliage and growth resemble that of *M. sinensis*. Beautiful with late Monkshoods. 'Malepartus' is of only half the height.

★ —**'Variegatus'** *c.* 1873 (*M.s.* 'Vittatus'). While all these varieties have a pale grey midrib to lighten their greenery, this is prettily striped with white for the whole length of the leaf. A perfect companion to *Hibiscus syriacus* 'Blue Bird'.

373

● ★ —'**Zebrinus**' 1877. The Tiger Grass has leaves of the same size and width as the species, but by the end of July they become markedly variegated, with yellow bands across the blades. A highly desirable garden plant, a lovely background for phloxes, and it regularly produces in October beautiful feathery terminal sprays of silky, pinky brown, drying indoors to grey-brown fluff. There are more erect forms of this and 'Variegatus', known as 'Strictus', which are more suitable for smaller gardens.

"It seems desirable to have, next to grass, some foliage of rather distinct and important size and form. For this the Megaseas [Bergenias] are invaluable."—GJ

MOLINIA, Gramineae.

caerulea
| 60 × 60 cm | [5–9] | Purplish | Autumn | | D |
2 × 2 ft

Europe, Britain, etc. The Purple Moor Grass is able to put up with extreme cold, dampness and acidity, but the variegated form seems happy in most gardens and is highly decorative. *M.c. altissimum* 'Fountain' has conspicuous, upright, yellow stems; *M.c.* 'Windspiel' arises to 1.8 m (6 ft).

—'**Heidebraut**'. A good plant for autumn and winter effect; the prim erect stems are straw yellow with yellow seed heads. 1.2 m × 60 cm (4 × 2 ft).

—'**litoralis**'. Under this name, and also under *M.c. altissima*, are some much taller variants of the type, with wide-branching or arching purplish sprays. 1.2 m (4 ft) or more. *M. litoralis* (of gardens).

—'**Moorhexe**'. A small variant with neat upright stems. 46 × 30 cm (18 in × 1 ft).

—'**Variegata**' ★
60 × 30 cm · Purplish · E. Autumn · P · D
2 × 1 ft

This forms dense tufts, slowly increasing, composed of limp, narrow arching leaves, conspicuously striped lengthwise with cream. The flower spikes are held well aloft on creamy stalks, the flowers are decorated with purple stigmas and anthers. This grass, faded to parchment tint, is conspicuously beautiful in the winter sunlight.

PANICUM, Gramineae.

virgatum
1.2 m × 60 cm · [5–9] · Brownish · Summer · P · DS
4 × 2 ft

North America. 1781. This is not in the first flight of grasses, but it makes an elegant clump crowned by wide, dainty, feathery panicles. *P.v.* 'Rubrum' has reddish brown tinted foliage in late summer and red-brown flowers; it is far more attractive. *P. amarum* [5–9], also from North America, is an autumn-flowering species, with drooping sprays of purplish tint just over the greyish leaves; 90 cm (3 ft). Invasive.

PENNISETUM, Gramineae. All of these are for our warmer counties, in full sun.

374

alopecuroides ●

| 90 × 46 cm | [5–10] | Indigo | Autumn | P | D |
| 3 ft × 18 in | | | | | |

E. Asia, E. Australia. 1820. *P. japonicum, P. compressum.* A bigger plant than *P. orientale,* with normal grassy leaves. In September or October, after a warm moist summer, the indigo bottle-brushes appear, each with a white tuft at the end. The spikes are some 12.5 × 5 cm (5 × 2 in) long and are distinctive for cutting. Its clump of sere, parchment-coloured leaves is an asset in the winter garden. 'Woodside' (1971) is a free-flowering form.

macrourum

| 1.5 m × 60 cm | [9–10] | Green | Summer | P | DS |
| 5 × 2 ft | | | | | |

South Africa. *Gymnothrix caudata.* Those who like the Timothy Grass of our meadows will approve of this, with its pencil-long, pencil-thick, cylindrical green spikes. The flowers drop unless the spikes are picked while fresh and green. Clumps of 90-cm (3-ft) grass. Highly ornamental.

orientale ● ★

| 46 × 46 cm | [6–9] | Purplish | Summer | PF | D |
| 18 × 18 in | | | | | |

S.W. Asia, N.W. India. The narrow, light green, hairy leaves form a dense dwarf clump; slowly increasing. Well above these the flower spikes appear, each like a huge hairy caterpillar, or bottle-brush, of soft mauve-grey, the colouring being intensified by long projecting hairs of rich amethyst-purple; they dry off later to a greyish brown. A first-class flowering plant, beautiful with *Sedum spectabile,* with a very long flowering period. It creates an unusual effect in the Old Garden at Hidcote, Gloucestershire. It needs protection in cold districts and should not be divided until growth starts in late spring. Sometimes labelled *P. setaceum.*

villosum ●

| 46 × 46 cm | [8–10] | White | Autumn | P | DS |
| 18 × 18 in | | | | | |

N.E. Africa. 1891. *P. longistylum* (of gardens). The clump of grassy leaves might well be pulled up for a weed before the lovely display of flower tufts, composed of long white awns. Hardy in warm sheltered borders. Successful in heavy soil at Sissinghurst, Kent.

PHALARIS, Gramineae.

arundinacea

| 90 × 60 cm | [4–9] | Creamy | Summer/ | P | D |
| 3 × 2 ft | | | Autumn | | |

Northern Hemisphere. *P.a.* 'Picta' (1596) ('Elegantissima'), is the Ribbon Grass or Gardener's Garters. It is conspicuous in the summer owing to its white-striped leaves, and it is lovely as a contrast to purple-leafed plants. The invasive roots soon form a dense clump, and when it is suited it may get as tall as 1.5 m (5 ft), seldom needing support. Pale biscuit-coloured and very effective in winter.

PHLEUM, Gramineae. The Timothy Grasses all have appeal; I single out this species for special attention. It is easy to grow in sun in any fertile soil.

phleoides

60 × 40 cm	*[7–10]*	*Green*	*Summer*	P	DS
2 ft × 18 in					

Europe, Asia, N. Africa. *P. boehmeri, P. phalaroides.* Unexciting grassy tufts produce long, dense, cylindrical spikes of green, carried erect.

PHRAGMITES, Gramineae. A well-known sight in fen country. *P. communis* is the Norfolk Reed, used for thatching.

communis

1.8–3.6 × 3.6 m	*[4–10]*	*Purplish*	*L. Summer*	P	D
6–12 × 12 ft					

Cosmopolitan. *P. australis.* This is not a plant for the garden. There is no denying the beauty of the silky, feathery heads of purplish maroon flowers, but its far-questing rootstock rules it out. Where there is room in a marsh of vast size the form with leaves striped with creamy yellow, 'Variegata', is effective.

SORGHUM, Gramineae. For our warmer counties, in full sun.

halepense

1.8 × 1.2 m	*[7–10]*	*Purplish*	*L. Summer*	P	DS
6 × 4 ft					

Mediterranean Region. *Holcus halepense.* The Johnson Grass is a freely spreading plant for large gardens. The broad rich green leaves have a narrow white midrib. The open branching panicles of bloom are purplish brown and carried well aloft on leafy stems.

SPARTINA, Gramineae.

pectinata

1.8 m × 90 cm	*[5–9]*	*Greenish*	*Autumn*	P	D
6 × 3 ft					

North America. *S. michauxiana.* The clone 'Aureo-marginata' (1904) of the Prairie Cord Grass has long, graceful, ribbon-like foliage striped with yellow, and narrow flower spikes of green hung with masses of purple stamens. It has an invasive root and prefers a moist soil.

STIPA, Gramineae.

arundinacea ●

46 cm × 1.2 m	*[5–10]*	*Green*	*Summer*	P	D
18 in × 4 ft					

New Zealand. 1882. *Calamagrostis* or *Apera arundinacea.* When out of flower this evergreen grass—which assumes soft brownish tones after the young leaves have hardened—might be considered rather ordinary, though attractive, making a dense mass of arching leaves. The 90-cm–1.5-m (3–5-ft)-long flowering stems are hair-fine, arching and drooping, soft brown. Needs a good soil, and is best displayed so that its glistening, tumbled, maiden's tresses can hang down from a vantage point, as at Trengwainton, Cornwall. I have not found it successful in cold dry gardens, nor does it appreciate poor dry soils, but will seed itself in heavy soils as far north as Yorkshire.

> "The Pheasant's-tail Grass as it is called—goodness knows why, as it is no more like a pheasant's tail than a pig's—is one of the most beautiful of all light Grasses."—EAB

calamagrostis ●

90 × 90 cm	*[6–10]*	*Greenish*	*Summer/*	PF	DS
3 × 3 ft			*Autumn*		

S. Europe. *S. lasiagrostis*. Profuse-flowering, the arching, long, dense feathery sprays make a waving mass of green, turning to golden brown by autumn. Conveys the summery delight of a shimmering field of barley to the garden scene. In order to achieve this beauty one must put up with its lax growth and use the ground around it for spring bulbs. It needs a little support, such as that recommended for peonies, *q.v.*; if staked it will ascend to 1.2 m (4 ft) or 1.5 m (5 ft).

"... soft and feathery ... as they dry they turn to a pleasing light buff and last on the plant all the Winter."—EAB

capillata

1.2 m × 30 cm	*[6–9]*	*White*	*L. Summer*	P	DS
4 × 1 ft					

S. Europe, Asia Minor. 1815. A thin tuft of inconspicuous leaves, forming a tight clump. The white, wispy, curled and delicate flower-heads have some appeal for the flower arranger, but are scarcely substantial enough for garden effect. Grey stems. Closely related to *S. barbata* [6–9].

gigantea ● ★

1.8 m × 90 cm	*[6–9]*	*Purplish*	*Summer*	P	D
6 × 3 ft					

Spain. This resembles the oat but is a true perennial, with huge heads of flowers, glistening purple on opening, but turning to a real harvest yellow. Every flower terminates in a long awn. The tall stems withstand wind without staking, and the foliage makes a weed-proof clump.

"... flower stems bear long awns arching out on either side in a way that gives it an air of its own."—EAB

pennata

90 × 60 cm	*[7–9]*	*White*	*Summer*	PF	DS
3 × 2 ft					

Europe, Siberia. 1696. Feather Grass. In spite of its distribution, the plants in cultivation are seldom reliably perennial, but it is worth raising afresh for the beauty of its long wispy white flower-heads (25 cm (10 in)) long, over thin grassy tufts. Full sun and a warm position.

Chapter 12

Alphabetical List of Ferns

A hundred years ago the amazing Victorian craze for ferns and fern culture was on the wane. Many books had been published and many woods and hillsides had been scoured, not only for plants for sale to town-dwellers but also for any freak or abnormality of nature. These freaks were given fantastically long strings of names, one of the longest being *Polystichum angulare divisilobum plumosum densum erectum*! The craze gathered way quickly and died out equally quickly—rather like the Tulip craze in Holland in the early seventeenth century. All this and more can be read in D. E. Allen's *The Victorian Fern Craze*; the decline was due in great part to boredom, in part to the unscrupulous vendors of plants. But the craze resulted in some great books being written, some great collections being made and the inception of the British Pteridological Society, which still guides and interests enthusiasts. The names of Druery, Stansfield, May, Lowe—and later, Perry—stand out from the period, and some of their plants are still with us.

One enters into a new world in growing ferns. One speaks of fronds, not leaves; stipes not stalks; pinnae not leaf-sections; spores not seeds. The mystique is furthered by the strange fact that the plants we grow and admire are not the main, sex-divided life-cycle, but comparable with the mushroom, whose real life is lived underground. The true fern plant, which results from a germinating spore, is a tiny green thing like a liverwort, which has a very short life, occasionally intermarries and produces the next part of the cycle—the spore-bearing plant that we grow in our gardens. They are difficult to classify and names like "Shield Fern" and "Buckler Fern" refer to the shapes of the covering of the tiny spore clusters—indusia—on the back of the frond.

In Victorian times the hunt was up for every variant and peculiarity—each a minutely different collector's piece. Today I like to think we are interested mainly in species of ferns which will add to our resources for clothing beautifully the different parts of our gardens, and adding to our plantings the grace and delicacy which are the prerogative of most ferns.

I dealt with certain ferns in my book *Plants for Ground-Cover*, selecting mostly those which would spread; but we may say, I think, that all the larger ferns create good ground-cover and mulch the soil with their own quickly decomposing fronds, except some of the evergreens. The following selection covers ferns which I have grown successfully in Surrey, together with a few for the warmth and shelter of western coombs. The list does not include any of the extraordinary crested and bizarre forms of yesteryear. These strange freaks of nature are surely to be considered as malformations, since not one of them can be said to improve on Nature's perfection. Nor have I included any of the very small ferns such as *Asplenium trichomanes, Blechnum penna-marina, Ceterach officinarum, Gymnocarpium* species, *Crytogramma crispa,* and the dainty little hardy Japanese Hare's Foot Fern, *Davallia mariesii*; these are for the rock garden and other areas where tiny garden toys are treasures, such as peat walls, where in sheltered gardens *Pallaea atropurpurea* may thrive also.

The cultivation of ferns presents little difficulty provided that you do not live on the heaviest clay, a windswept heath or a hot chalky slope. They are very tolerant of any reasonable garden soils so long as they are open-textured and well mixed with humus—leaf mould, peat or compost. For bog, waterside and very moist ground we should choose *Matteuccia, Onoclea, Osmunda* and *Thelypteris*. The following require a certain amount of moisture throughout the season if they are to give of their best: *Asplenium scolopendrium, Athyrium filix-femina, A. niponicum, Blechnum chilense, Dryopteris aemula, D. dilatata* and *Woodwardia. Blechnum spicant* seems to tolerate considerable moisture or drought. For the driest soils we can choose *Dryopteris pseudomas, D. filix-mas, Polypodium vulgare* and *Polystichum setiferum*. The remainder need just the cool conditions one would try to give them. They are all tolerant of lime except *Blechnum* and *Thelypteris*. The *Dicksonia,* and certain species of *Woodwardia* and *Cyrtomium,* are only suitable for our warmest counties, and the first, the Tree Fern, needs continued dampness of soil and atmosphere.

Though many of the above will tolerate dryness when the fronds have fully developed, their size is reduced by spring drought; particularly is this so of the daintier *Polystichum setiferum* forms. In this connection a fortnight of dry east wind in early summer is as bad as dryness at the root. In fact, though I have to grow them in a garden much open to east wind, they are obviously of far better quality in valleys and sheltered gardens.

Invasive ferns, running freely or slowly at the root, are found in *Adiantum, Blechnum chilense, Dennstaedtia, Thelypteris palustris, Hypolepis, Matteuccia, Onoclea* and *Polypodium*. Their fronds intermingle and make interlacing greenery, with one exception, *Matteuccia*. In this each crown produces a separate shuttlecock of leaves. The same may be said of *Asplenium scolopendrium, Athyrium, Cyrtomium, Dryopteris, Osmunda, Polystichum* and *Woodwardia*; but as these increase one shuttlecock grows into the next and the lovely outline is somewhat lost. Purists try to remove side-shoots while young to avoid this, and there is no doubt that a single crown of, say, *Polystichum,* is worth a great deal of trouble to keep in perfect shape.

In Surrey several ferns are good evergreens, unless we are beset with very severe winter weather. The most evergreen sorts are *Asplenium, Blechnum, Cyrtomium, Polypodium* and *Polystichum*. In more sheltered areas these will retain their greenery until spring, and will be joined by most *Dryopteris* species. Beautiful as they are in spring and early summer, with their unfurling fronds and fresh greenery, they come into their own again in early autumn, because they do not succumb to autumn weather—except *Matteuccia* and *Athyrium*. When most of the herbaceous plants have flopped on the ground or stand sere and gaunt, and deciduous shrubs have dropped their leaves, most ferns provide a wonderful touch of unique greenery, and last until severe frost spoils them.

When one can be so choosy, it is best to plant or transplant or divide ferns in late September or in the spring. I find the adiantums particularly dislike deep planting, in fact nothing destroys *Adiantum venustum* so quickly as 7.5 cm (3 in) of soil over its spreading roots. On the other hand some of the others, *Polystichum* especially, tend yearly to grow higher and higher out of the soil and need either a good top-dressing or eventual replanting. In addition to initial preparation of the soil with humus, all ferns like a good mulch of humus in the spring; their own dead leaves help towards this. Many of the commoner sorts will sow themselves on damp mossy boulders or rotten wood, or solid peaty banks; the Royal Fern, even, has sown itself with *Kalmia latifolia* and *Gentiana asclepiadea* quite freely in the moss on a piece of absorbent sandstone in my garden. Spores can be raised by sowing very thinly on peat in a closed frame or box-and-glass, under a glass jar or in a green house; but it is a lengthy process.

They should be kept permanently cool and moist. The polystichums, which produce buds on their stems, can be helped by pinning down the stems, or cutting them off and pinning them on some peaty soil in a frame and treating them as for spores.

"Nature has provided other forms of beauty than mere brilliancy of colour, and after a feast of this the appreciative eye turns ... to the contemplation of the delicate tracery of verdant foliage ... such as the Fern world presents in surpassing degree."—C. T. Druery: *The Book of British Ferns.*

"The marriage of the fern and flower garden is worth effecting, our many hardy evergreen Ferns being so good for association with hardy flowers."—WR

ADIANTUM, Filices, to which Family all the following genera belong.

pedatum ★

46 × 30 cm	*[3–8]*	*Deciduous*	DS
18 in × 1 ft			

Northern Hemisphere. *c.* 1656. A choice and exquisite plant. A slowly increasing rootstock sends up black wire-like stems bearing fronds of maidenhair-fern-like delicacy, shaped like a branching crozier. Worthy of sheltered positions among choice small plants, although quite hardy. *A.p. japonicum* (of gardens) is noted for its rosy brown young foliage, which turns green on maturing. It is a variable species, and two very dwarf forms have been named: *A.p. subpumilum* (*A.p.* 'Aleuticum' of gardens) with horizontal fronds of rather glaucous green, and the true *A.p. aleuticum* which has vertical fronds, also somewhat glaucous.

venustum ★

23 × 23 cm	*[4–8]*	*Deciduous*	DS
9 × 9 in			

Himalaya. This closely resembles the Maidenhair Fern of our greenhouses, but is smaller. The lacy filigree of the fronds, tinted with brown when young, is the perfect foil for interplanting with *Cyclamen neapolitanum.* Worthy of every care but it appears to be quite hardy. The same cultivation as for *A. pedatum.* Do not plant deeply and do not top-dress heavily.

ARACHNIODES

simplicior

46 × 60 cm	*[7–9]*	*Evergreen*	DS
18 in × 2 ft			

Japan. *A. aristata variegata.* An intriguing fern whose fronds have a yellowish band on each side of the midrib. Slow growing.

standishii ★

46 × 60 cm	*[6–8]*	*Evergreen*	DS
18 in × 2 ft			

Japan. Korea. *Lastrea standishii.* Like so many of the species from the Far East this is a beautiful shining evergreen, with extra daintily divided fronds which, on a stem of some 23 cm (9 in), arch outwards or are held somewhat horizontally. A gem worth seeking, but rare.

ASPLENIUM

scolopendrium ★

30 × 30 cm   *[4–8]*   *Evergreen*   DS
1 × 1 ft

Northern Hemisphere, Britain. *Phyllitis scolopendrium, Scolopendrium vulgare.* The Hart's Tongue Fern. Broad, undulating, rich green strap-shaped fronds produced in shuttlecock formation. An ornament to any garden and a contrast to almost any vegetation; hardy and easy to grow in any soil, even on chalk, but intolerant of drought. An excellent contrast to the filigree of daintier ferns and also to the round leaves of hostas.

★ —'Crispum'. A rare form with beautifully undulate margins to the fronds as if they have been well goffered. One called 'Golden Queen' will develop rich yellowish colouring in sunny positions.

"... the goffered edge of the fronds is as perfect as those my old nurse used to produce for the frills of her caps."—EAB

ATHYRIUM

filix-femina

60 × 60 cm   *[4–9]*   *Deciduous*   DS
2 × 2 ft

Cosmopolitan, Britain. The Lady Fern is a moisture-loving species which will also thrive in fairly dry ground. Fresh green, divided into distinct small pinnae, the fronds create a lovely lacy effect; in general outline it resembles the Male Fern (*Dryopteris filix-mas*) but is much more refined. At its best in spring and summer; by September the fronds start to wither. It sows itself freely on moist peaty ground. *A.f.* 'Percristatum' is one of the few crested forms in which I can take an interest; the cresting is regular and heavy, and the stems on my plant are red-brown.

—'Minor'

30 × 30 cm   *Deciduous*   D
1 × 1 ft

Increases very readily at the base, and is only half the height of the Lady Fern. A highly desirable, neat fern. *A.f.f.* 'Minutissimum' is a size smaller. The Lady Fern has given rise to numerous beautiful forms in the past, now very rare. Some forms are worth searching for, producing most elegant daintily divided fronds in light green, and are classed under the name *Athyrium filix-femina* 'Plumosum'.

niponicum

30 × 46 cm   *[3–8]*   *Deciduous*   DS
1 ft × 18 in

Japan. *A. goeringianum.* The form I grow is less vigorous than its variety. The fronds are rich green, coarsely divided, distinguished by a maroon stalk and a maroon flush on the pinnae nearest the stalk.

—'Pictum' ★

60 × 46 cm   *Deciduous*   DS
2 ft × 18 in

The Japanese Painted Fern is unique among hardy ferns because of the colour of its fronds. The maroon stalk and flush are there as in the species, but the rest of the pinnae are of a grey, even glaucous, hue, making a lovely blend with *Anemonopsis macrophylla.*

otophorum
> 60 × 46 cm   *[3–8]*   *Semi-evergreen*   **DS**
> *2 ft × 18 in*

Japan, China. *Diplazium otophorum.* A bold and beautiful fern with handsome, broad, bipinnate leaves, pale green, almost glaucous. The spores are in indusia of maroon colouring, noticeable in late summer. This is a species to covet.

vidalii
> 60 × 46 cm   *[5–8]*   *Deciduous*   .   **DS**
> *2 ft × 18 in*

Far East. *Asplenium vidalii, A. commixtum.* In its dark stems, dark veins, and the overall shape of the fronds it resembles *Asplenium adiantum nigrum,* but it is infinitely more dainty and charming, and of course taller. This is one of the most elegant of ferns.

BLECHNUM

chilense ★
> 90 × 60 cm   *[8–10]*   *Evergreen*   **D**
> *3 × 2 ft*

Chile, etc. This is well known in gardens on our south and west coasts as *B. tabulare* or *Lomaria magellanica,* which two names are synonyms, and I have distributed it for years as such, erroneously. *B. chilense* is a much larger plant and is one of the most handsome of ferns, hardy in sheltered districts, in moist soils. In cold districts it can be protected by a thick mulch. The roots are slowly but steadily invasive, the arching fronds broad and massive, divided into finger-wide pinnae. The fertile fronds are conspicuous, each pinna recurving like a ram's horn. *B. tabulare* has narrower pinnae, much smaller fronds and the pinnae of fertile fronds do not recurve so much; I have not seen it in British gardens.

> "... the deep green leathery-fronded *Blechnum chilense* ... will wander about in rather widely disposed tufts."—ATJ

spicant
> 46 × 30 cm   *[4–8]*   *Evergreen*   **DS**
> *18 in × 1 ft*

Northern Hemisphere, Britain. Hard Fern. One of the prettiest of hardy ever-greens, it makes a good clump of neat, dark green shining fronds with regular pinnae. Above them are the taller, more slender, spore-bearing fronds. Ideal under shrubs and trees, on banks and in rotted stumps and walls. Lime-free soil, dry or wet.

CONIOGRAMME

japonica
> 60 × 60 cm   *[7–9]*   *Deciduous*   **D**
> *2 × 2 ft*

Japan, Taiwan. 1863; 1933. From the creeping rootstock the wide-spraying, arching fronds arise, elegant and prettily divided. Also known as *Gymnogramme japonica.*

CYRTOMIUM

falcatum
  60 × 46 cm   *[7–9]*   *Evergreen*   W   DS
  2 ft × 18 in

Far East. The Japanese Holly Fern is not reliably hardy in Surrey, but is quite at home in the warmer south and west. The dark, shining green, broad segments of the frond earn its name and it is to be treasured as a contrast to the dainty fresh green of athyriums and polystichums.

There are several named forms or subspecies, such as the larger *caryotideum,* with long-pointed pinnae, and *fortunei,* with narrower pinnae; this seems reliably hardy. Since the distribution of the species extends from Hawaii to Japan, plants or spores from colder districts of Japan would be best for our gardens.

CYSTOPTERIS

bulbifera
  46 × 23 cm   *[3–7]*   *Deciduous*   *Bulbils*
  18 × 9 in

North America. 1638. A dainty, hardy, small fern with bright green leaves on chestnut-brown stalks. An unusual habit is the bearing of bulbils under the leaves, which will sow themselves in the cool areas where the plant grows well.

fragilis
  30 × 23 cm   *[2–7]*   *Deciduous*   D
  1 ft × 9 in

Temperate Regions, Britain. 1762. Similar to *C. bulbifera,* but with green stems and no bulbils. Extremely dainty, slowly forming dense groups.

DENNSTAEDTIA

punctilobula
  60 × 30 cm   *[3–8]*   *Deciduous*   D
  2 × 1 ft

North America. 1811. *Dicksonia pilosiuscula.* It bears no real resemblance to the Tree Ferns, in spite of its synonym. It is just a very pretty, very neatly divided fern of bright fresh green, for the choicest of company. It spreads vigorously underground. Often confused with *Hypolepis millefolium, q.v.*

DICKSONIA

antarctica
  3 × 3 m   *[9–10]*   *Evergreen*   W   S
  10 × 10 ft

Australia. 1786. This giant, with great trunks covered in brown root-fibre, supporting a huge umbrella of magnificent foliage, thrives—and even sows itself—in the sheltered coombs of Cornwall and other equally mild places on the west coast and in Ireland. It is superb at Glendurgan, Trelissick and Trengwainton, all in Cornwall. I include it, though rather out of the scope of this book, being tree-like, to call attention to yet another tender plant that can add so much to warm and sheltered gardens. If it gets too tall all you have to do is to saw off as much of the lower stem (and root) as is necessary, and replant the upper portion.

DRYOPTERIS

aemula
60 × 30 cm   *[3–7]*   *Evergreen*   DS
2 × 1 ft

Northern Hemisphere, Britain. *Lastrea aemula.* The Hay-Scented Buckler Fern derives its name from the fragrance of the fading fronds, which are beautifully cut and elegant, of a luxuriant quality. Upright habit.

carthusiana
60 × 30 cm   *[4–8]*   *Deciduous*   DS
2 × 1 ft

Northern Hemisphere, Britain. *D. spinulosa.* While the other species of *Dryopteris* mentioned increase slowly from the crown, this seems to be slightly spreading in habit. The fronds are dark green, dainty, borne on thin wiry upright stems.

cristata
90 × 60 cm   *[3–7]*   *Deciduous*   DS
3 × 2 ft

Europe, W. Siberia, N. America. *Lastrea* or *Nephrodium cristatum.* Crested Buckler Fern. Not crested in any way, so this name is confusing, and the plant comes somewhere between the boldness of *D. goldieana* and the Male Fern. Mid-green.

dilatata
60 × 60 cm   *[3–8]*   *Deciduous*   DS
2 × 2 ft

Cosmopolitan, Britain. *Dryopteris aristata, Lastrea dilatata.* The Broad Buckler Fern. Easily grown and beautiful; graceful, wide-spreading fronds, broad and deeply segmented. A good contrast to the Hart's Tongue Fern. It will put up with considerable moisture.

erythrosora ★
60 × 30 cm   *[5–9]*   *Evergreen*   DS
2 × 1 ft

Japan, China. A bold-leafed plant whose main attraction is the warm rosy brown of the young leaves; they gradually turn to rich rather glossy green later. The reverse of the frond is decorated with scarlet spore-capsules, hence its name. This is a most beautiful and rare species.

> "... with fronds 18–24 inches long, of a beautiful bronzy red colour when young and of a deep dark green hue when mature."—WR

filix-mas
90 × 90 cm   *[4–8]*   *Deciduous*   DS
3 × 3 ft

Cosmopolitan, Britain. *Lastrea filix-mas.* Male Fern. This common fern is a splendid shade-bearing plant for almost any soil that is not boggy, thriving even in quite dry ground in any untoward place. It makes a graceful sheaf of elegant, freely divided leaves, which remain evergreen in sheltered districts. Very hardy. Good ground-cover. It sows itself freely on moist peaty ground and is in fact, like the German Iris, one of the most long-suffering of plants. It thrives in my garden in a sterile place at the foot of a hedge, and even so achieves fronds

1.2 m (4 ft) high yearly. There are many crested, fancy and peculiar forms. *D. abbreviata* [3–7] is a smaller, related species, from mountain districts. The pinnae lobes are crenate as opposed to serrate in *D. filix-mas*. The beautiful *D.* × *remota* [4–8] is a hybrid with *D. carthusiana*.

goldieana
90 × 60 cm   *[4–8]*   *Deciduous*   DS
3 × 2 ft

N. America. Large boldly divided leaves, achieving 90 cm–1.2 m (3–4 ft) in moist cool conditions, and adding to the general greenery a yellowish tint in spring, becoming pale green later.

hirtipes
60 × 46 cm   *[4–8]*   *Deciduous*   DS
2 ft × 18 in

Far East. *Lastrea atrata*. A very distinguished-looking fern of smooth regular outline and verging towards emerald green. Sometimes labelled *D. cycadina*.

pseudomas
1.5 m × 90 cm   *[4–8]*   *Evergreen*   DS
5 × 3 ft

Old World, Britain. *D. borreri*. The Golden Scaled Male Fern is one of the most vigorous and beautiful of all hardy ferns. It frequents open places, hedgerows, etc, in the west, and in the spring can be picked out from a distance owing to the golden green of the young fronds, unfolding like croziers from the golden brown scaly stems. The great fronds are a model of smooth, handsome regularity, and remain richly green until really severe frost. A magnificent plant of considerable landscape value, far more beautiful than the equally adaptable *D. filix-mas,* though they may be confused at first sight. It is much to the fore at Mount Stewart, Northern Ireland. *D.p.* 'Pinderi' is a small form with very pointed fronds. The species is also known as *D. affinis*.

wallichiana ★
1.5 m × 90 cm   *[6–8]*   *Deciduous*   DS
5 × 3 ft

Himalaya to Japan. *D. paleacea, D. doniana*. Apart from the Royal Fern, this I consider the most magnificent of all ferns hardy in Surrey; even surpassing our native and closely related *D. pseudomas*. This has the same brilliant raw-sienna, or golden-green (the tint of young oak leaves) of the unfolding fronds in spring, and the same smooth and handsome regularity of the greenery, but in addition the stems are clothed in sepia scaly hairs. One of the most magnificent of all hardy plants, but I have known it suffer in severe winters.

HYPOLEPIS

millefolium
30 × 60 cm   *[7–9]*   *Deciduous*   D
1 × 2 ft

New Zealand. Often grown in gardens under the name of *Dennstaedtia punctilobula, q.v.* It may best be described as a very dwarf bracken. The freely questing roots produce a dense cover of extremely dainty fronds up to 30 cm (1 ft) high in sun or shade. They are dark green and hairy, and with widely separated divisions as in bracken. It thrives in full sun on the rock garden at Edinburgh. Invasive and not for choice peat beds.

MATTEUCCIA. Invasive roots extending by long underground shoots.

orientalis
60 × 60 cm   *[5–8]*   *Deciduous*   DS
2 × 2 ft

Far East. *Onoclea* or *Struthiopteris orientalis*. A rare plant differing from the next mainly in its coarser leaves and the fact that the fertile fronds arch outwards. Exquisite autumn colour.

struthiopteris ★
90 × 60 cm   *[2–8]*   *Deciduous*   D
3 × 2 ft

Northern Hemisphere. *c.* 1766. *Onoclea* or *Struthiopteris germanica, S. pennsylvanica; Pteretis nodulosa*. Ostrich Plume Fern. Very dependent on moisture, and happy even at the waterside in boggy soil, this is an unusual plant, being the only hardy fern to make a slight stem. These stems grow to about 23 cm (9 in) in time and annually produce an exceptionally regular shuttlecock of erect, dainty fronds, exquisite in their fresh spring greenery, but intolerant of drought and drying winds. The fronds are usually past their best by the end of August. A lovely sight at Hidcote, Gloucestershire, in the Stream Garden. The fertile fronds are dark brown and stand stiffly erect all the winter, achieving 60 cm (2 ft) in extra favourable conditions.

ONOCLEA

sensibilis ★
46 × 90 cm   *[4–8]*   *Deciduous*   D
18 in × 3 ft

N. Asia, North America. 1799. A marsh-loving fern, with freely-running rootstock, making good ground-cover. Bold, arching, broadly-segmented leaves of light, fresh green, continually renewed during the summer. A handsome plant where an invasive fern can be accommodated, under trees or tall shrubs. It is happy in most soils which remain damp. Very good for pressing.

"It has such a tender oak-leaf green of its own all the Summer, and turns a pleasant foxy-brown in Autumn ..."—EAB

ONYCHIUM

japonicum ★
46 × 46 cm   *[7–9]*   *Deciduous*   DS
18 × 18 in

China, Japan. 1924. Slowly increasing clumps produce some of the most finely lacy fronds imaginable. The ideal foil for hardy orchids, *Dactylorrhiza* species. Reintroduced from Sichuan by Dr A. Leslie.

OREOPTERIS

limbosperma
60 × 46 cm   *[5–8]*   *Deciduous*   DS
2 ft × 18 in

N. and S. Hemispheres, Britain. *Thelypteris limbosperma, Dryopteris oreopteris, Lastrea montana*. The Mountain Fern frequents dripping banks in nature but is happier in drier situations in the garden so long as the soil is lime-free. Dainty, finely divided pinnae which when unfolding are covered with creamy grey scales, giving an unusual touch to the prevailing spring greenery.

OSMUNDA. All osmundas need moist conditions. The first two species have fronds resembling, more or less, the Male Fern, but *O. regalis,* and its forms, is something apart—bolder, larger in every way.

cinnamomea
1.2 m × 60 cm   [4–9]   *Deciduous*   DS
4 × 2 ft

North America. The unfurling fronds are covered with creamy brown woolly fluff, and open out into tall, well-poised greenery of fresh tint. The fertile fronds are separate and wither away in summer.

claytoniana
1.2 m × 60 cm   [4–9]   *Deciduous*   DS
4 × 2 ft

North America. 1772. *O. interrupta.* The Interrupted Fern derives its name from the clusters of brown fertile pinnae borne in the middle portion of the whole frond: the greenery is thoroughly interrupted.

regalis
1.2 m × 90 cm   [3–9]   *Deciduous*   DS
4 × 3 ft

Cosmopolitan, Britain. Well named the Royal Fern, for it is the largest and most handsome that can be grown outdoors in England, delighting in moist peaty bog or stream- or pond-edges, or any soil that remains moist in summer. Extremely elegant leaves, exquisite when unrolling in crozier form in spring, when they are tinted with coppery brown, and they add bright yellow and snuff-brown to the autumn scene. Admirable for pressing and drying.

Spores germinate reasonably well if sown as soon as ripe, but in spite of this osmundas remain comparatively rare plants. Rare forms are occasionally seen. A dainty variety called *O.r. gracilis* (1827), seldom achieving more than 90 cm (3 ft), has young fronds of coppery colour, and has sown itself more than once on a mossy rock for me. This American is undoubtedly the most beautiful Royal Fern for the smaller garden. 'Purpurascens' is much taller, with fronds coppery tinted when young and retaining a rather glaucous tint for most of the summer, and lasting green well into the autumn. 'Cristata' is less beautiful than the typical species but has frilled pinnae.

O. regalis grows in many British boggy areas, and it is a wonderful experience to see this great fern growing wild with Yellow Flag on Sedgemoor, Somerset. All the osmundas build up their clumps with a mass of peaty roots, and the only way to divide them is to cut the crown apart with a spade—a harrowing business and only to be done for one's very best friend.

"... having in the middle of the great and hard wooddy part thereof some small whitenesse, which hath beene called the heart of *Osmund* the water-man."—GH

PAESIA

scaberula
30 × 30 cm   [7–9]   *Deciduous*   P   W   D
1 × 1 ft

New Zealand. 1882. *Pteris scaberula.* A very charming, delicate-looking fern which grows happily at Washfield Nursery, Hawkhurst, increasing freely underground. Branching fronds of tender lacy green. Somewhat tender.

POLYPODIUM, Polypody.

vulgare
30 × 30 cm	*[5–8]*	*Evergreen*	DS
1 × 1 ft			

Temperate Regions, Britain. Common Polypody. A first-rate colonizer, creating an ornamental and effective ground-cover of mid-green deeply cut leaves. For dry positions. This often grows on tree branches in the moister west. The fronds are long and narrow, seldom more than 7.5 cm (3 in) wide.

★ —'Cornubiense'. The lovely Cornish variant whose fronds are divided into small segments, achieving a lacy effect. It is apt to revert to the original; these fronds should be removed at once. One of the most beautiful sights in the August garden, when its leaves are a lovely fresh spring-green.

Botanists observe two closely related species, or forms of the one, *P. australe* and *P. interjectum*. Both have much broader fronds, particularly the former, to which 'Cambricum' the Welsh Polypody belongs; it is equally beautifully divided as in 'Cornubiense'. 'Longicaudatum', with attenuated fronds, 'Trichomanoides', with daintily modelled fronds, and other collectors' pieces are all charming variants. All of these ferns are ideal lowly cover whose new leaves do not appear before summer, when they bring lovely fresh greenery, and last until late winter, when they should be cut off.

POLYSTICHUM, Shield Fern.

acrostichoides
60 × 60 cm	*[3–9]*	*Evergreen*	DS
2 × 2 ft			

E. North America. Sword Fern or Christmas Fern—on account of its evergreen beauty. Less handsome than *P. munitum,* but the frond tips are narrowed to a point, bearing the fertile pinnae, and this no doubt earns its name of Sword Fern.

aculeatum ★
90 × 60 cm	*[4–8]*	*Evergreen*	DS
3 × 2 ft			

Europe, Britain. *P. lobatum.* Hard Shield Fern. Long, graceful, daintily cut fronds of yellowish green in spring, developing into rich shining green later. One of the most elegant. It reaches a very high degree of elegance in *P.a.* 'Pulcherrimum' and its forms, which should be sought and propagated. *P.a.* 'Plumosum' is also to be sought.

adiantiforme
90 × 60 cm	*[7–9]*	*Evergreen*	DS
3 × 2 ft			

South America, South Africa, New Zealand. A beautiful glossy evergreen fern, with neat, hard frond divisions. It seems to be hardy in Surrey but the leaves are damaged by frost.

braunii
60 × 46 cm	*[4–8]*	*Deciduous*	DS
2 ft × 18 in			

Europe and America. 1919. Prickly Shield Fern or Braun's Holly Fern. Handsomely cut fronds, beautifully silvery when young, bristly when mature. Highly desirable for moist shade.

discretum ★

60 × 90 cm	[6–8]	Evergreen	DS
2 × 3 ft			

Far East. *P. setosum*; *Dryopteris varia setosa*. The neatly and deeply divided fronds are hard and shining and of rich green. This is likely to become a favourite when better known. Severe frost damages the fronds in exposed gardens.

"... the handsome *Polystichum setosum*, with beautiful dark green, shining foliage." WR

lonchitis

46 × 30 cm	[2–8]	Evergreen	DS
18 in × 1 ft			

Arctic and Temperate Regions. *Aspidium lonchitis*. Holly Fern. It has proved difficult to grow in Surrey, but is easier in cooler and moister districts. Hard, dark green, simple pinnate leaves, like a small edition of *P. munitum*. It is less entitled to its vernacular name than *Cyrtomium falcatum*.

munitum ★

90 × 90 cm	[5–8]	Evergreen	DS
3 × 3 ft			

W. North America. Christmas Fern, Sword Fern. The finest evergreen hardy fern, making big clumps of radiating fronds, long and often beautifully curved, with multitudes of regular, narrow, undivided pinnae, of shining dark green. A great asset to any shady or half-shady garden, especially in winter, and a good contrast to hellebores and snowdrops. The crowns increase steadily, making a large clump. It is a very variable plant in nature, forms from the coastal ranges being the most luxuriant—though not necessarily the hardiest—and one such is distinguished by the name 'Inciso-serratum'. Like *P. acrostichoides* of the Eastern States, it is also known as Christmas Fern.

"... a good specimen is as beautiful as any fern."—EAB

polyblepharum ★

60 × 60 cm	[5–8]	Evergreen	DS
2 × 2 ft			

Japan and South Korea. Only less glittering than *P. squarrosum*. A very beautiful dark green fern, distinctively cut fronds.

setiferum ★

1.2 m × 90 cm	[5–8]	Evergreen	DS
4 × 3 ft			

Europe, Britain. *P. angulare*. The Soft Shield Fern. Apart from a few of the most elegant forms of the Lady Fern, these are the queens of the tribe; unlike the Lady Ferns they are noticeably tolerant of dry conditions, and will thrive almost anywhere. They retain their freshness until late winter. *P. setiferum* 'Acutilobum' is even quite at home in paved paths in full sun. *P. setiferum* itself has a luxuriance and poise of frond not found in other species; the stems are encased in shaggy pale brownish grey scales, and the fronds are of soft dull green. It is exquisite in tint when unfurling.

—'Acutilobum' ★

60 × 60 cm   *Evergreen*   Bulbils
2 × 2 ft

1852. *P.s.* 'Proliferum'. Some forms of *P. setiferum* occasionally produce a bud on the leaf-stem from which they may be propagated, but this bears several regularly. It is fortunate that this prolific form is of such exquisite beauty, and is so tolerant of cultivation almost anywhere. The long pointed fronds of dark green are arranged in a spiral pattern around the crown and are extremely daintily divided.

—'**Dahlem**'. A particularly prettily cut, light green form, newly from Germany. Plentiful "buds" on the stems. 90 cm (3 ft).

★ —'**Divisilobum**'. For sheer elegance the forms bearing this name are hard to beat, the form known as 'Bland' being tall, dark green, infinitely graceful and finely divided.

★ —'**Densum**'. A name given to a number of forms which sometimes produce leaf-buds, and are extremely plumose in quality. Each segment of the frond is doubled until the effect is like a dense parsley-green feather. As in many *P. setiferum* forms the fronds develop a spiral twist around the crown. The ultimate is 'Plumosum Densum Erectum'; the last term refers to the raised pile of featherings on the fronds.

—**gracile**. An exceedingly finely cut and elegant form.

—'**Herrenhausen**'. Another comparatively new form from Germany with mid-green daintily cut fronds. Like those of 'Acutilobum' they produce "buds" along the stems which form a speedy means of increase. 90 cm (3 ft).

rigens

46 × 46 cm   *[5–9]*   *Semi-evergreen*   DS
18 × 18 in

Japan. Comparatively light green fronds, broadly divided at the base, simply pinnate above. Rigidly erect, with chestnut coloured scales on the stems. Handsome.

squarrosum ★

60 × 60 cm   *[6–9]*   *Evergreen*   DS
2 × 2 ft

Himalaya, China. The distinctly lobed and cut fronds are remarkable for their shining, very dark green tint. Arching and graceful.

tsusimense ★

30 × 30 cm   *[6–8]*   *Evergreen*   DS
1 × 1 ft

Far East. *Polystichum monotis*. This bears considerable resemblance to *P. discretum* in its evergreen neat hard leaves of shining green, and is equally desirable.

THELYPTERIS

palustris

60 × 60 cm   *[5–8]*   *Deciduous*   D
2 × 2 ft

Northern Hemisphere, Britain. *Lastrea* or *Dryopteris thelypteris*. The Marsh Fern has dainty erect fronds. It is unassuming but is included because of its tolerance for the marshy fringe of pools, etc. where its wandering roots will quickly spread.

WOODWARDIA

radicans

90 × 90 cm	*[9–10]*	*Evergreen*	W	Bulbils
3 × 3 ft				

Canaries, S. Europe, China, N. India, etc. 1779. A very graceful tender fern for really sheltered gardens in the west, where its fronds may achieve 1.8 m (6 ft) in length. Of exceptional beauty. Each magnificent, long, arching, light green, boldly divided frond bears a bud at the tip which, if secured by a stone, will take root. *W. orientalis* (*W. radicans orientalis*) is of similar appearance and probably of equal hardiness; it lacks the tip-buds.

virginica

46 × 46 cm	*[6–9]*	*Deciduous*	DS
18 × 18 in			

Canada, E. United States. *Anchistea virginica*. Erect fronds, of bold outline, arising from a creeping rootstock. The pinnae are deeply lobed. It needs moist soil.

Chapter 13

Cuttings from My Notebook

We are never too young or too old to start an *aide-mémoire* and I hope that the following lists, tables and suggestions will be helpful to intending planters. It should be remembered that the plant names refer to species mentioned in Alphabetical Lists in this book, and not to other species.

1. Frontal Plants
A big omission from this book is the numerous plants which are suitable for the fronts of borders and beds, mostly less than 30 cm (1 ft) in height, or thereabouts. Their inclusion in detail would have resulted in a book of excessive size and cost. The bulk of them are described and prescribed for in my *Plants for Ground-Cover*, so I will do no more here than provide a list of names.

E = Evergreen.
H = Shade-loving plants.

Ajuga reptans and other species 'Jungle Beauty' is a very tall new American Hybrid.	E
Alchemilla conjuncta	
Alyssum saxatile	E
Arabis	E
Armeria maritima	E
Armeria corsica (of gardens)	E
Asarum europaeum	H
Astilbe glaberrima	
Aubrieta	E
Campanula poscharskyana; 'Stella' is more compact than the species.	E
Carlina	
Cerastium tomentosum	E
Chrysogonum virginianum	
Corydalis cheilanthifolia	
Fuchsia 'Tom Thumb'	
Gentiana septemfida, G. gracilipes	
Heloniopsis	
Hypericum rhodopaeum and others	E
Iris chamaeris, I. ruthenica and others	
Lamium maculatum	EH
Liriope spicata	
Mitella diphylla	E
Omphalodes cappadocica	H
Omphalodes verna	H
Pachyphragma macrophyllum (often	

wrongly labelled *Cardamine asarifolia*).	H
Penstemon diffusus	E
Penstemon scouleri and others	E
Phlox subulata	E
Polygonum affine	
Potentilla alba	
Primula, all kinds of primroses, polyanthus and the like.	H
Prunella grandiflora, and varieties.	
Sanguinaria canadensis	H
Saponaria ocymoides	
Saxifraga geum	EH
Saxifraga × urbium forms and hybrids	EH
Sedum anacampseros	E
Sedum ewersii	
Sedum 'Ruby Glow'	
Sedum spurium and varieties	E
Sisyrinchium angustifolium	
Solidago 'Golden Thumb'	
Tiarella cordifolia; *T. wherryi*	EH
Viola labradorica	
Viola odorata	E
Viola septentrionalis	
Waldsteinia ternata	E

Grasses—see introduction to Chap. 11
Ferns—see introduction to Chap. 12

2. Sub-shrubs

Though our borders and beds of perennials may well have shrubs as a background to give height and to augment the colour schemes, I should find it difficult to make a satisfactory display without the use of some of the following little bushy plants. Most are included in detail in my book *Plants for Ground-Cover.*

E = Evergreen.
G = grey foliage.
H = will tolerate continuous or passing shade other than overhead shade.
W = need warm positions in Surrey.

Ballota pseudodictamnus	G	*Iberis sempervirens*	EH
Berberis thunbergii 'Atropurpurea Nana'		*Potentilla fruticosa* 'Beesii'	
		Potentilla fruticosa 'Clotted Cream'	
Cheiranthus and *Erysimum*	E	*Potentilla fruticosa* 'Elisabeth'	
Convolvulus cneorum	EGW	*Potentilla fruticosa* 'Tangerine'	
Dorycnium hirsutum	GW	*Potentilla* 'Manchu'	
Erodium macradenum and *E. trichomanefolium*		*Ruta graveolens* 'Jackman's Blue' EG	
		Salvia officinalis and varieties,	
Hebe albicans	EGH	grey, purple and variegated	E
Hebe pinguifolia 'Pagei'	EGH	*Santolina*	EG
Hebe rakaiensis	EH	*Satureja montana*	E
Helianthemum, some are grey-leafed; double-flowered varieties keep their petals until nightfall.	E(G)	*Teucrium chamaedrys*	
		Thymus citriodorus and varieties	E
		Thymus nummularius	E
		Thymus vulgaris and varieties	E
Hyssopus officinalis	E		

Although various heathers (*Calluna, Daboecia* and *Erica*) are of the right height and would provide good colour through the entire year from foliage and flower in full sun, they do not associate well with perennials either aesthetically or practically. Much the same applies to dwarf rhododendrons and azaleas, though these are useful in parts of the garden given to woodland plants.

3. Evergreen Perennials

However we may thicken up our beds or borders with shrubs, the usual run of perennials cannot but appear uninteresting in the winter. The following plants retain their foliage through the winter and help to clothe the bare ground.

W = need warm positions; see description in Alphabetical Lists.

Achillea, some		*Dianthus*	
Aciphylla	W	*Dierama*	
Agave	W	*Doronicum* 'Miss Mason'	
Aloe	W	*Epimedium*, some	
Anthemis cupaniana		*Erigeron glaucus*	
Artemisia, several		*Eryngium*, American species	
Aspidistra	W	*Euphorbia*, several	
Bergenia		*Fascicularia*	W
Beschorneria	W	*Galax*	
Campanula latiloba		*Helleborus*, most *Heuchera*	
Campanula persicifolia		× *Heucherella*	
Celmisia	W	*Iris confusa*	W
Chrysanthemum coccineum (Pyrethrum)		*Iris foetidissima*	
		Iris tectorum	
Dianella	W	*Iris wattii*	W

Kniphofia 'Atlanta' and other large kinds	*Phormium*	
	Pulmonaria, most	
Kniphofia caulescens	*Puya*	W
Kniphofia northiae	*Reineckia*	
Kniphofia uvaria	*Sisyrinchium*	
Libertia	*Speirantha*	
Limonium	*Stachys olympica*	
Liriope	*Tellima*	
Marrubium	*Tulbaghia*	W
Moraea	*Verbascum phoeniceum*	
Morina	*Yucca*	
Penstemon, partially W	*Ferns*, several	
Phlomis russeliana		

There are several useful evergreen types also among the plants in Lists 1 and 2.

4. Biennial Plants

This book would not be complete without brief reference to a number of popular plants which usually flower in their second summer when raised from seeds and then die. They have a special temporary value for filling gaps while awaiting growth of permanencies. In addition they are used in rotation with other plants, i.e. Wallflowers, Sweet Williams and Canterbury Bells, can, after flowering, be replaced with Chrysanthemums and Dahlias, which in turn can be lifted at the end of October when a repeat of the spring-flowering crop will be ready for planting.

Biennials are normally raised from seeds sown in early summer, transplanted into nursery rows and put into their appointed places in early autumn. To the few mentioned above can be added:

Adlumia fungosa. A climbing plant for trailing over bushes; the leaves are dainty, and the flowers are mauve, both *Corydalis*-like. Shade.

Angelica archangelica. A study in green, of the Cow Parsley family. The Angelica of commerce. 1.2 m (4 ft). Sun.

Cirsium eriophorum and *C. velenowskyi.* Two handsome thistles with flower buds covered with silver cobwebs. 1.2 m (4 ft). Sun.

Dianthus. Many seed-strains, also two species which have wiry stems ending in dense heads of small flowers; *D. carthusianorum* (pink) and *D. knappii* (yellow). 60 cm (2 ft). Sun.

Digitalis officinalis. The common Foxglove is normally soft mauve-pink, the flowers hung on a one-sided spike. The white form is exquisite. Always pull up the mauve ones before they seed if you want to preserve the white strain; further, the plants can be distinguished in spring: the white will have pale green leaf stalks, the mauve are purplish-tinted. Unfortunately the grace of the common Foxglove has been destroyed in the modern large spotted strains with flowers borne all around the stems. 1.5 m (5 ft). Shade.

D. ferruginea. A startling plant with small flowers of brown with white lips. 90 cm (3 ft).

Eryngium giganteum. Affectionately known as "Miss Willmott's ghost", this has wonderful white thistle-flowers. The legend has it that Ellen Willmott used to drop a few seeds in gardens that she visited and thus it sprang up in her wake. 90 cm (3 ft). Sun.

Euphorbia lathyrus. The Caper-Spurge has white juice of blister-making propensity. Architectural in winter and masses of green flowers and pods. 1.2 m (4 ft). Sun or shade.

Geranium anemonifolium. Only suitable for our warmest counties. A superb display of rosy lilac flowers over handsome leaves. 90 cm (3 ft) high and wide. Sun.

Glaucium flavum.   The Horned Poppy; grey crinkly foliage and red or yellow flowers followed by long pods. 60 cm (2 ft). Sun.

Hedysarum coronarium.   Like a red clover. 1.2 m (4 ft). Sun.

Isatis tinctoria.   The Woad produces a mass of tiny yellow flowers in gypsophila-like profusion, followed by shining black pods (for drying they should be picked immediately they turn black). 90 cm (3 ft). Sun.

Lunaria annua.   Honesty is normally mauve, and there is also a strain with white-variegated leaves. 'Munstead Variety' is rich crimson-purple. All have silvery white pods in autumn. 90 cm (3 ft). Sun or shade.

Meconopsis regia, M. napaulensis, M. superba, M. paniculata, and others. Sumptuous rosettes, often clad in golden or silver fur, give rise to stately stems bearing silky blooms of blue, purple, yellow or red. For sheltered woodland gardens on lime-free soil. 1.8 m (6 ft). Shade. They sometimes take three or more years to flower.

Michauxia campanuloides and *M. tchihatcheffii.*   Though related to campanulas, they more resemble lily-flowers of extreme delicacy of design and colour. 1.2 m (4 ft). Sun.

Onopordon acanthium.   The Scotch Thistle presents a great sight, with handsome large grey leaves, and grey stems bearing big mauve thistles. 2.2 m (7 ft). Sun.

Salvia sclarea turkestanica.   The Vatican Sage is a big smelly plant creating a lovely pinky-mauve patch for many weeks. 1.2 m (4 ft). Sun.

Smyrnium perfoliatum.   Greenery-yallery flowers like those of *Euphorbia* at first sight. 60 cm (2 ft). Shade.

Verbascum olympicum.   A huge, statuesque, yellow-spiked Mullein, with a great rosette of grey leaves. 1.8 m (6 ft). Sun.

V. bombyciferum. (*V.* 'Broussa').   Silvery woolly basal leaves and slender silvery woolly stems with clear yellow flowers. 2.4 m (8 ft). Sun.

Several other plants are short-lived and are best treated as biennials to get the best out of them; these are noted in the body of this book, under *Aquilegia, Coreopsis, Althaea rosea, Hesperis,* etc.

5. Plants with Handsome Foliage

B = broad, rounded, or with large lobes.
L = lacy or filigree, much divided and fern-like.
R = grassy or sword-like.
C = cut foliage will last reasonably well in water when mature.

There are all dignified plants whose foliage makes a basal pile and looks well for most of the growing season at least. Though some are tall, these plants should not be obscured by others growing in front of them; although the heights of some might indicate anything but frontal positions it is here that they are best appreciated. If bolstered by plants of equal or greater height behind them they will not look out of place.

GREEN LEAVES			
		Aruncus	L
Acanthus	B	*Astilbe*	L
Alchemilla	BC	*Baptisia*	C
Anemone × hybrida	B	*Begonia*	B
Anemone tomentosa	B	*Bergenia*	BC
Aralia	L	*Brunnera*	B
Arisaema	C	*Buphthalmum speciosum*	B
Arum	C	*Caltha*	B

395

Canna	BC	*Hosta*	BC
Cardiocrinum	B	*Iris*	CR
Cautleya	RC	*Kirengeshoma*	B
Celmisia		*Ligularia*	B
Centaurea, several	BC	*Liriope*	CR
Cimicifuga	BL	*Macleaya*	B
Corydalis	CL	*Megacarpaea*	L
Crambe	B	*Morina*	CR
Crocosmia	CR	*Musa*	B
Curtonus	CR	*Myrrhis*	L
Dianella	CR	*Paeonia*	BC
Dicentra	CL	*Peltiphyllum*	B
Dierama	CR	*Phlomis*	B
Diphylleia	B	*Phormium*	CR
Dracunculus	BC	*Podophyllum*	B
Epimedium	B	*Ranunculus aconitifolius*	BC
Eryngium, some	R	*Rodgersia*	B
Ferula	CL	*Sauromatum*	BC
Filipendula	B	*Selinum*	CL
Foeniculum	CL	*Senecio tanguticus*	L
Galax	BC	*Silphium terebinthinaceum*	BC
Geranium, several	BC	*Speirantha*	BC
Gladiolus	CR	*Symplocarpus*	BC
Glaucidium	B	*Thalictrum*	CL
Gunnera	B	*Trachystemon*	B
Hedychium	BR	*Veratrum*	B
Helianthus salicifolius		*Verbascum*	B
Helleborus	BC	*Yucca*	CR
Hemerocallis	CR	*Zantedeschia*	BC
Heracleum	B	Grasses	CR
Heuchera	BC	Ferns	L

VARIEGATED LEAVES

Plants with yellow-variegated leaves are best in full sun.
Plants with yellow-flushed leaves are best in part shade.
Plants with white-variegated leaves are best in shade.

These general notes must be used in conjunction with the species' individual requirements mentioned in the Alphabetical Lists.

Acorus	CR	*Phlox paniculata* 'Harlequin'	
Arum italicum 'Pictum'	BC	*Phlox paniculata* 'Norah Leigh'	
Astrantia, one	B	*Phormium tenax* 'Variegatum'	CR
Brunnera, forms	B	*Polygonatum*, two	C
Filipendula ulmaria 'Aurea'	B	*Pulmonaria saccharata* and	
Fuchsia magellanica		varieties	B
'Variegata'		*Scrophularia*	B
Geranium punctatum	B	*Sedum alboroseum* 'Variegatum'	B
Hosta, several	BC	*Sisyrinchium striatum* 'Aunt	
Humulus	BC	May'	R
Iris, some	CR	*Symphytum*	B
Liriope	CR	*Tovara*, two	B
Oenothera tetragona fraseri			

COPPERY-PURPLE LEAVES

'Purple' and 'copper' are horticulturally used to denote leaves which in the darkest sorts are as richly coloured as those of a Copper Beech. The best tinting occurs in full sun; shade results in a greenish tint.

Astilbe, some	L	*Rodgersia*, some	B
Canna, some	BC	*Saxifraga fortunei* 'Wada's	
Clematis recta 'Foliis Purpureis'		Variety'	BC
Crocosmia 'Solfatare'	CR	*Sedum maximum atropurpureum*	B
Galax (in winter)	BC	Grasses: *Imperata cylindrica*	
Heuchera americana	BC	'Rubra'	R
—*diversifolia* 'Palace Purple'		*Melica altissima* 'Atro-	
Ligularia dentata forms	B	purpurca'	R
Oenothera glaber		Ferns: *Adiantum pedatum*	
Phormium tenax 'Purpureum'	R	*japonicum*	L
Rheum palmatum form	B	*Dryopteris erythrosora*	L

GREY LEAVES

Some have silky or woolly leaves, others are glaucous and smooth. They all prefer full sun and well-drained soil except *Anaphalis* and *Hosta*; both prefer a moist soil and hostas thrive in shade. These two, together with the *Fuchsia* and *Athyrium*, are useful for providing a greyish tint in shady places.

Achillea, several	CL	*Lychnis flos-jovis*	
Anaphalis		*Lysimachia ephemerum*	
Anthemis cupaniana	L	*Mertensia*, two	
Aquilegia vulgaris nivea	BC	*Perovskia*	
Artemisia, most	CL	*Potentilla*, several	BC
Beschorneria	CR	*Puya*	R
Crambe maritima	B	*Romneya*	
Cynara	CL	*Rudbeckia maxima*	BC
Dianthus		*Salvia argentea*	B
Eryngium maritimum		*Sanguisorba*	CL
Fuchsia magellanica		*Scabiosa graminifolia*	
'Versicolor'		*Sedum*, several	B
Hieracium lanatum	B	*Senecio cineraria*	CL
Hosta fortunei hyacinthina	BC	*Sisyrinchium striatum*	CR
Hosta sieboldiana	BC	*Stachys olympica*	B
Hosta tokudama	BC	*Thalictrum speciosissimum*	CL
Iris longipetala and hybrid	CR	*Veronica incana*	
Iris ochroleuca	CR	*Yucca*, several	CR
Iris spuria	CR	Grasses, several	CL
Kniphofia caulescens	R	Ferns: *Athyrium goeringianum*	
Lupinus ornatus		'Pictum'	
Lychnis coronaria			

6. Trees and Shrubs with Handsome Foliage, green, variegated or coppery. These are often needed to augment colour schemes and lists will be found in nurserymen's catalogues and various books. I recommend my books *The Art of Planting* and *Ornamental Shrubs, Climbers and Bamboos.*

7. Shade

Many plants, though sun-loving, will grow well in part or full shade so long as there are no tree branches overhead. The following prefer or will thrive in shade from overhanging branches, or shade from buildings. In the cooler north and west of the British Isles many that would need shade in Surrey will grow perfectly well in part shade or full exposure.

T = plants which will tolerate dry shade; this is often a difficult proposition. It occurs under greedy-rooted trees, at the side of greedy-rooted hedges, and on the shady side of high buildings where the prevailing wind does not bring rain, and under overhanging eaves. Most need humus mixed in the soil; see Alphabetical Lists.

Actaea		*Hyacinthoides*	T
Allium stipitatum		*Hylomecon*	
Anemone nemorosa	T	*Iris foetidissima*	T
Aquilegia alpina and *vulgaris* strains		*Kirengeshoma*	
Arum italicum		*Lamium*	
Aruncus		*Leucojum*	
Aspidistra	T	*Lilium martagon* and hybrids	
Aster macrophyllus		*Lunaria*	T
Astilbe		*Meconopsis*	
Begonia		*Melittis*	
Bergenia		*Myrrhis*	
Brunnera		*Nomocharis*	
Campanula latifolia	T	*Ourisia*	
Cardiocrinum		*Paeonia emodi*	
Chamaelirium		*Paeonia veitchii*	
Cimicifuga		*Paris*	
Clintonia		*Phlox paniculata* (species)	
Codonopsis		*Podophyllum*	
Convallaria		*Polygonatum*	T
Cortusa		*Polygonum*	
Corydalis		*Primula*	
Cypripedium		*Pulmonaria*	
Dactylorrhiza		*Saxifraga fortunei*	
Deinanthe		*Scopolia*	
Dentaria		*Smilacina*	
Dicentra		*Smyrnium*	T
Diphylleia		*Speirantha*	T
Dodecatheon		*Streptopus*	
Eomecon		*Stylophorum*	
Epimedium	T	*Symphytum grandiflorum* and hybrids	
Epipactis		*Tellima*	
Eupatorium ageratoides		*Trachystemon*	T
Euphorbia robbiae T, and some others		*Trillium*	
		Uvularia	
Galax	T	Grasses: *Carex pendula*	T
Gentiana asclepiadea		*Luzula*	
Geranium, several		*Milium*	
Glaucidium		Ferns: *Dryopteris*	T
Helleborus		*Polypodium*	T
× *Heucherella*		*Polystichum*	T
Hosta		others	

8. Moisture-loving Plants

H = shade-loving kinds.
Y = plants for boggy or wet ground.

Acorus	Y	*Lythrum*	Y
Astilbe	Y	*Meconopsis*	H
Caltha	Y	*Mimulus,* some	Y
Cardiocrinum	H	*Monarda didyma*	
Cautleya		*Nomocharis*	H
Cimicifuga		*Ourisia*	H
Darlingtonia	Y	*Peltiphyllum*	Y
Decodon	Y	*Podophyllum*	
Deinanthe	H	*Polygonum,* some	
Diphylleia	H	*Primula*	Y
Dodecatheon		*Ranunculus,* some	
Eomecon	H	*Rodgersia*	Y
Euphorbia griffithii		*Sarracenia*	Y
Euphorbia sikkimensis		*Schizostylis*	
Filipendula, most	Y	*Senecio smithii*	Y
Gentiana asclepiadea	H	*Stenanthium*	
Glaucidium	H	*Trollius*	Y
Gunnera	Y	*Veratrum*	H
Hedychium		*Xerophyllum*	
Hosta	H	*Zantedeschia*	
Iris kaempferi	Y	Grasses: *Carex riparia*	
Iris laevigata	Y	*Carex stricta*	
Iris pseudacorus	Y	*Cyperus longus*	Y
and some others		*Glyceria*	Y
Kirengeshoma	H	*Phalaris*	
Leucojum aestivum		*Phragmites*	Y
Ligularia	Y	Ferns: *Athyrium filix-femina*	H
Lilium, some		*Matteuccia*	H
Lobelia, some		*Onoclea*	HY
Lysichitum	Y	*Osmunda*	HY
Lysimachia		*Oreopteris*	HY

9. Early and Late-flowering Perennials: Perennials of Special Colours, Heights. The "line of facts" following the species' name in the Alphabetical Lists will make it possible to pick out plants for particular schemes without trouble.

10. Tender Perennials for use in our warmest counties.
These are marked W in the 'line of facts' in the Alphabetical Lists. See also Chapter 5.

11. Herbs

It is not always realized that space can be saved in small gardens by doing away with a special area for herbs and growing their various variegated forms as ornamental plants. The variegated forms are just as tasty for culinary purposes as their green types. This especially applies to Sage (*Salvia officinalis*); Marjoram (*Origanum vulgare*); Mint (*Mentha × gentilis* and *M. × rotundifolia*) and Lemon Balm (*Melissa officinalis*). The last three are in the main Alphabetical List; for *Salvia* see Cuttings from My Notebook, List 2. The yellow and the variegated-leafed varieties of *Thymus vulgaris* are also useful.

12. Plants for Naturalizing in Grass

Areas of rough mown grass—in the open or under trees—which are beautiful in spring with bulbs, are lost and forlorn until September when colchicums and autumn crosuses spring up. It is wisest not to attempt to grow summer-flowering bulbs as well, because their growth interferes with summer mowing. The following plants will hold their own in all but very coarse grass, on account of their running roots or dense leafage; the clumps are highly decorative in summer, to be mown down in autumn.

H = shade tolerant.
N = full sun.
M = demand moisture.
D = highly decorative foliage and clump.
U = running roots.

Acanthus mollis	NDU	Heracleum	D
Acanthus spinosus	NDU	Hosta, strong growers	HD
Althaea cannabina	N	Inula hookeri	NU
Anemone tomentosa	NDU	Inula magnifica	ND
Aralia cachemirica	ND	Iris 'Ochraurea'	N
Aruncus dioicus	D	Iris pseudacorus	M
Astilbe biternata	U	Lactuca	NU
Buphthalmum speciosum	DU	Lathyrus latifolius	N
Camassia		Ligularia	MND
Campanula latiloba	HD	Lupinus arboreus	N
Centaurea macrocephala	HD	Macleaya microcarpa	NU
Cephalaria gigantea	HD	Papaver orientale	NU
Chrysanthemum macrophyllum	HD	Petasites	HU
Chrysanthemum uliginosum	U	Phormium (evergreen)	ND
Crambe cordifolia	ND	Phytolacca	D
Crocosmia crocosmiiflora	U	Polygonum, some	MDU
Curtonus	ND	Rheum	ND
Datisca	ND	Rodgersia	MND
Doronicum pardalianches	HU	Rudbeckia, tall kinds	N
Echinops, strongest growers	ND	Salvia glutinosa	U
Eryngium pandanifolium	ND	Senecio tanguticus	NU
Eupatorium purpureum	D	Solidago 'Golden Wings'	NU
Euphorbia griffithii	U	Verbascum vernale	ND
Euphorbia sikkimensis	MU	Yucca, tall species	ND
Filipendula purpurea	MD	Grasses: Arundo	NDU
Filipendula rubra	MD	Carex pendula	HD
Foeniculum	ND	Cortaderia	ND
Galega	NU	Miscanthus	ND
Geranium psilostemon	ND	Stipa gigantea	ND
Gunnera	MD	Ferns: strongest growers	HD
Hemerocallis fulva and varieties and vigorous hybrids	NU		

13. Plants for Coastal Gardens and Maritime Districts

Though the seaside with its strong winds and salt-laden air can make gardening difficult, it has its benefits in usually providing milder conditions than those inland. Especially is this true of our south and west coasts. Apart from the rearing of sheltering shrubs, the main plants to avoid are those which normally require staking or are tall growers. By keeping to plants of compact growth much can be achieved. Unless your garden is in a wooded coomb it is best to concentrate on sun-lovers, and many of the border plants mentioned in Chapter 5 will thrive in the warmest districts.

Perennials which may be expected to prove tough and hardy for general coastal plantings include the following:

Achillea	*Lathyrus*
Aconitum × bicolor 'Bressingham Spire'	*Lavatera*
	Libertia
Agapanthus	*Limonium*
Allium christophii	*Linaria*
Allium cernuum	*Lychnis-flos-jovis*
Armeria	*Melissa*
Alstroemeria	*Mertensia virginica*
Amaryllis	*Mimulus*
Anemone	*Morina*
Anthemis	*Myosotideum* (tender)
Anthericum	*Nerine*
Artemisia	*Oenothera*
Aster, short-growing kinds	*Origanum*
Bergenia	*Osteospermum*
Campanula, short-growing kinds	*Penstemon*
Catananche	*Perovskia*
Celmisia	*Phormium*
Centaurea	*Phygelius*
Centranthus	*Physostegia* 'Vivid'
Chrysanthemum, short-growing kinds	*Polygonum bistorta*
Crambe	*Potentilla*
Crocosmia	*Pulsatilla*
Cynoglossum	*Romneya*
Dianthus	*Salvia*, short-growing kinds
Dierama	*Scabiosa*
Echinops	*Schizostylis*
Erigeron	*Scrophularia*
Erodium	*Sedum*
Eryngium	*Senecio pulcher*
Euphorbia	*Sisyrinchium*
Fascicularia	*Stachys*
Filipendula hexapetala	*Stokesia*
Geranium	*Tritonia*
Gypsophila	*Veronica*
Heuchera	*Viscaria*
Hieracium	*Yucca*
Iris	*Zantedeschia*
Kniphofia	Grasses, short-growing kinds

In addition to the above plants seaside gardens can draw upon the vast range of fuchsias, hydrangeas and hybrids of *Hebe speciosa*; also *Lupinus arboreus,* gazanias, *Convolvulus cneorum, Ruta, Santolina, Potentilla fruticosa* and lavenders, and many more sub-shrubs.

14. Plants for Dry Sunny Places

This would make a long list. A selection can be made, however, by comparing the lists of plants in Nos. 2, 5 (grey leaves), 10, 11, 13, with the descriptions in the Alphabetical Lists.

15. The Non-stop Border

We all long for flowers for as long as possible. In the first half of the year plants tend to flower for a short period only; after July there are many which go on flowering for many weeks. The following, coupled with variously coloured foliage from plants and shrubs, may each be relied upon in most districts to provide flower for the months of July, August, September and into October.

Acanthus spinosus
Aster × frikartii 'Flora's Delight'
Aster × frikartii 'Mönch'
Aster thomsonii 'Nanus'
Fuchsia, all
Geranium 'Russell Prichard'

Geranium wallichianum 'Buxton's Variety'
Indigofera gerardiana, pruned as recommended
Lavatera olbia varieties

To these may be added shrubby *Potentilla fruticosa* varieties, *Hydrangea macrophylla* and *H. serrata* varieties, together with Floribunda and Polypom roses.

16. Colour Schemes

Whether for small groups or for whole borders, this book seeks to help in assembling plants for blending or contrast, in style, height and colour. Everyone must arrange his or her plants according to taste. To the several hints in the descriptive lists I add below a few combinations that have pleased me through the years. Please also refer to Chapter 5.

WINTER/SPRING

Helleborus atrorubens under *Hamamelis mollis* 'Pallidus'
Mahonia japonica surrounded by *Crocus tomasinianus*.
Bergenia × schmidtii near to *Erica carnea* 'Springwood White'.
Pulmonaria rubra and *Crocus* 'Vanguard' under *Corylopsis pauciflora*.
Symphytum grandiflorum under *Cornus alba* 'Elegantissima' or *C. alba* 'Sibirica'.
Honesty (*Lunaria annua*) with late white *Narcissus* and bluebells and *Erica mediterranea* 'Brightness' near a pink cherry or *Magnolia × soulangiana*. A scheme of soft tints.
Doronicum 'Miss Mason' or *plantagineum* 'Excelsum' with *Euphorbia polychroma, E. characias, Chaenomeles japonica* (*C. maulei*) and *Milium effusum* 'Aureum' and young foliage of *Hemerocallis* of the *fulva* type. A scheme of sharp tints.
Dentaria pinnata with *Skimmia* 'Rubella' and *Bergenia × schmidtii*.
Helleborus corsicus, Colchicum foliage, *Philadelphus coronarius* 'Aureus', *Fritillaria imperialis* (yellow) and *Milium effusum* 'Aureum'.

LATE SPRING/EARLY SUMMER

Euphorbia griffithii 'Fireglow', *Berberis darwinii*, Munstead Honesty and some coppery foliage. A scheme of hot contrasts.
Lunaria rediviva, Kerria japonica and bluebells. Delicate tones.
Smilacina with dicentras (white) and lemon *Trollius*.
Dicentras (pink), *Aquilegia* 'Hensol Harebell', *Geranium sylvaticum*.
Geranium sylvaticum, Paeonia mlokosewitschii, Potentilla fruticosa varieties.
Geranium magnificum under Rose 'Nevada'.
Geranium 'Johnson's Blue' under Rose 'Frühlingsgold' or 'Golden Wings'.
Rheum palmatum 'Atrosanguineum' with *Dryopteris borreri, Ranunculus acris* 'Plenus', *Hemerocallis dumortieri* and *Geum* 'Borisii'. A vivid grouping.

Symphytum × *uplandicum* and camassias, with grey foliage.
Iris longipetala, Paeonia officinalis, Anthericum algeriense.

EARLY SUMMER
Baptisia australis with *Centaurea hypoleuca* 'John Coutts', *Anthericum liliago* and *Dictamnus*, backed by old roses. Soft tones.
Geranium psilostemon, Alchemilla mollis and *Thalictrum speciosissimum* (foliage).
Alchemilla mollis with purple irises, *Nepeta* and grey foliage.
Campanula latiloba, Philadelphus 'Belle Etoile', *Diervilla florida* 'Purpurea'.
Alstroemeria, Tropaeolum polyphyllum, Iris pallida dalmatica (foliage), and *Allium christophii*, backed by coppery leaves and *Senecio* 'Sunshine'.

MIDSUMMER
Rose 'Cerise Bouquet', *Philadelphus* 'Beauclerk', *Penstemon campanulatus* 'Garnet', *Geranium pratense* doubles, *Stachys olympica*. Strong contrasts.
Lavatera olbia 'Rosea', *Eryngium tripartitum, Aconitum* × *bicolor* 'Spark's Variety', *Gypsophila paniculata*. Soft tinting.
Echinops ritro with *Tritonia rosea* and grey foliage.
Early heleniums, *Genista aetnensis, Macleaya microcarpa* 'Coral Plume', *Philadelphus incanus*, golden privet and white achilleas. Yellow dominates.

LATE SUMMER
Inula magnifica, Hemerocallis in strong red or yellow, coppery foliage and brilliant orange-red Floribunda roses. Hot enough for the hottest days.
Crocosmia masonorum, Ceanothus 'Gloire de Versailles', *Hemerocallis* 'Marion Vaughn', silver foliage and white phlox. Brilliant but cool.
Aster × *frikartii* 'Mönch', *Monarda didyma* 'Croftway Pink', *Echinops niveus, Lonicera korolkowi* (grey-blue foliage). A soft collection.
Phlox, vivid orange-red, with *Miscanthus sinensis* 'Zebrina', *Crocosmia* and *Bergenia* foliage.

LATE SUMMER/EARLY AUTUMN
Hydrangeas with *Hosta sieboldiana* and 'Thomas Hogg' foliage, *Astilbe taquetii. Acanthus*, Japanese Anemones and Fuchsias of all tints. Long-lasting richness.
Ligularias with *Lobelia* × *vedrariensis, Kniphofia* 'Wrexham Buttercup' and *Curtonus paniculatus, Lilium tigrinum fortunei*, yellow variegated *Cornus alba*. Strong and refreshing contrasts.
Aster × *frikartii* 'Mönch', *Sedum* 'Autumn Joy', *Calamintha nepetoides, Miscanthus japonicus* 'Silver Fern', *Buddleja fallowiana* 'Alba'. A cool collection.

EARLY AUTUMN
Nerina bowdenii, Liriope spicata, with silvery foliage, and *Kirengeshoma* in the shade nearby.
Aconitum × *carmichaelii, Cimicifuga ramosa, Aster* 'Climax', *Vernonia* and *Chrysanthemum* 'Anastasia'. Late in the season but highly satisfying.

17. Notes for the Flower Arranger
This book has been written very much with Arrangers in mind, and as a consequence I have been at pains to devote a column to their needs, marking plants as follows in the Alphabetical Lists:

P = these plants will last reasonably in water when in flower.
F = these have fruits or seed-heads which last when cut.

With regard to the cut flowers, obviously with care and expert attention almost any flower will last for a day or two in water, provided one can spare them from the garden—that is, one does not need them for the seeds they produce or they are not too choice—but practically all those marked P I have found to last satisfactorily at one time or another. A few like rodgersias are inclined to droop when in flower, but are more lasting when mature and in seed, and they are therefore only marked F.

Those marked F are not necessarily striking in seed or fruit but even small sprays of dry capsules have some appeal. Flowers will usually have improved lasting powers in water when woody stems are slit or crushed, and all big basal leaves are removed; they should be cut in the evening if possible and deeply steeped in water overnight in a cool place. When taking them out of water to arrange them always cut off a portion of stem and slit or crush again, and at once put them into their places. Many a flower show has been spoiled by neglect of this; it applies particularly to shrubs and woody stemmed plants. If travelling *any* distance by car, try to keep the cut stalks in water all the time.

With regard to leaves, without which we can make neither garden nor arrangement, a glance down List 5 will indicate those plants whose foliage is notable in shape, colour or size.

When cutting stems of plants like peonies and some bulbs it should be remembered that leaves are there to take in the health-giving sunshine through the summer. Therefore do not cut more stems and leaves than is absolutely necessary from one clump.

18. Plants which are Favoured by Bees

Allium	*Helianthus*
Alstroemeria	*Heliopsis*
Althaea	*Hyssopus*
Anchusa	*Inula*
Anemone	*Lavandula*
Asclepias	*Lavatera*
Aster	*Ligularia*
Calamintha	*Lupinus*
Camassia	*Lythrum*
Campanula	*Malva*
Centaurea	*Melittis*
Chrysanthemum	*Mirabilis*
Clematis	*Monarda*
Coreopsis	*Nepeta*
Cosmos	*Oenothera*
Dahlia	*Origanum*
Delphinium	*Polemonium*
Doronicum	*Potentilla*
Echinacea	*Rudbeckia*
Echinops	*Salvia*
Epilobium	*Scabiosa*
Eryngium	*Sedum*
Fuchsia	*Senecio*
Galega	*Sidalcea*
Galtonia	*Stachys*
Gypsophila (single)	*Verbascum*
Helenium	*Veronica*

19. Plants which Attract Butterflies

On a summer's day a few brilliant fluttering insects are a great asset to a garden. They seem to prefer to sip nectar from a head of small flowers rather than from a large bloom. Besides the following perennials, some much appreciated shrubs are buddleias of all kinds, lavenders, *Caryopteris, Syringa* (Lilac) and *Hebe*. Many annuals such as Marigolds, Candytuft and Sweet Alyssum are freely visited. *Create a Butterfly Garden* by L. H. Newman and M. Savonius is for further reading. Double flowers are of course useless to butterflies.

Armeria	*Helenium*
Aster	*Hesperis*
Calamintha	*Knautia*
Centranthus	*Lunaria*
Cephalaria	*Melissa*
Chrysanthemum	*Mentha*
Coreopsis	*Nepeta*
Echinacea	*Phlox*
Echinops	*Scabiosa*
Erigeron	*Sedum*
Eryngium	*Solidago*

20. Rabbit-proof Plants

In rabbit-infested areas, where it is impossible to provide a wire-netting boundary fence, the following perennial plants may be tried. The list is taken in part from one devoted to shrubs as well as plants prepared by the Royal Horticultural Society.

Aconitum	*Epimedium*
Aegopodium	*Eupatorium*
Agapanthus	*Euphorbia*
Alchemilla	*Fuchsia*
Anaphalis	*Gentiana asclepiadea*
Anemone	*Geranium*
Aquilegia	*Hedychium*
Asphodeline	*Helenium*
Asphodelus	*Helianthus*
Aster	*Helleborus orientalis*
Astilbe	*Hemerocallis*
Bergenia	*Hosta*
Brunnera	*Houttuynia*
Buphthalmum	*Iris*
Campanula lactiflora; latifolia	*Kirengeshoma*
Cardiocrinum	*Kniphofia*
Centaurea steenbergii	*Lamium*
Clematis	*Leucojum*
Colchicum	*Luzula*
Convallaria	*Lysimachia*
Cortaderia	*Malva*
Corydalis	*Melissa*
Crinum	*Miscanthus*
Crocosmia	*Nepeta*
Cyclamen	*Omphalodes*
Cynara	*Orchis*
Digitalis	*Paeonia*
Doronicum	*Papaver*

Phormium
Phytolacca
Polygonatum
Polygonum
Pulmonaria
Rhazia
Rheum
Romneya
Saxifraga geum, S. × umbrosa
Sedum

Stachys olympica
Tellima
Tradescantia
Trillium
Trollius
Vancouveria
Vinca
Yucca
Zantedeschia

21.   Plants resistant to deer

The following perennial plants are not usually eaten by deer, but deer are choosey, chancy animals and what may repel them one year may attract them later. Having little experience of deer myself I gratefully acknowledge help in compiling this list from the Royal Horticultural Society and Pacific Horticulture.

Acanthus
Aconitum
Agave
Allium
Amaryllis
Artemisia
Arum
Arundo
Astilbe
Campanula
Carex
Centaurea
Ceratostigma
Chrysanthemum maximum
Cortaderia
Crinum
Crocosmia
Dicentra
Digitalis
Epimedium
Euphorbia
Ferns
Festuca glauca
Filipendula
Gaillardia
Geranium
Gerbera
Gunnera
Helianthus
Helichrysum
Hosta
Iris

Kniphofia
Leucojum
Liriope
Lychnis coronaria
Melianthus
Melissa
Melittis
Mentha
Mirabilis
Myosotis
Nepeta
Origanum
Paeonia
Papaver
Phormium
Polygonatum
Potentilla
Pulmonaria
Romneya
Rudbeckia
Salvia
Satureia
Scabiosa
Sisyrinchium
Tellima
Thalictrum
Tiarella
Trillium
Veratrum
Vinca
Ferns

22.   Specialist Societies

The following Societies exist for those interested in perennials:

The Hardy Plant Society

Delphinium Society

The British National Carnation
  Society
The National Chrysanthemum Society

British Iris Society
Alpine Garden Society

The Hardy Plant Society publishes a Hardy Plant Directory (*The Plant Finder*), containing sources of supply for thousands of plants. Distributed by Moorland Publishing Co. Ltd, Moor Farm Road, Airfield Estate, Ashbourne, Derbyshire DE6 1HD, England.

23. The Index Hortensis, Vol. 1   Perennials, Alpines, Bulbs, is published by Piers Trehane, Hampreston Manor, Wimborne, Dorset, BH21 7LX. It attempts to place on record correct nomenclature for some 26,000 plants offered by nurserymen in northern Europe.

24. NCCPG.
The National Council for the Conservation of Plants and Gardens was set up in 1978. The Secretariat is at R.H.S. Gardens, Wisley, Ripley, Woking, Surrey. There are many Groups throughout the country and numerous genera are being conserved in many different districts. These "living museums" are mostly on view to members.

Chapter 14

Pests and Diseases

Many books on plants go to excessive lengths, it seems to me, to make gardeners develop a "pest complex"; it is almost a disease in itself! I want to avoid this attitude, but think it only right to call attention to the few diseases which normally affect perennials and a few pests which are occasionally troublesome.

The important principle to grasp is that a healthy plant is less likely to suffer from disease or pest than one which is just existing and hanging onto life; furthermore, the species of plants, native or exotic, and their close varieties, are as a rule less likely to succumb than the multitudinous and overbred man-made hybrids, selected forms and strains. It is obvious that, by expecting as we do such a varied selection of plants to grow in our gardens, some will be more suitable to our particular microclimate than others, and therefore some will be less healthy than others. The conclusion to be drawn is that if we ensure that every plant in our garden is a good, vigorous type, not in- or over-bred, and is growing in conditions suitable for it, pests and diseases will trouble us little. It is far bettter to cope with the whole matter in this rational way than to douse everything with noxious sprays and powders—and far more pleasant and rewarding. Towards all this I would stress that a balanced diet (not an excess of nitrogen) with a suitable supply of humus for the needs of the type of plant in question, should be the gardener's aim for all his plants.

Pests

Everything with two or more legs can be a pest at times, from our biggest mammals down to the microscopic eelworm. Those with two legs and a walking-stick can also be troublesome. No gardener enjoys the attentions of deer, hares, rabbits, dog or cats; our feathered "friends" like peafowl and lesser types will peck and make dust baths, while the depredations of bullfinches and sparrows are well known. Mice will eat hellebore buds, lily leaves and buds, and devour seeds on tall stems almost before they are ripe; they are fond of early anemone and columbine leaves. Little can be done to safeguard plants from such as these apart from trapping and shooting, nets, and naphtha balls for mice.

Hostas are particularly prone to slug- and snail-damage, but there are appetizing and lethal preparations on the market for them.

A number of caterpillar-like grubs are found in the soil; so long as these are slow-moving they may be regarded as enemies of our plants and destroyed. They eat roots and are sometimes a serious menace in weedy, ill-cultivated land. Their control is difficult.

There are plenty of preparations, systemic and otherwise, on the market to control greenfly or aphides, frog-hoppers and the occasional caterpillars on the portions of the plants above ground. These not only spoil the leaves, growing shoots and flowers, but are also apt to spread virus diseases. Capsid is a small greenish insect which is elusive and seldom seen, but its punctures spoil growing tips of *Fuschia* and *Caryopteris* among other plants, and a suitable spray once a fortnight in July and August will usually control them. A nicotine preparation should be used when leaves of such plants as *Chrysanthemum* and *Aquilegia* become netted with a pale or brownish pattern caused by leaf-miners. The growing tips of Michaelmas Daisies—especially forms of *Aster novi-belgii*— are often rendered abortive by mites, and I think the best answer is to grow the more resistant species, though a lime-sulphur spray can be used.

Eelworms are too small to be seen by the naked eye and are found inside live plants; they get the upper hand sometimes in unhealthy or weak plants of *Phlox decussata, Paeonia, Chrysanthemum*, etc. It is best to purchase clean stock and to see that the plants are given good conditions in the garden. A badly infested clump should be burned and new plants tried elsewhere in the garden. The symptoms are wispy, deformed leaves and swollen stems.

In Surrey and Berkshire the Lily Beetle is a great nuisance. An eagle-eye should be kept open for the oblong scarlet beetles from spring onwards. Later their disgusting grubs devour the foliage and must be picked off or sprayed with any preparation used against caterpillars.

Diseases

Here again there is no doubt whatever that a well-nurtured plant, so long as it is not given excess nitrogen but rather a balanced diet, will resist the many diseases, whether fungus or virus, which are found in the soil and in the air. Just as aphides blow for miles on the wind, minute fungus spores of the various mildews and rusts are airborne to a degree almost incomprehensible. There are hundreds of different species of mildew, so that if you have a mildewed shoot of *Aster*, for instance, it need not be concluded that it will spread to other genera which "enjoy" their own particular brand!

Fortunately the vast majority of hardy perennials survive successfully the constant battle against these fungi, but troubles occur in *Paeonia* and *Helleborus* (wilting and spotting of foliage and flowers and stems), *Lilium* (Botrytis causing spotting and wilting of foliage and stem, and virus causing mottling and distortion), *Iris* (rhizome-root and leaf-spot), *Althaea* (rusty patches mainly on reverse of leaves) and *Aster* and many other plants (grey mildew). There are many copper compounds on the market which will help to cure most of these troubles which, in addition to initial unhealthiness in, or starvation of, the plants, are often caused by chilly damp early summer weather; mildew on the other hand is more inclined to occur later in the year when the soil has become too dry and the foliage is damped by dew and light rain.

In spite of the discouraging particulars in this chapter, garden perennials are well worth growing, and in my experience probably about 2 per cent of plants succumb to pests and diseases, except in gardens which are neglected in all ways.

Bibliography

ABRAMS, Leroy, *Illustrated Flora of the Pacific States*. Stanford University Press, California, 1923 *et seq.*

ALLEN, D. E., *The Victorian Fern Craze*. Hutchinson, 1969.

ARENDS, Georg, *Mein Leben als Gartner und Züchter*, 1951.

BAILEY, L. H., *Gentes Herbarum*. New York, 1920 *et seq.*

—— *The Standard Cyclopedia of Horticulture*. Macmillan, New York, 1927

BAILEYA, various papers. Cornell University. New York, 1953 *et seq.*

BELL, C. R. *See* JUSTICE.

BERGMANN, J., *Vaste Planten and Rotsheesters*. Haarlem, 1924.

BLOOM, Alan, *Hardy Perennials*. Faber & Faber, 1957.

BOOM, B. K., *Flora der Geweekte Kruidachtige Gewassen* II. Veenman & Zonen, Wageningen, Holland, 1970.

'BOTANICAL REGISTER, THE.' Ridgeway, London, 1815–47.

BRITTON, Nathaniel Lord and BROWN, Hon. Addison, *Illustrated Flora of the Northern United States*. New York Botanic Garden, 1936.

BROWN, Hon. Addison. *See* BRITTON.

CAMBRIDGE UNIVERSITY, *Flora Europaea*. C.U.P., 1964 *et seq.*

CODD, L. E., "*The South African Species of Kniphofia*" *Bothalia*, vol. 9, October 1968, Department of Agricultural Technical Services, South Africa.

COHEN, Victor A., *A Guide to the Pacific Coast Irises*. The British Iris Society, 1967.

DYKES, W. R., *A Handbook of Garden Irises*. Martin Hopkinson & Co Ltd, London, 1924; and other writings.

—— *The Genus Iris*. Cambridge University Press, 1913.

EDGAR, E. *See* MOORE.

ENGLER, Adolph, *Das Pflanzenreich*. Wilhelm Engelmann, Leipzig, 1900 *et seq.*

EUROPEAN GARDEN FLORA, The, S. M. Walters et al. Cambridge University Press, 1984–.

'GRAY'S MANUAL OF BOTANY', 8th edn. New York, 1950.

GREY, C. H., *Hardy Bulbs*.William & Norgate, London, 1938.

HADFIELD, Miles, in *Quarterly Bulletin of the Alpine Garden Society*, June 1966. (*Anemone nemorosa*.)

HANSE, R., *Namen der Stauden*. Ullmer, Stuttgart, 1972.

HEGI, Gustav, *Illustrierte Flora von Mittel-Europa*. Lehmans Verlag, Munich, 1906 *et seq.*

HENSEN, K. J. W., *Preliminary Registration Lists of cultivar names in Hosta*, Tratt. H. Veenman & Zonen, Wageningen, Holland, 1963.

HIRAO, Shuichi, see Kuribayashi.

HYLANDER, Nils, *The Genus Hosta in Swedish Gardens*. *Acta Horti Bergiani*, Band 16, no. 11. Uppsala, 1954.

JEKYLL, Gertrude, *Colour Schemes for the Flower Garden*. Country Life, London.

JELITTO-SCHACHT, *Die Freiland Schmuckstauden*. Ullmer, Stuttgart, 1963.

JUSTICE, W. S., and BELL, C. R., *Wild Flowers of North Carolina*. University of North Carolina Press, USA, 1968.

KERNER, Antonio, *Monographia Pulmonaria*. University Library, Wagneria, Oeniponte, 1878.

KRUSSMANN, G., SIEBLER, W., and TANGERMANN, W., *Winterharte Gartenstauden*. Parey, Berlin, 1970.

KURIBAYASHI, Motojiro and HIRAO, Shuichi, Eds. *The Japanese Iris*. Asiatic Shimbun Publishing Co., Tokyo, 1971.

LEIGHTON, F. M., "The Genus *Agapanthus* L'Heritier". *Journal of South African Botany*, 1965.

LYNCH, R. Irwin, *The Book of the Iris*. John Lane, London, 1904.

MAEKAWA, F., *The Genus Hosta*. Tokyo, 1940.

MATHEW, Brian, *A Gardener's Guide to Hellebores*. The Alpine Garden Society, London.

MILDE, J., *Monographia Generis Osmundae*. Nuremberg, 1868.

MOORE, L. B., and EDGAR, E., *Flora of New Zealand*. Shearer, Wellington, New Zealand, 1970.

'NEW FLORA AND SILVA', vols. 1–12, 1929 *et seq*. Dulau, London.

NEW YORK BOTANIC GARDEN, *Addisonia*. 1916 *et seq*.

OHWI, Jisaburo, *Flora of Japan*. Smithsonian Institution, New York, 1965.

PERRY, Frances, *Border Plants*. Collins, London, 1957.

POLUNIN, Oleg, *Flowers of Europe*. Oxford University Press, 1969.

ROBINSON, William, *The English Flower Garden*. 15th edn. John Murray, London, 1934.

ROYAL BOTANIC GARDENS, KEW, *The Botanical Magazine*, 1786 *et seq*.

ROYAL HORTICULTURAL SOCIETY, *The Dictionary of Gardening*. Oxford University Press, 1951; Supplement, 1969.

——— *The Journal The Garden*, 1975–.

SIEBLER, W. *See* KRUSSMANN.

SILVA TAROUCA, Ernst, *Unsere Freiland-Stauden Anzucht*. F. Tempsky, Vienna, 1910.

STEARN, W. T., Various writings (in the R.H.S. *Dictionary of Gardening, Journal*, etc.).

STOUT, A. B., *Daylilies*. Norwood, Massachusetts, 1934.

SYNGE, Patrick M., *Collins Guide to Bulbs*. Collins, London, 1961.

TANGERMANN, W. *See* KRUSSMANN.

TAYLOR, G., *An Account of the Genus Meconopsis*. New Flora & Silva Ltd, London, 1934.

TREHANE, P., *Index Hortensis*. Quarterjack Publishing, Wimborne, Dorset. 1989.

TRELEASE, W., *The Yuccaceae*. 1902. In 13th Annual Report, Missouri Botanic Gardens, St Louis, Mo., USA.

WEHRHAHN, H. R., *Die Gartenstauden*. Parey, Berlin, 1931.

WILSON, C. Grey, *The Genus Iris: subsection Sibiricae*. The British Iris Society, 1971.

Gardening Books for Further Study

Alan Bloom's Hardy Perennials, 1991. Batsford.

Border Plants, Frances Perry, 1957. Collins.

A Chalk Garden, J. C. Stern, 1960. Nelson.

Colour in the Winter Garden, Graham Stuart Thomas, 1984. Dent.

Colour Schemes for the Flower Garden, Gertrude Jekyll, 1910. Country Life.

The Damp Garden, Beth Chatto. 1982. Dent.

The Dry Garden, Beth Chatto. 1977. Dent.

Flowers and their Histories, Alice M. Coats, 1956. Hulton Press.
Gardening in Britain, Miles Hadfield, 1960. Hutchinson.
Gardening on Clay, Howard Hamp Crane, 1963. Collingridge.
Gardening on Lime, Judith M. Berrisford. 1963. Faber.
Gardening on Sand, Christine Kelway, 1965. Collingridge.
Gardening in the Shade, Margery Fish, 1972. Collingridge.
The Golden Age of Plant Hunters, Kenneth Lemmon, 1968. Phoenix (Dent).
Hardy Ferns, Reginald Kaye, 1968. Faber.
Hardy Perennials, Alan Bloom, 1957. Faber.
Moisture Gardening, Alan Bloom, 1966. Faber.
The Peat Garden and its Plants, Alfred Evans, 1974. Dent.
Perennials for Trouble-free Gardening, Alan Bloom, 1960. Faber.
Plants for Ground-Cover, Graham Stuart Thomas, 1977. Dent.
The Quest for Plants, Alice M. Coats, 1969. Studio Vista.
Seaside Gardening, Christine Kelway, 1962. Collingridge.
The Victorian Fern Craze, D. E. Allen, 1969. Hutchinson.
Welsh Ferns, Hyde, Wade & Harrison, 1969. National Museum of Wales, Cardiff.
Wood and Garden, Gertrude Jekyll, 1899. Longmans.

Lists of Nurserymen Specializing in Perennials

(Notes of any omissions or inaccuracies will be appreciated for further editions.)

Britain
Austin, David, Roses, Bowling Green Lane, Albrighton, Wolverhampton. (Peonies, Irises etc.).
Blackmore & Langdon, The Nurseries, Bath, Somerset (Delphinium and Phlox).
Blackthorn Nursery, Kilmeston, Alresford, Hampshire SO24 0NL.
Blom, Walter, & Son Ltd, Leavesden, Watford, Herts (bulbs).
Bloom's Nurseries Ltd, Bressingham, Diss, Norfolk.
Ann and Roger Bowden, Cleave House, Sticklepath, Okehampton, Devon. (Hostas a speciality.)
Bressingham Gardens, Diss, Norfolk.
Brewhouse Plants, Pilgrims Way, Boughton Aluph, Ashford, Kent.
Brook Cottage Nursery, Warehorne, Ashford, Kent.
Burncoose and Southdown Nurseries, Gwennap, Redruth, Cornwall.
Cally Gardens, Gatehouse of Fleet, Castle Douglas, Scotland DG7 2DJ.
Carlile, T., Loddon Nurseries, Twyford, Berkshire.
Chatto, Beth, White Barn House, Elmstead Market, Colchester, Essex.
Christian, Dr P., Pentre Cottages, Minera, Wrexham, Clwyd, N. Wales. (Rare bulbs.)
Daisy Hill Nurseries, Newry, Co. Down, Northern Ireland.
Four Seasons Nursery, Forncett, St Mary, Norwich, Norfolk.
Derek Fox, 54 Woodlands Road, Hookley, Essex, S25 4PY. (Lilies.)
Diana Gilbert, 25 Virginia Road, South Tanerton, Whitstable, Kent.
Goldbrook Plants, Hoxne, Eye, Suffolk.
Great Dixter Nurseries, Northiam, Sussex.
Hadspen House Gardens, Castle Cary, Somerset.
Hillier & Sons, West Hill Nurseries, Winchester, Hampshire.
Hoecroft Plants, Sheringham Road, West Bookham, Holt, Norfolk.
Holden Clough Nursery, Holden, Botton-by-Bowland, Clitheroe, Lancashire.
Home Meadows Nursery Ltd., Martlesham, Woodbridge, Suffolk. (Korean Chrysanthemums.)
Hydon Nurseries Ltd, Hydon Heath, Godalming, Surrey.
Ingwersen, W. E. Th., Ltd, Birch Farm Nursery, Gravetye, East Grinstead, Sussex (Alpine and other plants).
Jackamoor's Hardy Plant Farm, Enfield, Middlesex.
Jackman, George, Ltd, Woking Nurseries, Woking, Surrey.
Kaye, Reginald, Ltd, Waithman Nurseries, Silverdale, Carnforth, Lancs.
Kayes' Garden Nursery, 33 Mill Road, Rearsby, Leicester.
Kelway & Son Ltd, Langport, Somerset.
Langthorne's Plantery, High Cross Lane West, Little Canfield, Dunmow, Essex.
Lawley, Mrs M., 2 Dovecote, Wallington, Cambo, Morpeth, Northumberland.
Linnegar, Sidney, 5 New Road, Ruscombe, Twyford, Reading, Berkshire (Irises).

Longacre Nurseries, Perrywood, Selling, Faversham, Kent.
Longstock Park Nursery, Stockbridge, Hants.
Monksilver Nurseries, Oakington Road, Cottenham, Cambridge CB4 4TW.
Notcutt, R. C., Ltd, The Nurseries, Woodbridge, Suffolk.
Old Court Nurseries Ltd, Colwell, Malvern, Worcestershire.
Ponton, J. R., Kirknewton, Midlothian, Scotland.
Robinson's Hardy Plants, Greencourt Nurseries, Crockenhill, Swanley, Kent.
Rock Farm Nurseries, Gibbs Hill, Nettlestead, Maidstone, Kent.
Sandwich Nurseries Ltd., Dover Road, Sandwich, Kent.
Scott, John & Co., Royal Nurseries, Merriott, Somerset.
Southcombe Gardens, Widecombe-in-the-Moor, Devon.
Thompson & Morgan Ltd, Ipswich, Suffolk.
Toynbee's Nurseries Ltd, Barnham, Sussex.
Treasures of Tenbury Wells, Worcestershire.
Treseder's Nurseries Ltd, Truro, Cornwall.
Wallace & Barr Ltd, Marden, Kent (Hemerocallis, Iris, bulbs).
Washfield Nurseries, Hawkhurst, Kent.
Williamson, H., Wyevale Nurseries, King's Acre, Hereford.

Australia
Norgates' Plant Farm, Trentham, Victoria 3458.
Thomson, D. M., Mount View Nursery, Summertown, South Australia 5141.

Canada
Alpenglow Gardens, 11328 King George Highway, North Surrey, B.C., Canada.

Denmark
Abbing, Postbus 500, Zeist.
Andersen, A. L., Planteskole, Nyborgvej 284, 5700 Svendborg.
Buhl, Th., Planteskole, Harridsley, 8900 Randers.
Christensen, H., Virum Staudegartneri, Bakkevej 43, 2830 Virum.
Nørgaards Stauder, Hovedvej 10, Lilballe, 6000 Kolding. (Ferns.)
Petersen, Paul V., "Bakkely", Vasby, 2640 Hedehusene.
Vergmann, Ole, Planteskole, Skovvangsvej Sosum, 3670 Vekso.

France
Croux et Fils, Le Val d'Aulnay, 92290 Chatenay-Malabry.
Delaunay, Francois, 100 Route des Ponts-de-Ce, 49000 Angers.

Holland
Abbing Boomkwekerij, Postbus 500, Zeist.
Koninklijke Kwekerij Moerheim, Dedemsvaart. (Export wholesale only.)
Lubbe, G. en Zn., Postbus 42, 2160 AB, Lisse.
Stam, G. & E., Tuincentrum-Kwekerij, 44 R.I. Straat 10, 4051 AR Ochten.
Tubergen van BV., Postbus 86, 2160 AB, Lisse.

New Zealand
Dow, Peter B. & Co., South Pacific Seeds, Gisborne.
Duncan & Davies, Christchurch.
Harrison & Co. Ltd, P.O. Box 1, Palmerston North.
Liddle, D. J., Ltd, Ngarara Road, Waikanae.
Winstone, F. M., Ltd, Remuera 5, Auckland.

United States

Kurt Bluemel, Inc., 2740 Greene Lane, Baldwin, MD 21013. (Ornamental Grasses)

Canyon Creek Nursery, 3527 Dry Creek Road, Oroville, CA 95965.

Carroll Gardens, P.O. Box 310, 444 East Main Street, Westminster, MD 21157.

Cooley's Gardens, 11553 Silverton Road NE, P.O. Box 126, Silverton, OR 97381. (Bearded Iris)

Garden Place, 6780 Heisley Road, P.O. Box 388, Mentor, OH 44061.

Holbrook Farm & Nursery, Rt. 2, Box 223B, Fletcher, NC 28732.

Chas. Klehm & Son Nursery, Rt. 5, 197 Penny Road, S. Barrington, IL 60010. (Peonies, Hostas, Daylilies, Irises)

Louis Smirnow & Son, 85 Linden Lane, Brookville, NY 11545.

Melrose Gardens, 309 Best Road South, Stockton, California 95205.

Schreiner's Gardens, 3625 Quinaby Road NE, Salem, OR 97303. (Bearded Iris)

Siskiyou Rare Plant Nursery, 2825 Cummings Road, Medford, OR 97501–1524. (Woodland Plants)

Ty Ty Plantation, Box 159, Tyty, GA 31795. (Warm zone bulbs)

Andre Viette Farm & Nursery, RT. 1, Box 16, Fisherville, VA 22939.

Wayside Gardens Hodges, SC 29695–0001.

Gilbert H. Wild & Sons, Inc., HPB–84 1112 Joplin Street, Sarcoxie, MO 64862–0338. (Peonies, Daylilies, Iris)

Woodlanders, Inc. 1128 Colleton Avenue, Aiken, SC 29801. (S.E. USA Natives)

West Germany

Arends, Georg, Staudenkulturen, 56 Wuppertal-21, Ronsdorf.

Hagemann, H., Staudenkulturen, 3001 Krahenwinkel, bei Hannover.

Heinz Klose, 3503 Lohfelden bei Kassel, Rosenstrasse 10.

Kayser & Siebert, Odenwalder Pflanzenkulturen, 6101 Rossdorf bei Darmstadt.

Karl Wachter, Holsteinische Staudenzucht, 2081 Pinneberg-Etz, Schlweswig-Holstein.

von Zeppelin, Gräffin, Laufen/Baden, D7811 Sulzburg-Laufen.

Dutch Plant Names

Aardaker	*vide*	*Lathyrus tuberosus*	
Absinth		*Artemisia absinthium*	
Adderwortel		*Polygonum bistortum*	
Akelei		*Aquilegia*	
Akkerklokje		*Campanula rapunculoides*	
Alant		*Inula*	
Alsem		*Artemisia absinthium*	
Andoorn		*Stachys*	
Anemoon		*Anemone*	
Anjer, Anjelier		*Dianthus*	
Aronskelk		*Arum*	
Artisjok		*Cynara*	
Asperge		*Asparagus*	
Bereklaw		*Heracleum*	
Bergamotplant		*Monarda*	
Bernagie		*Borago*	
Blauw Schapegras		*Festuca*	
Blauwe Distel		*Eryngium*	
Blauwe Papaver		*Meconopsis*	
Blauwe Strobloem		*Catananche*	
Bloedrode Ooievaarsbek		*Geranium sanguineum*	
Bloemriet		*Canna*	
Boomlupine		*Lupinus arboreus*	
Boompapaver		*Romneya*	
Bosdruif		*Clematis*	
Boterbloem		*Ranunculus*	
Brandende liefde		*Lychnis*	
Christoffelkruid		*Actaea*	
Citroenkruid		*Artemisia abrotanum*	
Citroenmelise		*Melissa*	
Cupressenkruid		*Santolina chamaecyparissus*	
Daglelie		*Hemerocallis*	
Damastbloem		*Hesperis*	
Distel		*Cirsium*	
Donkere Ooievarsbek		*Geranium phaeum*	
Dotteerbloem		*Caltha*	
Dovenetel		*Lamium*	
Drakekop		*Dracocephalum*	
Duikfruid		*Scabiosa*	
Duizenblad		*Achillea millefolium*	
Duizendknoop		*Polygonum*	
Ereprijs		*Veronica*	
Ezelsoren		*Stachys olympica*	
Gamander		*Teucrium*	
Ganzerik		*Potentilla*	
Geitebaard		*Aruncus*	
Gele Kamille		*Anthemis tinctoria*	
Gele Lis		*Iris pseudacorus*	
Gentiaan		*Gentiana*	
Gewone Akelei		*Aquilegia vulgaris*	
Geirstgras		*Milium*	
Gipskruid		*Gypsophila*	
Gladiool		*Gladiolus*	

Glidkruid	*v.*	*Scutellaria*
Groot Hoefblad		*Petasites*
Guldenroede		*Solidago*
Havikskruid		*Hieracium*
Heilingenbloem		*Santolina*
Helmbloem		*Corydalis*
Hemelsleutel		*Sedum telephium*
Herfstaster		*Aster novi-belgii*
Hondstong		*Cynoglossum*
Hoornpapaver		*Glaucium*
Hop		*Humulus*
Hyssop		*Hyssopus*
Ijslandse Papaver		*Papaver nudicaule*
Ijzerhard		*Verbena*
Jacobsladder		*Polemonium*
Jupiterbloem		*Lychnis flos-jovis*
Kaapse Fuchsia		*Phygelius*
Kaapse Hyacinth		*Galtonia*
Kaasjeskruid		*Malva*
Karmozijnbes		*Phytolacca*
Kattestaart		*Lythrum*
Keizerskroon		*Fritillaria imperialis*
Klaproos		*Papaver*
Klaver		*Trifolium*
Klokbilzekruid		*Scopolia*
Klokje		*Campanula*
Kluwenklokje		*Campanula glomerata*
Knoldragende boterbloem		*Ranunculus bulbosus*
Koeieoog		*Buphthalmum*
Koekoeksbloem		*Lychnis*
Kogeldistel		*Echinops*
Korenbloem		*Centaurea*
Kruis Distel		*Eryngium*
Kruiskruid		*Senecio*
Lampionplant		*Physalis*
Lamsoren		*Limonium*
Leeuweklauw		*Alchemilla*
Lelie		*Lilium*
Lepelblad		*Cochlearia*
Leverkruid		*Eupatorium*
Liesgras		*Glyceria maxima*
Lijnzaad		*Linum*
Lis		*Iris*
Longkruid		*Pulmonaria*
Look		*Allium*
Lupine		*Lupinus*
Luizenbloem		*Coreopsis*
Malrove		*Marrubium*
Margriet		*Chrysanthemum*
Marjolein		*Origanum*
Maskerbloem		*Mimulus*
Moederkruid		*Chrysanthemum parthenium*

Moerasgentiaan	*vide*	*Gentiana*
		pneumonanthe
Moerasspiraea		*Filipendula ulmaria*
Moeraswolfmelk		*Euphorbia palustris*
Monnikskap		*Aconitum*
Montbretia		*Crocosmia*
Munt		*Mentha*
Muskuskaasjeskruid		*Malva moschata*
Naald van Cleopatra		*Eremurus*
Nachtschone		*Mirabilis*
Nagelkruid		*Geum*
Nieskruid		*Helleborus*
Ooievaarsbek		*Geranium*
Oosterse Papaver		*Papaver orientale*
Ossetong		*Anchusa*
Palmlelie		*Yucca*
Pampasgras		*Cortaderia*
Pantoffelplant		*Calceolaria*
Parelgras		*Melica*
Pepermunt		*Mentha*
Pimpernel		*Sanguisorba*
Pinksterbloem		*Cardamine*
Pioen		*Paeonia*
Poelruit		*Thalictrum flavum*
Prikneus		*Lychnis coronaria*
Rapunzel		*Phyteuma*
Reuzenriet		*Arundo*
Rhabarber		*Rheum*
Ribzaad		*Chaerophyllum*
Ridderspoor		*Delphinium*
Rietgras		*Phalaris arundinacea*
Roomse Kamille		*Anthemis*
Roomse Kervel		*Myrrhis*
Ruit		*Ruta*
Ruit		*Thalictrum*
Salie		*Salvia*
Salomonszegel		*Polygonatum*
Scharnierplant		*Physostegia*
Scherpe boterbloem		*Ranunculus acris*
Schoenlappersplant		*Bergenia*
Siberische Lis		*Iris sibirica*
Sleutelbloem		*Primula*
Slijkgras		*Spartina*
Smele		*Descampsia*
Standelkruid		*Orchis*
Standkruid		*Armeria*
Steenbreek		*Saxifraga*
Steentijm		*Satureja*

Stinkende Gouwe	*v.*	*Chelidonium*
Stinkend Nieskruid		*Helleborus foetidus*
Teunisbloem		*Oenothera*
Toorts		*Verbascum*
Trilgras		*Briza*
Tuinsalie		*Salvia officinalis*
Twaalfgodenkruid		*Dodecatheon*
Valeriaan		*Valeriana*
Veldbies		*Luzula*
Veldsalie		*Salvia pratensis*
Venkel		*Foeniculum*
Vetkruid		*Sedum*
Vijfbladig		
Kaasjeskruid		*Malva alcea*
Vingergras		*Panicum*
Vingerhoedskruid		*Digitalis*
Vlamboem		*Phlox*
Vlas		*Linum*
Vlasleeuwebek		*Linaria*
Vlotgras		*Glyceria*
Voetblad		*Podophyllum*
Vogelmelk		*Ornithogalum*
Voojaarszonnebloem		*Doronicum*
Vrouwenmantel		*Alchemilla mollis*
Vrouwenschoentje		*Cypripedium*
Vuurpijl		*Kniphofia*
Vuurwerkplant		*Dictamnus*
Wederik		*Lysimachia*
Wespenorchis		*Epipactis*
Wilde Bertram		*Achillea ptarmica*
Wildemanskruid		*Pulsatilla vulgaris*
Wilgeroosje		*Epilobium*
		angustifolium
Wolfsmelk		*Euphorbia*
Zandhaver		*Elymus*
Zee-Distel		*Eryngium maritimum*
Zeekool		*Crambe*
Zeepkruid		*Saponaria*
Zegge		*Scirpus*
Zevenblad		*Aegopodium*
Zijdeplant		*Asclepias*
Zilverkaars		*Cimicifuga*
Zoethout		*Glycyrrhiza*
Zomerklokje		*Leucojum*
Zonnebloem		*Helianthus*
Zwaardlelie		*Gladiolus*
Zwarte Dahlia		*Cosmos*
Zwenkgras		*Festuca*

French Plant Names

Absinthe	*vide*	*Artemisia absinthium*
Agrostemma		*Lychnis flos-jovis*
Ail		*Allium*
Alkekeng		*Physalis*
Amour en Cage		*Physalis*
Ancolie		*Aquilegia*
Aneth		*Foeniculum, Ferula*
Armoise		*Artemisia*
Asperge		*Asparagus*
Aunée		*Inula*
Avoine persistante		*Avena sempervirens*

Baguenaude	*Physalis*
Balisier	*Canna*
Bananier	*Musa*
Barbe de Jupiter	*Centranthus*
Barbeau Vivace	*Centaurea*
Baton blanc	*Asphodelus albus*
Baton de Jacob	*Asphodeline lutea, Campanula persicifolia*
Baton royal	*Asphodelus albus*
Bec de Grue sanguin	*Geranium sanguineum*
Bechin rouge	*Centranthus*
Belladonne d'Automne	*Amaryllis*
Belle de Nuit	*Mirabilis*
Belsombra	*Phytolacca*
Benoite	*Geum*
Berce Géante	*Heracleum*
Bétoine	*Stachys betonica*
Bluet Vivace	*Centaurea*
Bois de réglisse	*Glycyirrhiza*
Bonnet d'Évêque	*Epimedium*
Boule azurée	*Echinops*
Boule d'Or	*Trollius*
Bouton d'Argent	*Achillea ptarmica*
Bouton d'Argent	*Chrysanthemum parthenium*
Buglosse	*Anchusa*

Calamplis	*Eccremocarpus*
Calla	*Zantedeschia*
Camomile jaune	*Anthemis tinctoria*
Campanule	*Campanula*
Campanule à fleur de pêcher	*Campanula persicifolia*
Canne de Provence	*Arundo donax*
Capuce de moine	*Aconitum*
Capuchon	*Aconitum*
Capucine	*Tropaeolum tuberosum*
Cardinale	*Lobelia cardinalis*
Casque, Aconit	*Aconitum*
Cazon d'Olympe	*Armeria*
Centaurée	*Centaurea*
Cerise d'hiver	*Physalis*
Cerise en chemise *vide*	*Physalis*
Char de Vénus	*Aconitum*
Chardon bleu	*Eryngium*
Chardon des Alpes	*Eryngium* and *Echinops*

Chasse punaises	*v.*	*Actaea spicata*
Christophorine		*Actaea spicata*
Coccigrue		*Physalis*
Cœur de Jeannette		*Dicentra spectabilis*
Cœur de Marie		*Dicentra*
Coquelicot		*Papaver*
Coquelourde		*Lychnis*
Coqueret		*Physalis, Phlox*
Couronne Impériale		*Fritillaris imperialis*
Croix de Jérusalem		*Lychnis chalcedonica*
Croix de Malte		*Lychnis chalcedonica*
Cupidone		*Catananche*

Dentèlaire	*Ceratostigma plumbaginoides*
Digitale	*Digitalis*
Doronic	*Doronicum*

Échelle de Jacob	*Polemonium*
Échinope	*Echinops*
Enothère	*Oenothera*
Épervière	*Hieracium*
Éphémère de Virgil	*Tradescantia*
Épiaire	*Stachys*
Épiaire laineuse	*Stachys byzantina*
Étrangle loup	*Aconitum*
Eulalie	*Miscanthus*

Faux acore	*Iris pseudacorus*
Flambe	*Iris*
Flambe d'eau	*Iris pseudacorus*
Fleur de Jupiter	*Lychnis*
Fleur des Veuves	*Scabiosa*
Fougères	*Ferns*
Fraxinelle	*Dictamnus*

Galane	*Chelone*
Galanga des marais	*Acorus calamus*
Georgine	*Dahlia*
Gerbe de Bouc	*Aruncus*
Germandrée	*Teucrium chamaedrys*
Gesse vivace	*Lathyrus latifolius*
Girarde	*Hesperis*
Giroflée	*Cheiranthus*
Giroselle	*Dodecatheon*
Glaieul	*Gladiolus*

Hélénie		*Helenium*
Herbe à Becquet		*Geranium sanguineum*
Herbe aux Charpentiers		*Achillea millefolium*
Herbe aux chats		*Nepeta*
Herbe aux poux		*Actaea spicata*
Herbe de Pampas		*Cortaderia*
Herbe de St Christophe		*Actaea spicata*
Herbe de Saint Jean	*v.*	*Artemisia*
Herbe du Vent		*Anemone*
Hoteia		*Astilbe*

Iris d'Angleterre	*Iris xiphioides*
Iris d'Espagne	*Iris xiphium*

Iris du Japon	*vide*	*Iris kaempferi*	
Iris faux acore		*Iris pseudacorus*	
Jacinthe du Cap		*Galtonia*	
Jacobée Blanche		*Cineraria maritima*	
Julienne		*Hesperis*	
Ketmie		*Hibiscus*	
Ketmie de marais		*Hibiscus moscheutos*	
Laiche		*Carex*	
Lanterne Japonnais		*Physalis*	
Lavatère d'Hyères		*Lavatera olbia*	
Liatride		*Liatris*	
Lilas d'Espagne		*Centranthus*	
Lin		*Linum*	
Lin de la Nouvelle Zélandie		*Phormium*	
Lis de St Bernard		*Anthericum*	
Lis de St Bruno		*Paradisea*	
Lis des Incas		*Alstroemeria*	
Lis des Vallées		*Convallaria*	
Lis jaune		*Hemerocallis*	
Lis rouge		*Hemerocallis*	
Lobelie Écarlate		*Lobelia*	
Lunaire		*Lunaria*	
Lychnide		*Lychnis*	
Lysimaque rouge		*Lythrum*	
Marguerite		*Chrysanthemum*	
Marguerite de Transvaal		*Gerbera*	
Marguerite Grande		*Chrysanthemum maximum*	
Marjolaine		*Origanum*	
Matricaire		*Chrysanthemum parthenium*	
Mauve		*Malva, Hibiscus and Lavatera*	
Mélisse		*Melittis*	
Menthe du Chat		*Nepeta*	
Menthe poivrée		*Mentha*	
Mignardise Blanche		*Dianthus*	
Millefeuille		*Achillea*	
Molène		*Verbascum*	
Monnaie du Pape		*Lunaria*	
Montbretia		*Crocosmia*	
Muguet de Bois		*Convallaria*	
Napel		*Aconitum*	
Œil du bœuf		*Anthemis tinctoria*	
Œil du Christ		*Aster amellus*	
Œillet		*Dianthus*	
Œillet mignardise		*Dianthus plumarius*	
Oignons à fleurs		*Allium*	
Orpin		*Sedum*	
Osmonde		*Osmunda*	
Pangue		*Gunnera*	
Panicaut		*Eryngium*	

Panis	*v.*	*Panicum*
Pavot d'Orient		*Papaver orientale*
Pavot en arbre		*Romneya*
Persicaire		*Polygonum sachalinense*
Pervenche		*Vinca*
Petit chêne		*Teucrium*
Phalangère de lis		*Anthericum liliago*
Pied d'Alouette		*Delphinium*
Pigamon		*Thalictrum*
Pivoine		*Paeonia*
Plume de Pampas		*Cortaderia*
Poids de Senteur Vivace		*Lathyrus grandiflorus*
Polalyre		*Baptisia*
Polypode		*Asplenium scolopendrium*
Populage des marais		*Caltha*
Pyrèthre rose		*Chrysanthemum coccineum*
Reine des Alpes		*Filipendula*
Reine Marguerite		*Aster, Chrysanthemum*
Renouée		*Polygonum cuspidatum*
Rhubarbe		*Rheum*
Richardia		*Zantedeschia*
Rose de Noël		*Helleborus*
Rose tremière		*Althaea rosea*
Roseau à plumes		*Cortaderia*
Roseau à quenouille		*Arundo donax*
Roseau aromatique		*Acorus calamus*
Rue de Chèvre		*Galega*
Saique-nez		*Achillea millefolium*
Salicaire		*Lythrum*
Sanguinaire		*Geranium sanguineum*
Sauge		*Salvia*
Saxifrage peltée		*Peltiphyllum*
Sceau de Salomon		*Polygonatum multiflorum*
Senecon de la Plata		*Senecio pulcher*
Soleil Vivace		*Helianthus*
Souci d'eau		*Caltha*
Spirée		*Filipendula*
Stenactis		*Erigeron*
Tritoma		*Kniphofia*
Tuberose bleu		*Agapanthus*
Tue Loups		*Aconitum*
Ulmaire		*Filipendula*
Valeriane des Jardins		*Centranthus ruber*
Valeriane Grecque		*Polemonium*
Vendangeuse		*Aster*
Verge d'Argent		*Cimicifuga*
Verge de Jacob		*Asphodeline lutea*
Verge d'Or		*Solidago*
Vergerette		*Erigeron*
Vergerette de Californie		*Erigeron speciosus*

419

German Plant Names

Aaronstab	*vide* *Arum, Arisaema*	Dreiblatt	*v.* *Trillium*
Adonisröschen	*Adonis*	Dreiblattspiere	*Gillenia*
Affodil	*Asphodelus*	Dreimasterblume	*Tradescantia*
Akelei	*Aquilegia*		
Alant	*Inula*	Edeldistel	*Eryngium*
Artischocke	*Cynara*	Edelraute	*Artemisia*
Aster	*Aster*	Ehrenpreis	*Veronica*
Attich	*Sambucus*	Eibe	*Aconitum*
		Eibisch	*Hibiscus*
Baldrian	*Valeriana*	Eidechsenblume	*Sauromatum*
Ballonblume	*Platycodon*	Eisenhut	*Aconitum*
Ballonglocke	*Platycodon*	Eisenkraut	*Vernonia*
Bärenklau	*Acanthus*	Elfenblume	*Epimedium*
Bartfarden	*Penstemon*	Engelsüss	*Polypodium*
Bärwurz	*Meum*	Engelsüssfarn	*Polypodium*
Battunge	*Stachys*	Enzian	*Gentiana*
Baumannswurz	*Gillenia*	Erdrauch	*Corydalis*
Becherfarn	*Matteuccia*	Erdwurz	*Geum*
Becherglocke	*Adenophora*	Etagenerika	*Physostegia*
Beifuss	*Artemisia*		
Belladonna	*Amaryllis*	Fackellilie	*Kniphofia*
Bergenie	*Bergenia*	Falsche Alraunwurzel	*Tellima*
Bergkamille	*Anthemis*	Falscher Drachenkopf	*Physostegia*
Bergminze	*Calamintha*	Farn	*Ferns*
Berufskraut	*Erigeron*	Federborstengras	*Pennisetum*
Beschreikraut	*Erigeron*	Federgras	*Stipa*
Bienenbalsam	*Monarda*	Federmohn	*Macleaya*
Bilbernell	*Pimpinella*	Federnelke	*Dianthus*
Binsenlilie	*Sisyrinchium*	Feder-Pfriemengras	*Stipa capillata*
Blasenfarn	*Cystopteris*	Feenglocke	*Disporum*
Blasenkelch	*Physostegia*	Feinstrahl	*Erigeron*
Blattspiere	*Rodgersia*	Felberich	*Lysimachia*
Blauernpfingstrosse	*Paeonia*	Fettblatt	*Sedum*
Blauglöckchen	*Mertensia*	Filzkraut	*Phlomis*
Blauhafer	*Helictotrichon*	Fingerhut	*Digitalis*
Blaulilie	*Agapanthus*	Fingerkraut	*Potentilla*
Blaustrahlhafer	*Helictotrichon*	Flachs	*Linum*
Blaustrandhafer	*Elymus*	Flammenblume	*Phlox*
Bleiwurz	*Ceratostigma*	Fliegendes des Herz	*Dicentra*
Bletille	*Bletia*	Flockenblume	*Centaurea*
Blutrösle	*Geranium sanguineum*	Frauenfarn	*Athyrium filix-femina*
Blutweiderich	*Lythrum*	Frauenherz	*Dicentra*
Brandkraut	*Phlomis*	Frauenmantel	*Alchemilla*
Braunwurz	*Scrophularia*	Frauenschuh	*Cypripedium*
Brennende Liebe	*Lychnis*	Freilandprimeln	*Primula*
Brennender Busch	*Dictamnus*	Freilandwinteraster	*Chrysanthemum*
Bronzeblatt	*Galax*	Frühlingswaldwicke	*Lathyrus*
		Fuchsie	*Fuchsia*
Chinaschilf	*Miscanthus*	Fünffaden	*Penstemon*
Christophskraut	*Actaea*	Funkie	*Hosta*
Christrose	*Helleborus*		
Cupidopfeil	*Catananche*	Gamander	*Teucrium*
Cypergras	*Cyperus*	Gartenlilie	*Lilium*
		Gauklerblume	*Mimulus*
Diptam	*Dictamnus*	Gefiederähre	*Pennisetum*
Doppelmalve	*Sidalcea*	Geissbart	*Aruncus*
Doppelsporn	*Dicentra*	Geissraute	*Galega*
Dost	*Origanum*	Gelbweiderich	*Lysimachia punctata*
Dotterblume	*Caltha*	Gelenkblume	*Physostegia*
Drachenkopf	*Dracocephalum*	Gemswurz	*Doronicum*
Drachenkopf falscher	*Physostegia*	Germer	*Veratrum*

420

Gichtrose	*vide* *Paeonia*	Krugglocke	*v.* *Adenophora*
Gipskraut	*Gypsophila*	Krugpflanze	*Sarracenia*
Gladiole	*Gladiolus*	Küchenschelle	*Pulsatilla*
Glanzgras	*Phalaris*	Kugeldistel	*Echinops*
Glockenblume	*Campanula*		
Glockenkraut	*Codonopsis*	Lampen-	
Gloxiniestauden	*Incarvillea*	putzergras	*Pennisetum*
Goldbandleistengras	*Spartina*	Lampionflor	*Physalis*
Goldmargerite	*Buphthalmum*	Lampionflanze	*Physalis*
Goldmelisse	*Monarda*	Lauch	*Allium*
Goldrute	*Solidago*	Lein	*Linum*
Goldwurz	*Asphodeline*	Leinkraut	*Linaria*
Götterblume	*Dodecatheon*	Leopardblume	*Belamcanda*
Graslilie	*Anthericum*	Leopoldslilie	*Belamcanda*
	Paradisea	Lerchensporn	*Corydalis*
Grasnelke	*Armeria*	Lichtnelke	*Lychnis*
Grindkraut	*Scabiosa*	Lilie	*Lilium*
		Lilienschweif	*Eremurus*
Haargras	*Elymus*	Lungenkraut	*Pulmonaria*
Habichtskraut	*Hieracium*		
Hahnenfuss	*Ranunculus*	Mädesüss	*Filipendula*
Hainsimse	*Luzula*	Madonnenlilie	*Lilium candidum*
Hakenlilie	*Crinum*	Maiapfel	*Podophyllum*
Helmkraut	*Scutellaria*	Maiblume	*Convallaria*
Herbstanemone	*Anemone*	Maidchenauge	*Coreopsis*
Herbstaster	*Aster*	Maiglöckchen	*Convallaria*
Herculeskraut	*Heracleum*	Malve	*Malva, Althaea*
Herkulesstande	*Heracleum*	Mammutblatt	*Gunnera*
Herzblume	*Dicentra*	Mannstreu	*Eryngium*
Himmelsleiter	*Polemonium*	Marbel	*Luzula*
Hirschzunge	*Phyllitis*	Margaretenblume	*Chrysanthemum*
Hirse	*Panicum*		*coccineum*
Hopfen	*Humulus*	Margrite, Margerite	*Chrysanthemum*
Hornmohn	*Glaucium*	Marjoram	*Origanum*
Hornnarbe	*Ceratostigma*	Mauerpfeffer	*Sedum*
Hundskamille	*Anthemis*	Meerkohl	*Crambe*
Hundszunge	*Cynoglossum*	Meerzwiebel	*Endymion*
		Megasea	*Bergenia*
Immenblatt	*Melittis*	Mertensie	*Mertensia*
Immergrün	*Vinca*	Milchstern, Milkstern	*Ornithogalum*
Indianernessel	*Monarda*	Minze	*Mentha*
Indigolupine	*Baptisia*	Mittelfarn	*Athyrium filix-femina*
Indigostrauch	*Indigofera*	Mohn	*Papaver*
Inkalilie	*Alstroemaria*	Montbretien	*Crocosmia*
Islandsmohn	*Papaver nudicaule*	Morgensternsegge	*Carex grayi*
		Moschusmalve	*Malva*
Jakobsleiter	*Polemonium*	Moskitogras	*Bouteloua*
Judenkirsche	*Physalis*	Myrrhe	*Myrrhis*
Junimargrite	*Chrysanthemum*		
	coccineum	Nabelnuss	*Omphalodes*
Junkerlilie	*Asphodeline*	Nachtkerze	*Oenothera*
		Nachtviole	*Hesperis*
Kaiserkrone	*Fritillaria*	Nelke	*Dianthus*
Kalmus	*Acorus*	Nelkenwurz	*Geum*
Kaphyacinthe	*Galtonia*	Nieswurz	*Helleborus*
Kapuzinerkresse,			
Hochrote	*Tropaeolum*	Ochsenauge	*Buphthalmum*
Kardendistel	*Morina*	Ochsenzunge	*Anchusa*
Katzenminze	*Nepeta*	Offenscheide	*Lysichitum*
Kaukasusvergiss-		Osterluzie	*Aristolochia*
meinnicht	*Brunnera*		
Kermesbeere	*Phytolacca*	Palmlilie	*Yucca*
Kleopatranadel	*Eremurus*	Pampasgras	*Cortaderia*
Knabenkraut	*Orchis*	Pechtnelke	*Lychnis*
Knöterich	*Polygonum*	Perlfarn	*Onoclea*
Kokardenblume	*Gaillardia*	Perlflötchen	*Anaphalis*
Königsfarn	*Osmunda*	Pfahlrohe	*Arundo*
Königskerze	*Verbascum*	Pfeifengras	*Molinia*
Königslilie	*Lilium*	Pfennigkraut	*Lysimachia*
Kornblume	*Centaurea*	Pfingstrose	*Paeonia*
Kornrade	*Lychnis coronaria*	Platterbse	*Lathyrus*
Kreuzkraut	*Ligularia*	Prachtglocke	*Codonopsis*
Kronlichtnelke	*Lychnis coronaria*	Prachtscharte	*Liatris*
Krötenlilie	*Tricyrtis*	Prachtspiere	*Astilbe*

421

Prairiemalve	*vide*	*Sidalcea*
Primel		*Primula*
Punktfarn		*Polystichum*
Purpurglökchen		*Heuchera*
Quamaschilie		*Camassia*
Radblume		*Lychnis coronaria*
Raketenblume		*Kniphofia*
Reisenbrandgras		*Phalaris*
Reisensteinbrech		*Bergenia*
Reitgras		*Calamagrostis*
Rhabarber		*Rheum*
Riesenfenchel		*Ferula*
Riesengras		*Miscanthus*
Riesenhyacinthe		*Galtonia*
Riesenkreuzkraut		*Ligularia*
Rindsauge		*Buphthalmum speciosum*
Rippenfarn		*Blechnum spicant*
Rispenfarn		*Osmunda*
Rittersporn		*Delphinium*
Rodgersie		*Rodgersia*
Rotmäulchen		*Monarda*
Rutenhirse		*Panicum*
Salbei		*Salvia*
Salomonssiegel		*Polygonatum*
Schafgarbe		*Achillea*
Schattenblume		*Smilacina*
Schaublattspiere		*Rodgersia*
Schaumkraut		*Cardamine*
Scheinaster		*Boltonia*
Scheincalla		*Smilacina*
Scheinhanf		*Datisca*
Scheinmohn		*Meconopsis*
Scheinziest		*Stachys officinalis*
Schildblatt		*Peltiphyllum*
Schildblume		*Chelone*
Schildfarn		*Polystichum*
Schilf, Chinesisches		*Miscanthus*
Schirmblatt		*Diphylleia*
Schirmsteinbrech		*Peltiphyllum*
Schlangenkopf		*Chelone*
Schlangenkraut		*Cimicifuga*
Schlangenwurz		*Arum dracunculus*
Scheierkraut		*Gypsophila*
Schlüsselblume		*Primula*
Schmiele		*Deschampsia*
Schmucklilie		*Agapanthus*
Schneemohn		*Eomecon*
Schneerose		*Helleborus*
Schuppenkopf		*Cephalaria*
Schwaden		*Glyceria*
Schwalbenwurz		*Asclepias*
Schwalben- wurzenzian		*Gentiana asclepiadea*
Schwertlilie		*Iris*
Schwingel		*Festuca*
Segge		*Carex*
Seidenpflanze		*Asclepias*
Siefenkraut		*Saponaria*
Siegwurz		*Gladiolus*
Silberblatt, Silberling		*Lunaria*
Silberkerze		*Cimicifuga*
Simse		*Luzula*
Sinngrün		*Vinca*
Skabiose		*Scabiosa*
Sockenblume		*Epimedium*
Sommerhyacinthe		*Galtonia*
Sonnenauge		*Heliopsis*
Sonnenblume		*Helianthus*
Sonnenbraut		*Helenium*

Sonnenhut	*v.*	*Rudbeckia*
Spätsommeraster		*Aster*
Sperrkraut		*Polemonium*
Spierstaude		*Filipendula*
Spiräen		*Astilbe*
Spornblume		*Centranthus*
Staudengloxinie		*Incarvillea*
Staudenimmortelle		*Anaphalis*
Staudenlobelie		*Lobelia*
Staudenlupine		*Lupinus*
Steckpalmenfarn		*Cyrtomium*
Steinbrech		*Saxifraga*
Steppenlilie		*Eremurus*
Sternblume		*Aster*
Sterndolde		*Astrantia*
Stinkkoln		*Symplocarpus*
Stockmalve		*Althaea rosea*
Stockrose		*Althaea*
Storkenschnabel		*Geranium*
Strandflieder		*Limonium*
Strandhafer		*Elymus*
Strandschleierkraut		*Limonium*
Strauchmalve		*Lavatera*
Straussfarn, Straussenfarn		*Matteuccia*
Sumpfdotterblume		*Caltha*
Sumpffarn		*Onoclea*
Sumpfstendel		*Epipactis*
Süssgras		*Glyceria*
Süssholz		*Glycyrrhiza*
Taglilie		*Hemerocallis*
Taubenkropf		*Corydalis*
Taubnessel		*Lamium*
Telekie		*Buphthalmum*
Tigerlilie		*Lilium tigrinum*
Tranendes Herz		*Dicentra*
Traubenfarn		*Osmunda*
Trauerglocken- blume		*Uvularia*
Trollblume		*Trollius*
Trompetenblume		*Incarvillea*
Truthahnbart		*Xerophyllum*
Tulpen		*Tulipa*
Tupfelfarn		*Polypodium*
Turkenbund		*Lilium martagon*
Turkenmohn		*Papaver orientale*
Veilchen		*Viola*
Venushaarfarn		*Adiantum*
Vergissmeinnicht, Kaukasus		*Brunnera*
Wachsglocke		*Kirengeshoma*
Waldgeiffbart		*Aruncus sylvester*
Waldrebe		*Clematis*
Waldschmiele		*Deschampsia*
Waldweidenröschen		*Epilobium angustifolium*
Waldwicke		*Lathyrus*
Wallwurz		*Symphytum*
Wasserdost		*Eupatorium*
Wasserweide		*Decodon*
Weidenkraut		*Lysimachia*
Weidenroschen		*Epilobium*
Weiderich		*Lythrum*
Weisenraute		*Thalictrum*
Weisswurz		*Polygonatum*
Wermuth		*Artemisia absinthium*
Wicke		*Lathyrus*
Wiesenhafer		*Helictotrichon*
Wiesenknopf		*Sanguisorba*
Windblume		*Anemone*
Windröschen		*Anemone*

Witwenblume	*vide*	*Scabiosa*	Zergspiere	*v.*	*Astilbe*
Wolfsbohne		*Lupinus*	Zierlauch		*Allium*
Wolfsmilch		*Euphorbia*	Zierspargel		*Asparagus*
Wucherblume		*Chrysanthemum*	Zieste		*Stachys*
Wunderblume		*Mirabilis*	Zitronenmelisse		*Melissa*
Wurmfarn		*Dryopteris,*	Zittergras		*Briza*
		Polystichum	Zweilingsblatt		*Plagiorrhegma*
			Zweisporn		*Dicentra*
Zahnwurz		*Dentaria*			

Indexes

Index

PLANT NAMES AND SYNONYMS IN LATIN AND ENGLISH

It will be realized how many plants in cultivation suffer a complexity of names due to botanical authorities having different views or working in ignorance of the findings of others. I have therefore included in this index the authority after each name, thus indicating whose nomenclature I have adopted throughout the book for each species.

435

441

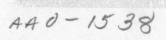